SUSTAINABILITY, CIVIL SOCIETY
AND INTERNATIONAL GOVERNANCE

T0079627

Global Environmental Governance Series

Series Editors: John J. Kirton and Konrad von Moltke

Global Environmental Governance addresses the new generation of twenty-first century environmental problems and the challenges they pose for management and governance at the local, national, and global levels. Centred on the relationships among environmental change, economic forces, and political governance, the series explores the role of international institutions and instruments, national and sub-federal governments, private sector firms, scientists, and civil society, and provides a comprehensive body of progressive analyses on one of the world's most contentious international issues.

Sustainability, Civil Society and International Governance
Local, North American and Global Contributions

Edited by
JOHN J. KIRTON
University of Toronto
PETER I. HAJNAL
University of Toronto

Routledge
Taylor & Francis Group
LONDON AND NEW YORK

First published 2006 by Ashgate Publishing

Reissued 2018 by Routledge
2 Park Square, Milton Park, Abingdon, Oxon OX14 4RN
711 Third Avenue, New York, NY 10017, USA

Routledge is an imprint of the Taylor & Francis Group, an informa business

First issued in paperback 2018

© John J. Kirton and Peter I. Hajnal 2006

John J. Kirton and Peter I. Hajnal have asserted their right under the Copyright, Designs and Patents Act, 1988, to be identified as the editors of this work.

All rights reserved. No part of this book may be reprinted or reproduced or utilised in any form or by any electronic, mechanical, or other means, now known or hereafter invented, including photocopying and recording, or in any information storage or retrieval system, without permission in writing from the publishers.

A Library of Congress record exists under LC control number: 2006921289

Notice:
Product or corporate names may be trademarks or registered trademarks, and are used only for identification and explanation without intent to infringe.

Publisher's Note
The publisher has gone to great lengths to ensure the quality of this reprint but points out that some imperfections in the original copies may be apparent.

Disclaimer
The publisher has made every effort to trace copyright holders and welcomes correspondence from those they have been unable to contact.

ISBN-13: 978-0-815-39728-1 (hbk)
ISBN-13: 978-1-138-62074-2 (pbk)
ISBN-13: 978-1-351-14828-3 (ebk)

Contents

vi   *Sustainability, Civil Society, and International Governance*

List of Figures

List of Tables

List of Contributors

Diane Bartlett is a doctoral student at the Department of Sociology at the University of Toronto, completing her dissertation on civil society participation in international food safety regulation.

Stefanie J. Bowles studied Peace and Conflict Studies at the University of Toronto and completed an MSc in Environment and Development at the London School of Economics and Politics, and now works for Environment Canada.

Stephen Clarkson is a professor of political economy at the University of Toronto and was a co-investigator with 'Strengthening Canada's Environmental Community through International Regime Reform' (the EnviReform project).

Michael E. Cloghesy is President of the Conseil patronal de l'environnement du Québec (CPEQ), known in English as the Business Council on the Environment. The CPEQ was one of the social partners of 'Strengthening Canada's Environmental Community through International Regime Reform: Exploring Social Cohesion in a Globalizing Era' (the EnviReform project).

Sarah Davidson Ladly studied political science at the University of Toronto and is pursuing a Juris Doctor degree at the University of Toronto's Faculty of Law.

Debbie Field is the Executive Director of FoodShare Toronto, which works to improve access to affordable, healthy food from field to table. FoodShare was a social partner of 'Strengthening Canada's Environmental Community through International Regime Reform' (the EnviReform project).

Harriet Friedmann is a professor of sociology at the University of Toronto and was a co-investigator with 'Strengthening Canada's Environmental Community through International Regime Reform' (the EnviReform project).

Bill Graham, Minister of National Defence, served as Canada's Minister for Foreign Affairs from 2002 to 2004 and Minister of Defence from 2004 to 2006, and is Interim Leader of the Opposition.

Peter I. Hajnal is a Research Fellow at the Munk Centre for International Studies of the University of Toronto and Adjunct Professor in the Faculty of Information Studies at the University of Toronto. He was also a co-investigator in 'Strengthening Canada's Environmental Community through International Regime Reform' (the EnviReform project).

John J. Kirton is an Associate Professor of Political Science and Director of the G8 Research Group at the University of Toronto, and was Principal Investigator of 'Strengthening Canada's Environmental Community through International Regime Reform' (the EnviReform project).

Sonia Labatt is an associate faculty member at the Institute for Environmental Studies at the University of Toronto.

Ian Thomas MacDonald is studying philosophy and politics at the University of Toronto and political economy at York University.

Virginia Maclaren is Associate Professor in the Department of Geography and Program in Planning at the University of Toronto and Associate Director of the Institute for Environmental Studies. She was a co-investigator in 'Strengthening Canada's Environmental Community through International Regime Reform' (the EnviReform project) at the University of Toronto.

Désirée M. McGraw is Director of Policy and Senior Policy Advisor to Canada's Minister of International Cooperation.

Angela Morris is a graduate of the Geography and Environmental Studies Collaborative Master's Programme at the University of Toronto.

Jennifer Leah Mullen has studied aboriginal issues as well as history and politics at the University of Toronto.

Ken Ogilvie is the Executive Director of Pollution Probe, one of Canada's most distinguished environmental groups. Pollution Probe was a social partner of 'Strengthening Canada's Environmental Community through International Regime Reform' (the EnviReform project).

Sylvia Ostry is Distinguished Research Fellow at the University of Toronto's Centre for International Studies. She was a co-investigator in 'Strengthening Canada's Environmental Community through International Regime Reform' (the EnviReform project) at the University of Toronto.

Louis W. Pauly is Professor of Political Science and Director of the Centre for International Studies at the University of Toronto. He was a co-investigator in 'Strengthening Canada's Environmental Community through International Regime Reform' (the EnviReform project) at the University of Toronto.

Sheila Risbud is Senior Policy Advisor for Environment Canada in Edmonton, responsible for monitoring the ministry's activities in the Manitoba, Saskatchewan, Alberta, the Northwest Territories, and Nunavut.

Alan M. Rugman holds the L. Leslie Waters Chair in International Business at the Kelly School of Business at Indiana University in Bloomington, Indiana. He was a research collaborator in 'Strengthening Canada's Environmental Community through International Regime Reform' (the EnviReform project) at the University of Toronto.

Julie Soloway is an associate with Blake, Cassels & Graydon LLP, practising competition law. She was a collaborator on 'Strengthening Canada's Environmental Community through International Regime Reform' (the EnviReform project) at the University of Toronto.

Carlton Thorne is a student in the combined Juris Doctor/Master's in International Relations Programme involving the Faculty of Law and the Department of Political Science at the University of Toronto.

Chris Tollefson is Associate Professor at the Faculty of Law of the University of Victoria and a member of Canada's NAAEC National Advisory Committee. He served on the board of the Sierra Legal Defence Fund and is a fellow of Leadership through Education and Development International (LEAD), both of which were social partners of 'Strengthening Canada's Environmental Community through International Regime Reform', the EnviReform research project. He was also a co-investigator of the project.

Michael J. Trebilcock is University Professor and Professor of Law and Economics at the University of Toronto. He was a co-investigator on 'Strengthening Canada's Environmental Community through International Regime Reform' (the EnviReform project) at the University of Toronto.

Scott Vaughan is director of the Office for Sustainable Development and Environment at the Organization of American States.

Alain Verbeke holds the McCaig Chair in Management at the Haskayne School of Business, University of Calgary, and is an Associate Fellow of Templeton College at the University of Oxford.

Preface and Acknowledgements

This is the eighth volume in Ashgate Publishing's Global Environmental Governance series, and continues the tradition of exploring the central issues and contemporary challenges of integrating trade liberalisation, environmental protection, and social cohesion in a globalising age. The book's insights come at a particularly timely moment, as the world embarks on the second decade of constructing an environmentally and socially sustainable global economy, based on the foundation of the World Summit on Sustainable Development in 2002 and following on from the World Trade Organization's Doha Development Agenda of that same year, as well as the subsequent ministerial meetings at Cancun and Hong Kong.

This volume is based on the work of the University of Toronto–based project on 'Strengthening Canada's Environmental Community Through International Regime Reform' (the EnviReform project). This project brought together experts from the scholarly, nongovernmental, business, labour, and government communities, to examine the role of civil society in global governance in the 21st century. They drew on a wealth of disciplinary traditions and fields: political science and political economy, law and regulation, economics, environmental studies, labour studies, and management studies.

This volumes draws heavily on the contributions of the EnviReform project's participating scholars and its several social partners. Many of the project's ten scholars are represented in this volume: Stephen Clarkson, Harriet Friedmann, Peter Hajnal, John Kirton, Sylvia Ostry, Louis Pauly, Alan Rugman, Michael Trebilcock, and Chris Tollefson, as well as collaborator Julie Soloway. Responding to their contributions are several of the project's social partners: Michael Cloghesy of the Centre patronal de l'environnement du Québec, Debbie Field of FoodShare, Ken Ogilvie of Pollution Probe, and Chris Tollefson in his capacity as a representative of the Sierra Legal Defence Fund of Canada as part of the broader, global Leadership for Environment and Development (LEAD) network. In addition, the volume benefits from the contributions from senior officials in the Canadian government, including the Honourable Bill Graham, former Minister of Foreign Affairs, and in the international organisation community.

Acknowledgements

In producing this volume, we have enjoyed the exceptional support of those who have contributed in many different ways. We are grateful in the first instance to the Social Sciences and Humanities Research Council of Canada, under its strategic grant program on 'Social Cohesion in a Globalizing Age', for its award to the

University of Toronto's EnviReform project.

We are further grateful to the Centre for International Studies at the Munk Centre, and its director, Professor Louis Pauly, who oversaw the EnviReform project, served as a member of its scholarly project team, and imparts wisdom and collegiality that have been a constant and indispensable source of sound advice and support. Beyond the University of Toronto, we recognise the valuable and vital part played in the EnviReform project by our social partners: the Commission for Environmental Cooperation, the Centre patronal de l'environnement du Québec, LEAD Canada, the Canadian Auto Workers, Pollution Probe, Foodshare, and the Sierra Legal Defence Fund. We are also pleased and proud to acknowledge the critical contribution of our international partner, the Woodrow Wilson Center for International Studies in Washington DC, under the leadership of its Director of Canadian Studies, David Biette.

Many others have contributed to the success of the EnviReform project. At the Centre for International Studies, Mary Lynne Bratti, Diane Granato, Nancy Fortin, Tina Lagopoulous, and Scott Bohaker worked tirelessly and efficiently in support of our work. Helen Walsh of ThinkContent has been instrumental in supporting our knowledge transfer efforts. In addition we were well served by many exceptional research assistants and student volunteers including Daniella Aburto Valle, Rachel Bendayan, Elizabeth Ben-Ishai, Gillian Clinton, Bob Papanikolaou, Caroline Saint-Mleux, and Amy Schwartz.

We owe a particular word of thanks to one individual, Madeline Koch, who as Managing Editor of the EnviReform project and the Global Environmental Governance Series worked with her usual superb skill and dedication to produce this book.

We are also most grateful to our colleague Professor Michael Donnelly, who oversaw the process of having this manuscript anonymously refereed. We are further grateful to the dedication, thoroughness, and insight of our anonymous referees, whose important comments have been taken fully into account.

As always we reserve a special word of thanks for Kirstin Howgate and her colleagues at Ashgate for recognising the value of producing this volume and for working so effectively, and with appropriate understanding, to ensure the smooth adoption and speedy publication of the manuscript.

We acknowledge, as always, the patience and support of our families as we laboured to organise our conference, produce our own initial papers, and convert rough drafts into finished chapters. Above all, we thank our students for their endless enthusiasm, constructive criticism, intellectual contributions and challenges, and continuing commitment to the causes dealt with in this book. It is to them that we dedicate this work.

John J. Kirton and Peter I. Hajnal
January 2006

List of Abbreviations and Acronyms

4D	Dossiers et débats pour le développement durable
AFL-CIO	American Federation of Labor and Congress of Industrial Organizations
AFN	Assembly of First Nations (Canada)
APEC	Asia-Pacific Economic Co-operation
APR	African personal representatives of the G8 leaders
ATTAC	Association pour une Taxation des Transactions financières pour l'Aide aux Citoyens (Association for a Taxation of Financial Transactions and for Assistance to Citizens)
BIAC	Business and Industry Advisory Committee of the Organisation for Economic Co-operation and Development
BIT	bilateral investment treaty
BP	British Petroleum
BSE	bovine spongiform encephalopathy (mad cow disease)
CAAF	contrat d'approvisionnement et d'aménagement forestier (forest supply and management agreement)
CADTM	Comité pour l'annulation de la dette du tiers-monde
CAFTA	Central American Free Trade Agreement
CAP	Common Agricultural Policy
CAPs	community advisory panels
CBD	Convention on Biological Diversity
CCFD	Comité catholique contre la faim et pour le développement
CEC	Commission for Environmental Cooperation
CEMSA	Marvin Roy Feldman Karpa
CEO	chief executive officer
CETLAC	Centro de Estudios y Taller Laboral, A.C.
CG18	Consultative Group of Eighteen
CIA	United States Central Intelligence Agency
CIDA	Canadian International Development Agency
CITES	Convention on International Trade in Endangered Species
CITT	Canadian International Trade Tribunal
CLC	Commission for Labor Cooperation
CMA	Chemical Manufacturers' Association (United States)
COCOPA	Comisión de Concordia y Pacificación (Peace and Concord Commission of Mexico)
CONGO	Conference of Non-Governmental Organizations in Consultative Relationship with the United Nations
CPC	Canada Post Corporation

CRID	Centre de Recherche et d'Information pour le Développement
CTE	Committee on Trade and Environment (of the World Trade Organization)
CTM	Congreso de Trabajadores Mexicanos (Confederation of Mexican Workers)
CUFTA	Canada-U.S. Free Trade Agreement
CWGs	committees and working groups
DATA	Debt AIDS Trade Africa
DEA	Drug Enforcement Agency
DFAIT	Department of Foreign Affairs and International Trade (Canada)
DOT	United States Department of Transportation
ECOSOC	United Nations Economic and Social Council
ENGO	environmental nongovernmental organisation
EPA	United States Environmental Protection Agency
ESAF	enhanced structural adjustment facility
FAO	Food and Agriculture Organization
FAT	Frente Auténtico del Trabajo (Authentic Workers' Front)
FBI	United States Federal Bureau of Investigation
FDA	United States Food and Drug Administration
FDI	foreign direct investment
FIM	Montreal International Forum/Forum international de Montréal
FIPA	Inter-Parliamentary Forum of the Americas
FOE	Friends of the Earth
FOGS	Functioning of the GATT System
FSA	firm-specific advantage
F/T	foreign to total sales
FTAA	Free Trade Agreement of the Americas
G6B Summit	Group of Six Billion People's Summit
G7	Group of Seven (G8 without Russia)
G8	Group of Eight (France, United States, United Kingdom, Russia, Germany, Japan, Italy, Canada)
G10	Group of Ten (G8 plus Belgium, the Netherlands, Sweden, Switzerland, plus the Bank for International Settlements, the European Commission, the International Monetary Fund, and the Organisation for Economic Co-operation and Development)
G77	Group of Seventy-Seven
G90	Group of Ninety (the poorest developing countries)
GATS	General Agreement on Trade in Services
GATT	General Agreement on Tariffs and Trade
GDP	gross domestic product
GHG	greenhouse gas
GMO	genetically modified organism
GNP	gross national product
HIPC	heavily indebted poor country
ICFTU	International Confederation of Free Trade Unions

ICSID	International Centre for the Settlement of Disputes
ICT	information and communication technology
IFI	international financial institution
IGO	intergovernmental organisation
ILO	International Labour Organization
IMF	International Monetary Fund
ISO	International Organization for Standardization
ITC	International Trade Canada
ITO	International Trade Organization
JPAC	Joint Public Advisory Committee of the Commission for Environmental Cooperation
LTSS	Land Transportation Standards Subcommittee
MAI	Multilateral Agreement on Investment
MDG	Millennium Development Goal
MEA	multilateral environmental agreement
MEPP	Middle East Peace Process
MFN	most-favoured-nation
MMT	methylcyclopentadienyl manganese tricarbonyl
MNC	multinational corporation
MOU	memorandum of understanding
MSF	Médecins Sans Frontières
MTBE	methyl tertiary butyl ether
NAAEC	North American Agreement on Environmental Cooperation
NAALC	North American Agreement on Labour Cooperation
NAEWG	North American Energy Working Group
NATO	North American Treaty Organization
NAFTA	North American Free Trade Agreement
NEPAD	New Partnership for Africa's Development
NFU	National Farmers Union (Canada)
NGO	nongovernmental organisation
NIEO	New International Economic Order
NLRB	National Labor Relations Board (United States)
NT	national treatment
NTB	non-tariff barrier
OAS	Organization of American States
OECD	Organisation for Economic Co-operation and Development
OLF	other legitimate factors
PCB	polychlorinated biphenyl
Pemex	Petróleos Mexicanos
POPs	persistent organic pollutants
PRI	Partido Revolucionario Institucional
PRSP	Poverty Reduction Stategy Paper
RMALC	Red Mexicana de Acción Frente al Libre Comercio (Mexican Action Network on Free Trade)
RCMP	Royal Canadian Mounted Police

Rio+10	Johannesburg World Summit for Sustainable Development (ten years after the World Summit for Sustainable Development at Rio de Janeiro)
SAF	structural adjustment facility
SAL	structural adjustment loan
SBU	strategic business unit
SDR	special drawing rights
SE	Secretaría de la Economía (Mexico)
SMEs	small and medium-sized enterprises
SPAM	Sommet pour un autre monde (Summit for Another World)
SPS	sanitary and phytosanitary measures
STRM	Sindicato de Telefonistas de la República Mexicana (Telecommunications Union of Mexico)
TBT	technical barriers to trade
TCG #1	Transportation Consultative Group on Cross-Border Operations and Facilitation
TRIMS	Trade-Related Investment Measures
TRIPS	Trade-Related Aspects of Intellectual Property Rights
TOES	The Other Economic Summit
TPRM	Trade Policy Review Mechanism
TUAC	Trade Union Advisory Committee of the Organisation for Economic Co-operation and Development
UE	United Electrical, Radio, and Machine Workers of America
UNCED	United Nations Conference on Environment and Development
UNCITRAL	United Nations Commission on International Trade Law
UNCTAD	United Nations Conference on Trade and Development
UNDP	United Nations Development Programme
UNECE	United Nations Economic Commission for Europe
UNEP	United Nations Environment Programme
UNESCO	United Nations Educational, Social, and Cultural Organization
UNFCCC	United Nations Framework Convention on Climate Change
UNGA	United Nations General Assembly
UNSC	United Nations Security Council
UNT	Unión Nacional de Trabajadores (National Workers' Union)
UPS	United States Postal Service
USTR	United States Trade Representative
WHO	World Health Organization
WMD	weapons of mass destruction
WMO	World Meteorological Organization
WSSD	World Summit on Sustainable Development
WTO	World Trade Organization
WWF	World Wildlife Fund

PART I:
INTRODUCTION

Chapter 1

Introduction, Observations, and Conclusions

John J. Kirton and Peter I. Hajnal

The Civil Society Challenge to Global Governance

As the 20th century gave way to the 21st, the established, state-centric, international institutions of global governance faced a new rebellion and, potentially, a revolution from the streets. The 25 000 protestors at the 1999 ministerial meeting of the World Trade Organization (WTO) in Seattle, followed by the 250 000 protestors at the G8's 2001 Genoa Summit, dramatically demonstrated civil society's fervent rejection of the old order and its firm demand for greater democratic influence and participation in the international institutions linking economic, environmental, and social concerns. The protestors at the Quebec City Summit of the Americas in April 2001 (whose number has been estimated between 20 000 and 60 000), and the many thousands in Calgary for the G8's June 2002 Kananaskis Summit and in the vicinity of the June 2003 Evian Summit, showed that Canadians, as well as Americans and Europeans, were equally engaged in this cause and that both governors and civil society activists could move beyond violent confrontation toward civil dialogue and creative responses to the new challenges they faced together. Yet the September 11 terrorist attacks on America, and the new concern with national security that followed, led to a diminished civil society presence at some global governance conferences (although not others such as the WTO ministerial meeting in Cancun in September 2003). Indeed, at the U.S.-hosted G8 Summit in Sea Island, Georgia, in June 2004, civil society had virtually disappeared.

Has civil society's growing demand for direct influence and involvement in the institutionalised centres of global governance been a passing fad that has foundered in the face of the Westphalian fundamentals once again rendered visible by the shock of the attacks on 11 September 2001? Or, in this 21st-century world, in which nation-states are more vulnerable and old intergovernmental organisations are more likely to fail in meeting human security needs, has September 11 merely stalled, or temporarily diverted, the rising presence of civil society as a direct participant in institutionalised global governance?

Until now, the traditionalists have dominated the discourse on these questions. Their immediate reaction to the proliferation of mass protests had been to insist that, in the work of intergovernmental institutions, citizens should only be involved at home within their sovereign, national jurisdictions. Reinforcing this argument was the claim that democracy could now be better practised at home on a global scale, given the post–Cold War spread of democratic practice to many formerly undemocratic regimes that now accept the rule of law, basic norms of public participation, and dialogue and participation between government and civil society. At the same time, at the multilateral level, there arose a new generation of much more powerful multilateral institutions such as the WTO, created in 1994, as well as a reinforced International Monetary Fund (IMF) and a growing G8 system that raised the locus of decisions on critical trade, finance, environmental, and social concerns – and the relationships among them – up to the international level. Here, at the insistence of traditionalists and to the dismay of critics, dialogue, direction setting, and decision making must take place largely in closed sessions, often among unelected officials, following the institutionalised processes, principles, and procedures of old. At the regional level, the North American Free Trade Agreement (NAFTA) was born in 1994 as a traditional intergovernmental trade agreement, with little significant citizen participation to guarantee direct democracy in a growing North American community and to find a better balance among the economic, environmental, and social values its citizens share. Indeed, it was largely left to the subsequently negotiated side arrangement of the North American Agreement on Environmental Cooperation (NAAEC) and the creation of the Commission for Environmental Cooperation (CEC) to experiment with more innovative mechanisms for civil society involvement. Only at the national level, as many issues long considered local in nature assumed transnational dimensions in a rapidly globalising era, did a rich repertoire of innovative, well-developed techniques for multi-stakeholder, consensus-oriented, democratic decision-making arise within communities to connect civil society and governors, to forward the values of sustainability shared by both. The traditionalists' argument, and the continuing constraints of Westphalianism, seemed fully confirmed.

Yet such a conclusion may be misleading, for it largely flows from those looking in the wrong places. While the vigorous and sometimes violent mass demonstrations at G8 summits and WTO ministerials may have disappeared, this may reflect in large part the ability of both sides to develop more institutionalised and effective ways to come together peacefully in an ultimately shared cause. Moreover, the hard law multilateral organisations born by the Westphalian formula, such as the WTO, built on the foundation of the General Agreement on Tariffs and Trade (GATT), may be the wrong place to look for rapid innovation in civil society's incorporation in global governance. Rather, apart from the limited advances made long ago by the International Labour Organization (ILO) and the Organisation for Economic Co-operation and Development (OECD), it may be the more flexible, informal intergovernmental institutions that are best able to adapt to the new demands and to move from a monolithic Westphalian world to a multi-stakeholder one. Even in older, more traditional intergovernmental organisations, there has been a move from formal to more effective informal arrangements. And at a time when the global is ever more tightly connected to the local, it may be that the wealth of innovation at the regional, national, and local levels is increasing, and will move faster and more fully to bring civil society into the institutions and processes of global governance as a whole. In short, civil society may already have shifted emphasis from the noisy outside to the effective inside of institutionalised global governance in the 21st century.

Purpose

This book explores how civil society has moved into institutionalised global governance. It examines the role now being played by civil society actors in the international institutions that most affect the presence of economic, ecological, and social sustainability in today's world. It analyses how civil society and global governors have, could, and should come together in new ways to improve the links, the balance, and the synergies among economic, environmental, and social values. It thus has three central purposes.

Its first purpose is descriptive: to describe and critically evaluate the rich recent record of what has been done. It thus analyses many new processes of civil society engagement that have been introduced at the local, regional, and global levels to identify how – and how well or badly – they have worked, particularly for those in the trade and environmental communities.

Its second purpose is explanatory: to assess why some new processes have developed and flourished and thus what could be done under varying conditions to strengthen the productive partnerships between civil society and global governors. To construct such an inventory, the book draws on the extensive record of existing practices in the local, regional, and multilateral spheres as well as community-based alternatives. It highlights those that have worked well, the conditions that have fostered their success, and the possibilities of their adoption by other institutions at similar or different jurisdictional levels.

The book's third purpose is prescriptive: to identify what should be done, based on a critical assessment of how particular mechanisms for civil society participation in global governance have enhanced or impeded specific desired economic, environmental, and political outcomes.

The Contribution

This volume thus seeks to contribute to the evolving scholarly debate on the role of civil society in global governance and sustainability in several ways. The first is by directly addressing and assessing the involvement and impact of civil society organisations and movements on global governance and sustainability at the level of intergovernmental institutions.

Thus far, the proliferating literature on civil society's place in international relations in an era of globalisation has focussed largely on the longstanding issue, which emerged in the 1970s, of whether the world is witnessing 'sovereignty at bay' and a 'retreat of the state' (Angell 1969; Brown 1974; Mansback, Ferguson, and Lampert 1976; Vernon 1971; Strange 1996). That debate led to a second about whether the beneficiaries of a diminished state have been the hard law, multilateral organisations that have moved global governance beyond the nation-state, or the various civil society actors and networks that have rendered both forms of formal, hierarchical, organised Westphalian-grounded governance obsolescent in the face of new problems and empowered citizens (Haas 1968).

More recently, the end of the Cold War and advent of globalisation in the 1990s have revived interest in the role of civil society in international relations, and extended that interest to include global governance as a whole (Scholte 2000). Scholars have thus explored whether civil society networks have been increasingly effective in altering nation-state behaviour on international issues either within their own national political processes or through the 'boomerang effect' of going abroad to bring international pressure to bear on unresponsive governments at home (Keck and Sikkink 1998). They have also broadened their dependent variables to include the impact of civil society and social movements not just on sovereign states but also on large-scale processes of authority and behaviour centred in economic actors such as corporations and consumers, or empowered individuals themselves (Wapner 1995). Scholars and citizens have also concentrated on how a new generation of international institutions with supranational and even constitutional characteristics has become an effective centre of governance for a broad array of economic, environmental, and social policy fields that were once the preserve of national politics and that have thus eroded the vibrant democratic debates and processes that lay within (Clarkson 2002). This attention has been especially evident in the trade field, with the emergence in the 1990s of more powerful international institutions with a wide-ranging reach, starting with the WTO, NAFTA, and the many other regional and bilateral free trade arrangements that have come in their wake.

Thus far, these claims about the growing relevance of civil society have evoked the predictable counterarguments. Some have argued that even in fields where civil society influence should have flourished, notably the global governance of the internet, great power governments still prevail over the most empowered civil society experts and economic interests, and over the longest established multilateral organisations such as the International Telecommunication Union (Drezner 2004). Others have pointed to the way in which civil society engagement with the states and secretariats at the centre of international governance can lead to co-optation as civil society activists seeking influence come to adopt the technical rational knowledge and discourse that keep a neo-liberal corporate order in place (Ford 2003). Yet neither side of this debate has looked beyond civil society's impact on the principles, policies, or broader regimes established by international institutions. The question is not raised of whether civil society is acquiring a more institutionalised, legitimate, and influential involvement in the ongoing operation and management governance of the international institutions themselves.

Has civil society gone from being an actor on the outside, pressuring or bypassing the institutionalised centres of global governance, to being a more equal actor on the inside of the international institutions that are increasingly the source of effective global governance? In addressing this question, scholars have thus far largely looked

at a very limited array of venerable historical examples. The influential involvement of civil society in international governance dates back to the medieval era, when the intelligentsia from the universities were given a vote, alongside princes and bishops, at the Council of Constance that ended in 1415 (Wight 1977, 131–133). In the modern period, the engagement of transnational advocacy movements in international conferences arose in 1907, when the International Council of Women and another private international organisation were received by the president of the Second Peace Conference at the Hague (Keck and Sikkink 1998, 55).[1] Then came the ILO and, much later, the OECD, with their Trade Union Advisory Committee (TUAC) and Business and Industry Advisory Committee (BIAC) respectively. Here, however, there has emerged no 'green' environmental advisory committee alongside those 'blue' and 'red' bodies, despite the environmental civil society and intergovernmental organisations that have proliferated since the 1970s. Moreover, recent innovations relevant to environmentalists, such as the World Bank's Independent Inspection Unit, suggest that civil society remains largely an add-on to the major multilateral organisations established in the distant past.

This limited record has left the overall impression that civil society's direct place in the centre of global governance has remained minimal, and will remain so. This conclusion is reinforced by the relative impermeability of the old multilateral institutions in the face of the formidable pressures of the rapid globalisation of the 1990s, global financial crises that showed the inadequacies of the old multilateral organisations, and new demands to bring the values of environmental and social cohesion into the trade and financial liberalisation organisations of old. The shock of September 11, the new premium on national security, and the revival of the 'garrison state' all suggest that at the outset of the 21st century, the role of civil society has been further reduced. The virtual absence of any civil society activists at the 2004 G8 Sea Island Summit, in sharp contrast to the quarter million who gathered at the G8 Summit in Genoa three years earlier, seems to show that civil society itself, as well as its influence, has been forced out of the centres where effective global governance takes place.

This book challenges this conventional wisdom. It looks well beyond the few traditional hard law bodies and models from the faraway past to survey the rich experience and experimentation occurring across the much broader array of international institutions that have been newly constructed or reformed to meet the demands of the rapidly globalising 21st century. Its first focus is on the major economic bodies for trade and finance, notably the WTO, the IMF, and NAFTA, which were created or reformed in the 1990s with few visible innovations to include civil society, despite the rising visibility and voice of civil society. It also concentrates on those major environmental bodies that have become newly important in the 1990s, notably the governance centres of the United Nations Framework Convention on Climate Change (UNFCCC) and its Kyoto Protocol, and the Food and Agriculture Organization (FAO), where the inclusion of civil society similarly seems slight.

The second contribution of this volume is to explore the place of civil society in global governance not only in the fixed, formal, hard law multilateral organisations

of the UN galaxy, but also in the more informal, soft law, intergovernmental institutions that have arisen since (Kirton and Trebilcock 2004). Here particular attention is given to the G8 major market democracies created in 1975 and to the Codex Alimentarius, which has emerged as an important centre for governing global food. Such informal bodies should have greater flexibility to involve civil society actors, especially when these bodies are dominated by democratic states with open societies that need to respond to their citizens' demands, not just for generic voice and representation, but also for better ways to meet their new human security needs. Since the 1990s, starting with its new Global Information Society ministerial forum, the G8 has pioneered several new multi-stakeholder bodies in which national governments, intergovernmental organisations, and civil society activists from business, nongovernmental organisations (NGOs), and other component communities have come together as equals to met new needs. Starting at the Okinawa Summit in 2000, the G8 has also attempted to include civil society more directly in its leaders-level forum. While more recent summits have made little visible progress in this regard, it remains to be seen whether the inclusion of civil society by the G8 or other informal intergovernmental institutions is a process that has been slowed down or even stopped by September 11, or channelled in different ways.

A third contribution of this volume is to look below the multilateral level to the regional, to explore the interface between civil society and international governance in the more restricted domains where greater innovation and experimentation can take place. Here the North American experience in the 1990s is particularly interesting, and potentially relevant on a global scale (Kirton and Maclaren 2002). To be sure, NAFTA was a traditional trade agreement, in which the three sovereign governments of the U.S., Canada, and Mexico resisted the creation of an international organisation that could constrain their freedom. But they did create a wealth of official-level bodies with an ability and incentive to reach out to involve civil society stakeholders in their work (Kirton and Fernandez de Castro 1997). Moreover, they added pioneering investment provisions that enabled aggrieved corporations direct access to an international governance institution to sue national governments, with NAFTA's sovereign national governments unable to stop them in any way. Furthermore, NAFTA produced the NAAEC, which gave environmental NGOs (ENGOs) a similar if more limited ability to bring complaints against their national governments. It also came with a regional organisation, the CEC, which created the Joint Public Advisory Committee (JPAC) as part of its governance structure and included civil society actors in all parts of its work. As these features of the NAFTA model have been infused into the many other free trade agreements signed by the U.S., Canada, and Mexico with a growing array of partners, they have acquired an operational and potential significance for global governance as a whole.

A fourth contribution of this volume is to connect the global and the local, in a reciprocal two-way flow. The book examines how the global affects the local, by tracing the effects of the mechanisms for civil society inclusion in international governance on the efficacy of civil society actors, individual citizens, and social cohesion at the local level. It also examines how the local affects the global, by

exploring how processes of civil society and government inclusion at the local level can serve as an influential model for governance arrangements at the global level. In doing so, the volume examines not only how existing models of global governance inhibit democratic participation and social cohesion at the national and local levels, but also how innovations can move upward to make the institutions of global governance themselves more democratic, legitimate, and effective.

A fifth contribution of this work is to broaden the concept of civil society to include the activities of individual citizens beyond NGOs, other civil society organisations, or social movements that are aroused to take an interest in issues that affect them locally and engage in global governance, on an *ad hoc* basis, by influencing the functioning of the global governance institutions themselves. Thus far, the literature has offered a wide array of conceptions of what civil society is at its core and what the category contains. Some focus on the elite business, professional, research, or association groups and empowered individuals that assemble at intergovernmental conferences, while others include the radical, oppositional social movements enduringly devoted to broad causes of social justice on a global scale (Ford 2003). Still others regard civil society as 'that arena of social engagement which exists above the individual yet below the state' in a 'complex network of economic, social, and cultural practices based on friendship, family, the market, and voluntary affiliation' (Wapner 1995, 313). In these views, civil society becomes global civil society through 'the conscious association of actors, in physically separated locations, who link themselves together in networks for particular and social purposes' (Lipschutz 1992, 393), or through 'associational life which exists above the individual and below the state but also across national boundaries' (Wapner 1995, 313). This volume extends the meaning to include ordinary citizens with *ad hoc*, local concerns, whose activities have an impact on international governance regardless of whether they consciously form or use transnational networks for their cause. Global civil society thus includes ordinary citizens coming together at a local level within a state to use international centres of governance in ways that will make a difference to their own and others' daily lives. International institutions that include individual citizens and are directly accessible to them for help with their local problems are part of what makes civil society global, too.

The Approach

To make these contributions, this volume assembles the work of leading scholars from several disciplines and fully combines it with the insights of practitioners in the trade and environment community at the local, regional, and multilateral levels. Its chapters represent the scholarly research and results of the ongoing dialogue among scholars and community partners in the EnviReform project based at the University of Toronto, which explored ways to enhance social cohesion through the reform of the major international institutions for trade and financial liberalisation, and environmental protection. The project featured a dialogue among the research project's ten scholarly investigators, their seven community partners from critical constituencies across Canada, and leading individuals from the new generation of policy makers involved in the key institutions of global governance, which was extended through association with the Woodrow Wilson International Center for Scholars in Washington DC.

This book thus combines the work of several scholarly disciplines directly related to the subject, notably those of political science, economics, law, sociology, and geography. It integrates their contributions with those of community partner practitioners from several, similarly relevant professional fields, notably business, law, NGOs, international organisations, and national governments at the official and ministerial level. The authors from both the scholarly and practitioner communities are united by a common concern with the Canadian experience, both as it highlights the impact of the current global governance and civil society practices relating to sustainability and as it forms a foundation for securing desirable reforms. Yet they also bring a rich array of international experience through their work with a broad range of international organisations, countries, and civil society. The book thus unites as equals the work of scholars and practitioners, members of civil society and their governors, and Canadians and their fellow citizens of the global community as a whole.

In keeping with this commitment, the book contains the work of scholars and practitioners alike in full formal chapters, and contains their contributions throughout the book, so that each may bring his or her insights to bear on a common issue. It opens with this introductory chapter by two scholars and ends with a chapter by one of Canada's leading practitioners of international affairs. While the contributions of the practitioners usually do not flow from the formal research programs and methods that are standard for the scholarly community, their operational knowledge, intimate familiarity with the social, economic, and political worlds, critical perspectives, and sense of the possible are integral, important, and innovative features of this work.

The Analyses

To conduct its analysis, this book undertakes a multilevel examination of the civil society–global government nexus. It begins at the local level, focussing in Part II on 'Local and Transboundary Networks and Co-operation'. It then moves to the regional level, examining it in 'North American and Hemispheric Experiences' in Part III. From there, it considers the international level. Part IV focusses on 'The Multilateral Trade and Finance Systems'; Part V moves to the comprehensive, fully global level with a discussion of 'The G8 and United Nations Systems'. In keeping with the commitment to combine the insights of scholars and practitioners, the volume concludes, in Part VI, with a contribution from the Honourable Bill Graham, who, as a scholar of the international trade system, a parliamentarian specialising in international affairs and a former Cabinet minister for foreign affairs and defence, has been at the forefront of understanding and enhancing the connection between citizens in civil society and governors engaged in global governance.

Beginning at the local level, in Chapter 2, 'Engaging Local Communities in Environmental Protection with Competitiveness: Community Advisory Panels in Canada and the United States', Virginia Maclaren, Angela Morris, and Sonia Labatt explore the similarities and differences in the effectiveness of the roles played by private sector citizen advisory committees (CACs) to the chemical industry in the U.S. and Canada under the Responsible Care programme, which probably has the largest number of CACs of any industrial sector. Given the paucity of empirical research on such committees in the private sector, the authors draw on the literature on such committees in the public sector to identify factors that may influence effectiveness in the private sector. They also consider the regulatory and policy environment and other contextual factors that can lead to differences in the effectiveness of community advisory panels (CAPs) in the U.S. and Canada. To obtain data, they conducted a survey that secured responses from 56 community members and 17 company members representing 15 Canadian CAPs, and followed the results up with semi-structured interviews with four key informants.

The results show very similar views from the two countries and from company and community representatives on CAP effectiveness in communicating with the larger community, as only about 40 percent of respondents in each case felt that CAPs were effective. However, Canadian community members gave higher evaluations of CAC influence on corporate environmental performance (75 percent) and on health and safety (63 percent) than their American counterparts (43 percent) had in an earlier study on a combined measure of health, safety, and environment. Company representatives from both countries responded similarly, at substantially lower rates than their community member counterparts. On a third measure of effectiveness – a CAP's ability to represent a diversity of community viewpoints – Canadian community members give a high 80 percent rating and U.S. members gave a low 57 percent rating, just as Canadian company members give a high of 71 percent and U.S. members a low of 45 percent. Canadian CAPs have fewer industry group and more environmental group representatives than American ones. On the measure of making the company aware of community concerns, more Canadian community members (89 percent) than American ones (77 percent) felt that CAPs are effective, while three quarters of company representatives from both Canada and the U.S. felt that CAPs are effective or very effective in raising awareness. The respondents suggested that differences in the political, regulatory, and cultural context in the two countries were less important causes of differences in the effectiveness of the two sets of CAPs than CAP specific factors, above all the commitment of the plant manager to the CAP and his or her influence on the diversity of membership on the committee.

In Chapter 3, 'Precaution Versus Sound Science: Risk Discourses and Civil Society Participation in International Food Safety Negotiations', Diane Bartlett and Harriet Friedmann explore the risk contest over food safety in international organisations for trade and environment. They focus on how much the discourse on risk and uncertainty has created opportunities for public participation in the decision-making process, or restricted it to so-called experts. The authors introduce theories of risk and discourse, explore the institutional field of inter-state and inter-issue negotiations created in the 1990s, and examine the key terms of precaution, sound science, and substantial equivalence. Furthermore, they consider the implications of the current contest for the future of public participation in decisions about food safety.

Bartlett and Friedmann conclude that discourse contests over regulatory frames for genetically modified foods, notably 'risk' and 'precaution', have continued into the 21st century. Here the trade community and the U.S., as the leading exporter of agricultural biotechnology, prefer the concept of substantial equivalence, while environmentalists and the European Union, as the leading importer, remain attached to the precautionary principle. At issue in this standoff is the very process of taking risk decisions. Here, the contested risks of introducing genetically modified crops into the environment and food supply may lead from 'reflexive scientisation' to a 'reflective democracy' with greater political involvement by citizens in whether and how to introduce, manage, and evaluate the effects of genetically modified seeds and foods. Even as governments argue endlessly in international organisations, corporations are producing a 'practical harmonisation' of standards by spreading plantings of genetically modified crops throughout the world. The resulting widespread contamination and effects on human bodies and food supplies raise potentially greater risks than any so far faced by human societies, and thus the possibility that the environment and the Cartagena Protocol on Biosafety will prevail and trade will accommodate the EU framing of precaution.

In Chapter 4, 'Continentalism from Below? Trinational Mobilisation among Labour Unions, Environmental Organisations, and Indigenous Peoples', Stefanie J. Bowles, Ian Thomas MacDonald, Jennifer Leah Mullen, and Stephen Clarkson ask whether the trade liberalisation and extensive international institutional development brought by NAFTA have produced a corresponding inclusion of civil society in the new continental governance. They explore, in turn, the differing effects of NAFTA on mobilising three distinct categories of sociopolitical actors – organised labour, the environmental movement, and indigenous communities – that often shared a common opposition to trade liberalisation but did not all share the same reaction to NAFTA. By examining their disparate programmatic responses in relation to their differing ideological perspectives, organisational structures, and social capacities, these three case studies explore whether there is indeed any real North American governance from below.

Bowles and her colleagues find that NAFTA has had adverse but uneven effects on civil society. Each sector's reactions reflect its respective ideology and socioeconomic capacity. Organised labour, in particular, with its ideology and economic incentives of trilateral solidarity, an autonomous social base and much greater financial resources, has the greatest potential for exercising governance from below at the continental level.

In Chapter 5, 'The Emergence of Environmental Movement–Government Partnerships', Ken Ogilvie, the executive director of Pollution Probe, reflects in turn on the evolution of the environmental movement and environmental or sustainability principles, the international experience of Pollution Probe in relation to the

International Organization for Standardization (ISO) 14000 series of environmental management standards, and the experience under NAFTA in North America.

Ogilvie shows how the environmental movement began at the very local level in the 1960s, with Pollution Probe starting as a student group at the University of Toronto concerned primarily with issues of garbage and the creation of environment ministries in provincial and national governments. On that foundation, the institutions and defining principles of global environmental governance were progressively constructed, with the 1970s bringing the Stockholm Conference, the United Nations Environment Programme (UNEP) and the polluter pays principle, the 1980s the Brundtland Commission, the principle of sustainable development and the 1992 United Nations Conference on Environment and Development (UNCED), and the subsequent decade the struggle for the precautionary principle in a world in which no commensurate advances in institutionalised global governance have taken place. In practice, Pollution Probe has thus focussed its international energies on the multi-stakeholder, private sector–driven ISO, trying to create an NGO task group to bring an environmental voice to balance that of business on Technical Committee 207, which oversees the development of the ISO 14000 series of environmental management systems standards. Despite the limited involvement of NGOs, the open architecture for civil society involvement of the ISO has enabled environmentalists to be very effective on a few standards. This experience suggests that they should have a major role in the mechanisms for measuring, monitoring, and verifying greenhouse gas (GHG) emissions under the UNFCCC. It further suggests that even on a regional basis, as in the NAFTA negotiations, the mobilisation of a transnational environmental movement could be compromised by deep differences in national political culture, with the consensus-based, multi-stakeholder, inclusive Canadian policy-making system and style clashing with the legalistic, adversarial approach that prevails in the United States. The way forward, on both the national and international levels, is thus to assemble horizontal multi-stakeholder coalitions in which civil society organisations from the environmental, consumer, labour, indigenous, business, and even local government communities can come together in a common cause, rather than creating coalitions of different environmental groups.

In Chapter 6, 'Local Nongovernmental Organisations, Global Governance, and the Challenges of a Global Movement for Sustainable Food and Agriculture', Debbie Field, the Director of FoodShare, asks in what ways have social movements built alliances and effectively contested the global neo-liberal agenda in the post-NAFTA period. In seeking the answer, she examines, in turn, the success of some social movements in building new grassroots alliances at the regional level in regard to NAFTA and increasing globalisation, relevant developments in agriculture and food movements, and the organisation of effective resistance movements for the future.

Field argues that it was programmatic unity, more than organisational capacity or material resources, that led labour, in contrast to the environmental and indigenous movements, to organise cross-border, regional resistance to NAFTA. While NAFTA promoted greater transnational networking for all social movements, the environmental movement still needs to develop a common cause among local citizens around simple ideas such as no war, clean water, and safe food. In the realm of food, such an approach has been pursued by the local organisation FoodShare and by the Via Campesina, a global network of such organisations. The latter succeeded in helping stop the liberalising agenda at the WTO's 1999 Seattle ministerial meeting and has helped stop the spread of genetically modified foods and seeds. The key causes of success in such cases, and in future struggles, are the establishment of organisations and campaigns from below at the most local level, popular, and multi-class support from 75 percent of the public, international, and professional organisational capacity, and strong regulatory frameworks in government and the private and voluntary sectors.

Part III opens with Chapter 7, 'A North American Community of Law with Minimal Institutions: NAFTA's Committees and Working Groups'. Sarah Davidson Ladly, Carlton Thorne, and Stephen Clarkson focus on the 30 trilateral 'micro bureaucracies' known as committees and working groups, which were designed to oversee the application of NAFTA's various chapters. They examine the behaviour of these administrative bodies in order to make some inferences about the viability of the bold proposal for a community of law without major institutions for building the next generation of North American governance. The authors discuss the theory behind the bodies, and the ideals embodied within them, as well as the past and current status, activities, and dynamics of these largely invisible entities, and how this first experiment in a minimally institutionalised community reflects on the prospects of a post–September 11 attempt to achieve another grand bargain of continental integration without structures.

They find that these bodies have been largely underused and are relatively insignificant as continental institutions, due to the incongruity between their trilateral, professional, and symmetrical nature and the bilateral, political, and asymmetrical reality of Canada's and Mexico's relationship with the United States. Regional issues are, in fact, bilateral and thus inappropriate for the trinational bodies; the political stakes are too high to be left to apolitical, technocratic institutions based on formal legal equality, which can deal only with low-level, low-interest disputes, rather than those that require political sensitivity, flexible processes, and compromise. Their experience suggests that, while a community of law can deal with some of the problems that currently dominate the American agenda, such as terrorism, it cannot deal with the broader issues that lie ahead.

In Chapter 8, 'Regional Multinational Corporations and Triad Strategy', Alan M. Rugman and Alain Verbeke look directly at the business sector in a regional and global context. They focus on inherently international multinational corporations (MNCs) that serve as flagship firms. These firms lead, direct, co-ordinate, and manage the value-added activities of partner firms in a business network, including key suppliers, key customers, and the non-business infrastructure, involving key components such as professional associations, research centres, and educational institutions. The authors examine the extent to which the clusters of flagship firms are regionally based, in North America, the EU, and Asia, the significance of MNCs in various sectors, the regional location of business networks, the possibilities of global corporate strategies as opposed to regional ones for MNCs, and how firms and service organisations for small, open economies fit into these spatial clusters. Rugman and Verbeke conclude that the majority of even the most 'global' MNCs actually operate on a triad-centred regional basis. Indeed, only six of the world's 20 most global MNCs are truly global with a global strategy. The rest are MNCs based in their home sector of the triad and need regional strategies. With such key actors and their networks so regionally centred, civil society's relationship to regional governance, rather than global governance, should be a primary concern.

In Chapter 9, 'NAFTA's Chapter 11: Investor Protection, Integration, and the Public Interest', Julie Soloway examines the area of NAFTA that most directly and innovatively gave MNCs a major place in international governance. NAFTA's Chapter 11 contains provisions on investment that define the treatment of an investment or investor from one signatory country by another and allow the affected investor to initiate an international dispute-settlement proceeding should a signatory adopt a measure that breaches an obligation contained in the chapter. Despite the predictability for business and the economic growth that these rules were designed to encourage, they are being challenged due to their perceived effects in inhibiting government regulation for environmental and social protection. Soloway evaluates the claim that Chapter 11 has undermined environmental regulation in North America.

She concludes that, for the most part, the concern has been overstated. To date, NAFTA's Chapter 11 has not threatened the progress of environmental regulation in North America. Rather, the jurisprudence of Chapter 11 shows that it respects the state's 'police powers' – its right to protect the environment, consumers, and public health. The cases decided under Chapter 11 during NAFTA's first eight years did not restrict governments' ability to act in the public interest. Yet certain changes to the process may still be warranted in order to address some of the weaknesses of the current institutional architecture. In particular, there is a need for greater transparency, openness, public and NGO participation, and appellate review, and even the creation of a new NAFTA institution in the form of a permanent appellate body similar to that of the WTO.

In Chapter 10, 'NAFTA's Chapter 11: The Case for Reform', Chris Tollefson closely scrutinises three key elements in Soloway's analysis: that Chapter 11 has had no demonstrable chilling effect on regulatory activity; that, in any event, regulators have no legitimate reason to be concerned about the impact of Chapter 11 on their activities; and that Chapter 11 jurisprudence shows that the chapter poses no real threat to legitimate, non-discriminatory environmental protection measures. To assess these claims, he examines the architecture and jurisprudence of Chapter 11 and considers in some detail the tribunal decision in *Metalclad*.

Tollefson concludes that the discretion that Chapter 11 places in tribunals is ill defined and too broad and that this discretion has already led, in several cases, to highly questionable interpretive results. He concludes that as momentum builds for reforming Chapter 11, especially in the U.S., Canada must redouble its efforts to ensure that investor rights do not unnecessarily compromise domestic policy autonomy, whether under NAFTA or in future trade and investment agreements.

In Part V, the book's analysis rises from the regional to the global level, with a functional focus on the two key issue areas of trade and finance that are driving the contemporary globalisation process and raising critical concerns from those concerned with social cohesion.

In Chapter 11, 'What Are the Necessary Ingredients for the World Trading Order?', Sylvia Ostry addresses the urgent need for reform in the world trading system, at a time when the very sustainability of the rules-based multilateral system is at stake and the reformers are nowhere to be seen. She begins with a brief overview of the background to the formidable challenges to the WTO and proceeds to offer some suggestions for its reform.

Ostry argues that the current challenge facing the WTO arises from both the previous Uruguay Round and current Doha negotiations for multilateral trade liberalisation. The Uruguay Round moved from negative regulation of border barriers to positive regulation for domestic social and environmental policy and thus 'touched the exposed raw nerve of sovereignty'. It also produced a small, member-driven institution with very strong judicial but very weak legislative and executive powers. The November 2001 ministerial meeting in Doha started to turn the WTO into a development institution, but undertook no reforms to correct the imbalance left by the Uruguay Round. The needed reform agenda must improve both the WTO's internal functioning and its external relations with stakeholders. What is required is an informal, voluntary initiative, based on the Trade Policy Review Mechanism (TPRM), to discuss national trade policy-making processes in the WTO under the broad rubric of transparency. Such participatory processes produce better policy outcomes, more legitimate policy, and more compliance with norms and laws.

In Chapter 12, 'Trade Liberalisation, Regulatory Diversity, and Political Sovereignty', Michael J. Trebilcock addresses the dilemma posed by the move of contemporary trade liberalisation beyond the border to confront domestic regulatory differences among countries. This raises calls for international harmonisation or mutual recognition, and arouses concerns from consumer, environmental and civil society groups, and developing countries, about the harmful effects therefrom. He reviews in turn the major areas where such regulatory issues arise, as trade intersects with the environment, health and safety standards, labour standards, human rights, intellectual property, competition policy, investment, services, and culture.

Trebilcock argues for a conservative approach to the harmonisation or convergence of domestic regulatory standards, in contrast to those who want the WTO to assume responsibility for environment, labour, and competition policy. He shows how a faithful application of the basic trade principles of national treatment (NT) and most favoured nation (MFN) status can serve well in all these areas. By this logic, the better-than-NT status bestowed on foreign investors by NAFTA's Chapter 11 in the case of expropriation stands out as an unwelcome anomaly. Nor do the EU's supranational governmental mechanisms apply outside the region. This is partly because in the multilateral system, voluntary agreements among firms and industries, and the work of voluntary standardisation in bodies such as the ISO or Codex Alimentarius can solve many problems in the absence of WTO-centred intergovernmental harmonisation. Elsewhere, the venerable trade principles of NT and MFN will suffice.

In Chapter 13, 'Civil Society and the Roots of Structural Conditionality in the World Bank and the International Monetary Fund', Louis W. Pauly turns from trade to finance, where powerful international organisations have also come to intrude very deeply into the sovereign domestic polities and politics of member states on a broad range of social and environmental issues where local civil society stakeholders have long had a direct involvement and concern. He offers an overview of the evolution of the practice of structural conditionality and the financial instruments within which it is embedded in the IMF and the World Bank, the leading international financial institutions (IFIs) of the contemporary period. On this foundation, he proposes a political explanation for the emergence and elaboration of the practice during the watershed decade of the 1980s.

Pauly argues that important ideological changes affecting the structures of governance within the political economy of the U.S. took place at the time that structural conditionality arose. In the wake of these ideological changes in the U.S., the World Bank, and the IMF sought new ways to reinforce America's political commitment to progressive internationalism, especially after the Cold War came to an end. In the earlier years, the move toward structural conditionality was driven by changing coalitions of economic actors within civil society, largely in the United States. More recently, U.S. attention has been heightened by the advocacy work of special-interest NGOs that have promoted the elaboration of structural conditionality in the IMF and the World Bank. But, in all, the evolution of structural conditionality within the two institutions has been 'almost perfectly attuned' to the continuing interest of a complex American state and society in ensuring stability abroad without paying its full cost.

In Chapter 14, 'World Trade Organization Gridlock and Alternative Regimes to Pursue an International Social Clause', Scott Vaughan examines the major issues that arise from the expanding mandate, universal membership, and rigid internal governance structures of the WTO. He explores the governance of the organisation, the substantive links between trade and non-trade policies (notably labour and environment), and the lessons that the WTO debate can draw from critiques that confront the World Bank and the IMF as discussed by Pauly in the Chapter 13.

Vaughan argues that the WTO has exhibited internal confusion and a lack of clarity about the mandate of the organisation itself in dealing with the relationship of the trade regime to labour and the environment. The mixed messages sent by the WTO to other legal regimes seeking the most effective enforcement mechanisms to pursue their objectives make it timely to examine these relationships. The international labour and human rights regimes very much need strengthening, along the lines of the model of the Montreal Protocol on Substances that Deplete the Ozone Layer, which maximises effectiveness and equity in the environment. The alternative of piling more and more agenda items onto the already impossibly crowded agenda of the WTO will mean that the crisis facing that institution will only deepen, while desperately needed institutional strengthening in the labour, human rights, environmental and other regimes will be postponed as uncertainty about trade measures continues.

Part V considers the global level in a comprehensive fashion, with a discussion of the two major international institutional galaxies for global governance, the G8 and the UN. In Chapter 15, 'Civil Society, the United Nations, and G7/8 Summitry', Peter I. Hajnal compares the relationship of NGOs and other civil society organisations and coalitions with the UN and, in the context of summitry, with the G8. He concludes with nine proposals for furthering civil society influences, and the lessons learned about civil society's role in the UN and G8.

Hajnal's analysis shows that civil society, present at the very start in the UN system, has come to acquire a widespread involvement and influence, both at periodic UN summits and in the ongoing operation of the organisation itself. In contrast, civil society's interest and involvement in the G7/8 was slower to start, but made major advances from 1995 through to the violence-scarred Genoa Summit in 2001. Kananaskis 2002 and Evian 2003 suggest that a productive, mutually beneficial relationship is back on track. Although it suffered a serious setback in 2004, there are early indications that the Sea Island Summit was an anomaly and with Gleneagles in 2005 civil society involvement will again be back on track as both G8 governors and civil society activists are learning what makes for success. Looking ahead, Hajnal states that informal new arrangements at the UN and civil society relations with the informal G8 – rather than the somewhat sterile formal mechanisms of the UN – may be where the most productive connection can be made between civil society and global governance, although civil society's role is legitimate, likely, and necessary across the board. He concludes that intergovernmental institutions and civil society share the responsibility to ensure that their interaction is meaningful and productive, and that meeting this challenge will be a true test of the viability of both intergovernmental organisations and responsible civil society movements.

In Chapter 16, 'Building Democratic Partnerships: The G8–Civil Society Link', John J. Kirton takes issue with the trend of the post–September 11 G8 summits to retreat to remote, isolated locations for meetings where the G8 are cut off from the media and civil society as a whole. In doing so, he argues, G8 governors are 'making a major mistake'.

Kirton offers an 11-point programme for G8 governments to connect with civil society more effectively. His recommendations include better public information about the G7/8, with an important role for parliamentarians and a G8 interparliamentary group; better work with the news media; bringing civil society closer to the summit through multistakeholder civil society forums and other endeavours; and using G7/8 ministerial meetings to promote dialogue with civil society.

In Chapter 17, 'Civil Society Engagement: A Case Study of the 2002 G8 Environment Ministers Meeting', Sheila Risbud examines a meeting of G8 environment ministers in Banff, Alberta, as a detailed case study of civil society engagement in the G8 process. She describes the various techniques used to engage civil society, highlighting both the successes achieved and the improvements needed in the Canadian government's outreach and engagement program in the leadup to the

2002 Kananaskis Summit. She also addresses lessons learned from this event and how they can be applied to future ministerial meetings and summits.

Risbud concludes that the meeting represented a significant step forward for civil society engagement. Groups wanted to be part of the process, wanted to be involved, and were brought in. There was value in their involvement. Citizen participation helped inform deliberations at the ministerial level and served to diffuse the propensity for violent protest. Yet the Banff experience showed there is much more to be done. It is important to ensure that outreach and engagement not be seen as attempts on the part of the government simply to placate civil society, but as a genuine commitment to citizen involvement. In particular, further thought should be given to the role that host communities can play in planning future meetings.

In Chapter 18, 'Canada and the Kyoto Protocol: Beyond Ratification to Implementation', Désirée M. McGraw examines, from a Canadian perspective, the adoption of a key instrument of sustainable development and international governance – the Kyoto Protocol to the UNFCCC that emerged from the 1992 Rio Summit. She addresses the Canadian debate surrounding the accord's ratification and implementation according to five themes: competitiveness, credibility, consultations, commitment, and consistency in public and foreign policy.

McGraw concludes that Canada took too long to ratify the Kyoto Protocol, taking five years from a 1998 commitment to do so until 9 December 2002, when Prime Minister Jean Chrétien issued an executive order-in-council to do so. The delay cost Canada in the difficult task of implementing its commitments. Behind the delay lay a federal government process of consultation with civil society that failed to consult the right people on the right question at the right time. It featured selective discussions with elites, experts, and special interest groups on whether to ratify Kyoto, rather than consulting Canadians directly on how to implement the accord from the start. As the domestic implementation process will be dynamic, if not equally divisive, it is important to engage civil society properly and move quickly to meet the Kyoto targets.

In Chapter 19, 'The Globalisation of the Marketplace', Michael E. Cloghesy asks whether the globalisation of the marketplace helps improve the quality of the environment in developing countries and what role governments, business, and other civil society actors have in helping it to do so. He begins from the premise that environmental improvements are not an automatic consequence of opening a national marketplace to the world.

Cloghesy concludes that industrialisation, especially in its early stages, can degrade the environment in developing countries. Globalisation of the marketplace is not a guaranteed solution, but depends on other forces to help. Of particular importance are good governance, stable government, realistic legislation, an appropriate regulatory infrastructure, and resources to enforce the law. Also useful is responsible corporate behaviour from MNCs. These are especially likely if the local government has endorsed the concept of sustainable development and is prepared to work with industry and civil society to set objectives that will enhance the quality of the environment and ensure a viable economy at the same time. Civil society, both within and beyond the business community, plays an important role in developing countries to ensure that their national governments move in these directions.

Part VI's Chapter 20, 'Civil Society and Institutions of Global Governance', ends the volume with a contribution from Canada's former foreign minister, the Honourable Bill Graham, who as a scholar, parliamentarian, and former Cabinet minister has been at the forefront of enhancing the connection between civil society and global governors. He concludes that problems of global scope are felt locally all around the world. Such interdependence and complexity require strong institutions of global governance, which alone can guide and co-ordinate efforts to address global crises. At all levels of governance, civil society is vital for ensuring the integrity and soundness of policy making. At the international level, civil society plays a key role in supporting the institutions of global governance and in fostering the climate of public opinion necessary for these institutions to succeed.

Conclusions

In pursuit of its threefold purpose – descriptive, explanatory, and prescriptive – this book addresses a number of questions about civil society involvement in governance on the local, regional and global levels, particularly in the institutional setting. How has the influence of civil society arisen and how has it changed over time? What are the goals and prospects of civil society in international governance? How much impact have civil society organisations had? Are there cross-sectoral and cross-country differences in the functioning and influence of those organisations? What are the benefits and costs of civil society participation?

In terms of the first question of how the role and influence of civil society in international governance has evolved, Bowles, MacDonald, Mullen, and Clarkson find that, in a trinational North American context, NAFTA has affected the three civil society sectors of labour, the environmental movement, and indigenous groups negatively but in different ways: NAFTA's Chapter 11 has privileged corporations over labour rights, resulting in dislocations, low wages, and a loss of bargaining power; indigenous communities have suffered from resource marginalisation and land dispossession; and from the perspective of ecologists, NAFTA and its environmental side agreement have addressed the trade-environment nexus inadequately. In response, the labour movement has shifted toward continentalisation, indigenous coalitions have tended to retain their focus on local and national issues, and environmental groups, which endorsed the side agreement, have found accommodation for solidarity in the CEC. Expectations of an increasing social policy role for civil society have, however, run up against limitations of resources and other capacities.

On the global level, Ostry notes that the WTO has become 'a magnet for anti-corporate globalisation' involving NGOs of various types: development groups, advocacy NGOs seeking to shape policy (NGOs that have become a 'virtual secretariat' for countries of the South), and mobilisation networks concentrating on dissent. Pauly, writing about the Bretton Woods institutions, comments on the deep intrusion of these financial organisations, particularly through structural conditionality, into the domestic economic, political, and social lives of member states – areas in which civil society has long been involved. He asserts that in earlier years structural conditionality was catalysed by coalitions within American civil society and that, more recently, special-interest NGOs, having undergone ideological and structural changes, have come to advocate further elaboration of structural conditionality in the World Bank and the IMF. Thus, developments in structural conditionality reflect the support of both the U.S. state and parts of U.S. civil society, the U.S. having been the foremost proponent of stability in other countries. Vaughan argues that, similar to the experience of the Bretton Woods institutions, the WTO's expanding agenda has resulted in increasing questioning of the trade organisation's legitimacy, accountability, and transparency on the part of civil society and others concerned with human rights, labour rights, the environment, animal welfare, and other issues. Citing Jeffrey Sachs and Andrew Warner, Vaughan observes that trade policy has become the single most important catalyst for all kinds of reforms.

Hajnal traces the emergence and evolution of civil society relations with the UN and with the G7/8 system. The UN has had a long-standing, structured relationship with a large number of designated NGOs. Over the decades, the rigidities of these formal arrangements became clear. It was during the major UN conferences of the 1990s, starting with the Rio Summit in 1992 that civil society organisations became major stakeholders. Environmental, development-oriented, and other organisations have since expanded their influence on the UN and its member governments – a trend that has continued into the 21st century. The recognition of these new realities prompted the UN to recommend, in 1996, changes to NGO relations, notably by extending NGO ties to the General Assembly and beyond. The more ambitious proposals have stalled for lack of political will. In June 2004 a UN Panel of Eminent Persons emphasised that constructive engagement with civil society was no longer simply an option but a necessity for the UN if it wished to reinvigorate intergovernmental relations, and that in order to obtain civil society support the UN needed to champion meaningful reforms of global governance. The panel offered 30 proposals to enhance relations between the UN and civil society so that they reflect the growing capacity and influence of nonstate actors, foster multi-stakeholder processes, and improve policy and operational partnerships. It remains to be seen how well the panel's ambitious proposals fare, given the UN's political, financial, institutional, and human resource constraints. In contrast with the UN, the more flexible and informal G7/8 system has had a slow start but an increasingly sophisticated relationship with civil society. Civil society organisations were the first to recognise the importance of the G7/8 in global governance. Civil society actions have ranged from dialogue with summit country leaders and officials, through demonstrations, advocacy, and compliance monitoring to parallel summits. The G7/8, for its part, has reflected civil society's increasing role and influence in its deliberations, documents, dialogue, and multistakeholder task forces.

Second, with regard to the goals and prospects of civil society in global governance, Bartlett and Friedmann note that in the area of food safety and biotechnology, faith in scientific and technological expertise is fading and the public is demanding greater decision-making power. The discourse on risk has given rise to a conflict, especially since the 1990s, that has led to uncertainties over the appropriate roles of actors in trade- and environment-related intergovernmental negotiations: how can citizen and advocacy groups achieve the same clout as corporations in these negotiations? Bartlett and Friedmann find some cause for optimism should the precautionary principle prevail over substantial equivalence in negotiating trade agreements; precaution facilitates a greater role for civil society inherent in the inclusion of health and environmental criteria in the discourse over genetically modified food. Field sees the long-term strategic goal for the Canadian environmental and agriculture/food movement to be a combination of local community building and efforts to democratise governance structures at the municipal, provincial, and federal levels, while also addressing global problems of ecology and capital – an ambitious goal indeed.

Trebilcock states that consumer, environmental, and other NGOs seek to resist constraints imposed by international trade agreements on domestic political sovereignty; these constraints would prevent importing countries from imposing more stringent regulatory standards than those of exporting countries. Such civil society organisations also favour the imposition of trade sanctions on exporting countries with weaker standards in order to induce the raising of those standards. He argues, however, that where there are linkages of trade with domestic policy issues of the environment, health and safety standards, human rights, intellectual property, competition policy, investment, trade in services, and culture, the solution lies in the harmonisation or convergence of domestic regulatory standards rather than in the WTO taking on responsibility for such extraneous issues. He concludes that the two non-discriminatory trade principles of NT and MFN are sufficient to discipline protectionist domestic policies yet allow scope for domestic policy sovereignty and preferences, as well as competitive, accountable, and democratically legitimate governments.

Kirton criticises the post–September 11 G8 summits for convening in isolated locations, and thus depriving media and civil society of access to summit events and officials. He concludes that the leaders' choice in this matter will determine whether G8 meetings become a summit of retreat or a summit of reaching out.

Graham, in the concluding chapter, stresses that international institutions, if they are to be recognised as legitimate and effective, must move beyond secret meetings of experts. He asserts that civil society's support is vital for sound policy making of integrity at all levels of governance.

Third, on the subject of the impact of civil society organisations on international governance, Maclaren, Morris, and Labatt find that the effectiveness of CAPs in environmental protection is mixed. It remains contingent on several variables: there are important differences in the impact of civil society organisations in Canada and the U.S., due to differing regulatory and policy regimes in the two countries as well as to the particularities of the local context in which CAPs operate. Moreover, perceptions of effectiveness differ in both countries between the more optimistic community members and the more pessimistic company representatives – a difference due, perhaps, to the companies' lesser commitment to CAPs.

Bowles, MacDonald, Mullen, and Clarkson observe that the reactions to NAFTA of the three civil society sectors they examine reflect different ideologies and capacities, the labour movement having the strongest potential to affect governance on the continental level and the indigenous communities the weakest. Because NAFTA lacks effective regulatory institutions, organised labour acts more effectively outside that formal institution of governance, using its ability to exercise power through lobbying and legal processes. Indigenous groups have engaged in pressuring formal governing structures using blockades and other forms of confrontation. But environmental groups, concerned with standards and enforcement, must depend on institutions and regulatory regimes. With all the variations among the three sectors, the authors conclude that 'civil society's capacity to engage at the continental level in effective governance from below in order to combat the degradation of workers' conditions – or to protect indigenous peoples' ancestral rights or to enhance environmental sustainability – is dangerously limited'. Looking at 'continentalism from above', Davidson Ladly, Thorne, and Clarkson question the democratic legitimacy of NAFTA's committees and working groups, and note that the near-total lack of transparency of these groups 'prevents individual citizens' or civil society organisations from providing a counterpoint to private sector access.

Field notes that transboundary civil society networks have a better chance of success if they are able to link their multiple activities on the local and global levels. This is difficult to achieve in the case of agriculture and food, given the lack of consistent forums to debate and resolve tensions between food rights (a concern of Northern civil society organisations) and food sovereignty (paramount for the South). But the experience of the Via Campesina movement shows that a successful link can be forged between sovereignty over agricultural and food resources, on the one hand, and food rights, on the other hand. Fundamental political and social changes can be brought about if there is sufficient popular support built on an understanding of the food system and of the associated social and ecological issues, and if the necessary organisational capacity and regulatory frameworks are established in all three sectors (government, private sector, and the community).

Discussing the second sector, namely clusters of regional MNCs, Rugman and Verbeke state that these clusters embrace civil society groups such as professional associations, research centres, and educational institutions. In their view, regional, not global, governance is the first concern in business–civil society relationships.

Ostry asserts that NGOs have had an impact on the WTO's agenda in several ways. The emphasis on development in the Doha round of trade negotiations is due at least in part to NGOs taking up issues with moral resonance. And the Doha special declaration on global health is a victory for the campaign led by Oxfam and Médecins Sans Frontières to make it easier for developing countries to have access to affordable life-saving medicines in the face of pressures from large pharmaceutical companies with strong patent protection.

Risbud reviews the various techniques to interact with local citizens and broader civil society in the lead-up to the 2002 G8 environment ministerial meeting. As host, the Canadian government decided well in advance to develop an inclusive strategy: an informational town hall session for residents and other stakeholders was held, followed by one-on-one meetings of interested individuals or groups with senior officials, and a roundtable discussion where Canada's environment minister, representatives of other G8 delegations, and UNEP's executive director met with a whole gamut of stakeholders – business, labour, environmental, indigenous groups, and others. There was also a youth forum, meetings with local authorities and briefing sessions for local media. Risbud concludes that the Banff meeting was a significant step forward for engaging civil society, but it was only the first step. She emphasises that G8 outreach and civil society engagement should represent real government commitment to citizen participation.

In a contrasting case study of Canadian engagement with the Kyoto Protocol, McGraw examines five themes of the Canadian debate around ratification, and notes that Canada took far too long to ratify the agreement. Even after ratification, Canada lacks a clear, credible, comprehensive action plan.

Cloghesy explores whether globalisation of the marketplace is a positive factor in improving the quality of the environment in developing countries. He endorses the view that governments, business, and other stakeholders, including environmental organisations, all play a role if environmental conditions are to improve along with economic progress including free trade. He concludes that what is needed for enhanced environmental quality and a vibrant economy in developing countries is a set of factors: globalisation of the marketplace along with good governance, stable government, eradication of corruption, appropriate and enforceable legislation, sound regulatory infrastructure, responsible corporate behaviour, and multi-stakeholder involvement. Local governments need to aim for sustainable development and need to work with industry and civil society in order to move toward sound economic and environmental goals.

It emerges from several contributions to this book that perhaps the greatest potential impact of NGOs and civil society organisations on negotiations occurs when these organisations offer specific knowledge, expertise, or information that governments do not possess or have not placed in the centre of their attention. The greater the expertise of these NGOs, the more seriously governments take them, regardless of the governments' normative position on actual negotiations. Many NGOs and civil society organisations have played this role very well, benefiting themselves as well as the overall bargaining process. This type of impact is stronger than the display of power in a confrontational situation. Moreover, some contributors view civil society effectiveness as more of a Northern than a Southern phenomenon.

Fourth, on cross-country and cross-sectoral differences in the functioning and influence of civil society organisations, in contrast with the sectoral analysis of Bowles her his colleagues, Ogilvie focusses on national differences between the apparent Canadian tendency for consensus-based policy making and the more legalistic U.S. system, and the implications of these differences for the methods of mobilisation of Canadian and U.S. civil society organisations: the environmental NGO Pollution Probe 'fights for a policy statement in Canada [while] in the U.S. NGOs fight for a legal process'. In addition, there is a major difference in resources between the relatively well-funded U.S. groups and the generally much poorer Canadian ones, leading to a huge imbalance of relative capabilities. Also, in contrast with Clarkson and his co-authors who concentrate on labour-to-labour or aboriginal-to-aboriginal coalitions, Ogilvie concludes that building horizontal coalitions – where environmental groups interact with industry, municipalities, and other stakeholders – result in the greatest potential for policy influence by civil society organisations.

Field takes this divergence a step further. She points out that the differences between strong organised labour and newer environmental, indigenous, and agriculture/food movements go beyond resources and organisational capacity. While labour tends to be programmatically united, with common goals, strategies, and political objectives that can spread across borders, similar commonalities have not occurred in some of the newer, grassroots movements.

Fifth, with respect to the benefits and costs of civil society influence, Ostry asserts that public policy making contributes not only to the legitimacy of international organisations and governance but also to better compliance with laws and norms as well. A participatory consulting process allows governments to inform stakeholders on a continuing basis, and makes it less likely that stakeholders will reject the entire regime. There are also costs for governments engaging in public consultation – in terms of time, expertise, and financial resources.

Hajnal argues that the UN–civil society relationship has been mutually beneficial. Civil society participation has provided the UN with technical expertise on the environment, development, human rights, women's issues, disarmament, emergency assistance, and other areas. Civil society organisations have also increased public awareness of global issues, and contributed to greater democracy, transparency, and accountability on the part of UN member governments. For NGOs, the UN nexus has provided an opportunity to engage, within political and resource limits, in policy formulation, standard setting, operational activities, and advocacy. In the G7/8 context, it has been demonstrated that the G7/8 can work in partnership with responsible, constructive civil society groups rather than confronting them as adversaries, as long as all parties work to muster the political will and to find ways to develop such partnerships in a meaningful and mutually beneficial manner.

Risbud notes that engaging civil society and other stakeholders is crucial. The ideas of these stakeholders on good governance and environment-health linkages provided valuable input for the Canadian government as host of the 2002 G8 environment ministerial; the results of the consultations were then conveyed to the host minister and his counterparts.

McGraw concludes that the long delay to ratify the Kyoto Protocol has resulted in costs to Canada in implementing its commitments under the agreement. During the five years from Canada's commitment to ratify until actual ratification, the federal government failed to consult the right people on the right question at the right time. It had a selective dialogue with elites, experts, and special interest groups – rather than with broader civil society – a dialogue that, moreover, was framed in terms of whether to ratify Kyoto, rather than how to implement it. And failure to meet global climate change commitments may well become a self-fulfilling prophecy.

Finally, the contributors to this book offer a number of reform and policy proposals both for civil society and for institutions of international governance. Soloway, writing about investor protection and the public interest under NAFTA's Chapter 11, concludes that NGO participation would be useful in developing more robust rules governing transparency. She further suggests that a permanent appellate body (following the pattern of the WTO's Appellate Body) would provide more consistency in the application of Chapter 11 in the public interest. Tollefson challenges Soloway's contention that Chapter 11 jurisprudence poses no real threat to legitimate, non-discriminatory environmental protection measures. He asserts that Chapter 11 tribunals have too broad and ill-defined discretion, leading to questionable interpretations. It is these interpretations, rather than the language of Chapter 11 itself, that gives Tollefson concern over whether environmental or public health measures would survive an investor challenge – a concern at the heart of some civil society criticism. Building his analysis on the *Metalclad* case affecting domestic Mexican law, he concludes that it is necessary to be mindful of the democratic price of erecting and maintaining such sweeping investor protections residing in essentially unaccountable tribunals. Reform of Chapter 11 is clearly needed and Tollefson calls on Canada, in particular, to work for such reform in order to achieve a better balance between investor rights and domestic policy preferences.

On the global level, Ostry proposes modest reform of the WTO, namely a voluntary initiative based on the TPRM. More transparency would promote opportunities for greater participation by stakeholders, including civil society organisations. This could be achieved (notwithstanding significant opposition by Southern governments and other countries) by such means as a research network connecting the WTO secretariat not only with intergovernmental organisations but also with academic, business, labour, environmental, and other institutions. A further step might be an infrastructure for meetings where this collective knowledge could be disseminated and debated; monitoring of policy performance could follow.

Commenting on Ostry's proposals, Vaughan argues that the greatest challenge to the WTO's expanding mandate and structural problems comes from inside the organisation rather than from outside critics. He concludes that the time has come to clarify the relationship among various regimes – trade, labour, human rights, and environment. Reacting to Trebilcock's proposal that the WTO incorporate core labour standards in its trade policies, Vaughan envisions the possible shape of such a nexus, which would make it conceivable to use WTO help enforce core labour and environmental standards. Yet he cautions that adding to WTO's already overcrowded agenda would only deepen the crisis facing that organisation.

Hajnal offers a list of ideas for civil society that could potentially enhance relations with the G7/8 in order to promote social, economic, and other global goals: better networking; awareness of linkages of various issues; building on successes and learning from mistakes; knowing thoroughly the international institutions with which they interact; taking advantage of the convergence of their priorities with those of international governors; isolating potentially violent elements that cause harm to civil society organisations; analysing the costs and benefits of participation versus self-exclusion; and developing alternative strategies when faced with non-receptive international governors. Kirton, in a complementary set of 11 proposals, suggests how G8 governments can interact with civil society more effectively: upholding the 1975 founding rationale of the G7 as a group of heads of open democratic societies; giving civil society a real voice in the lead-up to each summit; informing the public about the G8 so as to promote transparency; inclusion of parliamentarians in the summit process; forming G8 study centres in each G8 country or region to promote local access to and analysis of the G8; sponsoring scholarships to expose students to the G8 all year; educating the broad citizenry using the internet and other information and communication technologies; not restricting media access to the leaders; keeping or restoring the communiqué (and keeping it clear and credible); inclusion of civil society on the summit site in a multi-stakeholder forum allowing access to the leaders; and mobilising the G8 ministerial meetings to promote dialogue with civil society.

Amidst the rich diversity in analysis in this volume, there emerges a broad and deep consensus on some fundamental points. All authors agree that the debate is no longer over whether civil society should be involved in international governance, but rather on how much and how it should. There is widespread agreement that civil society should be involved directly at the international level, rather than left exclusively at home. Although there are disadvantages to doing so, these are more hypothetical than the sensitivity, expertise, capacity, compliance, and regime effectiveness brought by an internationally engaged civil society. Probably the greatest current challenge is to bring about a better balance, by building on the substantial voice of business and labour groups and civil society organisations from the North, to give ENGOs, women's groups, and indigenous groups – especially from the impoverished South – greater weight. Doing so will engender the inclusive, multi-stakeholder, consensus-oriented decision making that, despite its frustrations, brings better results over the long term. And in bringing about a new generation of global governance that realises this ideal in the 21st century, the field of ecological and social sustainability is the proper place for steady incremental progress to take a great leap forward.

Note

1   Keck and Sikkink (1998, 55) note: 'This may be the earliest example of the now established practice of granting nongovernmental organizations a special role in international conferences.'

References

Angell, Robert (1969). *Peace on the March: Transnational Participation.* Van Nostrand Reinhold, New York.

Brown, Seyom (1974). *New Forces in World Politics.* Brookings Institution, Washington DC.

Clarkson, Stephen (2002). *Uncle Sam and Us: Globalization, Neoconservatism, and the Canadian State.* University of Toronto Press, Toronto.

Drezner, Daniel W. (2004). 'The Global Governance of the Internet: Bringing the State Back In'. *Political Science Quarterly* vol. 119, no. 3, pp. 477–498.

Ford, Lucy (2003). 'Challenging Global Environmental Governance: Social Movement Agency and Global Civil Society'. *Global Environmental Politics* vol. 3, no. 2, pp. 121–134.

Haas, Ernst B. (1968). *Beyond the Nation-State: Functionalism and international Organization.* Stanford University Press, Stanford CA.

Keck, Margaret E. and Kathryn Sikkink (1998). *Activists Beyond Borders: Advocacy Networks in International Politics.* Cornell University Press, Ithaca.

Kirton, John J. and Rafael Fernandez de Castro (1997). *NAFTA's Institutions: The Environmental Potential and Performance of the NAFTA Free Trade Commission and Related Bodies.* Commission for Environmental Cooperation, Montreal.

Kirton, John J. and Virginia W. Maclaren, eds. (2002). *Linking Trade, Environment, and Social Cohesion: NAFTA Experiences, Global Challenges.* Ashgate, Aldershot.

Kirton, John J. and Michael J. Trebilcock, eds. (2004). *Hard Choices, Soft Law: Voluntary Standards in Global Trade, Environment, and Social Governance.* Ashgate, Aldershot.

Lipschutz, R.D. (1992). 'Reconstructing World Politics: The Emergency of Global Civil Society'. *Millennium* vol. 21, pp. 389.

Mansback, Richard, Yale Ferguson, and Donald Lampert (1976). *The Web of World Politics: Nonstate Actors in the Global System.* Prentice Hall, Englewood Cliffs NJ.

Scholte, Jan Aart (2000). *Globalization: A Critical Introduction.* Palgrave, Houndsmills.

Strange, Susan (1996). *The Retreat of the State: The Diffusion of Power in the World Economy.* Cambridge University Press, Cambridge.

Vernon, Raymond (1971). *Sovereignty at Bay: The Multinational Spread of U.S. Enterprises.* Basic Books, New York.

Wapner, Paul (1995). 'Police Beyond the State: Environment Activism and World Civic Politics'. *World Politics* vol. 47, no. 3, pp. 311–340.

Wight, Martin (1977). *System of States.* Leicester University Press, Leicester.

PART II:
LOCAL AND TRANSBOUNDARY NETWORKS AND CO-OPERATION

Chapter 2

Engaging Local Communities in Environmental Protection with Competitiveness: Community Advisory Panels in Canada and the United States

Virginia Maclaren, Angela Morris, and Sonia Labatt

In 1984, an accidental release of methylisocyanate from a Union Carbide plant in Bhopal, India, killed more than 2000 people and injured almost 200 000. This incident resulted in widespread public distrust of the chemical industry, not only in India but also around the world. Bhopal demonstrated that irresponsible environmental risk management by a single company could damage the reputation of an entire industry. The chemical industry's response to Bhopal, and to potentially stricter regulation by concerned governments, was the creation of the Responsible Care programme, a voluntary code meant to improve the industry's environmental performance. The programme originated in Canada in 1985 and was adopted, with minor changes, by the American Chemical Manufacturers' Association (CMA) in the United States in 1988. American chemical manufacturers with operations in Canada were the first to make the CMA aware of the programme and encourage its adoption in the United States (Nash and Ehrenfeld 1996).

The programme has now spread to 52 countries, although not all chemical companies in participating countries have sought verification under Responsible Care (International Council of Chemical Associations 2005). For example, only 50 percent of chemical companies in Japan and 17 percent in India have achieved certification as Responsible Care companies (Prakash 2000). In contrast, Responsible Care members in the U.S. account for about 90 percent of the country's chemical industry output (Prakash 2000). Canadian members account for about 95 percent (Shearing 2003).

The Responsible Care programme is built on a series of codes of practice that vary slightly from country to country in both number and content. To become certified as a Responsible Care member, a company must demonstrate that it has all of these codes of practice in place and that it is seeking their continual improvement. A key component of the programme in Canada and the U.S. is the Community Awareness and Emergency Response code of practice. Among other things, this code of practice requires companies to establish a regular process of communication with the local community (American Chemical Council 2005; Canada's Chemical Producers 2005). This process is intended to ensure that the company becomes aware of community concerns about the hazards and associated risks of company operations and that the company responds to those concerns. Although the code does not specify the type of process that should be followed, most companies have chosen to establish community advisory panels (CAPs) to meet this requirement.

CAPs are a type of citizen advisory committee, which can be defined as 'a relatively small group of people who are convened by a sponsor for an extended period of time to represent the ideas and attitudes of various groups and/or communities for the purpose of examining a proposal or issue or set of issues' (Lynn and Busenberg 1995, 148).

Normally these committees are not given decision-making authority by their sponsor; rather, they only have an advisory role. Citizen advisory committees have been employed extensively as a method for public participation in public sector policy-making, but private sector citizen advisory committees are relatively rare. The Responsible Care CAPs are probably the largest set of citizen advisory committees to be found in any industrial sector.

There have been a number of reviews of the effectiveness of the Responsible Care programme as a self-regulation tool for the chemical industry, but they have paid little or no attention to the effectiveness of CAPs (c.f. Prakash 2000; Nash and Howard 1995; Gunningham 1995). One exception is a wide-ranging study of more than 60 CAPs in the U.S., conducted in the late 1990s (Lynn *et al.* 2000). This study examined the effectiveness of CAPs, as perceived by community CAP members and company representatives, across several different measures. It concluded that CAPs perform well on some measures, such as building trust between CAP members and the company and helping companies to anticipate issues of concern to the community. It also found, however, that CAPS are not as effective in their representativeness of the community, in influencing health, safety, and environmental performance at the company, in providing the company with feedback on proposed changes to the plant, or in communicating about the company to the larger community.

This chapter examines similarities and differences in the effectiveness of the roles played by private sector citizen advisory committees to the chemical industry in the United States and Canada. Since there has been almost no empirical research on private sector advisory committees, other than the aforementioned study, this chapter draws on the literature on public sector advisory committees to identify factors that may influence effectiveness in the private sector. It also discuss several contextual factors, such as the regulatory and policy environment, that may lead to differences in the effectiveness of CAPs in the U.S. and Canada.

Differences in Effectiveness

There is a vast normative literature on the effectiveness of participation in public sector decision making. One of the fundamental points made in this literature is that effectiveness or success depends on both the process of participation and the outcomes of that activity (Lynn and Busenberg 1995; Chess and Purcell 1999). It is generally agreed that one of the most desirable outcomes from the perspective of participants is the ability to influence decisions made by the sponsor (Rowe and Frewer 2000; Hampton 1999). A key process measure is how well the individuals involved in the participation process represent the values and interests of the broader public (Rowe and Frewer 2000; Hampton 1999; Lynn and Kartez 1995; Smith and McDonough 2001). A second important process measure, one that particularly applies to citizen advisory committees, is how well participants reach out to the local community that they represent. Communicating with the local community and maintaining links to that community help the committee to retain its legitimacy as a representative body (Smith and McDonough 2001).

Empirical research has shown that citizen advisory committees have been both successful (Beltsen 1995) and unsuccessful (Knaap, Matier, and Olshansky 1998) in achieving representation. Success on this measure appears to depend on efforts made by the sponsor during membership recruitment, whether members are self-selected or appointed, and the level of community interest in the issues to be addressed by the committee. Advisory committees have also been both successful and unsuccessful in reaching out to the communities that they are meant to represent (Knaap, Matier, and Olshansky 1998). Success here may depend on the resources allocated to the committee and whether the committee has a specific outreach goal. Finally, advisory committees have been both successful and unsuccessful in influencing decision making.[1] There are strong links between successful outcomes and an effective process. Ultimately, the overall effectiveness of an advisory committee depends on the intentions of the sponsor in establishing the committee (Lynn and Busenberg 1995). Was the intention to solicit advice and act on recommendations, or to create a body that would simply appear to legitimise decisions already made by the sponsor (Rowe and Frewer 2000)? These mixed results suggest that it may be difficult to predict the effectiveness of private sector advisory committees based on the public sector experience. However, the public sector experience does point to important indicators that should be considered when judging effectiveness.

Are there likely to be differences in effectiveness between CAPs in the United States and Canada? They were both established under very similar circumstances and have almost identical goals, according to the statements found in each country's Community Awareness and Emergency Response code of practice. However, there are differences in the two countries' approaches to environmental policy making and regulation that might lead to differences in effectiveness between the two sets of CAPs. While Canadian policy makers often search for collaborative, consensus-based solutions to environmental problems, Americans tend to rely more on judicial processes (Rabe 1994; Piette 1988). In the U.S., environmental groups may be reluctant to collaborate with industry for fear of weakening their own position in any potential litigatory actions (Gray and Hay 1986). Hence, representation by environmental groups on CAPs may be lower in the U.S. than in Canada.

Methodology

For this study, data were collected by means of a questionnaire survey of a sample of Canadian CAPs. Because a list of all CAPs in Canada was unavailable, an initial set was identified with the assistance of knowledgeable individuals in government and environmental organisations in Canada and by reviewing corporate literature and sources on the internet. A company representative was contacted at each CAP to request permission to send a questionnaire to all members of that CAP, including company representatives. If permission was granted, the representative or the committee's facilitator was asked to distribute the questionnaires at the next meeting. All of the companies contacted agreed to participate in the survey. CAP members were asked to return the completed questionnaire in a self-addressed envelope. The questionnaire was pre-tested on three companies and then refined, with a few questions added for the final survey.

The survey obtained responses from 56 community CAP members and 17 company CAP members representing 15 Canadian CAPs. It is difficult to assess the response rate for the survey because some company contacts asked for more questionnaires than they needed. For example, one company had CAPs at several of its factories and, because the company contact was not exactly sure how many individuals were on each CAP, considerably more questionnaires were sent to that company than were requested by other company representatives. In total, 166 questionnaires were sent and 73 were returned, so the estimated total response rate was at least 35 percent. There was very little difference between the estimated response rate for community members (34 percent) and company representatives (39 percent).

Both company and community members were asked to evaluate the effectiveness of their CAPs on four different measures. These results were compared with those from the 2000 U.S. study, which had 473 responses from community members and 146 from company representatives (see Lynn *et al.* 2000). Three of the four measures that were compared with the American study were identical, but the fourth was slightly different. The authors of the U.S. study asked respondents to rate the effectiveness of their CAP in influencing health, safety, and environmental performance at the company. In the Canadian survey, this question was broken down into two parts, the first asking respondents about the CAP's influence on health and safety, and the second asking about the influence on environmental performance. The common measures for the two studies included effectiveness of the CAP in communicating with the larger community, in representing a diversity of viewpoints, and in making the company aware of community concerns.

After completing the CAP survey, semi-structured interviews were conducted with four key informants in order to develop a better understanding of the reasons underlying similarities and differences between the two sets of CAPs. One respondent had worked extensively with CAPs in both the United States and Canada, while the other three had worked almost exclusively in either Canada or the United States.

Results and Discussion

The results of the comparative study reveal very similar views from the two countries on CAP effectiveness for one of the four measures we evaluated. Only about 40 percent of CAP members in the two countries felt that CAPs are effective or very effective at communicating with the larger community (see Figure 2.1). Both company and community representatives held similar views on this issue.

Interviews with key informants identified several specific reasons for the low rating. Two informants suggested that communicating with the community was not necessarily a primary goal of the CAP. One respondent said that he did not set up CAPs with the expectation that they would reach out, but rather that the CAP would be the 'touchstone of the community'. If membership is broad and representative, then this was sufficient for obtaining community views. The same respondent noted that not all CAPs have the same view of community outreach. He suggested that some CAPs from smaller communities actually perform quite well on this measure. Single-company CAPs typically were more community-oriented and there was a tendency for people to get more excited about CAPs in smaller communities in the U.S. For example, small community CAPs often engage in outreach at local fairs.

Figure 2.1   Evaluation of CAP Effectiveness

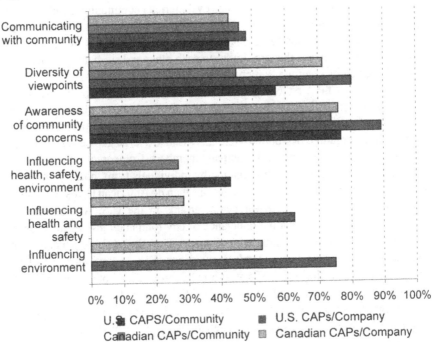

However, the respondent noted that this is more of a southern and rural phenomenon in the U.S. and that it can also be found in small communities in Western Canada. Unfortunately, it was not possible to confirm this assertion from the Canadian data set because the sample was not large enough to generalise about the characteristics of Western Canadian CAPs.

Our second respondent suggested that CAP-community feedback becomes more important as the CAP evolves. She said that at the start of a CAP, this is not a priority. Only after a while might the CAP want to extend to the community. In her view, communicating with the larger community at this point was a critical part of making the CAP process as meaningful as possible.

The third respondent commented on the challenges facing CAPs that do want to reach out to the community. Members have a dilemma of not wanting to appear as cheerleaders for the company. They also have little personal time to engage in outreach and face a lack of community interest, unless there has been a recent incident. The problems of personal time commitments and lack of community interest can also be serious barriers to attracting new members to the CAP (Sim 2001).

It is somewhat difficult to compare the two sets of CAPs on the second measure because the question on health, safety, and environment was different from the one in the American study. However, the effectiveness ratings given to their CAPs by Canadian community members are higher for their influence on corporate environmental performance (75 percent) and their influence on health and safety (63 percent) than the effectiveness ratings by American community members on the combined measure of health, safety, and environment (43 percent). Another notable finding is that the company representatives from both countries give effectiveness ratings on these measures that are similar to each other and substantially lower than the ratings given by community members.

In contrast to the first two measures, a fairly wide gap exists between the effectiveness ratings given by Canadian (80 percent) and U.S. community members (57 percent) for the third measure, which asks about a CAP's ability to represent a diversity of community viewpoints. Here there is also a large gap between Canadian (71 percent) and U.S. (45 percent) company members. Compared to the U.S. study, Canadian CAPs have lower representation by individuals from industry groups and higher representation by environmental groups than do American CAPs. This finding of lower representation by environmental groups in the U.S. is consistent with previous research on the relative reluctance of environmental groups to co-operate with industry in the U.S., compared to Canada. Two Canadian respondents noted that environmental nongovernmental organisations (ENGOs) are often reluctant to sit on CAPs because they see CAPs as a form of co-option. Another respondent said that he had seen environmental groups in the U.S. joining CAPs many times over the past 15 years 'just so that they can make a dramatic resignation'. The respondents with experience in Canada said that resignations by environmental groups are not as common.

One respondent felt that another reason for the difference in diversity was that being asked to sit on a CAP in the United States has more status than in Canada and participants may join to get 'CV points'. In Canada, being a member of a CAP is more run of the mill. He attributed this difference to what he considered a cultural trait in the U.S. for 'aggrandising small events'. On a similar note, a second respondent commented that she often saw CAPs dominated by white middle-aged males in the United States and speculated that this occurs because people were seeking membership for status.

On the fourth measure, there is a small but important difference between community members from U.S. and Canadian CAPs in terms of their ability to make the company aware of community concerns. More Canadian CAP members (89 percent) felt that CAPs were effective or very effective in this task than did U.S. CAP members (77 percent). This result may be due to the lower level of diversity found on American CAPs. However, Canadian company representatives were less positive than their fellow community members about CAP effectiveness on this measure. Like U.S. community members, about three quarters of company representatives from both countries felt that CAPs were effective or very effective in raising awareness.

All of the respondents noted, with varying degrees of emphasis, that differences in the political, regulatory, and cultural contexts in the two countries were not the only factors that led to differences in the effectiveness of the two sets of CAPs. They felt that CAP-specific factors can be equally important or, in certain situations, can be the only influence on effectiveness. Of most significance is the commitment of the plant manager to the CAP and his or her influence on the diversity of membership on the committee. If a committee is to be effective, then the plant manager will foster diversity. If the committee is more of a legitimation tool, then the plant manager will not want diversity but rather will choose people that he or she feels comfortable with. One respondent claimed that CAP-specific factors could override broader contextual factors. She suggested that despite the litigious culture in the United States, if a CAP builds a high level of trust between the committee and the company, then participants may be willing to continue as members or express views that would otherwise put them in a vulnerable position.

Arguments that broader contextual factors are more or less important than CAP-specific factors are not necessarily in conflict with one another. The two sets of influences are interlinked. For example, the plant manager's style, attitude, and approach may all be shaped to some extent by the country's regulatory and policy regime.

Conclusion

According to this study, the degree to which advisory committees established by the private sector, such as Responsible Care CAPs, are perceived to be effective is contingent on a variety of factors that operate on a range of scales. Like the public sector experience, the effectiveness of private sector CAPs tends to be mixed, depending on the measure used.

A few important differences between the effectiveness of CAPs in the U.S. and Canada were identified, some of which may be due to differences in the regulatory and policy regimes in the two countries, and some of which could be attributed to characteristics of the local context in which the CAP operates.

Although the main purpose of this study was to compare U.S. and Canadian CAPs, a significant finding was that in both countries company representatives were often less optimistic about the effectiveness of their CAPs than community members. Very little has been written about diverging opinions on effectiveness between sponsor and community members on public sector committees. The reasons for these differences in both the public and private sector need further investigation, including detailed interviews with company representatives. One possible explanation is that companies have less of a commitment to the committees than community representatives. The company representatives may perceive the role of the committee to be a sounding board for decisions that have already been made.

Note

1   For a discussion of successful committees, Knaap, Matier, and Olshansky (1998) and Beltsen (1995). For a discussion of unsuccessful committees, see Plumlee, Starling, and Kramer (1985), Stewart, Dennis, and Ely (1984), and Hannah and Lewis (1982).

References

American Chemical Council (2005). 'Responsible Care'. <www.americanchemistry.com> (November 2005).

Beltsen, L. (1995). *Assessment of Local Stakeholder Involvement*. Western Governors' Association, Denver.

Canada's Chemical Producers (2005). 'The Responsible Care Codes of Practice'. <www.ccpa.ca/ResponsibleCare/Codes.aspx> (November 2005).

Chess, Caron and Kristen Purcell (1999). 'Public Participation and the Environment: Do We Know What Works?' *Environmental Science and Technology* vol. 33, no. 16, pp. 2685–2691.

Gray, Barbara and Tina M. Hay (1986). 'Political Limits to Interorganizational Consensus and Change'. *Applied Behavioral Science* vol. 22, no. 2, pp. 95–112.

Gunningham, Neil (1995). 'Environment, Self-Regulation, and the Chemical Industry: Assessing Responsible Care'. *Law and Policy* vol. 17, no. 1, pp. 57–109.

Hampton, Greg (1999). 'Environmental Equity and Public Participation'. *Policy Sciences* vol. 32, no. 2, pp. 163–174.

Hannah, Susan B. and Helena S. Lewis (1982). 'Internal Citizen Control of Locally Initiated Citizen Advisory Committees: A Case Study'. *Journal of Voluntary Action Research* vol. 11, no. 4, pp. 39–52.

International Council of Chemical Associations (2005). 'Responsible Care: Who We Are'. <www.responsiblecare.org> (November 2005).

Knaap, Gerrit J., Debra Matier, and Robert Olshansky (1998). 'Citizen Advisory Group in Remedial Action Planning: Paper Tiger or Key to Success?' *Journal of Environmental Planning and Management* vol. 41, no. 3, pp. 337–354.

Lynn, Frances M. and George Busenberg (1995). 'Citizen Advisory Committees and Environmental Policy: What We Know, What's Left to Discover'. *Risk Analysis* vol. 15, no. 2, pp. 147–162.

Lynn, Frances M., George Busenberg, Nevin Cohen, *et al.* (2000). 'Chemical Industry's Community Advisory Panels: What Has Been Their Impact?' *Environment Science and Technology* vol. 34, no. 10, pp. 1881–1886.

Lynn, Frances M. and Jack D. Kartez (1995). 'The Redemption of Citizen Advisory Committees: A Perspective from Critical Theory'. In O. Renn, T. Webler and P. Wiedermann, eds., *Fairness and Competence in Citizen Participation: Evaluation Models for Environmental Discourse*. Kluwer Academic Publishers, Boston.

Nash, Jennifer and John Ehrenfeld (1996). 'Code Green'. *Environment* vol. 38, no. 1, pp. 16–20, 36–45.

Nash, Jennifer and J. Howard (1995). 'The U.S. Responsible Care Initiative: The Dynamics of Shaping Firm Practices and Values'. Paper presented at the International Research Conference on the Greening of Industry Network, 12–19 November. Toronto.

Piette, Jean (1988). 'La protection de l'environnement au Canada et aux États-Unis'. *Cahiers de Droits* vol. 29, pp. 425–445.

Plumlee, J. Patrick, Jay Starling, and Kenneth W. Kramer (1985). 'Citizen Participation in Water Quality Planning: A Case study of Perceived Failure'. *Administration and Society* vol. 16, no. 4, pp. 455–473.

Prakash, Aseem (2000). 'Responsible Care: An Assessment'. *Business and Society* vol. 39, no. 2, pp. 183–209.

Rabe, Barry G. (1994). *Beyond NIMBY*. Brookings Institution Press, Washington DC.

Rowe, Gene and Lynn J. Frewer (2000). 'Public Participation Methods: A Framework for Evaluation'. *Science, Technology, and Human Values* vol. 25, no. 1, pp. 3–29.

Shearing, David J. (2003). Personal communication. February.

Sim, Peck Hwee (2001). 'Searching for New Members'. *Chemical Week* 4–11 July.

Smith, Patrick D. and Maureen H. McDonough (2001). 'Beyond Public Participation: Fairness in Natural Resource Decision Making'. *Society and Natural Resources* vol. 14, no. 3, pp. 239–249.

Stewart, Thomas R., Robin L. Dennis, and Daniel W. Ely (1984). 'Citizen Participation and Judgement in Policy Analysis: A Case Study of Urban Air Quality Policy'. *Policy Sciences* vol. 17, no. 1, pp. 67–87.

Chapter 3

Precaution Versus Sound Science: Risk Discourses and Civil Society Participation in International Food Safety Negotiations

Diane Bartlett and Harriet Friedmann

The emergence of biotechnology in the late 1980s provoked a heated global debate over the management of new technologies. Whether these new technologies represent progress or a problem depends on how proponents and opponents succeed in constructing frames for defining the issues. Even basic terms such as 'risk' and 'danger' are socially constructed and constantly evolving, through 'meaning-making' contests (Hannigan 1995). The debate over agricultural biotechnologies takes place at two levels. Although the media rhetoric of 'miracle seeds' and 'Frankenfoods' stays outside the doors of international negotiating sessions, these form frames that act as background pressure on states and thus help to shape the continuing impasse in agricultural trade negotiations. Beneath the bland vocabularies of risk assessment and precaution lie deep disagreements about how decisions about risks will be made.

These debates reflect fresh uncertainty about the relationship between public policy and science. In the past, debates over the safety of technological developments would have been resolved quickly (or even bypassed) by a traditional constellation of scientific experts. However, recent social theories suggest that faith in science is waning and the public is demanding a more active role in the decision-making process. The result, for agricultural biotechnology, has been a lingering stalemate in international organisations over the principles of regulation and the types of actors that should be legitimately involved in risk decisions. The stalemate expands beyond different national interests to include profound questions about the appropriate role of corporations and social movements in defining government positions and international decisions. Will the meaning of terms such as 'precaution' and 'risk' locate decisions with traditional 'experts' who decide how to apply (necessarily selective) scientific findings? Or will the meaning of these terms include not only botanical and chemical research findings, but also social, environmental, and health considerations, which open decisions about assessment and management of risks to a wider public discussion?

Conflicts over how to assess genetic engineering risks take place in an institutional field that was transformed in the 1990s. The impacts of plant genetic engineering

– which are possibly far-ranging – cut across distinct regulatory issues, particularly trade and environment. The tasks of regulating trade and environment are charged to institutions created in the 1990s, such as the World Trade Organization (WTO) and the bodies established at the 1992 United Nations Conference on Environment and Development (UNCED). The co-ordination of these different bodies remains unsettled. In the arena of food safety, states jockey over definitions of important terms such as 'precaution' within and across trade and environment organisations, while at the same time they wrestle with the demands of civil society actors. Some of these actors, mainly corporate representatives, carry considerable clout in national delegations; others, such as citizens and advocacy groups, have gained observer status but press for more involvement and empowerment.

This chapter explores the risk contest over food safety in international organisations for trade and environment. Its main concern is the degree to which the discourse contest over risk and uncertainty has created opportunities for public participation in the decision-making process, or restricted participation to (also contested) experts. After introducing theories of risk and discourse, the chapter examines the institutional field of inter-state and inter-issue negotiations created in the 1990s. It then turns to the three key terms in discourse contests over the meaning of precaution for trade and environment: 'precaution', 'sound science', and 'substantial equivalence'. Finally, it considers the implications of the contest thus far, for the future of public participation in decisions about food safety.

Risk and Discourse in International Politics

Recent social theorists have suggested that as the negative consequences of industrial society intensify, the foundations of policy decision-making are being restructured. Industrial society was dominated by 'primary scientization' (Beck 1995) where scientific experts held a monopoly on risk definition and were highly trusted by the public. In this period, the lay public was involved in the decisions only as knowledge takers who were communicated to. Over time, industrial processes, which initially reduced risks such as hunger, cold, and disease, began to create new risks. The globalised and unmeasurable nature of these new risks now strain the limits of traditional science to secure public trust. This crisis of legitimacy has the potential to move into a period of reflexive scientisation or reflexive democracy where discussions and reframing of the relation of science and policy and civil society take place. Whether civil society is empowered or marginalised is decided through contests over the meanings of powerful terms, such as precaution and risk assessment, and the way they are connected to other terms.

Maarten Hajer (1995) has applied discourse analysis to environmental politics, focussing on how it brought into public debate the relationship between science and politics. He defines discourses as 'a specific ensemble of ideas, concepts, and categorizations that is produced, reproduced, and transformed in a particular set of practices and through which meaning is given to physical and social realities' (264).

Competing discourses are socially constructed and perpetually in contest, but at some moments provisional understandings can emerge through discourse coalitions including states and civil society actors.

The key idea is the ensemble of ideas. For example, Hajer uses the term 'ecological modernization' to describe how the acid rain controversy of the 1980s served to reduce the politically complex issues of air pollution into a manageable policy issue. This resolution was the result of discourse alliances between specific environmental groups, policy officials, scientists, and industry groups. Ecological modernisation was the language that contained the potential contradiction between progress and risks of industrial society itself, that is, between 'ecological' and 'modernisation', or more commonly, between 'sustainable' and 'development'.

The international discourse of sustainable development led to a practical shift toward new concepts such as 'risk analysis', 'polluter pays', and the 'precautionary principle'. These replaced the former implicit assumption that environmental protection should be an industrial afterthought epitomised by end-of-pipe technologies. Although ecological modernisation reinforced beliefs in industrial progress, it nonetheless also created the potential for changes in participation by new actors such as environmental organisations and local residents, as well as changes in policy-making practices, such as the consultation of nongovernmental organisations (NGOs) (Hajer 1995, 29).

In the 1990s, a protracted contest was waged in the arena of agricultural regulation. Risk and precaution, both terms identified by Hajer as characteristic of ecological modernisation, were the objects of struggle in debates over politically sensitive agro-food safety challenges such as biotechnology and bovine spongiform encephalopathy (BSE). The stakes of these meaning-making contests are high because they will decide who will be given the right to make globally binding regulatory decisions. Discourses can be shaped so that they cognitively and practically open up (or close off) avenues to participation (Hajer 1995, 25). The focus of this exploration of official genetic-engineering discourses is the degree to which they challenge or defend participation by non-state actors such as corporations and transnational advocacy networks.

The Contested Field of International Institutions

Corporations, professional associations, and transnational advocacy networks have entered into international discussions previously reserved for states. They have been able to do so partly because the regulatory spaces for food safety and other matters related to agricultural biotechnology are in flux. This section identifies the international organisations with (conflicting) mandates for food safety before turning to the discourses whose outcomes will determine the balance of citizen participation.

A series of important changes and agreements that took place in the 1990s set the stage for a reconfiguration of the discourses of precaution and risk in food and agriculture. At the 1992 UNCED, often referred to as the Earth or Rio Summit, many states signed the Rio Declaration that affirmed their commitment to the concept of sustainable development. This meeting created the Convention on Biological Diversity (CBD) and started the process that would lead to the creation of the Cartegena Protocol on Biosafety for the regulation of living modified organisms (Le Prestre 2002). In 1994, after years of difficult negotiation, the WTO was created. One of its chief products, the Agreement on Agriculture, subjected food and agriculture for the very first time to negotiations committed to liberalisation of trade. This agreement had consequences beyond the WTO when it named a marginal organisation – the Codex Alimentarius – as the legitimate referent for food safety standards. During the 1990s, the structures and governing principles of these global organisations were hotly negotiated. Indeed, there is still no consensus on how these institutions fit within a single hierarchy of authority in situations where their mandates overlap.

World Trade Organization

In 1986, at the beginning of the Uruguay Round of the General Agreement on Tariffs and Trade (GATT), various interests converged to support liberalisation as a solution to a generally perceived crisis in agricultural trade. The United States perceived trade liberalisation in the Uruguay Round as essential to recovering its declining trade position and sought deep cuts (75–90 percent) in domestic subsidies and import controls, mainly targeting the Common Agricultural Policy (CAP) of the European Union (Moyer and Josling 2002). Although politically unpalatable, discussions of reform and liberalisation were stimulated in the EU by the swelling budget of the CAP in the late 1970s and the impending access of new countries (Tracy 1990, 22). The EU welcomed more modest cuts (around 30 percent) and policies that were flexible and retractable (Skogstad 1994, 252). The countries of the South hoped for access to Northern markets and an end to the dumping of agricultural products by both U.S. and EU, which undermined both domestic agriculture and their position in international markets. A key lobby was the Cairns Group of agricultural exporters, which came together in August 1986 in order to influence the Uruguay Round of negotiations toward open trade and the abolition of subsidies. The Cairns Group was supported by the G7 and by the Organisation for Economic Co-operation and Development (OECD), both representing the North.

Yet beyond a vague agreement, rifts existed between North and South, within the North, and within the South. The Cairns Group of major exporting countries linked some South countries, notably Argentina, Thailand, and South Africa, with countries of the North – Canada and Australia – through a shared interest in removing unfair competition from domestic and export subsidies by the U.S. and EU. However, the largest Southern exporter, Brazil, belonged to both this group and – in environmental organisations – to the Miami Group, which opposed most Cairns members on issues related to agricultural trade in genetically engineered crops. Thus the global South is divided, just as the North is divided by the U.S.-EU (and Japan) impasse. Moreover, North and South are divided over the failure of the

North to fulfil its promise to open Northern markets to Southern agricultural goods. Indeed, U.S. subsidies have been increased to historic levels. State interests are not clearly aligned. This leaves space for civil society politics, both corporate lobbies and social movements.

The WTO acknowledges the right of nations to set food safety standards. Yet, as a trade organisation, it seeks to limit food safety regulations to those that are the 'least trade restrictive'. Within the WTO, the Agreement on Sanitary and Phytosanitary Measures (SPS) concerns health and safety regulations, while the agreement on Technical Barriers to Trade (TBT) deals with abuse of safety standards, as well as packaging, marking, and labelling, that could be used as a disguised form of protection. Divergent national rules offer considerable space for disagreement over the legitimacy of national standards with respect to trade. At the same time, environmental issues, which have emerged as newly important to food safety, were delegated to the WTO's Committee on Trade and the Environment (CTE).

Of course, states are not equal. The WTO relies on a dispute-resolution system that privileges powerful states with the capacity to produce scientific research and policy documents. The WTO is intended to be a multilateral organisation; however, food safety disputes are launched bilaterally and often resolved the same way. Only rich countries can mount complaints effectively and weather the kinds of sanctions required by a settlement. As a comparison, when the EU lost the WTO dispute over beef hormones, in 2003 the WTO approved U.S. retaliatory trade sanctions of US$116 million a year on sensitive European products such as Danish ham, German chocolate, and French mustard (Osborn 2003). Canada imposed its own sanctions of C$11 million per year. By contrast, when Sri Lanka issued a precautionary ban on living modified organisms based on biodiversity concerns and concerns over traceability, veiled threats of a WTO dispute by the U.S. led to suspension of the law (Parmentier 2001).

Codex Alimentarius

Codex Alimentarius was cast into a crucial new role in 1995 because of references made in the WTO Agreement on Agriculture. The Codex Alimentarius ('food code') was created in 1963 as a joint initiative of the World Health Organization (WHO) and Food and UN's Agriculture Organization (FAO).[1] It emerged out of concern in the 1950s and 1960s that multiple and variable national food regulations impeded trade and provided inadequate health protection for consumers. These issues were particularly a concern for the countries of the South. Powerful Northern countries were able to develop strong and, of course, specific domestic regulations. Codex attempted the role of facilitating developing country access to developed nations' markets. This goal was frustrated by strong import restrictions imposed by countries in the North. As well, the voluntary nature of Codex standards meant that governments of the North were under no obligation to disrupt their individualised and highly elaborated food control systems to conform to a Codex standard. Before the WTO, Codex was a marginal organisation oriented mainly to creating ready-made standards and national food safety infrastructure for developing countries that lacked these abilities (Jukes 2000, 182).

Now Codex standards matter. Given that Codex was the only organisation that had done work on food safety codes, the SPS and TBT agreements of the WTO were set up to recognise Codex standards as the appropriate benchmarks against which all national measures should be evaluated (FAO and WHO 1999). Countries that set higher standards invite challenge through the WTO dispute panel. The burden then falls on the national government to prove that harm exists. Without a legitimate scientific rationale for the higher standard, the offending country risks retaliation, such as hefty trade sanctions or payment of compensation. Although the WTO does not enforce Codex standards directly, violating those standards could prove costly and difficult. In one stroke, Codex Alimentarius – a marginal, inadequately funded, consensus-oriented organisation – became linked to the WTO's adversarial and power dominated systems of resolution. Even the anticipation of the WTO transformed Codex into a key crucial political arena for discursive struggles over the principles of biotechnology regulation.

Cartagena Protocol on Biosafety

The new importance of genetic resources stemming from biotechnology has shifted the interests of the South as a whole. This is reflected in the politics of the CBD. The South had opposed the concept of sustainable development when it was first formulated at the 1972 UNCED, the Stockholm Conference. The Southern countries viewed it as an attempt to prevent them from catching up to Northern countries through economic growth.

The South reversed its position between 1972 and 1992. Many of the poorest countries now find themselves as guardians and potential beneficiaries of the overwhelming majority of sources of biodiversity, including food crops. Many (but not all) countries of the South advocate sovereign control over flows of commodities that might affect biodiversity. Their ecosystems and farming systems have the most to lose from genetic pollution and they have reason to fear that their countries will be used to experiment with unknown novel organisms and foods (Lehmann 2002). At the same time, they wish to capitalise on their advantage in genetic diversity as resources for food and other industries, such as pharmaceuticals. The 1992 Rio Declaration addressed another problem of developing states by acknowledging the different capabilities of governments.

The Cartagena Protocol on Biosafety was initiated by the CBD, which came into force in December 1993. The work of the protocol has been slowed several times by the Miami Group of grain-exporting nations (U.S., Canada, Australia, Argentina, Chile, and Uruguay), which feared it would affect their export markets. This group attempted to have the agreement exclude genetically engineered seeds and even agriculture entirely. In 1998, a U.S. delegate said his goal was 'to avoid undue interference with world trade because this is as much a trade agreement as an environmental agreement' (cited in Friends of the Earth 1999). There is disagreement on the exact relationship of the Cartagena Protocol to the WTO. The U.S. and the Miami Group view the CPB as an exception to the WTO rules, while the EU believes the protocol cannot be subordinated to any other agreement.

On 11 September 2003, the CPB entered into force. The EU has included a concept of precaution in its constitution, which remains to be ratified. It continues to advocate specific measures, such as independent and specific documentation of all living modified organisms in international trade, in alliance with many countries of the South, particularly the Africa Group led by Ethiopia. The U.S., the Cairns Group, and the Miami Group, including non-signatories (that continue to participate in discussions) continue to block specific precautionary measures. In 2005, the Experts' Meeting on Traceability for the Cartagena Protocol on Biosafety resulted in a refusal to require stand-alone documentation of shipments containing living modified organisms, in favour of a statement on commercial invoices accompanying shipments of grains intended for food, feed, and processing stating that a 'shipment may contain living modified organisms not intended for intentional introduction into the environment' (CBD 2005, 15). The final report, at the insistence of Ethiopia and other countries of the South, as well as the EU and Norway, included statements refusing to agree that the chair's report reflected consensus or even a majority of governments (Ching 2005).

Each of these international arenas is too important to ignore. None has a settled framework for regulating food safety. The highly fragmented and overlapping issues of environment and trade create a fluid field for discourse contests.

Civil Society

Along with a changing field of inter-state negotiations, transnational advocacy networks have also changed in the decade since Rio. NGOs opposed to agricultural biotechnologies have particularly affected the EU. Divisions occur, for instance, between professional societies, consumer organisations (in both cases, some favour genetically engineered foods and others oppose them) and environmental advocacy networks (usually opposed). Corporate lobbies have played an important role in defining the U.S. position. Indeed, biotechnology corporations have contributed to writing U.S. national legislation and regulations, which are often promoted by U.S. delegations to international bodies, and corporations are often directly represented on U.S. negotiating teams. The United States hopes that the lead of U.S. biotechnology companies will strengthen its dominance in international trade.

Civil society organisations of both kinds work internationally. These non-state actors complicate definitions of national interests and inter-state alliances, as they participate in contests over the framing of regulations, inside and outside of international organisations. The outcomes of these contests have implications not only for national interests, but also for the breadth and depth of public participation. The degree to which risk is acknowledged to be unknowable in principle – and thus subject to public debate and democratic decision – depends on how it is defined in relation to science, and specifically in relation to the new vocabulary of precaution.

Contested Discourses: What is the Meaning of Precaution?

Major discourse contests have arisen among states over how to frame risk. These contests take place through the terms 'precaution', 'sound science', and 'substantial equivalence'. Although states negotiate within the WTO, CBD, and Codex, their positions are only partly about national interests. The contest over the framing of precaution has implications for public participation in genetic engineering policy, and thus for the relation between science and democracy.

Framing Precaution: European Origins

The word 'precaution' in this context emerged in the 1960s from public concern over environmental damage due to pollution from industry, including industrial agriculture. In Europe, the term was part of a new regulatory discourse shifting responsibility onto polluters instead of the public, targeting risky processes rather than risky outcomes, and moving regulation to prior assessment rather than end-of-pipe measures. Precaution was a key term in the discourse that channelled the profound ecological critique of economic growth as an overarching social goal (and thus of capitalism itself) into a manageable policy issue. Depending on the country and its political culture, various combinations of policy innovators in government, minority scientists, and advocacy groups helped governments to find a way to transform a radical challenge into a technical approach to assess and manage risks (Hajer 1995). Even as it tamed the radical critique, however, the idea of precaution contained an implicit recognition of the limits of scientific prediction and the necessity for widening risk assessment and management to social concerns and to public participation.

Precaution arose with environment as a specialised policy field in European countries. Both precaution and the environment emerged via political and scientific challenges to the traditional pragmatist orientation to industrial pollution (Hajer 1995), which consisted of localised efforts to 'identify, clean up and repair' damage. By the late 1980s, this policy discourse had shifted to one of 'anticipate' and 'prevent'. For example, the OECD began to promote a loose idea of precaution very similar to prevention. This was consistent with its general economic mandate to 'achieve the highest sustainable economic growth', 'contribute to the development of the world economy,' and 'contribute to the expansion of world trade' (Long 2000, 4). The OECD, which promoted a shift from national to international regulation, based its outlook on an assumption of the possibility of an integration of economic and environmental concerns. The key question was who should pay for pollution. Nonetheless, the OECD recognised situations 'when there appears to be no immediate harm … and where the longer-term effects are only speculative' (38). In such situations it was necessary to ask what criteria should govern public action. This opened up the question of how strong or weak precaution should be and how, if at all, it should be embedded in law.

At the same time, a more expansive understanding of precaution was being developed in the 1970s in Germany. This would eventually become the precautionary principle. Many analysts locate the origin of the term 'precautionary principle' with the German concept of *Vorsorge* or 'forecaring,' which was used in the 1970s to justify cutting emissions to curb forest devastation, despite the absence of concrete scientific proof. In German environmental law, this approach became *Vorsorgeprinzip:* 'the forecaring, or precautionary, principle' (Pollan 2001). While, as Volker Lehmann notes, the German approach was balanced with a concern with 'economic viability' (Lehmann 2002, 7), it nonetheless promoted precautionary action in the absence of scientific proof.

In the EU, the precautionary principle has been increasingly interpreted as inherently political and thus more conducive to the wider participation of civil society and a lively democracy. The principle enshrined in the Treaty on European Union requires action to protect against risk even in the absence of scientific proof. In 2000, the EU's Communication from the Commission on the Precautionary Principle stated that precaution entails acceptance of the provisional nature of scientific evidence, so that 'decisions to act (or not) are ultimately political' (Lehmann 2002, 12). This leaves open the implicit shift in the burden of proof of safety. It recognises that a precautionary measure might be taken to place the burden of proof upon the producer, manufacturer, or importer, although doing so cannot be made a general rule. It distinguishes between 'risk management' where precaution applies, from the caution used in 'risk assessment'. This shift may be a conservative backtracking on where politics belongs in the decision chain.

With respect to agricultural biotechnologies, the EU's interpretation lends itself to giving attention to the unique characteristics of living organisms and ecosystems. This argument for the precautionary principle claims to be more realistic than reliance on supposedly conclusive science, because it accepts that absence of scientific knowledge is the norm in regulatory decision making. It permits, and may even require, the type of discretion that is challenged by advocates of sound science as protectionist (Cosbey 2000). Because the precautionary principle acknowledges the profoundly political nature of decisions to introduce genetically modified crops, it also opposes strong interpretations of harmonisation of rules. However, Regulation 178/2002 of the European Parliament establishes the Food Safety Authority as responsible for scientific and policy questions relating to genetically modified foods. It specifies that the precautionary principle means that scientific uncertainty requires risk management, but measures are to be the 'least restrictive'. The balance between expertise and politics in EU regulation remains in flux.

Framing Precaution Internationally: Environment

Internationally, precaution has, not surprisingly, been most strongly represented in environmental agreements. The 1992 Earth Summit instituted precaution in international environmental law. Precaution had been turned into a principle governing European inter-state policy in the 1987 Declaration of the Second International North Sea Conference, which used the term 'precautionary principle' for the first time in such a document and stated that 'a precautionary approach is necessary which may require action to control inputs of such substances even before a causal link has been established by absolutely clear scientific evidence' (North Sea Conference 1987). Although the South had opposed the related idea of sustainable development in 1972, in 1982 the precautionary principle appeared in the World Charter for Nature adopted by the UN General Assembly, where Southern governments are a majority (Lehmann 2002). In these documents, the terms 'precautionary approach' and 'precautionary principle' were interchangeable.

The Cartagena Protocol gave governments the right to refuse 'living modified organisms' in cases of uncertainty or lack of scientific consensus. In the text, the protocol makes use of the word 'approach' exclusively: 'In accordance with the precautionary approach contained in Principle 15 of the Rio Declaration on Environment and Development' (CBD 2000, art. 1). The protocol is clearly intended to provide a more formal endorsement of the spirit of precaution contained in the original text of the Convention on Biological Diversity, which states: 'Where there are threats of serious or irreversible damage, lack of full scientific certainty shall not be used as a reason for postponing cost-effective measures to prevent environmental degradation' (UNCED 1992, art. 15).

Implications for harmonisation of domestic regulations, later promoted by the WTO, were potentially significant. It is thus clear that the word 'approach' is meant strongly: 'the precautionary approach shall be widely applied by States according to their capabilities' (UNCED 1992, art. 15). In 1992, the fine rhetorical differences between precautionary principle and precautionary approach, which later came to characterise discourse contests at the WTO, were still three years away. In the CBD, the precautionary approach therefore has the meaning of precautionary principle in trade discourse.

Framing Precaution Internationally: Trade

In trade debates, the EU advocates a strong precautionary principle in all institutional forums responsible for regulating agricultural trade: the WTO Committees on Agriculture and on Trade and Environment, the SPS Agreement, and, outside the WTO, the Codex Alimentarius. The U.S., supported by the Cairns Group, has stood opposed (WTO 2000). One of the rhetorical strategies used by the U.S. is to make a distinction between principle and approach, advocating approach to weaken precaution to the point of meaninglessness.

In trade regulation, any version of precaution is suspected of hiding trade barriers. Within the WTO, there is tension between the SPS Agreement, which is concerned with safety, and the TBT Agreement, whose very name carries the presumption that precaution will be abused. In this context, precaution can more easily be put on the defensive. Although the SPS Agreement is the first instance of precaution in the WTO agreements, it is also the source of weaker definitions of precaution than those promoted by the EU and the Rio Declaration. Precautionary language enters via Article 5.7 of the SPS Agreement, which allows provisional measures to be taken in situations where there is an absence of scientific data (WTO 1995). The absence of scientific data, however, is presumed rare via the more specific discursive challenge of sound science, which is discussed in the next section.

While discussions have taken place in all WTO forums, the most important one is in Codex Alimentarius. As Codex is responsible for creating binding safety standards for all its member nations, principles and procedures have been the major focus of recent deliberations. Yet Codex is caught between its original mandate of food safety and consumer health and its new mandate to create binding standards for the WTO. As a result, arguments for precaution within Codex are at a disadvantage because they must refer to WTO texts for justification.

An example of the dispute can be seen in the argument that unfolded when the EU tried to have the precautionary principle explicitly written into the procedural manual during the 1999 Codex meeting on general principles. The EU argued that the text of the SPS Agreement was sufficient for writing the precautionary principle into the Codex procedural manual. According to SPS, 'where relevant scientific evidence is insufficient, a Member may provisionally adopt sanitary or phytosanitary measures on the basis of available pertinent information' (WTO 1995, art. 5.7). The U.S., pointing to the Article 5.7, objected on the grounds that caution was already built into risk assessment. The U.S. stated, 'if such factors are explicitly considered by Codex in risk assessments, any country could justify trade barriers on virtually any product for virtually any reason ... We believe precaution is already the basis for what is done in Codex, and therefore a "principle" is unnecessary' (Grocery Manufacturers of America 2001). Thus disagreement between the EU and the U.S. at Codex was argued through disagreement over interpretation of the SPS provisions in the WTO. The 2004 report of the Codex Committee on General Principles acknowledges a 'lack of consensus' on the precautionary principle (Codex 2004).

One of the goals of Codex Alimentarius is to determine the extent to which countries support the precautionary principle. However, the review published FAO says very little about the principle. It states: 'The [Codex Alimentarius] Commission has recognized that precaution is an element of risk analysis, but has not defined or agreed to the use of the "precautionary principle" within the framework of Codex' (FAO 2002, para. 50). The issue remains highly contentious. The extraordinary circumlocution of the commission's position, enunciated in 2001, expresses the impasse in negotiations: 'When there is evidence that a risk to human health exists but scientific data are insufficient or incomplete, the Commission should not proceed to elaborate a standard but should consider elaborating a related text, such as a code of practice, provided that such a text would be supported by the available scientific evidence' (Codex 2001).

Discussions of the precautionary principle continued to stall discussions in the WTO Committee on Agriculture, until the whole issue was sidelined by a renewed focus on commitments to agriculture and export subsidies and import restrictions at the 2003 ministerial meeting in Cancun. In 2002, the EU and Switzerland said they would not negotiate until there was more discussion on issues such as the precautionary principle (International Centre for Trade and Sustainable Development [ICTSD] 2002). The EU explicitly asked for an interpretation of the Agreement on Agriculture to include precautionary measures, instead of allowing these issues to be worked out in the dispute mechanisms or requiring an amendment to the SPS Agreement. They asked for the Committee on Agriculture negotiations to clarify situations where the use of precaution was appropriate and were supported by Norway, Korea, and Japan. However, they were challenged by the U.S., Cairns Group members, and China, who felt this was an SPS issue. Even in the preparatory document for the 2003 meeting, there was no mention of precaution and the whole issue was dropped at the WTO as the North-South cleavage over subsidies took centre stage.

Although precaution was marginalised at the WTO, its link to public participation was clear in the years before Cancun. For instance, at a 2001 meeting of the WTO Committee on Trade and Environment, in response to a typical EU request for clarification of the relationship between the precautionary principle and WTO rules, the U.S. (and several other countries) asked how civil society and consumer concerns would be integrated and how minority scientific opinions would be managed (Department of Foreign Affairs and Trade [Australia] 2001). In the Codex exchange described above, the U.S. position was supported by industry. The observer from the Confederation of the Food and Drink Industries of the EU wanted the clear guidelines on the principle to avoid constraints to technological innovation. The European Food Law Association requested definition and clarity on the issue of burden of proof. By contrast, Sweden and EU governments claimed the precautionary principle was relevant for risk management and essential for building consumer confidence in the risk assessment process. These views were supported by consumer organisations in Europe. EU support for strong precautionary language also corresponded to a more democratic (although highly ambivalent) set of rules and procedures for managing risks, while the U.S. opposition also corresponded to a reliance on traditional experts outside the sphere of politics. The reframing of risk in this case was a direct challenge to precaution in favour of sound science and substantial equivalence.

Sound Science

Sound science is a discursive strategy to reframe risk assessment. The latter was originally joined to precaution in the 1980s as an alternative to previous regulation based on expert predetermination of safe levels of dangerous substances. This shift was what Maarten Hajer called the shift from traditional pragmatism to ecological modernisation. The challenge to precaution attempts to deny the political nature of risk decisions and to return to reliance on experts, now positioned as dispensers of sound science. The reframing thus attaches risk assessment to the very phenomenon it originally displaced, that is, the assumption of clear predictability of risks.

The official discussion frames risk in a phrase 'other legitimate factors' (OLF), including environmental and social risks. These are accepted to be relevant only at a stage after risk assessment, namely risk management. A further stage in the process is risk communication, namely public relations. In other words, public participation is pushed down the decision chain as much as possible, from determining what limits should be place on introduction of a technology to implementing that technology to manipulating public opinion. All this is necessary because faith in experts cannot return. Therefore, a strategy to reintroduce expert decisions (which must contain political agendas), in place of democratic politics, shifts the debate into science and anti-science, rational and Luddite, and, at the level of official discourse, sound science and junk science. The juxtaposition is used by the U.S. to separate out all social and political considerations.

The main venue for arguments between the precautionary principle and sound science has been the Codex Committee on General Principles. Sound science, which completely altered the original Codex mandate, entered the Codex framework several years before creation of the WTO. Codex principles since 1961 had been defined in relation to consumer health, with the motivation of helping Southern countries meet the standards of Northern regulators. As a result, Codex had few financial or administrative resources and, given protection against agricultural imports in Northern countries, little success in helping Southern food exports to the North. Codex therefore had inadequate staff and little appropriate institutional experience for the new tasks assigned by the WTO. It is not surprising that principles were applied inconsistently during deliberations in the subsidiary committees (Jukes 2000). To address the inconsistency, in 1991 an international food standards conference considered the implications of a WTO/Codex relationship. The FAO recommended that all existing standards be reviewed to determined 'their current relevance and sound scientific basis' and requested that all Codex committees work to ensure that their risk assessments were consistent and based on 'suitable scientific principles' (182).

Two years later, in 1993, risk analysis was first discussed by the Codex Alimentarius Commission. Thus, risk analysis was repositioned in a framework of science rather than in its original framework of precaution. Within this new framework, all discussions of precaution are disadvantaged. The U.S. and its allies reject inclusion of a precautionary principle because of its absence (as such) in the Rio Declaration, the CBD, or the SPS Agreement. Sound science acquires a sacred status.

Meanwhile, in continuing to refine its own use of the precautionary principle, the EU elaborated the related concept of risk analysis. Its 2000 Communication stated that the principle should be 'considered within a structured approach to the analysis of risk which comprises three elements: risk assessment, risk management, risk communication. The precautionary principle is particularly relevant to the management of risk' (Commission of the European Communities 2000, 3). Management is explicitly distinguished from assessment and, thus, precaution is moved to the middle rung of risk analysis. At this level, 'judging what is an acceptable level of risk is "ultimately" a political responsibility' and one that will involve a consideration of public concern (4). The precautionary principle is 'not simply an economic cost-benefit analysis: its scope is much broader, and includes non-economic considerations, such as the efficacy of possible options and their acceptability to the public' (5).

In 2002, when the EU brought the precautionary principle to Codex, the U.S. responded from a stance of sound science. The U.S. 'agree[d] that precaution can be an integral component of regulatory decisions, and that decisions usually need to be made in the face of uncertainty' (United States Food and Drug Administration [FDA] 2000). Nonetheless, in this view risk assessment was based on science, and proceeds with caution, so the U.S. demanded to know how it could be improved by the EU intention to use 'all pertinent factors (e.g., socio-economic)' in introducing a precautionary principle. The U.S. then challenged the commitment of the EU to science, asking whether the commission's guidelines placed consumer and political concerns on the same level as scientific information. It contested the EU statement that the decision to act or not – that is, to exercise precaution or not – was a 'political decision', which it maintained implied that the decision need not also be based on science. Finally, regarding risk communication – where the public was a passive receiver even for the EU – the U.S. asked what role the EU envisioned for governments in communicating distinctions between levels of risks as perceived by the public versus risks as evaluated by scientists.

Thus, despite the shared origins of the terms 'risk' and 'precaution', the rhetorical strategy of the U.S. is to break the link and reconstruct them as opposing ideas. These arguments appropriate risk analysis, now opposed to precaution, through appeal to a new term, sound science. Science now needs a modifier to do the work of re-legitimating expertise. It is opposed to junk science, namely, opinions challenging those of legitimate experts. It therefore works to de-legitimate some scientists, particularly those working with civil society organisations to challenge legitimate experts. Sound science consequently attempts to restore trust in experts in the midst of disputes over expertise. Experts are in turn opposed to an uninformed public.

The next step in the argument is to apply sound science to trade rules. This is the work of the term 'substantial equivalence'.

Substantial Equivalence

Substantial equivalence applies sound science to the regulation of genetically engineered food. The principle involves comparing the novel food with a conventional counterpart on a limited number of characteristics. Substantial equivalence allows (certain) experts to apply minimal criteria to evaluate the safety of novel products. The minimal approach privileges 'practicality' in regulating trade. Substantial equivalence constructs a particular definition of expertise that is shaped by industries' interest in the least restrictive trade.

Substantial equivalence originated in a U.S. federal regulatory guideline for medical equipment. It was first applied to agriculture with the genetically altered Flavr Savr™ tomato to facilitate its market launch in 1994 in the U.S. (Schauzu 2000, 1). Since then, the doctrine of substantial equivalence has been advocated by U.S. biotechnology companies to avoid subjecting genetically engineered foods to regulatory processes that exist for other novel compounds, such as pharmaceuticals, pesticides, or food additives. Those regulations might lead to regulatory specification of restrictions on acceptable daily intakes. They would require expensive toxicological experiments that could add five years and about US$25 million to the research and development costs of a new product. This particular classificatory move allowed genetically engineered foods to be novel enough to require patents, but not novel enough to require extensive safety testing.

Substantial equivalence appears widely in national regulations of the EU as well as of the U.S. and Canada. It began to appear in international discussions as early as 1993, when an OECD report stated that substantial equivalence to 'analogous food products' was 'the most practical approach' to determine the safety of 'foods and food components from organisms developed by the application of modern biotechnology' (Apel 2000). This report was endorsed by the FAO and WHO in 1996 (FAO and WTO 1996).

But controversy arose quickly. Academics and civil society groups publicly criticised substantial equivalence. In 1999, Erik Millstone, Eric Brunner, and Sue Mayer (1999) argued that it is not possible, using only the chemical composition of a novel food, to be certain about its biochemical and immunological effects. They concluded that 'relying on the concept of "substantial equivalence" is therefore just wishful thinking: it is tantamount to pretending to have adequate grounds to judge whether or not products are safe'. A member of the British Royal Society argued that 'the presumption of safety of novel GM [genetically modified] plants based on substantial equivalence lacks scientific credibility, given modern expectations of standards of evidence' and cannot underpin a regulatory framework strong enough to inspire public confidence (Bainbridge 2001, 1).

Substantial equivalence was introduced into Codex documents despite objections by civil society observers. The Codex Ad Hoc Intergovernmental Task Force on Foods Derived from Biotechnology had its first meeting in 2000 to develop principles for risk analysis of foods derived from biotechnology. The Task Force – despite objections from Consumers International – found the principle to be 'useful' (FAO and WHO 2002). In 2002 the Working Group went further, in spite of objections from Greenpeace, to state: 'Rather than trying to identify every hazard associated with a particular food, the intention is to identify new or altered hazards relative to the conventional counterpart' (Codex 2002, 47). Most critics believed that substantial equivalence was used by the U.S., and by U.S. corporations, to circumvent a full safety assessment. The Council for Biotechnology Information, having succeeded in getting industry language into international documents, began to refer to substantial equivalence as a 'globally accepted principle' (Council for Biotechnology Information, 2).

Doubt soon spread to the OECD itself, which had introduced the concept into international circles. In a report published in 2000, the OECD described uncertainties and ambivalence about the 'commonly used tool' of substantial equivalence, and proposed 'after six years of using the tool, to undertake a more detailed review' (OECD 2000a, 3). This review would expand the number of voices in the debate: 'The means for carrying out a transparent review – which should acknowledge the need to include the various interest groups – should be worked out between the various international bodies active in the field. Namely, the new Codex Alimentarius Task Force, the OECD, the FAO and the WHO' (OECD 2000b, 8). Concern about the concept of substantial equivalence spread to national governments. Although some governments tentatively incorporated the principle into their domestic regulatory systems, many kept the concept under review and showed a desire to find more comprehensive methods of evaluation.[2] This reflected, in part, a realisation of the intrinsic limits to standardised comparisons. Substantial equivalence as an approach relies on the existence of a comparator with a well-documented history of use. Second-generation genetically modified products may have no suitable reference product.

Substantial equivalence, as the practical application of the term 'sound science', has been used to exclude public participation by opposing the precautionary principle. Yet the original unity of precaution and risk has reasserted itself, even at the OECD. A recent statement from the OECD brings in environment and brings back Precaution: 'the concept of a precautionary approach to risk assessment, recognised in the Cartagena Protocol on Biosafety, has the potential to be worked up into a practical way to accommodate the new approaches consumers, the public at large, special interest groups, and scientists request from a risk assessment and management system' (OECD 2000b, 8).

Conclusion

Discourse contests over regulatory frames for genetically engineered foods ended the 1990s without resolution. The key terms of 'risk' and 'precaution' remain the focus of argument. This analysis has shown how the risk contests have taken place at two levels simultaneously. At one level, the stand-off between positions for the precautionary principle and for substantial equivalence must be seen as more than a matter of national interests. The reason for the impasse also has to do with domestic politics. Underlying apparently coherent national interests – the U.S. as leading agricultural biotechnology exporter versus the EU as leading importer – are domestic politics with divergent implications for civil society participation in risk decisions.

At the other level, the sociology of risk leads to a deeper question about the political space in contention: will critical understandings of technology and power be reduced to discourse coalitions that find accommodation with existing power relationships? This is the thrust of attempts to find compromises, such as possible agreement on labelling as an emblem (Hajer 1995) that can reduce complex issues to a single policy (Patterson and Josling 2002; Browne, Chaitoo, and Hart 2000). Yet although discourse coalitions might succeed in achieving agreement, the deeper issues prevent a coalition capable of resolving the wider conflict over risk decisions for genetic technologies.

If a discourse coalition seems unlikely to resolve the framing of precaution, it is because at issue is the very process of taking risky decisions. Will the unprecedented risks of introducing genetically engineered crops into the environment and food supply lead to greater political involvement by citizens in whether and how to introduce, manage, and evaluate the effects of genetically engineered seeds and foods? This is what Ulrich Beck (1992) anticipated more than a decade ago as a new phase of reflexive scientisation in turn entailing reflexive democracy in risk decisions. The precautionary principle advanced by the EU, while retaining the ambiguity about expertise built into the original concept described by Hajer, nonetheless opens the door to civil society actors by including social and environmental criteria along with economics in cost-benefit analysis. The precautionary principle is used extensively by civil society groups in challenges to expert and corporate dominance in setting rules within international organisations.

Disputes over precaution also raise the complex issue of the balance between trade and environment, including the mutual influence of discourse contests in different international organisations. A key term in this field is 'harmonisation' – a fundamental principle for trade institutions. In the WTO and Codex, the U.S. has worked to recapture precaution in order to reinforce a model of decision making characterised as primary scientisation, that is, faith in experts now framed as sound science capable of determining substantial equivalence between novel and familiar entities. This entails resistance to the precautionary principle, instead framing precaution in international texts as an 'approach' or (a still greater weakening) as equivalent to the simple caution that may be presumed to be exercised by experts. This framing reinforces existing power relations – of the U.S. as dominant exporter and corporations as dominant agents – by legitimating an expert form of analysis, management, and communication of risk. The EU's framing of the precautionary principle, by contrast, shifts attention away from standard safety rules toward harmonising processes of risk decision – who should decide according to what criteria? Therefore, as the U.S. consistently argues, the precautionary principle sits uncomfortably with trade institutions whose mandate is to standardise. With U.S. negotiators taking the lead, the framing of precaution in international trade policy has so far been shaped by corporate biotechnology interests.

Precaution is more securely grounded in environmental issues and organisations. Thus in the CBD even the term 'precautionary approach' has a meaning equivalent to the strength of precautionary principle in the WTO and Codex. The U.S. and its allies (called the Miami Group) are more defensive in their attempts to preserve traditional constellations of risk managers and contain the idea within risk assessment. Of course, despite its powerful role in the CBD and the Cartagena Protocol, the U.S. has not ratified either agreement. These are nonetheless significant as part of the discursive field shaping how precaution affects the practice of genetic engineering. Indeed, the EU may include the CBD in domestic law, which would further strengthen its commitment to the precautionary principle and reinforce the impasse on agricultural trade negotiations.

Meanwhile, the stalemate over regulation has allowed corporations to create a new reality on the ground without being restricted by precaution. Delay in establishing a regulatory framework and agreed-upon principles allows corporations to proceed in the absence of rules. While governments argue endlessly in international organisations, delay has permitted what might be called a practical harmonisation by spreading plantings of genetically engineered crops throughout the world. Between 1996 and 2000, the planted area of genetically engineered crops rose from 1.7 million hectares to 43 million hectares (Rural Advancement Fund International 2000). Widespread contamination of conventional crops threatens to destroy alternatives to genetic engineering, including organic crops. Even countries with *de facto* bans, such as Brazil, face contamination. Brazilian farmers who fear being non-competitive smuggle in genetically engineered seed from neighbouring Argentina and Uruguay, facilitated by Monsanto's artificially low seed prices. Contamination of Brazil's southern region is estimated to be between 60 percent and 80 percent.

Contamination raises new risks that must be included in the mix of negotiated issues. As pollution, it fits more easily into the old problems of industrial pollution of air and water. The opportunity to find a way to assess and regulate risk before the fact has already passed. The problem of managing risks of contaminated crops, however, is not likely to fall easily into the rules for managing other industrial pollution (which themselves, *vide* Kyoto, remain far from settled). The effects on living organisms, both human bodies and food supplies, raise potentially greater risks than any so far faced by human societies. This raises the possibility that the present balance between international organisations could tilt toward environment and the CBD, and that trade will be forced to accommodate something closer to the EU's framing of precaution.

Hope lies in both the emerging contradictions in practice of substantial equivalence, and in alliances between states and civil society reframing trade and precaution in the new discourse of health. Substantial equivalence will likely be of limited use beyond the first generation of novel plants and foods. At the same time, international politics in the related field of pharmaceuticals suggest that a discourse alliance might emerge with greater support for a strong version of precaution to somehow find discursive resolution. The South, torn between a desire for development and the advantage of genetic resources, sits uneasily in the stand-off between the EU and the U.S. in agricultural trade negotiations. The South agreed to the WTO's Agreement on Trade-Related Aspects of Intellectual Property Rights (TRIPS Agreement) because it expected the Agreement on Agriculture to open Northern markets up to Southern exports. The impasse at the WTO and the increased U.S. agricultural subsidies dashed that expectation and opened the way for other alliances. These have come from international NGOs. Several organisations, led by Médecins Sans Frontières and Oxfam, successfully mobilised a campaign against the TRIPS Agreement with regard to international pharmaceuticals because of the prohibitive cost of HIV/AIDS drugs and other medicines to poor countries. As a result, at its ministerial meeting at Doha the WTO declared public health to be a legitimate grounds for limiting trade. It remains to be seen whether this alliance will extend to agricultural biotechnologies, and perhaps even to related issues such as indigenous intellectual property in seeds and medicines, as other NGOs intend (Shiva 1995). The alternative may well be the violent and desperate opposition of farmers in the South revealed in the uprooting of crops in Brazil and attacks on Monsanto facilities in India. If so, inclusion of civil society in risk decisions in international organisations has consequences for the legitimacy and future relevance of the institutions themselves.

Notes

1 Additional information on the Codex Alimentarius can be found at <www. codexalimentarius.net>.
2 The OECD reports influenced the approach of several national governments. Canada's 'Guidelines for the Safety Assessment of Novel Foods' are based on OECD approach of substantial equivalence but review the concept (Health Canada 1994). Other countries such as Norway asked that 'particular attention is given to possible measures of unintended effects of the genetic modification, for instance through a broader measure of the concept substantial equivalence' (OECD 2002). The UK also used substantial equivalence but hoped that in the future that new techniques (genomic, proteomic, and metabolic profiling approaches) will 'further increase the robustness of the substantial equivalence principle as a safety evaluation tool' (OECD 2000). In the 2000 'Report of the Task Force for the Safety of Novel Foods and Feeds', the OECD referred to substantial equivalence as one of 'a number of internationally established scientific principles' but noted that it is not applied the same in each nation or region (OECD 2000c). The OECD said that it might be difficult to apply this principle in the future when the modifications involve more than one gene.

References

Apel, Andrew (2000). '"Substantial Equivalence" and the Precautionary Principle: A Challenge to Risk Assessment'. AgBiotech. <www.biotech-info.net/risk_assessment_challenge. html> (November 2005).
Bainbridge, Janet (2001). 'The Use of Substantial Equivalence in the Risk Assessment of GM Food'. Royal Society <www.royalsoc.ac.uk/trackdoc.asp?id=1050&pId=2144> (November 2005).
Beck, Ulrich (1992). *Risk Society: Towards a New Modernity*. Sage Publications, London.
Beck, Ulrich (1995). *Ecological Politics in an Age of Risk*. Polity Press, Cambridge.
Browne, Dennis, Ramesh Chaitoo, and Michael Hart (2000). 'Can Eco-Labelling Undermine International Agreements on Science-Based Standards?' In G.B. Doern and E.J. Reed, eds., *Risky Business: Canada's Changing Science-Based Policy and Regulatory Regime*, pp. 120–130. University of Toronto Press, Toronto.
Ching, Lim Li (2005). 'No Agreement at Biosafety Protocol Experts' Meeting'. Third World Network Biosafety Information Service. <www.twnside.org.sg/title2/service178.htm> (November 2005).
Codex Alimentarius Commission (2001). 'Summary and Conclusions'. 24th Session, Geneva, 2–7 July. ALINORM 01/41. <www.codexalimentarius.net/cac24/alinorm0141/ summarye.htm> (November 2005).
Codex Alimentarius Commission (2002). 'Report of the Third Session of the Codex Ad Hoc Intergovernmental Task Force on Foods Derived from Biotechnology'. ALINORM 03/34. <www.codexalimentarius.net/download/report/75/al03_34e.pdf> (November 2005).
Codex Alimentarius Commission (2004). 'Report of the Twentieth Session of the Codex Committee on General Principles'. ALINORM 04/27/33A. <www.fao.org/docrep/ meeting/008/j2469e/j2469e01.htm> (November 2005).

Commission of the European Communities (2000). 'Communication from the Commission on the Precautionary Principle'. COM(2000) 1. 2 February. <europa.eu.int/comm/dgs/ health_consumer/library/pub/pub07_en.pdf> (November 2005).

Convention on Biological Diversity (2000). 'Cartagena Protocol on Biosafety'. <www.biodiv.org/biosafety/protocol.asp> (November 2005).

Convention on Biological Diversity (2005). 'Report of the Open-Ended Technical Expert Group on Identification Requirements of Living Modified Organisms Intended for Food or Feed, or for Processesing'. UNEP/CBD/BS/COP-MOP/2/103, 30 March. <www.biodiv.org/doc/meetings/bs/mop-02/official/mop-02-10-en.pdf> (November 2005).

Cosbey, Aaron (2000). 'A Forced Evolution? The Codex Alimentarius Commission, Scientific Uncertainty, and the Precautionary Principle'. International Institute for Sustainable Development, Winnipeg. <www.iisd.org/pdf/forced_evolution_codex.pdf> (November 2005).

Council for Biotechnology Information (2001). 'Substantial Equivalence in Food Safety Assessment'. <www.whybiotech.com/html/pdf/Substantial_Equivalence.pdf> (November 2005).

Department of Foreign Affairs and Trade (Australia) (2001). 'World Trade Organization: Meeting of the Committee on Trade and Environment (CTE), 13–14 February 2001'. <www.dfat.gov.au/trade/negotiations/environment/wto_cte_feb01.html> (November 2005).

Food and Agriculture Organization (2002). 'Report of the Evaluation of the Codex Alimentarius and Other FAO and WHO Food Standards Work'. <www.fao.org/docrep/meeting/005/ y7871e/y7871e00.htm> (November 2005).

Food and Agriculture Organization and World Health Organization (1996). 'Biotechnology and Food Safety'. Report of a Joint FAO/WHO Consultation. FAO Food and Nutrition Paper No. 61. <www.fao.org/es/ESN/food/risk_biotech_food_en.stm> (November 2005).

Food and Agriculture Organization and World Health Organization (1999). 'Understanding the Codex Alimentarius'. <www.fao.org/docrep/w9114e/w9114e00.htm> (November 2005).

Friends of the Earth (1999). 'Memorandum Submitted by Friends of the Earth'. Select Committee on Environmental Audit Minutes of Evidence, United Kingdom Parliament, 25 November. <www.parliament.the-stationery-office.co.uk/pa/cm199900/ cmselect/cmenvaud/45/9110909.htm> (November 2005).

Grocery Manufacturers of America (2001). 'Precautionary Principle'. <www.gmabrands.com/ publicpolicy/docs/whitepaper.cfm?docid=301> (November 2005).

Hajer, Maarten A. (1995). *The Politics of Environmental Discourse: Ecological Modernization and the Policy Process*. Clarendon Press, Oxford.

Hannigan, John A. (1995). *Environmental Sociology: A Social Constructionist Perspective*. Routledge, London.

Health Canada (1994). 'Guidelines for the Safety Assessment of Novel Foods'. <www.hc-sc.gc.ca/food-aliment/mh-dm/ofb-bba/nfi-ani/e_nvvlie.html> (November 2005).

International Centre for Trade and Sustainable Development (2002). 'Split on GIs Overshadow Market Access talks at WTO's Agriculture Committee'. *Bridges* vol. 6, no. 30. <www.ictsd.org/weekly/02-09-13/story1.htm> (November 2005).

Jukes, David (2000). 'The Role of Science in International Food Standards'. *Food Control* vol. 11, no. 3, pp. 181–194.

Le Prestre, Philippe G., ed. (2002). *Governing Global Biodiversity: The Evolution and Implementation of the Convention on Biological Diversity*. Ashgate, Aldershot.

Lehmann, Volker (2002). 'From Rio to Johannesburg and Beyond: Globalizing Precaution for Genetically Modified Organisms'. Heinrich Böll Foundation. Washington. <www.boell.org/520.asp> (November 2005).

Long, Bill L. (2000). 'International Environmental Issues and the OECD, 1950–2000: An Historical Perspective'. Organisation for Economic Co-operation and Development, Paris. <cdnet.stic.gov.tw/ebooks/OECD/29.pdf> (Maerh 2005).

Millstone, Erik, Eric Brunner, and Sue Mayer (1999). 'Beyond "Substantial Equivalence"'. *Nature* no. 401, p. 525–526.

Moyer, H. Wayne and Tim Josling (2002). *Agricultural Policy Reform: Politics and Process in the EU and U.S. in the 1990s*. Ashgate, Aldershot.

North Sea Conference (1987). 'Ministerial Declaration Calling for Reduction of Pollution'. 25 November, 27 ILM 835. London.

Organisation for Economic Co-operation and Development (2000a). 'Chairman's Report'. GM Food Safety: Facts, Uncertainties, and Assessment, OECD Edinburgh Conference on Scientific and Health Aspects of Genetically Modified Foods, 28 February–1 March. <www.oecd.org/dataoecd/4/25/1897032.pdf> (November 2005).

Organisation for Economic Co-operation and Development (2000b). 'Rapporteurs' Summary'. GM Food Safety: Facts, Uncertainties, and Assessment, OECD Edinburgh Conference on Scientific and Health Aspects of Genetically Modified Foods, 28 February–1 March. <www.oecd.org/dataoecd/4/25/1897056.pdf> (November 2005).

Organisation for Economic Co-operation and Development (2000c). 'Report of the Task Force for the Safety of Novel Food and Feeds'. C(2000)86/ADD1. <www.olis.oecd.org/olis/2000doc.nsf/LinkTo/C(2000)86-ADD1> (November 2005).

Osborn, Andrew (2003). 'EU Revives Row over Hormone Beef Ban'. *The Guardian*, 16 October, p. 20.

Parmentier, Rémi (2001). 'David and Goliath Travel to Qatar'. Greenpeace. <archive.greenpeace.org/politics/wto/Doha/html/remi_oped.html> (November 2005).

Patterson, Lee Ann and Tim Josling (2002). 'Regulating Biotechnology: Comparing EU and U.S. Approaches'. European Policy Paper No. 8, University of Pittsburg Center for International Studies. <www.ucis.pitt.edu/cwes/papers/poli_series/TransatlanticBiotech.pdf> (November 2005).

Pollan, Michael (2001). 'Precautionary Principle'. Science and Environmental Health Network. <www.sehn.org/pollan.html> (November 2005).

Rural Advancement Fund International (2000). 'Speed Bump or Blow-Out for GM Seeds?' 21 December. <www.etcgroup.org/text/txt_article.asp?newsid=13> (November 2005).

Schauzu, Marianna (2000). 'The Concept of Substantial Equivalence in Safety Assessment of Foods Derived from Genetically Modified Organisms'. *AgBiotech* vol. 2, pp. 1–4. <binas.unido.org/binas/reviews/Schauzu.pdf> (November 2005).

Shiva, Vandana (1995). 'Biotechnological Development and the Conservation of Biodiversity'. In V. Shiva and I. Moser, eds., *Biopolitics: A Feminist and Ecological Reader on Biotechnology*. Zed Books, London.

Skogstad, Grace (1994). 'Agricultural Trade and the International Political Economy'. In R. Stubbs and G.R.D. Underhill, eds., *Political Economy and the Changing Global Order*. McClelland and Stewart, Toronto.

Tracy, Michael (1990). 'The Political Economy of Agriculture in the European Community'. In H.J. Michelmann, J.C. Stabler and G.G. Story, eds., *The Political Economy of Agriculture and Trade Policy: Towards a New Order for Europe and North America*. Westview Press, Boulder.

United Nations Conference on Environment and Development (1992). 'Rio Declaration on Environment and Development'. <www.unep.org/Documents/Default.asp?DocumentID=78 &ArticleID=1163> (November 2005).

United States Food and Drug Administration (2000). 'A U.S. Government Submission to the Committee on General Principles of the Codex Alimentarius Commission for the Committee's April 10–14, 2000, Meeting'. <www.fsis.usda.gov/OA/codex/confpaper.htm> (November 2005).

World Trade Organization (1995). 'The WTO Agreement on the Application of Sanitary and Phytosanitary Measures'. <www.wto.org/english/tratop_e/sps_e/spsagr_e.htm> (November 2005).

World Trade Organization (2000). 'TE/033 – 10 July 2000'. Environment: Trade and Environment News Bulletins. <www.wto.org/english/tratop_e/envir_e/te033_e.htm> (November 2005).

Chapter 4

Continentalism from Below? Trinational Mobilisation among Labour Unions, Environmental Organisations, and Indigenous Peoples

Stefanie J. Bowles, Ian Thomas MacDonald, Jennifer Leah Mullen, and Stephen Clarkson[1]

In *The Great Transformation,* Karl Polanyi (1957) argued that the creation of a liberalised market economy in the 19th century generated a 'double movement', when opposition from social forces pressed national governments to strengthen their institutional capacity and reduce the insecurities occasioned by markets that had been freed of government controls.

The current phase of globalisation may be replicating this tension at the international level. Institutionalists see the emergence of transnational policy making both globally in the World Trade Organization (WTO) and continentally in the European Union as part of a process to re-regulate liberalised transnational markets. Observers of social movements detect a double movement in the development across borders of civil society networks that are grappling with social policy concerns, because traditional territorial states are no longer able to address these issues satisfactorily (Munck 2002).

Whether the new international governance institutions can serve the interests of transnationally organised citizens becomes a leading issue. It does so not just for democratic theorists of the new globalism (Risse-Kappen 1995). It does so also for the practical strategising of the activists involved in such issues as defending labour rights or resisting threats to the earth's ecology. Within continental North America, there has been considerable institutional development in the last 15 years. The corresponding inclusion (or exclusion) of civil society in the new continental governance is thus of critical concern.

It would be difficult to conceive of a more elite-driven process than the negotiation and implementation of the North American Free Trade Agreement (NAFTA), which came into effect in 1994 (Cameron and Tomlin 2000). Like all social institutions, however, NAFTA has encouraged the emergence of contradictory and potentially powerful forces that connect with a countermovement to the neo-liberal agenda as it expands to global arenas.

A burgeoning literature has sought to understand this civil society mobilisation against North American neo-liberal integration in terms of the movements' structural characteristics (Dreiling 2001), contestation tactics (Ayres 1998; Cook 1997; Foster 2005), and its historical context (Aaronson 2001). Yet has there been the development of a 'continentalism from below' through the transnational solidarity of civil society organisations? To provide an answer, this chapter analyses the differing effects that NAFTA has had on mobilising three distinct categories of socio-political actors: organised labour, the environmental movement, and indigenous communities. As a market player, labour is directly implicated by any rules affecting trade. Native peoples, by contrast, are barely even mentioned in trade agreements. At various positions between these extremes of complete involvement and virtual exclusion, environmentalists' trade concerns vary by shades of green. These three sets of groups have thus assumed varying levels of involvement in continental structures of contestation. While often sharing a common opposition to trade liberalisation, the three civil society sectors do not react to NAFTA in a common way. This chapter considers their disparate programmatic reactions in relation to their differing ideological perspectives, organisational structures, and social capacities. This analysis should help assess whether the notion of North American 'governance from below' has any real substance as a countermovement resisting neo-conservative globalisation.

Labour

Experience with NAFTA has confirmed the initial fears of Canadian and American unionists that the deal would bring damaging competitive pressures to bear on their memberships and has strengthened their resolve to oppose further trade liberalisation. More telling has been the reversal of the mainstream Mexican labour movement's original support for NAFTA. While Canadian and American unions unanimously rejected the agreement, including its labour side accord, the Mexican government had initially secured broad union support for the agreement due to its promise of job and wage gains and an effective mechanism to enforce labour rights. Belying the premise accepted in the free trade debate, which assumed Mexican workers would gain at the expense of Canadian and American workers, Mexican labour has fared the worst of the three under the agreement. This 'lose-lose-lose' scenario, combined with the manifest failure of the North American Agreement on Labour Cooperation (NAALC) to protect workers' rights, has served to promote a common, continental opposition to trade liberalisation among labour unions (Graubert 2002).

The destructive impacts of the agreement on labour and the coalescing of a common opposition to the project form only half the story. Completely unintentionally, NAFTA has introduced a creative-destructive process that, in many ways, has helped revitalise the North American labour movement. Most significantly, NAFTA has brought the issue of continental labour co-operation to the forefront of labour union strategy, not as a well-meaning moral duty or an empty political slogan, but as a practical tactic to deal with regionalised production systems.

Many labour market analysts have put forward the thesis that free trade pits protectionist workers in the global North against workers in the South, with the latter demanding the elimination of industrialised countries' tariffs and voicing suspicions of the motivations behind the social rights clauses advocated by their Northern brothers and sisters.[2] It is commonly understood that free trade agreements increase competitive pressures in an expanded labour market. Given a surprisingly wide range of analytical frameworks, this dominant view emphasises the cross-border conflict that competition engenders between national working classes.

This 'impossibility thesis' reduces labour unions to simple interest groups that defend the economic interests of their members.[3] But workers form unions in order to withdraw the price and conditions of their labour from market competition. Historically, this has been done first within a specific trade and then along industrial lines. Unionised workers are inclined to support the unionisation of other workers, as this strengthens their bargaining power through reducing the threat posed to their living standards by less expensive, non-union labour. Unions are thus not competitive but anti-competitive agents, which resist attempts to enlarge and deregulate labour markets. In circumstances where such resistance has failed, they continue to support the organisation of workers in the new, larger market, with the consistent goal of removing labour from competition.

NAFTA has powerfully underscored this logic. Staggering wage differentials across the North-South divide in continentalised production systems are largely the product of the weak bargaining position of Mexican workers who are hamstrung by corrupt unions and persistent violations of labour rights. In the automotive sector, for example, Mexican workers are just as skilled and disciplined and work with the same technology as their American counterparts but are paid one fourteenth the wage (Moody 1997, 71). Wage differentials of this magnitude, in turn, undermine the bargaining strength of workers north of the Rio Grande. By the very logic of neo-liberal integration, Canadian and American unions are encouraged, in defending their own members' interests, also to support the struggles of Mexican workers in their struggles for unionisation for improved wages and working conditions. Thus, far from exposing a rift between Northern and Southern unions, NAFTA has in fact revealed the importance of continental labour co-operation (Macdonald 2003). This hypothesis is evaluated below through an examination of NAFTA's effects on each country's working class and the development of organised labour's reaction to this impact.

The strictly economic impacts of NAFTA on North American workers have been relatively uneven, reflecting both nationally specific labour market conditions and the disproportionate shift in investment flows occasioned by the agreement.[4] As NAFTA has had a minimal impact on the redirection of Canadian foreign investment and trade toward Mexico compared to the shift in the United States, American workers have suffered higher levels of NAFTA-related job and wage loss than Canadian workers. Although a low Canadian dollar has to some extent mitigated the effects of tariff reduction and investment redirection on job loss, a report by D. Peter Dungan and Steven Murphy (1999, 98) for Industry Canada established that, due to free trade, imports displace relatively more jobs than are added by exports. In the U.S., the Economic Policy Institute has argued that NAFTA eliminated 766 030 actual and potential U.S. jobs between 1994 and 2000 (Scott 2001). Lawrence Mishel, Jared Bernstein, and John Schmitt (2001, 172) have established in an exhaustive study of the American labour market that increased U.S. foreign trade 'has been an important factor in both slowing the growth rate of average wages and reducing the wage levels of workers with less than a college degree'. In Mexico, wages in the manufacturing sector have declined by 10 percent, while real minimum wages have fallen by 24.8 percent since 1994 (Bensusan 2002, 5). While labour productivity in Mexican manufacturing surpassed Canadian and American levels by 1999, wages failed to keep pace due in part to Mexico's compromised official unions, which keep wages low in concert with the government's macro-economic strategies (5).

Arguably, the most devastating impact of NAFTA on Canadian and American workers has been a pronounced increase in capital mobility, encouraged by tariff elimination and the continental constitutionalisation of transnational corporate property rights. The ability of corporations to shift production and investment to Mexico, where wages are low, labour rights are ignored, and workers in the *maquiladora* sector are controlled by *charro* (corrupt) unions, has further undermined the bargaining position of Canadian and American labour. NAFTA has made such threats more credible and evidence suggests that the threat of disinvestment in a particular workplace or community can be an effective instrument to extract wage concessions and government subsidies and to discourage workers from organising. In a study commissioned by the Commission for Labor Cooperation (CLC), Kate Bronfenbrenner (1997, 8) found that, when confronted by a unionisation drive, 50 percent of corporations threatened to relocate to Mexico, and 12 percent followed through on their threat once a union was successfully formed. A strong correlation of this phenomenon to NAFTA can be made as the 15 percent post-1994 relocation rate tripled its pre-NAFTA level (8).

The NAALC was intended to address labour union fears that NAFTA would lead to these erosions of working conditions. As the NAALC failed to establish any common minimum standards and lacked a sanctions-based mechanism to enforce respect for core labour union rights, Canadian and American unions have come to regard it as ineffectual. Critics of the process have nevertheless noted one positive, if unintended, effect. Due to the requirement that a labour rights violation be related to trade, a complaint against a delinquent government must be filed with that government's NAFTA partner, a process that has fostered the establishment of cross-border alliances of interested parties (Graubert 2002, 3; Rosen 1999).

Notwithstanding their criticisms of the agreement, unions across the continent have shown some willingness to use the process as a way to publicise labour-rights abuses. The first cases pursued by the small, independent Mexican labour central, the Frente Auténtico del Trabajo (Authentic Workers' Front [FAT]) and the United Electrical, Radio, and Machine Workers of America (UE) were followed by increasingly sophisticated complaints filed by large coalitions involving the main Canadian and American labour federations, independent Mexican unions, and nongovernmental labour-rights organisations. The role of the CLC in fostering trinational and cross-sectoral links, however, cannot be divorced from the actual inability of the institution to secure fundamental labour rights. From a high of ten complaints filed in 1998, CLC's case load has dropped off dramatically, with one filed in 2000, two in 2001, none in 2002, three in 2003, and none in 2004. Due to the limited outcomes of the process and the high costs of filing complaints, unions have become increasingly reluctant to participate. Whereas the UE and the FAT are still open to the possibility of filing further cases, arguing that the institution remains the best means available for condemning labour rights violations in Mexico, the American Federation of Labour–Congress of Industrial Organizations (AFL-CIO) and the Canadian Labour Congress are no longer participating (Beaty 2002).

More significant in promoting continental union co-operation have been the increased competitive pressures occasioned by NAFTA itself. These pressures would have led to the elaboration of co-operative strategies even in the absence continental governance structures. But CLC promoted continental contestation by revealing the futility of tying labour rights clauses to free trade deals. In its policy paper on the matter, the Canadian expressed its opposition to future trade liberalisation, with or without social clauses (Katz-Rosene 2002). Not only has the CLC's failure hardened union attitudes toward neo-liberal globalisation, but it has also left a concrete, autonomous international struggle in the workplace to leverage union governance from below as their only viable alternative.

The NAFTA-related emergence of trinational co-operation among labour unions has taken several forms, ranging from broad educational coalitions to industry-based alliances for confronting common employers. Typically, the civil society networks that emerged to oppose the signing of the agreement fostered links among unions that later matured into formal agreements to co-operate in collective bargaining and organising campaigns. The process is best exemplified by the activity of the Red Mexicana de Acción Frente al Libre Comercio (Mexican Action Network on Free Trade [RMALC]), formed by the independent FAT along with environmentalists, teachers' unions, and progressive intellectuals in 1991 (Hathaway 2000, 173). Federations such as the FAT and the Unión Nacional de Trabajadores (National Workers' Union [UNT]) were concerned that a free trade agreement would lock in neo-liberal policies, entrench corporate power, and have an adverse impact on the well-being of their members.

RMALC conferences established contacts between Canadian and American unions and the FAT, which had experienced difficulty in interesting Northern unions in trinational co-operation before the threat of NAFTA. The UE had lost 10 000 manufacturing jobs to Mexico during the 1980s and thus decided to conclude an alliance with the FAT to bargain collectively with common employers (Carr 1999, 53). By 1992, the first targets of their 'strategic organising alliance' were American-owned *maquiladoras* along the Mexican-American border, such as a General Electric plant in Ciudad Juarez and a Honeywell plant in Chihuahua (Townsend 2002). When employers reacted to the drive by firing pro-union workers, the alliance brought a complaint before the CLC. As the favourable ruling failed to result in the reinstatement of the illegally fired workers, the alliance shifted its focus to other sectors where the FAT had a stronger base and established a union school (called a Centro de Estudios y Taller Laboral, A.C. [CETLAC]) to 'conscientise' *maquiladora* workers (Carr 1999, 53).

Within the broader labour movement, NAFTA also led to an alliance of the Sindicato de Telefonistas de la República Mexicana (Telecommunications Union of Mexico [STRM]) with the Communications Workers of America and the Communications, Energy, and Paperworkers of Canada. The original alliance was reached after the signing of Canada-U.S. Free Trade Agreement (CUFTA) to combat Nortel's anti-union activities (Carr 1999, 53). The STRM was asked to send organisers to a Sprint call centre in San Francisco, where most of the workers were Mexican Americans. The organising drive was successful, but Sprint closed the plant before a contract was signed. The communications alliance filed a complaint under CLC in 1995, alleging the violation of the right to association. The complaint was successful, with the U.S. National Labor Relations Board (NLRB) finding that the plant closing was indeed motivated by anti-union animus and ordering Sprint to reopen the plant. Sprint subsequently appealed the ruling to the U.S. Court of Appeals, however, which overturned the NLRB ruling. Ministerial consultations followed and a report was commissioned on NAFTA-related plant closings. Disappointed with the outcome of the proceeding, the communications alliance redirected its focus to autonomous strategies (Torres 2002).

The explicit goal of the communications alliance is wage parity, based on the principle of equal pay for work of equal value. Proposals for concrete co-operative tactics include, for example, Canadian and American unions putting pressure on employers with satellite operations in Mexico not to sign agreements with the official labour central, the Congreso de Trabajadores Mexicanos (CTM) (Torres 2002). The STRM can also learn how to deal with the pressures of technology and productivity changes, which Canadian and American unions are more likely to deal with first in their collective bargaining. More broadly, international labour co-operation in the telecom sector can lead to a common understanding of global and regional challenges, including the elaboration of a unified approach to resistance. The participation of a large delegation of the STRM in the 2001 Porto Alegre Social Forum in Brazil was instrumental in formulating the union's opposition to the proposed Free Trade Area of the Americas (FTAA) (Torres 2002; Friedmann 2002).

NAFTA has led to a considerable shift in the AFL-CIO's foreign policy. Since the traditional ally of the American labour movement in Mexico – the CTM – promoted NAFTA and has shown little willingness to fight for wage gains, the AFL-CIO has widened its relations with the entire Mexican labour movement, including the more radical FAT. This represents a significant change for the federation, which had previously ignored FAT's overtures. Although the Canadian Labour Congress has never had close ties with the CTM, except for an uncomfortable relationship through the International Confederation of Free Trade Unions, the Canadian union movement is increasingly willing to co-operate with Mexican independent unions. The persistent decline of union density in the United States and the strength of corporatist unionism in Mexico, however, temper the effectiveness of organised labour's programmatic shift to international strategies.

In revealing the logic behind the common interests of North American workers, continental neo-liberal integration has promoted a more internationalist perspective within the labour movement. This shift is not merely discursive. Indeed, labour movements have backed an emerging internationalist discourse with a re-evaluation of union policy toward international orientation, political action, immigration, trade policy, and organising strategies. They have sought to broaden their appeal to the working class in general and to other groups opposed to liberalisation. If they take hold and deepen, international labour alliances in the Americas promise to profoundly reshape the trajectory and the social content of continental and hemispheric integration.

Indigenous Peoples

While indigenous movements have challenged neoliberal economic policies and structures such as NAFTA, they have done so within an indigenous analysis that focusses on colonisation.[5] Indigenous struggle seeks to replace colonial systems and influences in their communities.[6] This is at once a far more local and more international process than a strictly continental response to NAFTA. This difference in outlook modifies the expectations one would have of indigenous continental governance–from-below developing as a result of NAFTA.[7]

Transnational linkages among indigenous nations and their organisations are certainly evident throughout North America, although these have yet to develop significantly. Despite NAFTA's obvious effects on indigenous peoples, the agreement has not generated anything that might be called continental governance. Just as indigenous analysis of NAFTA differs from that of other sectors' understandings of the agreement, so too do the goals and aims of indigenous peoples differ from those of mainstream activists. State actors maintain the ability to exert far greater control over indigenous peoples than any international institution or multilateral agreement, so activists must direct their efforts toward national government structures.

The Effects of NAFTA on Indigenous Peoples

The uprising in Chiapas, Mexico, is the best known indigenous response to NAFTA. The Zapatista rebellion, which broke out on 1 January 1994 – the implementation date of NAFTA – was explicitly linked to trade liberalisation, because the Mexican government had removed the protection for communal ownership of *ejido* land under Article 27 of the Constitution to make way for private property and foreign investment in capitalist agriculture.[8] That said, to portray NAFTA as the only cause of the revolt is misleading. The Zapatistas had been training for more than a decade, and many other factors, from economic marginalisation to the Mexican government's colonial policies, led to the push for self-determination and autonomy.[9] In the final analysis, the Zapatistas, like indigenous peoples in Canada and the United States, must negotiate with their own state, not with NAFTA, which has no mechanism to protect the rights of indigenous peoples.

Softwood lumber illustrates NAFTA's potential to affect the economic viability of logging on indigenous lands. For instance, the Algonquins of Barriere Lake in Quebec experienced degradation of their land without having input into its use and were forced to negotiate with the federal and provincial governments a trilateral agreement covering a territory of 10 000 square kilometres of their lands. Provisionally, sensitive areas in cutting zones were to be identified and protected, and attempts were made to harmonise forestry operations with the Algonquins' way of life through greater community input and consultation. But in 2001, the Canadian government withdrew funding, effectively ending negotiations and Barriere Lake input despite good political will on all sides (Diabo 2002).

Russell Diabo, who represented Barriere Lake in these negotiations, expressed concern that if the softwood lumber tariffs imposed by the United States are lifted following dispute settlement under NAFTA, lumber companies would move in to log according to forest management and supply contracts, or *contrats d'approvisionnement et d'aménagement forestier* (CAFs), without Barriere Lake permission, creating the potential for conflict and more blockades.[10] The Canadian government has little interest in encouraging Algonquin work on this issue as it looks at NAFTA as only a trade agreement, without considering its social or cultural impacts. Past victories of Canada at NAFTA tribunals and the movement of the softwood dispute to the WTO carried concerns not only of economic and environmental impacts but also of sociocultural impacts as title to, usage, and control of traditional indigenous lands are usurped.

Institutional Absence of Indigenous Rights

The weakness of continent-wide indigenous organisation is related to the lack of institutional structure affecting indigenous peoples within NAFTA. Labour and environmental concerns were at least acknowledged in side agreements to NAFTA; indigenous concerns and issues did not even register with NAFTA's negotiators. Dean Jacobs (2002), executive director of the Walpole Island Heritage Centre and former band councillor for the Walpole Island First Nation, noted that 'there was some hope at the time that NAFTA could improve the WIFN [Walpole Island First Nation] economically by creating international opportunities. It seems to me that only big corporate players benefit the most. Environmentally, we have been impacted as a result of upstream companies moving their operations south'.

The strongest institutional attention indigenous concerns received in NAFTA came in Annex II: Reservations for Future Measures, which made explicit exemptions to NAFTA and the trade rules laid out in chapters 11 and 12 of the agreement.[11] Canada, in part, 'reserves the right to adopt or maintain any measure denying investors of another Party and their investments, or service providers of another Party, any rights or preferences provided to aboriginal peoples' (NAFTA Secretariat 1994, annex 2, schedule for Canada). This exemption is supported by similar reservations made by Mexico and the U.S., although it contains less recognition of indigenous peoples as a collective. Adam Bailey (2002), legislative associate at the National Congress of American Indians noted that there are 'different levels of response'. According to him, 'while most tribes in the United States are more concerned with building their own economies and focusing a lot on home communities, just trying to get up to basic levels, there are some economically successful tribes that are starting to respond to NAFTA and now crossing borders in the Americas is creating both business opportunities and opportunities for them to interact with other Indigenous communities'. The question then becomes whether what is written into NAFTA responds to indigenous communities from the standpoint of their needs as developing economies.[12]

Lacking channels to participate in NAFTA, indigenous peoples must interact with the colonial governments of the three member parties.[13] One indigenous activist, concerned with the possible impact of this situation on internal relations between indigenous peoples and the state, commented that sometimes 'forces such as NAFTA in Canada are actually pushing Native people to engage more with the state structures ... people begin to see their lands more and more usurped so it pressures them to accept the current limited frameworks of land claim negotiations' (Tabobondung 2002).

The declaration of the Indigenous Peoples Summit of the Americas linked the exclusion of indigenous peoples from NAFTA to violations of their human rights and called for their inclusion in the negotiation of the FTAA (Indigenous Peoples Summit of the Americas 2001). The declaration also called for an intensification of social, political, and economic relationships among indigenous peoples throughout the hemisphere. The issues relating to the declaration also illustrate the division that exists within indigenous communities, particularly those afforded recognition by states as indigenous. Accusations of co-optation, particularly in the U.S. and Canada, were common at the summit, because most of the representatives were elected under systems put in place by national governments, which are not recognised by traditional peoples and which are not considered particularly responsive to ordinary indigenous citizens. While the National Congress of American Indians is independently funded, the Assembly of First Nations (AFN), its Canadian counterpart and host of the Indigenous Peoples Summit, is funded by the federal government and is thus susceptible to allegations of working within a government agenda. It is interesting that after National Chief Matthew Coon Come mentioned the 'systemic racism' faced by Canadian indigenous peoples at the World Conference against Racism in Durban, South Africa, funding for the AFN was cut, resulting in the layoffs of 70 employees and the elimination of a further 24 positions that had been vacant, amounting to 64 percent of its workforce (AFN 2001).

In Mexico, the government's claim to address indigenous rights was hotly disputed after the passage in 2001 of the indigenous rights law as originally proposed by the Comisión de Concordia y Pacificación (Peace and Concord Commission [COCOPA]). The reform, approved by 16 of the 31 Mexican state congresses, disappointed indigenous peoples and human rights organisations as it was severely watered down following 'little or no consultation [with indigenous peoples] regarding the significant alterations to this initiative after President [Vicente] Fox submitted it to Congress' (Miguel Agustin Pro Juarez Human Rights Centre [Miguel Agustin Pro] 2001a, 2). Efforts by indigenous peoples, organisations, and nongovernmental organisations (NGOs) have included protesting procedural violations in calculating state decisions, submitting 'constitutional controversies' to Mexico's Supreme Court, launching several *amparos* (legal challenges) to actions resulting from the reform, and making submissions to the International Labour Organization (ILO) that stated that 'the constitutional reform does not comply with the international obligations that were assumed by the Mexican government when it ratified Convention 169' (Miguel Agustin Pro 2001b, 2).[14] In August 2001, the ILO requested a report from the government detailing Mexico's compliance with Convention 169.[15] Opposition to the law, which included the resubmission of the original COCOPA bill to Congress, did not provoke any meaningful response from the Mexican government (see Rojas 2002a, 2002b).

Due to the changes to the COCOPA proposal, the Zapatistas terminated negotiations, which had only recently started again after being broken off in 1996. Paramilitary groups still operate in the region – the Miguel Agustin Pro Juarez Human Rights Centre reported that the special office created to investigate and prosecute paramilitaries in Chiapas arrested eleven members of the Peace and Justice paramilitary in November 2000. Reports of paramilitary attacks and activity in connection with the Zapatistas and their supporters have continued into 2005 (Social Justice Committee 2002; Immigration and Refugee Board of Canada 2003; Chiapas Support Committee 2005). The centre notes that, 'the Fox administration has not taken any concrete steps towards disbanding paramilitary groups and prosecuting their members' (Miguel Agustin Pro 2001b, 8). Indigenous activists in Mexico were also concerned by the Plan Puebla Panama, which covers southern Mexico and the seven countries of Central America. It promotes 'investment in infrastructure in the areas of energy and others such as water and communications. This plan is governed by two legal frameworks that have been widely promoted by the Mexican government: the Free Trade Agreement of the Americas (FTAA) and constitutional reform regarding the Indigenous people, which place restrictions on Indigenous autonomy, particularly in the area of land rights' (Miguel Agustin Pro 2002, 9). The plan supports investment in *maquiladoras*, some of which are already being built around San Cristobal de Casas in Chiapas, to draw upon indigenous labour, as well as development projects such as dry canals (railways and highways) that cut across indigenous land.[16]

Indigenous peoples have no reason to support NAFTA, which has done little to further their causes. It is true that many foreign companies have easier access to resources on, or use of, indigenous lands as a result of the trade agreement. But it must be remembered that domestic corporations, which operated on those lands before, are in many ways as alien to a people struggling for self-determination under colonial rule as so-called foreign ones. Indigenous lands were exploited prior to

NAFTA, just as they have been exploited after the agreement was signed. It is also true that many of the priorities of indigenous communities do not relate to NAFTA's trade provisions. While indigenous peoples are attempting proactively to affect the content of new agreements such as the FTAA, they are also heavily involved in developing draft declarations on indigenous rights of both the United Nations and the Organization of American States, activities that more accurately reflect the concerns and priorities of their communities (Tullberg 2002). To many activists, NAFTA is not the issue. Rather, colonisation is. As Cristina Fernandez commented at the World Social Forum in Porto Alegre, 'indigenous peoples in the Americas have been resisting globalization for 500 years'.[17] It is in this light that weak continental indigenous governance should be viewed. NAFTA is only a manifestation of indigenous problems and attacking it does not address the root issue.

The Environment

Because such trade-related issues as energy, transportation, agriculture, and investors rights have environmental consequences, the natural environment and economic liberalisation are inextricably linked. Which perspective is privileged when approaching this nexus between environment and trade has proven to be a critical barrier to productive dialogue.[18] Groups that took the integrity of the natural environment as their mandate were faced with difficult choices when North American free trade negotiations were announced. While some engaged in cross-border alliance building to resist what they feared was a development model in which essential regulatory measures would be jeopardised, other large environmental groups in the U.S. publicly endorsed NAFTA as ecologically friendly. This high-profile environmental endorsement of the agreement lent crucial support for its passage through U.S. Congress and dealt a crippling blow to the entire anti-NAFTA movement.[19]

Since this deep rift in 1994, there have been two important but subtle shifts in the responses of environmental nongovernmental organisations (ENGOs) to free trade agendas in North America. A widespread consensus has developed with regard to NAFTA's detrimental environmental impact due to the devastating impact on environmental regulation of Chapter 11 investor-state disputes and because of the perceived ineffectiveness of NAFTA's environmental institution, the Commission for Environmental Cooperation (CEC). However, this consensus on the deleterious effects of NAFTA no longer translates into opposition to free trade. Neither does it necessarily generate trinational projects and campaigns. Groups that previously opposed free trade on environmental grounds, such as the Sierra Club and Friends of the Earth, now advocate the inclusion of environmental standards as part of the core text of trade agreements, leaving North American ENGOs at odds with their more radical counterparts in Latin America that stand in opposition to the FTAA. And while institutionally sponsored trinational co-operation has increased since NAFTA, trinational campaigns, lobbying, and solidarity appear to have diminished.

Many of the environmental and social justice battles over NAFTA were fought during the negotiations of CUFTA. Although Americans greeted NAFTA's precursor with a 'collective yawn' (Aaronson 2001), the Canadian debate was intense and spoke passionately to issues at the heart of the Canadian identity, such as the safeguard of sovereignty, the survival of the social welfare system, and the control of natural resources. The first contact between Canadian and American environmental activists occurred in 1988, when, after repeated dismissals by U.S. ENGOs, Mark Ritchie, president of the Institute of Agriculture and Trade Policy, invited Steven Shrybman, legal counsel to the Canadian Environmental Law Association, to talk about the trade-environment nexus to an audience of grassroots activists in Washington DC. Most groups reacted with indifference, arguing that they did not see the connection (Ritchie 1992, 143). A few organisations, including the National Toxics Campaign, Friends of the Earth, Greenpeace, and Clean Water Action, expressed an interest, but no binational solidarity emerged at this time.

In Mexico, environmental action was even slower to develop. In the past, issues that raised the most concern involved the U.S.-Mexico border: the sewage problems in Tijuana, inadequate waste disposal at the *maquiladoras*, and the smelting activities in Sonora and Arizona. Environmentalism was perceived as elite terrain, and up until 1980, small groups rallied sporadically and mostly in urban areas to oppose specific developments (Ezcurra *et al.* 1999). In the wake of the devastating 1985 earthquake in Mexico City, environmentalism ceased to concern only academics, and there was a surge of *organizaciones de barrios* (community organisations), leading to a discussion of environmental risks and prompting a growth of environmental associations. Mexican ENGOs were subject to consistent harassment and co-optation by the government in order to minimise opposition that might have undermined the authority of the ruling Partido Revolucionario Institucional (PRI). Despite the repressive nature of Mexico's political climate, an unprecedented increase in the number and activity of ENGOs in Mexico occurred while NAFTA was being negotiated.[20] Environmentalists were quick to identify the dangers of free trade by using pollution in the U.S.-Mexico border region as a case in point. They argued that the liberty to pollute that *maquiladoras* had enjoyed could be extended under NAFTA to include the whole country (Fronteras Comunes/CECOPE and Keresztesi 1992). In a strong example of trinational environmental solidarity, environmental groups from all three countries organised protests against the dumping of toxic waste in the *maquiladoras* in March 1992 (Ayres 1998). The presence of American and Canadian representatives undoubtedly served as a deterrent to an otherwise repressive Mexican police force accustomed to harassing, imprisoning, and even threatening to kill activists.

Given their experience with CUFTA, Canadian activists proved to be highly influential consultants to their environmental counterparts in Mexico (Dreiling 2001). Many Mexicans looked to their Canadian allies as mentors in the mobilisation against NAFTA, seeking to emulate inter-sectoral coalition-building strategies developed in the fight against CUFTA (Gutierrez-Haces 1996). In October 1990, a key exchange between 30 Canadian organisations and 60 Mexican groups inspired the formation of the RMALC (Fronteras Comunes/CECOPE and Keresztesi 1992). This coalition evolved into a significant voice pressing for democratic participation and has expanded to include more than 100 organisations.

Canadians were to play a large role in trinational coalition building for another more tangible reason. Brian Mulroney's election victory in 1988 created a political climate that was resistant to another fervent free trade debate. With the domestic arena so heavily constrained for environmental objections to NAFTA and in the face of a concerted, trinational business campaign, environmental (and other social justice groups) began to consider 'developing trinational co-operative education and strategic links across the North American community' (Ayres 1998, 12).

These emerging networks opposed to NAFTA were facing a formidable opponent: a coherent, extremely well-funded, and enormously leveraged lobbying group entitled USA*NAFTA. This coalition of 2300 corporate members, 46 trade associations, and numerous law firms created in all 50 states what were known as 'State Captain' NAFTA defenders whose purpose was to lobby intensively. In the six months prior to the NAFTA vote, USA*NAFTA lobbied the Hill from an office inside the Capitol building itself (Dreiling 2001, 95).

The continental dimension of the far less leveraged anti-NAFTA fight was composed of alliances whose actions took a variety of forms, including site visits, educational tours and workshops, meetings attended by trinational representatives, regular communication and information exchanges, joint political strategising, and the lobbying of government officials (Cook 1997). Likely as a result of the U.S. congressional system and its overwhelming political and economic power on the continent, the main NAFTA battleground was Washington.[21] This resulted in U.S. ENGOs taking on a central role in the NAFTA fight. As such, the great rift that was their internal division profoundly fragmented and weakened the multi-issue, trinational coalitions.[22] To get past their protectionist image, oppositional environmental groups engaged in trinational citizens' presentations and collaboration with key Democratic congressional offices and at congressional committees. Lobbying in the halls of the U.S. Senate and the House developed in 1992 and 1993. On the eve of the vote 'corporate lobbyists celebrated under chandeliers inside the U.S. Congress, while the trinational coalition huddled outside on the steps of the Capitol building in damp defeat' (Foster 2005, 213).

After ten years under NAFTA, the environmental movement's response could no longer be classified as deeply divided, although tactical and ideological differences persisted. Even groups that originally endorsed NAFTA, such as the National Wildlife Federation, came out against the Chapter 11 investor-state provisions because they were used to eviscerate governments' environmental regulations. There has also been broad environmental opposition to fast-track procedures for further trade negotiations. Echoing the perspectives of David Waskow of the Friends of the Earth, Claudia Saladin of the World Wildlife Fund, and others, the Sierra Club's Dan Seligman (2003) stated: 'There is no credible environmental position that would argue NAFTA has been environmentally sound, given the failure of the side agreement and the impact of the investor-state rulings.'

The perceived failure of the environmental side agreement to fulfil its promises has been central to this widespread denunciation of NAFTA. Most environmentalists raise questions about the ability of an appended side agreement to address core issues such as regulatory chill, competitive deregulation, energy subsidies, and the persistent ambiguity over whether a regulation is an unfair barrier to trade or an essential health or environmental measure. Many perceive the CEC's citizen submission process (Article 14-15) as an unjustifiable demand on their often meagre resources (Hansen-Kuhn 2003). Ten out of the fifty cases submitted to the CEC since 1995 have survived the bureaucratic process, only to produce a factual record. None resulted in legally binding action. The independence of the institution's secretariat is also questionable: the Council of Ministers (the environment ministers of the three member countries) rejected the secretariat's requests for factual records on at least two occasions (Kirton 2003).

However, the side agreement on the environment has proven successful in specific ways. The CEC created an ongoing forum for discussion with environmentalists in academic and nongovernmental communities in all three countries, culminating in the North American Symposium on Trade and Environment in the Americas in March 2003. The CEC's grant program (the North American Fund for Environmental Cooperation) has supported more than 150 projects since 1997, many of which have trinational or binational dimensions. Its high-quality reports have provided the first data for the whole continent using comparable measurements. The 'North American Mosaic: A State of the Environment Report' documented declines in ecosystem health and biodiversity and garnered front-page news (CEC). On the U.S.-Mexico border, the Border Environment Cooperation Commission and its fellow institution, the North American Development Bank, have funded travel for activists from both sides of the border to meet with regional policy advocates to discuss specific projects (Browne 1997).

While the CEC has financially facilitated collaboration on many specific projects, ENGOs have quietly questioned the effectiveness of trinational coalition building. The consensus that NAFTA has been environmentally destructive does not translate into tactical unity, and coalitions appear to be decreasing in intensity. Environmental groups express solidarity and work with broad-based coalitions only for key fights such as opposition to fast-track trade promotion authority, and then return to their individual roles, or 'niche markets', in the political system.[23] The ENGOs that consistently participate in coalition strategies are the Center for International Environmental Law, Public Citizen, the American Lands Alliance, and the Canadian Environmental Law Association (Hansen-Kuhn 2003).

In the early 1990s, the U.S. environmental community placed much more emphasis on working with organisations in Canada and Mexico (Seligman 2003). The Sierra Club, then a strong coalition partner, has since lost confidence in the effectiveness of such coalitions. Calling networks 'distracting' and 'not very grounded', it considers its limited resources better spent nationally than internationally. Revealingly, a recent strategy of Friends of the Earth (a central environmental member of the Hemispheric Social Alliance and one of the strongest proponents of coalition strategy) has been to concentrate on 'leapfrogging' trade agreements completely by introducing a bill in Congress which forces foreign companies to declare their international practices (Waskow 2003).

Within the U.S., environmental groups that deal with trade meet monthly or bimonthly in what are called 'green groups', but there has been no initiative to develop a similar forum continentally (Waskow 2003). Some see the lack of a continental legislative body that could be lobbied as central to why no concerted trinational environmental strategy has developed (Seligman 2003).[24] Others recognised the benefits of such solidarity, but quickly acknowledged its improbability, given the ideological divisions within the environmental community (Waskow 2003). Karen Hansen-Kuhn (2003) of the Alliance for Responsible Trade argues that because environmental groups are so ideologically divided about whether to work within the system, labour unions are more prominent in trade-related fights. Yet there is evidence of occasional co-operation: in 2003, the National Environmental Defense Fund, the World Wildlife Fund, the Sierra Club, and others signed an agreement entitled 'Trade and Environment Principles', which stated that trade agreements should support – not undermine – environmental protection, encourage environmental progress, and require democratic procedures (American Lands Alliance *et al.* 2005).

It is also difficult to isolate environmental organisations that work exclusively within North America. Greenpeace and the Friends of the Earth act transnationally but do not stop at the continent's periphery. The Sierra Club, perhaps the most active ENGO in the U.S. and Canada, is also working in South and Central America. Friends of the Earth has no office in Mexico, but does have some small ones in Canada. In Mexico, environmental organisations have mobilised internally through the Red para el Desarrollo Sostenible de México. Financed by the United Nations Development Programme (UNDP), its main objective is to facilitate communication among organisations by providing information on government programs, sending out electronic bulletins, providing directories of ENGOs, and listing environmental standards. This network for sustainable development is not linked with other exclusively North American groups, but provides possibilities for connecting with the UN's Food and Agricultural Organization (FAO), the UN's Environmental Programme (UNEP), and the International Union for the Conservation of Nature (Ezcurra *et al.* 1999).

Faced with the FTAA negotiations, North American civil society coalitions formed as a result of NAFTA have expanded to include countries such as Brazil and Chile (Hansen-Kuhn 2003). The 2003 CEC-sponsored symposium on trade and environment in the Americas was immediately followed by a hemispheric congress sponsored by UNEP, underlining the importance of the hemispheric dimension. This adds another complicating dynamic: many Latin American ENGOs are firmly opposed to free trade ideologically and politically. Although many U.S., Canadian, and Mexican ENGOs sympathise with the anti–free trade critique, few openly endorse it. As late as 1997, the Citizens Trade Campaign was pushing for NAFTA's repeal under the NAFTA Accountability Act, which had more than 100 co-sponsors in the U.S. House of Representatives, while the Alliance for Responsible Trade and

RMALC pushed for modifications ('Fair Trade Networks after NAFTA' 1996). By 2003, the Citizens Trade Campaign was no longer pursuing this goal for fear of committing political suicide.[25]

Since the great rift in 1994 over whether to oppose or endorse NAFTA, there have been two important but subtle shifts in ENGO responses to the free trade agenda. Even among those who initially endorsed NAFTA, there is a recognition that NAFTA's Chapter 11 investor-state disputes and the weakness of the CEC have resulted in a regulatory situation where the environment is compromised. However, this consensus on the deleterious effects of NAFTA no longer translates into opposition to free trade. Instead, the focus is to mainstream environmental concerns in existing agreements. This raises questions about how far Karl Polanyi's double movement can be said to include the bulk of North American ENGOs, which in contrast to their Latin American counterparts, no longer stand in stark opposition to neoliberal agendas as traditionally understood. And while CEC-sponsored collaboration has increased, the more organic trinational projects, lobbying, and solidarity appear to have diminished. Although the environmental community remains divided about tactics and has branched to fill different functions in the political system, the environmental crisis still holds a very public profile. While the CEC remains effective in specific ways, a significant amount of reform will be needed before the bulk of environmental opinion sees the environment-trade nexus as reconciled.

Conclusion

NAFTA has had adverse but uneven effects on the various elements of civil society in Canada, the U.S., and Mexico. For labour, the agreement has meant a dislocation of employment, stagnant or falling wages for many workers, a loss of bargaining power, and the entrenchment of a neo-liberal regime that has privileged corporate rights over labour rights. Millions of dollars have been paid out following Chapter 11 investor-state disputes, yet the labour side agreement has proven toothless. Indigenous peoples have been affected by intensified resource marginalisation, land dispossession, and diminishing political accountability. For ecologists, neither NAFTA nor its side agreement effectively addressed the heart of the environment and trade nexus, in particular the chilling impacts of the Chapter 11 investor-state disputes.

Despite NAFTA's negative effects, the reactions of these sectors reflected their respective ideologies and socioeconomic capacities. Organised labour responded to NAFTA with its own form of continental restructuring. Along with the strictly economic dynamics of free trade, the broken promise of labour rights enforcements and the unexpected co-operation sparked by the CLC process have promoted labour's continentalising shift. Although indigenous groups were involved in umbrella coalitions opposing liberalisation, their focus remained on local and national issues, for the lack of continental structures has resulted in a merely symbolic continental engagement. While labour unions and indigenous peoples overwhelmingly rejected NAFTA, a large majority of the environmental community actually endorsed the agreement, resulting in a diluted and fragmented mobilisation. Continental environmental solidarity after NAFTA is almost entirely the work of the CEC. Of these three movements, organised labour therefore enjoys the greatest potential for exercising governance from below at the continental level, moving beyond the limitations of Polanyi's state-focussed double movement.

Disaggregating these oppositional coalitions also reveals the role of fiscal disparities among them. As the regulatory power of the state is increasingly constrained, pressure on civil society organisations to fill sophisticated social policy and corporate surveillance roles is growing. NAFTA's labour and environmental commissions exercise some watchdog functions, but they depend on their governments for their funds. Need does not determine capacity. The critical problem of the capacity of civil society organisations forces many social agents to approach organised labour for financial support, and may result in an increasingly dependent and one-sided relationship.[26] As pressure mounts for increased integration in a North America obsessed with security against terror, pressures to harmonise on various policy levels could increase both oppositional grievances and funding requirements.

This analysis reveals significant inter-sectoral differences in transnational civil society mobilisation in the absence of democratically structured supranational institutions. The ability of labour to use cross-border co-operation as a means of leveraging its governing power, despite the lack of effective regulatory institutions under NAFTA, speaks to labour's relatively independent social power. While organised labour does engage in lobbying and legal processes, its ability to stop production in the marketplace allows it to act effectively outside of formal governance structures. Indigenous peoples do have the ability to exert pressure on formal governing structures through blockades and low-intensity warfare, as exhibited by the Zapatistas and various Warrior's Societies throughout Canada and the United States. This tactic, however, is extremely resource-intensive and strains communities already facing a number of internal divisions regarding relationships with the state. This lack of institutionalisation concerning indigenous issues in NAFTA only strengthens pre-existing regimes governing indigenous rights and land tenure. Most environmental groups consistently emphasise the essential importance of high standards and their enforcement. This dependence on strong regulatory regimes focusses their strategies on institutional concessions. Although their following is considerable, their ideological fragmentation allows for practically any initiative to be passed off as 'green', thereby eliminating the need for tradeoffs and diluting their potentially powerful political influence.

The CLC and the CEC were both created in response to the relative clout of the American labour and environment movements *vis-à-vis* other social agents such as the indigenous peoples, whose omission reveals the variations in North America's structures of inclusion and exclusion. Civil society's capacity to engage at the continental level in effective governance from below in order to combat the degradation of workers' conditions – or to protect indigenous peoples' ancestral rights or to enhance environmental sustainability – is dangerously limited.

Appendix 4.A: Civil Society Sources Interviewed

Labour

Beaty, Tim. Deputy Director, International Affairs Department, American Federation of Labour – Congress of Industrial Organizations (AFL-CIO). Washington DC, 11 April 2002.

Beckman, Steve. Assistant Director, Governmental and International Affairs, International Union, United Automobile, Aerospace, and Agricultural Implement Workers of America (UAW). Washington, 10 April 2002.

Gindin, Sam. Former Research Director, Canadian Auto Workers (CAW). Toronto, 13 January 2002.

Hameed, Yavar. Labour lawyer, Caroline Engelman Gottheil. Mexico City, 16 February 2002.

Hubbard, Gary. Director, Public Policy, United Steelworkers of America (USWA). Washington DC, 10 April 2002.

Humphrey, John. President, United Steelworkers of America (USWA) Local 5338. Toronto, 20 January 2002.

Katz-Rosene, Sheila. National Representative, International Department, Canadian Labour Congress. Mexico City, 17 February 2002.

Lee, Thea. Director, International Affairs, American Federation of Labour – Congress of Industrial Organizations (AFL-CIO). Washington DC, 11 April 2002.

Medina, Salvador. Director, International Affairs, Congreso de Trabajadores Mexicanos (CTM). Mexico City, February 2002.

Ramsaroop, Chris. Former organiser, American Farmworkers. Toronto, 3 February 2002.

Rowlinson, Mark. Lawyer, United Steelworkers Canada. Toronto, 8 February 2002.

Stanford, Jim. Economist, Canadian Auto Workers (CAW). Toronto, 13 February 2002.

Torres, Eduardo. Editor, Sindicato de Telefonistas de la República Mexicana (STRM). Mexico City, 16 February 2002.

Townsend, Chris. Political Action Director, United Electrical, Radio, and Machine Workers of America (UE). Washington DC, 11 April 2002.

Indigenous

Bailey, Adam. Legislative Associate, National Congress of American Indians. 10 April 2002.

Bobiwash, Rodney. III Encounter Organizing Committee and attendee; II Encounter. 22 November 2001.

Diabo, Russell. Algonquins of Barriere Lake. 16 March 2002.

Hernandez, Fernando. Food for Chiapas. 28 March 2002.

Jacobs, Dean. Executive Director, Walpole Island Heritage Centre. 12 March 2002.

Page Hall, Munford. Dorsay Witney LLP. 9 April 2002.

Roman, Dick. III Encounter Organizing Committee and II Encounter Attendee. 18 March 2002.

Tabobondung, Rebeka. III Encounter Organizing Committee. 10 March 2002.

Tullberg, Steven. Indian Law Resource Centre. 9 April 2002.

Waboose, Don. Former AIM member. 20 March 2002.

Environment

Audley, John. Senior Associate and Director, Trade, Environment, and Development Project, Carnegie Endowment for International Peace (formerly of the Sierra Club). Washington DC, 11 April 2002.

Cooper, Ernie. National Representative, Traffic North America (World Wildlife Fund Canada). Toronto, 21 March 2002.

Donini, Gabriela. Inter-American Strategy for the Promotion of Public Decision-Making for Sustainable Development, Organization of American States. Washington DC, April 2002.

Hansen-Kuhn, Karen. Program Co-ordinator of the Americas, Development Group for Alternative Policies. Washington DC, 28 January 2003.

Huber, Richard M. Principal Environmental Specialist, Unit for Sustainable Development and Environment, Organization of American States. Washington DC, 8 April 2002.

Krist, William K. Senior Policy Scholar Environmental Change and Security Project, Woodrow Wilson International Center for Scholars. Washington DC, 13 April 2002.

Ogilvie, Ken. Executive Director, Pollution Probe. Toronto, 19 March 2002.

Parga, Ceser. Trade Unit Consultant, Organization of American States. Washington DC, 11 April 2002.

Seligman, Dan. Director, Responsible Trade Program, Sierra Club. 6 February 2003.

Saladin, Claudia. Trade Lawyer, World Wildlife Fund USA. Washington DC, 10 April 2002.

Steiner, Melanie. Trade Lawyer, World Wildlife Fund Canada. Toronto, 21 March 2002.

Waskow, David. Trade Lawyer, Friends of the Earth. Washington DC, 31 January 2003.

Wenzler, Mark. Environmental Lawyer, National Environmental Trust and the Sierra Club, Washington DC Chapter. Washington DC, 10 April 2002.

Notes

1   The authors would like to thank the University of Toronto's Department of Political Science and Faculty of Arts and Science, for their generous research support, especially Dean Carl Amrhein whose financial support allowed them to conduct their research in Washington DC, where they were hosted by the Woodrow Wilson International Center for Scholars. This chapter is largely based on interviews conducted with the civil society representatives and activists in Canada, the United States, and Mexico listed in the appendix.

2   See for example Bob Milward (2000, 16). For an elaboration of the argument, see Milward (2004) as well as Sylvia Ostry (2001).

3   This conception was first expounded by John R. Commons, founder of the Wisconsin school of trade union theory; see Simeon Larson and Bruce Nissen (1987, 132).

4   Canada-Mexico trade, while it has doubled in volume since NAFTA, remains at a modest 3 percent of Canada-U.S. trade (Jackson 1997). U.S. imports from Mexico, in contrast, increased by 240 percent since NAFTA, creating a US$24.2 billion trade deficit (American Federation of Labor–Congress of Industrial Organizations 2000).

5   Ward Churchill, a Keetoowah Cherokee AIM activist and professor at University of Colorado at Boulder, speaking on 17 January 2002 in Toronto, stressed the need for all activists, indigenous or otherwise, to address issues of colonisation in order to combat global trade structures effectively.

6   See Patricia Monture-Angus (1999) for an excellent discussion of the impact of colonialism in law and James Tully (1995) who works toward the reconciliation of 'Canada' with self-government and determination.

7   Anishinaabe activist Rebeka Tabobondung (2002) expresses this when she stated that 'NAFTA and colonization cannot be separated. The value systems that allowed colonisation to take place are the same that allowed NAFTA to materialise.'

8   Under the *ejido* system, land was distributed to those who worked it, allowing peasants to have land, however marginalised it was. The removal of *ejido* protection and the implementation of NAFTA acted as the final straw to many indigenous people in Chiapas, and the Zapatistas chose the date of NAFTA's implementation as the start of their revolution. Subcomandante Marcos referred to the revision as the 'detonating factor in the Zapatista decision to go to war' (Ross 1995, 241). The Zapatista demanded a return to Article 27 not just to its original 1917 constitutional language but to the language of Emiliano Zapata's much tougher 1915 agrarian reform law.

9   According to Tzotzil Mayan activist Fernando Hernandez (2002), the uprising was part of Mayan prophecy and was rooted in understanding the uprising as part of a centuries-old struggle.

10 A 1991 Barriere Lake briefing note stated: 'There is no mechanism for modifying the 25-year Forestry Management Agreements, which thereby constrain our efforts to make any meaningful changes to land use practices in La Verendrye Wildlife Reserve' (Algonquins of Barriere Lake 1991). The concerns of 1991 exist today as articulated by Russell Diabo (2002).

11 The annex reads in part: '1. The Schedule of a Party sets out, pursuant to Articles 1108(3) (Investment) and 1206(3) (Cross-Border Trade in Services), the reservations taken by that Party with respect to specific sectors, sub-sectors or activities for which it may maintain existing, or adopt new or more restrictive, measures that do not conform with obligations imposed by: a) Article 1102 or 1202 (National Treatment); b) Article 1103 or 1203 (Most-Favored-Nation Treatment); c) Article 1205 (Local Presence); d) Article 1106 (Performance Requirements); or e) Article 1107 (Senior Management and Boards of Directors)' (NAFTA Secretariat 1994, annex 2, art. 1). While Canada had a specific reservation listed under Aboriginal Affairs, both Mexico and the United States have reservations under Minority Affairs. Mexico's states it 'reserves the right to adopt or maintain any measure according rights or preferences to socially or economically disadvantaged groups' (NAFTA Secretariat 1994, annex 2, schedule of Mexico), while the U.S. reserves 'the right to adopt or maintain any measure according rights or preferences to socially or economically disadvantaged minorities, including corporations organized under the laws of the State of Alaska in accordance with the *Alaska Native Claims Settlement Act*' (NAFTA Secretariat 1994, annex 2, schedule of the United States). The overall thrust of institutionalisation regarding indigenous peoples is perhaps further illustrated when one considers that the *Alaska Native Claims Settlement Act* is essentially legislation setting up indigenous corporations and business interests.

12 Even this institutionalisation, which in theory should protect indigenous business interests, is extremely weak, as illustrated by Mexico and the United States' lack of explicit guidelines for indigenous businesses. However, Jacobs's comments would suggest that Canada's more detailed guidelines have had little impact on cross-border links with other indigenous communities: 'locally, I would say [there has been] only marginal change since NAFTA. Economically we still face borders and barriers' (Jacobs 2002).

13 Indigenous people are involved in NAFTA's institutions – for instance, the Commission for Environmental Cooperation's Joint Public Advisory Committee has had several indigenous members from Canada and Mexico (such as Don Christmas and Mindahi Crescencio Bastida-Muñoz), although none from the United States. However, this participation does nothing to address systemic political concerns exacerbated by NAFTA or issues of indigenous rights.

14 By 26 September 2001, the closing date for submissions of constitutional controversies, Mexico's Supreme Court had received 329 (Miguel Agustin Pro 2001a, 2–3).

15 In May 2001 *La Red de Defensores Comunitaros*, an indigenous organisation composed of representatives from nine regions in Chiapas, began Project 169. By October, the organisation had 'filed the first of 3 formal complaints against the Mexican Government before the International Labour Organization … through Convention 169 … The first complaint challenged the validity of the Foxista farce known as the "Constitutional Reforms on Indigenous Matters", the 2nd complaint dealt with paramilitary activity and state complicity; and the 3rd complaint will dispute the presidential land expropriations & consequent militarisation in the Chiapaneco zone of conflict' ('"In Our Own Defense" Campaign in Support of La Red de Defensores Comunitaros' 2002).

16 See Francisco Rojas (2002b; 2002a). Other sources include Miguel Agustin Pro Juarez Human Rights Centre (2002) and Fernando Hernandez (2002).

17 Cristina Fernandez's comments were made in response to presentations by members of the Socialist Workers Party at the workshop on 'The Anti-Globalization Movement after Seattle and New York' on 3 February 2002.

18 So much so that the International Institute for Sustainable Development (2000) prefaced *Environment and Trade: A Handbook* with a chart comparing the central tenets of each viewpoint.

19 'The simple fact of their support effectively eliminated the environment as a political problem of NAFTA. For pro-NAFTA corporations seeking to break the large anti-NAFTA effort, a well-organized counter-mobilization, including the corporate environmental courtship, secured the passage of NAFTA' (Mayer 1998, 291).

20 However, Claudia Shatan (2000) argues that the causal effect of NAFTA in raising the profile of the environment in Mexico is unclear. Other major events occurred around the same time as NAFTA: the deadly 1992 gas station explosions, the Earth Summit at Rio, the adhesion of Mexico to the Organisation for Economic Co-operation and Development (OECD) in 1994. Not only did the number of environmental groups increase, but the Mexican government also implemented a host of environmental legislation.

21 'In general, both Canadians and Mexicans placed more expectations on the possibilities for obstructing, changing, or defeating the NAFTA project in the US Congress than in either the Mexican political structure or in the Canadian Parliament' (Foster 2005, 216). Also 'because the U.S. political dynamic revolved around specific congressional decisions, such as yes-or-no votes on fast track and then NAFTA itself, nationalist and internationalist NAFTA critics, as well as the right and left, could come together in an intense, short-term campaign' (Brooks and Fox 2002, 35).

22 Those environmental groups that came out in support of the NAFTA (such as the National Wildlife Federation, the National Audubon Society, the World Wildlife Fund, the Natural Resources Defense Council, the Environmental Defense Fund, and Conservation International) largely supported the goals of the member states and hence did not require any sort of oppositional coalition building. Enjoying an open political structure, large amounts of public support, and good media coverage, their 'liberal environmentalism'

type agenda (after Bernstein 2001) was something that could be mandated from the top down, and did not necessitate grassroots mobilisation of any kind. Naturally, there would be no transnational mobilisation where these organisations were concerned; they actively criticised the other environmental groups with accusations of protectionism and sent caustic letters to the Sierra Club. Indeed, the extent of the disagreement caused by NAFTA led some to call it the most vicious fight the environmental movement has ever been through (Seligman 2003).

23 The term 'niche markets' is how Ken Ogilvie (2002) of Pollution Probe described the various functions of environmental groups, that is how some work within the system by working directly with corporations (for example), while others work outside the system by performing street theatre, organising protests, and so on.

24 It is worth reiterating that during the NAFTA campaigns, Washington was the focus for the trinational coalition's efforts, rather than the legislatures of Canada or Mexico.

25 'Political suicide' are the exact words used by David Waskow (2003) of Friends of the Earth when describing the consequences of taking an anti–free trade position.

26 This tendency to turn to organised labour is exemplified by recent grassroots attempts at building (or re-building) the 'Teamster Turtle Alliance' where turtles are the symbolic representation of a host of social justice groups looking for support from organised labour's Teamsters.

References

Aaronson, Susan A. (2001). *Taking Trade to the Streets: The Lost History of Public Efforts to Shape Globalization.* University of Michigan Press, Ann Arbor.

Algonquins of Barriere Lake (1991). 'Barriere Lake Update'. <www.native-net.org/archive/nl/91a/0002.html> (November 2005).

American Federation of Labor–Congress of Industrial Organizations (2000). 'NAFTA's Seven-Year Itch: Promised Benefits Not Delivered to Workers'. <www.aflcio.org/mediacenter/resources/upload/naftabenefitsnotdelivered.pdf> (November 2005).

American Lands Alliance, Center for International Environmental Law, Consumer's Choice Council, *et al.* (2005). 'Trade and Environment Principles'. <www.citizen.org/trade/wto/ENVIRONMENT/articles.cfm?ID=5555> (November 2005).

Assembly of First Nations (2001). 'AFN Undergoes Massive Staff Layoffs Following Drastic Budgetary Cuts'. <www.afn.ca> (May 2002).

Ayres, Jeffrey McKelvey (1998). *Defying Conventional Wisdom: Political Movements and Popular Contention against North American Free Trade.* University of Toronto Press, Toronto.

Bailey, Adam (2002). Interview. National Congress of American Indians, 10 April.

Beaty, Tim (2002). Interview. International Affairs Department, AFL-CIO, Washington DC, 11 April.

Bensusan, Graciela (2002). 'Labor: Impacts and Outlooks'. Paper presented at the meeting of the Trinational Labour Lawyer Association, 22 February. Mexico City.

Bernstein, Steven (2001). *The Compromise of Liberal Environmentalism.* Columbia University Press, New York.

Bronfenbrenner, Kate (1997). 'We'll Close! Plant Closings, Plant-Closing Threats, Union Organizing, and NAFTA'. *Multinational Monitor* vol. 18, no. 3, pp. 8–13. <multinationalmonitor.org/hyper/mm0397.04.html> (November 2005).

Brooks, David and Jonathan Fox, eds. (2002). *Cross-Border Dialogues: Mexico-U.S. Social Movement Networking.* Center for U.S.-Mexican Studies, University of California, San Diego, La Jolla CA.

Browne, Harry, ed. (1997). *Cross Border Links: Environmental Directory.* International Relations Centre, Silver City NM.

Cameron, Maxwell A. and Brian W. Tomlin (2000). *The Making of NAFTA: How the Deal Was Done.* Cornell University Press, Ithaca.

Carr, Barry (1999). 'Globalization from Below: Labour Internationalism under NAFTA'. *International Social Science Journal* vol. 51, no. 1, pp. 49–50.

Chiapas Support Committee (2005). 'International Women's Day in Chiapas'. 27 March. <www.chiapas-support.org> (November 2005).

Commission for Environmental Cooperation (2001). 'The North American Mosaic: A State of the Environment Report'. <www.cec.org/files/PDF/PUBLICATIONS/soe_en.pdf> (November 2005).

Cook, Maria Lorena (1997). 'Regional Integration and Transnational Politics: Popular Sector Strategies in the NAFTA Era'. In D.A. Chalmers, C.M. Vilas, K. Hite *et al.*, eds., *The New Politics of Inequality in Latin America: Rethinking Participation and Representation.* Oxford University Press, Oxford.

Diabo, Russell (2002). Interview. Algonquins of Barriere Lake, 16 March.

Dreiling, Michael C. (2001). *Solidarity and Contention: The Politics of Security and Sustainability in the NAFTA Conflict.* Garland Publishing, New York.

Dungan, D. Peter and Steven Murphy (1999). 'The Changing Industry and Skill Mix of Canada's International Trade'. Perspectives on North American Free Trade Paper No. 4. Industry Canada, Ottawa.

Ezcurra, Exequiel, Marisa Mazari-Hiriart, Irene Pisanty, *et al.* (1999). *The Basin of Mexico: Critical Environmental Issues and Sustainability.* United Nations University Press, Tokyo.

'Fair Trade Networks after NAFTA' (1996). *Borderlines* vol. 4, no. 7. <www.americaspolicy.org/borderlines/1996/bl26/bl26ntwk_body.html> (November 2005).

Foster, John W. (2005). 'The Trinational Alliance against NAFTA: Sinews of Solidarity'. In J. Bandy and J. Smith, eds., *Coalitions Across Borders: Transnational Protest and the Neoliberal Order.* Rowman and Littlefield, Lanham MD.

Friedmann, Harriet (2002). 'The World Social Forum at Porto Alegre and the People's Summit at Quebec City: A View from the Ground'. *Studies in Political Economy* vol. 66, pp. 85–106.

Fronteras Comunes/CECOPE and Nick Keresztesi (trans.) (1992). 'Fighting Free Trade, Mexican Style'. In J. Sinclair, ed., *Crossing the Line: Canada and Free Trade with Mexico.* New Star Books, Vancouver.

Graubert, Jonathan (2002). 'Emergent Soft Law Channels for Mobilization Under Globalization: How Activists Exploit Labour and Environmental Side Agreements'. Presented at the EnviReform Conference on 'Hard Choices, Soft Law: Combining Trade, Environment and Social Cohesion in Global Governance', 8–9 November. Toronto.

Gutierrez-Haces, Teresa (1996). 'Globalization from Below: The Awakening and Networking of Civil Societies in North Americas'. Paper presented at the First Biennial Association for Canadian Studies in the United States in Canada Colloquium, 8 November. Toronto.

Hansen-Kuhn, Karen (2003). Interview. Development Groups for Alternative Policies, Washington DC, 28 January.

Hathaway, Dale A. (2000). *Allies Across the Border: Mexico's "Authentic Labor Front" and Global Solidarity.* South End Press, Cambridge MA.

Hernandez, Fernando (2002). Interview. Food for Chiapas, 28 March.

Immigration and Refugee Board of Canada (2003). 'Mexico: Update to MEX37620. E of 12 September 2001 on the Treatment of the Zapatista National Liberation Army (EZLN) by the Mexican Government'. 20 May. <www.irb-cisr.gc.ca/en/research/ndp/ref/ ?action=view&doc=mex40054e> (November 2005).

'"In Our Own Defense" Campaign in Support of La Red de Defensores Comunitaros' (2002). 19 February. <chiapas.indymedia.org/print.php3?article_id=102131> (April 2002).

Indigenous Peoples Summit of the Americas (2001). 'Declaration of the Indigenous People Summit of the Americas'. 31 March, Ottawa. <www.dialoguebetweennations.com/ dbnetwork/english/declation.pdf> (November 2005).

International Institute on Sustainable Development and United Nations Environment Programme (2000). 'Environment and Trade: A Handbook'. <www.iisd.org/pdf/ envirotrade_handbook.pdf> (November 2005).

Jackson, Andrew (1997). 'Impacts of the Free Trade Agreemet and the North American Free Trade Agreement on Canadian Labour Markets and Labour and Social Standards'. Canadian Labour Congress, 20 November. <action.web.ca/home/clcpolcy/en_issues. shtml?x=14935> (November 2005).

Jacobs, Dean (2002). Interview. Walpole Island Heritage Centre, 12 March.

Katz-Rosene, Sheila (2002). Interview. International Department, Canadian Labour Congress, Mexico City, 17 February.

Kirton, John J. (2003). 'NAFTA's Trade-Environment Regime and Its Commission for Environmental Cooperation'. *Canadian Journal of Regional Science* vol. 25, no. 2, pp. 135–163.

Larson, Simeon and Bruce Nissen, eds. (1987). *Theories of the Labor Movement.* Wayne State University Press, Detroit.

Macdonald, Ian Thomas (2003). 'NAFTA and the Emergence of Continental Labour Co-operation'. *American Review of Canadian Studies* vol. 33, no. 2.

Mayer, Frederick (1998). *Interpreting NAFTA: The Science and Art of Political Analysis.* Columbia University Press, New York.

Miguel Agustin Pro Juarez Human Rights Centre (2001a). 'Constitutional Reform on Indigenous Rights Approved'. *Focus: Human Rights in Mexico* no. 8.

Miguel Agustin Pro Juarez Human Rights Centre (2001b). 'Initial Trends in the Fox Administration'. *Focus: Human Rights in Mexico* no. 8.

Miguel Agustin Pro Juarez Human Rights Centre (2002). 'Human Rights Defenders in Mexico'. *Focus: Human Rights in Mexico* no. 9. <www.sjsocial.org/PRODH/Focus/ PDFS_FOCUS/Focus%20CompactoAmarillo.PDF> (November 2005).

Milward, Bob (2000). 'On the Consequences for the Empowerment of Labour in the Era of Globalization: A Marxian Perspective'. Paper presented at the 18th World Congress of the International Political Science Association, August. Quebec City.

Milward, Bob (2004). *Globalisation? Internationalisation and Monopoly Capitalism: Historical Processes and Capitalist Dynamism.* Edward Elgar, Cheltenham.

Mishel, Lawrence R., Jared Bernstein, and John Schmitt (2001). *The State of Working America, 2000–2001.* Cornell University Press, Ithaca.

Monture-Angus, Patricia (1999). *Journeying Forward: Dreaming First Nations' Independence.* Fernwood, Halifax.

Moody, Kim (1997). *Workers in a Lean World.* Verso, New York.

Munck, Ronaldo (2002). 'Globalization and Democracy: A New "Great Transformation"?' *Annals of the American Academy of Political and Social Science* vol. 581, no. 1, pp. 10–21.

NAFTA Secretariat (1994). 'North American Free Trade Agreement'. <www.nafta-sec-alena. org> (November 2005).

Ogilvie, Ken (2002). Interview. Pollution Probe, Toronto, 19 March.

Ostry, Sylvia (2001). 'A Clarion Call to Whatever'. *Literary Review of Canada* vol. 9, no. 6, p. 6.

Polanyi, Karl (1957). *The Great Transformation: The Political and Economic Origins of Our Time*. Beacon Press, Boston.

Risse-Kappen, Thomas (1995). *Bringing Transnational Relations Back In: Non-state Actors, Domestic Structures, and International Institutions*. Cambridge University Press, New York.

Ritchie, Mark (1992). 'Fighting NAFTA U.S. Style'. In J. Sinclair, ed., *Crossing the Line: Canada and Free Trade with Mexico*. New Star Books, Vancouver.

Rojas, Francisco (2002a). <chiapas.indymedia.org/display.php3?article_id=102273> (April 2002).

Rojas, Francisco (2002b). 'Interview with Chris Trefer, Global Exchange'. <chiapas.indymedia.org/display.php3?article_id=102294> (April 2002).

Rosen, Fred (1999). 'The Underside of NAFTA: A Budding Cross-Border Resistance'. *NACLA Report on the Americas* vol. 32, no. 4, pp. 37–42.

Ross, John (1995). *Rebellion from the Roots: Indian Uprising in Chiapas*. Common Courage Press, Monroe ME.

Scott, Robert E. (2001). 'NAFTA's Hidden Costs: Trade Agreement Results in Job Losses, Growing Inequality, and Wage Suppression for the United States'. Economic Policy Institute, April. <www.epinet.org/content.cfm/briefingpapers_nafta01_us> (November 2005).

Seligman, Dan (2003). Interview. Sierra Club, 6 February.

Shatan, Claudia (2000). 'Lessons from the Mexican Environmental Experience: First Results from NAFTA'. In D. Tussie, ed., *The Environment and International Trade Negotiations: Developing Country Stakes*. St. Martin's Press, New York.

Social Justice Committee (2002). 'More Violent Attacks on Zapatista Autonomous Municipalities in Chiapas'. 29 August. <www.s-j-c.net/English/mexicocaua/pastactions/pua9.htm> (November 2005).

Tabobondung, Rebeka (2002). Interview. III Encounter Organizing Committee, 10 March.

Torres, Eduardo (2002). Interview. Sindicato de Telefonistas de la República Mexicana, Mexico City, 16 February.

Townsend, Chris (2002). Interview. United Electrical, Radio, and Machine Workers of America, 11 April.

Tullberg, Stephen (2002). Interview. Indian Law Resource Centre, Washington DC, 9 April.

Tully, James (1995). *Strange Multiplicity: Constitutionalism in an Age of Diversity*. Cambridge University Press, Cambridge.

Waskow, David (2003). Interview. Friends of the Earth, Washington DC, 31 January.

Chapter 5

The Emergence of Environmental Movement–Government Partnerships

Ken Ogilvie

Over the past three or four decades, the environmental movement has developed considerably in North America. This development has been paralleled by an evolution in the basic principles underlying environmental sustainability. The 1970s witnessed the development and partial implementation of the polluter pays principle. By the 1980s, the pollution prevention principle was emerging. Sustainable development became as the dominant principle by the end of the 1990s, and the new millennium opened with the precautionary principle under vigorous debate. This chapter traces the evolution of environmental and sustainability principles and looks briefly at the international experience of a single Canadian environmental nongovernmental organisation (ENGO) in relation to the ISO 14000 series of environmental management standards. It concludes with a short commentary on chapters 2 and 4 in this volume. Indeed, this chapter is not based on research; rather, it reflects some of the views of its author in his role as executive director of Pollution Probe, one of Canada's leading ENGOs.

The Development of the Environmental Movement and Principles

The emergence of the environmental movement in North America, and its role in the debate over the North American Free Trade Agreement (NAFTA), is reflected in a brief historical perspective of Pollution Probe. Pollution Probe was formed in 1969 as a student movement on the campus of the University of Toronto. It dealt with issues that ranged from the local, such as cleaning up Toronto's Don River, to the global, such as a ban on the use of DDT. Pollution Probe also worked on establishing political accountability for the environment within government. Ministries of the environment were put in place in Canada only in the early 1970s, at both the federal and provincial levels. In those early years, there was not enough institutional capacity to deal broadly with the environment and there were few good laws, and very few international agreements, with an environmental component. Most of the issues at that time were local, although global issues were emerging in the scientific literature. Pollution Probe started with questions about litter and garbage, which later developed into the issue of waste management. But even as the terminology changed, the issues remained largely local: Pollution Probe focussed on paper recycling and other local and regional topics, such as the poor performance of waste incinerators in the province of Ontario.

The environmental movement grew rapidly throughout the 1970s, especially following the 1972 Stockholm Conference on the Human Environment – the first conference at which world leaders gathered to talk about environmental issues. The legislative base and government institutional capacity also grew and there was some international movement in this direction. However, the global movement picked up in the mid 1980s. For its first 15 years, Pollution Probe devoted most of its energy on the domestic scene, or on the Canada–United States issues (especially on transboundary issues, such as the Great Lakes and acid rain).

Since the 1960s, the environmental approach has moved 'from red tape to smart tape' as some of the key issues have become much more global in nature (Ogilvie 2002). Each decade has had a dominant environmental principle. The polluter pays principle was the dominant principle in the 1970s. It emphasised the need to regulate industry and internalise some of the costs of reducing pollution, usually through 'end-of-pipe' technologies that treat the products of polluting systems. In industry there is generally no way to recapture that money, so it became a cost paid by industry.

In the 1980s, a industry backlash grew, particularly in the U.S., in response to the increasing cost per tonne of removing certain types of pollutants. Once 90 to 95 percent of those pollutants are removed, the cost of further emission reductions begins to rise dramatically. There was some examination of market mechanisms and the development of emissions trading systems in the U.S., but pollution prevention was the dominant principle in the 1980s. From an industrial point of view, pollution prevention means finding ways to recycle materials and reuse energy in ways that also increase industry's return on investment, or that at least minimise the impact on its bottom line.

By the 1990s, globalisation was really starting to roar. The World Commission on Environment and Development (known as the Brundtland Commission) had presented its report in 1987 to the United Nations General Assembly and the term 'sustainable development' had become *au courant* (World Commission on Environment and Development 1987). It is an interesting and ambiguous term. But its timing was not particularly good for the environmental movement, for in the 1990s the economy took a dive. If one considers tradeoffs (which are broadly implied by the term), the economy became the dominant concern. The fear of globalisation and apprehensions about international competitiveness trumped the environmental agenda. This led to an environmental 'stalling' in Canada, so much so that by the late 1990s governments at the federal and provincial levels cut environment ministries and undermined their capacity to do even some essential work, such as enforcing their regulations. This situation was compounded by a few disasters toward the end of the decade and into the new millennium, such as the Walkerton disaster in Ontario in 2000, in which the town's water became contaminated by *E. coli* that claimed seven lives and made more than 2000 people sick. The dominant principle had become sustainable development, which would knit the environment and economy together. However, the environment lost out more often than not.

Since 2000, the precautionary principle has dominated. Even today, it still needs to be worked out in policy and practice. The difficult debate over the principle continues, with the European Union leading the way. Canada is looking for ideas internationally on how to deal with this principle. Of course, every new principle and every new set of issues build on the previous decade and the previous principles, which were never fully worked out before each new principle took hold. Nonetheless, these first years of the 21st century are shaping up to be the decade of the precautionary principle. Consequently, environmental policy will change profoundly in Canada and around the world.

The Work of Pollution Probe in the NAFTA Era

In the years leading up to the implementation of NAFTA in 1994, Pollution Probe participated in multi-stakeholder meetings and various committees leading to the negotiation of agreement. Janine Ferretti, then the organisation's executive director, helped develop the environmental side agreement that resulted in the creation of the Commission for Environmental Cooperation. Pollution Probe has always been heavily involved in stakeholder dialogues, having evolved from an organisation that, in its early years, led the ENGO movement in theatrics to one that is a leader in partnership building. Today, Pollution Probe works to bring together government, industry, nongovernmental organisations, health groups, and others to deal with policy issues and on moving those issues forward with broad societal support.

ISO 14000

Although Pollution Probe still focusses on domestic issues, it has also done some international work, particularly on the issue of environmental standard setting under the International Organization for Standardisation (ISO). Under the auspices of the ISO, countries come together, more as private sector–driven groups than as states, to set standards that help international trade. Pollution Probe has a large domestic role in this area, but also gets involved in the international plenaries of TC207, the body that oversees the ISO 14000 standards. Civil society's engagement in ISO 14000 standards is interesting. In general, there is very little engagement of the environmental community in the process of developing standards. Pollution Probe has been involved since 1998 and a few other NGOs participate from around the world. Pollution Probe has helped to create an NGO Task Group (now called the NGO Forum) to address issues related to increasing the involvement of the environment community in ISO standards because those standards affect trade by industry. They also influence public policy (and hence the public interest).

There is criticism of ISO and the environmental management system standards in the literature (Morrison *et al.* 2000; Ogilvie 2002; Pollution Probe 2002), but there is also discussion about corporate social responsibility and about a number of other areas in which the public interest and environmental interests are likely to be cross-linked (Kirton and Trebilcock 2005). If the environmental movement is not involved in these issues, they suddenly spring out on the world resulting in a huge controversy and backlash. Pollution Probe and other NGOs are trying to avoid that from happening, if possible, or at least to get the most important environmental concerns included in the process before it results in unacceptable standards. Despite their limited engagement in the ISO standard-setting process, NGOs have been very effective in a few instances.

Concluding Observations

The analysis in Chapter 4 by Stefanie Bowles, Ian Thomas MacDonald, Jennifer Leah Mullen, and Stephen Clarkson suggests that a kind of ideological bifurcation has occurred within the environmental movement in North America and that this undermines the effectiveness of the groups dealing with environmental issues. Yet has this, in fact, weakened the movement's ability to deal with the NAFTA, or are other factors at play? Here it is important to explore the difference between the apparent Canadian desire for consensus-based policy making (even though the reality may be somewhat different) and the more legalistic system of the United States. These differences have major implications for the way Canadian groups interact with U.S. groups in terms of mobilisation.

Pollution Probe gets involved on certain issues in the United States, such as the Midwest Coal Campaign and the Clean Air Network. It was deeply engaged with U.S. NGOs in the past on the issue of acid rain. But in such involvement, Pollution Probe finds it is dealing with a much larger system, one that lays out its process in fairly definitive legalistic terms, unlike the Canadian policy process. One illustrative case is the Ontario debate on coal plants led by the Ontario Clean Air Alliance (of which Pollution Probe is a member). Another is the policy debate in Canada over emissions trading. There are no clear lines laid out for these processes: they wander around, erupt into the public, recede behind the scenes where Pollution Probe discusses them with industries, governments, and NGOs, and then become public again – whereupon, suddenly, political commitments and promises are made. This process is foreign to the United States. It is of no interest to U.S. NGOs if there is no legal basis in Canada for the political statements that result. Pollution Probe fights for a policy statement in Canada; in the U.S. NGOs fight for a legal process.

Thus, the Canadian world of working together to influence policy is a different world altogether than the U.S. scene. In Canada, it takes a huge amount of effort and time and is like an iceberg that is 98 percent below the surface. It is necessary to understand the different decision-making systems and the relative weakness of Canadian environmental groups compared to the larger U.S. groups. Some of the U.S.

groups are well funded and may have half a dozen high-powered lawyers on staff. Canadian NGOs usually have a part-time person responsible for an issue (as well as maybe six or seven other issues at the same time). There is a huge imbalance in the relative capacities of the two countries to engage in policy and legal processes.

To be sure, the consensus-based approach preferred by Canadians has its limits. In Chapter 2, Virginia Maclaren, Angela Morris, and Sonia Labatt suggest that community advisory panels (CAPs) are very effective in building trust between the community and the company. Yet they also suggest that CAPs are not quite as effective at communicating with the large community in which they operate. Significant challenges exist in reaching out to the broader communities and dealing with barriers such as the lack of outreach mechanisms, limited personal time, and community interest.

The question of local networks and coalitions is extraordinarily important. What is usually understood by the term 'networks' is that they are often networks of labour with labour, NGOs with NGOs, aboriginal groups with aboriginal groups, and so on. The most powerful networks, however, may be the horizontal ones. In this regard, Pollution Probe works to build coalitions not just with environmental groups, but also with industry, municipalities, and others, in order to find ways to reach agreement on common goals. There will always be stakeholders that disagree, but building horizontal coalitions is where policy making is most powerful. Raising public awareness is very influential with single-focus coalitions because the media can clearly define who is talking. But from the point of view of government policy making, horizontal coalitions of support are truly necessary for new policies.

References

Kirton, John J. and Michael J. Trebilcock, eds. (2005). *Hard Choices, Soft Law: Voluntary Standards in Global Trade, Environment, and Social Governance*. Ashgate, Aldershot.

Morrison, Jason, Katherine Kao Cushing, Zoe Day, *et al*. (2000). 'Managing a Better Environment: Opportunities and Obstacles for ISO 14001 in Public Policy and Commerce'. Pacific Institute for Studies in Development, Environment, and Security, Oakland CA. <www.pacinst.org/topics/globalization_and_environment/public_policy/isoes.pdf> (November 2005).

Ogilvie, Ken (2002). 'From Red Tape to Smart Tape'. Presentation to IPAC Research's conference on 'Red Tape to Smart Tape', 25–27 September. Toronto. <www.smarttape.ca/files/Ken_Oglivie-Pollution_Probe.ppt> (November 2005).

Pollution Probe (2002). 'Environmental Non-governmental Organization (ENGO) Participation in National Standards Setting'. Toronto. <www.pollutionprobe.org/Reports/standardssetting.pdf> (November 2005).

World Commission on Environment and Development (1987). *Our Common Future*. Oxford University Press, Oxford.

Chapter 6

Local Nongovernmental Organisations, Global Governance, and the Challenges of a Global Movement for Sustainable Food and Agriculture

Debbie Field

In what ways have social movements built alliances and effectively contested the global neoliberal agenda since the implementation of the North American Free Trade Agreement (NAFTA) in 1994? In Chapter 4, Stefanie Bowles, Ian Thomas MacDonald, Jennifer Leah Mullen, and Stephen Clarkson ask whether social movements have succeeded in building new grassroots alliances at the regional level in regard to NAFTA at a time of increasing globalisation. After commenting on this important question, this chapter examines developments in the food and agriculture movement – the social movement home for a Canadian organisation, FoodShare. It concludes with observations about how resistance movements could be more effectively organised in the future.

The North American Experience

The analysis in Chapter 4 poses important questions about the conditions necessary to create solidarity across borders. It argues that organised labour has been most successful in cultivating new links and, to some extent, in building new organisational capacity under the NAFTA regime. The labour movement's relative success arises in great part from labour's comparatively greater resources. Well-financed unions, which already enjoyed a tradition of working together for many years, responded to the challenge of NAFTA by building cross-border labour networks.

There is no comparable history and there are no comparable resources within the environmental movement, indigenous peoples' movement, or the food and agriculture movement. These newer social movements lack the material capacity to strengthen their existing cross-border links quickly or easily, or to initiate new organisational structures specifically designed to contest the NAFTA regime.

The differences between organised labour and these other movements go beyond resources and organisational capacity. Whatever its limitations, organised labour is programmatically united. It shares common goals, strategies, and political objectives that can be adapted across borders in distinct national contexts. Thus labour has been able to seize the initiative to develop deeper programmatic unity across national borders and move toward a unified strategy of resistance to trade agreements. Yet the much-anticipated grassroots movement capable of halting the erosion of labour, environmental, and human rights has not materialised.

The Larger Challenge

Although that desired grassroots movement has not yet appeared, the question remains whether it is possible. What would an effective challenge to the NAFTA regime look like? What lessons are there from the limited, but relatively effective, response from organised labour? In the context of the environmental movement, what would it take to effect a global transition from the current unsustainable use and abuse of resources? What would it take to bring about locally based popular control over these resources? Given the experience of organised labour, the starting point for an effective environmental strategy must be a series of programmatic initiatives that effectively link multiple scales of struggle. The strategy needs to connect local community-building efforts with attempts to democratise state governance structures (municipal, provincial, federal), while addressing the daunting presence of global capital and global ecological problems.

This is a tall order. But it is also an absolute precondition for building a common international agenda that resonates within nations and communities. Just as labour's message of economic justice and the dignity of labour is as effective at the level of individual factories as it is across the whole North American continent, the environmental movement must build its international plan of action on issues that connect to the common sense of people in various diverse communities. This is the critical first step in transforming a group of activists and 'policy wonks' into an actual social movement comprising multiple groupings across national, cultural, language, and even class interests. After all, it is one common cause based on simple ideas – no war, clean water, safe food – that defines both the existence of a movement and its capacity for mobilisation and organisation.

Several observers have remarked that this mobilisation has not occurred as hoped for in the environmental movement. Virginia Maclaren, Angela Morris, and Sonia Labatt document a community process in Chapter 2 that was unable to halt or even manage the negative impact of the chemical industry. They record a relatively common experience of an ineffectual community-based organisation that is eventually overcome by powerful and well-organised business interests.

But the many failed examples of community organisation and resistance hardly prove that efforts to mobilise civil society are doomed to failure. In Ontario, there is the spectacular example of town of Walkerton, where systematic neglect and mismanagement of the water system caused death and suffering that triggered a vast mobilisation. From grassroots committees organised by residents of the town to province-wide networks to co-ordinated political action, the mobilisation that developed in the wake of the Walkerton tragedy forced a review of the regulatory framework for water management in Ontario. But beyond this, Walkerton has become the rallying cry for a host of campaigns that are battling the neoliberal retraction of the state that erodes critical public goods and services. It was arguably the most important factor that led Ontario premier Mike Harris to retire from public life.

This kind of grassroots organising makes a major difference in how governments govern. Change is not always commensurate with the perceived effort. There is sometimes an apparent disconnect or time lag between the peak of organising and mobilisation and the first real evidence of victory. But community-based mobilisation invariably opens new opportunities for struggle and builds the capacity to undertake new initiatives. In this sense, the mobilisation of civil society is best understood as a perpetual process in which the prospects for effective resistance cycle through peaks and troughs.

Many long-time activists in diverse social movements think it is now time to move beyond a focus on NAFTA, or any other specific trade agreement. The more interesting question is how social movements will be effective in a period in which politics moves increasingly to the global arena. There has been an almost myopic focus on the trade agreements as the significant problem, as though the period before them was a happy time of cross-border solidarity and co-ordinated grassroots organisation. That was not the case. Before NAFTA, international movements were largely unsuccessful in creating international forums and developing strategically coherent campaigns to fight for favourable regulatory regimes. Indeed, many social movements had even weaker global networks in the pre-NAFTA period than they have had in the ten years since NAFTA's birth in 1994. And although not forced to face the recent hurricane of globalisation, national social and environmental movements were subject to identical pressures from the international business community within their own nation-states even before NAFTA and the subsequent decade of trade agreements. The history of generations of social struggles illustrates that movements can only maintain and sustain policy changes when they stay active. This was as true a hundred years ago as it is today, regardless of the issue of concern. All movements must develop strategies to move their agenda forward internally in their own nation-state and then cross boundaries and unite with allies in other countries.

Many have argued that the most successful movement of the last hundred years is the women's movement. An analysis of its success shows a politics that worked successfully on multiple planes: rooting itself in grassroots movement, lobbying at the level of the nation-state, and eventually exercising agency in the global arena. Many of the limitations of other social movements result from restricting the focus to a singular scale of activity, such as seeking new laws. Of course, changes are needed at the regulatory level. But the laws are only as strong as the movements that are pushing for these changes.

The Development of the Food and Agriculture Movement

FoodShare Toronto has worked since 1985 with a variety of communities to improve access to affordable, healthy food, addressing a multitude of issues from field to table. Although FoodShare does not belong to any international nongovernmental food organisation, it has colleagues in cities all over the world trying to achieve similar goals. For at least a decade, neo-liberal policies have deregulated agriculture policies and limited the ability of sovereign states to set food and agriculture policies promoting food rights for their citizens. A fledgling peasant and small farmers' movement has organised to resist the loss of food sovereignty resulting from global trade agreements, and from the expanded commodification of common resources by multinational corporations (MNCs).

Many governments in the world, particularly in the member countries of the Organisation for Economic Co-operation and Development (OECD), have subsidised their food and agriculture sector for decades. These subsidies, along with structural adjustment programmes, investor and consumer pressures, and trade arrangements, have combined to pry open markets in developing countries to excess products from the North, lowering the price of foodstuffs and undercutting local market access for family farmers and peasants. The subsidies favour large multinational agro-business and lead to the displacement of small family and peasant farmers who are undercut in their local markets and unable to function in the international market dominated by economies of scale and market power.

To address these problems, an international small farmer and peasant network, the Via Campesina, was created in 1992. An invitation from the Nicaraguan peasant organisation brought together leaders from many progressive farm and peasant organisations that, in the face of negotiations over the General Agreement on Tariffs and Trade (GATT) and later the World Trade Organization (WTO) in agriculture, recognised an urgent need to protect the interests of peasant agriculture. The Via Campesina is one of the few international networks that have brought people together from different countries to develop strategies in ways similar to the labour movement. The National Farmers Union (NFU) represents Canada on the Via Campesina, and its former president, Nettie Wiebe, serves as the female co-ordinator for North America, including Mexico. The Via Campesina has been in part responsible for two of the few successes in the food and agriculture movement over the last decade, one with regard to the 1999 ministerial meeting of the WTO and the other with regard to genetically modified organisms (GMOs).

The Case of the Seattle Ministerial Meeting

The existence of the Via Campesina provided an opportunity for farmers from the North and peasant farmers from the South to meet and work out common positions, which they then took to international trade meetings, such as the 1999 ministerial meeting of the World Trade Organization in Seattle. Seattle is seen as a turning point in the politics of the last decade, in part because of the great outpouring of energy created by the youth mobilisation and the large demonstrations in the streets. But Seattle was also important because the agriculture movement came of age, as food producers from around the world halted the globalised trade agenda articulated by the United States. Via Campesina organisations from France, led by José Bové, worked in an alliance with peasant farmers from the developing world to block the trend toward agricultural deregulation. The attitude of Europeans toward food, farmers, and agriculture is very different from the attitude that prevails among U.S. policy makers and corporations. The Europeans were able to argue articulately for farm multi-functionality. In effect, they said to the U.S. that negotiators could talk all they wanted about the need to remove all trade barriers in agriculture, but the French government had been subsidising farmers for 400 years for many reasons and planned to continue to do so.

In Seattle, the future of agriculture policy was redirected because of the existence of an international network. The Via Campesina network is composed of dynamic grassroots organisations such as the Canada's NFU, alongside peasant and farmers' movements in the South.

Since 2000, the U.S., for its own internal reasons, which were connected partly to the dynamics of U.S. politics in the 2002 congressional election, has continued to spend billions subsidising its own agriculture sector. This will create even more havoc in the international arena about who will be 'allowed' to subsidise farmers and what kind of subsidies are good for small and peasant farmers. But the existence of the Via Campesina as an international forum means that farmers from around the world have a structure allowing them to meet. This network's organisational structure may allow the development of policies and strategies to advance the goals of food sovereignty and sustainability in individual countries, and at the global level.

The Case of Genetically Modified Organisms

The movement has had a second victory in halting the spread of genetically modified food and seeds. In this case there is no one organisation, no single global campaign, and very little money to fund resistance – particularly compared to the billions of dollars funding biotechnology. Some international organisations with resources are involved, such as Greenpeace, as are some strong national organisations such as the Council of Canadians in Canada. But the movement against GMOS is a good example of a grassroots civil society process that has stopped the globalisation process in its tracks. Rather than focussing on trade agreements first, the movement was a mobilisation of popular sentiment from below to stop the use of genetically modified products. It was also a very interesting cross-class alliance in which two groups that usually do not work together found common ground: peasant farmers in the South and health-conscious and environmental consumers in the North.

Farmers in the South rebelled against the pressure of multinational seed and pesticide companies to buy genetically modified seeds. They were concerned that the cost of the new seeds would lead to even more peasant bankruptcies and displacement. There was also a strong moral reaction that led peasant organisations, particularly in India, to object to giving up sovereign control over age-old seeds. At the same time, consumers in the North were worried about the potential dangers of putting untested genetically modified food into their bodies and about irreversibly polluting the broader ecosystem.

The Challenge for the Food and Agriculture Movement

Few could have predicted that these divergent interests could work together. The possibilities for uniting diverse groupings give hope for those interested in promoting global solidarity among grassroots social movements. It is not necessarily the same story moving different people against genetically modified foods. But this combination of diverse interests has slowed down the efforts of Monsanto and other major corporations. These are not total or absolute victories. But they demonstrate an example of what continentalism from below and transboundary networks could mean when strategy works to link multiple scales of activity between the local and the global. At the same time, the lack of cross-boundary mobilisation and organisation has resulted in less success at the 2003 World Food Summit in Rome. Delegates from nongovernmental organisations (NGOs) from the North and South could not agree on common demands, with the result that very little was achieved at that meeting.

Although there are United Nations forums that bring food and agriculture NGO representatives together, identifying common goals and programmes is difficult without a unifying cross-boundary strategy or consistent language. In the North, activists speak in individualist terms of food rights, while in the South, the discourse of 'food sovereignty' seems paramount in neo-colonial struggles over food. There are no consistent venues or forums to debate the tension between food rights and food sovereignty, nor are there ongoing local campaigns as developed by the anti-GMO movement.

This is beginning to change. Via Campesina organisations, and the food NGOs that agree with their analysis, are working together to understand how food rights can be embodied in the self-determination goals of food sovereignty. Through this dialogue, they articulate the need for access to and control over land, markets, and resources. Sovereign control at the community, regional, and national levels are considered essential elements in a meaningful food security agenda.

What would it take to win sovereign control over food resources, and guarantee food rights in a post-NAFTA, post-trade agreement global reality? First, there is a need to establish organisations and campaigns from below. In the prevailing political climate, the starting point for all successful movements for social change is a firm and vibrant popular base, whether it be a small neighbourhood committee next to a chemical plant or a major international movement against global warming. Laws do not change unless there are organisations dedicated to getting people involved and mobilised. Improvements to the regulatory framework do not occur when elites voluntarily decide to do so. Rather, governments decide to make changes when they feel people are pushing them. The only way to influence the policy framework and effect lasting progressive legislative change is by educating, organising, and mobilising the majority of society. The example of Walkerton illustrates this well.

Early in 2003, Saskatchewan farmer and NFU member Jim Robbins travelled to Mexico City to hold a joint press conference with members of a powerful Mexican farm coalition called El Campo No Aguanta Mas (The Countryside Will Not Take It Anymore). Speaking with Mexican farmers, Robbins identified common problems caused by the impacts of NAFTA in both Canada and Mexico. This, too, is a powerful example of what can be achieved when grassroots organisations work together across boundaries.

The second need is to look for opportunities of the 'politics of the 75 percent'. Lasting and fundamental progressive social and legal changes are the result of popular, multi-class support. This does not mean that unpopular positions must be avoided. It does mean, however, that it is necessary to find issues that will receive broad popular support and to push for winning outcomes on these fronts. It also means that movements must speak to people's common sense understanding of the industrial food system and its social and ecological problems, rather than preaching from a moral high ground.

To take one example, there is now a belief among 75 percent of Canadians that gays and lesbians should have full democratic rights. This belief did not exist a hundred years ago, or even fifty. How did this change come about? It did not come not from regulatory framework change in isolation from public education. Ideas changed as a result of vibrant debates in which diverse people clashed on the need of gays and lesbians to have democratic rights. Through these debates, straight people eventually made connections between an abstract discourse of 'rights' and their personal experiences with gay and lesbian relatives, friends, and colleagues. Eventually, a majority of Canadians came to agree that laws should be changed to deliver gay and lesbian rights. The gay and lesbian movement emphasised local roots and public awareness, while simultaneously understanding the need for a national regulatory framework to legislate these rights. The lesson is that social movements force laws to move.

The struggle for gay and lesbian equality is not over. There is still not a majority support on issues of gay adoption or marriage in Canada. Gay and lesbian organisations continue to raise these issues in public debates, but understand that legislative change will happen when that majority support exists. Activists simultaneously educate about less popular, complex issues while campaigning for legal changes on demands that are winnable. This kind of multi-scaled approach allows movements to be as radical as possible, pushing the boundaries in the public sphere, while seeking broad public consensus to develop campaigns that result in legal victories.

The third need is for international and professional organisational capacity. This includes communications, networks, campaigns, coalitions, and policy think tanks. Common demands and shared analysis and vision across boundaries are required to brand movements. This has yet to be done in the environmental or aboriginal movements. It has happened only minimally in struggles over labour and agriculture. EnviReform, a research project based at the University of Toronto from 1999 to 2004, is one example of this global process at the think tank level that allows dialogue across boundaries.

Finally, support must be built for a strong regulatory framework by working in all three sectors of society. There are specific roles for government, the private sector, and the community, or the 'third sector'. The government sector must have strong laws to protect human and environmental rights. At the same time, private sector partners need to support these principles in their organisations and join civil society movements to support government policies that protect these rights. Yet the engine of change in this process is often advocacy organisations and social movements in the third sector that push both government and the private sector by building a consensus for change. And it is third sector organisations that will lead campaigns to force chemical plants to disclose what they are doing to their community 'neighbours'.

PART III:
NORTH AMERICAN
AND HEMISPHERIC
EXPERIENCES

Chapter 7

A North American Community of Law with Minimal Institutions: NAFTA's Committees and Working Groups

Sarah Davidson Ladly, Carlton Thorne, and Stephen Clarkson[1]

In 2003, Canadians were contemplating their future in a North America to which their economy had become irrevocably integrated but in which their participation was held hostage to the United States administration's fixation on homeland security. At the same time, they were being exposed to a vigorous debate over deeper regional integration. At one extreme were those favouring national autonomy and arguing against any deepening of the continental dependence, which had made Canadians' well-being so vulnerable to the border blockade that had briefly paralysed Canada-U.S. trade following the terrorist attacks of 11 September 2001 (Hurtig 2002). At the other extreme were those favouring enhanced continental integration and arguing for a 'Big Idea', a grand bargain with Washington, to erase the remaining vestiges of the economic border between Canada and the U.S. (Dobson 2002).

This bold initiative would create what Allan Gotlieb (2003), former Canadian ambassador to the United States, called a 'community of law'. Inspired by the solidarity side of the European model but designed for the North American context, this grand scheme, he argued, would put in place a common competition law and tribunal (to replace the partners' trade-remedy legislation), a common external tariff (to eliminate rules of origin and the need for customs agents at the Canadian-U.S. border), and a common security perimeter (to alleviate U.S. concern about Canada's antiterrorism capacities). But in defiance of the structural side of the European model, Gotlieb's community of law would have neither legislature nor executive, neither administration nor court.

This conception of an entity created by the U.S. and Canada, and possibly Mexico, to transform intergovernmental relations on the continent without having law-making, law-applying, law-enforcing, or law-adjudicating mechanisms was both bold and controversial. Fortunately for North Americans, this proposal does not need to be evaluated in the abstract, since there is a recent and relevant precedent that can be assessed. This is the Canada-U.S. Free Trade Agreement (CUFTA) of 1989 and its trinational successor, the North American Free Trade Agreement

(NAFTA) of 1994. The latter broadened CUFTA to include Mexico while tightening its disciplines on the signatory governments' policy autonomy.

A big idea in its own right, NAFTA embodied a vision of continental economic integration by setting parameters for what would constitute legitimate policy in the three parties' systems. NAFTA went further than previous free trade agreements with regard to border barriers such as tariffs and quotas on goods physically crossing national boundaries. In contrast, NAFTA extended its normative reach beyond border controls. In addition to tariff elimination, it contained provisions on potential non-tariff barriers such as health or environmental standards, established new rights for foreign investors, and introduced to international trade law rules on services and intellectual property rights. In short, the agreement's wide-ranging norms asserted such intrusive authority over its members' domestic policy and regulatory capacities that it could be considered as having constitutional effect (Clarkson 2002, ch. 4).

As an external constitution, however, NAFTA was far from balanced, the civil society-oriented commissions on labour and the environment having proven largely ineffectual, two as explained in Chapter 4. It was much stronger in its normative dimensions strengthening corporate powers than in its institutional capacities that might enable democratic controls. While it did contain various adjudicatory mechanisms to promote the settlement of conflicts that might arise between its parties and investors, it had no coercive capacity to force compliance with these judicial rulings and no executive or legislative capacity beyond the so-called Free Trade Commission, which merely consisted of periodic short meetings of the three parties' trade ministers. In addition to this minimal law-adjudicating, non-existent law-enforcing, and negligible law-making capacity, NAFTA did boast two embryonic forms of institutionalisation. The first was a NAFTA secretariat that was given neither staff nor quarters but consisted of a minor office in each government's trade bureaucracy. The second was approximately 30 micro bureaucracies known as committees and working groups (CWGs), designed to oversee the application of the agreement's various chapters.

This chapter examines the behaviour of these trinational administrative bodies in order to make some inferences about the viability of the proposal for a community of law without major institutions that is on the agenda for reforming North American governance. It first discusses the theory behind the CWGs and the ideals embodied within them. It then reports the results of research on the past and current status, activities, and dynamics of these largely invisible entities. It concludes by evaluating this first experiment in a minimally institutionalised community of law in order to reflect on the prospects of a post–September 11 attempt to achieve another grand bargain of continental integration without structures.

This analysis finds that the CWGs set up under NAFTA have for the most part been under used and have remained relatively insignificant as continental institutions. This weakness is largely due to the incongruity between the working groups' trilateral, professional, and symmetrical nature and the bilateral, political, and asymmetrical reality that continues to characterise the relations of Canada and Mexico with their neighbouring colossus. In practice, purportedly continental issues turn out to be bilateral, so are of little interest to the third, uninvolved government, thus rendering the groups an inefficient mechanism through which to resolve disputes or discuss emerging issues. Furthermore, the stakes in these relations are generally too high for discussions and disputes to be channelled through apolitical, technocratic institutions built on the principle of formal legal equality. It appears that NAFTA-style CWGs can only deal with low-level, low-interest disputes. More politically sensitive controversies require a political arena with more appropriate representation of the interests involved and more flexible processes that provide room for compromise. Such bilateral and political realities constitute a serious impediment to the formation of active and effective continental institutions. This experience suggests that, while a putative grand bargain can hardly deal with the immediate problems, such as terrorism, that are on the protagonists' present agenda, it cannot deal with the issues that lie ahead, whatever they may be.

Committees and Working Groups in Theory

NAFTA has been described as an 'after-the-fact acknowledgement' that formalised the deep economic integration occurring between the U.S., Canada, and Mexico (Confidential interview 2002a). Although NAFTA is a trilateral agreement, the pattern of North American integration is more accurately understood as a 'hub and spokes' dynamic between the core power (the U.S.) and its two neighbours (Mexico and Canada) (Eden and Molot 1992, 67). Before NAFTA, a combination of geographical realities, market forces, state policies, and demographic and cultural patterns fostered two distinct but disconnected bilateral relationships rather than generating an integrated continentalism (71). These two elements formed a dyad defined by the asymmetries in power between the three states resulting from the hegemonic status of the U.S. in the world and its geographic centrality on the continent. The U.S. is the region's economic engine, the source of by far the largest share of its economic activity. In 1987, its economy was responsible for 85 percent of the region's exports and 91 percent of its imports (Brunelle and Deblock 1992, 125). Moreover, the gross national product (GNP) of the U.S. was 20 times larger than Mexico's and 12 times the size of Canada's in 1994, at the time NAFTA was signed (Salvatore 1994, 23).

There was marked resistance on the part of all three states' negotiators to complementing NAFTA's intrusive rules with institutions. Yet a meagre and highly decentralised structure was designed to deal with the sector- and policy-specific subjects that were likely to arise from the agreement and to foster the co-operation necessary for its implementation and administration (McKinney 2000, 14).

Most of NAFTA's chapters included provisions to establish committees and groups to monitor and direct their implementation. The CWGs were not supranational, but intergovernmental and, most important, explicitly professional. They were to be forums in which civil servants from the three countries' various ministries could exchange relevant information, resolve minor disputes, and discuss liberalisation. Their structure and composition were intended to favour objective analysis and the pre-emptive resolution of conflicts through the formation of small networks of experts (McKinney 2000, 17). It was hoped that the resulting epistemic communities would be inclined to treat issues objectively and focus on long-term benefits of increased economic activity that would be mutually rewarding, rather than short-term costs of immediate dislocations that might be politically contentious (22).

Indeed, the implicit corollary of 'professional' was 'apolitical'. The thinking behind the CWGs was grounded in a desire to create forums where all three parties could voice their interests and transmit them in a relatively de-politicised arena. Although 'political direction for the NAFTA work programme [was to be] provided by ministers through the Free Trade Commission', the groups were intended to be insulated from direct political pressures in their day-to-day activities (Carrière 2002). The CWGs also contributed to the de-politicisation of some public authority insofar as decision making would be vested in the hands of professional policy makers and diffused within a highly decentralised organisational structure. The basis for having autonomous but disconnected groups staffed by civil servants drawn from various agencies and ministries and selected for their detailed knowledge of the issue at hand – be it pesticides, trucking standards, or customs issues (Carrière 2002) – was the belief that NAFTA was more likely to adhere to its rules if their operation was at least partly removed from the sphere of domestic politics (McKinney 2000, 22). The CWGs were meant to engender intergovernmental trust, decrease diplomatic deception, create favourable conditions for generating objective solutions to policy conflicts, and increase the chances that member countries would abide by their commitments and implement the principles of the agreement (19).

Establishing the CWGs also acknowledged that commercial disputes tended to spring less from quarrels between states than from quarrels between increasingly transnational firms (Doran 2002). The creation of groups intended to generate 'an apolitical arena for the discussion of issues and, through early dialogue on contentious points, the possible avoidance of disputes' (Carrière 2002) spoke to this conviction on the part of trade bureaucrats that discussions relating largely to commercial matters ought to be led by professionals acting in forums that were relatively free of political power dynamics. It was in such an environment that these issues could be resolved on the merits of the arguments using stable legal and economic criteria. Under this new approach, efficiency and merit were to prevail over politics and emotion (Carrière 2002). While no one expected high-level issues to be handled by intergovernmental committees of experts, a prevailing functionalist view assumed that, as issues were resolved, these types of processes would gain more legitimacy and would in turn lead to more important issues being directed toward these problem-solving forums (Carrière 2002).

Central to the working groups' professional make-up was their trilateral composition. In the spirit of a new continentalism, they were created with a view to trilateralise relations by evaluating and even helping direct trade-related public policy within all three member states. The groups were mandated within the text of the agreement to meet from one to four times yearly, or as issues arose, to produce reports for the Free Trade Commission according to specific schedules established within the agreement. Meetings were to take place, in rotation, in Canada, the U.S., and Mexico (Carrière 2002). Trilateral forums were expected to be more likely to defuse binary conflicts and so provide a means to transcend the traditional bilateralism of North American trade politics. Third-party actors with specialised knowledge were explicitly encouraged to lend their voice to discussions on a member state's domestic policy. In this respect, the groups could be described as embryonic structures of continental governance. By fostering trilateral co-operation, the signatories hoped to prevent any party from unilaterally interpreting NAFTA's code of law. The groups were to hold member states accountable at a relatively low level, allowing the two other parties a chance to intervene before one's policy changes became entrenched.

Trilateralism had its own implicit corollary: symmetry. Symmetry represented a step in the direction of a new continental relationship founded on the ideal of legal equality. There was to be approximately equal representation of the three countries on each group, which was to be co-chaired by an official from each member state. The mere existence of such trilateral institutions could be expected to offset somewhat the immense asymmetry in power that existed between the United States and its neighbour-partners who would never be left to negotiate one on one with the hegemon. Additionally, participation in these groups would allow Canada and Mexico some influence over relevant aspects of U.S. regulatory policy and generally ensure that all three states were given 'voice opportunities' with which to make their views known and possibly give them effect (McKinney 2000, 14).

The CWGs' trilateral, professional, and symmetrical nature marked a significant innovation for North American relations. Whether the innovation had any substantive effect was another matter entirely.

Committees and Working Groups in Practice

The civil servants who staff NAFTA's committees and working groups are drawn from a range of departments and agencies. Typically a member state will have between two and ten members representing its interests on any committee or working group. One civil servant is designated as the national lead or contact for each group. Although trilaterally equal in principle, the U.S. tends to have the largest contingent of civil servants working on any specific CWG. Canada's and Mexico's lesser resources usually explain this discrepancy (Shigetomi 2002). Additionally, a minority of the CWGs also have as members who are volunteers from the private sector who offer particular expertise on an issue and represent a variety of nongovernmental interests. Representatives from standards organisations, scientists, and other technical experts may also serve (Trade Compliance Center 2001). The standards-related measures subcommittees are the most notable example of such private sector participation (according to one civil servant respondent).

In many cases, one bureaucrat is responsible to his or her government for the activities of several committees or working groups because the portfolio generally represents a very small portion of a civil servant's work load. One CWG official noted that he spent only about 3 percent of his time on his working group portfolio (Dutton 2002).[2] In the event that a meeting is imminent, the representatives will likely devote more time than normal to assignments related to their working group.

The CWGs operate in a highly autonomous fashion. Relations within the groups tend to be informal (Confidential interview 2002b). Much work is done over the phone or by e-mail rather than by convening formal meetings. In sociological terms, civil servants who staff the committees do not appear to think of themselves as members of a cohesive and stable group. The national members of the various working groups are likely to deal with their counterparts around the world in their respective epistemic communities on a frequent and informal basis regarding a variety of non-NAFTA issues. Their communication style does not change when the issue falls under the ambit of a NAFTA committee or working group (Dutton 2002).

The national sections of each CWG are ultimately accountable to their national government's trade policy agency – the International Trade Canada (ITC), which was known as the Department of Foreign Affairs and International Trade (DFAIT) until 2004; the Office of the United States Trade Representative (USTR); and the Secretaría de la Economía (SE) – but decisions made by the groups must also be cleared by the various departments and agencies represented within them.

Although the CWGs were instructed to produce regular reports for review by the Free Trade Commission, they do so infrequently (Dutton 2002). Although ITC's website proclaims that 'Canada has made a priority of strengthening the NAFTA work program to enhance the transparency, accountability and effectiveness of the NAFTA Working Groups and Committees' (ITC 2002), these CWGs rarely publish materials. The minutes of meetings are not made public (Confidential interview 2002b). Given that these groups appropriated a degree of national authority *vis-à-vis* policy or regulatory decision making in such areas as determining standards, defining rules of origin, and adjusting customs procedures, their obscure, inaccessible, and semi-privatised nature creates an obvious element of democratic deficit. However, the weakness of these institutions largely negates the significance of this problem.

Activities and Processes of the Committees and Working Groups

Just as the CWGs' mandates vary, so to do their actual processes and functions. Most groups are engaged in a combination of activities which fall into five categories: implementing or overseeing the implementation of the agreement; exchange of information; resolution of conflicts; harmonisation of regulations; and forums for relaying information between the governments and interested parties.

Implementing or Overseeing the Implementation of the Agreement The majority of the CWGs are involved to some extent in the oversight of NAFTA's implementation, insofar as they are mandated to deal with any issues in their field that arise during that process and to address ambiguities in the text as they appear. The group most directly and successfully involved in the implementation of NAFTA was the Committee on

Trade in Goods. Having completed all four rounds of its tariff acceleration mandate, it no longer meets regularly (Shigetomi 2002).

Exchange of Information All groups act as forums for the exchange of data among member states. This information sharing takes many forms, including tracking each country's administration or implementation of the agreement, formulating understanding of various problems, laying the groundwork necessary for generating further ideas for deeper integration and, more generally, understanding the needs and concerns of each country. This exchange sometimes results in the production of trilateral statements or reports and has become the groups' primary function (SICE 1997a).

Resolution of Conflicts Another expected function of the CWGs was the resolution of low-intensity disputes and so the limiting of the number and the nature of the conflicts to be dealt with by NAFTA dispute panels or by the Free Trade Commission. The groups have resolved or worked on low-level disputes concerning, for example, the appropriate classification of goods (Customs Subgroup of the Working Group on Rules of Origin) (SICE 1997c), increased Mexican duties on the importation of frozen Canadian geese and U.S. ducks (Committee on Trade in Goods), and the application of a merchandise-processing fee by the U.S. on imports of some Canadian textile products (Committee on Trade in Goods) (SICE 1997a).

Harmonisation of Regulations Some CWGs had explicit mandates to harmonise or to generate new regulations that would directly affect how NAFTA was implemented and administered. For example, the Working Group on Rules of Origin was to 'develop common regulations to govern the detailed interpretation, application and administration of the rules' (ITC 1994, 39) that are essential to the realisation of NAFTA's economic benefits, because they protect the parties against direct and indirect trade deflection. This working group was one of the most active in 2002, when it reconfigured and realigned seven NAFTA rules of origin, bringing them into conformity with changes in the worldwide Harmonized System announced by the WTO in January 2002 (Shigetomi 2002).

Forums for Relaying Information between the Governments and Interested Parties The final function of the committees and working groups is to facilitate the exchange of information and ideas between those responsible in the member governments for NAFTA's implementation and any interested nongovernmental players in the private sector. In this respect, the CWGs encourage a high level of private sector participation and appear to create new and more explicit access points for these interests, though not for civil society organisations.

The activities of the Telecommunications Standards Subcommittee of the Committee on Standards-Related Measures illustrates this relationship. One of the subcommittee's key responsibilities is the co-ordination of efforts and exchange of information with the Consultative Committee for Telecommunications, an organisation that represents North American telecommunications interests. The subcommittee's membership consists of two to three government officials from each of the NAFTA states. But since 1999, the chair and the vice-chairs of the Consultative Committee for Telecommunications have additionally been invited to all of the committee's meetings with the goal of enhancing the degree of feedback coming from the pertinent business communities of the three countries.[3]

Most CWGs operate as forums for relaying private sector concerns and ideas to government officials charged with interpreting and implementing NAFTA, but the degree of private sector participation and consultation varies from group to group (Dutton 2002). Although the involvement of private sector interests is appropriate in the context of a free trade agreement, CWGs blur the lines between consulter and consulted in some cases. Despite the fact that the level of consultation is 'nothing beyond the usual day-to-day interaction' for an administrative entity such as the U.S. Department of Commerce (*Ibid.*), the democratic legitimacy of these groups is questionable. Their near-total lack of transparency prevents individual citizens' or civil society organisations from providing a counterpoint to private sector access.

Current Levels of (In)activity

The CWGs have not become new agents of continental governance, for better or worse. Rather, they have proven largely inconsequential. Approximately 60 percent of them were inactive as of 2002. In the case of the Committee on Trade in Goods, inactivity symbolised success, because its final round of tariff acceleration, completed ahead of schedule, left it without an agenda. However, that committee stands out as the only example of a group that has completed, to the satisfaction of all three parties, the mission set out for it by NAFTA, which specified the items requiring tariff removal (Shigetomi 2002).

A more common cause of inactivity is a lack of political mandate for the particular working group. The Advisory Committee on Private Commercial Disputes Regarding Agricultural Goods and the Working Group on Trade and Competition are inactive largely because the three parties are unsure about what benefits work by these groups will produce. Due to the three countries' often conflicting objectives, finding trilateral agreement on the direction a specific group ought to pursue has been a major sticking point. With regard to the Working Group on Trade and Competition – which Canada hoped would replace national trade remedy laws through a continental approach – the USTR's Director for Mexico and NAFTA Affairs noted blandly that 'the U.S. feels it has completed its work [but] we have some disagreements with Canada, I believe, on what the future work in competition would be' (Shigetomi 2002).

If a CWG's mandate is too politically sensitive to be dealt with in such a forum, it becomes deadlocked and thus inactive. Some groups, such as the Committee on Trade in Worn Clothing and the Working Group on Emergency Action, were born out of the inability to reach consensus on certain controversial issues during the

NAFTA negotiations. To forestall delay in signing the agreement, many unresolved but contentious issues were assigned to working groups as a way to 'soften the failure of a lack of resolution' (Shigetomi 2002). In these cases, establishing working groups was simply a 'graceful way of pretending there would be more discussion' about a failed negotiation (Doran 2002). These CWGs encountered considerable difficulties as issues that were too contentious prior to 1994, and did not become any easier to navigate.

The Chapter 19 Working Group on Trade Remedies was established in 1993 as a face-saving device for Ottawa, for which eliminating the application of U.S. antidumping and countervailing duties to Canadian exports had been the prime objective when soliciting a trade agreement with Washington. The group was mandated 'seek solutions that reduce the possibility of disputes concerning the issues of subsidies, dumping, and the operation of trade remedy laws regarding such practices' (SICE 1997b). The exceptionally controversial nature of these issues ensured that the group would be unable even to approach them. Not surprisingly, the working group is completely inactive (Shigetomi 2002). Similarly, the Government Procurement Working Group, which was established 'resolve issues related to government procurement, to provide a forum for future negotiations, and to facilitate technical cooperation between the Parties' (ITC 1996), has been unable to do its work since 1999, although it had instructions from the Free Trade Commission to carry on with its mandate. This stasis results from the group's inability to 'reach trilateral agreement on how to proceed' due to the controversial nature of regulations surrounding government procurement for the three parties (Shigetomi 2002).

The Services and Investment Working Group's remit includes the notoriously controversial Chapter 11, which empowers NAFTA corporations to take legal action against a member state on the grounds of expropriating their assets. While these types of clauses are standard in bilateral investment treaties, NAFTA's Chapter 11 has been widely criticised for allowing transnational corporations to usurp national sovereignty. The working group was established to monitor the implementation of chapters 11 and 12, develop procedures for consultation and notification on relevant matters, and focus initially on actions required by the parties to implement the related commitments. However, the group has been inactive since 1999 and the politically charged discussions relating to investment under Chapter 11 have instead been assigned to *ad hoc* intergovernmental groups set up outside NAFTA's frail institutional system (Shigetomi 2002). Ultimately, it was the NAFTA's trade commission that issued an interpretative instruction to Chapter 11 tribunals.

Two particularly instructive cases of contentious bilateral issues that defied resolution through NAFTA's institutional framework are trucking and energy.

The Mexico-U.S. Trucking Dispute

In the NAFTA negotiations, the U.S. agreed to end the moratorium against Mexican trucking companies seeking to operate in the United States. Introduced in the *Bus Regulatory Reform Act of 1982*, the restrictions initially applied to both Canadian and

Mexican truckers. Whereas a presidential memorandum of understanding (MOU) quickly lifted the restriction against Canadian trucks, the presidential moratorium against Mexico was extended every two years. It did provide exemptions to certain categories of Mexican trucking companies and businesses, but most applicants were rejected (Condon and Sinha 2001, 236–237).

With NAFTA, it appeared that a compromise had been struck, because the U.S. agreed to phase out the moratorium and progressively allow Mexican trucks to obtain operating authority. This process was to have begun on 16 December 1995 and to have been completed by 1 January 2000 (Condon and Sinha 2001, 238). Although the Canadian and Mexican ministers of transportation signed MOUs permitting Canadian and Mexican truckers equal access within both countries, Mexico and the United States did not grant full access to each other's trucks (Condon and Sinha 2001, 237).

The restrictions were maintained by the Clinton administration because of strong domestic pressure stemming from interest groups benefiting from the *status quo*. American trucking unions argued that Mexican trucks would not sufficiently adhere to American safety standards. Financial considerations were substantial: the cross-border–trucking industry carried US$250 billion in Mexican-U.S. trade. If U.S. truckers were to be transporting fewer goods, the market share and profits of U.S. insurance companies would decrease (Condon and Sinha 2001, 235–236, 240).

In 1995, the Mexican government requested that a dispute resolution process be activated under the rules of NAFTA's Chapter 20. American manoeuvring managed to drag out the adjudicatory process. But finally, in February 2001, the panel ruled that the moratorium violated NAFTA and ordered the U.S. Department of Transportation (DOT) to begin considering all Mexican applications on their merits (Condon and Sinha 2001, 238).

The corollary of this long, unhappy episode was the failure of NAFTA's working group system. The Land Transportation Standards Subcommittee (LTSS) had been established under NAFTA's Chapter 9 'to address developments of more compatible standards related to truck, bus & rail operations and the transport of hazardous materials among the United States, Mexico and Canada' (ITC 1999). Within this general mandate, the LTSS established the Transportation Consultative Group on Cross-Border Operations and Facilitation (TCG #1) to deal with the Mexican-U.S. border issue. Since its inception, however, the group's most significant activity has been to arrange for 'a meeting of the trilateral *ad hoc* government-industry insurance group formed by TCG #1 two years ago' (*Ibid.*). Thus, the LTSS has primarily functioned to exchange information and study national regulatory systems, despite the fact that the NAFTA text explicitly states that 'the Subcommittee shall implement the following work program for making compatible the Parties' relevant standards-related measures for: (a) bus and truck operations ... (iii) no later than three years after the date of entry into force of this Agreement, for standards-related measures respecting vehicles, including measures relating to weights and dimensions, tires, brakes, parts and accessories, securement of cargo, maintenance and repair, inspections, and emissions and environmental pollution levels' (NAFTA Secretariat 1994, ch. 9, ann. 913.5.a-1).

These problems comprised many of the safety concerns expressed by the United States. The task of co-ordinating weight standards for bus and truck operations fell within the mandate of the LTSS, and as such, it was an issue that was meant to be resolved in a trilateral, professional fashion by a group of experts. The bilateral nature of the dispute is one reason why it did not function well in the trilateral framework. Canada remained involved in this issue only to the extent that it desired to be kept informed of developments, and that it wanted to see the dispute resolved. Despite being formally a NAFTA issue, it remained primarily a bilateral dispute (Decarme 2002).

The most important barrier to the working group's success was the highly politicised nature of the dispute, which prevented the LTSS from dealing with the issue in any meaningful way. Eventually, the increasing importance of Mexico in U.S. presidential and congressional politics necessitated a politically negotiated solution. As the issue was related to the U.S. government's refusal to act in the face of powerful domestic interests opposed to granting national treatment to Mexican trucks, a solution was required that would allow Mexican trucks into the U.S. while also taking into account the domestic political realities that had, until that point, impeded the U.S. administration's compliance with its NAFTA commitment. This issue was resolved – and could only have been resolved – by high-level negotiations between President George W. Bush and President Vicente Fox in 2001 (Dutton 2002).

The LTSS has since become reinvigorated as a result of the Bush administration's decision to honour the dispute panel's decision. Prior to this decision, it was noted in early 2002 that

> the motivation, if you will, for that committee to really do a lot of work has kind of stagnated ... the problem with gaining some momentum for that group's work has been, basically, in a practical sense, tied to an ability to foresee that we're actually going to implement these provisions of the agreement, because no one, up until about two months ago, had a real clear vision that we were actually going to do that (Decarme 2002).

The procedures for implementing the dispute panel's ruling were defined when the U.S. Congress set specific guidelines that the DOT was to follow. In November 2002, Bush modified the moratorium on granting operating authority to Mexican motor carriers and enabled the DOT to review the 130 applications already received from Mexico-domiciled truck and bus companies (DOT 2002). Ultimately, the LTSS had little to do with the resolution of this dispute. The U.S. conformity with its obligation was primarily determined by executive will and other political considerations such as a continuing obstruction through the U.S. trucking interests' use of the courts.

The U.S.–Mexico Energy Relationship

Energy has long been an important and contentious issue between the U.S. and Mexico. In the 1930s, President Lázaro Cárdenas made nationalisation of economic resources a symbol of Mexican sovereignty (Bacon 2002). Cárdenas argued that independence from the north required seizing the main levers of the country's economic life from the U.S. owners. In this spirit, Mexico nationalised U.S. and British oil facilities.

Consequently, public ownership of oil and electricity was written into the Mexican constitution. This effectively excluded foreign capital from developing the country's energy resources. Article 27 of the constitution says that the state has the exclusive right to generate, conduct, transform, distribute, and supply electrical energy for use in public service and in fact Article 28 requires the maintenance of a state-run monopoly in the energy sector.

The last 20 years have witnessed modest efforts toward privatisation on the part of different Mexican administrations. In 1992 President Carlos Salinas enacted several minor laws that, despite their contradictions with the constitution, allowed private companies to participate in a limited fashion in electricity generation (Bacon 2002). However, major changes to Mexico's electricity laws would require a constitutional amendment, which would, in turn, require the support by a two-thirds majority in the Mexican congress ('Bush Pressing Mexico to Open Energy Market on 1st Foreign Trip' 2001).

In May 2001 President Fox issued a set of energy proposals that would have amended the Mexican constitution by striking the requirement for a monopolistic energy sector from Article 28 and including a clause permitting exceptions to Article 27. But in April 2002 the Mexican Supreme Court struck down Fox's proposed changes and, moreover, cast doubt on the constitutionality of the 1992 legislation permitting a degree of private sector participation (Lindquist 2002).

Mexico has the second-largest proven crude oil reserves in the western hemisphere, after Venezuela ('Bush Pressing' 2001). Petróleos Mexicanos (Pemex) exported 1.4 million barrels of oil a day to the U.S. in 2000, making it the American's fourth-largest foreign source (Hebert 2001). With ever-increasing U.S. demand and shortages on the horizon, Bush viewed Mexico as a critical source of new supplies of natural gas and was anxious to increase U.S.-Mexico integration, linking Mexican electricity generation to the power grid and market in the U.S. southwest (Hebert 2001; Bacon 2002). He envisioned a North American energy market characterised by the free flow of natural gas, oil, and electricity across U.S. borders to the south and north (Hebert 2001). However, it was also clear that Bush's considerable interest in crafting the energy co-operation needed to develop a North American common market for energy was more than matched by Mexican resistance to such an arrangement (*Ibid.*).

The energy market is an important component of Mexico's economy. It represents 3 percent of the GNP and 8 percent of all exports, and it generates more than one third of the nation's tax income (Lindquist 2002). Since Mexicans view their energy resource base as part of their national heritage, the maintenance of a public sector oil industry remains symbolic of Mexican sovereignty. Strong political forces in Mexico oppose giving access to foreign corporations (Hebert 2001). Wary of job losses if foreign companies move back in, Mexico's electricity labour unions, with a combined membership over 100 000, oppose energy privatization (Lindquist 2002). So does Pemex, whose labour unions control 40 percent of the board of directors

('Bush Pressing' 2001). It was within this context that the U.S., anxious to bring Mexico into the same kind of energy interdependence it had achieved with Canada, pushed for a continental approach to energy policy development.

On 22 April 2001, at the Summit of the Americas in Quebec City, the North American Energy Working Group (NAEWG) was set up by the energy ministers of the three countries to build a deeper continental understanding regarding energy (Hartill 2002). Its mission was to help:

> foster communication and cooperation among the governments and energy sectors of the three countries on energy-related matters of common interest, and to enhance North American energy trade and interconnections consistent with the goal of sustainable development, for the benefit of all (NAEWG 2002).

Since its creation, the NAEWG has been very active and has been quite successful in accomplishing meaningful tasks at an early stage (Hartill 2002). As with NAFTA's CWGs, decisions within this new group are made informally and on a consensus basis. Most of the Canadian members come from Natural Resources Canada, although a small number work for International Trade Canada or serve on the National Energy Board (Hartill 2002).[3] The NAEWG's mandate is in the same spirit as that of the CWGs. Like them, it is a trilateral forum and performs a wide range of functions, one of which concerns information exchange and the harmonisation of statistical methodology among the three countries. The NAEWG serves an important purpose as an effective tool through which, for instance, Canada may promote significant bilateral goals such as advancing definitional concerns surrounding the U.S. classification of the Alberta oil sands (*Ibid.*).

Given NAFTA's extensive array of working groups, the question arises why the NAEWG, which chiefly explores issues relating to continental energy supply and the co-ordination of energy infrastructure and practices, was not set up under its aegis. NAFTA's Chapter 6 is about energy. The answer stems from energy's controversial and extremely important status among the three member governments. Chapter 6 establishes rules governing trade in energy and basic petrochemical goods among the parties, but it was not meant to facilitate the same degree of open and secure access as other chapters of the agreement. It adds to, and clarifies, existing principles set out in the General Agreement on Tariffs and Trade (GATT) covering the prohibition on the use of export taxes, 'national security' justifications for import or export restrictions, and proportional access requirements. However, Mexico is bound by neither the national security nor the proportional access provision, which forbids Canada from reducing its export of energy to the U.S. unless it cuts back its own consumption by the same proportion (SICE 2005). More than a third of the chapter consists of extensive reservations qualifying those provisions under which Mexico is obligated.[4] The first of five guiding principles listed states that 'the Parties confirm their full respect for their Constitutions' (NAFTA Secretariat 1994, ch. 6, ann. 601). It is evident from the text that not all three countries shared the same degree of enthusiasm for opening up this area of the economy.

Because of the sensitivities surrounding North American trade in energy, it is not handled under the ambit of NAFTA. As a Canadian official remarks,

> yes, we have a NAFTA energy chapter, yes it provides for national treatment ... but look through the system, look through the market, and you will find that five or six years on, not everyone has sort of taken this jargon into their daily workings, the way they carry out business. This is not like shoes, this is not like autos, this is not like even wheat, or other sectors that are covered by the trade agreement where people operate on the same basis, trade by the same rules (Hartill 2002).

The North American energy relationship remains highly politicised, involving long-term national security concerns and billions of dollars. The fact that the NAEWG was created on an *ad hoc* basis supports the contention that issues involving powerful interests do not get channelled through NAFTA institutions. To work within NAFTA on energy would place constraints on the member governments' policy options and could inflame domestic constituencies. Trilateral discussions on energy are more suited to forums where there is room for political compromise and negotiation, rather than forums in which the parties are subjected to a legalistic interpretation of each country's commitments under an international agreement. Energy continues to be an issue that cannot be assigned to relatively de-politicised institutional mechanisms.

The Resurgence of Committees and Working Groups

The CWG story is not all about decline. Some is about revival. Certain working groups have been revitalised as a result of a particular working group incorporating the continued bilateralism of North American relations. Some of the more active trilateral committees are those that deal with a certain issue on a bilateral basis, such as the Committee on Standards-Related Measures, the Temporary Entry Working Group, the Committee on Sanitary and Phytosanitary Measures, as well as the technical working groups recently set up to deal, for example, with pesticides and animal health. That these groups maintain fruitful information exchange and meet more regularly than some of their more exclusively trilateral counterparts is consistent with the view that bilateral realities continue to drive the North American relationship.

A further factor contributing to higher levels of CWG activity can involve political will redirecting activity from related areas of government policy. Since the negotiation and implementation of 'smart border' initiatives between the U.S. and Canada and Mexico following 11 September 2001, the Customs Subgroup of the Working Group on Rules of Origin has been largely concerned with issues of border security (Shigetomi 2002). The Working Group on Rules of Origin also appears to have been reinvigorated by event since September 11 (*Ibid.*). That extraneous political motivations recharged these groups' mandates suggests that the existence of a latent structure may generate an active function.

The Disjuncture between Theory and Practice in a Community of Law

In negotiating powerful economic rules for a continental community of law in the early 1990s, the U.S., Canada, and Mexico adopted a grand bargain that was complemented by the weakest possible political structure to oversee its evolution. The three parties achieved enough of what they wanted that they readily put aside any thought of creating a more robust structure for managing the agreement's implementation and for developing its norms than the series of committees and working groups whose flimsiness is now clear. As a result, a trinational North America has become more economically integrated through the increase of cross-border trade and cross-border production processes while remaining bereft of a capacity to manage its increased interdependence.

As Robert Pastor (2001) has demonstrated, the unintended consequences of economic success are such negative effects of increased vulnerability as Mexico's increasing economic and social disparities, which impinge on the U.S. in the form of an inexorable flow of immigrants, legal or illegal. Yet when negotiating their grand bargain, the three countries deliberately refrained from establishing mechanisms that might be in a position to address the problems that the continent's new rule book might engender. The minimalist institutions – a few dispute settlement mechanisms, an unstable executive, and a network of committees that have mandates that far exceed their capabilities for fulfilling them – have left NAFTA with a chronic disease that condemns its norms to atrophy for lack of a continuing supply of political energy. Major disputes are taken to the WTO for resolution rather than to NAFTA panels. New norms are negotiated at the global level in the Doha round of negotiations or at the hemispheric level in the FTAA, rather than in North America where there is no viable forum for deliberation and decision.

This experience suggests that, although a grand bargain can deal with the problems that are currently on the protagonists' agenda – yesterday, trade; today, terrorism – it cannot deal with tomorrow's issue, whatever that may turn out to be. Without institutions that can breathe life into the new community of law, tomorrow's issues will have to be addressed, if they are addressed at all, by yesterday's structures, namely the individual member states dealing with each other as needed and incrementally, using the same mainly bilateral channels through which they managed their affairs before the first Big Idea was turned into rules more than a decade ago.

Notes

1   The authors examined published reports listed on such government websites such as Canada's Department of Foreign Affairs and International Trade (DFAIT) and the United States Trade Representative (USTR), and sent out questionnaires pertaining to the tasks and responsibilities of the Canadian representatives on committees and working groups of the North American Free Trade Agreement (NAFTA) in early 2002. In addition to those at DFAIT who took the time to complete this questionnaire, the authors would like

to thank those who generously shared their experience and insights: Claude Carrière, Ricardo Del Castillo, and Carl Hartill of DFAIT; David Decarme of the U.S. Department of Transportation; Charles Doran, director of the Center of Canadian Studies at the Paul H. Nitze School of Advanced International Studies at Johns Hopkins University; Jeffrey Dutton of the Office of NAFTA and Inter-American Affairs at the U.S. Department of Commerce; Carlos Rico of the Mexican Embassy to the United States; Kent Shigetomi of the Office of the USTR; and Sidney Weintraub of the Center for Strategic and International Studies. They would especially like to thank Dean Carl Amrhein of the Faculty of Arts and Science at the University of Toronto for the generous financial support that allowed them to conduct their research in Washington DC, where they were hosted by the Woodrow Wilson International Center for Scholars.

2   By contrast, the majority of this U.S. official's time was spent working on the Free Trade Agreement of the Americas (FTAA).
3   Equivalent data for the U.S. and Mexico not given.
4   See Annex 602.3, Annex 603.6, Annex 605, Annex 607, and Annex 608.2 of the NAFTA text (NAFTA Secretariat 1994).

References

Bacon, David (2002). 'Mexican Workers Fight Electricity Privatization'. Global Exchange. <www.globalexchange.org/campaigns/mexico/energy/bacon010602.html> (November 2005).
Brunelle, Dorval and Christian Deblock (1992). 'Economic Blocs and the Challenge of the North American Free Trade Agreement'. In S.J. Randall, H.W. Konrad and S. Silverman, eds., *North America without Borders? Integrating Canada, the United States, and Mexico.* University of Calgary Press, Calgary.
'Bush Pressing Mexico to Open Energy Market on 1st Foreign Trip'. (2001). *Bloomberg*, 15 February.
Carrière, Claude (2002). Email correspondence. Trade Policy Bureau, Department of Foreign Affairs and International Trade (Canada), March.
Clarkson, Stephen (2002). *Uncle Sam and Us: Globalization, Neoconservatism, and the Canadian State.* University of Toronto Press, Toronto.
Condon, Bradly and Tapen Sinha (2001). 'An Analysis of an Alliance: NAFTA Trucking and the U.S. Insurance Industry'. *Estey Centre Journal for International Law and Trade Policy* vol. 2, no. 2, pp. 235–245.
Confidential interview (2002a). Mexican Embassy, Washington DC, 10 April.
Confidential interview (2002b). Secretaría de la Economía, Mexico City, 19 February.
Decarme, David (2002). Interview. Surface, Maritime, and Facilitation Division, United States Department of Transportation, Washington DC, 11 April.
Dobson, Wendy (2002). 'Shaping the Future of the North American Economic Space: A Framework for Action'. Commentary 162. C.D. Howe Institute. <www.cdhowe.org/pdf/commentary_162.pdf> (November 2005).
Doran, Charles (2002). Interview. Paul H. Nitze School of Advanced International Studies, John Hopkins University, Washington DC, 11 April.
Dutton, Jeffrey (2002). Interview. Office of NAFTA and Inter-American Affairs, United States Department of Commerce, Washington DC, 10 April.
Eden, Lorraine and Maureen Appel Molot (1992). 'The View from the Spokes: Canada and Mexico Face the United States'. In S.J. Randall, H.W. Konrad and S. Silverman, eds.,

North America without Borders? Integrating Canada, the United States, and Mexico. University of Calgary Press, Calgary.

Gotlieb, Allan (2003). 'A Better Way to Conduct Canadian-U.S. Relations'. Paper presented at the Borderlines Conference on Canada in North America, Woodrow Wilson Center for International Scholars, 27 February.

Hartill, Carl (2002). Interview. Canadian Embassy, Washington DC, 12 April.

Hebert, H. Josef (2001). 'Bush Expected to Push Energy-Market Idea'. *Associated Press*, 16 February.

Hurtig, Mel (2002). *The Vanishing Country: Is It Too Late to Save Canada?* McClelland and Stewart, Toronto.

International Trade Canada (1994). 'NAFTA: What It's All About'. <www.dfait-maeci.gc.ca/nafta-alena/what3-en.asp> (November 2005).

International Trade Canada (1996). '1994-1996 Report on the NAFTA Government Procurement Working Group'. <dfait-maeci.gc.ca/nafta-alena/report6-e.asp> (November 2005).

International Trade Canada (1999). 'Meeting of the NAFTA Land Transportation Standards Subcommittee'. Baltimore, 25–28 October. <www.dfait-maeci.gc.ca/nafta-alena/report13-e.asp> (November 2005).

International Trade Canada (2002). 'Institutions of the NAFTA'. <www.international.gc.ca/nafta-alena/inst-en.asp> (November 2005).

Lindquist, Diane (2002). 'Energy Reforms in Mexico Being Held Up by Politics, Observers Say'. *San Diego Union-Tribune*, 30 October. <www.signonsandiego.com/news/mexico/20021030-9999_1b30mexen.html> (November 2005).

McKinney, Joseph A. (2000). *Created from NAFTA: The Structure, Function, and Significance of the Treaty's Related Institutions.* M.E. Sharpe, Armonk NY.

NAFTA Secretariat (1994). 'North American Free Trade Agreement'. <www.nafta-sec-alena.org> (November 2005).

North American Energy Working Group (2002). 'North America: The Energy Picture'. <www2.nrcan.gc.ca/es/es/energypicture/index_e.cfm> (November 2005).

Pastor, Robert (2001). *Towards a North American Community.* Institute for International Economics, Washington DC.

Salvatore, Dominick (1994). 'NAFTA and the EC: Similarities and Differences'. In K. Fatemi and D. Salvatore, eds., *The North American Free Trade Agreement.* Alden Press, Oxford.

Shigetomi, Kent (2002). Interview. Office of the United States Trade Representative, Washington DC, 10 April.

SICE (1997a). 'March 1997 Report to the NAFTA Commission from the Committee on Trade in Goods'. <www.sice.oas.org/trade/nafta/reports/goods_e.asp> (November 2005).

SICE (1997b). 'NAFTA Trade Remedies Working Groups: Statements by the Governments of Canada, Mexico, and the United States'. <www.sice.oas.org/trade/nafta/reports/remed_e.asp> (November 2005).

SICE (1997c). 'Report to the Free Trade Commission Working Group on Rules of Origin (including Customs Subgroup): February 1997'. <www.sice.oas.org/trade/nafta/reports/origi_e.asp> (November 2005).

SICE (2005). 'OAS Overview of the North American Trade Agreement. Chapter Six: Energy and Basic Petrochemicals'. <www.sice.oas.org/summary/nafta/nafta6.asp> (November 2005).

Trade Compliance Center (2001). 'Exporter's Guides to U.S. Trade Agreements: Chapter Nine (Standards-Related Measures) of the North American Free Trade Agreement (NAFTA)'. <www.mac.doc.gov/tcc/e-guides/eg_naf09.html> (November 2005).

United States Department of Transportation (2002). 'U.S. Transportation Department Implements NAFTA Provisions for Mexican Trucks, Buses'. 27 November. <www.dot.gov/affairs/dot10702.htm> (November 2005).

Chapter 8

Regional Multinational Corporations and Triad Strategy

Alan M. Rugman and Alain Verbeke

Today, despite the appearance of globalisation, much economic activity in both manufacturing and services is location-bound. It takes place in clusters within the triad of the European Union, North America, and Japan. The geography of location has been summed up in the phrase 'sticky places'. These rigidities influence the strategic management decisions of firms, including multinational corporations (MNCs). In fact, the choice of entry mode and choice of location complement strategic management decisions of profound importance to MNCs.

This chapter builds on the insight from MNC scholars such as John H. Dunning (2001), Michael J. Enright (2002), and Alan M. Rugman and Alain Verbeke (2001b; 2001a), who find that in most triad clusters of value-added activities, MNCs are embedded as leading participants. The most far-reaching vision of this viewpoint is that of Alan Rugman and Joseph R. D'Cruz (2000): they argue that MNCs act as flagships to lead, direct, co-ordinate, and manage strategically the value-added activities of partner firms in a business network, including key suppliers, key customers, and the non-business infrastructure. While Dunning refers to flagships as leaders only of vertical clusters, as in automobiles, Rugman and D'Cruz also include horizontal clusters, as in textiles and financial services. Such clusters thus embrace not only MNCs and other private sector firms, but also other key components of civil society such as professional associations, research centres, and educational institutions.

This chapter examines the extent to which clusters are regionally based, in that they operate across the national borders of nation-states in the triad, in the spirit of Rugman (2000). Key cases will be examined from the North American context (specifically, the United States and Canada) and from within the EU. Coupled with this regional focus as clusters is an analysis of the past, present, and future roles of MNCs in such regional or triad geographical spaces. Here three questions stand out. First, what is the significance of MNCs as flagship firms in various sectors and to what extent are such business networks regionally located? Second, what are the implications of this for future strategy? Or, in view of the work by Vivay Govindarajan, and Anil K. Gupta (2001), can there be a global strategy that assumes an integrated, homogenous market, or are there triad-based regional strategies for MNCs? Third, how can firms and service organisations for small, open economies fit into these spatial clusters (if they do at all), and what are the past, present, and future links between such organisations and MNCs from the triad?

This chapter offers evidence that demonstrates that the majority of even the most global MNCs in reality operate on a triad-centred regional basis. Of the world's 20 most global MNCs, only six are truly global MNCs with a global strategy. The remainder are home- or nation-based and need regional strategies. With such key civil society actors and networks so regionally centred, it is the relationship of civil society to regional governance, rather than global governance, that should be the priority concern.

A Framework of Triad or Regional Business Activity

Figure 8.1 presents a framework that distinguishes among global, regional, and national strategies for MNCs with geographically strongly dispersed sales, assets, and employees. The vertical axis represents the actual product characteristics (*ex post*) of an MNC at these three levels: world (or global) product, region-based (or triad-based) product, and nation-based product.

The extent to which products are standardised at the global, regional, or national level represents the revealed preferences of MNCs to institutionalise a particular approach at the world scale or to adapt to the income, consumer demand, marketing, regulatory, and other requirements of national or regional markets. In contrast, the horizontal axis is more a reflection of stated preferences – that is, the extent to which MNC managers view strategic decision making as a process concentrated in one home base or dispersed across regions or countries.

More specifically, the horizontal axis represents the location of decision-making power (*ex ante*) for corporate, business, or functional strategies. Here, the question

Figure 8.1   A Framework for Analysing Globalisation

		Firm's Organisational Structure and Decision-Making Power		
		Corporate Headquarters	Regional Centres	National Subsidiaries
Firm's Product Characteristics	World (global) product	1 a	4 d	7 g
	Region-based (triad-based) product	2 b	5 e	8 h
	Nation-based product	3 c	6 f	9 i

to be answered is whether all of the MNC's key strategic decisions (such as choice of product or market niches, choice of strategic management tools to outperform rivals, and key choices made in each functional area, including research and development, production, marketing, distribution, human resources management) are taken in a single location, or whether at least a substantial portion of these decisions is taken in several home bases at the national or regional levels.

Figure 8.1 adapts the framework on global strategies developed by Rugman and Verbeke (1993). They argued that the truly important decisions to be taken by MNCs relate to two parameters. The first is the number of national (or home) bases with which they function – the number of locations where important strategic decisions are taken (equivalent to the horizontal axis). The second is the use of non-location–bound firm-specific advantages (FSAs) versus location-bound FSAs (equivalent to the vertical axis). The former allow various approaches to standardising the MNC's product offering across borders and to earn benefits of integration (related to scale, scope, and benefits of exploiting national differences). The latter provides the potential to gain benefits of national responsiveness.

To this resource-based perspective on the integration-national responsiveness model (Rugman and Verbeke 1993), the framework in Figure 8.1 explicitly introduces a regional dimension. This new dimension is now needed due to emerging empirical work that suggests that global strategies are not appropriate for most MNCs that actually operate on a regional or triad basis (Rugman 2000). More specifically, on the horizontal axis this regional dimension implies that a number of strategic decisions are left to region-based headquarters rather than to nation-based ones. The vertical axis implies the development of FSAs that are useful at the level of the set of nations that form the region. These are region-bound company strengths: they can contribute to survival, profitability, and growth beyond the geographic scope of a single nation, but they are still location-bound, in the sense that they cannot be deployed globally (Morrison, Ricks, and Roth 1991; Morrison and Roth 1992). In this context, the view that a global company 'has the capability to go anywhere, deploy any assets, and access any resources, and it maximizes profits on a global basis' may be a striking normative message (Yip 2003, 7). But in practice it applies to very few, in any, MNCs. Indeed, most rely largely on sets of location-bound and region-bound FSAs as the basis for their competitiveness.

Figure 8.1 helps identify some of the more important mistakes made by proponents, and critics, of globalisation and by advocates of a global strategy for MNCs. They view as a reflection of a global strategy not only cell *a*, but also cells *b*, *c*, *d*, and *g* (where strategies other than globalisation are required). In cells *b* and *c*, they focus on the decisions and actions of corporate leaders, typically the chief executive officer (CEO), the top management committee, and the board of directors. To be sure, most key financial decisions in MNCs are taken at that level. However, even if all major corporate strategy decisions are taken centrally, typically in the home country (the column headed 'Corporate Headquarters' of Figure 8.1), as is the case for many companies in the computer business (both hardware and software), cells *b* and *c* reflect respectively the existence of substantial regional and national responsiveness regarding the product offering (including its service component) that actually is provided to the market.

In other words, MNCs that tailor their product offering to regional and national circumstances do not pursue a simple global strategy as suggested by cell *a*. Considerable resources must be allocated to allow for the required level of sub-global responsiveness in terms of what is being delivered to the market. In addition, even if the MNC's product offerings are largely global, this does not necessarily imply that all important decisions on market penetration, distribution, advertising, and so on can be taken centrally. Bounded rationality constraints are likely to force corporate management to delegate important decisions to the regional and national levels, thereby positioning the firm closer to cells *d* and *g*.

This point is vitally important. At the other end of the academic and policy-oriented spectrum, many antiglobalisation critics suffer from a similar misperception. They view MNCs as centrally directed, profit-maximising entities, eager to sell standardised products around the globe. Antiglobalisation critics state that MNCs are insensitive to host country and host region demands, especially those of host country governments. In fact, the presence of intense international rivalry and the unfortunate reality that every MNC from one region does face an important liability of foreignness in the other regions of the world force MNCs to be particularly sensitive to the requirements of host country governments and other salient stakeholders (Rugman and Verbeke 1998). And because most MNCs rely on location-bound and region-bound FSAs for their competitiveness, the spectre of a global 'race to the bottom' conjured up by some analysts from nongovernmental organisations (NGOs) has little basis in fact.

Of course, this does not imply that MNCs can or should adopt an approach in cell 9, and be fully polycentric, with products carefully tailored to each national market and most strategy decisions left to subsidiary managers in the host country. Much conceptual and empirical evidence suggests that a 'multi-national' approach leads to overlapping efforts and duplication in innovation, inconsistent national strategies, opportunistic behaviour by subsidiary managers, and more generally a waste of resources and lack of clear strategic direction (Bartlett and Ghoshal 2000). The great strength of an MNC is to overcome market imperfections that characterise national markets and to develop systemic, network-related FSAs rather than asset-based FSAs (Dunning and Rugman 1985). Even for MNCs with a polycentric administrative heritage, cells 6 and 8 are likely much more relevant than cell 9. In cell 6, attempts are made to achieve decision-making synergies across markets, for example by developing pan-European or pan-American strategies in particular functional areas (Rugman and Verbeke 1992). In cell 8, economies of scale and scope are pursued by the national subsidiary managers themselves, through standardising at the regional level their product offering across those national markets that have strong similarities in demand. In that case, subsidiary initiative is critical (Birkinshaw 2000; Rugman and Verbeke 2001b).

The strategy and international management literature has done a good job of distinguishing between cells 1 and 9. But it has not addressed most of the other cells. The basic matrix of integration (cell 1) and national responsiveness (cell 9) popularised by Christopher Bartlett and Sumantra Ghoshal (1989) distinguished between a pure global cell 1 strategy and the 'act local' national responsiveness strategy of cell 9. In addition, the key contribution of their 'transnational solution' framework was the prescription that MNCs should usefully combine strategies in cells 1 and 9. They should attempt to develop appropriate strategies for each separate business, for each function within that business, and for each task within that function, and the capability to implement either a national or a global approach.

The Bartlett and Ghoshal framework thus can usefully explain cell 3 (centralised, global strategic decision making combined with local product offering) – that is, the think global–act local approach. It also allows the analysis of less common cases in cell 7, whereby rather powerful national subsidiaries are responsible for delivering global products, but choose themselves which products have the most potential in their national markets and largely take responsibility for the delivery. This approach is found in many global professional services companies. Yet their framework cannot handle the triad-based strategies of cell 5 very well, nor the intermediate cases of cells 2, 4, 6, and 8, that is, all cases whereby the regional level is important.

Yet an increasing number of MNCs operate largely at the regional level. Therefore regional elements are becoming increasingly important in many MNCs, either in terms of strategic decision making or of actual product offering. If many MNCs are at least partially operating in cell 5 on a triad basis, then any strategy-related analysis of the MNC's functioning first needs to take into account the need to decompose its strategic decision-making processes and product offering along global, regional, and national lines, building upon a more complex analytical tool than a conventional integration-national responsiveness matrix. Only then can a correct analysis be performed of the actual extent of triad-based decision-making power and can the rationale for region-based or adapted products and services from these MNCs be properly investigated. If the theoretical construct itself of a 'regional solution' (cell 5 in Figure 8.1) is neglected, little can be expected from empirical research on strategy and structure in MNCs to portray accurately the present importance and future potential of the regional approach.

The regional approach has sometimes been described as the mere outcome of a global strategy. Indeed, George Yip (2003, 222) argues that 'before deciding whether and how to do business in a region of the world, a company needs to have a clear global strategy [which includes] the core business strategy, the competitive objectives for the business, and the extent to which the business will be operated as one integrated business or a looser collection of geographically independent units. Next, a company needs to decide on the overall role of the region within the global strategy'. This view assumes a particular sequence and hierarchy in MNC strategic decision making. In practice, however, the global-regional sequence is unlikely to occur.

The regional solution of cell 5 should be viewed as an efficient corporate response to several factors. First, internal information processing requirements are critical. The rules of engagement may be different in each region, given a different industry structure, different regulatory system, different competitive position of the firm, different optimal expansion pattern, different product scope, and different strategy tools required to outperform rivals. If so, intra-regional information processing must be sufficiently dense so as to permit affiliates to cope optimally with shared external circumstances and to develop regionally consistent strategies. Second, customer requirements may vastly differ across regions depending upon the level of economic development, culturally determined preferences, and other factors. Third, region-based cluster requirements may impose specific types of behaviour on firms in order for these firms to be perceived as legitimate within the context of regional clusters, especially suppliers, related and supporting industries, and the non-business infrastructure. Here, region-based isomorphic flexibility may be critical for firms to function effectively as true insiders in the region. Finally, political requirements at the regional level are increasingly important. Regional co-operation agreements such as the North American Free Trade Agreement (NAFTA) and the European Union are single-market measures that mainly represent, some assert, the elimination of trade and investment barriers, and therefore allow a reduced attention devoted by MNCs to government policy. In fact, regional agreements usually imply not merely the elimination of national regulation, but a shift of regulatory authority to the regional level, and thereby the need to allocate firm resources to monitor and manage relationships at that level.

The rigidity of the triad has been explored in Rugman (2000). It is reinforced by the new trade regime of the World Trade Organization (WTO), which must devote enormous managerial resources to arbitrate triad-based trade disputes and trade-remedy law protectionism (as in the cases of bananas, beef hormones, export subsidies, and steel). The new protectionism of health, safety, and environmental regulations is preventing an open world market and reinforcing triad markets. NAFTA is being expanded into the Free Trade Agreement of the Americas (FTAA) and 13 countries are in negotiations to be added to the EU. These political developments reinforce the triad and the need for regional government policies and triad-based firm strategies.

Empirical Evidence on Triad Activity

As a test of the strength of the triad/regional focus of strategy, rather than a global strategy, one can consider the most favourable possible case for the global strategy viewpoint. This would classify as global all MNCs with a foreign to total sales (F/T) ratio above 50 percent or with some significant activity in each part of the triad. Such MNCs are easy to identify because the United Nations Conference on Trade and Development (UNCTAD) reports the F/T ratios for sales, assets, and employees annually for the world's 100 largest MNCs, ranked by foreign assets. The UNCTAD *World Investment Report* for 2001 lists the largest 100 MNCs by foreign asset size. For these 100 MNCs one can calculate the F/T sales ratios where foreign sales are sales by subsidiaries and exports by the parent MNC. Of these, the top 20 MNCs ranked by foreign to total sales are reported as F/T sales in Table 8.1.

These 20 MNCs have the highest F/T sales ratios among the 100 top MNCs. The 20 MNCs are mostly from small, open economies such as Canada, Australia, and Switzerland, or are in members of the EU such as Finland, France, the United Kingdom, Germany, and Sweden. There are no U.S. MNCs among the most international global firms. This is not all that surprising given the huge size of the U.S. home market. There is one Japanese MNC.

Yet Table 8.1 disguises a very important point. While these 20 MNCs have the majority of their sales outside of the home country, many are still very regional. Most of these foreign sales are still mainly in their home-triad regional market. This point is demonstrated in Table 8.2, where MNCs are ranked according to their intra-regional sales percentages. By intra-regional is meant sales within Europe (and usually within the 15 member states of the EU) for MNCs from those countries and within NAFTA (for Canadian and U.S.) MNCs. In the case of Asia-Pacific MNCs, intra-regional refers to Asia excluding Australia.

Table 8.1   The World's Most International MNCs

Rank	Company	Country	Foreign to Total Sales
1	Seagram	Canada	104.2
2	Roche	Switzerland	98.4
3	Nestle	Switzerland	98.3
4	ABB	Switzerland	97.5
5	Electrolux	Sweden	95.9
6	Philips	Netherlands	94.9
7	Thomson Corporation	Canada	94.8
8	AstraZeneca	United Kingdom*	94.7
9	Stora Enso	Finland	93.5
10	British American Tobacco	United Kingdom	91.2
11	News Corporation	Australia	90.2
12	Holcim	Switzerland	90.1
13	Volvo	Sweden	88.7
14	Unilever	United Kingdom	87.3
15	Diageo	United Kingdom	86.3
16	Michelin	France	86.2
17	Glaxo Wellcome	United Kingdom	85.5
18	Nippon Mitsubishi Oil Corporation	Japan	83.8
19	Akzo Nobel	Netherlands	81.8
20	DaimlerChrysler	Germany	81.1

Notes: *UNCTAD lists AstraZeneca as a U.S. company but its headquarters are in the United Kingdom.

This table is constructed from the UNCTAD (2001) source, which lists the world's 100 largest MNCs by foreign asset size. The foreign and total sales of these 100 MNCs are also reported so F/T sales ratios can be calculated. The top 20 MNCs on F/T sales are included in this table.

Source: UNCTAD (2001). Data are for 1999.

Table 8.2 reveals that about half of the world's allegedly most global MNCs are, in fact, operating mainly in the home-triad market. For example the French MNCs, Pernod Ricard (81.7 percent intra-regional sales) and Vivendi (68.0 percent) are clearly European MNCs in their sales, as more than two thirds of their business is within Europe. They need a European-based strategy, not a global one. The same is true for several other MNCs that are allegedly global; in fact, these MNCs operate in their home-base triad for the majority of their sales: Thomson Corporation (84.4 percent), Stora Enso (69.2 percent), Akzo Nobel (63.0 percent), Volvo (55.1 percent), ABB (54.0 percent), and Philips (53.2 percent). Two other MNCs, Electrolux (47.0 percent) and Michelin (47.2 percent), are very home triad–based. For one MNC these data could not be constructed (Nippon Mitsubishi Oil Corporation). This leaves only 10 of the top 20 (actually 21 included in Table 8.2 due to Vivendi's purchase of Seagram and then Pernod Ricard's purchase of part of Seagram's liquor business) as allegedly global MNCs that could possibly be global, with global strategies.

Table 8.2   Home Region Distribution of Sales of the World's Index of Multinational Corporations, 2001

Company	Home Country	2001 percent intra-regional	2001 percent extra-regional	1999 UNCTAD F/T
Vivendi*	France	68.0	32.0	NA
Pernod Ricard*	France	81.7	18.3	NA
Roche	Switzerland	37.0	63.0	98.4
Nestle	Switzerland	31.6	68.4	98.3
ABB	Switzerland/Sweden	54.0	46.0	97.5
Electrolux	Sweden	47.0	53.0	95.9
Royal Philips	Netherlands	53.2	46.8	94.9
Thomson Corporation	Canada	84.4	15.6	94.8
AstraZeneca	United Kingdom	32.0	68.0	94.7
Stora Enso	Finland	69.2	30.8	93.5
British American Tobacco	United Kingdom	26.3	73.7	91.2
News Corporation	Australia	9.0	91.0	90.2
Holcim	Switzerland	33.0	67.0	90.1
Volvo	Sweden	55.1	44.9	88.7
Unilever	Netherlands/UK	38.7	61.3	87.3
Diageo*	United Kingdom	31.8	68.2	86.3
Michelin	France	47.2	52.8	86.2
GlaxoSmithKline	United Kingdom	26.5	73.5	85.5
Nippon Mitsubishi Oil Corp.	Japan	NA	NA	83.8
Akzo Nobel N.V.	Netherlands	63.0	37.0	73.7
DaimlerChrysler	Germany	29.9	70.1	81.1

Notes: * Vivendi purchased Seagram in 2001 and later sold it to Diageo and Pernod Ricard. 'Intra-regional' refers to Europe in the case of European companies and North America in the case of North American companies. In the case of DaimlerChrysler, Europe refers to the EU. Ericsson reports Europe, Africa, and the Middle East as one region.

Sources: Individual annual reports, UNCTAD (2001).

Of these, several are highly focussed in one part of the triad, but not their home triad. These include U.S.-based MNCs such as:

- News Corporation (9 percent sales in Australasia, 74.7 percent in the United States, and 16.3 percent in the United Kingdom);
- AstraZeneca (32 percent in the United Kingdom, 52.8 percent in the United States, 5.2 percent in Japan, and 10 percent in the rest of the world);
- GlaxoSmithKline (26.5 percent in Europe, 52.5 percent in the United States, and 21 percent in the rest of the world); and
- DaimlerChrysler (29.9 percent in the EU, 60.1 percent in NAFTA, and 10 percent in the rest of the world).

The more balanced MNCs, operating across at least three regions of the triad, number only six in total (out of 21):

- Nestle (31.6 percent in Europe, 31.4 percent in the Americas, and 37 percent in the rest of the world);
- Holcim (33 percent in Europe, 22 percent in North America, 27 percent in Latin America, and 18 percent in the rest of the world);
- Roche (37 percent in Europe, 38 percent in North America, and 25 percent in the rest of the world);
- Unilever (38.7 percent sales in Europe, 26.6 percent in North America, 15.4 percent in Asia, 12.7 percent in Latin America and 6.6 percent in the rest of the world);
- Diageo (31.8 percent in Europe and 68.2 percent in the rest of the world); and
- British American Tobacco (26.3 percent in Europe and 73.7 percent in the rest of the world).

These six MNCs are much more diversified across the triad. They can be regarded as global firms and will have global strategies and structures. But they are the exception. In this exclusive set of 20 highly internationalised MNCs, only six are truly global and the others are either strongly home-triad based or are from small countries peripheral to the triad and are focussed in one of the other triad markets. Most of the other 80 of the top 100 MNCs are even less global and are either domestic or home-based MNCs. Location and region matter even to MNCs.

One possible modification to this triad-based strategy message is that, for some MNCs, the strategy may need to be adjusted by strategic business unit (SBU). While it is even more difficulty to find data on SBU sales by triad for the 100 largest MNCs, some examples may help.

Table 8.3 reports data on the SBUs of Vivendi Universal. Some SBUs, like CANAL+, are 96 percent in Europe, while others have a larger U.S. presence, such as the Universal Studios Group (57 percent U.S.), Publishing, (35 percent U.S.), and Music (42 percent in the United States and 40 percent in Europe). Vivendi's water business is part of the Environmental Services SBU, and this is still 73 percent in Europe.

The large retail organisations are even more triad based than the manufacturing MNCs. Table 8.4 reports data showing that the large U.S. retailers such as Wal-Mart, Sears, and K-Mart are all North American based. The latter two have no stores outside the United States, and Wal-Mart only has 10 percent of its stores and revenues outside of the NAFTA region.

In 2001, Wal-Mart had 4414 stores, of which 3,244 were in the United States, 196 in Canada, and 551 in Mexico. Only 423 were in international markets, constituting 9.6 percent of the total stores. Nonetheless, Wal-Mart was the most international large-scale retailer from the United States. Its foreign revenue as a percentage of total revenues was 16.26 percent (US$35.4 billion of a total of US$217.7 billion).

K-Mart has divested itself of its operations in Canada and Mexico. In 2001, its 2105 stores were all in the United States. There is a K-Mart Australia, but this is owned by an Australian company.

Elsewhere in the retail sector, Sears operates only in Canada and the United States. In 2001, Target had 1381 stores only in the United States, JC Penney had 3700 stores only in the United States. Daiei, mainly a Japanese operation but with stores in China

Table 8.3   Vivendi Universal 2001 Revenues by Region (percent)

Area	Europe	U.S.	Rest of World
Music	40	42	18
Publishing	55	35	10
Universal Studios Group	28	57	15
CANAL+ Group & Other	96	2	2
Telecoms	87	–	13
Internet	47	53	–
Total Media and Communications	62	26	12
Environmental services	73	19	8
Non-core businesses	67	–	33
Total Vivendi Universal	68	22	10

Note: Vivendi purchased Seagram in 1999 and the combined operations are reported here.
Source: Vivendi Universal Annual Report.

Table 8-4   The Largest U.S. Retailers, Number of Stores, 2001

Company	U.S.	Canada	Mexico	North Am. Triad %	International	%	Total
Wal-Mart	3118	174	499	90.5	398	9.5	4189
Sears	2167	511	–	100.0	–	–	2678
K-Mart	2105	–	–	100.0	–	–	2105

Note: In addition to Sears's Canadian retail stores, the company has more than 2157 Sears Catalogue Stores. These are independently owned catalogue stands that operate mostly in remote areas across Canada.

Source: Wal-Mart Annual Report 2001; Sears Annual Report 2001; <www.sears.com>; K-Mart Annual Report 2001.

and the United States, had 8609 stores (including 7432 convenience stores). Groupe Pinault-Printemps of France made 52.5 percent of its revenues outside of France. However, it only made 30 percent of its revenue outside of Europe. Carrefour of France had about 9200 stores in 30 countries; yet only 19 percent of Carrefour's revenues originated from outside of Europe (see Table 8.5). Clearly Carrefour must be analysed on a European regional level because it is not a global organisation.

Turning to financial services, Citigroup, the world's largest financial MNC, is also very regional. Table 8.6 reports Citigroup's consumer banking group, where total revenues are 72.7 percent in North America, accounts are 77.1 percent, and only deposits are more diversified, at 45.5 percent. Credit cards are part of the accounts in Citigroup's consumer banking group and over 76 percent of accounts in the United States are credit card accounts. While more than 70 percent of Citigroup's revenue and accounts are in the United States, only 45 percent of average consumer

Table 8.5   Carrefour's International Locations, 2001

Country/Region	Number of Stores	Percentage of Total
France	3367	36.6
Europe (excluding France)	4870	52.9
Spain	2719	29.6
Italy	918	10.0
Belgium	442	4.8
Greece	375	4.1
Portugal	332	3.6
Poland	62	0.7
Switzerland	11	0.1
Czech Republic	11	0.1
Total Europe	8237	89.5
Americas	645	7.0
Argentina	391	4.3
Brazil	226	2.5
Mexico	19	0.2
Colombia	5	0.1
Chile	4	0.0
Asia	109	1.2
China	27	0.3
Japan	3	0.0
South Korea	22	0.2
Taiwan	27	0.3
Thailand	15	0.2
Malaysia	6	0.1
Indonesia	8	0.1
Singapore	1	0.0
Other and nonspecified	209	2.3
Total	9200	100.0

Source: Carrefour Profile (Number of Stores) <www.carrefour.com> (June 2001).

deposits are there. Table 8.7 shows that this regionalisation is common across all the major business groups of Citigroup, except in commercial loans, which is 27 percent U.S.-based. While Citigroup has large commercial loans to foreign companies, it is not as active in foreign consumer loans, as 65.6 percent of consumer loans are in the United States. Overall, these data reveal a very home-based North American business. Indeed, Citibank became less global after the merger with Travellers in 1999. The latter's insurance business was very localised, and this offset much of Citibank's banking diversification in South America and Asia.

Conclusion

There is abundant empirical support for the Rugman (2000) proposition that large MNCs operate on a regional triad rather than a global basis. The old-fashioned view of global MNCs operating in an integrated and homogeneous world market with globalisation as the predominant form of international business needs to be replaced. The world's 100 largest MNCs are mainly triad-based regional players, not global

**Table 8.6   International Operations of Citigroup, 2001:
Consumer Banking Division (Percentage of Total)**

Country/Region	Revenue	Number of Accounts	Deposits
NAFTA	72.7	77.1	45.5
Japan	8.9	3.3	10.2
Other Asia	5.8	6.2	24.2
Western Europe	6.8	6.4	9.1
Latin America	3.6	4.5	7.1
Other	2.2	2.5	4.0
Total	100.0	100.0	100.0

Note: Numbers might not add up due to rounding.
Source: Citigroup Annual Report, 2001.

Table 8.7   Selected Indicators of Citigroup's International Scope

average volume in millions of dollars

Indicator	U.S.	Foreign	U.S. as a % of Total
Investments	95 781	38 822	71.2
Brokerage Receivables	25 058	2517	90.9
Trading Account Assets	81 241	37 304	68.5
Trading of Federal Funds and Securities	104 150	34 087	75.3
Consumer Loans	151 837	79 782	65.6
Commercial Loans	53 834	91 867	36.9
Employees	149 000	123 000	54.8

Source: Citigroup Annual Report, 2001.

ones. They operate on a strongly segmented regional/triad basis. A relevant framework to analyse MNC strategy needs to recognise this fact. In short, management strategy needs to refocus from a simplistic global strategy and globalisation perspective to the more empirically accurate one of triad market activity and the regional MNCs.

These findings are partially confirmed in work on the triad-based nature of the automobile sector by E.H. Schlie and George Yip (2000). However, they argue that most MNCs first follow a global strategy, and then some should selectively regionalise in a regionalisation that is a sequential process. This is not observed here. Rather, the triad strategies of MNCs in 2002 are very similar to the nature of triad strategies in John Stopford and John Dunning (1983).

References

Bartlett, Christopher A. and Sumantra Ghoshal (1989). *Managing Across Borders: The Transnational Solution*. Harvard Business School Press, Boston.

Bartlett, Christopher A. and Sumantra Ghoshal (2000). *Transnational Management: Text, Cases, and Readings in Cross-border Management*. 3rd ed. Irwin/McGraw Hill, Boston.

Birkinshaw, Julian (2000). *Entrepreneurship in the Global Firm*. Sage Publications, London.

Dunning, John H. (2001). *Global Capitalism at Bay?* Routledge, London.

Dunning, John H. and Alan M. Rugman (1985). 'The Influence of Hymer's Dissertation on the Theory of Foreign Direct Investment'. *American Economic Review* vol. 75, no. 2, pp. 228–232.

Enright, Michael J. (2002). 'The Globalization of Competition and the Localization of Competitive Advantage: Policies Towards Regional Clustering'. In N. Hood and S. Young, eds., *Globalization of Economic Activity and Economic Development*, pp. 330–331. Macmillan, Basingstoke, UK.

Govindarajan, Vivay and Anil K. Gupta (2001). *The Quest for Global Dominance*. Jossey-Bass/Wiley, San Francisco.

Morrison, Allen, David Ricks, and Kendall Roth (1991). 'Globalization versus Regionalization: Which Way for the Multinational'. *Organizational Dynamics* vol. 19, no. 3, pp. 17–29.

Morrison, Allen and Kendall Roth (1992). 'The Regional Solution: An Alternative to Globalization'. *Transnational Corporations* vol. 1, no. 2, pp. 37–55.

Rugman, Alan M. (2000). *The End of Globalization*. Random House, London.

Rugman, Alan M. and Joseph R. D'Cruz (2000). *Multinationals as Flagship Firms: Regional Business Networks*. Oxford University Press, Oxford.

Rugman, Alan M. and Alain Verbeke (1992). 'Europe 1992 and Competitive Strategies for North American Firms'. *Business Horizons* vol. 34, no. 6, pp. 76–81.

Rugman, Alan M. and Alain Verbeke (1993). 'Generic Strategies in Global Competition'. In A.M. Rugman and A. Verbeke, eds., *Research in Global Strategic Management, Volume 4. Global Competition: Beyond the Three Generics*, pp. 3–15. JAI Press, Greenwich, CT.

Rugman, Alan M. and Alain Verbeke (1998). 'Multinational Enterprises and Public Policy'. *Journal of International Business Studies* vol. 29, no. 1, pp. 115–136.

Rugman, Alan M. and Alain Verbeke (2001a). 'Location, Competitiveness, and the Multinational Enterprise'. In A. M. Rugman and T. Brewer, eds., *The Oxford Handbook of International Business*, pp. 150–180. Oxford University Press, Oxford.

Rugman, Alan M. and Alain Verbeke (2001b). 'Subsidiary-Specific Advantages in Multinational Enterprises'. *Strategic Management Journal* vol. 22, no. 5, pp. 237–250.

Schlie, E.H. and George Yip (2000). 'Regional Follows Global: Strategy Mixes in the World Automotive Industry'. *European Management Journal* vol. 18, no. 4, pp. 343–356.

Stopford, John and John H. Dunning (1983). *Multinationals: Company Performance and Global Trends*. Macmillan, London.

United Nations Conference on Trade and Development (2001). 'World Investment Report 2001: Promoting Linkages'. UNCTAD/WIR/2001.

Yip, George (2003). *Total Global Strategy II*. Prentice-Hall, Upper Saddle River, NJ.

Chapter 9

NAFTA's Chapter 11: Investor Protection, Integration, and the Public Interest

Julie Soloway[1]

The North American Free Trade Agreement (NAFTA) created an institutional environment that fosters economic integration among Canada, Mexico, and the United States. Since NAFTA has come into force, there has been substantial growth in trilateral trade and investment among those three countries (Hart and Dymond 2002, 132). The importance of both inward and outward foreign direct investment (FDI) for Canada is well known. FDI in Canada is responsible for 30 percent of all Canadian jobs and 75 percent of its manufacturing exports (Kirton 1998). The U.S. is Canada's largest source of inward FDI and more than one half of Canadian outward FDI goes to the United States. Increased investor protection is one reason that Canadian and U.S. direct investments in Mexico have boomed, from an annual flow of US$5.7 billion in 1994 to US$19.9 billion in 2001 (Secretaría de Economía 2001b, 2001a).

In general, a more predictable environment for investors will lead to increased investment (Drabek and Payne 1999). NAFTA's goals for integration, however, are relatively modest compared to those of many other regional trade agreements. The parties to NAFTA did not contemplate the creation of an European Union–style arrangement that provides for political and social integration. Rather, the NAFTA attempts to provide for economic integration among the three countries while, at the same time, preserving political autonomy and decision-making power in each country. Similarly, the NAFTA and its institutions were not designed to manage social welfare issues. As one commentator has noted, 'NAFTA was not designed with the intention to manage social welfare conditions. To the extent that the NAFTA has failed to address those conditions, this failure was built in to its institutions' (Abbott 1999).

The rules of NAFTA's Chapter 11 provisions on investment ideally create a secure and predictable framework for the unencumbered flow of investment within North America, and thus for substantial economic gains. Chapter 11 encodes certain obligations that define how a NAFTA government must treat an investment or an investor from another NAFTA country (see Table 9.1). If any one of NAFTA's governments adopts a 'measure' that breaches an obligation contained in Chapter 11, the affected investor may initiate a dispute settlement proceeding directly against a NAFTA government.[2]

Despite the economic growth that these rules are designed to encourage, their desirability in the context of an integrated North American marketplace is being seriously challenged, primarily because of the perceived effects that these rules are having, or could have, on public regulation. This chapter evaluates the claim that Chapter 11 has undermined environmental regulation in North America. It concludes that, for the most part, the concern has been overstated. To date, NAFTA Chapter 11 has not threatened the progress of environmental regulation in North America. It also suggests, however, that certain changes to the NAFTA Chapter 11 process may be warranted, to take account of some of the weaknesses of the current institutional architecture.

NAFTA's Chapter 11 Investment Provisions

The rules found in Chapter 11 are by no means novel in international economic law. The key legal principles are largely grounded in customary international law, as codified in a myriad of existing bilateral investment treaties (BITs). NAFTA is thus not a 'radically new departure from prevailing practice with respect to investment protection' (Wilkie 2002, 15). More than 2000 BITs currently exist worldwide.

Table 9.1   NAFTA Chapter 11 Obligations

The main obligations in NAFTA Chapter 11 upon which a claim may be based are:

1. national treatment (the obligation to treat investments or investors from a NAFTA country no less favourably than domestic investments or investors in like circumstances) (Article 1102);
2. most favoured nation treatment (the obligation to treat investments or investors no less favourably than investments or investors from any other country) (Article 1103);
3. minimum standard of treatment (the obligation to treat investments or investors in accordance with international law, including fair and equitable treatment) (Article 1105);
4. compensation for expropriation (the obligation not to expropriate, either directly or indirectly, or to take a measure tantamount to expropriation of an investment, without compensation) (Article 1110); and
5. performance requirements (subject to certain exceptions, the obligation not to impose performance requirements, such as a given percentage of domestic content, in connection with any investment) (Article 1106).

Through the use of reservations and exceptions, governments have excluded many important public services and a wide range of otherwise non-conforming existing measures from the national treatment and most favoured nation obligations, as well as from the obligation not to impose performance requirements.

For further detail on the rules of Chapter 11, see Jon R. Johnson (1997) and Christopher Wilkie (2002, 6–38).

Canada has no fewer than 21 foreign investment protection agreements – the equivalent of a BIT – currently in force.

BITs have historically been negotiated between developed and developing countries. Because of the inequality between the negotiating parties, many BITs were intrinsically asymmetrical (Wilkie 2002, 15). For example, while U.S. investors had significant foreign investment in Bangladesh, the same was not true for Bangladesh investors in the U.S. Thus, traditionally, BITs were a function of an economic relationship characterised by an investor and a recipient of that investment where the negotiating power almost always tilted in favour of the investor state. Moreover, BITs were generally based on developed-country concerns regarding legal fairness and access to justice. Investor-state dispute settlement provisions were a feature of BITs because once an investment was expropriated (whether for a legitimate public purpose or not) an investor generally had no standing in the courts of the host country. It would thus have to persuade its own government to pursue a claim. Investor-state dispute settlement provisions removed the decision of whether to initiate a claim from the government whose interests were directly at stake, or whose decision would be based on broader political considerations (Browne 2002, 39–43).

The application of this model to two countries with highly developed, mixed economies such as Canada and the U.S. is new. It has resulted in some unanticipated consequences. The nature of the disputes under NAFTA has differed from traditional challenges under BITs in the type of measure challenged. The application of rules governing, for example, expropriation and the minimum standard of treatment have hitherto not generally been used to challenge regulatory measures adopted by a developed country with a comprehensive regulatory environment. The U.S. sought to have a core set of principles imported from the BITs into the Canada-U.S. Free Trade Agreement (CUFTA) and ultimately into NAFTA. Compliance with these rules required significant adjustments to Mexican foreign investment rules. The U.S. was adamant that expropriation provisions be included in NAFTA in order to protect U.S. investors in Mexico from the possibility of expropriation of U.S.-owned assets without compensation or recourse to impartial dispute settlement. This was a U.S. reaction to the fact that Latin American countries had historically included a 'Calvo' clause in their constitutions. Named after a 19th-century Argentinian diplomat, these clauses limit foreign investors to domestic remedies in the case of a dispute (Daly 1994).

Other developing countries beyond Mexico had also confiscated U.S.-owned property in the past without compensation. It is interesting to note that the inclusion of these 'boilerplate' provisions did not attract any special attention during the NAFTA negotiations. What the parties failed to anticipate were the implications of these provisions between countries with highly developed regulatory regimes.[3] Even though significant changes were required by the NAFTA parties, those changes were considered vital in securing the protection that NAFTA offered from unfettered parochial political interests (see Table 9.2). In the case of Canada, because of its size, Canada has 'traditionally been at the forefront of countries ready, willing and able to undertake international commitments as the price of limiting the capacity of larger countries to impose arbitrary and unwanted restraints on Canadian trade, economic and other interests' (Hart and Dymond 2002, 130). Empowering a private investor to challenge a host government directly in principle depoliticises the dispute settlement process by removing it from the realm of state-to-state diplomatic relations. Under Chapter 11, a foreign investor has the comfort of knowing that a dispute concerning a foreign investment would be heard and adjudicated based on legal rules rather than political negotiations over a variety of matters not related to the investment in question. An investor would thus feel more confident in making a substantial investment in the context of this framework.

Subsequent Concerns about Chapter 11

However, as the Chapter 11 jurisprudence has emerged, several shortcomings have been revealed. They have called into question the ongoing viability of its rules in supporting and sustaining cross-border investment. Thus, while these rules do encourage investment and economic integration, many have asked what cost do they incur. If, ultimately, economic integration leads to social disintegration through reduced government regulation, it is neither desirable nor sustainable (Rodrik 1997, 2).

Table 9.2   NAFTA Investor-State Dispute Settlement

NAFTA's original investor-state dispute settlement mechanism allows investors to pursue a claim against a government that it believes has breached an obligation of Chapter 11, resulting in loss or damage. If the claim cannot be resolved by the parties themselves, the complainant has the choice of submitting the dispute to binding arbitration. A three-person tribunal (or arbitration panel) is then established under the existing rules of either the United Nations Commission on International Trade Law (UNCITRAL) or the International Centre for the Settlement of Disputes (ICSID).* Each party to the dispute appoints one of the arbitrators, and the parties agree on a third, presiding arbitrator. If the tribunal finds that the claim is founded, it can order that monetary compensation be made to the investor. NAFTA does not provide for the appeal of awards. Rather, each jurisdiction contains its own domestic rules that apply to the appeal of arbitral awards. In general, an appeal will be limited to judicial review of a decision, that is, a domestic court will not be entitled to review a decision on its merits, but rather, it may only rule on the much narrower legal question of whether the tribunal exceeded its jurisdiction in any way.

* NAFTA Article 1120 provides that an investor may choose from among the ICSID Convention, the ICSID Additional Facility Rules, and the UNCITRAL Arbitration Rules for making its claim. However, as neither Canada nor Mexico has ratified the ICSID convention, this option is currently not available to investors. Approximately half of the arbitrations that have been commenced have been under the ICSID Additional Facility Rules (a heretofore unused resource). The other half have proceeded under the somewhat more *ad hoc* UNCITRAL rules.

The concerns over Chapter 11 are part of a broader set of issues about the costs of globalisation – that is, increased global economic integration – and increased environmental concern and activism on the part of nongovernmental organisations (NGOs). The pace at which economic integration has taken place, facilitated in part by trade and investment liberalisation arrangements, has led to widespread anxiety among citizens who fear the loss of control over the forces and actors that govern their lives (Rodrik 1997, 2). This fear has fixed onto both the legal and procedural provisions of Chapter 11.

The first NAFTA Chapter 11 case to generate widespread controversy was the Ethyl case. Here, a U.S. investor in Canada, Ethyl Corporation, challenged a Canadian ban on the international trade of the fuel additive methylcyclopentadienyl manganese tricarbonyl (MMT), a ban ostensibly imposed for the purpose of protecting public health (Rugman, Kirton, and Soloway 1999). The case was settled for around CA\$19 million and resulted in the federal government retracting the trade ban on MMT before a decision was reached by the NAFTA tribunal. Yet the case became a lightning rod for widespread opposition to Chapter 11, sowing the seeds for controversy in later cases. The critique centred on three major issues, as follows.

First, the simple fact that a private investor could call into question a government's measure ostensibly protecting the public's health and welfare or the environment was objectionable to a wide range of civil society actors. They viewed this assault on national sovereignty by an international body and a foreign civil society business actor as a prime example of NAFTA favouring corporate interests over broader public concerns.

Second, the legal obligations provided for in Chapter 11 came under attack on substantive grounds. These rules were not viewed as neutral investment protection, but as inherently biased against environmental, health, or safety regulations. Most prominent among the substantive concerns were the expropriation provisions and the uncertainty surrounding the concept of regulatory expropriation. Absent a direct takeover of foreign-owned property, what lesser interference could constitute 'tantamount to expropriation' and thus amount to a compensable expropriation? Would it be enough for a government action merely to affect the benefits of a foreign investment? Or did the effect have to be so severe as to render the investment inoperable? And, even if a measure did put a foreign investor out of business, what if the measure addressed serious consumer or health concerns? Most critically, what would this mean for the future of environmental regulation in North America?

Not surprisingly, no immediate clear answers emerged. As the Chapter 11 jurisprudence began to develop, other concerns about the operation of NAFTA's investment protection rules emerged from the NGO community. NGOs have alleged that NAFTA panels' broad interpretations of the national treatment obligation (Article 1102) and the minimum standard of treatment obligation (Article 1105) exceeded the generally accepted interpretations of these concepts in international law (see, for example, Mann 2001). Critics argued that the uncertainty in how these rules would be interpreted would result in a 'regulatory chill' whereby governments would cease to enact public health and safety measures for fear of a NAFTA challenge.

A third major area of concern arose from the process under which challenges were brought and disputes were heard. The NAFTA Chapter 11 process is, for the most part, private. It does not provide a formal mechanism for public access.[4] In this way, it is argued that NAFTA was deficient, given that such arbitrations involved the interpretation of issues that define the relationship of foreign private investor rights to domestic public measures. By not providing an adequate framework for public participation, critics argued that Chapter 11 created a 'democratic deficit'.

Central to the view that Chapter 11 was inappropriate to arbitrate issues of public policy is the question of process transparency. While Sylvia Ostry (1998, 1) 'only partly in jest' describes the word 'as the most opaque in the trade policy lexicon', transparency, in particular, remains one of the key concerns among critics of a liberalised investment regime.[5]

In addition, critics argue that Chapter 11 does not provide for adequate participation in the arbitral process, for example, through the submission of briefs or other relevant information to the panel as a 'friend of the court' (*amicus curiae*). Critics view this as especially important as *ad hoc* arbitrators may not have 'sufficiently broad expertise to adjudicate issues outside of traditional trade law, with implications that transcend trade, entailing public policy analysis, and assessment of complex environmental and health issues' (Tollefson 2002).

Some may argue that such concerns are overblown, as the jurisprudence is still in its infancy. Until September 2002, there were 27 Chapter 11 complaints, only five of which led to actual decisions. Other cases remained pending or had been settled or withdrawn. Yet, in response to the NAFTA critique outlined above, changes are being made as a result of intense political pressure being put on the NAFTA governments. On 31 July 2001, the NAFTA Free Trade Commission, made up of the

---

**Table 9.3   NAFTA Free Trade Commission's Notes of
Interpretation of Certain Chapter 11 Provisions**

On 31 July 2001, the NAFTA Commission issued a statement on the interpretation of certain provisions of Chapter 11. It provided that each party shall make available to the public in a timely manner all documents submitted to, or issued by, a Chapter 11 tribunal, subject to redaction of: confidential business information; information that is privileged or otherwise protected from disclosure under the party's domestic law; and information which the party must withhold pursuant to the relevant arbitral rules, as applied. The parties also agreed on a clarification of Article 1105(1), which prescribes the customary international law minimum standard of treatment to be afforded to investments of investors of another party. In summary, the clarification provides as follows: 1) the concepts of 'fair and equitable treatment' and 'full protection and security' do not require treatment in addition to or beyond that which is required by the customary international law minimum standard of treatment of aliens, and 2) a determination that there has been a breach of another provision of NAFTA, or of a separate international agreement, does not establish that there has been a breach of Article 1105(1).

three signatory governments, issued an interpretive statement (see Table 9.3) as part of an ongoing clarification exercise, designed to 'give future tribunals clearer and more specific understanding of Chapter 11's obligations, as originally intended by the drafters'.[6] In this regard, Canada's Minister of International Trade, Pierre Pettigrew, stated that the NAFTA Commission is 'seeking to clarify some of the provisions ... such as expropriation disciplines, to ensure they properly reflect the original intent of the NAFTA Parties in the dispute settlement process'. Ongoing consultations with expert groups (including representatives from NGOs) are currently underway to further the clarification process.

It is important to evaluate the veracity of the diverse claims against NAFTA Chapter 11, as well as the appropriate policy responses. In undertaking this exercise, one should determine the problem that people are trying to cure, and best way to solve it. This means stepping back from reactionary or 'worst case' scenarios and taking a realistic look at the rulings of the cases to date, on the basis of their facts and rendered decisions.

NAFTA Chapter 11 Jurisprudence

There are five cases where a NAFTA tribunal has issued a final determination. Also relevant is the Methanex case, where there has been an award on jurisdiction only. Although many more cases have been filed or settled, it is important to identify patterns from actual decisions, in order to set the record straight and challenge some of the myths surrounding NAFTA.

Here, there is a vital distinction between the arguments of a claimant and the decision of the tribunal. Although there have been some sweeping and surprising challenges brought by certain investors, this does not mean that these challenges are valid. As one expert stated, 'the media and some commentators often confuse what is alleged to have occurred and what will be found by a Tribunal' (Thomas 2002, 127). For example, investors have lost on the issue of expropriation more often than they have won. In fact, to date there has been only one successful expropriation claim under Chapter 11.[7] To be sure, claimants will continue to push at the edges of international law in order to obtain compensation. But any analysis of possible NAFTA reform must be based on actual tribunal decisions, rather than on the investors' claims.

The Limits of Analysing the Jurisprudence

There are nevertheless limits to the value of analysing the jurisprudence because, under international law, Chapter 11 decisions do not establish precedents (*stare decisis*, in legal terms). A NAFTA arbitral tribunal's ruling is not binding on subsequent tribunals.[8] In one case, a NAFTA arbitral tribunal declined to follow a prior ruling, noting that the previous case was not 'a persuasive precedent on this matter and [this Tribunal] will not be bound by it'.[9] That said, panels will still consider the relevance of the decisions of past NAFTA and other trade tribunals

(Price 2000). Thus, while not binding, the case law is an important element guiding all concerned parties.

Azinian In March 1997, Robert Azinian and two other U.S. nationals who were shareholders of Desechos Sólidos de Naucalpan S.A. de C.V. (Desona), a Mexican corporation, filed a Chapter 11 Notice of Arbitration against the Mexican government seeking damages of US$14 million. In November 1993, Desona had entered into a concession contract with the City Council of the Municipality of Naucalpan, Mexico, for the collection of solid waste. A few months later, the municipality complained about several irregularities in the implementation of the concession contract and, in March 1994, cancelled the contract for nonperformance by Desona. Three levels of Mexican courts confirmed the legality of the contract's annulment under Mexican law.

Azinian argued unsuccessfully before a Chapter 11 tribunal that the actions taken by the municipality had resulted in a violation of both the obligation to provide the minimum standard of treatment under international law and the expropriation provisions of NAFTA.[10] In rejecting the claim, the tribunal noted that the claimants' fundamental complaint was that they were the victims of a breach of the concession contract. This was not by itself sufficient to support a claim under NAFTA. The tribunal noted that NAFTA does not 'allow investors to seek international arbitration for mere contractual breaches'.[11] Rather, a successful claim under Chapter 11 must be grounded in the breach of a specific treaty obligation.

Analysing the claim that the annulment of the contract resulted in an expropriation of Desona's contractual rights (Article 1110), the tribunal stated that because the Mexican courts found that the municipality's decision to 'nullify the Concession Contract was consistent with the Mexican law governing the validity of public service concessions, the question [was] whether the Mexican court decisions themselves breached Mexico's obligations under Chapter Eleven'.[12] The claimants, however, had not alleged that the prior court rulings had violated any NAFTA provisions. Accordingly, if the Mexican courts found the contract to be invalid and no objection was raised to those courts' decisions, there was by definition no contract to be expropriated.[13] The tribunal stated as follows:

> To put it another way, a foreign investor entitled in principle to protection under NAFTA may enter into contractual relations with a public authority, and may suffer a breach by that authority, and still not be in a position to state a claim under NAFTA. It is a fact of life everywhere that individuals may be disappointed in their dealings with public authorities, and disappointed yet again when national courts reject their complaints ... NAFTA was not intended to provide foreign investors with blanket protection from this kind of disappointment, and nothing in its terms so provides.[14]

The tribunal also rejected the argument that the breach of the concession contract violated the minimum standard of treatment provision (Article 1105) and stated that 'if there was no violation of Article 1110, there was none of Article 1105 either'.[15] The meaning of this statement is not clear; however, the tribunal may have intended to assert, as the S.D. Myers tribunal would later do (see below), that a violation of another provision of Chapter 11 automatically results in a violation of the minimum standard of treatment provision.

This case illustrates that the tribunal did not view itself as a 'court of appeal' for an investor disappointed with the outcome of a domestic court ruling. Rather, the tribunal showed a high degree of deference for the domestic process by refusing to substitute its ruling for that of a Mexican court. The tribunal limited the scope of a claim for expropriation by stating that NAFTA was not intended to protect against disappointments in dealings with public authorities. In no way has this decision expanded any of NAFTA's substantive provisions beyond the scope of those provisions in international law.

Waste Management In September 1998, a U.S.-based investor, Waste Management, filed a Notice of Arbitration against Mexico. The claim arose from a 15-year concession contract granted by the state of Guerrero and the municipality of Acapulco to Acaverde, the Mexican subsidiary of Waste Management.

Under the concession, Acaverde was required to clean the streets, collect and dispose of all solid waste in the area, and build a solid-waste landfill. In return, Acaverde would receive monthly payments from Acapulco. Waste Management contended that it provided the services agreed to for about two years, but it only received payment equivalent to five months of services rendered. Waste Management claimed that Acaverde's concession rights were unlawfully transferred to a third party. Waste Management also claimed that the Mexican public authorities did not accord its investment (Acaverde) treatment in accordance with international law, including fair and equitable treatment. In addition, the investor contended that the acts of the Mexican authorities constituted measures 'tantamount to expropriation because the investor was deprived of the income from its investment; and because the Mexican authorities' disregard of its rights effectively extinguished Acaverde's viability as an enterprise'.

In June 2000, the tribunal delivered an award, based not on these issues, but on a jurisdictional question raised by the government of Mexico. Under Article 1121 of Chapter 11, a complainant must abandon its right to initiate or continue other legal action in any other legal forum with respect to the issue before a NAFTA tribunal. This is done in the form of a written waiver submitted by the investor to the tribunal, acknowledging that it is not pursuing the same claim concurrently before any other court or tribunal. Mexico contended, and the tribunal accepted, that the waiver submitted by the investor did not comply with Article 1121, since concurrent domestic legal action had been pursued in violation of the waiver agreement. Accordingly, the tribunal found that it lacked jurisdiction to hear the case.

Pope & Talbot, Inc. In March 1999, Pope & Talbot, Inc., a U.S. investor, claimed that Canada's allotment of export quotas under the 1996 United States–Canada Softwood Lumber Agreement discriminated against Pope & Talbot's Canadian subsidiary, thereby violating the national treatment, minimum standard of treatment, performance requirements, and expropriation provisions of Chapter 11.[16] The softwood lumber agreement imposed quotas on duty-free exports (export duties were charged above the quota limit) from the four major producing provinces in Canada (referred to as the 'covered' provinces – British Columbia, Alberta, Ontario, and Quebec).[17] Pope & Talbot claimed damages of between US$85 and US$135 million.

Canada contended that because this issue concerned trade in goods, it did not fall within the scope of Chapter 11. Canada argued that the term 'investment dispute' applied only to disputes about measures 'primarily aimed at' investors of another party or investments of those investors. Canada also argued that if it is possible to categorise a measure as relating to trade in goods, the measure cannot be seen as relating to investors or investments, and the dispute over the measure cannot be considered an 'investment dispute'. Softwood lumber is a good; therefore, the dispute relates to trade in a good and should have been brought under the NAFTA's state-to-state dispute settlement provisions.

In a preliminary award, the tribunal addressed the interrelationship between NAFTA's Chapter 11 and Chapter 3 (trade in goods), stating 'there is no provision to the express effect that investment and trade in goods are to be treated as wholly divorced from each other'.[18] The tribunal rejected the idea that a 'measure aimed at trade in goods *ipso facto* cannot be addressed as well under Chapter 11'.[19]

Pope & Talbot claimed that the export quotas violated the national treatment obligation because they imposed different treatment on softwood lumber producers from the covered provinces, which had to pay a permit fee in order to export to the U.S., and exporters from the non-covered provinces, which did not.

The tribunal rejected this argument. It ruled that the measure, on its face, did not distinguish between foreign-owned and domestic companies, and did not otherwise unduly undermine the investment-liberalising objectives of NAFTA.[20] The tribunal determined that Canada's differential treatment of lumber producers from covered and non-covered provinces, existing and new producers, and holders of different levels of quotas under the agreement, and did not violate Canada's obligations under Chapter 11 in the absence of discrimination between similarly situated foreign and domestic investors. The tribunal also found that, in establishing different categories of producers, Canada was not motivated by discriminatory protectionist concerns.

Pope & Talbot also claimed that Canada breached its duty to treat investors in a fair and equitable manner (Article 1105) in its allocation of quotas. The tribunal found that, under Chapter 11, foreign investors are entitled to the international law minimum plus the fairness elements.[21] Based on this standard of analysis, it found that actions of officials in the Softwood Lumber Division of the Canadian Department of Foreign Affairs and International Trade (DFAIT) violated the minimum standard of treatment.[22] After the Chapter 11 complaint was initiated, certain Canadian government officials had insisted on a 'verification review' of Pope & Talbot's records in support of its export quota allocation in earlier years. Specifically, by ordering Pope & Talbot to transport all of its corporate and accounting records located at the company's head office in Portland, Oregon, to Canada, it violated the obligation to provide fair and equitable treatment under Chapter 11. In doing so, the tribunal characterised the actions of the Softwood Lumber Division as imperious, based on naked assertions of authority and designed to bludgeon the company into compliance.[23]

In this regard, it should be noted that verifications are routinely conducted in international trade matters, particularly in customs valuation, antidumping and countervailing duty cases. Here they generally take place at the venue where the company's records are located. Indeed, since a verification is essentially a form of audit, it would have made little sense to conduct such an exercise anywhere else. The Softwood Lumber Division's insistence that the company transfer several truckloads of records to Canada was not only highly unusual to anyone familiar with the administration of international trade laws and counterproductive to the goal of a verification review, but was also highly oppressive to the company. The tribunal concluded that the investor was 'being subjected to threats, denied its reasonable requests for pertinent information, required to incur unnecessary expenses and disruption in meeting [the Softwood Lumber Division's] requests for information, forced to expend legal fees and probably suffer a loss of reputation in government circles'.[24] Taken together with the tenor of division's communications with the investor, and the less than forthright reports to the minister regarding the situation between the investor and Softwood Lumber Division, the tribunal ruled that the verification episode amounted to a denial of fair and equitable treatment contrary to Article 1105.

The claimants also argued that, by reducing Pope & Talbot's quota of lumber that could be exported to the U.S. without paying a fee, Canada's export control regime had deprived the investment of its ordinary ability to sell its product to its traditional and natural market, constituting an expropriation. At the outset of its analysis of Article 1110, the tribunal noted that the 'investment's access to the U.S. market is a property interest subject to protection'.[25] It also noted that, contrary to Canada's assertions, under certain circumstances regulation may indeed result in expropriation; a blanket exception for regulatory measures would create a gaping loophole in international protections against expropriation.[26]

The tribunal went even further, stating that an expropriation may include 'nondiscriminatory regulation that might be said to fall within the police powers'.[27] The tribunal, however, found that there had not been an expropriation of property in this particular case. The ruling established that, in order to determine 'whether a particular interference with business activities amounts to expropriation, the test is whether that interference is sufficiently restrictive to support a conclusion that the property had been "taken" from its owner'.[28] In Pope & Talbot's case there was no such interference inasmuch as the company remained in control of its investment, continued to direct the day-to-day operations, was free of government interference with officers and employees, and continued to export substantial quantities of softwood lumber to the U.S. and to earn substantial profits on those sales.[29]

A second ruling dealing with damages and with the NAFTA Free Trade Commission's interpretive statement of Article 1105 (see Table 9.3), referred to above, was delivered on 31 May 2002. Canada had contended that, although the tribunal had already ruled on the matter of Article 1105 in April 2001, the interpretive statement was binding on the tribunal and, therefore, it should reconsider its findings in light of it.

At the beginning of its analysis, the tribunal focussed on answering the question of whether the Free Trade Commission's interpretation was in fact an interpretation or an amendment. Since the interpretation had been issued in July 2001, many commentators had considered whether future NAFTA tribunals would find that it was within their powers to question the nature of a commission's action. In the tribunal's view, it was within its power to consider this question and it could not simply 'accept that whatever the Commission has stated to be an interpretation is one for the purposes of Article 1131(2)'.[30]

In its analysis of the history of Article 1105, the tribunal determined that there was no reference to customary international law in any of the draft versions of Article 1105. According to the tribunal, one cannot conceive that NAFTA negotiators would not have known that, 'as is made clear in Article 38 of the Statute of the [International Court of Justice], international law is a broader concept than customary international law, which is only one of its components'.[31] In light of this, the tribunal noted that if it were to determine whether the commission's action is an interpretation or an amendment, it would choose the latter.[32] The tribunal, however, chose not to make such determination. After analysing the question, it decided to proceed assuming that the commission's action was an interpretation.

The next step was then to determine whether the tribunal's award of April 2001 was incompatible with the interpretation.[33] Such incompatibility, in its view, would exist only if it were determined that the 'concept behind the fairness elements under customary international law is different from those elements under ordinary standards applied in NAFTA countries'.[34] In order to rule on this matter, the tribunal had to determine the content of customary international law concerning the protection of foreign property. It rejected Canada's view that under customary international law a country would violate Chapter 11's minimum standard of treatment provision only if the treatment accorded to investors amounted to gross misconduct, an outrage, bad faith, wilful neglect of duty or to insufficiency of governmental action so far short of international standards that every reasonable and impartial person would readily recognize its insufficiency.[35] According to the tribunal, Canada's argument was based on a view of customary international law standards from the 1920s. Since then, customary international law has evolved and the range of actions subject to international concern has broadened beyond 'international delinquencies' to include the concept of fair and equitable treatment.[36] Despite these findings, the tribunal based its ruling on the fact that even if Canada's proposed standard were adopted, there would still be a violation of Canada's obligations as a result of the verification review. The tribunal found that the conduct of the Softwood Lumber Division in that episode was egregious and would shock and outrage every reasonable citizen of Canada.[37]

Some argue that the tribunal's interpretation of Article 1105 is inconsistent with the minimum standard of treatment in international law. However, international tribunals, like domestic courts, do not much care for high-handed and objectionable conduct on the part of litigants that appear before them. They are understandably inclined to find a remedy where the conduct in question offends the basic principles of justice and fair play. To the extent that the Chapter 11 panels have raised the bar with respect to Article 1105, this is arguably a positive development (see Thomas 2002).[38]

In May 2002, the tribunal awarded Pope & Talbot US$461 500, a relatively small award considering the original claim of US$508 million (or 0.0909 percent of the original damages claimed). Thus, only a fraction of the amount claimed was awarded. There is nothing in this case that constitutes the erosion of public interest regulation at the expense of a foreign investor.

Metalclad Metalclad, a California-based corporation, developed a hazardous waste disposal facility in the Mexican state of San Luis Potosi. All the required federal and state permits for the construction and operation of the site were issued to COTERIN, a firm that was later bought by Metalclad, by August 1993. Construction of the facility began in May 1994.

In October 1994, however, local officials ordered that construction of the facility cease due to the absence of a municipal construction permit. The Mexican federal government then told Metalclad that such a permit was not required. Relying on this assertion, Metalclad resumed construction of the facility. Work on the new facility was completed in March 1995. But at this point local authorities opposed the opening of the facility on environmental grounds. Demonstrators, sponsored by the state and local governments, abruptly interrupted the ceremony of inauguration of the landfill. After this episode, in an effort to ensure the opening of the site, Metalclad maintained constant dialogue with the federal government.

Negotiations between Metalclad and federal environmental authorities resulted in an agreement in which Metalclad agreed, *inter alia*, to make certain modifications to the site, to take specified conservation steps, to recognise the participation of a technical scientific committee and a citizen supervision committee, to employ local manual labour, and to make regular contributions to the social welfare of the municipality, including limited free medical advice.

Despite the agreement, and in the absence of any evidence of inadequacy of performance by Metalclad, the municipality denied a construction permit in a process that was closed to the company. The municipal government refused to permit operation of the plant on the grounds that the local geology made it likely that the waste treated at the plant would contaminate local water supplies. In addition, after Metalclad had initiated a Chapter 11 arbitration proceeding, in September 1997 the governor of San Luis Potosi issued an ecological decree declaring the area of the landfill to be a natural area for the protection of rare cacti. The decree foreclosed any hope of operation of the facility.

In its statement of claim, Metalclad sought compensation of US$43 million plus damages based on the assertion that the actions of the Mexican government violated the expropriation (Article 1110) and minimum standard of treatment (Article 1105) provisions of Chapter 11. In its Article 1105 claim, Metalclad argued that the actions of the federal, state, and municipal governments, including the lack of transparency of the requirements for authorisation of the site, constituted a denial of fair and equitable treatment. The tribunal accepted Metalclad's argument and ruled that the Mexican government had indeed violated its obligations. A significant finding, which would also play an important role on the tribunal's finding of expropriation, was that the claimant was entitled to rely on the representation of the federal officials who stated that a municipal construction permit was not a requirement. According to the tribunal, Mexico failed to provide 'a transparent and predictable framework for Metalclad's planning and investments'.[39] The absence of a clear rule concerning construction permit requirements in Mexico amounted, according to the tribunal, to a 'failure on the part of Mexico to ensure the transparency required by NAFTA'.[40]

Metalclad is the only NAFTA Chapter 11 case in which a tribunal made a finding of expropriation. The tribunal adopted a relatively expansive interpretation of expropriation, stating that

> expropriation under NAFTA includes not only open, deliberate and acknowledged takings of property, such as outright seizure or formal or obligatory transfer of title in favour of the host State, but also covert or incidental interference with the use of property which has the effect of depriving the owner, in whole or in significant part, of the use or reasonably-to-be expected economic benefit of property even if not necessarily to the obvious benefit of the host State.[41]

The facts in this case made for an easy determination that an expropriation had taken place. The tribunal held that the inequitable treatment of Metalclad by local Mexican authorities – with the tolerance of the federal government – the violation of representations made and the lack of basis in refusing a permit, which would bar the use of the landfill permanently, amounted to indirect expropriation.

In October 2000, Mexico filed a petition before the Supreme Court of British Columbia challenging the tribunal's ruling. This appeal was brought in that province because the hearings had been located in Vancouver.

As noted above, Chapter 11 of NAFTA does not provide for appeal or other forms of challenges to a tribunal award. Justice Tysoe of the British Columbia Supreme Court ruled, however, that Mexico's claim should be analysed under the *British Columbia International Commercial Arbitration Act*. Justice Tysoe noted that, under the act, the court was not allowed to review points of law decided by the arbitral tribunal. The issue rather was 'whether the Tribunal made decisions on matters beyond the scope of the submission to arbitration by deciding upon matters outside Chapter 11'.[42] In other words, the court could set aside only the decisions of the NAFTA tribunal that were beyond the scope of its jurisdiction.

Despite Justice Tysoe's determination that the court could not, under the *British Columbia International Commercial Arbitration Act*, review points of law, his analysis of the arbitral award essentially amounted to the same thing. First, the court determined that Chapter 11's 'fair and equitable treatment' requirement must be interpreted in accordance with international law. The Court found that the tribunal erred in basing its decision on the lack of transparency in the Mexican domestic legal process for approving hazardous waste sites. Instead, the court ruled that a lack of transparency is neither a violation of customary international law nor of Chapter 11. Accordingly, the court determined that the tribunal's finding of such a violation, based on lack of transparency, was beyond the scope of the submission to arbitration.[43]

In addition, the court found that the tribunal had also improperly issued a finding of expropriation on the same mistaken basis. The finding of expropriation, however, was not totally set aside, since the court considered that there was no error impugning the tribunal's finding that the state government's Ecological Decree constituted expropriation under Article 1110.[44] In the end, the court refused to set aside the tribunal's award in total, determining only that the interest portion of the award be calculated from the date of the Ecological Decree, rather than from the day of the actions that had led to the finding of unfair treatment.[45]

S.D. Myers In October 1998, S.D. Myers, an Ohio-based waste disposal company, which performed polychlorinated biphenyl (PCB) remediation activities, claimed that Canada had breached its Chapter 11 obligations, thereby damaging S.D. Myers' investment in Canada.[46] S.D. Myers had no PCB remediation facilities in Canada. Its investment in Canada consisted essentially of obtaining PCBs for treatment by its U.S. facility.

S.D. Myers' main complaint was that Canada breached its obligations under Chapter 11 as a result of a 1995 interim order banning the export of PCB waste to the United States. The U.S. border had, since 1980, been closed to the import of PCBs and PCB waste for disposal. But in October 1995 S.D. Myers received special permission from the U.S. Environmental Protection Agency (EPA) to import PCBs and PCB waste from Canada for disposal. The permission was valid from 15 November 1995 to 31 December 1997. The interim order was in force from November 1995 to February 1997, at which time Canada reopened its border by an amendment to the PCB Waste Export Regulations. According to S.D. Myers, Canada acted to protect its PCB treatment facility, Chem-Securities in Swan Hills, Alberta.

S.D. Myers presented four claims. First, it asserted that the measure discriminated against U.S. waste disposal firms that sought to operate in Canada, by preventing them from exporting PCB contaminated waste for processing in the U.S.[47] Second, S.D. Myers alleged that Canada had failed to accord treatment in accordance with the minimum standard of international law. Third, the claimant asserted that, by requiring it to dispose of PCB-contaminated waste in Canada, the interim order imposed performance requirements (namely that PCB disposal operators accord preferential treatment to Canadian goods and services and achieve a given level of domestic content). Finally, S.D. Myers claimed that Canada had indirectly expropriated its investment.

The tribunal accepted S.D. Myers' claim that the ban on the export of PCBs favoured Canadian nationals over non-nationals, violating Chapter 11's national treatment obligations (Article 1102). In fact, even before examining the specific allegations against Canada, in its analysis of the legislative history of the PCB ban, the tribunal concluded that the regulation was 'intended primarily to protect the

Canadian PCB disposal industry from the U.S. competition' and that 'there was no legitimate environmental reason for introducing [it]'.[48]

According to the tribunal, the interpretation of 'like circumstances' between foreign and domestic investors and investments that give rise to the national treatment obligation must take into account two important factors: first, the 'general principles that emerge from the legal context of the NAFTA, including both its concern with the environment and the need to avoid trade distortions that are not justified by environmental concerns', and second, 'the circumstances that would justify governmental regulations that treat [foreign investors] differently in order to protect the public interest'.[49] With this statement the tribunal recognised that environmental factors may provide a legitimate basis for finding circumstances to be unlike. The legal context for Article 1102 was determined to include the various provisions of NAFTA, its side agreement, the North American Agreement on Environmental Cooperation (NAAEC), and its principles.[50] Emerging from this context are, according to the tribunal, the following principles: states have the right to establish high levels of environmental protection and are not obliged to compromise their standards merely to satisfy the political or economic interests of other states; states should avoid creating distortions to trade; and environmental protection and economic development can and should be mutually supportive.[51] Accordingly, the tribunal analysed Canada's environmental obligations and concerns and decided that the bilateral or multilateral treaties governing the disposal of hazardous waste did not justify favouring domestic suppliers over S.D. Myers. In addition, it rejected Canada's defence that the order was designed to secure the economic strength of the Canadian industry in order to ensure Canada's ability to process PCBs within its territory in the future (taking into consideration that the U.S. could, at any time, close its border again).

The tribunal agreed that ensuring the economic strength of the Canadian industry was a legitimate objective, but condemned Canada's means of achieving it. It also applied a least-restrictive means test to determine whether the specific measure chosen by Canada to achieve that objective was, despite its adverse impact on foreign investors, consistent with NAFTA. The tribunal found that there were several legitimate ways by which Canada could have achieved that goal, but imposing a ban on the export of PCB was not one of them.[52] It largely based its ruling on documentary and testimonial evidence that Canada's policy was motivated by the intention to protect and promote the market share of Canadian-owned enterprises.[53]

In comparing like circumstances, the tribunal went beyond comparing the S.D. Myers investment in Canada, which provided marketing services, to other Canadian-based providers of PCB marketing services (Mann 2001). Instead, it applied the national treatment obligation to the full business line of S.D. Myers, including operations in the home and the host countries (the U.S. and Canada, respectively) (27).

The tribunal also accepted S.D. Myers' claim that Canada had breached the minimum standard of treatment (Article 1105). The only reason the tribunal presented for this finding was that on the facts of the case a 'breach of Article 1102 essentially establishes a breach of Article 1105 as well'.[54] On this point, arbitrator

Edward Chiasson dissented, noting that the breach of another provision cannot establish a violation of Article 1105; a violation of this provision must be based on a demonstrated failure to meet the fair and equitable requirements. The tribunal, nevertheless, made some interesting remarks on the scope of Article 1105:

> a breach of Article 1105 occurs only when it is shown that an investor has been treated in such an unjust or arbitrary manner that the treatment rises to the level that is unacceptable from the international perspective. That determination must be made in the light of the high measure of deference that international law generally extends to the right of domestic authorities to regulate matters within their own borders.[55]

Regarding S.D. Myers' claim of expropriation, the tribunal noted that the 'general body of precedent usually does not treat regulatory action as amounting to expropriation' and, therefore, regulatory action is 'unlikely to be the subject of a legitimate complaint under Article 1110 of the NAFTA'.[56] This statement, however, was weakened by the note that it did not rule out the possibility of regulatory action giving rise to a legitimate action under that article. The tribunal also stated that, when determining whether a measure constitutes expropriation, a tribunal must look at the substance of a measure and not only at the form. In addition, tribunals 'must look at the real interests involved and the purpose and effect of the government measure'.[57]

Under this analysis, the tribunal noted that regulations may be found to be expropriatory. To make such a determination, both the purpose and the effects of the measure must be analysed. As for the purpose, it ruled that the measure was designed with the objective of preventing S.D. Myers from carrying on its business. However, the effects of the measure were found not to be expropriatory: due to its temporality, the effect of the measure was only to delay an opportunity. Another important finding of the S.D. Myers tribunal was that the phrase 'tantamount to expropriation' in Article 1110 did not expand the meaning of expropriation in the NAFTA beyond customary international law.[58]

The tribunal also did not support S.D. Myers' claim that Canada had breached the article on performance requirements. In examining its wording, it found that the Canadian government had imposed no such requirements on S.D. Myers.

In February 2001, Canada filed an application before the Federal Court of Canada to set aside the tribunal's partial award. Canada based its application on the *Commercial Arbitration Act*, alleging that elements of the NAFTA tribunal's award exceeded the tribunal's jurisdiction and that the ruling conflicts with the public policy of Canada. In January 2004, the Federal Court upheld the award.

In October 2002, the tribunal ruled that the damages incurred by S.D. Myers amounted to more than CA$6 million plus interest. These damages amount to approximately 30 percent of the damages of CA$20 million sought S.D. Myers.

Methanex On 3 December 1999, Methanex, a Canadian company with a U.S. subsidiary, brought a Chapter 11 complaint against the U.S., claiming that an executive order providing for the removal of a gasoline additive known as methyl tertiary butyl ether (MTBE) violated U.S. obligations under Chapter 11. The impugned directive was based in large part on a study by the University of California that concluded that there are significant risks associated with MTBE, as it seeps into ground and surface water via leaky underground fuel tanks.[59]

Methanex claimed that the ban was not based on credible scientific evidence and that the University of California report was flawed in several aspects. In addition, the claimant alleged that the ban went far beyond what was necessary to protect any legitimate public interest and that the government failed to consider less restrictive alternative measures to mitigate the effects of gasoline releases into the environment. Methanex contended that the real problem was the leaking gasoline tanks.

Methanex does not manufacture MTBE. It produces and markets methanol, the principal ingredient of MTBE. Methanex fears that the measures taken by California will effectively end its methanol sales in California. Thus, Methanex argues, the California measure constitutes a substantial interference with, and taking of, Methanex's U.S. business and its investment in Methanex U.S., thus violating the expropriation provision of Chapter 11 (Article 1110).

Methanex has also claimed that the California measure violates the non-discrimination provision of Article 1102, as the ban was the result of a lobbying effort by the U.S. ethanol industry, specifically by Archer Daniels Midland, an ethanol producer. Methanex asserts that the discriminatory purpose can be seen on the face of the executive order, which not only banned MTBE but also sought to establish an ethanol industry in California. Moreover, the subsequent regulations that implemented the MTBE ban specifically name ethanol as the replacement product.

Methanex also claimed that the manner in which the legislative measure was established constitutes a violation of Chapter 11's minimum standard of treatment provisions (Article 1105). According to the company, because of the U.S. ethanol industry's lobbying, the California measures were arbitrary, unreasonable, and not in good faith.

Between August and October of 2000, four environmental NGOs (ENGOs) submitted petitions requesting the Ttribunal's permission to submit *amicus curiae* briefs, to make oral submissions, and to have observer status at oral hearings. Methanex opposed any *amicus* participation on three grounds. First, the tribunal had no jurisdiction to add a party to the proceedings without the agreement of the parties that already had standing. Second, Article 1128 (participation by a member state) of NAFTA already ensured the protection of the public interest and, if the petitioners were to appear as *amici curiae*, the parties to the dispute would have no opportunity to cross-examine the factual basis of their contentions. Third, were the petitioners allowed to participate, there would be a breach of the privacy and confidentiality of the arbitration process. Mexico also submitted a response to the *amicus* application, asserting that NAFTA did not provide for the involvement of persons other than the disputing parties and the other NAFTA signatory in matters related to the interpretation of Chapter 11.

The tribunal analysed separately each of the requests made by the NGOs. First, it declined the request to attend oral hearings of the arbitration, since Article 25(4) of the UNCITRAL rules provides that the oral hearings must be held in camera unless the parties agree otherwise. Second, it concluded that it had no power to accept the petitioners' request to receive materials generated within the arbitration, since confidentiality was determined by the agreement of the parties to the dispute. Third, the tribunal considered that allowing a third person to make an *amicus* written submission could fall within its procedural powers over the conduct of the arbitration, within the general scope of Article 15(1) of the UNCITRAL Arbitration Rules.[60] This decision was based on the fact that there is no provision in Chapter 11 that expressly prohibits the acceptance of *amicus* submissions. Although the tribunal concluded that it had the power to accept such submissions, it decided not to issue an order for the participation of *amici* in its January decision.

In August 2002, the tribunal issued a preliminary award on jurisdiction, that is, whether it was entitled to hear the case in the first place.[61] This ruling did not involve a consideration of any of the merits of the substantive claims before it. Nonetheless, it did not seem to offer Methanex much encouragement.

Chapter 11 rules apply only to measures adopted or maintained by a party relating to investors of another party, or investments (for example, subsidiaries) of investors of another party. Without establishing that a measure in question relates to either it or its investment, a foreign investor will not be able to pursue a claim under NAFTA.

In its award, the tribunal stated that there 'must be a legally significant connection between the measure [the ban on MTBE] and the investor or nature of the investment'.[62] The fact that Methanex is a producer of only one component of the additive to MTBE, which was the subject of the California regulation, was viewed as too indirect a connection between the measure and the investor/investment. The scope of impact of the measure was viewed as too broad to be the subject of challenge. A measure that merely affects the investor does not automatically mean that they are necessarily related.

At the same time, the tribunal ruled that to require that a measure be 'primarily aimed at' a foreign investor would be too high a hurdle for a foreign investor to bring a claim under Chapter 11. The only avenue left open for Methanex to submit a claim would be to establish that the measures in question were intended to discriminate against it in favour of a domestic competitor. This would be sufficient for the tribunal to rule that the case could proceed.

Reforming Chapter 11: The Issues

Has NAFTA Seriously Undermined Public Regulation?

The central concern over NAFTA has been the extent to which NAFTA has imposed substantive limits on the ability of governments to adopt *bona fide* regulatory and legislative measures for public welfare purposes (see Mann and Soloway 2002, from which this section draws heavily). Do the decisions to date support the concern about these provisions, or have critics overstated the risk?

This is a critical issue because it speaks to the ability of governments to regulate in the public interest. No part of Chapter 11, and especially not the article on expropriation, was intended to subvert the ability of governments to undertake legitimate public welfare measures. However, given the potential for self-interested parties to use environmental or other measures for protectionist purposes or to transfer economic benefits for reasons not related to the common good, it is important that investors maintain the ability to protect themselves against the abuse of regulatory power. Nonetheless, there is a good argument that Chapter 11 does respect a state's police powers; that is, the state's right to protect the environment, consumers, public health, etc., and that the cases decided to date under Chapter 11 have not demonstrated a restriction on governments to act in the public interest.

Regulatory Chill Critics of NAFTA have argued that the very fact that compensation has been paid to foreign investors has resulted in regulatory chill (see, for example, Mann 2001). The meaning of the term 'regulatory chill' is not clear. Does it mean that regulators are so fearful of a possible Chapter 11 challenge that they cease to adopt any new regulations and that the entire environmental regulatory framework grinds to a halt? Or does it mean, rather, merely regulatory prudence – that regulators must be mindful of not violating certain obligations when developing new regulations? Not only is the term 'regulatory chill' imprecise, but it is pejorative, leading one to conclude that regulatory chill exists as a negative force on regulators without any analysis or even understanding of what the term means. To the extent that regulators are required to take care in designing regulation to avoid unduly discriminating against foreign investors, that will not necessarily diminish the quality, quantity, or effectiveness of public regulation. Indeed, such constraints are entirely consistent with a range of similar existing constraints imposed on regulators by, for example, the Government of Canada's Regulatory Policy.[63] It is hard to imagine that, based on the cases to date, regulators would be inhibited from proposing *bona fide* environmental regulation. In NAFTA's first eight years, the cases only punished what tribunals considered to be outrageous behaviour on the part of government officials. Only three cases resulted in awards in favour of the investor: Metalclad, S.D. Myers, and Pope & Talbot. In each, the investor had significant evidence to the effect that the government had engaged in high-handed and capricious conduct to the detriment of the investor. In all three cases, the objectionable conduct was found sufficient to trigger liability on the basis of the minimum standard of treatment (and in Metalclad, liability for expropriation as well).

In examining the cases, it is important to ask what environmental regulation or value is at stake. A close examination of the cases leads to the conclusion that the so-called 'environmental cases' are not really environmental cases at all. In Metalclad, for example, a Mexican state governor used a sham environmental measure to prevent a hazardous waste disposal site from opening, despite the fact that it had been built in compliance with all applicable legal requirements. There was significant evidence pointing to the fact that the governor was using, or rather abusing, environmental regulation as a manipulative tool for self-serving and parochial interests. This type of capricious action on the part of a sub-national government is exactly the type of behaviour that NAFTA was designed to constrain. The panel fully addressed the evidence regarding the arbitrary nature of the alleged environmental measure in that case. Metalclad confirms that the mistreatment of foreign investors can take many forms, including the form of an environmental regulation. It does not support the proposition that *bona fide* environmental regulation can form the basis of a compensation award.

Similarly, in S.D. Myers, there was much evidence presented that the Canadian measure responded to protectionist interests, rather than those of environmentalists. There was no valid environmental justification for closing the border to the export of PCB waste. But there was a valid economic reason for doing so: to eliminate the competition to less efficient Canadian businesses. Again, this type of capricious, discriminatory, and high-handed behaviour is what NAFTA Chapter 11 sought to address.

Nor has *bona fide* environmental regulation been threatened by the precedential value of Chapter 11 jurisprudence. Rather, the cases demonstrate that what is threatened by Chapter 11 are discriminatory and unfairly protectionist measures. Tribunals have not been afraid to 'call it as they see it', despite the fact that the measure in question concerns an ostensible environmental, health, or safety measure. In other words, 'egregious conduct begs a remedy, and ... Tribunals will be inclined to find a remedy where the conduct in question offends basic principles of justice and fair play' (Barutciski 2002).

In the eight years since the advent of NAFTA, there has only been one finding of expropriation. Tribunals have not made findings of expropriation lightly. There must be a substantial deprivation for such a finding to be made. Tribunals have stated that the diminishment of profits is not sufficient for finding expropriation, Rather, there must be a measure that, in effect, renders an operating business inoperable, whatever form that measure may take. These cases have demonstrated that incidental interference with an investment is not sufficient to substantiate a claim, even where it has a negative financial impact on the investment. Rather, there must be unreasonable interference for a sustained period of time that results in a substantial and fundamental deprivation of an investor's property rights.[64]

The focus on the effect of NAFTA Chapter 11 on public regulation also obscures the fact that other important values are at stake. The ability to regulate in the public interest is not the only value important to the functioning of a democratic society. The principles contained in Chapter 11 are not new. It is important to consider all of the values at stake. These includes the fair treatment of investors and government accountability for their actions, and the principle that a government not abuse its discretionary powers.

Environment Canada lists all the new federal environmental acts and regulations enacted since NAFTA was passed in 1994 that it is responsible for administering.[65] Included are regulations under the *Canadian Environmental Assessment Act* and the *Fisheries Act*, including the *Migratory Birds Convention Act* (1994), the *Alternative Fuels Act* (1995), the *Canada Marine Act* (1998), the *Mackenzie Valley Resource Management Act* (1998), and the *Oceans Act* (1996). As the volume of new legislative instruments continues to expand, one can presume that the environmental regulatory framework continues to function in Canada (as it does in Mexico and the United States), despite the alleged chill that Chapter 11 has caused.

The literature supporting the contention that regulatory chill does exist is largely anecdotal and not adequately substantiated. Those who assert that regulatory chill is inhibiting new environmental regulation should keep in mind that more work could be usefully done on researching the degree, if any, to which Chapter 11 may have created a regulatory chill at federal, provincial, or state levels in Canada and the U.S.

Deregulatory Chill Concerns about NAFTA have also extended to 'deregulatory chill', described by Daniel Schwanen (2002, 44–46) as 'a phenomenon potentially inimical to economic efficiency and growth'. Schwanen posits that governments have faced increased political difficulties with deregulation and privatisation politically since NAFTA, since a government's ability to unwind, or roll back, any deregulation or privatisation initiative may be seen as compromised as a result of NAFTA.

Jon R. Johnson (2002) has explored this phenomenon in the context of Canada's public healthcare system. While some Chapter 11 obligations are subject to reservations for the public health system, such as NAFTA Articles 1102, 1103, 1006, and 1107, other Chapter 11 provisions are not. [66] The Chapter 11 provisions not subject to reservations are, most notably, the expropriation provisions (Article 1110) and the minimum standard of treatment provisions (Article 1105). While the status of measures subject to reservations is not totally clear, Johnson concludes that their potential inhibiting impact on government actions is 'reduced substantially' by the reservations. However, with respect to those obligations that are not subject to reservations, he concludes that the expropriation provisions of NAFTA would have 'major impact if the public component of the system were expanded in any way that adversely affects the businesses of private firms' (17). Johnson similarly concludes that the minimum standard of treatment provisions may 'affect any expansion of the public component of the system that is coupled with a denial of recourse to the courts by private firms'. Governments might thus fear to deregulate any part of the healthcare system, for fear that Chapter 11 would prevent them from protecting national providers and from re-regulating in the future if they so wished.

However, Chapter 11 does not really impose onerous obligations on governments wishing to deregulate. In a sense, the effect of these provisions is simply to require governments to treat foreign investors fairly and reasonably. If, by virtue of a government's decision to deregulate or privatise, a private firm makes an investment to operate a business, that firm should be compensated in the event of a sudden reversal of policy. There is nothing in the expropriation provisions that prevents a government from taking the regulatory action it desires. Rather, it must compensate a firm for that if the action is tantamount to expropriation. Similarly, the minimum standard of treatment provisions do not prevent a government from adopting any regulation or policy. Indeed, they require that government to treat firms with due process; for example, a government could not deny a foreign investor access to the court system, as this would constitute a denial of justice.

NAFTA as an 'Evolving Regime'

Despite this generally sound record, there is considerable pressure for changing Chapter 11's process and procedure (Molot 2002). What has emerged from the various decisions is a rather uneven patchwork of rulings on the issues of transparency, openness, public participation, and appellate review. These areas are most ripe for reform by NAFTA parties.

Transparency Central among the pressures for change is the transparency of the Chapter 11 process. The lack of transparency of the panel process mandated by Chapter 11 is viewed by many as undesirable, since Chapter 11 does address issues of broad public concern. It is notable that none of the elements of a case is required to be made public. Thus, there is no right of public access to the pleadings, the transcripts of the hearing, or the reasons for judgement. In contrast, rulings under NAFTA's two other dispute settlement mechanisms – Chapter 19 (for antidumping and countervailing duty challenges) and Chapter 20 (for general state-to-state breaches of NAFTA) – as well as those under the World Trade Organization (WTO), are publicly available and accessible.

To some extent, the concerns over transparency have been alleviated by the Free Trade Commission's interpretation of July 2001 (see Table 9.3). However, in March 2002, the Pope & Talbot tribunal ruled on the investor's request that the tribunal urge Canada not to release protected documents. Canada was seeking to make public transcripts of the hearings under the *Canadian Access to Information Act*. The tribunal noted that Procedural Order on Confidentiality No. 5 prohibited disclosing transcripts of the hearings. In addition, the ruling noted that the UNCITRAL rules require in camera hearings. The tribunal rejected Canada's claim that the notes of interpretation issued by the Free Trade Commission on 31 July 2001 required such disclosure under the *Canadian Access to Information Act*. In the tribunal's view, the commission's interpretation recognised the validity of the order as binding on Canada. Accordingly, the tribunal concluded that making the documents available violated not only Procedural Order on Confidentiality No. 5, but also NAFTA itself.[67]

In any event, the parties could go further in developing more precise rules that address the transparency of documents, pleadings, transcripts, and hearings. This would bolster the legitimacy of the NAFTA dispute settlement process. At the same time, however, it is important to maintain certain safety valves that protect the confidentiality of sensitive business information. The demand for openness must also be balanced with protection of confidential or privileged information.

NGO Participation There also have been ongoing calls for other institutional reforms to Chapter 11. Most significant has been the demand for participation in the tribunal proceedings themselves, by becoming a party to the litigation itself, and through the submission of *amicus* briefs and oral arguments.

NAFTA Article 1120 provides that whichever arbitral rules are chosen by the investor 'shall govern the arbitration except to the extent modified' by Chapter 11

(NAFTA Secretariat 1994). Article 1131(1) also provides that a tribunal 'shall decide the issues in dispute in accordance with this Agreement and applicable rules of international law'. Accordingly, any tribunal asked to consider participation by a non-party in a given arbitration must look first to the designated arbitration rules and then to any applicable NAFTA provisions or 'rules of international law' that may be relevant to the dispute if the parties are not able to come to an agreement on such participation. Both the Methanex and the United States Postal Service (UPS) tribunals ruled that they have the power to accept *amicus* submissions.

Participation by interested parties raises a number of complex issues.[68] On the one hand, interested parties may possess specialised knowledge on a particular issue and, given the public nature of these disputes, the participation of certain NGOs may enhance the perceived legitimacy of the process. On the other hand, just because a certain group claims to represent broad public interests, that is not necessarily so. Arguably a democratically elected government is best equipped to represent the public interest in Chapter 11 litigation. Moreover, the addition of parties to a dispute, or the requirement to read and reply to briefs submitted, can add significantly to the time and cost of the arbitration.

However, where a public interest value is at stake, there is no compelling reason why interested parties should not be able to, at a minimum, submit briefs for a tribunal's consideration. This was the opinion of the Methanex tribunal, which stated:

> There is an undoubtedly public interest in this arbitration. The substantive issues extend far beyond those raised by the usual transnational arbitration between commercial parties. This is not merely because one of the Disputing Parties is a State ... The public interest in this arbitration arises from its subject-matter, as powerfully suggested in the Petitions. There is also a broader argument, as suggested by the [United States] and Canada: the Chapter 11 arbitral process could benefit from being perceived as more open and transparent; or conversely be harmed if seen as unduly secretive.[69]

However, the tribunal also recognised that:

> There are other competing factors to consider: the acceptance of *amicus* submissions might add significantly to the overall cost of the arbitration and, as considered above, there is a possible risk of imposing an extra burden on one or both of the Disputing Parties.[70]

However, attempts to make NGOs party to the actual dispute have not been successful. In October 2001, the UPS tribunal delivered an award deciding against the Canadian Union of Postal Workers and the Council of Canadians' petitions for standing as parties to the Chapter 11 proceedings. The petitioners argued that they have a direct interest in the subject matter of this claim and it would be contrary to the principles of fairness, equality, and fundamental justice to deny them the opportunity to defend their interests in the proceedings.

In its analysis of the petitioners' request for standing as parties, the tribunal determined that Chapter 11 does not confer authority to add parties to the arbitration.[71]

As a tribunal has only the authority conferred on it by the agreement under which it is established, the tribunal found that it had no power to add a third party to the proceedings. Furthermore, Article 15(1) of the UNCITRAL rules, as a procedural provision, cannot grant the tribunal any power to add further disputing parties to the arbitration.

Article 15(1) does, however, allow a tribunal to receive submissions offered by third parties (*amici curiae*) with the objective of assisting it in the arbitral process. In other words, acceptance of written submissions is only appropriate at the merits stage of an arbitration. Accordingly, the tribunal denied the petitioners' request to make submissions concerning the place of arbitration and the jurisdiction of the tribunal. However, the tribunal found that the requirement of equality and the parties' right to present their case limit the tribunal's power to admit *amicus* submissions if these are unduly burdensome for the parties or unnecessarily complicate the tribunal process.[72]

Referring to Article 24(5) of the UNCITRAL rules, which provides that the hearings are to be held in camera unless the parties agree otherwise, the tribunal denied the petitioners' requests to participate in the hearings without the consent of the parties.[73] In July 2002, however, the UPS hearings were made completely open to the public.

It is clear that further development of the rules that govern NGO participation through the submission of *amicus* briefs is required. There would be much to be gained from a consistent set of rules governing the submission of such briefs in an agreed-upon and predictable manner. For example, further work and analysis could usefully be done to define the circumstances in which it would be appropriate for such submissions to be made (Bjorklund 2002). However, it would be important that these rules limit any attempts by intervenors to widen the dispute between the parties. This is a real risk that has been recognised in the context of the WTO. It may be prudent to limit submissions to issues on which an intervenor possesses specialised information and only in the context of the merits of the case (Bjorklund 2002). In addition, one must be mindful of the time and cost that the submission of *amicus* briefs imposes on the parties to the dispute, as well as the arbitrators. Significant work would have to be undertaken to define the rules and procedures that would govern third-party participation and the effect such participation would have on the confidentiality of the arbitral process.

Appeals from NAFTA Chapter 11 Decisions

There is also pressure for clarification of the process relating to the appeal of tribunal awards. The possibility of a permanent appellate body, much like the WTO Appellate Body, should be explored in further detail. A permanent appellate body could provide a sense of consistency and permanence currently lacking in the Chapter 11 process. The current patchwork of appeal processes, with different rules in different jurisdictions, has led to jurisdiction shopping and a sense of uneven application of the rules among different parties to an arbitration. This is poor policy. A permanent appellate body could be useful in bolstering the perceived legitimacy of Chapter 11 as an *ad hoc* process. As well, in the event that a rogue tribunal did interpret the substantive provisions of Chapter 11 in such a way that did go significantly beyond international law, the fear articulated by many NGOs, a permanent appellate body could rein in such excesses.

The Challenge of Clarifying Substantive Law

Despite the widespread calls for NAFTA clarification, legal clarification is not always something that can be pulled 'off the shelf' as an answer to the uncertainty over a given legal issue. The common law tradition of judicial interpretation necessarily allows for an adjudicator to interpret the law in the context of specific facts. This section examines the challenges in clarifying the NAFTA, first by examining the procedure for clarification, and second, by examining substantive issues inherent in clarifying legal rules, using the expropriation provision as a case study (see Soloway and Broadhurst 2002).

Amendment or Clarification?

Christopher Wilkie (2002, 25) notes that treaties are 'living documents that often have to respond to different constituencies in a number of jurisdictions with different concerns and policy priorities'. Nowhere is this more evident than in the context of the General Agreement on Tariffs and Trade (GATT) and its successor, the WTO, where ongoing clarification is part of how the trade agreements operate in practice (Jackson 1997, 122). Before the establishment of the WTO, from time to time GATT interpretations were made in short statements by the chairs of the contracting parties. Sometimes this was done on the basis of a 'consensus view' of the contracting parties and sometimes it was done simply on the basis of there being no objection from any contracting party. As for the status of such interpretive statements with regard to future disputes, John Jackson suggests that it was, in the language of the Vienna Convention on the Law of Treaties, one of 'practice ... establishing agreement' (123).

Under Article XXV of the GATT, legally binding interpretations may be made by representatives of contracting parties who may 'meet from time to time for the purpose of giving effect to those provisions of this Agreement which involve joint action and, generally, with a view to facilitating the operation and furthering the objectives of this Agreement' (GATT 1947). Whether this includes the power to interpret, especially in a case where only a majority of contracting parties agreed, remained an open question. Practice suggested that Article XXV did include such a power.

The creation of the WTO in 1994 appears to have clarified matters. Article IX, paragraph 2 of the Marrakesh Agreement Establishing the World Trade Organization appears to provide for an official authorisation of the creation of notes of interpretation. It states that the Ministerial Conference and the General Council shall have the exclusive authority to adopt interpretations of this Agreement and of the Multilateral Trade Agreements. In the case of an interpretation of a Multilateral Trade Agreement in Annex 1, they shall exercise their authority on the basis of a recommendation by the Council overseeing the functioning of that Agreement. The decision to adopt an interpretation shall be taken by a three-fourths majority of the Members. This paragraph shall not be used in a manner that would undermine the amendment provisions in Article X (WTO 1994).

In 2001, the NAFTA Free Trade Commission began a clarification exercise to 'give future tribunals clearer and more specific understanding of Chapter 11's obligations, as originally intended by the drafters' (Pettigrew 2001). On the agenda was the possibility of clarifying the expropriation provisions of NAFTA and some institutional areas, such as the submission of *amicus* briefs.

This could be achieved by way of a formal amendment or a binding interpretive note issued by the NAFTA Commission. A formal amendment of the text of NAFTA is probably not a politically realistic option, given the considerable political energy which would be required to conclude an amendment to a trade agreement.[74] A more realistic approach is for the NAFTA Commission to issue an interpretive note.

The question that follows is what kind of interpretive note would resolve the perceived inadequacies of Chapter 11? When he was Minister of International Trade in 2001, Pierre Pettigrew (2001) said

> we want the investor-state dispute settlement process to be more open and transparent, to make it work better. Indeed, Canada has already taken steps to make this process more transparent. The Department of Foreign Affairs and International Trade web site contains all the publicly available documents related to Chapter 11 arbitrations involving the Canadian government. We would like to make all documents public – while accepting certain limitations to protect commercially confidential information – and to open the hearings to the public.
>
> We are also seeking to clarify some of the provisions of the NAFTA Chapter 11, such as expropriation disciplines, to ensure they properly reflect the original intent of the NAFTA Parties in the dispute settlement process.

However, there are limits to what a clarification provision can achieve. Todd Weiler (2002) notes there are two reasons why Pettigrew's statement may not work:

> First, it is an open question as to whether any of the minister's proposed changes can be considered to be mere 'interpretations' of the NAFTA text, as opposed to outright amendments. Second, even if a particular tribunal determines that it must obey the minister's 'interpretation' under Article 1131(2), the changes may simply not have gone far enough to have the desired effects.

A future tribunal may not necessarily follow the clarification to Chapter 11, if it finds that it has narrowed the scope of protection under that section. The tribunal in

Pope & Talbot did not automatically accept that the interpretation was a clarification rather than an amendment, although it eventually declined to make this determination. This underscores the point that clarifications, or interpretations, will not necessarily be accepted as such by a tribunal, potentially making them ineffective tools for reform.

Expropriation

In trying to define a regulatory expropriation, NAFTA negotiators attempted to include language in the text of NAFTA to distinguish legitimate regulation from a taking (another term for expropriation) but, in the end, were unable to (Soloway 2002). As one negotiator stated, 'if the U.S. Supreme Court could not do it in over 150 years, it was unlikely that we were going to do it in a matter of weeks' (Price 2000, 111).

As a case study, the following section examines a number of options for an interpretive note for the clarifications of NAFTA's expropriation provisions. This section demonstrates that such a note will not be easy to draft. In fact, significant risks are involved with such a clarification, not the least of which is undermining investor protection. This section reviews five of the options that were reviewed in a working group led by the Government of Ontario in order to determine what form (if any) such an interpretive note would take (Ontario Ministry of Economic Development and Trade 2001).

The Domestic Law Approach

Under the Domestic Law approach, the NAFTA Free Trade Commission would mandate that tribunals reviewing a claim under Article 1110 must consider the domestic law of expropriation of the respondent party in their interpretation of NAFTA's expropriation provisions.

Supporters of this approach argue that the domestic law of expropriation of all the parties is well established and would thus provide a greater framework of predictability to both investors and governments implementing new measures. It would also serve to impose a discipline on investors' reasonable expectations. Tribunals would be able to presume that investors had taken the limits of domestic expropriation law into account prior to making their investment decisions.

A central issue with this approach, however, is that it undermines the rationale for including the rules regarding expropriation in NAFTA. One of the stated objectives of NAFTA is to 'increase substantially investment opportunities in the territories of the Parties' (NAFTA Secretariat 1994, art. 102[1][c]). Presumably, the drafters were of the view that domestic law alone was not sufficient to accomplish this goal. As noted above, an international standard for expropriation articulated in an international treaty provides investors some assurance with regard to their investment beyond that of a domestic legal regime.

Moreover, linking the international standard to the domestic law creates a risk that the expropriation provisions would cease to function properly to protect foreign investors. Even if a domestic law regime currently provides adequate protection for expropriation, governments could enact new laws with discriminatory expropriation standards.

The Safe Harbour Approach

The safe harbour approach would do just that: create a safe harbour for reasonable regulation by the state. An interpretive note providing it would state that any claim for expropriation shall not include reasonable interference by a party with the operation, enjoyment, management, maintenance, use, or disposal of an investment of an investor. This approach would create an explicit exemption from compensating expropriation if the impugned measure was 'reasonable'. This approach would justify certain regulatory actions taken by governments that do not constitute a complete deprivation of ownership interests and that are not taken to benefit the government.

The central issue with this approach is simply that it is too vague. It leaves considerable discretion in the hands of the tribunals, as it does not define what would constitute a reasonable interference. Moreover, this proposed interpretation does not differ substantially from the law on expropriation as it currently stands, which also does not require compensation for reasonable regulation by the state. The international law of expropriation recognises police powers, that is, the sphere in which a government may regulate without being required to compensate an investor (Wortley 1959). The legitimate or reasonable use of police powers by a government (for example, measures that are supported by domestic regulatory processes) has not created a situation whereby governments are required to pay compensation awards under Chapter 11. What it does do is prevent the use of police powers to masquerade discriminatory regulation, that is, a disguised restriction on foreign investment. In this way, the safe harbour approach is superfluous and would not solve any problem that actually exists.

The Large Safe Harbour Approach

The large safe harbour approach provides that safeguards against expropriation do not apply to such things as general policy measures, namely a change in the public interest rate, industrial policy (excluding those measures whose aims are to protect domestic industry), environmental policy, and consumer protection.

This approach would remove certain areas of government regulation completely from any potential expropriation claim, thereby creating a safe harbour for specifically agreed-upon measures. The problem with this approach is that it essentially eviscerates the protection afforded by Article 1110, as any measure could be easily designed to fall within one of the enumerated categories (such as industrial policy). Investors would have no recourse against discriminatory measures adopted by NAFTA governments within these specified categories. This approach is arguably one step short of removing 'expropriation' from the text of NAFTA altogether.

The Factors for Evaluation Approach

The factors for evaluation approach would establish a set of factors that a panel must consider when interpreting Chapter 11 on expropriation. One possible formulation of such an interpretive note would first establish whether an impugned measure passed a threshold test that would allow a tribunal hearing. For example, the interpretive note would state that a claimant must establish the following:

1. The measure in question has affected or is likely to affect the value of the investment.
2. It is appropriate to adjudicate the matter under international law; that is, there has been a breach thereof. Once this threshold is met, the tribunal would then consider the following factors to determine whether a measure constitutes an expropriation.
3. The measure in dispute is designed to deprive the investor of the value of the investment.
4. The measure has the effect of depriving the investor of economically beneficial or productive use of the investment.
5. The measure is a *bona fide* general taxation, regulation, or other action of the kind that is generally accepted within the police powers of states.
6. The investor adversely affected by the measure had a reasonable expectation of non-interference by the party.

The advantage of having an initial threshold is that it functions to weed out frivolous and vexatious claims. However, Chapter 11 already contains a number of safeguards to eliminate such claims. For example, Article 1116 states that an investor can only bring a claim if the party has breached an obligation and the investor 'has incurred loss or damage by reason of, or arising out of, that breach'. As noted above, Article 1121 states that in order to bring a claim, an investor must waive its right to initiate or continue before any court any proceedings with respect to the measure that is alleged to be the breach.

After the threshold is established, this approach provides substantial guidance to an arbitral tribunal on what constitutes a taking, reflecting principles that have been developed in domestic and international law. However, no guidance is offered as to whether the factors listed are dispositive. Nor is there any guidance on how these factors relate to each other. It is also unclear whether tribunals will be able to look at other relevant factors or if these are the only legitimate factors that can be considered.

More seriously, this approach introduces the requirement of intent on the part of the government adopting the measure. This would drastically narrow the scope of Chapter 11 to include only those acts that are aimed at specific investments. By requiring specific intent, such an interpretive note would actually provide foreign investors with less protection than domestic investors. Again, this would eviscerate the protection in the NAFTA and potentially discourage foreign investment.

The Guidance to Panels Approach

The guidance to panels approach is similar to the factors for evaluation approach. The main difference is that this type of interpretive note would provide principles to guide tribunals rather than enumerate factors that must be considered. In this way, tribunals could include any number of factors particular to the cases they are adjudicating, and could exclude factors that are not. A guidance to panels interpretive note could state that panels should only be guided by the following clarifications:

1. NAFTA was not intended to create new forms of expropriation.
2. Expropriation is the taking of property rights by government for its own use or benefit or for the use or benefit of a third party.
3. Indirect expropriation and measures tantamount to expropriation are intended to capture expropriation by other than direct means and are not intended to create new forms of expropriation.
4. Property rights may be restricted by government measures for a public purpose without compensation, even when there is a loss of property or diminution of value of property, for example, in order to enforce laws which require forfeiture for criminal activity, to raise revenue, or to protect health, safety, the environment, or the public welfare.
5. The purpose and effect of the measure must be judged in light of reasonable expectations of a property owner about the degree of government regulation of that economic sector or activity.
6. There is a presumption that governments are regulating, and not expropriating, when they say they are regulating. But neither the government's intent nor its characterisation of its measures is determinative. The onus is on the disputing investor to prove on a civil standard (not just a *prima facie* case) that the measure is an expropriation.
7. Other NAFTA provisions (such as Articles 1101[4], 1110[7] and [8], 1114[1], 1410, 1502, and 2103) do not create any presumption with respect to expropriation for any other government measure.

The first and third points are simply an attempt to make clear that the phrase 'tantamount to expropriation' does not create a *lex specialis* (special law) that differs from the international law of expropriation. This would essentially support the conclusions of the tribunals in Pope & Talbot and S.D. Myers.

The second point would make it explicit that, to constitute an expropriation, a measure must both deprive the investor of ownership rights and pass those benefits on to the government (or a third party). Requiring that the government or another third party benefit from the expropriation may narrow Article 1110 as a remedy, as such benefits will be difficult to prove practically. The effect of these first three points would appear to endorse the interpretations found in Pope & Talbot and S.D. Myers (as opposed to the findings of the tribunal in Metalclad).

The fourth point is little more than a restatement of the safe harbour approach. As already stated, this type of statement is unnecessary and could lead to unintended consequences that severely undermine the underlying goals of NAFTA. This could effectively eliminate any concept of indirect expropriation from its scope. It would also represent quite a radical shift in the international law of expropriation and would deny the kind of protection that is necessary to encourage foreign investment.

The sixth and seventh points are two further examples of attempts to fix problems that do not exist. There has been no case in which the investor has attempted to argue that the onus is not on it to demonstrate that, on the balance of probabilities, the measure in question constitutes an expropriation. Nor has a tribunal made such a ruling. Similarly, no attempt has been made to use the articles listed in the seventh point to create any type of presumption with respect to expropriation.

This suggested approach contains too much ambiguity and not enough clarity. For every interpretive question it answers, it seems to raise more questions. It addresses too many non-issues and suggests too many interpretive principles that have already been employed by the panels.

Conclusion: Toward a Better Understanding

It is important to be mindful that arbitral tribunals have ruled in only five cases in eight years. As J. Anthony VanDuzer notes, 'most of the noise surrounding Chapter 11 has been generated by the arguments advanced by counsel for complaining parties, by interest groups who appear to feel threatened by review of the issues placed before arbitral tribunals, or by governments forced to defend questionable policy choices' (Hart and Dymond 2002, 127). Simply put, none of the decisions has confirmed the worst-case scenarios. To quote VanDuzer (2002) again, 'while the broadly worded substantive obligations of NAFTA stated in Chapter 11 may be capable of being applied in a manner that would impose significant constraints on sovereignty, they have not been applied to do so. So far, only egregious state actions which were either arbitrary, clearly unfair or overtly protectionist have been found to be contrary to obligations under Chapter 11'.

It is premature for the commission to adopt an interpretive note relating to any of the substantive provisions of NAFTA. Again, it is important to focus on what is actually broken before attempting to fix it. For the most part, the substantive provisions of NAFTA have not been expanded beyond their meaning in international law. As well, moving too early on reforming Chapter 11 seriously risks undermining the investor protection benefits it affords. A solid case for reform based on the jurisprudence to date needs to be established before substantive reform should be undertaken. This has not been done.

Interpretive notes can be tricky. If they go too far, they become amendments and, absent being incorporated into NAFTA by way of the formal amending process, they risk being disregarded by tribunals.

In terms of Chapter 11's substantive provisions, one of the current concerns regarding Article 1105 is that it is being used as a 'catch-all' for arguments under Chapter 11. Article 1105 arguments were presented successfully by the claimants in Pope & Talbot, Metalclad, and S.D. Myers. In each of these cases, government entities behaved in a discriminatory and unfair way toward the investor. However, some concerns remain with respect to the interpretations to date, which have been dealt with for the time being by the NAFTA Commission's interpretive statement. It is not likely that the NAFTA parties will revisit the issue any time soon, although this may depend on how future tribunals take account of the interpretive statement.

Regarding Article 1102 (national treatment), some NGOs have argued that the term 'like circumstances' should be clarified in order to specify what types of operations will be compared to determine 'no worse' treatment (International Institute on Sustainable Development [IISD] 2001). There has been one ruling to date which has found a violation of Article 1102: S.D. Myers. In comparing like circumstances, one would think that the tribunal would compare similar operations located in the host country (Mann 2001). However, in this case, the tribunal did go beyond comparing the investment in Canada of S.D. Myers, which provided marketing services to other Canadian-based providers of PCB marketing services. The tribunal instead applied the national treatment obligation to the full business line of S.D. Myers, including operations in the home and the host countries (the U.S. and Canada, respectively) (27). However, a decision to reform Article 1102 on the basis of one ruling is premature.

Regarding the prohibition against performance requirements in NAFTA Article 1106, some NGOs have argued that this provision risks becoming a 'wide open back door for firms to litigate trade-related obligations in an investment agreement' (IISD 2001, 4). This argument is speculative, as not one tribunal has found that a measure has violated Article 1106 to date. In this instance, it is definitely too early to take any action.

Based on the interpretations adopted to date with respect to NAFTA's expropriation provisions, there is no clearly established need for change. Two of the three tribunals have been relatively conservative in their approach. In Metalclad, while the tribunal adopted a more expansive interpretation of the expropriation provisions, the facts strongly supported a finding of expropriation.

It is vital to remain mindful of why Chapter 11 was included in the NAFTA. The parties felt it was important to encourage investment, particularly in Mexico. It would be wrong to obliterate the substantive protections afforded by Chapter 11 based on the case law to date because of early jitters. Despite the lack of *stare decisis* in international law, the tribunals do look to the judgements of previous tribunals for guidance. Eventually, trends will emerge and carefully considered action may be appropriate at a later date.

However, there is scope for reform in the process by which Chapter 11 cases are adjudicated. Reform in this area probably has the most scope for success, as it is important that the rules of the game are as fair as possible. In this vein, a more robust set of rules governing transparency and NGO participation would be useful.

As well, the parties should seriously consider the possibility of a permanent NAFTA appellate body as a way to provide consistency in the appeal process from tribunal decisions.

A permanent appellate body could also provide consistency, to some extent, in the application of the substantive rules of Chapter 11 in a much more effective manner than would clarification of NAFTA provisions by the Free Trade Commission. An appellate body could rein in any possible future rulings by tribunals that interpreted the provisions of Chapter 11 in a way that went far beyond international law, thereby addressing the concerns that Chapter 11 decisions not impinge on the ability of governments to regulate in the public interest.

Notes

1   The author is grateful to Armand de Mestral, Stephen Brereton, and Daniel Schwanen for their insightful comments on earlier drafts of this chapter. The author also wishes to thank Michelle Grando, LL.M., University of Toronto, for her assistance in researching and drafting the case summaries.

2   A measure is quite broadly defined to include 'includes any law, regulation, procedure, requirement or practice' (NAFTA Secretariat 1994, art. 201).

3   In addition, the obligation not to differentiate between domestic and foreign investors has been controversial and represents a departure from traditional practice on the part of governments. This is particularly true in the case of Canada and Mexico, which in the past have been wary of some of the implications of high levels of foreign investment in the domestic economy and have used foreign ownership restrictions as a means by which to regulate and set policy. For example, Canada has used foreign ownership restrictions to protect its cultural and broadcasting industries and Mexico has used such restrictions to maintain control over its electricity and oil sectors. See Daly (1994).

4   Unlike the general rule in the Canadian court system that provides that proceedings are public unless a judge rules otherwise, NAFTA does not provide a positive obligation on the tribunals to make any part of the arbitration process open to the public, although parties to the dispute remain free to agree otherwise if they so choose.

5   As will be addressed later in further detail, in response Canada has since made the decision to publish Notices of Intent to Commence Arbitration (Article 1119), thereby giving the public some advanced notice of what claims may eventually be filed.

6   The interpretive statement provided 1) that each Party shall make available to the public in a timely manner all Chapter 11 documents (subject to certain exceptions) and 2) a clarification of what minimum standard of international law governs foreign investments under NAFTA.

7   Metalclad, Award on the Merits.

8   See Articles 38 and 59 of the Statute of the International Court of Justice.

9   *Pope & Talbot Inc. v. The Government of Canada Award on the Merits of Phase 2*, 10 April 2001.

10 *Azinian, Robert et al. and United Mexican States*. NAFTA/ICSID (AF) Tribunal, Case No. ARB(AF)/97/2, Final Award, November 1, 1999, 39 I.L.M. 537 (2000).

11 *Azinian*, para. 87.

12 *Azinian*, para. 97.
13 *Azinian*, para. 100.
14 *Azinian*, paras. 83-84.
15 *Azinian*, para. 92.
16 Canada-United States: Softwood Lumber Agreement. Canada and the United States, 29 May 1996, 35 I.L.M. 1195. *Commercial Arbitration Act*, R.S.C. 1985, c.17 (2nd Supp.). Pope & Talbot, Inc. and the Government of Canada. NAFTA/UNCITRAL Tribunal, Final Award on the Merits of Phase 2 by Arbitral Tribunal, 10 April 2001 <naftaclaims.com/Disputes/Canada/Pope/PopeFinalMeritsAward.pdf> (November 2005), para. 42; Pope & Talbot, Inc. and the Government of Canada, NAFTA/UNCITRAL Tribunal, Interim Award by Arbitral Tribunal (26 June 2000) <naftaclaims.com/Disputes/Canada/Pope/PopeInterimMeritsAward.pdf> (November 2005).
17 Softwood lumber is the subject of a longstanding dispute between Canada and the United States and remains unresolved. The softwood lumber agreement was a politically negotiated settlement between the countries, completely outside the context of NAFTA's trade remedy rules. For Canadian exporters, the agreement was better than the alternative, namely, unilateral action by the U.S. in the form of severely punitive tariffs and quotas. It is interesting to note that, absent the U.S. threat, there would be no softwood lumber agreement and Pope & Talbot investors would not have a basis for a Chapter 11 complaint. Ironically, the investor is using a provision in a free trade agreement against Canada, precisely because a co-signatory (the U.S.) refuses to allow free trade in this area.
18 Pope & Talbot, Inc. and the Government of Canada, NAFTA/UNCITRAL Tribunal, Award by the Arbitral Tribunal in Relation to Preliminary Motion by Government of Canada (26 January 2000) <naftaclaims.com/Disputes/Canada/Pope/PopeAwardOnMotionToDismiss1.pdf> (November 2005), para 26.
19 Pope & Talbot Award on Preliminary Motion, para. 34.
20 Under the standard of not distinguishing between foreign-owned and domestic companies, justifying differences in treatment requires showing that the differential treatment bears a reasonable relationship to rational policies not motivated by preference of domestic over foreign-owned investments (see Pope & Talbot Final Award, paras. 78, 79).
21 Pope & Talbot Final Award, para. 110.
22 The filing by Pope & Talbot of the Notice of Intent to Submit a Claim to Arbitration under Article 1119 triggered a review by the Softwood Lumber Division of the investor's claim that its investment had not received the quota allocation to which it was entitled.
23 Pope & Talbot Final Award, paras. 173–175.
24 Pope & Talbot Final Award, para. 181.
25 Pope & Talbot Interim Award, para. 96.
26 Pope & Talbot Interim Award, para. 99.
27 Pope & Talbot Interim Award, para. 96. Under customary international law, the term 'police powers' generally includes measures taken by a government under normal or common functions of governments to protect the environment and human health, to provide consumer protection, to regulate hazardous products, and so on. However, there remain a degree of uncertainty regarding what exactly falls within the police powers rule, much as there remains uncertainty regarding what falls within the rule on expropriation itself.
28 Pope & Talbot Interim Award, para. 102.
29 Pope & Talbot Interim Award, para. 100.
30 Pope & Talbot, Inc. and the Government of Canada, NAFTA/UNCITRAL Tribunal, Award in Respect of Damages by Arbitral Tribunal (31 May 2002) <naftaclaims.com/Disputes/

Canada/Pope/PopeAwardOnDamages.pdf> (November 2005), para. 23. Pursuant to Article 1131(2), the NAFTA Commission may issue an interpretation of a provision that is binding on a Chapter 11 tribunal.

31　Pope & Talbot Award on Damages, para. 46.

32　Pope & Talbot Award on Damages, para. 47.

33　According to the tribunal, the interpretation should be understood as requiring 'each Party to accord to investments of investors of the other Parties the fairness elements as subsumed in, rather than additive to, customary international law' (Pope & Talbot Award on Damages, para. 54).

34　Pope & Talbot Award on Damages, para. 56.

35　Pope & Talbot Award on Damages, para. 57, notes 40, 42.

36　Pope & Talbot Award on Damages, para. 60.

37　Pope & Talbot Award on Damages, para. 68.

38　Thomas (2002, 121) notes that an award of costs combined with a strong statement of disapproval would have been a better course of action to follow than the tribunal's decision under Article 1105.

39　*Metalclad Corporation v. The United Mexican States*, Award [unreported, ICSID Case No. ARB (AF)/97/1 (30 August 2000), para. 99.

40　Metalclad Award, para. 88. Chapter 11, however, does not contain any specific transparency obligation; its existence was inferred on the basis of NAFTA's Article 102 and Chapter 18. Accordingly, the ruling holds that lack of transparency and assurances by the federal government, which were relied upon by the foreign investor to its detriment, constituted denial of fair and equitable treatment to Metalclad.

41　Metalclad Award, para. 103.

42　*United Mexican States v. Metalclad*, 2001 BCSC 664, Full Reasons for Judgement, 22 May 2001 <www.canadianliberty.bc.ca/nafta/mexico_vs_metalclad.html> (November 2005), para. 67.

43　Metalclad Judgement, para. 73.

44　Metalclad Judgement, paras. 84, 91.

45　Metalclad Judgement, paras. 133–134.

46　PCB remediation consists of analysing equipment and oil to assess the level of contamination, the transportation of the oil or equipment to a facility, and the extraction of the PCBs from the materials so transported. The decontaminated components of the equipment and the oil are recycled. The extracted PCBs and PCB waste material is then destroyed.

47　S.D. Myers, Inc. and the Government of Canada. NAFTA/UNCITRAL Tribunal, Partial Award (13 November 2000) <naftaclaims.com/Disputes/Canada/SDMyers/SDMyersFinalAwardMerits.pdf> (November 2005), paras. 131–132.

48　S.D. Myers Award, paras. 194, 195.

49　S.D. Myers Award, para. 250.

50　Even before delivering a final decision on whether the interim and final orders violated Canada's obligation under Section A of Chapter 11, the tribunal had already discussed general principles for interpreting NAFTA in the context of environmental concerns. Its discussion of the relationship between the NAFTA and the NAAEC led to the conclusion that 'where a state can achieve its chosen level of environmental protection through a variety of equally effective and reasonable means, it is obliged to adopt the alternative that is most consistent with open trade' (S.D. Myers Award, para. 221).

51　S.D. Myers Award, para. 247.

52　S.D. Myers Award, para. 255.

53 S.D. Myers Award, para. 162. The following are some of the evidences presented by the tribunal in its ruling. Several documents prepared by officials in Environment Canada highlighted the benefits of opening the border from the Canadian side. According to those officials, such a policy would represent a technically and environmentally sound solution to the destruction of some of Canada's PCBs. Nevertheless, the position of the Minister of the Environment, especially after a meeting with senior officials of Canadian operators of hazardous waste facilities, was that PCB waste should be disposed of in Canada by Canadians (statement made in the House of Commons).

54 S.D. Myers Award, para. 266.

55 S.D. Myers Award, para. 263.

56 S.D. Myers Award, para. 281.

57 S.D. Myers Award, para. 285.

58 S.D. Myers Award, para. 285.

59 In addition, the study pointed out the possibility of health risks to the population resulting from the presence of MTBE in the environment. According to the study, it is an animal carcinogen with the potential to cause cancer in humans. However, the state of scientific knowledge with respect to MTBE's human health effects remains incomplete.

60 Methanex and United States of America, NAFTA/UNCITRAL Tribunal, Decision of the Tribunal on Petitions from Third Persons to Intervene as 'Amici Curiae' (15 January 2002) <www.international-economic-law.org/Methanex/Methanex%20-%20Amicus%20Decision.pdf> (November 2005), para. 31.

61 Methanex and United States of America, Preliminary Award on Jurisdiction and Admissibility, 7 August 2002 <www.state.gov/documents/organization/12613.pdf> (November 2005).

62 Methanex Preliminary Award, para. 139.

63 See Government of Canada Regulatory Policy, November 1999, Privy Council Office <www.pco-bcp.gc.ca/raoics-srdc/docs/publications/regulatory_policy_e.pdf> (November 2005). The policy requires, for example, that regulatory authorities demonstrate both that a problem or risk exists and that federal intervention is justified, that the benefits and costs of regulatory interventions under consideration be assessed and that benefits justify the costs, that intergovernmental agreements be respected, and so on.

64 A NAFTA tribunal cannot require that a measure's repeal: it can only award damages against the federal government once an unlawful expropriation is established. Governments remain free to adopt any environmental, health, or safety measure they deem appropriate.

65 See Environmental Acts and Regulations <www.ec.gc.ca/EnviroRegs/ENG/Default.cfm> (November 2005).

66 See NAFTA Annex I for reservations for provincial measures grandfathering all measures in effect at the time NAFTA entered into force on 1 January 1994 and NAFTA Annex II for sectoral reservations, which includes social services (including health).

67 Pope & Talbot, Inc. and the Government of Canada, NAFTA/UNCITRAL Tribunal, Second Decision on Confidentiality (11 March 2002) <naftaclaims.com/Disputes/Canada/Pope/PopeSecondDecisionOnConfidentiality.pdf> (November 2005), para. 18.

68 From a legal perspective, it is arguable that NAFTA did not provide for the involvement of anyone beyond the parties to the dispute themselves. Under Article 1128, the NAFTA parties have the right to make submissions in any dispute on questions of interpretation only. If the submission of *amicus* briefs were allowed, then the *amici* would have greater rights than the NAFTA parties themselves.

69 Methanex Amicus Decision, para. 49.
70 Methanex Amicus Decision, para. 50.
71 United Parcel Service of America Inc. and the Government of Canada, NAFTA/ UNCITRAL Tribunal, Decision of the Tribunal on Petitions for Intervention and Participation as Amici Curiae (17 October 2001) <naftaclaims.com/Disputes/Canada/ UPS/UPSDecisionReParticipationAmiciCuriae.pdf> (November 2005), para. 36.
72 UPS Award on Amici Curiae Petition, para. 69.
73 UPS Award on Amici Curiae Petition, para. 68.
74 The amendment provisions of NAFTA are set out in Article 2202. Any amendment would have to pass the formal treaty ratification process of all three parties. Obtaining agreement for such an amendment from the U.S. Congress may be particularly difficult, as it has consistently refused to grant enhanced negotiating authority (or so-called 'fast-track authority') to the executive branch. Although the House of Representatives granted President George W. Bush fast-track authority, the Bush administration was forced to agree to a series of protectionist measures and negotiating positions. Similar restrictions are expected in the future if the legislation is to pass in the Senate (see Alden 2001).

References

Abbott, Frederick M. (1999). 'The North American Integration Regime and Its Implications for the World Trading System'. Jean Monnet Program, New York University, New York. <www.jeanmonnetprogram.org/papers/99/990201.html> (November 2005).

Alden, Edward (2001). 'Trading Nations Count the Cost of Fast-Track'. *Financial Times*, 9 December.

Barutciski, Milos (2002). 'In the Eye of the Beholder: A Commentary on Investor Protection under NAFTA'. Unpublished.

Bjorklund, Andrea K. (2002). 'The Participation of Amici Curiae in NAFTA Chapter Eleven Cases'. Essay Papers on Investment Protection, Ad hoc Experts Group on Investment Rules. International Trade Canada. <www.dfait-maeci.gc.ca/tna-nac/participate-en.asp> (November 2005).

Browne, Dennis (2002). 'Commentary'. In L.R. Dawson, ed., *Whose Rights? The NAFTA Chapter 11 Debate*. Centre for Trade Policy and Law, Ottawa.

Daly, Justine (1994). 'Has Mexico Crossed the Border on the State Reponsibility for Economic Injury to Aliens? Foreign Investment and the Calvo Clause in Mexico after NAFTA'. *St. Mary's Law Journal* vol. 25, no. 3, pp. 1147–1193.

Drabek, Zdenek and Warren Payne (1999). 'The Impact of Transparency on Foreign Direct Investment'. Staff Working Paper ERAD-9902. Economic Research and Analysis Division. World Trade Organization, Washington DC. <www.wto.org/english/res_e/reser_e/ erad-99-02.doc> (November 2005).

General Agreement on Tariffs and Trade (1947). 'The General Agreement on Tariffs and Trade'. <www.wto.org/english/docs_e/legal_e/gatt47_01_e.htm> (November 2005).

Hart, Michael and William Dymond (2002). 'NAFTA Chapter 11: Precedents, Principles, and Prospects'. In L.R. Dawson, ed., *Whose Rights? The NAFTA Chapter 11 Debate*. Centre for Trade Policy and Law, Ottawa.

International Institute on Sustainable Development (2001). 'Note on NAFTA Commission's July 31, 2001, Initiative to Clarify Chapter 11 Investment Provisions'. <www.iisd.org/ pdf/2001/trade_nafta_aug2001.pdf> (November 2005).

Jackson, John H. (1997). *The World Trading System: Law and Policy of International Economic Relations*. 2nd ed. MIT Press, Cambridge, MA.

Johnson, Jon R. (1997). *The North American Free Trade Agreement: A Comprehensive Guide*. Canada Law Book, Aurora ON.

Johnson, Jon R. (2002). 'How Will International Trade Agreements Affect Canadian Health Care?' Commission on the Future of Health Care in Canada, Discussion Paper No. 22. <www.hc-sc.gc.ca/english/pdf/romanow/pdfs/22_Johnson_E.pdf> (November 2005).

Kirton, John J. (1998). 'NAFTA, Foreign Direct Investment, and Economic Integration: A Canadian Approach'. In Organisation for Economic Co-operation and Development, ed., *Migration, Free Trade, and Regional Integration in North America*, pp. 181–194. Organisation for Economic Co-operation and Development, Paris.

Mann, Howard (2001). *Private Rights, Public Problems: A Guide to NAFTA's Controversial Chapter on Investors Rights*. International Institute on Sustainable Development and World Wildlife Fund, Winnipeg. <www.iisd.org/pdf/trade_citizensguide.pdf> (November 2005).

Mann, Howard and Julie Soloway (2002). 'Untangling the Expropriation and Regulation Relationship: Is There a Way Forward?' Report to the Ad Hoc Expert Group on Investment Rules and the Department of Foreign Affairs and International Trade. <www.dfait-maeci.gc.ca/tna-nac/regulation-en.asp> (November 2005).

Molot, Maureen Appel (2002). 'NAFTA Chapter 11: An Evolving Regime'. In L.R. Dawson, ed., *Whose Rights? The NAFTA Chapter 11 Debate*. Centre for Trade Policy and Law, Ottawa.

NAFTA Secretariat (1994). 'North American Free Trade Agreement'. <www.nafta-sec-alena. org> (November 2005).

Ontario Ministry of Economic Development and Trade (2001). 'Discussion paper prepared for a working group on NAFTA Chapter 11 on options for an interpretive note for Article 1110'. 1 March. Unpublished.

Ostry, Sylvia (1998). 'China and the WTO: The Transparency Issues'. *UCLA Journal of International Law and Foreign Affairs* vol. 3, no. 1, pp. 1–22.

Pettigrew, Pierre S. (2001). 'The Importance of Investment and Investment Rules to Canada'. Speech to the House of Commons during a Motion on Investor-State Dispute Settlement. 1 May. <www.dfait-maeci.gc.ca/tna-nac/Min_S_Inv-en.asp> (November 2005).

Price, Daniel M. (2000). 'Chapter 11: Private Party vs. Government, Investor-State Dispute Settlement: Frankenstein or Safety Valve?' *Canada-United States Law Journal* vol. 26, pp. 107–114.

Rodrik, Dani (1997). *Has Globalization Gone Too Far?* Institute for International Economics, Washington DC.

Rugman, Alan M., John J. Kirton, and Julie A. Soloway (1999). *Environmental Regulations and Corporate Strategy: A NAFTA Perspective*. Oxford University Press, Oxford.

Schwanen, Daniel (2002). 'Commentary'. In L.R. Dawson, ed., *Whose Rights? The NAFTA Chapter 11 Debate*. Centre for Trade Policy and Law, Ottawa.

Secretaría de Economía, Subsecretaría de normatividad y servicios a la industría y al comercio exterior (Mexico) (2001a). 'Inversión de Canadá en México'. December.

Secretaría de Economía, Subsecretaría de normatividad y servicios a la industría y al comercio exterior (Mexico) (2001b). 'Inversión de Estados Unidos en México'. December.

Soloway, Julie and Jeremy Broadhurst (2002). 'What's In the Medicine Chest for Chapter 11's Ills?' *Canadian Business Law Journal* vol. 36, no. 3, pp. 388–404.

Soloway, Julie A. (2002). 'Expropriation under NAFTA Chapter 11: The Phantom Menace'. In J.J. Kirton and V. Maclaren, eds., *Linking Trade, Environment, and Social Cohesion: NAFTA Experiences, Global Challenges*, pp. 131–144. Ashgate, Aldershot.

Thomas, J.C. (2002). 'The Experience of NAFTA Chapter 11 Tribunals to Date'. In L.R. Dawson, ed., *Whose Rights? The NAFTA Chapter 11 Debate*. Centre for Trade Policy and Law, Ottawa.

Tollefson, Chris (2002). 'Games without Frontiers: Investor Claims and Citizen Submissions under the NAFTA Regime'. *Yale Journal of International Law* vol. 27, no. 1, pp. 141–191.

VanDuzer, J. Anthony (2002). 'NAFTA Chapter 11 to Date: The Progress of a Work in Progress'. In L.R. Dawson, ed., *Whose Rights? The NAFTA Chapter 11 Debate*. Centre for Trade Policy and Law, Ottawa.

Weiler, Todd J. (2002). 'NAFTA Investment Arbitration and the Growth of International Economic Law'. *Canadian Business Law Journal* vol. 36, no. 3, pp. 405–435.

Wilkie, Christopher (2002). 'The Origins of NAFTA's Investment Provisions: Economic and Policy Considerations'. In L.R. Dawson, ed., *Whose Rights? The NAFTA Chapter 11 Debate*. Centre for Trade Policy and Law, Ottawa.

World Trade Organization (1994). 'Marrakesh Agreement Establishing the World Trade Organization'. 15 April. <www.wto.org/english/docs_e/legal_e/04-wto_e.htm> (November 2005).

Wortley, Ben Atkinson (1959). *Expropriation in Public International Law*. Cambridge University Press, Cambridge.

Chapter 10

NAFTA's Chapter 11:
The Case for Reform

Chris Tollefson[1]

Is the furore that has come to surround Chapter 11, the most controversial provision of the North American Free Trade Agreement (NAFTA), largely unjustified? In her provocative chapter, Julie Soloway contends that Chapter 11 jurisprudence during NAFTA's first years suggests that it does nothing to undermine or constrain the right of NAFTA governments to enact measures to protect public health and the environment. She claims that in every case in which a NAFTA government has been held liable under Chapter 11, tribunals have quite appropriately sought to punish 'outrageous behaviour on the part of governmental officials'. Nor does she think that Chapter 11 has contributed to a regulatory chill that might stifle or fetter domestic policy development. It is thus premature to be seriously contemplating ways to fix Chapter 11. So far, she asserts, the chapter is working much as it was intended. Reforming it, as the NAFTA governments seem to be inclined to do, would do more harm than good.

Three elements of this analysis deserve closer scrutiny: the contention that Chapter 11 has had no demonstrable chilling effect on regulatory activity; the contention that, in any event, regulators have no legitimate reason to be concerned about the impact of Chapter 11 on their activities; and, finally, the contention that the Chapter 11 jurisprudence shows that it poses no real threat to legitimate, non-discriminatory environmental protection measures.

A careful look at the architecture of Chapter 11, and the jurisprudence under it, suggests conclusions quite different from those reached by Soloway. This chapter argues that the discretion Chapter 11 reposes in tribunals is ill defined and overly broad, and has already led to highly questionable results in several cases, including Metalclad, a decision discussed by Soloway in some detail. It concludes that as momentum for reforming Chapter 11 builds, Canada must redouble its efforts to ensure that investor rights do not unnecessarily compromise domestic policy autonomy, whether under NAFTA or under future trade and investment agreements.

Perceptions of Chapter 11 and the Regulatory Chill Hypothesis

To be sure, the rhetoric of some of the Chapter 11 critics has at times been hyperbolic. To some extent, however, this rhetoric is explicable by the pervasive secrecy surrounding the process – a secrecy that is strikingly at odds with the way that many citizens have come to expect government, let alone judicial or quasi-judicial decision makers, should operate.[2] It is thus encouraging to see support for reforms aimed at making the process more transparent and open to citizen participation.

Negative perceptions about Chapter 11 have also been fostered by the high level of uncertainty surrounding its legal meaning and its implications for domestic policy making and administration.[3] The discretion conferred on NAFTA tribunals to interpret the extraordinarily broad language of Chapter 11 is breathtaking, both in its scope and the degree to which it is insulated from appellate or judicial review. Unlike domestic courts, Chapter 11 tribunals are not bound by the doctrine of precedent. This means that, in effect, such tribunals not only apply law but also regularly make it. Moreover, also unlike courts and other international dispute resolution bodies, they are not subject to appellate review for errors of law or fact. Furthermore, tribunals are not even bound by official interpretive statements offered by the NAFTA Free Trade Commission as to the meaning of the chapter's provisions.[4]

Despite the clouds of uncertainty surrounding Chapter 11 and the evident incentives it provides to litigate the propriety of public policy decisions, Soloway insists that 'it is hard to imagine' that it might inhibit regulators from enacting legitimate, non-discriminatory environmental laws or regulations. In support of this claim, she points out that since NAFTA came into force, the Government of Canada has passed several dozen new environmental laws and regulations, asserting that the environmental regulatory framework 'continues to function' in all three of the NAFTA countries.

However, it is hazardous to drawing conclusions about Chapter 11's impact on, or irrelevance to, the appetite of governments to engage in policy innovation based on the volume, as opposed to the content, of regulatory measures. Were one to systematically research Chapter 11's impact on environmental regulation, one would need to look far beyond the regulatory docket of Environment Canada. Such an investigation would necessitate a rather sweeping analysis of decision- and policy-making authority across a wide spectrum of agencies and departments vested with environment-related responsibilities in such areas as public health, resource management, consumer protection, and land-use planning. Such an analysis would, of course, need to examine not only federal institutions, but also provincial and local decision makers whose actions can also trigger Chapter 11 liabilities.

Once the myriad of government bodies to be examined were identified, one would then be faced with the equally challenging prospect of establishing with any certitude why governments might forgo particular policy options. Given the tremendous difficulties involved in such an analysis, simply because the reality of such a regulatory chill has yet to be definitively established does not mean it does not exist.

It has also been argued that Chapter 11 chills the appetite of government to pursue deregulation. In this regard, Daniel Schwanen (2002, 46) contends Chapter 11 makes privatisation and deregulatory initiatives less attractive for governments. In contemplating such initiatives, he asserts that governments are mindful of the potentially costly compensation requirements that will be triggered should such an initiative subsequently falter and force government back onto the scene to pick up the pieces.

Soloway's essentially normative response is that one should not worry about this result because it is one that achieves fairness for firms whose investments may be adversely affected by such a policy change. This seems to concede that when deregulating or privatising, governments do indeed factor into the equation the cost of policy reversals. It follows that such a costing may well tilt the balance against policy innovation. Moreover, under Canadian law, property rights are not presumed to trump government's right to regulate in the public interest. This basic principle was reaffirmed in 1982 when Parliament decided not to enshrine property rights in the Constitution. This does not mean that governments routinely ignore the claims of investors or businesses for compensation. Rather, it means that governments reserve the right to determine the nature and amount of compensation that should be provided, having to regard not only investor fairness but also the broader public interest. Chapter 11 takes this determination out of the hands of government, vesting it with tribunals that are under no obligation to take these public interest considerations into account – and are poorly positioned to do so.

Should Regulators Be Worried? The Chapter's Architecture and Jurisprudence

Whether a regulatory (or \) chill exists is one thing; whether regulators have legitimate cause for concern is another. Soloway is firmly of the view that they do not. She claims that Chapter 11 jurisprudence suggests tribunals have carefully balanced the public and private rights that are invariably implicated in such cases and arrived at the right results.

It is important to be mindful of a key architectural feature of Chapter 11. Unlike the General Agreement of Tariffs and Trade (GATT), Chapter 11 does not contain a generally applicable provision that prescribes how competing public and private interests are to be balanced when they come into conflict in cases of this kind. Under the GATT, this balancing function is performed by Article XX (General Exceptions). This provision allows a state to justify a measure that would otherwise be inconsistent with its GATT obligations on the basis that it is 'necessary to protect human, animal or plant life or health' (GATT 1947). As such, Article XX provides the World Trade Organization (WTO) with a vehicle to balance the goal of trade liberalisation against domestically defined policy preferences in the realms of environment and health.[5]

There is no comparable balancing provision in Chapter 11. The closest analogue is Article 1114, which states: 'Nothing in this Chapter shall be construed to prevent a Party from adopting, maintaining or enforcing any measure *otherwise consistent with this Chapter* that it considers appropriate to ensure that investment activity in its territory is undertaken in a manner sensitive to environmental concerns' (NAFTA Secretariat 1994, emphasis added). The permissive nature of this language – in particular the caveat that such environmental measures must be 'otherwise consistent with this Chapter' – has prompted many trade experts to discount Article 1114 as merely aspirational and of no legal consequence (for example, see Appleton 1994, 195, and; Johnson 1998, 225). To date, while several governments have invoked Article 1114 as a defence against Chapter 11 claims (most notably in the Metalclad case), for the most part tribunals have chosen not to respond directly to such arguments.

Some civil society critics contend that the absence of a GATT-like justification provision, combined with the permissive language of Article 1114, means that NAFTA governments cannot defend against an investor claim on the basis that its actions were motivated by *bona fide* health or environmental concerns. The architecture of NAFTA does not compel this conclusion. Indeed such an interpretation is inconsistent with preambular language in NAFTA and with its environmental side agreement, both of which affirm that environmental protection and economic development should be mutually supportive. Nonetheless, it is highly uncertain whether in any given case legitimate, non-discriminatory environmental or public health measures will survive a Chapter 11 challenge.

Architectural concerns about the Chapter 11 are by no means assuaged by an examination of the jurisprudence that has emerged to date. This jurisprudence raises a host of concerns, including the extent to which Chapter 11 vests in tribunals the discretion to interpret its provisions in anomalous and inappropriate ways, and to ignore relevant legal arguments and evidence without meaningful appellate scrutiny.

When Chapter 11 came into force, it was generally believed that tribunals would interpret its provisions in a manner consistent with customary international law. To the surprise of many, recent rulings suggest that tribunals are interpreting its disciplines much more broadly. This phenomenon is illustrated by rulings in relation to Article 1105 (fair and equitable treatment) and Article 1110 (expropriation).

Within international law, the notion that a state owes a duty of fair and equitable treatment has, to date, been generally considered to provide foreign interests with a reasonable expectation that they will not suffer egregious abuses of state power. In Metalclad, however, the arbitral tribunal said that Article 1105 went much further. In its view, the article not only protected against egregious excesses but also imposed an affirmative 'transparency' obligation on host states to relieve investors of all legal uncertainties that might adversely affect their investments. In reaching this extraordinary conclusion, the tribunal imported into Chapter 11 'transparency' obligations articulated in distinct provisions in Chapter 18 of NAFTA (on publication, notification, and administration of laws), without offering any authority that 'transparency had become part of customary international law'.[6]

On judicial review, the tribunal's decision to transplant transparency obligations that were neither part of international law nor found in Chapter 11 was unequivocally rejected.[7] According to the review court, the tribunal's decision in this regard was not just legally wrong but so seriously wrong as to deprive the tribunal of jurisdiction. On the heels of this review, the NAFTA parties – through the Free

Trade Commission – sought to confirm the approach taken on review by issuing an interpretive statement aimed at precluding future tribunals from reading the article as creating state obligations beyond those found in international customary law (Tollefson 2002, 186). Despite this interpretive statement, however, in a subsequent decision a tribunal has sought to resurrect the approach to Article 1105 discredited by the review court in Metalclad, positing that it is not bound to 'accept ... whatever the Commission has stated to be an interpretation' if, in its wisdom, it deems the interpretation to amend the chapter.[8]

Tribunals have exhibited a similar willingness to embark on interpretive adventures in relation to Chapter 11's expropriation provisions. Under customary international law and under the domestic law of the NAFTA parties, it has generally been accepted that governments are entitled to take regulatory action that adversely affects the value of a property as long as they are acting in good faith. Thus, non-discriminatory local bylaws, taxation measures, and environmental laws that reduce a property's value are not normally considered to create a right to compensation unless such measures render the property entirely devoid of value (Tollefson 2002, 159–160). The standard rationale for this result is that to do otherwise would make it impossible for governments to carry out their legitimate functions and derogate seriously from domestic sovereignty (Johnson 1998, 224; Sornarajah 1994, 299–300).

Both in Metalclad and Pope & Talbot, however, tribunals took a radically different approach. According to these tribunals, the principle that governments are entitled to enact non-discriminatory regulation aimed at protecting the public interest without incurring an obligation to compensate affected property owners does not apply to claims under Chapter 11. Indeed, in Metalclad the tribunal insisted, without offering jurisprudential authority, that an obligation to compensate under Article 1105 arises whenever an investor suffers a 'covert or incidental interference with the use of property which has the effect of depriving the owner, in whole or in significant part, of the use or reasonably-to-be-expected economic benefit of property', regardless of whether the measure complained of benefits the host state.[9]

What is most striking about this formulation is that it purports to protect investors against measures in the nature of expropriation and also against any measures that interfere with property rights, regardless of the stated or actual purpose of such measures. This interpretation of the scope of the article has, not unexpectedly, generated significant controversy and is vulnerable to serious challenge in terms of its legal soundness and its ramifications for the fiscal capacity, political appetite, and legal ability of governments to regulate in the public interest (Tollefson 2002, 215).

The court charged with reviewing the decision in Metalclad was clearly mindful of the radical implications of the tribunal's interpretation of the scope and nature of Article 1110. It observed that the tribunal's definition of expropriation was 'extremely broad' and concluded that it would easily embrace 'legitimate rezoning of property by a municipality or other zoning authority'.[10] Nonetheless, the court concluded that it lacked jurisdiction to overrule the tribunal's purported definition as the legal correctness of this definition was a question of law and, as such, was immune from judicial review.

In these and other respects, the picture that emerges from the Chapter 11 jurisprudence is one that should rightly cause the NAFTA parties to be concerned, quite apart from how that jurisprudence has been received in civil society. In discharging their function, tribunals seem remarkably ready to push the interpretive envelope, offering decisions that go well beyond established norms of customary international law. Moreover, in the one instance where such a decision has come under judicial scrutiny, the reviewing court adopted a largely deferential attitude on the basis that such decisions should not be reviewed for their correctness in law, a posture that is in keeping with established norms surrounding private international arbitration. Furthermore, to the extent that the parties seek to clarify the applicable law through use of interpretive statements, there is reason to believe that their efforts may well be thwarted by the tribunals' power to characterise such clarifications as nonbinding amendments to Chapter 11.

Soloway suggests that Chapter 11 jurisprudence is a 'rather uneven patchwork'. However, she argues that the tribunals have, without exception, arrived at the correct result. But even by this generous standard, the jurisprudence to date does not pass muster. A careful analysis of the tribunal's decision in Metalclad strongly reinforces this impression.

Are Tribunals Getting It Right? The Troubling Case of Metalclad v. United Mexican States

Soloway characterises Metalclad as a case in which the American investor was subjected to 'high-handed and capricious' treatment by local authorities that insisted it secure a municipal construction permit before opening a hazardous waste landfill site. She further contends that the investor's rights were violated by a 'sham environmental measure' promulgated by the state government aimed at preventing the site from opening, 'despite the fact that it had been built in compliance with all applicable legal requirements'.

The actual facts of the case are much more complex, interesting, and, ultimately, troubling than Soloway suggests. Her depiction of the case appears to be based on the rather sparse set of facts recited in the arbitral tribunal's decision. Much of the academic commentary on this and other Chapter 11 cases has been similarly perfunctory and anecdotal (see Gaines 2002; Gantz 2001). A closer look at the evidence before the tribunal, particularly evidence submitted by the Government of Mexico but not addressed in the tribunal's decision, provides a strikingly different picture of the Metalclad story.[11]

The dispute centred on a proposal to build a hazardous waste disposal landfill in La Pedrera, a remote community in the municipality of Guadalcazar, located in the state of San Luis Potosi. The municipality is sparsely populated, impoverished, and largely desert-like. At all material times, the operation in question was owned by a Mexican company known as COTERIN. In 1990, COTERIN received federal approval to operate a hazardous waste transfer station in Guadalcazar. Contrary to the terms of this permit, it soon became apparent that COTERIN was illegally storing untreated hazardous waste in barrels that were left outside and exposed to the elements. Subsequent investigations by federal authorities and the Mexican Commission on Human Rights revealed that over 20 000 tonnes of waste (some 55 000 barrels) were being stored in this manner, giving rise to serious concerns about groundwater contamination. Just 18 months after the facility opened, the federal government therefore ordered COTERIN to cease operations and formally sealed the facility's entrance.

Over the next two years, COTERIN applied on two occasions to the municipality for permission to turn the transfer station into a hazardous waste landfill site. Local officials denied these applications, citing community opposition and the company's refusal to clean up pollution caused by the illegally stored waste.

In 1993, the owners of COTERIN were introduced to senior management of Metalclad by Humberto Rodarte Ramon, who was then a senior advisor to the head of Mexico's federal environmental authority. COTERIN and Metalclad subsequently negotiated a deal under which Metalclad obtained an option to purchase COTERIN once either local approval for the landfill had been received or a definitive judgement from the Mexican courts that such an approval was unnecessary had been secured. Upon completion of the deal, Rodarte stood to receive a commission from the vendor. In September 1993, even though neither of these conditions had been met, Metalclad exercised its option to purchase COTERIN, supposedly on the faith of representations made by Mexican officials, including Rodarte, that local approvals were unnecessary.

During 1994 and 1995, COTERIN proceeded with construction of the landfill facility, even though it had not secured a local construction permit. A protracted battle between the municipality and COTERIN ensued. In June and again in October of 1994, the local government issued stop-work orders, which were apparently ignored. While COTERIN managed to secure various federal and state approvals for the project, the local government continued to refuse to give its approval to the project on the basis of environmental concerns and COTERIN's refusal to address existing pollution issues.

In March 1995, with construction now completed, Metalclad sought to 'inaugurate' the site, even though it was still subject to the federal closure order issued in 1991. Demonstrations by locals at the facility's entrance ensued. When this closure order was lifted in early 1996, the municipality secured an injunction preventing the facility from receiving further waste until the site was remediated. Metalclad also went to court to challenge the municipality's right to reject its permit application. When this challenge was dismissed as having been filed in the wrong court, Metalclad commenced proceedings under Chapter 11.

While the arbitration of this claim was underway, the state governor issued an ecological decree that covered an area of almost 190 000 hectares, including the 814-hectare area on which the landfill was located (only 5 percent of which was to be used by landfill operations). The decree was based on scientific research that had been underway in the region dating back to the 1950s. This research suggested that the region possessed some of the highest concentrations of cactus species in the world, including several endemic and threatened species. The decree explicitly preserved existing permits and allowed new businesses to be established as long as sustainability of the cacti and compliance with all applicable laws and regulations were ensured.

In holding that the course of events prior to the decree constituted a violation of Metalclad's rights under Chapter 11, the tribunal made two key legal findings: that the federal government had assured Metalclad local approvals were unnecessary and that under Mexican law no such approvals were indeed necessary.

The only direct evidence from Mexican officials that Metalclad had been given such assurances were written statements by Rodarte who, by the time of the arbitration, had resigned from government and was working for a Metalclad subsidiary. Rodarte's version of events was vigorously disputed by testimony given by Mexican officials at the hearing. They contended that at no time had Metalclad been advised that local approvals were unnecessary. When Mexican government lawyers sought to cross-examine Rodarte on his written statements, they were told he was under criminal investigation for corruption and had exercised his right not to give evidence.[12]

The tribunal also heard considerable evidence with respect to whether, under Mexican law, local governments had a constitutional right to refuse to grant construction permits based on environmental considerations. In support of its contention that local governments possessed this jurisdiction, the Mexican government filed two legal opinions: one by the Institute of Legal Research of the Autonomous University of Mexico and the other prepared by two former justices of the Mexican Supreme Court and a senior Mexican legal scholar. The lead author of the report relied on by Metalclad was a University of Arizona law school graduate enrolled in a Master of Laws programme at a Mexican university. The tribunal also heard evidence that Metalclad had been informed in 1993 by its own Mexican lawyers that a municipal permit may be needed for construction.

The tribunal's ruling with respect to the decree also raises troubling questions about the manner in which it discharged its adjudicative and fact-finding functions. In determining that the decree constituted an unlawful expropriation, the tribunal concluded that the decree 'had the effect of barring forever the operation of the landfill'. This conclusion flies directly in the face of the express language of the decree, which preserved existing permits and authorisations and allowed for the establishment of new businesses as long as such enterprises did not compromise protection of the cactus species. Moreover, in its reasons the tribunal completely ignored the Mexican government's attempt to justify the decree by relying on Article 1114 that, as described earlier, purports to protect the right of host states to adopt any measure that it considers appropriate to ensure that investment activity in its territory is undertaken in a manner sensitive to environmental concerns.

Conclusion

Soloway suggests that it is 'hard to imagine' that Canadian regulators would 'be inhibited from proposing *bona fide* environmental regulation' due to concerns about Chapter 11 liabilities. Based on the Metalclad decision, the NAFTA architecture and the virtually unfettered and unreviewable discretion Chapter 11 vests in tribunals, on the contrary, it is difficult to imagine how they would not.

This said, some might argue that decisions such as Metalclad should be written off as unfortunate train wrecks on the rails to a more integrated, sustainable, and prosperous North America. However, whether ill-defined and open-ended investor protections move toward this goal remains very much an empirically questionable premise.[13] In the face of this uncertainty, it is important to be mindful of the democratic price of erecting and maintaining such sweeping protections. In the case of an unreformed Chapter 11, this price includes vesting in essentially unaccountable tribunals the authority to constitute themselves as courts of appeal with powers to adjudicate key domestic legal issues. This is precisely what occurred in Metalclad when the tribunal decided, as a matter of domestic Mexican law, that municipal governments have no right to insist that foreign investors address local environmental and public health concerns, even though this conclusion was strenuously disputed by the Mexican government.

In the face of widespread calls to clarify Chapter 11 and rein in the broad discretion it vests in tribunals, the Canadian government cannot simply sit back, as Soloway advocates, and wait for a 'solid case for reform' to be made. Indeed, the case for reform is already compelling and growing stronger. With negotiations for the Free Trade Agreement of the Americas (FTAA) underway and various new bilateral trade and investment treaties in the works, Canada has a significant stake in developing proposals aimed at ensuring that rules aimed at promoting trade and investment flows do not unnecessarily compromise domestic policy autonomy.

A highly instructive contribution to this debate comes from Michael Trebilcock. He argues for what he characterises as a 'relatively conservative view of the case for the harmonisation or convergence of domestic regulatory policies', an analysis that suggests one should view with considerable caution trade-related disciplines that go beyond the traditionally recognised duty not to discriminate (as reflected in the national treatment and most favoured nation treatment concepts) (see Chapter 12, notes 1, 2) To do otherwise, he contends, creates the potential that trade rules will undermine 'regulatory diversity', a concept that he considers synonymous with providing broad protection for 'domestic political sovereignty, distinctive policy preferences, and competitive and accountable governments'. He proceeds to argue that Chapter 11 imperils regulatory diversity by conferring on foreign investors far more than the right to complain about discriminatory state action. Indeed, as he points out, Article 1110 stands the national treatment discipline 'on its head' by requiring host countries to treat foreign investors 'more favourably than they are required to treat domestic producers whose investments may also be impaired by a change in regulatory policy'.

The imperative of focussing on options to reform Chapter 11 is also strongly suggested by developments in the United States. An American trade journal has reported that the Bush administration is developing new standards for future trade and investment agreements that elaborate, based on principles drawn from U.S. domestic law, in what circumstances foreign investors should be compensated for government regulatory action ('Administration Proposes Higher Thresholds for Investor Suits' 2002). These proposed expropriation standards are reported to be designed to achieve consistency with the objectives of the recently enacted federal trade promotion legislation, in particular its stipulation that foreign investor protections not exceed the rights of domestic investors under the U.S. Constitution.[14] The Bush administration is reportedly investigating options for incorporating these new principles into NAFTA.

Given the apparent momentum of the U.S. push to clarify Chapter 11 and the firmness of its commitment not to replicate it in future agreements, Canada can hardly sit on the sidelines of the growing debate about reforming Chapter 11 and, more broadly, rethinking the whole issue of investor rights. Equally, it would be short-sighted and inconsistent for Canada now to take the position that the provision does not need fixing. In fact, for some time now our senior trade representatives have been saying the opposite. For instance, in 2000, long before the current U.S. reform initiatives, as Minister of International Trade Pierre Pettigrew stated that Canada would not sign any new free trade deal – including the FTAA – that contains investor protections modelled on the language of Chapter 11 (Corcoran 2001; McKinnon 2000). Now is not the time for Canada to abandon either the cause of fixing Chapter 11 or the critical goal of achieving a better balance between investor rights and the domestic policy preferences.

Notes

1   The author wishes to acknowledge Nathaniel Amann-Blake, Andrew Newcombe, Cathie Parker, and Jamie Woods for their helpful comments on earlier versions of this chapter.

3   Throughout the Chapter 11 claim process, up to and including the arbitral award itself, the only mandatory public notification or disclosure occurs when the claimant is required to notify the NAFTA Secretariat of its desire to convene an arbitral panel. Upon receipt of this notice, the Secretariat must publish it on a public registry. See Tollefson (2002, 27).

3   An excellent primer on these issues is Howard Mann (2001).

4   Pope & Talbot, Inc. and the Government of Canada, NAFTA/UNCITRAL Tribunal, Award in Respect of Damages by Arbitral Tribunal (31 May 2002) <naftaclaims.com/ Disputes/Canada/Pope/PopeAwardOnDamages.pdf> (November 2005).

5   For an extended discussion of Article 1114, see Chris Tollefson (2002, 152–153). For a discussion of GATT's Article XX, see George Hoberg (2001) and Steve Charnovitz (2002, 92–101).

6 *United Mexican States v. Metalclad*, 2001 BCSC 664, Full Reasons for Judgement, 22 May 2001 <www.canadianliberty.bc.ca/nafta/mexico_vs_metalclad.html> (November 2005), para. 68.
7 Metalclad Judgement, para. 68.
8 Pope & Talbot Award, para. 23.
9 *Metalclad Corporation v. The United Mexican States*, Award [unreported, ICSID Case No. ARB (AF)/97/1 (30 August 2000), para. 103.
10 Metalclad Judgement, para. 99.
11 What follows is an attempt to offer a fuller account of the facts and evidence that were before the tribunal based on the author's review of briefs of argument submitted by the petitioner (the United Mexican States) and the respondent (Metalclad) in connection with the judicial review of the award heard by Mr. Justice Tysoe of the British Columbia Supreme Court. Additional background on the case can be found in Lucien Dhooge (2001).
12 Subsequent to the arbitration, while the case was under judicial review, Mexican lawyers led evidence that Rodarte's wife, Ratner, owned shares in a Mexican subsidiary of Metalclad two years before the latter purchased COTERIN. In 1993, Metalclad allowed her to exchange these shares for shares in Metalclad that were valued US$150 000, under an agreement that provided for further payments upon Metalclad receiving additional federal government approvals for its landfill operation. At the time, Rodarte was a special advisor to the president of the federal environmental permitting authority in Mexico City. The respondent did not dispute that the stock swap took place, but contends that at the time it was unaware that Ratner and Rodarte were married to one another.
13 For references to the literature on the welfare effects of harmonisation, see Chapter 12, note 4.
14 The *Bipartisan Trade Promotion Authority Act* of 2002, under which the U.S. president gained fast-track authority, provides *inter alia* that new trade agreements shall '[ensure] that foreign investors in the United States are not accorded greater substantive rights with respect to investment protections than United States investors in the United States'. See also Max Baucus (2004).

References

'Administration Proposes Higher Thresholds for Investor Suits' (2002). *Inside U.S. Trade* no. 20, 39, 27 September.

Appleton, Barry (1994). *Navigating NAFTA: A Concise User's Guide to the North American Free Trade Agreement.* Carswell Publishing, Toronto.

Baucus, Max (2004). 'Statement of Senator Max Baucus: Markup of Fast Track Legislation'. Washington DC, 12 December. <finance.senate.gov/hearings/statements/121201mb.pdf> (November 2005).

Charnovitz, Steve (2002). 'The Law of "PPMs" in the WTO: Debunking the Myth of Illegality'. *Yale Journal of International Law* vol. 27, no. 1, pp. 59–110.

Corcoran, Terence (2001). 'Ottawa's Campaign to Sabotage NAFTA'. *Financial Post*, 23 February, p. C14.

Dhooge, Lucien J. (2001). 'The North American Free Trade Agreement and the Environment: The Lessons of Metalclad Corporation v. United Mexican States'. *Minnesota Journal of Global Trade* vol. 10, no. 1, pp. 209–289.

Gaines, Sanford E. (2002). 'The Masked Ball of NAFTA Chapter 11: Foreign Investors, Local Environmentalists, Government Officials, and Disguised Motives'. In J.J. Kirton and V. Maclaren, eds., *Linking Trade, Environment, and Social Cohesion: NAFTA Experiences, Global Challenges*, pp. 103–130. Ashgate, Aldershot.

Gantz, David A. (2001). 'Reconciling Environmental Protection and Investor Rights Under Chapter 11 of NAFTA'. *Environmental Law Reporter* vol. 31, no. 7, pp. 10 646–610 668.

General Agreement on Tariffs and Trade (1947). 'The General Agreement on Tariffs and Trade'. <www.wto.org/english/docs_e/legal_e/gatt47_01_e.htm> (November 2005).

Hoberg, George (2001). 'Trade Harmonization and Domestic Autonomy in Environmental Policy'. *Journal of Comparative Policy Analysis* vol. 3, no. 2, pp. 191–217.

Johnson, Jon R. (1998). *International Trade Law*. Irwin Law, Toronto.

Mann, Howard (2001). *Private Rights, Public Problems: A Guide to NAFTA's Controversial Chapter on Investors Rights*. International Institute on Sustainable Development and World Wildlife Fund, Winnipeg. <www.iisd.org/pdf/trade_citizensguide.pdf> (November 2005).

McKinnon, Mark (2000). 'Canada Seeks Review of NAFTA's Chapter 11'. *Globe and Mail*, 13 December, p. B1.

NAFTA Secretariat (1994). 'North American Free Trade Agreement'. <www.nafta-sec-alena. org> (November 2005).

Schwanen, Daniel (2002). 'Commentary'. In L.R. Dawson, ed., *Whose Rights? The NAFTA Chapter 11 Debate*. Centre for Trade Policy and Law, Ottawa.

Sornarajah, M. (1994). *The International Law on Foreign Investment*. Cambridge University Press, Cambridge.

Tollefson, Chris (2002). 'Metalclad v. United Mexican States Revisited: Judicial Oversight of NAFTA's Chapter Eleven Investor-State Claim Process'. *Minnesota Journal of Global Trade* vol. 11, no. 1, pp. 183–234.

Tollefson, Chris (2002). 'Games without Frontiers: Investor Claims and Citizen Submissions under the NAFTA Regime'. *Yale Journal of International Law* vol. 27, no. 1, pp. 141–191.

PART IV
THE MULTILATERAL TRADE
AND FINANCE SYSTEM

Chapter 11

What Are the Necessary Ingredients for the World Trading Order?

Sylvia Ostry

What are the necessary ingredients for the effective operation of the world trading order? The short answer is leadership. While this is often the answer to many such questions, the world trading system is in dire need of reform. And the reformers – if they exist – are nowhere to be seen, either in Geneva or national capitals. The stakes are high, no less than the sustainability of the rules-based multilateral system.

This chapter begins with a brief overview of the background to the formidable challenges that face the institution that houses the trading system, the World Trade Organization (WTO). These challenges arise from the unintended consequences of the previous Uruguay Round of multilateral trade liberalisation negotiations, as compounded by the Doha negotiations. The chapter then turns to the issue of reform of the WTO. It offers some suggestions to improve both the WTO's internal functioning and its external relations with stakeholders.

The Political Economy of Trade Policy Making

The Uruguay Round was the eighth negotiation under the auspices of the General Agreement on Tariffs and Trade (GATT), created in 1948 as part of the post-war international economic architecture. The primary mission of GATT was to reduce or eliminate the border barriers that had been erected in the 1930s and contributed to the Great Depression and its disastrous consequences. The GATT reflected its origins in the post-war world in that it provided rules to buffer or interface between the international objective of sustained liberalisation and the objectives of domestic policy, primarily the Keynesian consensus on full employment and the creation of the welfare state. This accord was reached with little difficulty since few countries were involved. They were almost all developed countries. They could thus operate as a 'club' whose members broadly shared basic norms and values with respect to trade (Keohane and Nye 2001).

Before the Uruguay Round from 1986 to 1994, the GATT club worked very well. Tariffs and non-tariff barriers were significantly reduced. Trade grew faster than world output as each fed the other. Most rounds were essentially managed by the United States and the European Community. The developing countries, as players, were largely ignored. Agriculture was virtually excluded from negotiations. The transatlantic alliance, helped by the Cold War's constraint on trade frictions, was the effective manager of the international trading system.

The Uruguay Round was a watershed in the evolution of that system. For the first time, agriculture was at the centre of the negotiations. The European effort to block the launch of the negotiations to avoid coming to grips with its heavily subsidised and protected Common Agricultural Policy (CAP) went on for half a decade. This foot-dragging also spawned a new single-interest coalition – the Australian-led Cairns Group. It included Southern countries from Latin America and Asia. They were determined to ensure that liberalisation of agricultural trade would not be relegated to the periphery by the Americans and the Europeans, as it always had in the past.

But the role of a group of developing countries, tagged the G10 hardliners and led by Brazil and India, was in many ways even more important in the Uruguay Round's transformation of the system. The G10 were bitterly opposed to the inclusion of the so-called 'new issues' – trade in services, intellectual property, and investment – central to the American negotiating agenda.

Those so-called new issues are not identical – obviously negotiations on telecommunications or financial services differ from intellectual property rights. But they do have one common or generic characteristic. They involve not the border barriers of concern to the original GATT but domestic regulatory and legal systems embedded in the institutional infrastructure of the national economy. This deep degree of intrusiveness into domestic sovereignty bears little resemblance to the shallow integration of the GATT with its focus on border barriers and its buffers to safeguard domestic policy space. The WTO, created in 1994 at the end of the Uruguay Round, thus shifted from the GATT model of negative regulation – what governments must not do – to positive regulation – or what governments must do.

The inclusion of the new issues in the Uruguay Round was an American initiative. This policy agenda was largely driven by American multinational corporations (MNCs) that were market leaders in the services and high technology sectors. These corporations made it clear to the U.S. government that without a fundamental rebalancing of the GATT they would not continue to support a multilateral policy but would prefer a bilateral or regional track. But they did not just 'talk the talk'. They also 'walked the walk'. They organised business coalitions in support of services and intellectual property in Europe and Japan as well as some smaller members of the Organisation for Economic Co-operation and Development (OECD). The activism paid off. American MNCs played a key – perhaps even *the* key – role in establishing the new global trading system.

By the onset of the 1990s, a major change in economic policy was underway. The debt crisis of the 1980s and thus the new role of the International Monetary Fund (IMF) and the World Bank, plus the fall of the Berlin Wall, ushered in a major transformation in the economic policy paradigm of developing countries. Economic reforms – deregulation, privatisation, liberalisation – were now seen as essential elements for launching and sustaining growth. Economic regulatory reform is at the heart of the concept of trade in services. Even without the thrust from the Uruguay

Round, many developing countries began to see reform of key service sectors such as telecommunications as essential building blocks in the soft infrastructure underpinning growth. They saw the GATT as a means to further domestic reform.

Thus, well before the end of the Uruguay Round the hard-line coalition had disappeared. Coalitions of developing countries concentrated on liberalisation of agriculture and textiles and clothing. They were among the strongest supporters of the negotiations they had so adamantly opposed in the 1980s. A 'North-South Grand Bargain' was completed. It was quite different from the old-time GATT reciprocity of 'I'll open my market if you'll open yours'. It was essentially an implicit deal: the opening of the OECD markets to agriculture and labour-intensive manufactured goods, especially textiles and clothing, for the inclusion in the trading system of trade in services, intellectual property, and (albeit to a lesser extent than originally demanded) investment. Also – as virtually a last-minute piece of the deal – came the creation of a new institution, the WTO. It contained the strongest dispute settlement mechanism in the history of international law. Since the WTO consisted of a 'single undertaking', the deal was pretty much 'take it or leave it' for the Southern countries. So they took it, but without a full comprehension of the profoundly transformative implication of this new trading system. This incomprehension was shared by the Northern negotiators as well.

The Northern piece of the bargain consisted of some limited progress in agriculture, with a commitment to go further in new negotiations in 2000; limited progress in textiles and clothing with most of the restrictions to be eliminated later rather than sooner; and a rather significant reduction in tariffs on goods in exchange for deeper cuts by developing countries. The essence of the South side of the deal – the inclusion of the new issues – requires major upgrading and change in the institutional infrastructure of many or most Southern countries. These changes will take time and cost money. Implementation thus involves considerable investment often with uncertain medium-term results.

It is also important to note that the Uruguay Round Grand Bargain included not only economic but also social regulation. In the OECD countries, but not the South, social regulation on environment, food safety, labour, and similar issues had started in the late 1960s. It was driven in large part by environmental and consumer nongovernmental organisations (NGOs) and has been accelerating since then. Since the establishment of the WTO the most high-profile and contentious disputes have concerned social regulatory issues, especially on food safety and the environment. These are very sensitive in the OECD countries. This has emboldened the NGOs in their attack on the WTO's lack of transparency.

There were two significant unintended consequences to this Grand Bargain (or Bum Deal). One is a serious North-South divide in the WTO. While the South is hardly homogeneous, there is a broad consensus that the club model is no longer operational, that the asymmetry of the Uruguay Round must be ameliorated and must never be repeated, and thus that Southern countries must play a far more proactive role in all WTO activities. This was evident at the launch of the Doha negotiations. Many of the Southern countries are far better organised and informed, in part because of the rise of democracy and the growing awareness of trade policy issues in the general public and political institutions and the business community. But another cause is the role of a number of NGOs created in developing countries during the 1990s to provide information ranging from technical research to policy strategy papers. And since the mid 1990s the internet has accelerated the linkages of Southern NGOs with a number of Northern partners in both Europe and the U.S. These NGOs together act, in effect, as a 'virtual secretariat'.

The other, and equally important, unintended consequence of the Uruguay Round has been the rise in profile of the MNCs. This is in part due to their role in the round. Indeed, for the more paranoid the round was simply a conspiratorial collusion between American corporations and the U.S. government. In any case, the global current of deepening integration, accelerated by the Uruguay Round, evoked a counter-current focused both on the MNCs and the WTO.

In regard to the MNCs, the active role of the corporations in the Uruguay Round certainly raised their profile. It made them a magnet for anti-trade advocates and made the WTO a magnet for what came to be called anti-corporate globalisation. This was evident to anyone who watched the 'battle of Seattle' in late 1999 or the demonstrations at high-level international economic meetings in Washington or Prague or Genoa or Quebec City that followed.

But the most significant case concerns the pharmaceutical industry and the HIV/AIDS crisis in Africa. As a result of a well-orchestrated campaign led by Oxfam and Médecins Sans Frontières, pharmaceutical companies withdrew a lawsuit against South Africa, the U.S. abandoned a dispute against Brazil, and the Doha declaration included a remarkable political statement concerning the Agreement on Trade-Related Aspects of Intellectual Property Rights (TRIPS) and health emergencies.

The rise in the profile of the MNCs in the Uruguay Round helped make the WTO a magnet for anti-corporate globalisation. To be sure, there is no homogeneous set of institutions called NGOs. This is the case even if development groups in poor countries are separated from advocacy NGOs, whose main objective is to shape policy, for one must still divide the latter into several categories. For example, along with the new virtual secretariat for Southern countries, there has been a remarkable proliferation of groups centred on establishing business codes of conduct. There are also groups rich in technical and legal expertise that usually consult 'inside' the system.

All of these are rather different from the mobilisation networks, for which a major objective is to rally support for dissent at a specific event – a WTO ministerial meeting, the Summit of the Americas, a meeting of the World Bank and IMF, or the G8 summit. The main objectives of the mobilisation networks are to heighten public awareness of the target international institution's role in globalisation and, by doing so, to change its agenda and mode of operation – or, in the case of the more extreme members, to shut it down. While these networks are loosely knit coalitions of very disparate groups, an analysis of the networks at Seattle (in 1999), Washington, Bangkok, and Prague (in 2000), and Quebec City, Genoa, and Doha (in 2001) shows that there is a core group – what might be called 'dissent.com' – of mainly North

American and European NGOs but also including some from developing countries. These NGOs are headed by a new breed of policy entrepreneurs who have very effectively used the internet to create what could be termed a new service industry – the business of dissent. The dissent industry is largely a product of the internet revolution that provides advocacy NGOs with economies of scale and also of scope by linking widely disparate groups with one common theme: anti-corporate globalisation and pro-democracy. The main charge is that the WTO is dominated by the interests of the MNCs and that its rules and procedures are secretive and undemocratic.

Of course, individual members of these networks pursue many other advocacy routes including lobbying (greatly aided by the media) as a means of influencing national governments. But the strategy of the networks to focus on demonstrations at specific events was designed to influence public opinion and through that route initiate change in the policy processes of the international institutions. Has the dissent industry been successful? In the case of the WTO, while it is too early to tell fully, there has been an impact on the agenda. The emphasis on development as the core of the new Doha Round (or, rather, the 'development agenda') and the political statement on health emergencies in poor countries were both probably in part due to a shift in emphasis by NGOs to issues with strong moral resonance. The NGOs' consistent and insistent refrain of lack of transparency has, for some, struck at the heart of the WTO's legitimacy.

But the shift in NGO strategy was essential for other reasons. While there was destruction of property in Seattle and other meetings, there was nothing comparable to the 2001 G8 Summit at Genoa where one protestor was killed. A number of mainline NGOs stayed away from Genoa because they were fearful of being associated with the violence planned by the anarchist Black Bloc and neo-fascists. Although no one could have foreseen what took place, including the extraordinary brutality of the police, there is probably an inevitable tendency for all demonstrations to attract extremists. They offer a free ride that is hard to decline. Escalating violence generates the need for more police security, which likewise generates more violence and attracts more extremists. Genoa was hardly the end of the story.

The terrorist attack of 11 September 2001, while unrelated to the antiglobalisation movement *per se*, greatly added to the pressure for dissent.com to adopt a new strategy and changes are underway. In the U.S., attempts of the left to change into a peace movement – centred on attacking the war against terrorism and American support of Israel – is not attracting mainline NGOs or the labour unions. The April 2002 meetings of the IMF and the World Bank in Washington attracted few demonstrators. Those who marched and chanted were ignored by the media. But the impact of the NGO campaign on global health, as exemplified by the Doha declaration, may also be a signal of a new shift in strategy from dissent to dialogue. A report released by Oxfam International (2002) entitled 'Rigged Rules and Double Standards' asserted that international trade can benefit the poor if the rich countries would reduce their protectionist barriers, especially in agriculture and labour-intensive products. It then elaborates on a range of policy proposals. The report has been attacked by some NGOs that still prefer dissent to dialogue but welcomed as a basis for discussion by some governments and international institutions. It is too early to tell whether these examples – in effect centred on alleviating third world poverty and disease – will serve to unify or re-create the antiglobalisation movement. In any case, the name now appears to be 'the global justice movement'. It is also premature to declare that the movement died after September 11, as did a *Wall Street Journal* editorial headline 'Adieu Seattle'.[1] A new headline could perhaps be 'Bonjour Cancun'.

In sum, the Uruguay Round and its unintended consequences transformed the multilateral trading system and the political economy of policy making. The round initiated one small step in the creation of a global single market – a step for which a majority of its members were totally unprepared. The intrusiveness of the new system touched the exposed raw nerve of sovereignty. And yet, to undertake the formidable role of housing and sustaining the system, the negotiations produced a minimalist, member-driven institution with extremely weak legislative and executive powers and an extremely strong, judicialised dispute settlement system. This is an asymmetry that must be rectified. Clearly, the system is in dire need of reform.

Doha, Cancun, and the New Geography

Given the serious North-South divide engendered by the Uruguay Round it is more than symbolic that the outcome of the ministerial meeting in Doha, Qatar, in 2001 was termed a 'development agenda'. The main objective of Doha was to avoid another Seattle: thus its great success was that it did not fail. Both the EU and the U.S. visited Africa to woo ministers, and the declaration repeatedly refers to technical assistance and capacity building. As noted earlier, pushed by the successful NGO campaign about HIV/AIDS in Africa, the Americans even seemed willing to antagonise the big pharmaceutical industries. So Doha was unique in its focus on the South and development. But, of course, there were many other items on the Doha agenda, including agriculture and the so-called Singapore issues of competition, investment, government procurement, and trade facilitation. And – most important – the Doha declaration was a masterpiece of creative ambiguity. Too clever by half, one might say. The devil remained in the details of the negotiations. They went nowhere. All deadlines were missed. And that brings us to Cancun.

For the veterans of trade negotiations, the abrupt ending of the ministerial meeting at Cancun, Mexico, in September 2003 brought a strong sense of *déjà vu* all over again. Cancun was a mid-term ministerial, as was the 1988 meeting in Montreal during the Uruguay Round. On the last morning of the Montreal meeting, at around six in the morning, the bleary-eyed negotiators were waiting for the arrival of the EC and U.S. warriors, who had been up all night dealing with agriculture. When they arrived, they announced that it was too bad but they had not reached an agreement, so the negotiators should tidy up the other agenda items and finish the communiqué. A group of Latin American countries headed by Brazil said no: no agriculture, no agreement on anything. It was a moment of shock (and maybe awe for some others), but it was handled with great finesse by announcing that the meeting was adjourned and would be reconvened shortly in Geneva. No big headlines ensued.

In any case the *déjà vu* feeling at Cancun soon dissipated. The North-South divide had taken a different shape. There appeared to be an axial shift in the political economy of policy making that would require a fundamental reorientation of the players and the game. Two new coalitions of Southern countries were formed at Cancun. One, termed the G20, led by Brazil and India as well as China (the Big Three) and South Africa, included several Latin American countries. Its main focus at Cancun was agriculture, catalysed by an unacceptable draft proposal from the U.S. and EU. The G20 seemed an unlikely coalition since it included countries with varying views on economic policy and, indeed, on agriculture. But it did not collapse under pressure at Cancun and, despite losing members because of American bilateral pressure, it has survived thus far. And it or its leader, Brazil, has succeeded in challenging the Free Trade Agreement of the Americas (FTAA) to the chagrin of the U.S. Indeed, India and China are now exploring a free trade agreement, as are India and Mercosur.

The G20 was very active at the United Nations Conference on Trade and Development (UNCTAD) at Sao Paulo in June 2004 and, indeed, at that meeting a South-South round of negotiations was launched under special provisions of the original GATT, in which developing countries provided trade preferences for products from other developing countries. This was underlined as another example of the 'new geography' of the trading system by UNCTAD head Rubens Ricupero and the Brazilian president Luiz Inacio Lula da Silva.

Indeed, the new geography was evident at Cancun in the formation of another coalition – the G90. This included the poorest developing countries, mainly from Africa. After failing to convince the U.S. to eliminate cotton subsidies to help the poverty-stricken African exporters and to persuade the EU to remove the Singapore issues from the agenda, the G90 terminated the negotiations. It is important to note that at Cancun NGOs played a prominent role with respect to the G90. African NGOs were included in many official delegations and they provided ongoing information as well as research and policy analysis. They had regular briefing sessions from officials and ministers. This could also be part of the new geography. But unfortunately there is not enough information to explore this important development in more depth.

The formation of Southern coalitions will undoubtedly change the dynamics of the Doha negotiations, especially but not only on agriculture. But the outcome at present is shrouded in a fog of uncertainty. The G20 was actively engaged in the bargaining over a 'framework' agreement (a broad outline with minimal detail) before the 2004 summer break. This would, it is assumed, allow the real negotiations to start after the U.S. election later that fall and be concluded just a year later than the target date set at Doha. But there remained genuine concern about the future of the global system. There will not be another agriculture deal by the Big Two (U.S. and the EU) without the Big Three and perhaps the G90 as well. Indeed, splits between the G90 and other developing countries are being encouraged by the rich countries. The geography certainly makes trade policy more complex. Both the U.S. and the EU are using bilateralism and other policy instruments to weaken the G20 and provoke conflict with the G90.

Thus the new geography could result in transforming trade into a zero sum game. By blocking consensus, the G20 and Big Three can both exert power, but for what purpose? The G20 includes countries with considerable soft infrastructure, and the proliferation of NGOs and a more active UNCTAD are able to provide knowledge and policy analysis. But there is no evidence of a significant capability to exploit the power shift by generating a coherent flexible strategy. Unlike the situation for rich countries, there is no OECD. The strategic assets of that institution – that is, its soft power in the form of research capabilities, both governmental and nongovernmental, and diffused through meetings, conferences, publications, and so on – are essential for developing consensus on policy strategies through debate, dialogue, and peer group pressure. There is thus a fundamental asymmetry in the global system that goes beyond the structure and content of the WTO and reflects the established structure of the world. It will not remain that way forever, but it will take a long time to reconfigure. Nonetheless, while some grand new vision of global governance is hardly worth discussion, some important reform may be possible.

The World Trade Organization: Suggestions for Reform

While the subject of WTO reform has recently evoked some interest in the academic community, the same is not true in national capitals or in Geneva. After Seattle, there was some desultory discussion on internal and external transparency. This is 'WTO-speak' for internal reform to make the governance of the institution more open and inclusive and external reform including more access to information and more opportunity for stakeholder participation. After a few meetings of the General Council that revealed strong opposition from many member countries – especially Southern – even to discussing the issues, the subject was dropped. After Doha, the General Council, after four years of deliberation, agreed on a set of procedures to de-restrict documents and discussed some proposals for ministerial preparatory processes and meetings. These, if adopted, could impose a straitjacket on the consultation process and might 'drive the real negotiations underground and ultimately lead to a less transparent procedure' (WTO 2002a; International Centre for Trade and Sustainable Development 2002, 3). In any case nothing was agreed.

The WTO's executive (management) and legislative functions are extremely weak, especially when compared with its judicial procedures. This asymmetry in architectural design is grossly inappropriate to the broad and complex mandate imposed by the Uruguay Round. While there is no possibility of major institutional redesign in the foreseeable future, some modest incremental reform should not be ruled out. In this regard three priorities should be considered. The first two concern internal functions and the third deals with external transparency.

How Can the World Trade Organization Be Managed?

Both the Bretton Woods institutions of the IMF and World Bank included weighted voting, in order to ensure that the economic power of the U.S. and the UK – the founders – would be reflected in both policy and management in the finance field. This was not the case in the International Trade Organization (ITO) – the proposed institution in the trade field. This apparent anomaly stemmed from the U.S. view that since in the trade regime other countries had to implement the outcome of negotiations, it was better to adopt a consensus approach that, in the then small club of 23 members, would not be difficult to achieve. But to ensure effective management and avoid paralysis by consensus, the ITO charter included an executive board. The executive board was to consist of 18 members, with broad geographic representation. It should include 'Members of chief economic importance, in the determination of which particular regard shall be paid to their shares in international trade' (ITO 1948, art. 78).[2] There was provision for the rotation every three years of the ten members who were not classified as 'of chief economic importance'. The executive board was to be responsible 'for the execution of the policies of the Organization' (ITO 1948, art. 81).

When the ITO died and the GATT became the home of the multilateral trading system, the ITO charter became defunct. The WTO, its successor – with more than 148 members in 2005 and likely to reach over 170 in the near future – did not provide for an executive board. Indeed, if anything, the WTO rules provide less room for flexibility that did the GATT.

Article 9(1) of the WTO Agreement provides for 'the practice of decision-making by consensus followed under GATT 1947' (WTO 1994a). This 'consensus' (the word did not appear in the ITO charter or the GATT) has been 'elevated from its previous status as an unwritten practice to being enshrined as a rule' (Steger 2000, 153). And, as one WTO legal expert has noted, new rules were added which, *inter alia*, make decision making and amendments of the agreement 'considerably more complex than the previous GATT provisions' (Steger 2000, 151; see also Bronckers 1999). There was thus more flexibility for the Club of 23 than the diverse and often conflictual Coterie of 144, soon to climb to 170!

As the negotiations on Doha proceed, the examples of decision-making paralysis concerning even the most trivial matters are growing apace. There has been some informal discussion on how, for example, to separate out housekeeping operations from substantive issues. It is unlikely to yield results anytime soon, however, although if paralysis and bickering get bad enough perhaps reason may eventually prevail. Mike Moore, Director General of the WTO, raised the issue for discussion in his speech to the Public Symposium on the Doha Development Agenda in Geneva at the end of April 2002: 'How are we going to respect the "consensus principle" in about five years time when the organization will account for more than 170 Member governments? … shouldn't we soon start to discuss the need for some sort of managerial structure capable of taking care of the day-to-day business of the WTO?'

(WTO 2002b). It is worth noting that these questions are answered by a proposal made in a joint statement on the multilateral trading system in February 2001 by three former heads of GATT/WTO: Arthur Dunkel, Peter Sutherland, and Renato Ruggiero.

These former directors general proposed establishing 'management board which could take routine decisions not affecting members' rights' (not unlike an executive board but with a more politically correct title) (WTO 2001). Their proposal was intended to be included in the Doha agenda. It was not. They also made a second proposal that a 'senior level policy consultancy group' be established to debate current trade issues in a 'wider policy context'. This reads like a reformulated version of a policy forum – the CG18 (Consultative Group of Eighteen) – established in the GATT in 1975. A policy forum is essential if the WTO liberalisation momentum is to be sustained. A brief sketch of the history and function of the CG18 will help explain why this is so.

Policy Forum: CG18 Redux

A policy forum would provide the locus for discussion and debate of basic issues – such as the definition of domestic policy space to be safeguarded in the international system. The GATT implicitly defined a domestic policy space in a number of ways: an escape clause; Article 20 that spelled out exceptions to GATT rules for public policy objectives; a national security exemption; a balance of payments exception, among other things (Jackson 1997, 203–216). But these mechanisms designed to protect domestic sovereignty reflect the shared views of the Club in 1948 and obviously need to be reconsidered and redefined. This will, of course, hardly be easy. There is no longer a consensus, of a Keynesian, Washington or whatever kind. The only way to grapple with this most fundamental issue is through debate informed by policy-analytical research. There are a number of other examples of policy-related concerns: the relationship among trade, growth, and poverty; the effectiveness of capacity building in mainstreaming trade in development; the implications of neo-institutional economics for development; the improvement of international coherence in policy making; and the links between the trading rules and environmental rules. Then policy options could be proposed and, if a consensus is achieved, the proposal would be sent to the General Council, the governing arm of the institution. There was, indeed, such a forum in the GATT, which was the CG18. Was the number an echo of the ITO? But an attempt to establish a successor at the end of the Uruguay Round failed.

The CG18 was established in July 1975 not by trade ministries but as a result of a recommendation of the Committee of 20 Finance Ministers after the breakdown of Bretton Woods. The Committee of 20 also established the IMF's Interim Committee. The CG18's purpose was to provide a forum for senior officials from capitals to discuss policy issues and not, in any way, to challenge the authority of the GATT council. Because of the creation of the Interim Committee, the Committee of 20 felt the need for a similar body in the GATT to facilitate international coordination between the two institutions. The composition of the membership was based on a combination of economic weight and regional representation. But there was provision for other countries to attend as alternates and observers or by invitation. Each meeting was followed by a comprehensive report to the GATT Council.

Because it was a forum for senior officials from national capitals, it provided an opportunity to improve coordination of policies at the home base. This is now far more important because of the expansion of subjects under the WTO. Indeed there is no 'minister of trade' today but a number of ministries with concerns covered by the WTO. After the Tokyo Round, the CG18 was the only forum in the GATT where agriculture was discussed. In the long lead-up to the Uruguay Round, it was the only place that dealt with trade in services. The CG18 was the only forum for a full, wide-ranging, often contentious debate on the basic issues of the Uruguay Round. There was an opportunity to analyse and explain issues without a commitment to specific negotiating positions. Negotiating committees inhibit discussion because rules are at stake. Words matter and might be used, for example, in a dispute settlement ruling, as was a report by the Committee on Trade and the Environment (CTE) with a predictable chilling effect on constructive dialogue. Thus the absence of direct linkage to rules is essential to the diffusion of knowledge that rests on a degree of informality, flexibility, and adaptability.

Although establishing the policy forum would be a great step forward, it is unlikely to function effectively without an increase in the WTO's research capability. Analytical papers on key issues are needed to launch serious discussions in Geneva and to improve the diffusion of knowledge in national capitals. If it is to keep up to date and reasonably small in size, the WTO could not possibly generate all its policy analysis in-house. The WTO secretariat would have to establish a research network linked to other institutions. This knowledge networking should include academic, environmental, business, labour, and intergovernmental organisations such as the OECD, UNCTAD, the Bretton Woods institutions, and environmental institutions. Moreover, establishing a research or knowledge network can enhance the ability of the WTO director general to play a more effective role in leading and guiding the policy debate. This will be politically contentious but is essential. The 1980s debt crisis would have been quite a different situation had the head of the IMF had the authority of the head of the GATT. There would have been a series of meetings to discuss meetings while Latin America went down the drain.

In the terminology of the international regime literature, the policy forum would become a broad meta-regime founded on mutually agreed basic principles and fostered by a combination of strategic assets: a knowledge infrastructure in the form of a research capability; a meeting infrastructure for knowledge diffusion, debate, peer group pressure; and strategic planning and monitoring of policy performance. But it would have no hard power to make rules.

A key difficulty in establishing the forum would be to determine the membership. One formula already exists in the former CG18, which was never officially terminated. But it would probably be necessary to include the policy forum as part of a North-

South tradeoff. And that would require the big powers to agree that institutional reform was essential to the sustainability of the system. The *raison d'être* of the forum would be to inform, energise, and facilitate the rule-making capability of the WTO. Perhaps members should be reminded that there is another route to change, namely litigation. Being faced with that alternative might clarify some minds.

The second place where reform is needed is the dispute settlement system. This is also a matter of high priority. But here a number of recent proposals have generated a healthy debate, which need not be added to here. (An excellent source for information is the *Journal of International Economic Law*, which was launched shortly after the WTO was established.)

External Transparency

The third place where reform is needed relates to external transparency. The demand for greater transparency at the WTO has continued unabated since its establishment. It is now gaining broad support. The WTO has responded by providing information, speedily and effectively on its website, through informal secretariat briefings, and by engaging civil society groups in annual symposia and, in the case of the CTE, in discussion. But even these efforts have been opposed by a number of Southern countries.

Curiously, the issue of transparency and the participation at the national level has only recently been raised. The 'Open Letter on Institutional Reforms in the WTO' sent by a group of NGOs to members in October 2001 (just before the Doha ministerial meeting) included the 'development of guidelines for national consultation with relevant stakeholders' among a number of other proposals (World Wildlife Foundation *et al.* 2001).[3] Since reform issues were not on the table in Doha, there was no response. A similar silence greeted U.S. efforts, after the Seattle debacle in 1999, to discuss national policy processes in the WTO.

Yet the WTO may be an outlier in its rejection of the relevance of this issue. It is useful to use other institutions as a benchmark in the rapidly evolving international policy environment, for in a globalising world 'policy spillover' has become increasingly significant. A review of developments in the OECD and in international environmental and human rights law show how.

OECD: Transparency, Trade, Environment, and Development

In 1993, the OECD Joint Working Party on Trade and Environment proposed that 'Transparency and Consultation' be established as a principle of policy making in this domain. That this innovation in governance involved environmental policies was hardly a coincidence. The proposal was adopted by ministers, as was the initiative to undertake case studies of member governments' consultative mechanisms and practices. These case studies were published in 1999 and 2000 (OECD 1999; 2000b; 2000a). They revealed a wide diversity among the countries reflecting, *inter alia*, culture, history, and legal systems. They also underscored the importance of capacity – analytical and financial resources – as a factor in determining the nature of the process.

In July 2001, the OECD directorate responsible for research in public management (PUMA) published a policy brief outlining a number of principles for good governance. The title of the brief was 'Engaging Citizens in Policy-Making: Information, Consultation, and Public Participation' (OECD 2001). The lead paragraph provides the rationale for the initiative:

> Strengthening relations with citizens is a sound investment in better policy-making and a core element of good governance. It allows governments to tap new sources of policy-relevant ideas, information and resources when making decisions. Equally important, it contributes to building public trust in government, raising the quality of democracy and strengthening civic capacity. Such efforts help strengthen representative democracy, in which parliaments play a central role.

The reference to building public trust and enhancing the credibility of governments is of key significance in catalysing the OECD initiative and of particular relevance in the trade policy domain. The antiglobalisation movement reflects a more pervasive secular change underway since the mid 1970s in all OECD countries: a clear, marked decline in confidence in government and all political institutions (Ostry 2001a). (While in the U.S., the events of 11 September 2001 radically reversed this trend, it is not clear how this will affect, if at all, international economic policy.) There is less information on this phenomenon in non-OECD countries. But anecdotal evidence suggests that an alienation from the elite is growing in many Southern countries and in Central and Eastern Europe. This is likely to increase if the trade negotiations are seriously impaired by the U.S. farm bill given that agriculture is so dominant in these countries.

There are many different views on the reasons for this worrisome phenomenon. No doubt different factors are operative in different countries. But one response – and not only by the OECD – has been to foster 'ownership' of the policy process by increasing information, consultation, and active participation by a wider range of stakeholders. As the case studies and other OECD research have demonstrated, although information access has increased over the past decade, there are large differences in consultation. And 'active participation and efforts to engage citizens in policy-making ... are rare ... and confined to a very few OECD countries' (OECD 2001, 2). What follows in the brief are a number of policy suggestions and a set of ten guiding principles for OECD governments to engage citizens in policy making (OECD 2001, 5). While these principles are not binding on OECD governments – being a form of soft law – their adoption by ministers is not without significance.

The Aarhus Convention

The United Nations Economic Commission for Europe (UNECE) Convention on Access to Information, Public Participation in Decision-Making, and Access to Justice in Environmental Matters was adopted on 25 June 1998 in the Danish city of Aarhus at the Fourth Ministerial Conference of the 'Environment for Europe' process. It entered into force on 30 October 2001 with 40 signatories, including members of the Economic Commission for Europe as well as states with consultative status with that body (mainly Central and Eastern European countries) and the European Community. This move to the Aarhus Convention from the OECD's soft law is a move to hard law.

The Aarhus Convention is built on Principle 10 of the United Nations Conference on Environment and Development (UNCED) at Rio. It underlined the importance of a participatory process in formulating and implementing environmental policy at the national level (Ebbesson 1997, 51–53). The idea of transparency and participation is deeply rooted in the environmental movement and policy domain both domestically and internationally. This is because, as a number of international environmental law experts have pointed out, non-state actors frequently have more and better information than governments. These actors include private firms and various and diverse NGOs, all of which have stakes (albeit often competing) in outcomes either as objects or beneficiaries of regulation (Raustiala 1997, 537–586).

But the Aarhus Convention is radical in its content and also, perhaps, in its implications for international law. It is built on three pillars: access to information, participation, and access to domestic courts. It spells out in detail what each of these rights includes. It recognises that forms of participation must be adapted to different legal and institutional systems and are dynamic in concept – that is, they will and should evolve over time. The intention of the convention, however, is to identify basic or preliminary elements that would entail a participatory process. It also includes the need for follow-up monitoring of implementation measures, which should be transparent. And to ensure transparency, the public is granted access to judicial review procedures when their rights to information and participation have been breached.

Whether or not the Aarhus Convention will be endorsed by other countries, the implications for international law could be significant. There will no doubt be an effort by the proponents of transparency and participation to extend the Aarhus principles to customary international environmental law. But while the convention concentrates on legal and administrative procedures, namely on procedural rights, it also includes a reference to human rights in the preamble and in some other provisions (Ebbesson 1997, 69–72). Many NGOs are pushing for a rights-based approach in the environmental domain and the Aarhus Convention may have opened up a small window of opportunity. But that aside, the human rights channel to greater transparency and participation looks very plausible, Aarhus or not.

Human Rights and Participatory Democracy

The push for including human rights in the WTO is linked to the ongoing – and often heated – debate on customary international law. In international law, the status of a rule is determined by its source. Thus international conventions such as the hard law Aarhus Convention present rules and enforcement agreed by, and applicable only to, members. In contrast, customary law relates to obligations established from 'a general and consistent practice of states followed by them out of a sense of legal obligation' and binds all states (Howse and Mutua 2000, 7–10).

There is considerable disagreement over whether and which human rights have status as custom. The proposal that human rights should prevail over international trade law or, in other words, override those WTO rules that are alleged to violate basic human rights has generated a storm of controversy (Ostry 2001b, 11–13). The battle seems set to continue. Yet, as several experts have noted, recent Appellate Body rulings cite the Vienna Convention on the Law of Treaties, which allows for the emergence of new laws in the future (Howse and Mutua 2000, 9). Thus some legal experts have argued that the preamble of the WTO agreement, which refers to sustainable development and the need for the poorest countries to develop and grow, states values that could be interpreted as basic human rights (Petersmann 2001, 24–28).[4]

The legal (as opposed to the legislative) route to inserting human rights into the WTO was given a boost by another decision of a dispute settlement panel concerning the U.S. trade law of section 301. Included in the panel's decision was the statement that 'it would be entirely wrong to consider that the position of individuals is of no relevance to the GATT/WTO legal matrix. Many of the benefits to members which are meant to flow as a result of the acceptance of various disciplines under the GATT/WTO depend on the activity of individual economic operators in the national and global market places' and thus 'the multilateral trading system is, per force, composed not only of the States but also, indeed mostly, of individual economic operators'.[5]

This astonishing conclusion of the panel has certainly attracted the attention of WTO watchers in the legal community – although, evidently, not of member governments as one prominent legal expert noted:

I would venture to guess that if this particular proposition were put to a vote in the General Council of the WTO, it would be rejected by governments who want to preserve the WTO as a cozy club of trade bureaucrats. In accordance with the WTO procedures, however, the Section 301 decision was automatically adopted by the WTO Dispute Settlement Body. Thus, this cutting-edge decision will influence future WTO panelists and the *invisible college of international law* [emphasis added] in the years ahead' (Charnovitz 2001, 108).

Among the individual rights of interest to the invisible college is certainly the right of public participation in policymaking as, for example, specified in the Aarhus Convention. Indeed, an entire school of international law based on 'interactional theory' points that 'law is persuasive when it is perceived as legitimate by most actors' and legitimacy rests on inclusive processes (which) reinforce the commitments of participants in the system to the substantive outcomes achieved by implicating participants in their generation (Brunnée and Toope 2000, 53; see also Koh 1997). This sounds very much like the OECD approach, so that norms generated through inclusive processes of decision making enhance governmental legitimacy and enjoy a greater degree of compliance. To the spreading climate of ideas – or 'norm spillover' – the WTO is unlikely to be immune. The invisible college will not be silent or inactive.

If the legal route to inserting human rights law is chosen, the results will be profoundly traumatic for the WTO. Such a pervasive and open-ended transformation of the present system, determined by a panel or an appellate board, would be rejected by most if not all members and generate a furious backlash against the crown jewel of the WTO, namely the dispute settlement mechanism. The issue of the WTO and human rights is one for debate – in a new policy forum. If there is to be any change in WTO rules, it must be legislated not litigated.

World Trade Organization: 'Legislate' Don't Litigate

The word 'legislate' appears above in quote marks because the proposal based on this approach need not involve a change in the formal rules of the WTO, which is a most difficult and lengthy proposition. Rather, what is needed is an informal, voluntary initiative to incorporate discussion of the national trade policy-making processes into the WTO under the broad rubric of transparency, a pillar of the GATT/WTO system from its origins. There is a growing consensus among not only legal and policy-analytical communities but also a number of intergovernmental institutions that participatory processes improve policy outcomes and enhance the legitimacy of policy and compliance with norms and laws.

The relationship between the WTO and the trade policy stakeholders including the NGOs is as follows. At the April 1994 ministerial meeting in Marrakesh, which concluded the Uruguay Round, Article 5(2) of the agreement stated: 'The General Council may make appropriate arrangements for consultation and cooperation with non-governmental organizations concerned with matters related to those of the WTO' (WTO 1994a). In order to clarify the precise legal meaning of this broad directive, on 18 July 1996 the General Council spelled out a set of guidelines covering transparency including release of documents and *ad hoc* informal contracts with NGOs. Guideline 6 is most pertinent here:

> Members have pointed to the special character of the WTO, which is both a legally binding inter-governmental treaty of rights and obligations among its Members and a forum for negotiation. As a result of extensive discussions, there is currently a broadly held view that it would not be possible for NGOs to be directly involved in the work of the WTO or its meetings. Closer consultation and co-operation with NGOs can also be met constructively through *appropriate processes at the national level where lies primary responsibility for*

taking into account the different elements of public interest which are brought to bear on trade policy-making [emphasis added] (Marceau and Pederson 1999, 45).

Nothing happened with respect to the admonition to focus on the national level until after Seattle. At a meeting of the General Council in July 2000, which included a discussion on external transparency (under the agenda item 'other business'), the chair suggested that members might make written contributions on the subject after making informal consultations in the autumn. This suggestion was criticised by several members, as was the chair's decision to propose discussion under the heading of 'other business'. The chair explained that since there was strong opposition to place this issue on a formal agenda he had decided to raise it under that heading, but since some delegations did want to discuss external transparency 'he believed that it would be difficult to continuously postpone even an informal discussion' (WTO 2000b). After further discussion among the supporters and opponents of informal discussions, the meeting was adjourned.

On 13 October 2000, the U.S. made a submission to the General Council Informal Consultations on External Transparency. After noting that the 1996 guidelines suggested the consultations should take place at the national level and a brief review of U.S. processes in this respect, the U.S. delegation proposed that since all members 'could benefit from an exchange of information on national experiences and approaches ... members [should] be invited to provide information on their respective approaches to providing their public with information and opportunity for input on developments in the trading system' (WTO 2000c). On 9 November 2000 an informal general council meeting was convened to discuss external transparency (WTO 2000a). Nothing much happened. This was the end of the story.

The same countries (mostly developing) opposed to increasing transparency at the WTO level were also opposed to discussing the policy process at the national level. There has been criticism about the more powerful well-financed Northern NGOs demanding two bites of the apple. This is fair enough, but the issue nonetheless merits discussion. But how realistic is it, in light of the current state of affairs in the multilateral trading system, to suggest no bite of the apple? For those countries that reject even an informal discussion of their domestic policy processes, it is useful to spell out the benefits of such a project.

First and foremost it is very important to emphasise that a discussion about the national policy processes would be simply that: a means for informing other countries about one's own practices and learning about theirs. There is clearly no 'one size fits all' model but rather considerable diversity related to history, culture, legal institutions, level of development, and so on. A pilot project undertaken in cooperation with the Washington-based Inter-American Dialogue and the Inter-American Development Bank revealed very significant differences among the eight countries surveyed: Argentina, Brazil, Canada, Chile, Colombia, Mexico, United States, and Uruguay (Ostry, Hakim, and Taccone 2002). Of these, only Canada and the United States have established institutional arrangements involving both legislative bodies and a wide range of interested parties or stakeholders including business, farmers, unions, NGOs, and academics. This is not surprising since the OECD studies showed that participatory processes were rare in member countries. Moreover, a 1996 study by the Swiss Coalition of Development Organizations showed that of 30 countries surveyed (both developed and developing), only three – Canada, the U.S., and Switzerland – had formal mechanisms for consultation (Bellmann and Gerster 1996).

Nonetheless, given this North-South dichotomy (and there are significant differences between Canada and the U.S. because of differences in basic governance, as in a parliamentary versus a presidential system), the Latin countries were by no means homogeneous. Furthermore, in some an evolutionary process was underway partly in response to changes in trade policy such as Mercosur or the U.S. farm bill. The policy process should be evolutionary, reflecting systemic changes (such as the transformation from GATT to the WTO) and changes in the policy environment. A participatory consulting process allows governments to inform stakeholders on a continuing basis and, while they may not always like what they hear (trade policy at the best of times involves change and change produces winners and losers), they will be less likely to reject the entire regime.

Moreover, by sharing information on national processes, stakeholders in many countries without adequate technical or financial resources – such as small and medium-sized enterprises (SMEs) – gain useful information on market opportunities or other issues of interest. In a related point, it should be noted that lack of technical and financial resources for many stakeholders and also for some government ministries and parliaments was a major factor affecting the nature of the process in a number of Latin American countries.

While there are undoubtedly benefits accruing from a more participatory policy process, there are also costs. This is certainly one reason many countries are wary of the project. There are costs for governments in terms of time, expertise, and financial resources, and there are significant differences in resources among the stakeholders. Because business lobbies are better equipped than other groups, an insider-outsider mentality can develop and the media are always happy to highlight the battles. Or some stakeholders, simply by being engaged in the process, develop unrealistic expectations about outcome and are frustrated when all their demands are, inevitably, not delivered. For the wily 'statesman', secrecy is considered essential, especially as the negotiations move to closure and the idea of a participatory process is an oxymoron – unless it provides an opportunity for co-option. All these issues arose in the Western Hemisphere country studies. The discussion repeatedly made clear that there were no magic bullets; the policy process was complex and messy, and processes should be in a condition of continuing evolution. The bottom line in all this deserves stressing: it is the role of government to make policy, and transparency and participation do not replace governmental responsibility.

In the WTO context, weighing costs and benefits thus rests on the judgement of each member country. The arguments presented here suggest that there are likely to be significant systemic costs from doing nothing and these should be considered by members when rejecting any WTO initiative. The erosion of the multilateral system will affect the weaker more than the stronger because the alternative to a rules-based system is one based on power.

Transparency and the Trade Policy Review Mechanism

Given the case for a WTO external transparency initiative, how could it be launched? Transparency was one of the founding principles of the post-war trading system.[6] Article 38 of the Havana Charter for the ITO became Article 10 of the GATT, which survived the death of the ITO. The article was entitled 'Publication and Administration of Trade Regulations – Advance Notice of Restrictive Regulations' and was borrowed from the 1946 *U.S. Administrative Procedures Act*. Transparency was greatly expanded in the WTO with the inclusion of services and TRIPS. The word finally appears in the TRIPS agreement as a heading in Article 63.

In the U.S., the evolution of administrative law expanded the participatory role of stakeholders partly in response to the increase in regulation beginning in the 1970s and to the growing literature on the dangers of 'regulatory capture' (Raustiala 1997, 577). Many economists and legal scholars argued that the best antidote to the capture of regulatory agencies by those they regulate was to broaden the spectrum of interests whose voices should be heard before rules are laid down. This development is for the most part not reflected in the WTO, which focuses, with limited exceptions, on the rights and responsibilities of governments and not stakeholders (Marceau and Pederson 1999, 37–40).[7] So WTO external transparency begins at home. There is one major exception, the Trade Policy Review Mechanism (TPRM).

The TPRM was based on a recommendation of the Functioning of the GATT System (FOGS) negotiating group in the Uruguay Round. It was designed to enhance the effectiveness of domestic policy making through informed public understanding, that is, through transparency (Ostry 1997, 201–203). Section B spells it out:

> Domestic Transparency
> Members recognize the inherent value of domestic transparency of government decision-making on trade policy matters for both Members' economies and the multilateral trading system, and agree to encourage and promote greater transparency within their own systems, acknowledging that the implementation of domestic transparency must be on a voluntary basis and take account of each Member's legal and political systems (WTO 1994b).

In order to underline that the TPRM is voluntary and flexible in subject matter, the declaration of objectives in section A states that it is 'not … intended to serve as a basis for the enforcement of specific obligations under the Agreements or for dispute settlement procedures, or to impose new policy commitments on Members' (WTO 1994b).

The TPRM's origins and objectives clearly embrace the policy-making process and thus seems the logical venue for launching this project – on a voluntary basis and as a pilot to be assessed after an agreed period. The WTO secretariat is already seriously overburdened. Thus it might be necessary for the volunteers to provide some funding. If the pilot took off and a number of developing countries became involved, the issue of more permanent funding would have to be faced since there would be capacity in terms building and technical assistance requirements. But these latter costs should clearly come under the arrangements agreed at Doha on capacity building. Enhancing capacity to improve and sustain a more transparent trade policy process sounds like a good investment. It is hardly a new idea. In the 1970s, during the Tokyo Round, a U.S. official remarked to an academic researcher that the advisory committees established under the 1974 *Trade Act* were working extremely well because 'when you let a dog piss all over a fire hydrant he thinks he owns it' (Winham 1986, 316). That is a rather less felicitous version of today's concept of ownership.

Conclusion

The multilateral rules-based trading system is under severe strain. Even under the best of circumstances the WTO, a minimalist, legalistic, member-driven institution, lacks the necessary infrastructure to carry out its ever-expanding mandate. The alternatives to multilateralism are quite clear: increasing bilateralism (especially by the U.S.) and regionalism. A growing fragmentation in a world of ever-deepening integration represents more than a threat to trade. The Cold War involved a spillover from 'high' to 'low' policy. The opposite may well be the case in the future.

Thus the need for reform of the WTO seems obvious. Except to its members, that is. The modest proposals suggested here would require no fundamental renegotiation of rules – just a little foresight. But as Machiavelli so wisely noted: all reform of a system is 'doubtful of success. For the initiators have the enmity of all who would profit by the preservation of the old system and merely lukewarm defenders in those who would gain from the new one.' It is to be hoped that some of the princes prove him wrong.

Notes

1 See also Greg Rushford (2002, 7): 'What began with a sizzle in Seattle has now fizzled ... Maybe the actual day that the anti-globalist movement fizzled was September 11, 2001'.
2 For an analysis of the U.S. position on weighted voting, see Elizabeth McIntyre (1954).
3 The NGOs were the World Wildlife Foundation, the Center for International Environmental Law, Oxfam International, the Institute for Agriculture and Trade Policy, ActionAid, and Friends of the Earth International.
4 The ruling of the appellate body in an environment trade dispute cited the preamble in adopting an 'updated' interpretation of the term 'exhaustible natural resources' to include endangered species because of recent evolution of international environmental law.
5 See sections 301–310 of the *Trade Act of 1974*, Report of the Panel, 22 December 1999, WT/DS/152/R, paras. 7.72 and 7.76.

6   The discussion on transparency is taken from Sylvia Ostry (1998).
7   The exceptions cited include the Subsidies and Countervail Agreement, Dumping Safeguards, TRIPS, and the General Agreement on Trade in Services (GATS) all of which provide for some procedural participatory rights.

References

Bellmann, Christophe and Richard Gerster (1996). 'Accountability in the World Trade Organization'. *Journal of World Trade* vol. 30, no. 6, pp. 31–75.

Bronckers, Marco (1999). 'Better Rules for a New Millennium: A Warning against Undemocratic Developments in the WTO'. *Journal of International Economic Law* vol. 2, no. 4, pp. 547–566.

Brunnée, Jutta and Stephen J. Toope (2000). 'International Law and Constructivism: Elements of an Interactional Theory of International Law'. *Columbia Journal of Transnational Law* vol. 39, pp. 19–74.

Charnovitz, Steve (2001). 'The WTO and the Rights of the Individual'. *Intereconomics* March/April.

Ebbesson, Jonas (1997). 'The Notion of Public Participation in International Environmental Law'. In J. Brunnée and E. Hey, eds., *Yearbook of International Environmental Law*. Oxford University Press, Oxford.

Howse, Robert and M. Mutua (2000). 'Protecting Human Rights in a Global Economy: Challenges for the World Trade Organization'. International Centre for Human Rights and Democratic Development, Montreal.

International Centre for Trade and Sustainable Development (2002). 'WTO Updates Info Dissemination, Discusses Internal Transparency'. *Bridges* vol. 6, no. 18, pp. 2. <www.ictsd.org/weekly/02-05-15/story1.htm> (November 2005).

International Trade Organization (1948). 'Charter of the International Trade Organization'.

Jackson, John H. (1997). *The World Trading System: Law and Policy of International Economic Relations*. 2nd ed. MIT Press, Cambridge, MA.

Keohane, Robert and Joseph Nye (2001). 'The Club Model of Multilateral Cooperation and Problems of Democratic Legitimacy'. In R.B. Porter, *et al.*, eds., *Efficiency, Equity, and Legitimacy: The Multilateral Trading System at the Millennium*, pp. 264–294. Brookings Institution Press, Washington DC.

Koh, Harold Hongju (1997). 'Why Do Nations Obey International Law'. *Yale Law Journal* vol. 106, no. 8, pp. 2599–2659.

Marceau, Gabrielle and Peter N. Pederson (1999). 'Is the WTO Open and Transparent?' *Journal of World Trade* vol. 33, no. 1, pp. 5–50.

McIntyre, Elizabeth (1954). 'Weighted Voting in International Organizations'. *International Organization* vol. 8, no. 4, pp. 484–497.

Organisation for Economic Co-operation and Development (1999). 'Transparency and Consultation on Trade and Environment: National Case Studies'. Volume 1. COM/TD/ENV(99)26/FINAL, 16 October.

Organisation for Economic Co-operation and Development (2000a). 'Transparency and Consultation on Trade and Environment in Five International Organisations'. COM/ENV/TD(99)96/FINAL.

Organisation for Economic Co-operation and Development (2000b). 'NGO Consultation Summary Record'. Summary Record of the Consultation of the Joint Working Party on Trade and Environment with NGOs, 16 May. COM/ENV/TD/M(2000)83.

Organisation for Economic Co-operation and Development (2001). 'Engaging Citizens in Policy-Making: Information, Consultation, and Public Participation'. OECD Public Management Policy Brief No. 10.

Ostry, Sylvia (1997). *The Post–Cold War Trading System: Who's on First?* University of Chicago Press, Chicago.

Ostry, Sylvia (1998). 'China and the WTO: The Transparency Issues'. *UCLA Journal of International Law and Foreign Affairs* vol. 3, no. 1, pp. 1–22.

Ostry, Sylvia (2001a). 'Global Integration: Currents and Counter-Currents'. Walter Gordon Lecture, Massey College, 23 May. <www.utoronto.ca/cis/GlobalIntegration.pdf> (November 2005).

Ostry, Sylvia (2001b). 'Dissent.com: How NGOs are Remaking the WTO'. *Policy Options* no. June, pp. 6–15. <www.irpp.org/po/archive/jun01/ostry.pdf> (November 2005).

Ostry, Sylvia, Peter Hakim, and Juan José Taccone (2002). 'The Trade Policy-Making Process: Level One of the Two Level Game – Country Studies in the Western Hemisphere'. Occasional Papers 13. Inter-American Development Bank and Institute for the Integration of Latin America and the Caribbean. <www.thedialogue.org/publications/program_reports/trade/trade_policy1.pdf> (November 2005).

Oxfam International (2002). 'Rigged Rules and Double Standards: Trade, Globalisation, and the Fight Against Poverty'. <publications.oxfam.org.uk/oxfam/display.asp?isbn= 0855985259> (November 2005).

Petersmann, Ernst-Ulrich (2001). 'Human Rights and International Economic Law in the 21st Century: The Need to Clarify Their Interrelationships'. *Journal of International Economic Law* vol. 4, no. 1, pp. 3–39.

Raustiala, Kal (1997). 'The "Participatory Revolution" in International Environmental Law'. *Harvard Environmental Law Review* vol. 21, no. 2, pp. 537–586.

Rushford, Greg (2002). 'The Intolerant Left: Fizzles and Fissures'. *The Rushford Report*, May, pp. 2, 6–7. <www.rushfordreport.com> (November 2002).

Steger, Debra P. (2000). 'The World Trade Organization: A New Constitution for the Trading System'. In M. Bronckers and R. Quick, eds., *New Directions in International Economic Law: Essays in Honour of John H. Jackson.* Kluwer Law International, The Hague.

Winham, Gilbert R. (1986). *International Trade and the Tokyo Round Negotiation.* Princeton University Press, Princeton.

World Trade Organization (1994a). 'Marrakesh Agreement Establishing the World Trade Organization'. <www.wto.org/english/docs_e/legal_e/04-wto_e.htm> (November 2005).

World Trade Organization (1994b). 'Trade Policy Review Mechanism'. <www.wto.org/english/docs_e/legal_e/29-tprm_e.htm> (November 2005).

World Trade Organization (2000a). 'Informal Consultations on External Transparency'. 9 November. Sent to author in response to request for information.

World Trade Organization (2000b). 'Minutes of Meeting'. General Council, 17 and 19 July. WT/GC/M/57.

World Trade Organization (2000c). 'Submission from the United States'. General Council Information Consultations on External Transparency, 13 October.

World Trade Organization (2001). 'Joint Statement on the Multilateral Trading System'. WTO News, 1 February. <www.wto.org/english/news_e/news01_e/jointstatdavos_jan01_e.htm> (November 2005).

World Trade Organization (2002a). 'Procedures for the Circulation and Derestriction of WTO Documents'. Decision of 14 May. WT/L/452. <docsonline.wto.org/DDFDocuments/t/WT/L/452.doc> (November 2005).

World Trade Organization (2002b). 'Moore Stresses Development Role at WTO'. Speech to the Public Symposium on Doha Development Agenda and Beyond, Geneva, 29 April. Press/290. <www.wto.org/english/news_e/pres02_e/pr290_e.htm> (November 2005).

World Wildlife Foundation, Center for International Environmental Law, Oxfam International, *et al.* (2001). 'Open Letter on Institutional Reforms in the WTO'. October. <ciel.org/Publications/Reform.pdf> (November 2005).

Chapter 12

Trade Liberalisation, Regulatory Diversity, and Political Sovereignty

Michael J. Trebilcock

It is a commonplace observation in contemporary trade policy circles that the very substantial success of the General Agreement on Tariffs and Trade (GATT) and various regional economic arrangements over the post-war years in dramatically reducing the level of tariffs and other border measures, such as quotas, have increasingly led to a focus in current liberalisation efforts on 'within the border' regulatory policies. Here divergences and policies from one country to another are often perceived as an impediment to the free movement of goods, services, capital, and people. The increasing focus on regulatory divergences as potential non-tariff barriers (NTBs) has substantially heightened both domestic and international political conflicts as trade policy linkages have increasingly involved domestic policy domains previously thought to lie largely outside the arena of trade policy. These include trade and the environment, trade and health and safety standards, trade and labour standards, trade and human rights, trade and intellectual property, trade and competition policy, trade and investment, trade in services, and trade and culture.

Conflicts over NTBs have drawn new domestic political constituencies into debates over trade policy. Consumer and environmental groups and other nongovernmental organisations (NGOs) seek to resist the imposition of constraints by international trade agreements on domestic political sovereignty, at least where these constraints would prevent importing countries from imposing more stringent regulatory standards than those that have been adopted by exporting countries. In other contexts, some of these same constituencies (not always consistently) favour the imposition of trade sanctions on exporting countries with standards that are perceived to be 'too lax', as a form of inducement to raise their standards.

Another at least as potentially divisive political fault-line relating to many of these issues has emerged between developed and developing countries. Many interests in developed countries see the much more relaxed environmental and labour standards that often prevail in developing countries as a threat to their more stringent standards and as risking a 'race to the bottom'. However, many interests in developing countries view the insistence by interests in developed countries that they should adhere to the same standards as those that prevail in many developed countries ('a race to the top') as a frontal assault on essential features of their international comparative advantage.

This chapter argues for a relatively conservative view of the case for the harmonisation or convergence of domestic regulatory policies (see Trebilcock and

Howse 2000). It stands in sharp contrast to the view of some commentators that the mandate of the World Trade Organization (WTO) should be dramatically broadened to encompass multilateral regulations over the environment, labour, and competition policy (see, for example, Guzman 2001). This general orientation is influenced by at least four basic premises. First, the issue of regulatory barriers to trade is complicated in many cases by both theoretical and empirical uncertainty over their effects on social welfare (given the wide array of values and concerns that domestic policies are designed to serve). In this respect, regulatory barriers stand in sharp contrast to traditional impediments to trade, such as tariffs and quotas. These can be shown, both theoretically and empirically, to be net welfare-reducing in almost all cases, from both a global and a domestic perspective (see Sykes 1995; see also Sykes 1999 and, more generally, Irwin 1996). Thus, it is emphatically not the case that international harmonisation of domestic policies will always increase both domestic and global welfare. Indeed, depending upon how harmonisation is induced, it may often have the opposite effect.[1]

Second, proponents of more sweeping or extreme forms of international harmonisation of domestic policies in the interests of creating more open and competitive international markets in goods and services appear to severely discount the importance of what Albert Breton (1996) calls 'competitive governments'. In contrast to a view of government as a monolith or monopoly, whose policies are typically viewed by public choice theorists as the product of rent-seeking behaviour by special interest groups that have captured Leviathan, Breton argues that governments in most democracies are intensely competitive in a wide variety of dimensions: opposing parties compete for political office (competition for the market in Harold Demsetz's terms – see Demsetz 1968), agencies within government compete with each other over policy priorities and claims on resources, lower houses compete with upper houses and both compete with constitutional courts, central governments compete with sub-national levels of government and with nonprofit organizations, sub-national levels of government compete among themselves, and national governments compete with other national governments. In Breton's thesis, these competitive features of government serve a crucial demand revelation function and yield a more benign view of public or collective provision of goods, services, or public policies than that of public choice theorists. This is because they establish links between revenue and expenditure decisions of the kind that earlier economists such as Knut Wicksell and Erik Lindahl viewed as a precondition to efficient public policies (see also Wittman 1995). While political markets are unlikely to function perfectly competitively, rendering governments vulnerable on occasion to rent-seeking behaviour (political market failure), one should not assume (as many public choice theorists tend to) that all government policies are explicable in these terms.[2] Thus, from this perspective, it would be a major and unfortunate irony if the price of adopting rules that are designed to remove constraints on and enhance competition in international goods and services markets is the adoption of rules or institutions that have the effect of monopolising or cartelising government policy making – that is, enhanced competition in economic markets at the price of reduced competition in political markets.

A third premise that motivates the relatively conservative view taken here of harmonisation driven by trade policy is the distinction between unilateralism and consensus-based approaches. The basic ground rules adopted in international trade treaties and the like pertaining to domestic policies as potential NTBs should minimise the extent to which harmonisation can be induced by supranational, quasi-judicial fiat, on the one hand, or threats of unilateral sanctions, on the other. This would attenuate the 'threat points' of nation-states in interactions with each other and increase the scope for mutually beneficial agreements on policy convergence. However, if the multilateral system is not to degenerate into a thicket of discriminatory managed trade arrangements, there must be additional ground rules about the form that such agreements may take, such as the application of an unconditional or conditional most-favoured-nation (MFN) principle, so that international discrimination among trading partners is constrained (Nicolaïdis 1997).

A final premise that motivates this relatively conservative orientation to the trade policy-based case for international harmonisation is the uniqueness of the European experience. Whatever view one takes of the European experience, the crucial shift that occurred in Europe with the enactment of the *Single European Act of 1986* – with a shift from an emphasis on negative integration (rules proscribing what domestic policy measures countries may not adopt) to positive integration (supranational regulations and directives prescribing what domestic policies member states must adopt) – is simply not feasible in most other institutional contexts. Deep economic integration among nation-states is typically predicated either on the existence of a hegemonic power with the ability to impress its will on other smaller and weaker states (the U.S. in the immediate post-war years), or on the willingness of member states to cede substantial aspects of their domestic political sovereignty to supranational political institutions, a willingness that for the most part is likely to be conditional on a reasonably egalitarian distribution of political influence and a common interest in overarching political objectives (in the case of Europe, the mitigation of conflicts that had devastated the continent militarily and economically over the first half of the 20th century) (see Trebilcock and Howse 1999, 129–134). Neither of these conditions is likely to apply in the foreseeable future outside of the European context, either with respect to other regional trading blocs or with respect to the multilateral system at large. For example, under the North American Free Trade Agreement (NAFTA), it is inconceivable that Canada and Mexico would be prepared to allow the U.S. to impose its domestic macroeconomic and microeconomic policies on them. Conversely, it is equally inconceivable that the U.S. would accept the creation of supranational political institutions with substantial legislative authority over major aspects of macroeconomic and microeconomic policies in the three countries, on the basis of a relatively egalitarian sharing of political influence in these institutions. These impediments to deep economic integration are likely to be compounded several times over at the multilateral level.

This suggests that in these other institutional contexts the focus of attention on domestic policies that may constitute NTBs to trade should relate principally to two objectives, one adjudicative, the other legislative. The first objective, with respect to the adjudicative (dispute settlement) function, is to elaborate on the principles of negative integration that have historically characterised the approach of the GATT to these issues, namely the application of the national treatment (NT) principle in Article 3 of the GATT to domestic policy measures of member states (requiring that products of foreign countries receive no less favourable treatment than that accorded to like products of national origin), and to elaborate the criteria currently contained in Article 20 of the GATT that justify exceptions to this basic obligation of non-discrimination and the constraints thereon, in particular constraints on disguised or unjustified forms of discrimination. Second, with respect to the legislative (treaty-making) function, the objective is to structure the ground rules pursuant to which mutually beneficial agreements between member states can be reached over policy harmonisation or convergence that are both non-coercive and non-discriminatory *vis-à-vis* other trading partners (in other words, an unconditional or conditional MFN principle). In short, one should be slow to abandon – in favour of governing principles of harmonisation, mutual recognition, or managed trade – well-established principles of non-discrimination in international trade law as the primary analytical framework for addressing the consequences for international trade of domestic regulatory diversity.

The following elaboration of these premises emphasises how a negative integration or non-discrimination perspective can structure evaluations of regulatory diversities or conflicts as potential NTBs to trade while at the same time being sensitive to issues of domestic political sovereignty and to distinctive policy preferences on many regulatory issues from one country to another.

Trade Policy and Domestic Policy Linkages

Trade and the Environment

This policy linkage has been a matter of intense controversy at least since the GATT panel decisions in the two tuna/dolphin cases in the early 1990s, and again in the decisions of the WTO panel and Appellate Body in the shrimp/turtles case.

Countries of origin should have no right to complain of more stringent environmental standards that they must meet in markets of countries of destination than the standards prevailing in their own countries, provided that the standards in the country of destination are non-discriminatory in the sense embodied in the NT principle in Article 3 of the GATT, which in effect requires equality of treatment between domestic and foreign producers of like or competitive products (see Trebilcock and Howse 1999, ch. 15; Trebilcock and Howse 1996). In turn, countries of destination should have no right to complain of less stringent environmental policies in countries of origin than their own, unless these less stringent standards are the source of cross-border environmental externalities or pose a threat to the global commons, for example to endangered species. In particular, countries of destination should have no right to complain that less stringent environmental standards entail lower regulatory compliance costs for exporters in countries of origin, and hence provide the basis for an 'unfair' form of competition. If countries of destination wish to impose trade restrictions or sanctions on countries of origin on account of policies that generate cross-border externalities or a threat to the global common, these restrictions or sanctions should again be required to satisfy the first limb of the non-discrimination test – the NT principle – in that domestic sources of similar externalities or threats to the global common should not be treated more favourably than foreign producers. In addition, countries of destination should also be required to meet the second limb of the non-discrimination principle – the MFN principle – by demonstrating that they have treated foreign sources of such externalities or threats to the global commons even-handedly and in ways consistent with the environmental rationale for the restrictions. Both these limbs of the non-discrimination principle are reflected in Article 20 of the GATT (the exceptions provision), which, while recognising exceptions for a variety of domestic measures, including various environmental measures, in its chapeau prohibits the invocation of such measures where these would entail an arbitrary on unjustifiable form of discrimination between countries where the same conditions prevail (MFN) or a disguised restriction on trade (NT).

The Appellate Body's initial decision in the shrimp/turtles case and its subsequent decision in compliance proceedings under Article 21.5 of the Dispute Settlement Understanding are largely consistent with these principles. First, the Appellate Body recognised the right of an importing country to impose trade restrictions on imports from countries of origin where fishing methods in the latter posed a threat to the global common, provided that the country of destination had also taken similar measures with respect to its own domestic producers. But in addition it required that the country of destination demonstrate it had dealt even-handedly with countries of origin in terms of the objectives of the measures in question – that is, that countries of origin were not arbitrarily included within or excluded from the trade restrictions except on a basis consistent with the rationale for the restrictions in the first place.

Trade and Health and Safety Standards

By parity of reasoning with that applied above to trade and environmental measures, countries of origin should have no right to complain of more stringent health and safety standards in countries of destination than those in their own countries unless these standards are discriminatory in either of the two senses identified above – that is, that they impose more stringent standards on products from countries of origin than apply to domestic producers of like or competitive products (the NT principle), or the standards are applied in a way that discriminates amongst countries of origin in ways that are inconsistent with the health or safety rationale for the measures in question. In turn, countries of destination should have no right to complain of less stringent health or safety standards in countries of origin than their own, unless these less stringent standards constitute a violation of international human rights (as discussed more fully below). In particular, countries of destination should have no right to complain of less stringent health or safety measures in countries of origin on the grounds that these constitute an unfair form of competition because of lower regulatory compliance costs.

The Technical Barriers to Trade Agreement (TBT Agreement) and the Agreement on Sanitary and Phytosanitary Measures (SPS Agreement) negotiated during the Uruguay Round embody these two non-discrimination principles.[3] But they elaborate on them by imposing certain minimum requirements on countries adopting health and safety measures (such as under the SPS Agreement) to adopt measures that conform to international standards or in the case of the measures that adopt more stringent standards ensure that they are based on a risk assessment, are not more trade restrictive than is necessary to realise their objectives and do not entail inconsistent standards from one context to another.

There should be a relatively deferential standard of review by international trade dispute settlement bodies in reviewing domestic health and safety measures against these requirements, again with a view to respecting domestic political sovereignty and distinctive preferences from one country to another as to health and safety risks that citizens are prepared to bear (Trebilcock and Soloway 2002). In other words, these more fully elaborated requirements should be interpreted in a way that is consistent with the two limbs of the non-discrimination principle, and not seek to promote harmonisation or convergence of regulatory policies as an end in itself. Broadly speaking, recent Appellate Body decisions under the SPS Agreement are consistent with this perspective.

Trade and Labour Standards

While much heat and somewhat less light has been generated by recent debates surrounding the linkage between trade policy and labour rights, the principles of non-discrimination identified above provide a valuable starting point for evaluating the linkage. Countries of origin should not be entitled to complain of less stringent labour standards in countries of destination (in contrast to more stringent standards in the case of environmental and health and safety standards) simply on the grounds that these less stringent standards make it more difficult for firms in countries of origin to compete with producers in countries of destination. In turn, countries of destination should not be entitled to complain of low labour standards in countries of origin, in particular on the grounds that these constitute an unfair form of competition by firms in countries of origin, unless the labour standards in countries of origin constitute a violation of international human rights.

Certain core labour standards such as freedom from forced labour, freedom from child labour, freedom of association, and freedom from discrimination in the workplace are widely viewed today as a subset of international or universal human rights (analogous to environmental threats to the global commons), and countries of destination are entitled to restrict imports from countries where these human rights are not respected (Trebilcock 2004). Trade restrictions may be justifiable even if the offending practices do not occur in traded goods sectors. On the other hand, countries of destination invoking this human rights exception should be required to show, if measures are challenged in dispute settlement proceedings, that these measures are consistent with both limbs of the non-discrimination principle – that is, that their own domestic producers are required to respect such norms and foreign producers are not being treated less favourably in this respect (the NT principle), and (more controversially) that the country of destination is being even-handed in its treatment of countries of origin in that countries are not included in, or excluded from, applicable trade restrictions in ways that are inconsistent with the rationale for the measures in question. For example, banning imports made from child labour in sectors where the country of destination has a competing industry but allowing imports produced with child labour in sectors where the country of destination does not have a competing industry would raise suspicions under the NT principle. Moreover, banning imports of both classes from one country while exempting or ignoring imports in both classes made with child labour from another country, for geopolitical or other reasons, would raise questions under the MFN principle and under the chapeau to Article 20 of the GATT, which prohibits measures that would otherwise fall under the exceptions enumerated under Article 20 where these measures entail an arbitrary or unjustifiable form of discrimination between countries where the same conditions prevail.

Trade and Human Rights

By extension of the arguments relating to a linkage between trade policy and labour standards (where at least some subset of labour standards can properly be assimilated to international human rights), other international human rights violations may also justify trade restrictions or sanctions (Trebilcock 2004; Cleveland 2002). While the scope and content of international universal human rights are controversial, violations of core civil and political rights, such as freedom from torture, freedom from arbitrary detention without trial, or freedom from genocide, where violated may justify countries of destination imposing trade restrictions or sanctions on imports from countries of origin in violation of these standards, even where the violations do not occur in the sector to which the trade restrictions relate. However, the country of destination should be required to demonstrate that such restrictions are not only imposed where it has a domestic industry to protect but in other cases where it is contrary to its material interest to impose such restrictions, because of adverse impacts on consumers without offsetting benefits to domestic producers, in order to meet the spirit of the NT principle and to satisfy the condition in the chapeau to Article 20 that prohibits disguised restrictions on trade. In addition, the country of destination should be required to prove that it is acting even-handedly in imposing these restrictions and not including in, or excluding from, the scope of the restrictions countries on a basis that is inconsistent with the claimed human rights rationale for the restrictions.

Trade and Intellectual Property

The TRIPS Agreement negotiated during the Uruguay Round requires all members of the WTO to adopt domestic international property laws that provide minimum substantive and procedural protection to intellectual property rights largely equivalent to the standards prevailing in developed countries. It has provoked much controversy both in the course of its negotiation and subsequently, in large part because it requires developing countries to adopt intellectual property standards of similar stringency to those prevailing in developed countries (a 'race to the top'), even though their comparative advantage may, in many contexts, lie in imitation rather than innovation, given their level of economic development. Many of these controversies have focussed on protection of proprietary pharmaceuticals under this agreement and the restrictions that this protection entails for developing countries in either developing a generic drug industry of their own for essential pharmaceuticals, such as AIDS vaccines, or importing such generics from other countries.

There should be deep scepticism about the wisdom of this form of international harmonisation of domestic regulatory standards (Trebilcock and Howse 1999, ch. 12). While it may be true that lax intellectual property standards in developing countries deprive exporters in countries of origin of export opportunities, the NT principle is respected if a country of destination adopts similar intellectual property standards for both foreign producers and domestic producers, even if these standards are lax, in just the same way that countries of destination adopting more stringent standards are entitled to insist that imports entering their markets respect these more stringent intellectual property standards. In addition, of course, countries of destination, whether adopting lax or stringent standards, should be required to demonstrate that these are applied even-handedly to imports from countries of origin and do not discriminate amongst these countries on bases unrelated to their rationale for intellectual property policy (the MFN principle and the chapeau to Article 20, which prohibits unjustifiable forms of discrimination between countries where the same conditions prevail).

It may be argued that a country of destination that has adopted lax intellectual property standards, on the grounds that its comparative advantage lies in imitation rather than innovation, even if it applies the same lax standards to both domestic and foreign producers, is engaging in a disguised restriction on trade that violates the NT principle and the condition in Article 20 that prohibits disguised restrictions on trade in the case of measures otherwise falling within the exceptions clauses of Article 20. Such an expansive interpretation of the NT principle and the prohibition on disguised restrictions on trade in Article 20 should be strongly resisted in that its implicit rationale is international harmonisation of all kinds of domestic regulatory standards, often around the most stringent standards prevailing anywhere in the world in a particular context. For example, by the same token, it would be arguable that countries of destination or origin that have much lower wages and concomitant minimum wage laws (if any) are depriving firms in either countries of origin or countries of destination of economic opportunities either in their own markets or in foreign markets. But to accept this would be to deprive developing countries of one of their principal sources of comparative advantage in many cases – low cost labour. In short, the NT principle creates a negative duty not to adopt laws that discriminate against foreign producers; it does not create an affirmative duty to adopt laws that enhance their access to the markets of countries of destination – no intellectual property laws at all are consistent with the NT principle.

The TRIPS Agreement highlights in dramatic form the reasons for a cautious approach to international harmonisation of domestic regulatory standards either directly (as in the case of the negotiation of the TRIPs Agreement) or indirectly through ill-considered interpretation by adjudicative bodies in dispute settlement proceedings of applicable provisions in the covered agreements under the WTO (or similar provisions in regional trade agreements).

Trade and Competition Policy

A new link between trade and domestic policy that is emerging in international forums is in the realm of trade competition. Here some argue that wide differences in domestic competition (or anti-trust) policies from one country to the next constitute a significant NTB.

Again, the proper approach should be similar to that adopted in the previous contexts (Trebilcock 1996; Trebilcock and Howse 1999, ch. 17). A country of origin should not be entitled to complain of more stringent competition laws in countries of destination than its own jurisdiction, provided that these are framed and enforced in a non-discriminatory fashion. For example, exporters from countries of origin to countries of destination should not be entitled to complain that they face much more severe sanctions for price fixing in the latter's markets than in their own. Conversely, countries of origin should not be able to complain of much less stringent competition laws in countries of destination than in their own jurisdictions, provided again that these are framed and applied in a non-discriminatory fashion that respects both the NT principle and the MFN principle. In the case of export cartels or anti-competitive mergers in countries of origin that affect markets in countries of destination where all or some of the output of the cartel or merger is sold, countries of origin should not be entitled to object to countries of destination applying more stringent or different laws than in the countries of origin to these arrangements, provided again that these laws as framed and enforced are non-discriminatory in a NT and MFN sense. To be sure, in the case of transnational mergers this may confer jurisdiction on more than one country under the 'effects' doctrine and risks inconsistent procedural requirements and substantive outcomes from multi-jurisdictional review of such mergers (a kind of 'race to the top'). This arguably requires some co-ordination of the review process in countries of destination, perhaps through choice of law or choice of forum rules that focus on the jurisdiction where most of the merged entity's output is sold (and where effects are greatest).

Trade and Investment

The Agreement on Trade-Related Investment Measures (TRIMS Agreement) negotiated during the Uruguay Round defines the scope of the trade-investment linkage quite narrowly by prohibiting a small number of restrictions that countries of destination might seek to impose on foreign direct investors where these conditions are likely to distort trade in associated goods markets, for example local sourcing requirements and minimum export requirements. But the aborted Multilateral Agreement on Investment (MAI) sponsored by the OECD and Chapter 11 of NAFTA go much further. While Chapter 11 of NAFTA adopts in articles 1102 and 1103, both a NT and a MFN principle (as it should), Chapter 11 goes much further than this. In Article 1105 it imposes on member countries an obligation to extend fair and equitable treatment in accordance with international law to foreign investors; it prohibits in Article 1106 a long list of performance requirements and, in Article 1110, direct and indirect forms of expropriation and measures tantamount to expropriation of investments of foreign direct investors by countries of destination.

The last provision, in particular, has proven controversial. It has exposed countries of destination to international arbitral proceedings initiated by private complainants, under Chapter 11, with substantial compensatory damages as the potential outcome, in cases of regulatory 'takings' where governments in countries of destination have adopted new environmental or health and safety regulations that impair the value of a foreign direct investor's interests in the country of destination. There is room for debate as to whether the measures that have been challenged to date are genuinely environmental or health and safety measures (for which Chapter 11 oddly makes no exception analogous to Article 20 of the GATT), or alternatively disguised restrictions on trade. But in principle the expropriation provision (Article 1110) in Chapter 11 is problematic in the framework developed here. In effect, it stands the NT principle on its head by requiring countries of destination to treat foreign direct investors more favourably than they may be required to treat domestic producers whose investments may also be impaired by a change in regulatory policy. The NT principle, which Chapter 11 has adopted, standing alone would ensure that if domestic producers would receive compensation for expropriation under domestic laws in a given context, then foreign investors should be treated no less favourably in such a context. But if domestic investors would not receive compensation in like circumstances, nothing in the non-discrimination principle requires that foreign investors be treated more favourably (again a 'race to the top'). The NT principle in Chapter 11 is itself subject to exceptions where parties enter reservations in their schedules, but these reservations are presumably subject both to the initial and ongoing negotiations. The MFN principle adopted in Chapter 11 would presumably prohibit countries of destination from playing favourites amongst foreigners by treating foreign investments from some countries of origin more favourably than foreign investments from other countries of origin.

It is not clear that Chapter 11 should embrace anything more than these two principles, unless one views the prohibition of various performance requirements in Article 1106 as little more than an elaboration of the NT principle. But even here the prohibition seems to go further than this in that even if a country were to impose similar performance requirements on its own domestic investors, it would not be entitled to impose such restrictions on foreign investors.

Trade in Services

The General Agreement on Trade in Services (GATS) negotiated during the Uruguay Round of the GATT adopts both the MFN and NT principles (articles 2 and 17), but in respect of the latter only with respect to commitments inscribed in members' schedules and only then subject to any conditions and qualifications set out therein.

This is, in effect, an opt-in regime, in contrast to the opt-out regime reflected in Chapter 11 of NAFTA. Exactly what NT implies in the case of domestic regulation of service sectors is far from clear – much less clear than what NT implies for foreign direct investors (for example, the absence of foreign ownership restrictions in particular sectors). Thus an opt-in regime for services and an opt-out regime for foreign direct investment (FDI) may make sense. But in either case, subject to initial and ongoing negotiations over commitments and reservations, countries are properly permitted wide latitude to pursue their own domestic policy preferences.

Trade and Culture

There are limited exceptions in the GATT for cultural industries (Article 4 permitting cinematographic screen quotas for national content). Moreover, Canada enjoys a qualified exemption for cultural industries under Article 2106 and Annex 2106 of NAFTA (preserving the provisions of the Canada-U.S. Free Trade Agreement in this respect). Yet concerns continue to be voiced about the threat to indigenous cultural industries and forms of expression from free trade and unrestricted FDI.

Again, as in other contexts reviewed, the MFN and NT principles (with an opt-in or opt-out option as in the GATS or Chapter 11 of NAFTA) are adequate to the task of disciplining disguised protectionism or favouritism among foreigners and facilitating negotiations over commitments or reservations over opt-in or opt-out options, while allowing substantial latitude for distinctive policy preferences in this context.

Conclusion

That policy divergences remaining after the application of non-discrimination principles will have an impact on trade cannot be gainsaid. However, in some cases, requiring policy convergence or equivalence reduces trade (such as antidumping, countervailing duty laws, environmental and labour policies). In others, it may expand trade by reducing multiple compliance costs, permitting the realisation of economies of scale in production and distribution and the attainment of network efficiencies, avoiding the costs of regulatory duplication and permitting the realisation of regulatory economies of scale and specialisation. The costs associated with remaining policy divergences may often be worth incurring as the price of maintaining competitive governments and respecting distinctive policy preferences from country to country. An indiscriminate attack on so-called 'system frictions' subordinates the value of competitive politics entirely to the value of competitive markets (Ostry 1993).

However, this is not to oppose consensual forms of harmonisation where mutual benefits are to be derived from policy convergence because they reduce the costs of divergence.[4] Much regulatory harmonisation is likely to occur as a result of private initiatives, either at the firm or industry level. In many contexts, firms have private incentives to minimise product incompatibilities if they wish to maximise access to export markets. Private or public-private standardising organisations, national and international, can often promote standards that avoid pointless incompatibilities. However, in some cases, incompatibilities are an unavoidable, indeed desirable, byproduct of product innovation and differentiation. However, in other cases, both firms and national governments may face incentives to promote strategic standard setting, such as technical interfaces in network industries, in order to realise first-mover advantages and possibly monopoly profits. In such cases, international standardising bodies are likely to encounter difficulties in achieving a voluntary consensus on appropriate standards (Sykes 1995, 110–117).

However, even intergovernmental harmonisation efforts, outside the context of the European Union, must necessarily be consensual in nature. Evidence from the early history of the EU and elsewhere suggests that state-to-state negotiations will often be slow and limited, at least when they occur between countries with roughly symmetric bargaining power. Nevertheless, it is important to recall that it was the concept of reciprocity – carrots, not sticks – that facilitated tariff reductions (the GATT's greatest achievement), albeit over half a century, by changing the domestic political dynamics of trade protectionism and more closely aligning them with the economics of trade liberalisation by enlisting a new political constituency in favour of liberalisation (exporters) (Sykes 1995, ch. 1). Tariff reductions were achieved, by and large, not by legal fiat or by threats of unilateral trade sanctions but by providing acceptable *quid pro quos* for other countries' tariff concessions. In the NTB context, countries may well be prepared to make similar concessions to reduce the costs of policy divergences, to increase competition and innovation in their domestic markets, to attract increased foreign investment by making credible regulatory commitments and to increase access to foreign markets, even if these gains require some compromise of legitimate policy objectives previously served by the policy measures being modified. Within the EU, this bargaining has been facilitated through EU supranational institutions and the adoption of qualified majority rules that mitigate the strategic hold-out problem while still respecting reasonable equality of influence of member states. Outside the EU, in the absence of supranational institutions with paramount legislative authority, a more purely consensual approach is likely to dominate. However, to the extent that greater reliance is placed on standards generated by international standard setting bodies, such as the International Organization for Standardization (ISO) and the Codex Alimentarius Commission, the decision-making processes of these institutions, which often do not involve direct government-to-government negotiations, will attract greater scrutiny in the future than in the past, given the status that these standards enjoy under the TBT and SPS agreements, in terms of the relative influence of various stakeholders, public transparency, and democratic legitimacy. In the case of government-to-government negotiations, plurilateral rather than multilateral (single undertaking) agreements, perhaps governed by a conditional MFN principle, may offer the best prospects of progress, as exemplified to some extent by the WTO agreement on government procurement and the two-track approach to economic integration that is beginning to emerge in the EU. The WTO/TRIPS Agreement is a confounding, and unfortunate, example of the alternative approach.

However, when negotiations over alleged NTBs take place bilaterally between countries with asymmetric bargaining power, as arguably exemplified by the Strategic Impediments Initiative between the United States and Japan, they carry the serious risk of gross over-reaching by one country into the domestic policy affairs of another (for example, domestic savings rates, public investment policy, land costs). Moreover, they are likely to result in managed trade arrangements that are antithetical to a non-discriminatory multilateral trading system. Out of frustration with the prospects of achieving extensive policy harmonisation, some commentators (principally the so-called American revisionists) argue for 'black boxing' domestic systems by relying on managed trade (results-oriented or 'crowbar'–based trade policy), to achieve more balanced economic relations (Kahler 1996). However, this both flatly denies fundamental elements of the theory of comparative advantage and often constitutes gross interference in the domestic affairs of countries who are parties to such arrangements, whose governments are required to orchestrate domestic economic activities in extraordinary detail in order to meet these targets, while at the same time typically discriminating against other member states (as exemplified by the Semiconductor Agreement between Japan and the United States). On the other hand, liberal traders who find themselves unattracted by the concept of managed trade and who feel frustrated at the likely pace of international policy harmonisation, and who propose instead that a central role be assigned to a relatively unqualified principle of mutual recognition (at least where not complemented by negotiated harmonisation of minimum standards) fail to acknowledge that such a principle would confer major forms of extra-territorial jurisdiction on countries of origin when exporting goods or services (and their policies with them) to other countries that may well have legitimate reasons for maintaining distinctive policies of their own, provided that they meet basic principles of non-discrimination (Nicolaïdis 1997).

In summary, the two limbs of the non-discrimination principle appropriately discipline protectionist domestic policies while allowing a large scope for domestic policy sovereignty, distinctive policy preferences, and competitive and accountable governments. The goals of international trade policy should not be more ambitious than this. In particular, they should not confuse the objective of disciplining protectionism (negative integration) with creating a single global market (positive integration).[5] The *Single European Act* is not a model that can be extrapolated to the world at large or sustained or defended on a global basis.

Notes

1   For insightful discussions of the welfare effects on harmonisation, see Jagdish Bhagwati (1996; 1993), David Leebron (1996), and Alan Sykes (1999).

2   The author has been guilty of this tendency in the past: see Trebilcock, Hartle, Prichard and Dewees (1982) and Trebilcock (1982); but see Trebilcock (1993; 1999).

3   The TBT Agreement in Article 2.1 requires that products imported from any member shall be accorded treatment no less favourable than that accorded to like products of national origin and to like products originating in any other country. The SPS Agreement in Article 2.2 requires members to ensure that their SPS measures do not arbitrarily or unjustifiably discriminate between members where identical or similar conditions prevail, including between their own territory and that of other members; SPS measures may not be applied in a manner that would constitute a disguised restriction on trade.

4   An excellent overview of the issues and approaches of importance in consensual harmonisation is to be found in Scott Jacobs (1994).

5   A distinction that Cass Sunstein (1992) argues has been maintained (albeit imperfectly) in the U.S. dormant commerce clause constitutional jurisprudence relating to inter-state NTBs to trade.

References

Bhagwati, Jagdish (1993). 'Fair Trade, Reciprocity, and Harmonization: The Novel Challenge to the Theory and Policy of Free Trade'. In D. Salvatore, ed., *Protectionism and World Welfare*. Cambridge University Press, Cambridge.

Bhagwati, Jagdish (1996). 'The Demands to Reduce domestic Diversity among Trading Nations'. In J. Bhagwati and R.E. Hudec, eds., *Fair Trade and Harmonization: Prerequisites for Free Trade?* MIT Press, Cambridge MA.

Breton, Albert (1996). *Competitive Governments*. Cambridge University Press, New York.

Cleveland, Sarah (2002). 'Human Rights Sanctions and International Trade: A Theory of Compatibility'. *Journal of International Economic Law* vol. 5, no. 1, pp. 133–189.

Demsetz, Harold (1968). 'Why Regulate Utilities?' *Journal of Law and Economics* vol. 11, no. 1, pp. 55–65.

Guzman, Andrew T. (2001). 'Global Governance and the WTO'. Boalt Working Papers in Public Law, University of California. <repositories.cdlib.org/boaltwp/83> (November 2005).

Irwin, Douglas (1996). *Against the Tide: An Intellectual History of Free Trade*. Princeton University Press, Princeton NJ.

Jacobs, Scott (1994). 'Regulatory Co-operation for an Interdependent World: Issues for Government'. Organisation for Economic Co-operation and Development, Paris.

Kahler, Miles (1996). 'Trade and Domestic Differences'. In S. Beiger and R.P. Dore, eds., *National Diversity and Global Capitalism*. Cornell University Press, Ithaca.

Leebron, David (1996). 'Lying Down with Procustes: An Analysis of Harmonization'. In J. Bhagwati and R. Howse, eds., *Fair Trade and Harmonization: Pre-requisites for Free Trade?* MIT Press, Cambridge MA.

Nicolaïdis, Kalypso (1997). 'Mutual Recognition of Regulatory Regimes: Some Lessons and Prospects'. Jean Monnet Working Papers. <www.jeanmonnetprogram.org/papers/97/ 97-07.html> (November 2005).

Ostry, Sylvia (1993). 'Beyond the Border: The New International Policy Arena'. In E. Kantzenbach, H.-E. Scharrer and L. Waverman, eds., *Competition Policy in an Interdependent World Economy.* Nomos, Baden-Baden.

Sunstein, Cass (1992). 'Protectionism, the American Supreme Court, and Integrated Markets'. In R. Bieber, R. Dehousse, J. Pinder *et al.*, eds., *One European Market? A Critical Analysis of the Commission's Internal Market Strategy.* Nomos, Baden-Baden.

Sykes, Alan (1995). *Product Standards for Internationally Integrated Goods Markets.* Brookings Institution, Washington DC.

Sykes, Alan (1999). 'Regulatory Protectionism and the Law of International Trade'. *University of Chicago Law Review* vol. 66, no. 1.

Trebilcock, Michael J. and Douglas Hartle (1982). 'The Choice of Governing Instrument'. *International Review of Law and Economics* vol. 29, no. 2,

Trebilcock, Michael J., Douglas Hartle, Robert Prichard, *et al.* (1982). *The Choice of Governing Instrument.* Economic Council of Canada, Ottawa.

Trebilcock, Michael J. (1993). *The Limits of Freedom of Contract.* Harvard University Press, Cambridge MA.

Trebilcock, Michael J. (1996). 'Competition Policy and Trade Policy: Mediating the Interface'. *Journal of World Trade* vol. 30, no. 4, pp. 71–107.

Trebilcock, Michael J. and Robert Howse (1996). 'The Fair Trade–Free Trade Debate: Trade, Labor, and the Environment'. *International Review of Law and Economics* vol. 16, no. 1, pp. 61–79.

Trebilcock, Michael J. (1999). 'Lurching around Chicago: The Positive Challenge of Explaining the Recent Regulatory Reform Agenda'. In R. Bird, M.J. Trebilcock and T. Wilson, eds., *Rationality in Public Policy.* Canadian Tax Foundation, Toronto.

Trebilcock, Michael J. and Robert Howse (1999). *The Regulation of International Trade.* 2nd ed. Routledge, New York.

Trebilcock, Michael J. and Robert Howse (2000). 'A Cautious View of International Harmonization: Implications from Breton's Theory of Competitive Governments'. In G. Galeotti, P. Salmon and R. Wintrobe, eds., *Competition and Structure: The Political Economy of Collective Decisions.* Cambridge University Press, Cambridge.

Trebilcock, Michael J. and Julie Soloway (2002). 'International Trade Policy and Domestic Food Safety Regulation: The Case for Substantial Defence by the WTO Dispute Settlement Body under the SPS Agreement'. In D. Kennedy and J. Southwick, eds., *The Political Economy of International Trade Law.* Cambridge University Press, Cambridge.

Trebilcock, Michael J. (2004). 'Trade Policy and Labour Standards: Objectives, Instruments and Institutions'. In J.J. Kirton and M.J. Trebilcock, eds., *Hard Choices, Soft Law: Voluntary Standards in Global Trade, Environment, and Social Governance*, pp. 170–185. Ashgate, Aldershot.

Wittman, Donald (1995). *The Myth of Democratic Failure: Why Political Institutions Are Efficient.* University of Chicago Press, Chicago.

Chapter 13

Civil Society and the Roots of Structural Conditionality in the World Bank and International Monetary Fund

Louis W. Pauly

When a state joins the International Monetary Fund (IMF) and the World Bank, it accepts certain obligations to bring external considerations into its internal policymaking. At the very least, members of the IMF are bound to submit to a formal apparatus of surveillance over the economic consequences for other members of a full range of macroeconomic policies. When they accept financial assistance from the IMF or the World Bank, moreover, the nature and scope of the obligations assumed can expand significantly. Conditionality is the term used to describe the practice of establishing those obligations and promoting compliance. The conferees at Bretton Woods in 1944 did not invent the practice, but the two institutions they helped establish later proved eminently adaptable. Over the past 25 years, members have enlarged the scope of conditionality in both institutions and used it to encourage ever deeper adjustments in a wider range of policies. Members requiring high levels of financial assistance over long periods of time have found themselves drawn into an elaborate practice now commonly labelled 'structural conditionality'. The practice rendered such assistance conditional on negotiating and agreeing to implement plans for profound reform and adjustment in important national systems affecting economic stability and prospects for future prosperity. Since the boundary lines among the economic, political, and social realms blur at this level, structural conditionality has sparked intense controversy.

This chapter provides an overview of the development of that practice and the financial instruments within which it was originally embedded in the IMF and the World Bank.[1] Against this background, it proposes a political explanation for the emergence and elaboration of the practice during the watershed decade of the 1980s. That explanation emphasises the importance of prior ideological and structural change mainly inside the U.S. state and its civil society.

The Puzzle of Structural Conditionality

International financial assistance conditional on structural adjustment can seem like an instrument of enforcement to its targets. Its development is puzzling in a world where sovereignty remains a key organising principle and where global government is not obviously on the horizon (see Krasner 1999; Caporaso 2000). Even if that principle has often been honoured in the breach, for the strong to attempt direct deep domestic transformation in the weak has been rare since the end of the European colonial era. The inter-war experience of the League of Nations in certain Central European countries, the post–World War II experience of occupied Germany and Japan, and more recent interventions of an intrusive nature in certain failed states stand out as exceptions that prove the rule (see Santaella 1993). In the absence of military or humanitarian emergencies, international efforts aimed at recasting internal social and political arrangements within sovereign states have occurred very infrequently – that is, until recently. During the 1990s, it became commonplace to see images of international financial diplomats apparently forcing the leaders of developing countries, states in transition from socialism, or newly industrialising states to abandon traditional policies, open markets, and break domestic logjams to the kinds of reforms deemed necessary to integrate their national economies into a rapidly emerging global economy.

Why were the strong, who have led the Bretton Woods institutions since their inception, now so overtly trying to construct such an economy? And why were they weak, often despite public displays of resentment, now apparently more willing to go along? The way in which structural conditionality evolved within the IMF and the World Bank suggests that the practice was driven by prior ideological and policy changes within their dominant member state, the United States. The crucial decade for those changes was the 1980s. In the end, the core challenge for the institutions and their key supporters was to draw lessons from the experience of that decade and apply them to debtor states. The principal underlying objective of that two-pronged effort, however, was to keep the U.S. engaged in the progressive internationalist project, which the IMF and the World Bank had represented ever since World War II. The Cold War obscured the nature of that project, but the denouement of that twilight struggle brought it back to the fore. It also brought back to prominence in U.S. public policy debate longstanding conservative opposition to that project. Structural conditionality needs to be understood in this light. The key issue remained defining and maintaining the essential place of the U.S. in a globalising economy. Changes within the U.S. as the Cold War stabilised and then receded needed to be accommodated if the overarching experiment giving rise to that economy was to endure. At the heart of that experiment was an attempt to reorient American foreign policy away from the pursuit of national interests narrowly defined and toward positive world order transformation guided by core American values. In the 1980s, the fundamental struggle inside the U.S. was over the redefinition of those values. For U.S. conservatives, the issue of reconstructing the most effective means for defending those values arose in this context. For progressives, an agenda continuing to emphasise global transformation implied new mechanisms for promoting those values in a politically feasible way.

Contemporary Money Doctors as Students, Then as Teachers

In the early years after World War II, when the seeds of contemporary international markets were first sown, many hoped that the resumption of exports, imports, and accommodating portfolio investment would render recovering national economies interdependent. There was nothing automatic about this return to what some probably thought of as 'normalcy'. As careful analysts have convincingly shown, the dream of a liberal post-war order naturally moving a more fully capitalist world along a more peaceful path soon met the reality of communist intransigence, of new claims for the right of national self-determination, of irresistible demands for social protection at the national level, and of the necessity of coherent international leadership rooted in an adequate base of popular support. It would be convenient if the resulting experiment in reconstituting world order had proven neat and tidy. But history often seems messy and untidy. The record indicates that the elements of an intentional experiment emerged, especially after 1947. It was centred on active and continuing U.S. engagement in the wider world, an engagement not simply conditioned on a narrow calculation of American national interests. It also succeeded in substantial part, at least if the avoidance of a reversion to global depression and great-power war may be taken as a reasonable indicator. Even with the advantage of historical hindsight, however, there seems no avoiding the conclusion that the experiment was an ideological and political muddle. Sympathetic scholars have tried to capture its essence with such evocative phrases as liberal internationalism, 'the compromise of embedded liberalism', multilateral collaboration, democratic capitalism, the extension of Franklin Roosevelt's New Deal to the world, and 'an empire by invitation' (see Cooper 1968; Kindleberger 1973; de Cecco 1976, 1979; Keohane and Nye 1977; Ruggie 1983; Burley 1993; Ikenberry 2001). And even opponents admit its existence, even if they favour terms such as 'hegemony' and 'neo-imperialism'.

The experiment rested on a deeply rooted, and still open, debate within the U.S. about its proper role in the world. Isolationism is commonly taken to inform one side of that debate, while the vision of the world converging inexorably toward the American way has long seemed to capture the other. As historians have convincingly demonstrated, however, if this sort of idealised ideological confrontation may once have had relevance, World War I rendered it irrelevant. The real debate inside the U.S. polity after 1918 was between progressive internationalists, who saw the need for deep engagement far beyond U.S. borders aimed at nothing less than positive world-order transformation, and conservative internationalists, who wanted to keep foreign interventions limited and carefully calibrated to bounded and realistically conceived U.S. interests.

The meandering path of this debate after World War I saw the progressive side losing decisively in the struggle over U.S. participation in the League of Nations, the conservative side recalibrating its world view in the midst of the storm unleashed by global depression and a new world war, a more 'realistic' but still recognisably progressive vision coming to the fore at the start of the Cold War, and a conservative reaction to an open-ended external commitments as it came to an end (Knock 1992; Trachtenberg 1999; Friedberg 2000; Kennedy 1987; Nau 2001). The brief case histories presented below are consistent with just such a reading. Their interpretation here rests on a sense that the ebb and flow of that debate still shapes the changing character, scope, and authority of international institutions such as the IMF and the World Bank.[2]

During the 1970s, expanding international trade as well as foreign direct investment (FDI) and mushrooming short-term capital flows intensified pressures on idiosyncratic domestic structures and created markets that rewarded conformity to certain expectations of behaviour broadly aligned with U.S. norms. For countries seeking economic growth and prosperity, this now seemed to imply eventual agreement on more than the kinds of basic liberal economic rules associated with the 1944 Bretton Woods Agreement that creating the IMF and the World Bank. The alternative of revolutionising the emerging structure of a globalising economy itself was attempted during the troubled decade of the 1970s. Plans for a 'New International Economic Order' (NIEO), one privileging local autonomy, national difference, and at least the possibility of assigning higher priority in national policies to social justice than to economic efficiency, came to naught. Whether the subsequent triumph of market liberalism in one developing country after another truly reflected a silent revolution within those countries remains the subject of debate. In any event, the trajectory of policy change seemed thereafter to imply convergence toward the way business is done, if not precisely as it is in the U.S., then at least generally in conformity with liberal-market norms now shared across the richest countries in the system – not to mention the fact that certain specific and important business practices often differed among those countries (see, for example, Berger and Dore 1996), or the fact that idiosyncratic economic structures in the developing world reflected distinct histories, cultures, and politics, or the fact that colonialism left persistent legacies across much of that world.

By the late 1980s, the main architects of the global economy – a handful of leading industrial states under the sometimes wavering but never seriously contested leadership of the U.S. – had constructed a system where international economic organisations appeared ever more assertively to promote deep structural change in countries needing financial assistance. By the end of the 1990s, the World Bank and especially the IMF were apparently now authorised to promote an expansive agenda of 'sound economic policies' and 'good governance'. As the IMF's managing director stated in speech after speech at the time, such a rubric now covered not simply prohibitions on outright corruption, but also prescriptions for financial market operations organised around objective commercial criteria, transparency in industrial conglomerates and in government-business relations more generally, the dismantling of monopolies, and the elimination of government-directed lending and procurement programmes (see, for example, Camdessus 1998).

The emerging global economy now seemed to require not simply voluntary adjustment in the context of gradually deepening interdependence across national economies, but also the external imposition of quite detailed normative standards in return for desperately needed financing. To radical critics from the left, what came to be known as structural conditionality as elaborated by the IMF and the World Bank now cloaked a new form of imperialism. To their counterparts on the right, the tool of financing conditioned on deep domestic reform proved a handy vehicle for the self-interested agendas of international bureaucrats, whose original purpose was rapidly being rendered obsolete by the liberated operation of private financial markets. To observers of a more moderately liberal persuasion, it seemed a defensible and rational response to new realities, a response embedded in a profound transformation in the ideological orientations of national policy makers in developing countries.[3] To political realists, it was simply a handy mechanism with which creditor states were trying to make the world safer for themselves.

Uncomplicated radical, liberal, or realist explanations may be attractive, but they are ultimately unsatisfying. The overarching questions are clear, but the easiest answers seem facile. Why did intergovernmental organisations of nearly universal membership and a founding ethos of political neutrality become the apparent enforcers of political preferences identified most clearly with a few rich countries, and especially with the U.S.? In a world where political authority remains dispersed but economic power is concentrated, why did a particular form of liberal internationalism develop whereby intermediaries originally organised precisely to allow members to retain a substantial degree of autonomy now became the guardians of a universal orthodoxy? Why did the strong not simply allow market forces to overwhelm those intermediaries and force adjustment among the weak? If their political autonomy meant anything anymore, why did the weak not continue to resist?

The story of the emergence of structural conditionality in the World Bank and the IMF revolves around such questions and sheds light on the interaction of international institutions, leading states, and dominant civil societies.[4] It also helps to deconstruct some of the images now associated with that nearly mystical word 'globalisation'. Important ideological changes affecting the structures of governance within the political economy of the U.S. occurred in the decade when structural conditionality first emerged. Viewed in historical perspective, the connection seems more than coincidental. Of course, much more work would have to be done to prove a causal connection, but an exploration of the essential plausibility of just such a linkage is a necessary first step. Such a step would lead to the suggestion that in the wake of those ideological changes, new ways had to be found to reinforce the U.S. political commitment to progressive internationalism. Attentive to important shifts on both Wall Street and Main Street in the United States ever since the end of World War II, the IMF and the World Bank adapted themselves to a new environment.

Mixed motives abound in the real world of policy. But adjustment in the roles of those institutions had long been an important element in the fluid U.S.-led experiment in world-order transformation first conceived while great-power war still raged in Europe and in the Pacific. A key objective, especially after the post-war experiment was reconceived in the mid 1970s, was the construction of a collaborative system of economic policy making in which states would increasingly defer to signals emanating from more open markets, now including markets for money. Even though this new emphasis was quintessentially conservative (that is, in the unique way Americans use that term; 'liberal' in the sense that Europeans use it), progressives could continue to support the experiment as long as the actual operation of those markets did not entail a stark separation between social justice and economic efficiency, and as long as no more feasible mechanisms could promise peace, expanding prosperity and increasing equity. The ultimate impact of more open markets remained unknowable, but the experiment itself continued to depend on U.S. willingness to define national interests much more broadly than they had before 1940. In concrete terms, it required institutions capable of bridging the gap between conservative and progressive views of those interests.

From their earliest days, international financial institutions (IFIs) played an important role both in buffering and in bolstering American engagement in the wider world. Not coincidentally, they had to be Janus-faced. On one side, their existence limited the liability of American policymakers and their civil society when other countries ran afoul of international markets. On the other side, they made those markets seem to the citizens of other states more cosmopolitan, less associated with particularistic national or class interests.

If the Americans did not desire an imperial order after 1945, even one mediated by the indirect instrumentality of markets, others did not desire market-based neo-colonialism. International financial markets ever more intensively linking still-national economies together confronted a particular kind of legitimacy problem, a problem that institutions such as the IMF and the World Bank promised to help assuage. The fact that their fundamental political role has never been entirely clear, the fact that jurisdictional disputes have always bedevilled them, and the fact that their operations have become more intrusive over time, reflect deeper changes in the structure of power and authority within the United States. Adaptation within those institutions, in turn, reflect shifts in a long and continuing internal debate over the relationship between that structure and the international system as a whole. In a sense, the students of the strong become teachers of the weak. But as any teacher knows, learning is rarely a straightforward or transparent process.

Structural Conditionality at the World Bank

In 1979, the World Bank first broke its standard practice of lending mainly for specific projects and began offering structural adjustment loans. A major, and continuing, adaptation in its focus and mandate commenced. But the initial policy shift did not come out of the blue.

Financial conservatism had genetic roots in the World Bank, roots that were embedded in the soil of American financial markets. The need to maintain its AAA credit rating, however, did not render the World Bank into an automaton. Just as ancient 'sound money' orthodoxy did dominate national economic policy making in Britain and the United States in the 1940s, 1950s, and 1960s, neither did the character of financial markets leave the World Bank without room to manoeuvre. It needed that room, for it was a creature of its leading member states, few of which would have appreciated the bank foisting American values on them through policy-based lending. The World Bank was forced to tread a fine line between satisfying the financial expectations of its funders and respecting the sovereign authority of its main clients.

The World Bank had been decidedly Keynesian in its formal and informal policy advice right through the 1960s.[5] Although stable macroeconomic frameworks inside client states were sought, that meant a reasonable equilibrium between internal and external balances. Excessive inflation, as in Brazil in the 1960s, could lead the bank to halt its lending to that country. But the World Bank did not question the legitimacy of the efforts of clients to steer markets, adopt and implement indicative economic plans, and control incoming and outgoing investment (Mason and Asher 1973, 662). It supported the IMF's mission of building up a global macroeconomy characterised by unified national exchange rate systems aimed at the kind of financial stability that promised to facilitate the expansion of international trade and long-term investment through well-functioning markets. Without compromising such objectives, however, the World Bank was pragmatic in its judgement of the full range of policies now labelled microeconomic. It was also generally cautious in its attempts to use financial leverage to encourage specific changes in macro policies.

A shift began to occur in the World Bank when Robert McNamara assumed the presidency in 1968. But it was not a shift toward what one might call 'Wall Street' values. In this respect, it is worth recalling the ideological baseline. In American political terms, the World Bank and the IMF were emanations of Franklin Roosevelt's New Deal.[6] The original plans for both institutions were anathema on Wall Street, for obvious reasons. After recovery from the ravages of war had occurred, as providers of financial assistance to countries in need the two institutions would be competitors to private financiers, and competitors with the very potent advantage of tacit safety nets from leading creditor states. Consequent distrust and resentment would pose larger challenges for the World Bank than for the IMF, for the former was made dependent on private investors willing to hold its bonds while the latter was provided with substantial 'own resources' through the quota subscriptions of its member states. That the World Bank would attempt to accommodate Wall Street orthodoxies, therefore, is not as puzzling as the fact that it resisted such accommodation at all. In practice, its early presidents articulated a conservative vision and kept it focussed on projects of relatively limited scale not often directly competitive with the interests of private finance.

While in 1968 some may have expected the incoming president, McNamara, to steer the institution in an even more conservative direction, the opposite seems to have been his own intention. As McNamara made clear in later interviews with the World Bank's historians, he always opposed fiscal indiscipline in client states. But he also moved quite deliberately to expand the World Bank's direct engagement with large-scale issues of poverty reduction, population control, and environmental-quality improvement. By way of implication, this engagement included the institution's commitment to harness and channel greater financial resource flows, involving loans at concessionary rates effectively subsidised by creditor governments and the necessity for the World Bank to seek leverage points to guide allocation decisions inside client states. These two objectives existed in tension with one another and success in raising new resources overshadowed aspirations for enduring policy influence.

During the heady and turbulent decade following McNamara's arrival, a vast expansion in the World Bank's size and scope sought to keep pace with the rising expectations linked to rising demands for a NIEO and to simultaneously rising financing 'gaps' associated with unprecedented oil price shocks. 'The net result was that the 1970s (until their final year) were a period in which most of the Bank's policy-influencing efforts were upstaged and ineffective' (Kapur, Lewis, and Webb 1997, 472). Inside, nevertheless, the ground was prepared for the World Bank one day to refocus and reinvigorate an agenda for policy reform in its client states, not least because clients desperately seeking cash infusions during the 1970s had opened the door.

The 'great bend in events', as the World Bank's historians call it, occurred between 1979 and 1981. The cast of characters in the drama on the world stage is well known – Margaret Thatcher, Paul Volcker, Ronald Reagan, Milton Friedman, and Walter Wriston. Against a changing ideological background, McNamara continued in his quest to increase the World Bank's lendable resources, increasingly to be targeted at anti-poverty programmes. (Curiously, McNamara's memoirs are silent on this period of his life, but speculation on his motivations at the time frequently and plausibly highlight the importance of his searing experience as U.S. Defense Secretary during the Vietnam War and its legacy of regret and atonement [McNamara and Vandemark 1996].) Advising him and writing speeches for him were such well-known pro-development, anti-poverty activists as Mahbub ul Haq, later Pakistan's finance minister. The World Bank's chief economist, Hollis Chenery, helped construct the intellectual links between resource claims and deeper policy conditionality. Ernest Stern, the chief operating officer after 1978, combined pragmatism with a clear vision of the need for policy reform inside the institution's clients.

The World Bank's new drama opened on 10 May 1979, with what must at the time have seemed like a fairly innocuous speech by McNamara to the United Nations Conference on Trade and Development (UNCTAD) meeting in Manila:

> In order to benefit fully from an improved trade environment, the developing countries will need to carry out structural adjustments favouring their export sectors. This will require appropriate domestic policies and adequate external help. I would urge that the international community consider sympathetically the possibility of additional assistance to developing countries that undertake the needed structural adjustments for export promotion in line with their long-term comparative advantages. I am prepared to recommend to the Executive Directors that the World Bank consider such requests for assistance, and that it make available program lending in appropriate cases (Kapur, Lewis, and Webb 1997, 506–507).

During the next year, structural adjustment loans (SALs) would be formalised just as demand for them would grow in tandem with rising balance-of-payments deficits occasioned by the second oil price shock.

The World Bank's board approved the new initiative early in 1980 and authorised structural adjustment lending in the range of US$700 million during 1981. The board had also authorised an increase in capital stock from US$41 billion to US$85 billion. Individual SALs were to adopt the 'programme' model then used by the IMF. They were to be policy-based, not project-based. They would be phased in on a multi-year basis and would aim at basic reforms in longer-term economic structures. The IMF, with which the World Bank pledged to co-ordinate its SALs, would continue to emphasise short-term adjustments needed to correct external payments imbalances. World Bank documentation on the thinking behind SALs provided a broad set of examples of the types of policies that might be targeted for reform: policies shaping incentives, infrastructure, and marketing to encourage export diversification, policies affecting domestic resource mobilisation, price incentives, and efficient resource use, and policies protecting inefficient industries and preventing the emergence of more competitive industries (Kapur, Lewis, and Webb 1997, 510).

As the SAL instrument developed, the irony is that what was originally advocated by anti-poverty activists trying to increase resource flows to developing countries soon proved quite attractive to parties long associated with economic orthodoxy. As if to symbolise the World Bank's new enthusiasm for the reform agenda to be promoted through the instrument of SALs, a leading proponent of neo-classical economics, Ann Krueger, was appointed chief economist in 1982.[7] Between then and 1986, the Research Department led by her would undergo a major transformation, and its work would provide the rationale for the adoption of market-friendly policies by developing countries (Rodgers and Cooley 1999, 1405).

Stern later recalled that this new form of lending was intended to accomplish three main things. It would 'support a program of specific policy changes and institutional reforms designed to reduce the current account deficit to sustainable levels, assist a country in meeting the transitional costs of structural changes in industry and agriculture by augmenting the supply of freely usable foreign exchange, and act as a catalyst for the inflow of other external capital to help ease the balance of payments situation' (Stern 1983, 189). This emphasis on the payment balance effectively subordinated World Bank programmes to IMF programmes, but this apparently did not bother Stern. In practical terms, the actual procedures put in place to administer a World Bank programme mirrored those of the IMF. Stern described the underlying procedures that 'may be called conditionality' as follows:

> The Bank must reach a firm understanding with each government on the monitorable action programs, specifying both the steps to be taken and the studies required as a basis for further progress. The practice for this understanding is to be spelled out in detail in a Letter of Development Policies that is explicitly referred to in the loan agreement. The tranching of disbursement involves the identification of a few key actions that are specified

as preconditions before the release of the second tranche. However, satisfactory progress on the implementation of the overall program is also a requirement (101).[8]

The practical shift allowing policy-based lending to occur through the World Bank reflected a clear tradeoff. New resources from creditor states implied new opportunities for constituents within those same states. Creditor states, mainly through the institution's private financiers based within them, were expected to increase the net resources at the disposal of the bank. They needed an incentive of their own. Even if policy reform could be depicted as inherently good for the World Bank's clients, whether they welcomed it or not in the short run, the reform agenda itself bolstered a supportive coalition of beneficiaries within the creditor states. Exports implied imports. The building and rebuilding of infrastructure in developing countries promised opportunities for bankers, engineers, and equipment manufacturers in developed countries. Antiprotectionism in poor countries opened markets for businesses based in rich countries. Moreover, as services became more important in the economies of creditor states, the range of markets needing to be opened in 'emerging' countries broadened. The line between portfolio capital flows needed to lubricate the machinery of trade-in-goods and flows constituting in themselves trade-in-financial services began to blur.

There was nothing cynical about the new tradeoff. No conspiracy theory is needed to explain it. Opening markets for goods and services in the World Bank's client states promised to open markets for financing in its creditor states. Market interdependence, not open national treasuries, promised to breed opportunities for mutual gain. Capitalism tempered by a progressive internationalist vision, the economic core of the post-war U.S.-led experiment in world order transformation, framed the bank's operations from the beginning. As those markets strengthened, and neither the U.S. Treasury nor the U.S Congress showed any interest in vastly expanding the role of direct governmental sources of development financing, the World Bank adapted to the new situation. Progressives and conservatives could both claim victory. That its legacy would come mainly to be associated with conservatives, however, would be a function of the ideological shading of its leaders finally catching up to that of mainstream Washington in the 1980s.

The first use of the World Bank's new structural lending tool happened to coincide with a significant transition in its leadership, a transition that paralleled a much broader ideological shift within its leading creditor state as well as in Great Britain, a key player inside the Bretton Woods institutions since the beginning. Reflecting on the images of Margaret Thatcher and Ronald Reagan, journalists at the time commonly described the shift in terms of the death of Keynesianism and the re-emergence of *laissez-faire* liberalism and of classical 'sound money' orthodoxy. In retrospect, that distinction is too stark. Excessive inflation, deepening fiscal imbalances, and threatened financial panics certainly shaped a new policy consensus across many member states of the Organisation for Economic Co-operation and Development (OECD). But Keynesianism, as conventionally conceived, survived. Indeed, in the U.S. it was given an enhanced military character and it thrived. Similarly, much to

Friedman's annoyance, an accompanying new monetarist fillip across much of the OECD was never truly orthodox nor absolute. Still, classical economics came back into fashion – in the North American academy, in Washington policy circles, on Wall Street and in the City of London, and, hardly coincidentally, in a World Bank now led by the former chief executive officer of the Bank of America. The SAL was a tool readily remoulded in its light.

A reduced economic role for governments, an expanded role for more open markets, export expansion, import liberalisation, the privatisation of public enterprises, more flexible exchange rates, fiscal austerity, monetary targeting, expanding reliance on private financing flows and foreign direct investment (FDI) – all of these policy reforms constituted the new agenda. And all implied deeper institutional change inside the World Bank's client states. If the leaders of those states had once thought that structural adjustment loans represented a low-cost vehicle for increasing net inward resource transfers, they soon realised their mistake. Expanded bank conditionality and a subtly threatened evolution of cross-conditionality with IMF lending programmes promised heightened domestic political pressures. Likewise, however, free marketeers forecasting the dawn of a new, post-Keynesian era where efficient markets would ineluctably constrain such pressures would soon also be disappointed.

SALs in practice turned out to be few, relatively small, and far between during the earliest phase of their implementation. An adapted version, targeted to specific sectors of a client's economy, also did not usher in a complete revolution in the way the World Bank did its main business. Borrowers, unsurprisingly, turned out to be chary of accepting policy conditions deemed too intrusive, even when they needed the money badly. Before the debt crisis of the 1980s came into its fullest bloom, moreover, many middle-income countries most suitable as candidates for policy-based, reform-oriented loans enjoyed access to other sources of financing – mainly foreign commercial bank loans, which generally came with no conditions except repayment with interest. What the World Bank had done when it invented SALs, however, was to create a relatively quick-disbursing vehicle for partially replacing such sources of capital if and when they dried up.

Within the World Bank, SALs had a number of consequences during the 1980s. For one, their logic implied, and their character allowed, a proliferation in policy objectives. Getting incentives right inside client economies meant deeper and deeper structural adjustment. From a bureaucratic point of view, the short-term costs for the World Bank to add conditions to its loans seemed very low. If those conditions were not met or if they were regularly ignored, their long-term costs in terms of the bank's own legitimacy could turn out to be very high. In fact, they deepened the necessity for expanded co-ordination between World Bank and IMF programmes. Money is fungible, and certain limited ideological, functional, and even cultural conflicts forced the two institutions to define and redefine their respective turfs over time.

The key example of where such conflicts could lead occurred in 1988 and 1989 over Argentina (de Vries 1987, 528–531; Polak 1997; Boughton 2001, ch. 11). The IMF was trying to negotiate an adjustment programme with Argentina that included tough fiscal austerity. New loans from the World Bank, for a brief period and likely because of direct political pressure from the U.S. Treasury on its president (by then Barber Conable, who had served in the U.S. Congress from 1965 until 1984), took the pressure off the Argentinean government of the day. From the IMF's point of view, this new financing set back the cause of reform and financial stability. Others, including sitting members of the U.S. Congress whose voices the U.S. Treasury does not even need to hear before it crafts pre-emptive policies, felt that it represented an emergency lifeline for a struggling democracy. When the pressure receded, however, the World Bank reversed course, and a new rapprochement (glorified in a document labelled a 'Concordat') between the two institutions was quickly negotiated on the basis of a now-traditional but always ambiguous distinction between the IMF's expertise in the area of relatively short-term balance-of-payments stabilisation and adjustment and the bank's expertise in long-term adjustment and development (see Ahluwalia 1999). The incident focussed attention on the receding difference between the two mandates. It reminded creditor states of the irrationality of holding back public financing with one hand while providing it with another. More importantly, however, it underlined the new context. Public moneys merely primed the pump of private financing. Official creditors needed a strong and compelling rationale for pumping public money into a debtor country while private money was flowing out. Private markets themselves had become the central instrument available for creditor states committed to channelling increased financial flows to debtors. The World Bank facilitated the process and, at the same time, buffered creditor states from more direct demands for financial resources. It should be emphasised in this regard that the leading creditor remained the U.S., even if the actual source of most development financing had long since migrated from the Treasury and the Congress just up the street from the World Bank to global networks with a principal node in downtown New York City.

It is worth quoting in substantial part the conclusion of the World Bank's historians on the implications of the emergence of structural conditionality on the bank itself.

> The turn toward heavier practice of macropolicy influence had major effects on the World Bank as an institution. It shaped the thrust of the Bank's work and program and surely gave many staff and managers a sense of power exercised. But the costs were heavy. With a higher profile, the institution was more exposed to attack ... The Bank helped cross-reference policy discussion across countries, and the loans that carried [policy] messages sometimes tipped decision balances or facilitated implementation of reform ... One reason the Bank was interesting as a policy promoter was that it was directed to be, and in considerable measure became, a financially powerful political eunuch ...The zone of independence around the Bank diminished, when first ... the Bank began to draw substantial public revenues, and second, began intruding more aggressively into their policymaking (Kapur, Lewis, and Webb 1997, 588–589).

Structural Conditionality in the International Monetary Fund

The IMF was originally designed to monitor and defend a global exchange rate system. The underlying aim was to promote the expansion of world trade. Its financial role followed from the need to provide adequate resources in the short term to enable countries with external payments imbalances to adjust without resorting to system-destructive policies such as competitive currency depreciation. Balance-of-payments adjustment was the key. In practice, the kinds of policy conditions that began to be attached to IMF credit in the mid 1950s focussed on the stabilisation of foreign exchange reserves. As practicable means for accomplishing such stabilisation were sought, path-breaking research inside and outside the IMF pointed to the key role played by excessive domestic credit expansion. This soon translated into IMF programming aimed at the soundness of macroeconomic policies having the most obvious impact on that variable. In its early days, then, the words 'growth' and 'development' had no special place in the IMF lexicon (Polak 1991).[9]

The situation began to change very gradually after the first concessionary lending facility was created in 1963 in an attempt to help commodity-dependent countries stabilise their export proceeds in the face of increasingly turbulent international markets. There followed various adaptations in the IMF's standard lending arrangements: commodity financing facilities, buffer stock facilities, oil facilities, extended IMF facilities, and 'enlarged access' to routine funding. A relatively straightforward line of policy development essentially moved the practice from an ethic that equated payments adjustment with monetary stabilisation to one that attempted in principle to balance stabilisation with long-term economic growth. That line starts with the inception in 1976 of a trust fund, essentially new financial resources for developing countries garnered from the sale of one sixth of the IMF's gold reserves.

The U.S. Treasury proposed the trust fund in 1974, mainly as a relatively inexpensive means of building support among developing countries for its belated plan to legalise the post-1971 system of flexible exchange rates. It also had the additional attraction of not requiring significant new commitments that needed to be authorised by the U.S. Congress. Developing countries were about to be disappointed by the refusal of the main creditor states to increase net aid flows by way of the free allocation of the IMF's fiat money, special drawing rights (SDRs). That refusal, in turn, was rooted in concerns about global inflation induced by excess liquidity and the preference of the U.S., Canada, Germany, and others not to obfuscate the issue of increasing foreign aid budgets directly. Loans granted under the terms of the trust fund did build in an aid element, however, for they were priced at below-market rates and came with relatively easy access conditions.

Ten years later, in 1986, when the original loans from the trust fund began to come due, the members of the IMF created a 'structural adjustment facility' (SAF) to recycle the funds to the poorest developing countries, all of which were asked to submit three-year adjustment programmes to correct macroeconomic and structural problems impeding balance-of-payments adjustment and economic growth. As Harold James (1996, 526) puts it, 'the new programs reflected the conviction that if adjustment were to succeed, it would require a medium-term orientation toward resumption of growth. This would be more feasible if a macroeconomic stabilization plan were associated with microeconomic reforms to stimulate enterprise and initiative at the local level'. One year later, the 'enhanced structural adjustment facility' (ESAF) was established with grants from Japan, Canada, and others to provide financing at low cost and with long maturity periods to the poorest countries in the world, which soon numbered 40.

By this time the public rationalisation for such facilities was to foster growth as well as to promote sustainable international payments balances. Such a rationalisation signalled a potentially far-reaching shift in mandate. Economic growth – a profoundly political matter in both its causes and its consequences – had now achieved something like equivalence with the traditional balance-of-payments objectives of the IMF. Long criticised for forcing financial stringency on countries really requiring a stimulus to establish a virtuous cycle of economic growth, inward capital flows, and productive investment, the IMF would now be forced to move its adjustment time-horizons outward. Sustainable payments positions and sustainable development were acknowledged as interdependent goals. The IMF remained a global 'monetary institution', but by increments it was also becoming an international development agency. For the true believers in politically neutral international organisations, such a transformation presaged much bigger dilemmas in the future. What constituted economic growth? A long series of ancillary questions arise from whatever answer is given. Not least, the following: if growth and development were now the appropriate targets for IFIs, could questions of economic justice be avoided?

The basic set of stabilisation and adjustment policies the IMF had commonly come to advocate found their ultimate rationale during the 1980s in the idea of stable, long-term growth – 'high quality' growth was the term later used by the IMF's managing director. The fact that the term was not innocuous can only be appreciated in retrospect. Traditionally, and in the simplest terms, the typical country coming to the IMF for assistance was driven there by an excess of its international payments over its international receipts, a cash shortfall that it could not easily finance on its own. The IMF was then charged with determining whether the shortfall was temporary, thus justifying the straightforward extension of short-term credit, or fundamental, thus requiring an adjustment programme likely facilitated in part by longer-term IMF credit. In either case, the alternative – assuming private financing, bilateral official development assistance (ODA), and other sources of funding were not available in sufficient amounts – was an immediate reduction in outgoing payments, typically payments for imports. In the case of fundamental problems, the ultimate implications for policies giving rise to them were generally the same. As the IMF's monetary approach to the balance of payments asserted, fundamental current account imbalances implied that underlying policies were generating excessive financial claims. Common sense seemed to lead to the conclusion that monetary stabilisation required macroeconomic adjustments to address the imbalance, for example, cuts in government spending, monetary tightening to rein in excess credit creation, and, if payments deficits were truly fundamental, changes in exchange rates to benefit exporters and discourage importers.

It takes little imagination to extrapolate the internal political consequences in the typical developing country exporting commodities and unfinished goods and importing finished goods, technology, equipment, and services. From the IMF's point of view, such consequences were inevitable, likely to be worsened in the absence of IMF financing, and, in any event, very much matters for 'internal' distributive politics to manage.

Common sense met hard experience in the 1980s, when middle-income developing countries, mainly in Latin America, confronted acute debt crises. As two respected critics of the IMF put it, the IMF's traditional approach risked 'overkill' if reciprocal processes of adjustment were not undertaken in countries generating current account surpluses, or if the deeper causes of macroeconomic policy problems were 'structural' in nature (Diaz-Alejandro 1981; Dell 1983; see also Dell 1981). The latter term was already in use by the IMF to refer to difficulties not attributable to normal business cycles and generally resolvable only in the medium (three to five years) or longer term. Throughout the 1980s and into the 1990s, notwithstanding its public image to the contrary, the IMF's staff, management, and executive board – often in conflict with one another – took such criticism seriously. The evolution of special financing facilities and more generalised adaptations in the actual practice of conditionality must be viewed in this light.

Small libraries were filled with analytical and policy research coming out of the Latin American debt crises of the 1980s. The standard view now holds that the basic problem in its early phase was misdiagnosed. As foreign bank lending, which dominated flows into many countries throughout the 1970s, suddenly dried up, the IMF and the world's main creditor countries thought they were dealing with a liquidity problem, albeit a serious one. The solution – embedded in the 'Baker plan' named for its chief architect, James Baker, then U.S. Treasury Secretary – was to bolster the confidence of private lenders, co-ordinate plans to lengthen debt maturities, and, in some cases, coerce lenders into continued lending. Baker himself put the plan's three main elements more diplomatically: the debtors 'should adopt comprehensive macroeconomic and structural policies', the IMF should play a central role 'in conjunction with increased and more effective structural adjustment lending by the multilateral development banks in support of the adoption of market-oriented policies for growth', and private banks 'should increase their lending in support of comprehensive economic adjustment programs' (cited in Boughton 2001, 417). In the absence of an international lender of last resort, the IMF was available to act as the co-ordinator of efforts on the part of creditor governments to keep money flowing. Economic growth would eventually return, and a rising tide was clearly expected lift all boats. The problem, after all, had occurred on Ronald Reagan's watch.

Alas, optimism can sometimes be excessive, even in the United States. Sufficient and enduring growth did not return to Latin America and the problem deepened. Moreover, the IMF had difficulty adapting to its emerging mandate of structural adjustment. Beyond its staff justifiably feeling out of their depth on microeconomic matters – from bank regulation to tax reform, to public procurement, to legal reform – sceptics in its management and executive ranks clearly saw the institutional risks inherent in the IMF setting itself up for a job that could prove impossible. The staff also considered themselves to be formally restricted by conditionality guidelines adopted by the IMF's board in 1979, which specified a continuing focus on macroeconomic policies. Under the leadership of a dynamic managing director, who identified the urgent necessity for pragmatic adjustment within the institution itself, those guidelines were to prove flexible. But disquiet remained among those who cherished the IMF's apolitical self-image.

The Baker plan, in the end, met with very limited success, especially from the point of view of indebted countries unable to hold policy lines that continued to build up trade surpluses while growth sputtered and domestic political coalitions began to crumble. (Of course, it met with very great success if the core threat really arose from the probability of financial panics in the creditor countries, for the plan clearly gave the implicated banks enough time to get their developing country exposure down to manageable levels in relation to their capital resources.) Diagnosticians both inside and outside the IMF began to conclude that many heavily indebted countries faced solvency crises, not liquidity ones.

As in any domestic context, insolvency seemed necessarily to imply debt restructuring, a euphemism for outright debt reduction to sustainable levels. Such a solution lay at the heart of the next 'plan' to resolve the regional crisis, this one identified with the name of Nicholas Brady, who had replaced Baker as U.S. Treasury Secretary. In the absence of an international bankruptcy court, the IMF was again called upon to co-ordinate national efforts, but this time to construct the functional equivalent of such a court. In short, creative debt workouts generally occurred under the umbrella of a IMF stand-by arrangement, which conditioned effective debt reductions on policy adjustment programmes emphasising macroeconomic matters but increasingly encouraging changes in deeper internal economic structures. In practical terms, this entailed co-ordinating, even mutually negotiating, letters of agreement between the borrowing country and the IMF and between the borrowing country and the World Bank. After 1989, moreover, many programmes had longer time-horizons and were also implicitly linked to new money flows directly from creditor treasuries.

The adequacy of such flows is a matter of dispute to the present day, especially for the poorest debtor countries. But few involved in the debt crises of the 1980s emerged happy, and everyone confronted but never clarified the fundamental political, economic, and legal ambiguities inherent in the core problem.[10] When economic growth returned in many of the indebted Latin American countries in the 1990s, optimists concluded that international cooperation had worked. This included many U.S. banks, which did not face ruin from having their shareholders' equity completely wiped out by Latin American defaults, and members of the U.S. Congress, who were never called upon to help those banks directly and who never permitted themselves to be pushed in the direction of vastly increasing the official resources available to the IMF.[11] Pessimists, conversely, contended that the problem had merely gone into remission. They agreed, on balance, that bankers and their regulators in creditor countries, as well as certain elites in debtor countries, had emerged as the true winners. In between those positions were the perplexed, who were left with a simple counterfactual issue to ponder. Would mass populations in Latin America have been better off under any other scenario? However they answered such a question, neither optimists nor pessimists could help observing that the trauma of the Latin American debt crises of the 1980s had profoundly transformed the IMF.

The capital-recycling mechanism at the heart of the global system of economic growth and adjustment could not be reformed. Its underlying norms and rules could not be addressed explicitly. In short, no formal rules equivalent to those governing world trade could be agreed for world finance. Private intermediaries, regulated by national authorities, could not be regulated at the international level. No single international arbiter could be chosen. The die had been cast long ago, when financial regulatory authority was taken off the multilateral negotiating table and reserved for national governments, and when those governments began using that authority to give more liberty to non-domestic intermediaries than to domestic ones (see Helleiner 1994). The subsequent policy priority assigned to financial markets in allocation of international resources for development, a priority most clearly enshrined in U.S. policy, was reinforced as most governments of rich countries intentionally reduced the relative and absolute volumes of public financing available for direct foreign aid. The consequences of increasingly free international capital flows through private channels could and would be addressed with available tools adapted for the purpose.

The historical record of international financial turmoil in the 1980s will be subject to interpretation and debate for many years to come. As it stands now, however, most interpretations place the Latin American debt crisis at its centre. In that context, they also strongly suggest that the expansion of the IMF's mandate into the realm of structural adjustment during that decade did not have a single, easily traceable source. It is true that strategic thinkers on the IMF's staff, most prominently in the Research Department, began arguing in the early 1980s that supply-side reforms were necessary to put leading debtor states onto a more sustainable financial track. Certainly not coincidentally, such views paralleled new thinking coming into vogue down Pennsylvania Avenue at a U.S. Treasury Department then led by firm supporters of the Reagan revolution.[12] Nevertheless, more than one executive director and many line staff members charged with designing and implementing actual country programmes firmly rejected calls for a formal expansion in the IMF's responsibilities in this area. The record also indicates reticence on the part of the executive board to give Jacques de Larosière, Managing Director during the first half of the decade, its full and enthusiastic support for projecting the organisation willy-nilly into the centre of a crisis that was beginning to require major adjustments in some basic economic and political structures somewhere. Clearly, structures deep inside weak countries desperate for capital looked the most vulnerable. In 1981, 1986, 1987, and 1988, the board directly addressed the question of explicitly including in its conditional lending instruments performance criteria related to those structures. Each time, however, it refused to authorise a formal, binding role for the organisation.

In 1981, Ariel Buira, then Mexico's Executive Director at the IMF, eloquently captured the scepticism the U.S.-led ideological shift to the right was then engendering in the developing world. In reaction to a staff paper recommending a limited economic role for the state, he noted that with regard to the 'nineteenth century liberal concept in which the state has ... no development responsibilities, [my authorities] did not expect Fund guidance on this matter' (IMF Executive Board Meeting Minutes, 20 April 1981, cited in Boughton 2001, 588–589). By the end of the decade, however, enough directors from the developing world were in agreement to authorise the staff, in conjunction with their counterparts at the World Bank, to experiment with the concept of deeper adjustment in specific cases where structural reform appeared 'essential for the achievement of external viability' (managing director cited in Boughton 2001, 590).

Gradual movement in the direction of embedding a structural reform agenda into IMF lending programmes did occur, however, for many Latin American debtors. Other significant cases bolstering the constituency for such an agenda include some ironies. In the case of South Africa, for example, the IMF designed a stand-by arrangement that wrapped a cloak of political neutrality and economic reasoning around an attack on labour market inefficiencies directly attributable to apartheid. Supporting structural adjustment in this sense was a broad constituency that included many developing countries. More controversially, signal programmes for Kenya, Tanzania, Uganda, and the Philippines during the 1980s edged very close to the inclusion of requirements for anticorruption, privatisation measures, and other structural measures, but formal performance criteria along these lines proved too controversial. Enforced policy liberalisation, or market-oriented reform, would have to wait until the next decade. The necessity to adjust unsustainable current account deficits overrode rhetorical commitments to 'adjustment *with* economic growth' at least in the short run. Formal commitments could still only be tied to that necessity. Throughout the decade, spokesmen for debtor nations continued to echo Buira's point, albeit with apparently declining enthusiasm: even if structural reforms were needed in many countries, it was beyond the authority and the competence of the IMF to enforce domestic institutional change. The IMF's historian puts the matter simply:

> Despite a universal agreement that growth was a 'primary objective of economic policy' and that adjustment would often fail if growth was too long in coming all efforts to link adjustment with growth foundered on this simple dilemma. Lacking a well-established and validated model of economic growth, the Fund could not require structural reforms as a condition of its credits. Not until domestic political support emerged for these reforms in their own right – not until the silent revolution was won – would the dichotomy between growth and stability finally fade away (Boughton 2001, 614).

That may be, but it is again worth recalling that the adjective 'structural' was used throughout the 1980s by IMF directors from poorer countries to refer not just to internal impediments to growth but also to external constraints on that growth. Low commodity prices, oil price shocks, turbulent exchange rates among leading currencies, closed markets for exports, and, again, the vagaries of privatised international finance – these surely constituted 'structures' as well. Could reform of such structures really not be linked to adjustment strategies in developing countries? Apparently not. But special funds and enhancements in standard financing arrangements could be established in the IMF partly to compensate for the one-sidedness of the process.

The institution's historian sums up the experience of the organisation during the 1980s in the following terms:

The reliance of many low-income countries on short and medium-term financing from the Fund in the early 1980s and the attempt of many middle-income developing countries to rely on macroeconomic policy reforms in the mid-1980s exposed weaknesses in the coordination of multilateral assistance. Efforts by the Fund, the World Bank, and other agencies to collaborate more fully in the second half of the decade were only partially successful. That effort did, however, help prepare the institutions for the much greater level of coordination that would be required in the 1990s, when countries in transition from central planning would have to make comprehensive structural and macroeconomic reforms in a very short period of time ... Throughout the 1980s, the Fund circumscribed its own scope for action by limiting explicit conditionality to macroeconomic policies and avoiding interference with policies that could be construed as politically rather than economically motivated. The initial success of countries that liberalized on their own – the silent revolution – drew the Fund out of that reluctance in ways that would enable it to play a more active role in promoting structural reform in the 1990s (Boughton 2001, 50).

While the latter contention is plausible, it again begs the question of where the norms embedded in actual reform programmes had come from, and why alternatives were infeasible. The continuation of the story into the 1990s draws attention back ever more insistently to the earlier and hardly silent 'revolution' that had occurred in the United States.

The Bretton Woods Institutions in the 1990s and Beyond

The 1990s are still too fresh in historical memory to permit a balanced assessment. Key events included a remarkable boom in the U.S. economy, a bursting financial bubble in Japan, a decisive move toward monetary union in Western Europe, the rise of what the Chinese called their socialist market economy, and an equally decisive shift away from socialism in Central and Eastern Europe. Linking those regional developments together was the vast expansion and increased volatility of international capital flows, but with continuing national-level experiments with various measures to control or influence such flows (Armijo 1999; Andrews, Henning, and Pauly 2002). In this context, the seeds of deliberate efforts to encourage, even to force, structural adjustment in developing countries that were sown in the 1980s flowered upon the terrain tended by the World Bank and the IMF. This occurred despite a relative decline in the financial size of either organisation relative to those burgeoning international capital flows and despite rising political attacks on both of them from the right and left sides of the political spectrum inside their leading member state.[13] Why? The story of the 1980s recounted above provides a clue.

There is no shortage of simple explanations on offer for the apparent emergence of the IMF and the World Bank as the enforcers of structural adjustment in a new global regime. Even if not to the exclusion of all other factors, public choice analysts continue to emphasise the preservationist and expansionist instincts of their senior managers and employees. Historians of both organisations assign significant weight to the conversion of national authorities in developing countries to sound economic orthodoxy as alternative strategies failed. Sceptics surmise a grand design orchestrated by the U.S. Treasury, or by faceless private financiers pulling the Treasury's strings.

Any such reading, on its own, does not fit comfortably with the full story of the 1980s. Taken together, they only help redescribe the mixed motivations of the 1980s and the ambiguous outcomes of the 1990s. Such an amalgamation does little to advance a deeper understanding, nor does it help anticipate future developments.

In the early post–World War II period, the U.S. Congress needed to be convinced that U.S. taxpayers would not be left with the full bill for reconstructing economies destroyed by the war or for easing the transition of European colonies to political independence. In the absence of guarantees to that effect, the Bretton Woods institutions would never have seen the light of day. During each succeeding round of legislation required to allow those institutions to develop, new guarantees were required mainly to convince U.S. legislators that public monies would not be wasted and that they would supplement, not substitute for, private financing. Conditionality itself was shaped in this context. Its strengthening and broadening into 'structural' variants correlate almost perfectly with increasing reliance on private financial markets as the world's principal source of development finance and with a declining U.S. interest in IFIs except as they connected to those markets or were needed to compensate for deficiencies in those markets (Kahler 1990).

In many member states, policy changes needed to participate in bolstering the resources of the World Bank or adapting the formal mandate of the IMF are usually handled by the finance minister, the central bank governor, and a small set of elite bureaucrats.[14] Keeping national treasuries open and legislatures supportive is relatively easy. In the U.S., this has never been the case. Over time, moreover, U.S. financial officials had greater difficulty in maintaining control over such issues, much less in fostering strategic consistency. As the Cold War receded, the situation became even more difficult as Congress came ever more obviously to the fore, while the relative power of the presidency seemed to erode. Simultaneously, financial markets became much more prominent as the mechanisms through which key distributive decisions were taken within U.S. society as a whole. Those markets also became much more important as mechanisms through which the U.S. polity linked the interests of that society with the interests of both developed and emerging economies around the world.

U.S. attention to the IMF and the World Bank now clearly ebbs and flows with the absence or presence of crises in financial markets, or the absence or presence of security crises that can be addressed in part through easing the impact of financial market pressures. In other words, it correlates most obviously with the existence of external challenges that have become threatening enough to justify some kind of financial response but not yet so urgent as to demand far less economical recourse to direct, unilateral aid from the U.S. Treasury. An upswing in this cycle occurred once again in the late 1990s, when the institutions were enlisted to oversee the orderly reduction of financial obligations in heavily indebted poor countries (the so-called HIPC Initiative). It also occurred in the wake of terrorist attacks in September 2001. In recent years American attention has sometimes also been heightened by the advocacy work of special-interest nongovernmental organisations (NGOs). Close observers have demonstrated how such advocacy has actually promoted the further elaboration of structural conditionality in the IMF and the World Bank.[15]

Conclusion

On the assumption that the U.S. continues to lead in the contemporary international system, the narrative histories outlined above suggest the following counterfactual question. Without the discourse on conditionality and structural adjustment, would the U.S. political commitment to the IMF and the World Bank increase? It seems unlikely. Indeed, the reverse seems much more plausible. Throughout the 1980s, the discourse itself arose directly out of U.S. political debates on issues of world order. Both on the 'left', with McNamara's commitment to poverty reduction, as well as on the right, with the rise of supply-side economics, the discourse of structural adjustment engaged or attempted to engage core U.S. interests. Throughout the 1980s, certain interests became obvious as U.S. financial intermediaries faced the prospect of catastrophe arising from their Latin American portfolios. In the 1990s, similar interests would be undeniable when countries in transition from communism as well as dynamic East Asian countries confronted a situation of sudden and catastrophic capital flight.

Across the cases touched on in this chapter, demands for ever deeper structural change in borrowing countries became more insistent. As Miles Kahler (1998, 21) points out, 'assuring the confidence of investors and nudging government toward prudent policies in the new environment had become the central task of multilateral institutions and industrialized-country governments in the 1990s'. This nudging really entailed promoting norm-governed behaviour, with the norms drawn from an idealised version of U.S. economic history and a close reading of contemporary U.S. economic policy.[16] The IMF's managing director appealed directly to such norms whenever he advocated 'financial market operations organized around objective commercial criteria, transparency in industrial conglomerates and in government-business relations more generally, the dismantling of monopolies, and the elimination of government-directed lending and procurement programs' (Camdessus 1998). In truth, such norms described the actual history of no industrial country, including the United States. They did, however, coincide clearly with the vision for a global market-system that came to be advocated by both government and business in the U.S. after World War II, and especially after the Cold War began to fade. The shift from 'government managed to market-based mode of governance' within the international system has been widely noted (Kahler 1998). The view that this was logical, inevitable, and even unstoppable came to be widely embraced during the 1990s. Some analysts of the implications and prospects for developing countries have nevertheless adopted a less determinist position. Devesh Kapur, for example, sums up one such argument:

> Norms can ... serve as a fig-leaf for more prosaic material interests. There is understandable skepticism that richer countries are long on norms when they are short on resources, and the increasing attention to norms of governance even as development budgets decline is perhaps not entirely coincidental. As long as the Cold War was on, 'crony capitalism' in Indonesia was not considered a problem. Nor was it a problem while the East Asian 'miracle' was being trumpeted. But when the Asia crisis of 1997–98 erupted, 'norms' of corporate governance were strenuously advanced to deflect attention from broader issues of the nature and quality of international financial regulation (Kapur 2000, 17).[17]

As it relates to the recent phase in the expansion of structural conditionality in the World Bank and the IMF, Kapur's position appears eminently supportable. Pushing reflection on the larger post–World War II experience one step further, however, promises deeper insight into both the most significant cause of the shift toward market-based governance and the most likely challenges ahead. In short, the narrative of this chapter suggests that the shift mirrored precisely the central struggle within contemporary U.S. capitalism since the early 1980s. That struggle may reasonably be interpreted as concerning the reconstruction of the middle-ground inside the U.S. between an enduring commitment to a still-national economy and a decided preference for openness in the cause of system stabilisation, at the very least, and in the cause of system transformation, at most. Consistent with a longstanding theme in American economic history, the customs, institutions, and processes involved in that reconstruction quite deliberately rendered opaque the borderlines between state and society. To a considerable extent, the struggle now revolved around questions concerning the appropriate limits of strict market principles within U.S. society. In more concrete terms, it focussed on the place of financial markets within that society, with all that this implies in terms of measuring important political and social outcomes in narrowly financial terms.

To be sure, the struggle did not begin when Ronald Reagan won the White House. Its terms had antecedents going back to the founding of the country. During the post–Great Depression period and right up to the 1970s, one set of answers to the principal dilemma created a relatively stable equilibrium: competitive markets centred on private corporations with diffuse (non-bank) ownership, fragmented financial markets (key parts of which now rested on implicit or explicit government guarantees) and an overarching ideology combining free enterprise with an expansion of public funding for social welfare, health, and educational programmes. Often obscured but always highly significant was the role of government as system regulator, promoter of a massive defence-industrial base, and guarantor of a modicum of social equity (see Roe 1994; Doremus *et al.* 1998). In the 1980s, a new set of answers coursed through the U.S. debate, the end result of which was to favour greater degrees of economic concentration, much less fragmented financial markets, a reduction of social welfare programmes, and an ethic of underlying market supervision by government instead of overt market regulation. Occurring at the same time was a complicated expansion in the scale of implicit financial guarantees provided by government agencies and a deepening sense of disquiet about the moral hazards thereby entailed. When in 1998 the Federal Reserve and the Treasury facilitated the massive financial operation that stabilised and then in an orderly fashion unwound the Long-Term Capital Management hedge fund, that sense of disquiet became quite palpable.

The rise of private intermediaries as the key providers of external financing for developing countries tracks a deeper transformation within the world's dominant economy. Here is the true taproot for the changing mandates of the main IFIs. The elaboration of their practice of structural conditionality makes little sense if it is divorced from this context. Ideological and structural change within the system leader implies the need for accommodating change among those who seek to benefit from the system it leads, and who sense on the basis of experience little prospect for the near-term construction of an alternative system.

Certain outcomes are undeniable – the tiering of developing economies in terms of their creditworthiness, the increasing desperation of those countries deemed uncreditworthy, mounting pressures on national policies aimed at mitigating income inequality, and the expansion in possibilities for exit for the owners of liquid capital. All such outcomes raise difficult international as well as domestic political problems, and those outcomes themselves summon a political response. The IMF and the World Bank arose in the context of an experiment aiming to foster international economic interdependence without simultaneously creating a global government.[18] The contemporary elaboration of their mandates is a political response consistent with that experiment, even as it now relies on financial markets for its motor force.[19]

Since asymmetries of power are hard to overlook, difficult for the weak to accept, and important for the strong to obscure, international political buffers are necessary even in 'market-led' systems.[20] In this light, the IMF and the World Bank may be viewed as a gift of history, one that would be difficult to replicate if they had to be created today *ab initio* today. They are led by the strong, but give voice to the weak. They can learn lessons at leading members, and they can teach those lessons to followers. They can deflect blame and play the role of scapegoats when things do not go smoothly. They are useful surrogates for the imagined collectivity commonly now referred to by politicians and journalists as 'the international community'.

Because of their relatively modest size and their ambivalent record in actually serving as catalysts to private market solutions for basic economic problems, both institutions can actually do little on their own to move the system toward what their founders called 'symmetry' (see, for example, Hurrell and Woods 1999).[21] It is not implausible to argue, however, that international economic inequities would be even worse in their absence. Such a view, of course, would be contentious, but the most sweeping positions currently being taken in related arguments over a new international financial architecture are surely misguided and misdirected. Scepticism is the appropriate response to calls for the abolition of the World Bank and the IMF from the ideological left or the ideological right, to calls for a radical refocussing of institutional mandates across the two organisations, and to calls for their massive expansion. All of such demands profoundly misunderstand the political underpinning of the international economy as it evolved after 1945.

A process of institutional adaptation at the international level has long been part of the experiment that began over half a century ago. In retrospect, it is but a step from the IMF's trust fund of 1976 to the HIPC Initiative of today, and from the World Bank's first SALs to today's Poverty Reduction Strategy Papers. The evolution of the practice of structural conditionality within both institutions has been almost perfectly attuned to developments within the state that continues in its role as leading proponent of that experiment. Those developments are not easily attributable to any one agency of U.S. government or to any one sector of its national economy. They mainly reflect instead the abiding interest of a complicated state and civil society in stability abroad but chary of paying its full cost.[22] At times, the historical record offers a glimpse of an aspiration deep within that state and society for a progressive transformation of world order. Whether it takes the Wilsonian form of trying to 'make the world safe for democracy', or the more mundane form of promoting the American way of doing business, periodic expressions of that aspiration seem quickly to elicit a conservative reaction. That reaction is often mistaken for isolationism; in the contemporary period it is in practice the reassertion of a still internationalist but more realistic impulse to correlate feasible ends with available means.

During the 1980s, the U.S. moved decisively to expand the scope for markets to resolve internal distributive problems. Other states and societies having recovered prominent positions in the hierarchy of world power since 1945 moved in a similar direction. But the system that bound them still required a leader, and the leader still required support from its civil society for a durable policy of external engagement. Support could not be mustered inside the U.S. for the unambiguously progressive policy advocated by many NGOs today, say one that could work only through significantly expanded and more open multilateral institutions. But neither could support be maintained for a consistently conservative retrenchment.[23] The continuing effort to strike a balance between these two positions within American civil society still shapes the deeper structure now encouraging adjustment elsewhere. The operations of more open capital markets and the ever more intimately related lending policies of leading IFIs remain rooted in that structure.

Notes

1 For earlier versions of this chapter, see Pauly (2003b) and Pauly (2003a). For constructive comments on drafts, the author is grateful to Albert Berry, Eric Helleiner, Richard Webb, Gerry Helleiner, Barry Herman, Gustavo Indart, John Kirton, Peter I. Hajnal, Marc Flandreau, Jérôme Sgard, and Nicholas Jabko. The Social Sciences and Humanities Research Council of Canada provided much-appreciated financial support.

2 For application of such an analysis to the IMF's core mandate, see Pauly (1997).

3 'There is no separate economic truth that applies to developed, or to developing countries' (James 1996, 609).

4 On the latter theme, seeScholte (1998), Woods (2001), O'Brien (2000), and Scholte (2003).

5 For a subtle explication of this part of the original Keynesian vision itself, see Skidelsky (2000).

6 The fullest exploration of this theme can be found in Ruggie (1998).

7 Krueger was appointed Deputy Managing Director of the IMF in 2001, following the retirement of Stanley Fischer, who left shortly after Michel Camdessus stepped down as Managing Director.

8 See also de Vries (1987, ch. 6).

9 Polak was a principal architect of the IMF's monetary approach; see Polak (2001).

10 For an excellent exposition of these issues, see Cohen (1986).

11 In this regard, note the assertion by Boughton (2001, 44) that 'the single greatest problem for the Fund in the 1980s was to garner the financial resources to meet the demand for its services'.

12 Richard Erb, who held the key role of IMF Deputy Managing Director after 1984, began his policymaking career as staff assistant to Richard Nixon in 1971. After 1974, he worked intermittently at the U.S. Treasury and the conservative American Enterprise Institute. In 1981, he became U.S. Executive Director at the IMF (see Boughton 2001, 1044).

13 The critiques are thoroughly set out in the report of the International Financial Institutions Advisory Commission (Meltzer 2000), especially chapters 2 and 3. See also Bordo and James (2000).

14 The situation is similar in many developing countries, where the role of the central bank in particular has recently been gaining in political importance (Maxfield 1997).

15 On the link between NGOs and U.S. Congress–U.S. Treasury and its impact on structural conditionality in the World Bank, see Wade (2001).

16 On the notion of norm-governed behavioural change, see Ruggie (1983).

17 See also Woods (1998; 2001).

18 On the original political bargaining behind the Bretton Woods institutions, see Eichengreen (1996, ch. 4).

19 In this regard, the special session of the UN General Assembly on Financing for Development in 2002 was relevant. For background, see United Nations General Assembly (2000). For antecedent debates, see Krasner (1985).

20 The theme is cogently addressed in the international monetary arena in Cohen (1989).

21 Worth examining carefully are debt-reduction efforts organised under the HIPC Initiative creditor countries, which are co-ordinated through the IMF and the World Bank.

22 This theme is explored in much recent research on international institution building (see, for example, Luck 1999; Hoopes and Brinkley 1997).

23 Witness the mixed signals in the first year of the Bush administration. Against the backdrop of electioneering that asserted the necessity of reining in the World Bank and the IMF, and even after overseeing the installation of a more 'conservative' team at the top of the latter (including, again, Ann Krueger), a U.S. Treasury said to be hostile to structural conditionality as well as to any prominent role for either organisation, strongly supported a massive bailout of Turkey that involved detailed conditionality on a range of microeconomic issues (see IMF 2001b; 2001a). See *IMF Survey*, May 21, 2001 and August 13, 2001. Later, key elements of structural conditionality were embedded in the administration's newly created Millennium Challenge Account, which promised significantly expanded foreign aid for countries willing to commit themselves to measurable reforms in economic policymaking and internal governance (see Tarnoff and Nowels 2004; Brainerd 2003a; Radelet 2003; Brainerd 2003b).

References

Ahluwalia, Montek S. (1999). 'The IMF and the World Bank in the New Financial Architecture'. In United Nations Conference on Trade and Development, ed., *International Monetary and Financial Issues for the 1990s*, vol. 11, pp. 1–26. United Nations, New York.

Andrews, David, C. Randall Henning, and Louis W. Pauly, eds. (2002). *Governing the World's Money*. Cornell University Press, Ithaca.

Armijo, Leslie Elliott (1999). *Financial Globalization and Democracy in Emerging Markets*. St. Martin's Press, New York.

Berger, Suzanne and Ronald P. Dore, eds. (1996). *National Diversity and Global Capitalism*. Cornell University Press, Ithaca.

Bordo, Michael D. and Harold James (2000). 'The Internatoinal Monetary Fund: its Present Role in Historical Perspective'. NBER Working Paper No. 7724. <www.nber.org/papers/W7724> (November 2005).

Boughton, James (2001). *Silent Revolution: The International Monetary Fund, 1979–1989*. International Monetary Fund, Washington DC.

Brainerd, Lael (2003a). *The Other War: Global Poverty and the Millennium Challenge Account*. Brookings Institution Press and the Centre for Global Development, Washington DC.

Brainerd, Lael (2003b). 'Compassionate Conservatism Confronts Global Poverty'. *Washington Quarterly* vol. 26, no. 2, pp. 149–169.

Burley, Anne-Marie (1993). 'Regulating the World: Multilateralism, International Law, and the Projection of the New Deal Regulatory State'. In J.G. Ruggie, ed., *Multilateralism Matters*. Columbia University Press, New York.

Camdessus, Michel (1998). 'Good Governance Has Become Essential in Promoting Growth and Stability'. *IMF Survey* vol. 27, no. 3 (9 February), pp. 36–38. <www.imf.org/external/pubs/ft/survey/pdf/020998.pdf> (November 2005).

Caporaso, James A. (2000). 'Changes in the Westphalian Order: Territory, Public Authority, and Sovereignty'. *International Studies Review* vol. 2, no. 2, pp. 1–28.

Cohen, Benjamin (1986). *In Whose Interest? International Banking and American Foreign Policy*. Yale University Press, New Haven, CT.

Cohen, Wesley M. and D. Levinthal (1989). 'Innovation and Learning: The Two Faces of R&D'. *Economic Journal* vol. 99, no. 3, pp. 569–596.

Cooper, Richard N. (1968). *The Economics of Interdependence: Economic Policy in the Atlantic Community.* McGraw-Hill, New York.

de Cecco, Marcello (1976). 'International Financial Markets and U.S. Domestic Policy since 1945'. *International Affairs* vol. 52, pp. 381–399.

de Cecco, Marcello (1979). 'Origins of the Postwar Payments System'. *Cambridge Journal of Economics* vol. 2, pp. 49–61.

de Vries, Barend A. (1987). *Remaking the World Bank.* Seven Locks Press, Washington DC.

Dell, Sidney (1981). 'On Being Grandmotherly: The Evolution of IMF Conditionality'. Princeton Essays in International Finance No. 144. Princeton University Press, Princeton.

Dell, Sidney (1983). 'Stabilization: The POlitical Economy of Overkill'. In J. Williamson, ed., *IMF Conditionality.* Institute for International Economics, Washington DC.

Diaz-Alejandro, Carlos (1981). 'Southern Cone Stabilization Plans'. In W.R. Cline and S. Weintraub, eds., *Economic Stabilization in Developing Countries.* Brookings Institution, Washington DC.

Doremus, Paul N., William W. Keller, Louis W. Pauly, *et al.* (1998). *The Myth of the Global Corporation.* Princeton University Press, Princeton.

Eichengreen, Barry (1996). *Globalizing Capital.* Princeton University Press, Princeton.

Friedberg, Aaron L. (2000). *In the Shadow of the Garrison State.* Princeton University Press, Princeton.

Helleiner, Eric (1994). *States and the Reemergence of Global Finance: from Bretton Woods to the 1990s.* Cornell University Press, Ithaca, NY.

Hoopes, Townsend and Douglas Brinkley (1997). *FDR and the Creation of the UN.* Yale University Press, New Haven.

Hurrell, Andrew and Ngaire Woods, eds. (1999). *Inequality, Globalization, and World Politics.* Oxford University Press, Oxford.

Ikenberry, John (2001). *After Victory: Institutions, Strategic Restraint, and the Rebuilding of Order after Major Wars.* Princeton University Press, Princeton.

International Monetary Fund (2001a). 'IMF Approves Drawing under Stand-By Arrangement for Turkey, Commends Ambitious Economic Program'. *IMF Survey* vol. 30, no. 16, pp. 261–262. <www.imf.org/external/pubs/ft/survey/2001/081301.pdf> (November 2005).

International Monetary Fund (2001b). 'IMF Executive Board Approves $8 Billion Augmentation of Stand-By Credit for Turkey'. *IMF Survey* vol. 30, no. 10 (21 May), pp. 165–166. November 2005).

James, Harold (1996). *International Monetary Cooperation since Bretton Woods.* International Monetary Fund and Oxford University Press, Washington and New York.

Kahler, Miles (1990). 'The United States and the International Monetary Fund: Declining Influence or Declining Interest?' In M.P. Karns and K.A. Mingst, eds., *The United States and Multilateral Institutions*, pp. 91–114. Unwin Hyman, New York.

Kahler, Miles (1998). 'Introduction'. In M. Kahler, ed., *Capital Flows and Financial Crises.* Cornell University Press, Ithaca.

Kapur, Devesh, John P. Lewis, and Richard Webb (1997). *The World Bank: Its First Half Century.* Vol. 1. Brookings Institution, Washington DC.

Kapur, Devesh (2000). 'Processes of Change in International Organization'. Working Paper 00-02. <www.wcfia.harvard.edu/papers/164__Helsinki3.wcfia.pdf> (November 2005).

Kennedy, Paul M. (1987). *The Rise and Fall of Great Powers.* Random House, New York.

Keohane, Robert and Joseph Nye (1977). *Power and Interdependence: World Politics in Transition.* Little, Brown, Boston.

Kindleberger, Charles P. (1973). *The World in Depression, 1929–1939*. University of California Press, Berkeley.

Knock, Thomas J. (1992). *To End All Wars*. Princeton University Press, Princeton.

Krasner, Stephen D. (1985). *Structural Conflict: The Third World against Global Liberalism*. University of California Press, Berkeley.

Krasner, Stephen D. (1999). *Sovereignty: Organized Hypocrisy*. Princeton University Press, Princeton.

Luck, Edward (1999). *Mixed Messages: American Politics and International Organizations, 1919–1939*. Brookings Institution, Washington DC.

Mason, Edward S. and Robert E. Asher (1973). *The World Bank Since Bretton Woods*. Brookings Institution, Washington DC.

Maxfield, Sylvia (1997). *Gatekeepers of Growth: The International Political Economy of Central Banks in Developing Countries*. Princeton University Press, Princeton.

McNamara, Robert and Brian Vandemark (1996). *In Retrospect: The Tragedy and Lessons of Vietnam*. Vintage Press, New York.

Meltzer, Allan H. (2000). 'Report of the International Financial Institutions Advisory Commission'. United States Congress, Washington DC. <www.house.gov/jec/imf/meltzer.htm> (November 2005).

Nau, Henry (2001). *At Home Abroad*. Cornell University Press, Ithaca.

O'Brien, Robert, Anne Marie Goetz, Jan Aart Scholte, *et al.* (2000). *Contesting Global Governance: Multilateral Economic Institutions and Global Social Movements*. Cambridge University Press, Cambridge.

Pauly, Louis W. (1997). *Who Elected the Bankers? Surveillance and Control in the World Economy*. Cornell University Press, Ithaca.

Pauly, Louis W. (2003a). 'New Therapies from Contemporary Money Doctors: The Evolution of Structural Conditionality in the Bretton Woods Institutions'. In M. Flandreau, ed., *Money Doctors: The Experience of International Financial Advising, 1850–2000*, pp. 276–305. Routledge, London.

Pauly, Louis W. (2003b). 'Enforcing the Rules in a Global Economy: The Emergence of Structural Conditionality in the World Bank and the International Monetary Fund'. In A. Berry and G. Indart, eds., *Critical Issues in International Financial Reform*, pp. 237–262. Transaction Publishers, Rutgers NJ.

Polak, Jacques (1991). 'The Changing Nature of IMF Conditionality'. Princeton Essays on International Finance No. 184. Princeton University Press, Princeton.

Polak, Jacques (1997). 'The World Bank and the IMF: A Changing Relationship'. In D. Kapur, J.P. Lewis and R. Webb, eds., *The World Bank: Its First Half Century*, vol. 2. Brookings Institution, Washington DC.

Polak, Jacques (2001). 'The Two Monetary Approaches to the Balance of Payments: Keynesian and Johnsonian'. IMF Working Paper No. WP/01/100. Washington DC. <www.imf.org/external/pubs/ft/wp/2001/wp01100.pdf> (November 2005).

Radelet, Steven (2003). 'Bush and Foreign Aid'. *Foreign Affairs* vol. 82, no. 5, pp. 104–117.

Rodgers, Yana Van der Meulen and Jane C. Cooley (1999). 'Outstanding Female Economists in the Analysis and Practice of Development Economic'. *World Development* vol. 27, no. 8, pp. 1397–1411.

Roe, Mark J. (1994). *Strong Managers, Weak Owners: The Political roots of American Corporate Finance*. Princeton University Press, Princeton.

Ruggie, John G. (1983). 'International Regimes, Transactions, and Change: Embedded Liberalism in the Postwar Economic Order'. In S.D. Krasner, ed., *International Regimes*. Cornell University Press, Ithaca.

Ruggie, John G. (1998). *Constructing the World Polity: Essays on International Institutionalization*. Routledge, London.

Santaella, Julio A. (1993). 'Stabilization and External Enforcement'. *IMF Staff Papers* vol. 40, no. 3, pp. 584–621.

Scholte, Jan Aart (1998). 'The IMF Meets Civil Society'. *Finance and Development* vol. 35, no. 3, pp. 42–45.

Scholte, Jan Aart and Albrecht Schnabel (2003). *Civil Society and Global Finance*. Routledge, London.

Skidelsky, Robert (2000). *John Maynard Keynes: Fighting for Britain, 1937–1946*. Macmillan, London.

Stern, Ernest (1983). 'World Bank Financing of Structural Adjustment'. In J. Williamson, ed., *IMF Conditionality*. Institute for International Economics, Washington DC.

Tarnoff, Curt and Larry Nowels (2004). 'Foreign Aid: An Introductory Overview of U.S. Programs and Policy'. CRS Report for Congress. <usinfo.state.gov/usa/infousa/trade/files/98-916.pdf> (November 2005).

Trachtenberg, Marc (1999). *A Constructed Peace*. Princeton University Press, Princeton.

United Nations General Assembly (2000). 'Towards a Stable International Financial System, Responsive to the Challenges of Development, Especially in the Developing Countries'. A/55/187, 27 July. <www.un.org/documents/ga/docs/55/a55187.pdf> (November 2005).

Wade, Robert Hunter (2001). 'The U.S. Role in the Malaise at the World Ban'. Paper prepared for the annual meeting of the American Political Science Association, San Francisco, 28–30 August.

Woods, Ngaire (1998). 'Governance in International Organization: The Case for Reforming the Bretton Woods Institutions'. In United Nations Conference on Trade and Development, ed., *International Monetary and Financial Issues for the 1990s*, vol. 9, pp. 81–106. United Nations, New York.

Woods, Ngaire (2001). 'Making the IMF and World Bank More Accountable'. *International Affairs* vol. 77, no. 1, pp. 83–100.

Chapter 14

World Trade Organization Gridlock and Alternative Regimes to Pursue an International Social Clause

Scott Vaughan

This chapter examines some issues arising from the expanding mandate, universal membership, and rigid internal governance structures of the World Trade Organization (WTO). It addresses some of the governance issues related to the WTO, and specifically how the expansion of the WTO agenda to include disciplines covering an array of behind-the-border measures coupled with its promise of delivering measurable development benefits to least developed countries, has prompted concerns both about the 'mission creep' of the institution as well as intense public scrutiny regarding its legitimacy, accountability, and transparency of governance structures. The debate echoes similar public concerns about the World Bank and the International Monetary Fund (IMF) following the expansion of their mandates with the inclusion of new conditions attached to lending and structural adjustment programmes. However, the greatest challenge to the WTO comes not from criticism from the outside regarding the scope of its mandate, but rather from the inside because of the structural problems that hampers flexible decision making. The chapter comments on the prescriptive proposals of Sylvia Ostry, Louis Pauly, Michael Trebilcock, and others to streamline and improve the decision-making apparatus of the WTO. The chapter closes by discussing how the WTO can respond to the additional demands being placed upon it, including using the WTO to help enforce core labour standards and international environmental standards.

Big Sails and the Saragossa Sea

The completion of the Uruguay Round and launching of the WTO in 1995 significantly broadened the parameters of trade policy (Jackson 1997). The mandate of the General Agreement on Tariffs and Trade (GATT) gradually arose from a durable and narrow foundation of reducing tariffs. Through successive rounds of negotiations, additional measures intended to restrict or reduce an array of non-tariff measures were built upon that original foundation.

The Uruguay Round marked both the culmination of this incremental expansion of trade policy, as well as a dramatic departure into an unfamiliar territory of rule making. In the former area, examples include the inclusion of albeit weak rules covering agriculture, and a timetable to eliminate textile quotas: two areas that long eluded GATT trade negotiators. In the latter area, new rules covering trade in services, under the General Agreement on Trade in Services (GATS), have been dubbed among the 'chief accomplishments of multilateral trade diplomacy at the end of the twentieth century' (Organisation for Economic Co-operation and Development [OECD] 2002). The Uruguay Round also introduced rules covering intellectual property rights, patents, and copyright regulations, under the Agreement on Trade Related Aspects of Intellectual Property Rights (TRIPS), as well as disciplines establishing how risk assessment procedures for food safety ought to be conducted, under the Agreement on Sanitary and Phytosanitary Measures (SPS). In addition, the WTO established the most robust dispute settlement mechanisms to be found anywhere in international law.

With wind fillings its sails after its launching, the first ministerial meeting, held in 1996 in Singapore, saw the institutional ambitions of the WTO expand further, with the tentative introduction of investment, competition policy, and procurement issues into the WTO agenda for initial analysis and future consideration.

Since Singapore, the fortunes of the WTO have taken a dramatic downturn. Following the collapse of negotiations in Seattle in 1999, the Doha ministerial meeting saw some sails brought in, and the institution seemingly paralysed in a negotiating Saragossa Sea. Dubbed the Doha Development Agenda, the WTO sought to refocus attention toward ensuring that economic benefits accrued from trade liberalisation delivered measurable benefits to developing and least developed countries. Although some additional mandates were included (such as acknowledging the decade-old trade-environment agenda with a modest negotiating mandate), the gap between the ambitions of 1995 and the lowering of expectations in Doha were unmistakable.

One sign of this abrupt and dramatic shift was the decision in Doha to allow some developing countries to waive some patent protection laws enshrined in TRIPS in order to acquire cheaper drugs to combat some diseases, notably HIV/AIDS and malaria.[1] Although the vague wording of the original decision required two years of intense negotiations after Doha to clarify which countries, diseases, and conditions could weaken TRIPS obligations, the policy significance of that decision was crystal clear: developing countries made it known that, as full WTO members, they viewed the ever-widening trade agenda as premature in relation to their development stage, or altogether inappropriate.

The progression from lowering tariffs to tackling HIV/AIDS, introducing antitrust competition measures, weighing the compatibility of environmental policies with trade rules or carving out global standards for risk assessment is neither linear nor even logical. The WTO thus found itself in a dilemma of not being certain how to made good on its promises, something other international organisations – from the United Nations and G8 to regional bodies like the Organization of American States – are entirely comfortable with, but a practice quite foreign to the tradition of the GATT.

However, if the Doha Development Agenda was intended to prompt a kind of return to fundamentals, it created a more basic paradox than trying to do too much:

the link between trade and development tends to be tenuous, indirect, and weak. Trade liberalisation clearly exerts an unambiguous and positive impact on allocative efficiency based on comparative advantage, specialization, and scale economies, which are associated with higher rates of economic growth. (Put another way, there is a strong empirical correlation between the extent to which a domestic economy is open to trade, and corresponding rates of economic growth.) However, trade policy remains largely mute about how best to support other dimensions of the development agenda, from the support of social safety nets to closing income and equity gaps within and between countries.[2] Moreover, development hardly rests its sights on aggregate rates of economic growth, and instead looks to improve income distribution and wage equity, raise human health protection services and lower infant mortality rates, bolster education and literacy, and strengthen environmental protection.[3] Michael Finger (2004) has cautioned that the WTO development-trade promise has introduced a 'troubled approach to development' that has led to paralysis. With this expansion of the trade agenda, the WTO finds itself overlapping or interfering with a wide array of both domestic economic and altogether non-trade policies. A former WTO director general acknowledges this phenomenon:

> More than ever before, the trade system intersects with a growing list of issues and concerns that have a powerful impact on people's lives – from investment and competition policies, to environmental, development, human rights, labour standards, health, animal welfare, distribution of resources, ethical issues, and even security. More and more the WTO is under pressure to expand its agenda because more and more it is seen as the focal point for the many challenges and concerns of globalization (Ruggiero 1998).

One result of this policy intersection is the intense scrutiny that WTO decision-making processes now receive from communities concerned with environment, human rights, labour rights, animal welfare, and others. Indeed, since the day it opened for business, coalitions of nongovernmental groups with little in common have collective asked whether the WTO is accountable for its decisions, and, if so, accountable exactly to whom. If the WTO is in a position to affect a range of domestic laws weakly linked to trade, then what recourse does the public have in influencing those decisions?[4] This question is new to the trading system: the GATT carried out most of its work with little public scrutiny during most of its 47-year run. By contrast, since the WTO – unlike the GATT – has entered policy arenas as diverse as drug costs for HIV/AIDS and food safety, questions about governance and accountability have come to the forefront in the public debate about the WTO. This debate finds some similarities to the accountability, governance, and related debates that have followed the World Bank and the International Monetary Fund (IMF) since the expansion of their mandates in the 1980s. As Louis Pauly notes in Chapter 13, the World Bank and the IMF attached an array of conditions – many barely related to monetary policies – to country-lending and structural adjustment programmes. Devesh Kapur (2000) notes that 'both [the World Bank and IMF] embrace areas of policy it was *inconceivable* for them to touch prior to the 1980s' (emphasis added).

It is similarly inconceivable that trade ministers can make life-and-death decisions about which infectious diseases should benefit from generic-drug pricing schemes. Ngaire Woods (2001, 89) and others have argued that as the scope of policies enacted by the World Bank and IMF increased, questions about governance, mandates and accountability have intensified:

> In the past, when such institutions were required to perform a narrow range of technical functions, the problem [of accountability gaps] was less acute. Today, however, the international financial institutions are being required to perform a much wider range of tasks directly affecting a wider range of people; and the question of their accountability assumes correspondingly greater importance.

Pauly notes that the World Bank and the IMF face a 'lack of clarity' in their mandates, implementation policies, and division of labour, a condition that has prompted searing criticism from economists such as Joseph Stiglitz (2002), Jeffrey Sachs (1998), and Paul Krugman (1996). The same absence of clarity in its mandate now haunts the WTO. As the issues related to trade policy expand and deviate from what trade liberalisation can reasonably be expected to deliver, delineating where trade policy ends and domestic policies begin is impossible. For instance, on the table in the current round of GATS negotiations involving supply of services are visa and immigration permits, professional legal or accounting association requirements, support for local cultural goals, public education, pricing regimes for electricity, and many other areas that, not long ago, would have squarely been seen within the realm of domestic policies.

One result of this expansion of mandates is that WTO committee work – in which negotiations on all-important implementation matters take place – is very close to paralysis. The most mundane administrative matters are subject to a kind of *Sturm und Drang* atmosphere. For example, an apparently all consuming issue in Geneva was whether the United Nations Environment Programme (UNEP) should be granted observer status in the special session of the WTO Committee on Trade and Environment (CTE). The debate has almost nothing to do with UNEP and the CTE. It has almost everything to do with horse-trading in other committees. However, with so many agenda items now on the table, and over 140 countries involved, progress in Geneva is gridlocked.

One reason the WTO's ministerial meeting in Cancun in September 2003 was likely to fail was the deep discontent outside the WTO. Public demonstrations in Cancun threatened to be more passionate, inclusive, and disruptive than those that captured media headlines during the 1999 Seattle meeting. Indeed, before the meeting, Cancun was shaping up to be the rallying point for thousands of *campesinos* and indigenous peoples throughout Latin America who have been displaced or threatened by free trade, over and above the now ritualised cast of antiglobalisation demonstrators.[5]

However, the more likely reason Cancun would falter was found *within* the WTO. In early 2003, almost every WTO negotiating item – from market access to rules, TRIPS to agriculture – bogged down. One result of this decision-making paralysis was that the world's two largest trading blocks – the United States and the European Union – shifted their negotiating energies outside of the WTO, and toward tighter and more manageable negotiations. In the U.S., examples include Jordan, Chile, Singapore, the Central American Free Trade Agreement (CAFTA), the South African Customs Union, Morocco, and Australia. The U.S. Trade Representative argued that these trade initiatives outside of the WTO 'multiply the likelihood of success' (Zoellick 2002). In the case of CAFTA, which launched negotiations in early 2003, all six governments had signalled that a comprehensive trade deal would be completed before December 2003.

If the WTO does not find a way of alleviating its internal governance problems, then this fragmentation of the trading system through regional and bilateral agreements will make the WTO less and less relevant. Sylvia Ostry, in her chapter in this volume, prescribes some practical ways forward to address both external and internal accountability issues. In the former area, proposals include better access to information, regular engagement with civil society, and other entirely sensible goals that the WTO itself has already moved on. In the latter area, options include creating a kind of management board or executive body, to streamline decision making. One option is reinvigorating the 'Green Room' process, in which a small number of representative WTO members meet with the director general of the WTO, on an ongoing basis, as well as during the final stages of negotiations. However, challenges in pushing such an arrangement are not insignificant. They revolve around defining which countries represent collective or regional interests. During the Singapore ministerial meeting in 1996, small developing countries complained bitterly when their trade ministers were barred from gaining entry to the Green Room negotiations.

Curiously, the internal crisis facing the WTO has not affecting its symbolic importance for many countries. For example, a key foreign policy goal of the Russian Federation is to become a WTO member, in order to confirm its position as a full player on the world's economic stage. In addition, WTO membership is sought as a means to catalyse and codify domestic economic, legal, administrative, and other reforms that are weakly associated with trade, but that are difficult to move forward without an external reference point like WTO membership. China's Minister of Environment, Zhenhua Xie, noted that 'WTO membership signifies that China is now more integrated into the world economy, and this will have *far-reaching significance for China's social and economic development*' (emphasis added; Ye *et al.* 2002). Similarly, Chinese legal scholar Veron Mei-Ying Hung argues that China's entry into the WTO is accelerating the rule of law, by initiating and broadening judicial review from WTO-related administrative actions to slowly embrace system-wide changes in judicial reviews (Hung 2002).

In short, the WTO – despite its internal paralysis – has become emblematic of a country's partnership in globalisation, a claim neither the World Bank nor IMF – with their focus on assistance as opposed to equal membership – can make. Jeffrey Sachs and Andrew Warner (1995) argue that trade policy has now become the single most important catalyst for all kinds of reforms, noting that the 'international opening of the economy is the *sine qua non* of the overall reform process. Trade liberalisation not only establishes powerful direct linkages between the economy and the world system, but also effectively forces the government to take actions on other parts of the reform program under the pressure of international competition'.

Trade and Labour Standards

This leads to the question of whether trade liberalisation is codifying respect for core labour standards and universal human rights automatically, and whether the WTO, as an institution, should formally include core labour standards in its broad mandate. China is a good place to begin, since China and human rights concerns are largely inseparable when discussing the WTO (Nolt 1999).

Now that China has entered into the WTO, one could hardly claim that a dramatic breakthrough in human rights or core labour standards had occurred. According to the annual report of Human Rights Watch, China continued to block internet search engines and publications, harass journalists, tighten controls on satellite transmission, and hamper the work of academics and activists (Human Rights Watch 2003). According to the same report, the state obstructed the right of free association and 'ignored its commitments as a member of the International Labour Organization (ILO)' (219). High-profile cases in which labour leaders have been imprisoned for union activities (notably Hu Mingjun and Wang Sen) go directly against the most basic ILO provisions.

Given these and other examples, a reasonable expectation is that the UN bodies responsible for upholding core labour standards and human rights would have initiated some action toward China. However, there appears to be no references to any infractions of any ILO standards by China in the 285th meeting of the Governing Body of the ILO.[6] Likewise, the UN Commission on Human Rights did not forward any resolution on China in 2002. With China's entry into the WTO, coupled with the focus on security issues and Iraq after 11 September 2001, countries appear increasingly reluctant to temper economic and security issues with alleged violations of human rights and labour standards.

Michael Trebilcock and others have suggested that, precisely because its mandate is so broad and dispute settlement provisions so potent, the WTO should take on more non-trade issues, and in particular a 'social charter' that ties market access rights with a country's adherence to core labour standards.[7] Core labour standards are not part of any formal negotiation or informal work within the WTO.[8] However, linking trade and labour standards has been in the public debate for years. In the 19th century, arguments about 'pauper labour' were used by the United Kingdom and others to condition market access, both on humanitarian and competitiveness grounds. In 1840, the U.S. argued that tariff protection ought to remain high to stop imports from ill-paid workers in Europe. In the 1920s and 1930s, several countries – including Cuba, Czechoslovakia, and the UK – all introduced higher duties on imports produced by low-paid labour under inferior conditions of employment

(Charnovitz 1987). In 1930, the U.S. applied an international labour standard in its Smoot-Hawley tariff laws.

In the lead-up to the 1994 Marrakesh ministerial meeting that concluded the Uruguay Round negotiations and launched the WTO, the U.S. pushed for exploratory work to begin that examined links between trade and labour standards. That proposal prompted by far the most acrimonious debate at an otherwise self-congratulatory meeting. All developing countries denounced the proposal. One country argued that trade and labour standard linkage could only proceed if a discussion of trade and immigration policies also took place. Despite the opposition of developing countries, the U.S. continued to push the labour link in the WTO. At the 1996 Singapore ministerial meeting, the following declaration included a reference – albeit tepid – to core labour standards and the competence of the ILO thus:

> The International Labour Organization (ILO) is the competent body to set and deal with these standards, and we affirm our support for its work in promoting them. ... We reject the use of labour standards for protectionist purposes, and agree that the comparative advantage of countries, particularly low-wage developing countries, must in no way be put into question. In this regard, we note that the WTO and ILO Secretariats will continue their existing collaboration (WTO 1996a, para. 4).

In Seattle, trade and labour standards received considerable media attention after U.S. president Bill Clinton suggested that trade sanctions could be used against countries that failed to adhere to such standards. After that comment, from which almost all countries recoiled, the trade-labour linkage all but vanished in the WTO. In Doha, the reference to labour standards was minimalist:

> We reaffirm our declaration made at the Singapore Ministerial Conference regarding internationally recognized core labour standards. We take note of work under way in the International Labour Organization (ILO) on the social dimension of globalization (WTO 2001, para. 8).

Against this background, in Chapter 12 Trebilcock argues that the WTO should incorporate core labour standards. In essence, WTO members would be allowed to ban the imports of goods or services from other WTO member countries, if the latter are found to be in violation of human rights or core labour standards. This conditioning of market access need not be centred on the specific sector in which the offending practices occurred; for example, sweatshops in the textiles sector could legitimately trigger the denial of market access involving agriculture or trucks or financial services. Trebilcock notes that

> countries of destination invoking this human rights exception should be required to show, if measures are challenged in dispute settlement proceedings, that these measures are consistent with both limbs of the non-discrimination principle – that is, that their own domestic producers are required to respect such norms and foreign producers are not

being treated less favourably in this respect (the [national treatment] principle), and (more controversially) that the country of destination is being even-handed in its treatment of countries of origin in that countries are not included in, or excluded from, applicable trade restrictions in ways that are inconsistent with the rationale for the measures in question.

The reference to national treatment (NT) suggests that trade measures applied in response to human rights violations should be applied in a procedurally fair and transparent manner (Howse 1999). (One hopes that a country seeking to use trade sanctions in support of human rights would be predisposed to do so.) However, the substantive argument as to why core labour standards would trigger WTO-consistent trade sanctions is not elaborated, aside from the observation that core labour standards constitute 'international or universal human rights (analogous to environmental threats to the global commons)'.[9]

While Trebilcock does not explore this relationship in detail, a possible interpretation, based on the above reference, is thus: since the Universal Declaration of Human Rights (1948), the United Nations Charter, and ILO core labour standards all ensrhine universal rights, they somehow supersede WTO rules. Another commentator – in making the link between the WTO and the Universal Declaration – argues that Article 16(6) of the Marrakesh agreement, which established the WTO (WTO 1994a); it states that 'this Agreement shall be registered in accordance with the provisions of Article 102 of the Charter of the United Nations', thereby making an explicit reference to the charter. Since the Universal Declaration of Human Rights is the authoritative interpretation of the human rights principles and objectives of the UN Charter, the commentator argues that the 'WTO is therefore bound by the primacy of the Declaration under international human rights law' (People's Decade for Human Rights Education 1999).[10]

However, Article 102 of the charter merely sets out the administrative procedures related to the registration of legal texts, and neither Article 16(6) of the Marrakesh agreement nor Article 102 shed any light on the substantive relationship among the WTO, UN charter, and relevant conventions of the ILO.[11] One way to clarify this relationship is through the Vienna Convention on the Law of Treaties. One could argue, based on that treaty, that since the WTO was negotiated after the charter, covers areas substantively different from the charter, contains provisions more specific than those in the charter, and enjoys a similar level of universal support among states as the charter, then the WTO would likely prevail in the event of an inconsistency between its regime and goals set out in the charter.

However, the question Trebilcock raises is whether the WTO itself could be marshalled to enforce core labour standards, especially since the latter are hampered by a weak compliance and enforcement regime. In the ILO, there are two complaint procedures to address alleged violations of core labour standards. The first involves evidence that is examined by a tripartite committee named by the governing body. The committee can request clarifying information from the government concerned, and it can publish all representations. The second allows complaints to be examined by an independent commission of inquiry, or by the governing body itself (ILO

2000). The commission can issue recommendations, and the government in question can inform the governing body or the commission as to whether it accepts or rejects those recommendations.[12] If recommendations are rejected by the country, then the final recourse of complaint resides outside the ILO and in the International Court of Justice, under Article 36 provisions regarding all matters pertaining to treaties and conventions in force.[13]

In contrast to ILO procedures, the WTO has created one of the strongest dispute settlement systems to be found in any international legal regime. Decisions of the Dispute Settlement Body and Appellate Body are binding, while clear procedures are in place regarding the timetable for settling disputes and upholding decisions. In the latter area, the implementation of decisions by the Dispute Settlement Body likely require some kind of clarification by WTO members. One barometer of the importance of this mechanism is found in its frequency of use. By mid 2002, 248 cases had been completed during the seven-year history of the WTO up until that time. This compares with the approximately 150 cases that transpired during the full 47-year run of the GATT. Developing countries are initiating the Dispute Settlement Body on a roughly equal basis to their developed country counterparts.[14]

In comparing the compliance procedures of the ILO and WTO, there is little doubt that the WTO and its dispute settlement regime could be a potent force in enforcing core labour standards. However, it is the wrong approach for three reasons.

First, trade sanctions as a weapon to push labour standards and human rights might lead to the opposite outcome. Countries with blocked exports would face higher unemployment and uncertainty. This is especially so if there is no required correlation between the violating sector and the trade measure applied, no clear formula estimating the commercial value of the human rights abuse, nor any indication the duration in which the trade restriction would be imposed. Moreover, countries cast outside of the trading system by sanctions could be inclined toward greater abuses. Overall, the economic effects of closing markets may likely affect the poorest.[15] On the other hand, bilateral trade agreements that contain labour standards do appear to be lifting those standards upward. Tariff quota reductions conditioned upon core labour standards in the textiles sector have been seen as an effective and focussed labour-trade link at the regional or bilateral trade policy level. (For example, this link has been used in an agreement between the U.S. and Vietnam.)

Second, as discussed above, the WTO already risks collapsing under the weight of its current agenda. Indeed, there is a real risk that the paralysis and fragmentation that have gripped the WTO are now so profound that very little can be expected to save it. Adding labour to the WTO agenda – a political nonstarter in any event given that the overwhelming membership is from developing countries – would deepen the accountability and governance crisis.

Third, and most important, advocating that the WTO enforce core labour and human rights in essence means that any hope of strengthening enforcement provisions where they are most urgently needed – in the ILO and UN Commission on Human Rights – has been abandoned. Instead of giving up on these institutions, new approaches are needed to improve the enforcement of core labour standards, in a way that sees developing countries as partners rather than victims of a Northern agenda. Sandra Polaski (2003) has argued that rather than rehearsing the debate about the WTO and labour – a debate that has become 'stale and ritualized' – developing countries should take the initiative to construct a 'global labor standards regime that they themselves could help to enforce' (4).

Clearly, such a regime would have incentives for compliance that are balanced with credible enforcement measures, including the use of trade measures. One of the best models in the environmental arena that weaves real incentives with a credible threat of sanctions is the Montreal Protocol on Substances that Deplete the Ozone Layer. The protocol – negotiated in 1987 and amended and tightened four times since in response to scientific evidence about stratospheric ozone depletion – is composed of a highly innovative menu of instruments. These include trade measures that are applied between parties (including quotas, bans, and prior notification systems), measures disallowing trade with nonparties to stop free riders and address spillovers, and financial support to developing countries to help them achieve the standards set out in the protocol. By mid 2002, roughly US$1.2 billion had been transferred to developing countries. The protocol also has an innovative system to address noncompliance, including the use of trade sanctions. However, in practice, the response to those countries that have thus far not complied – notably the Russian Federation, Belarus, and Ukraine – has concentrated on tapping additional financial assistance through the Global Environmental Facility, to help bring them back into compliance (see, for example, Victor, Raustiala, and Skolnikoff 1998; Vaughan and Dehlaavi 1998). The trade sanctions have never been used, but remain a credible threat. The Montreal Protocol has emerged as the most effective international environmental instrument that exists, one that provides useful guidance to the labour agenda.

Trade and Environment

If the ILO or another body were able to negotiate a new regime that resembled the Montreal Protocol, how the WTO would respond to the use of trade measures? This question is the basis of the decade-long examination within the WTO of trade measures contained in the international environmental regime. The Uruguay Round Decision on Trade and Environment, which established the CTE, instructs it to undertake a 'surveillance of trade measures used for environmental purposes' (WTO 1994b).

After a decade of 'surveillance', the WTO at Doha in November 2001 launched formal negotiations intended to address 'the relationship between existing WTO rules and specific trade obligations set out in multilateral environmental agreements (MEAs). The negotiations shall be limited in scope to the applicability of such existing WTO rules *as among parties to the MEA in question*. The negotiations shall not prejudice the WTO rights of any Member that is not a party to the MEA in question' (emphasis added; WTO 2001).

The Doha mandate on MEAs is one of the most bizarre areas ever included in trade negotiations. The WTO will decide what it has to say about trade measures explicitly agreed to by the very same countries that are WTO members. Posturing and drawn-out negotiations on this issue began soon after the ministerial meeting. `Members have asked what a legitimate MEA is, and what typology of trade measures negotiations will cover. But the issue has already been basically settled. The 1996 Report of the Committee on Trade and Environment was the source of intense negotiations – even by WTO standards. The CTE was one of the most active of all WTO committees in the lead-up to the Singapore ministerial meeting. Formal and informal meetings stretched out over three months, with the final text emerging after a final 36-hour negotiating stretch. By far the most contentious issue involved the WTO and the use of trade measures in MEAs. The final text set down what Konrad von Moltke has called the rules of disengagement between the two legal regimes (European Commission 2002). In the conclusions and recommendations of the 1996 CTE report, the WTO (1996b) the negotiated the following regarding the use of trade measures between parties to an MEA:

> While WTO Members have the right to bring disputes to the WTO dispute settlement mechanisms, if a dispute arises between WTO Members, Parties to an MEA, on the use of trade measures they are applying between themselves pursuant to the MEA, they should consider trying to resolve it through the dispute settlement mechanisms under the MEA.

However, the question that the Doha decision dodged involving MEAs is also the one that is by far the most contentious: what had the WTO to say about trade measures applied against nonparties to an MEA? Such measures are contained, and have been highly effective, in supporting the implementation not only of the Montreal Protocol, but also the Convention on International Trade in Endangered Species (CITES) and, to a lesser extent, the Basel Convention on the Control of Transboundary Movement of Hazardous Wastes and Their Disposal. The 1996 CTE report noted that some WTO members are

> concerned with trade measures applied in MEAs which can affect WTO Members rights and obligations ... doubts have been expressed by some WTO Members about the WTO consistency of certain trade measures applied pursuant to some MEAs, in particular discriminatory trade restrictions applied by MEA Parties against non-parties that involve extra-jurisdictional actions (WTO 1996b).

There is no clear answer that emerged from these doubts and concerns. Instead, the 1996 CTE report addresses the nonparty issue by forwarding the briefest, and by far most controversial paragraph: '174(ii) In the negotiation of a future MEA, particular care should be taken over how trade measures may be considered for application to non-parties' (WTO 1996a).

The compromise of 174(ii) – skillfully negotiated with the assistance of Richard Eglin of the WTO secretariat – represented a minimalist outcome, balancing interests of developing and developed countries. While it can be read in a number of ways, it basically signalled to the environmental community that future MEAs should refrain from using trade measures against nonparties.

Six years later, one could find evidence of the effect that the 'particular care' advice upon MEA negotiations. No MEAs negotiated since the 1996 CTE contained a trade measure against nonparties. At the same time, 'particular care' has resulted in particularly confusing signals from environmental negotiators. For example, in the Stockholm Conference (2001), the preamble notes that measures to address persistent organic pollutants should be done 'without distorting international trade and investment'. In the Rotterdam Convention (1998), the preamble notes that

> nothing in this Convention shall be interpreted as implying in any way a change in the rights and obligations of a Party under any existing international agreement applying to chemicals in international trade or to environmental protection.

The Rotterdam Convention then notes that 'the above recital is not intended to create a hierarchy between this Convention and other international agreements'. The Cartagena Protocol on Biosafety has similar language regarding the rights and obligations of other agreements, and then notes that this reference is 'not intended to subordinate this Protocol to other international agreements' (Convention on Biological Diversity 2000). In the case of Cartagena, Aaron Cosbey and Stanley Burgiel (2000) have noted that since the savings clause and contradictory statement about subordination exist outside of the text, uncertainty persists as to where a dispute over trade measures would be held.

Conclusion

These kinds of confusion and mixed signals in other international regimes arise from, and reflect the internal confusion and lack of clarity of the mandate of the WTO itself. In spite of – or perhaps because of – the mixed messages that the WTO sends to other legal regimes that seek the most effective enforcement mechanisms to pursue their objectives, it is time to clarify the relationship between different regimes. The international labour and human rights regime desperately needs strengthening. Models such as the Montreal Protocol are ones that maximise effectiveness and equity. Rather than being called into question and confusion by the WTO, they should instead be encouraged for the self-interest of the trading regime. The alternative, a continued call to pile more and more agenda items onto the already impossibly crowded agenda of the WTO, will almost certainly mean that the crisis facing that institution will only deepen, while desperately needed institutional strengthening in the labour, human rights, environmental, and other regimes will be postponed as uncertainty about trade measures continues to no one's benefit.

Notes

1 On 20 December 2002, the TRIPS council failed to reach agreement on which infectious diseases would be covered so as to allow developing countries to import cheaper generics from countries where pharmaceuticals are patented. The United States was the only country that blocked consensus.

2 Ana Revenga (1997) has argued that trade liberalisation in Mexico from 1985 to 1987 – when it became a GATT contracting party – put a 'downward pressure on employment and wages' by reducing industry product and labour demand, resulting in a real decline in wages by 3 percent to 4 percent in real wages on average, and in some sectors a wage decline of as much as 14 percent (see also Edwards 1998).

3 In following up on the Doha agenda, the WTO secretariat has been faithfully engaged in capacity building and technical assistance for developing countries, in essence to help their negotiators become more effective in Geneva. However, this misses the point. The development round was not launched to expand technical assistance. Instead, it reflects the powerful misgivings of many developing countries that the benefits of trade liberalisation remain concentrated in industrialised countries, while the expansion of trade rules to include environment, investment, competition policy, TRIPS, and GATS reflects the interests of industrialised countries.

4 Defenders of WTO governance structures respond that its members are accountable to their domestic populace. Moreover, there are many domestic economic decisions that are not subject to transparency or public participation. For example, decisions by the U.S. Federal Reserve Bank about interest rates have a far greater impact on people globally than the WTO does. Yet interest rates decisions are by definition opaque.

5 In January 2003, Mexico City hosted thousands of displaced and threatened farmers, who protested against the North American Free Trade Agreement (NAFTA). At the time, the populist mayor of Mexico City, Lopez Obrador, said that 'these neo-liberal policies have harmed the *campesinos* deeply – [former] President Salinas and those who followed him preferred American bankers to Mexican *campesinos* ... What's going to happen to this country? People are leaving this country en masse. Fields are abandoned. Whole villages are abandoned' ('Populist Mayor Is President-in-Waiting' 2003).

6 In June 2002, the International Confederation of Free Trade Unions (ICFTU) asked the ILO's Committee on Freedom of Association to take up the cases of the labour activists detained in the northeast. Although the ILO is already involved in several technical assistance programs in China, including development of a social security project, China still has not responded to a June 2000 ILO request to send a direct contact mission to discuss freedom of association.

7 Over time, the meaning of internationally recognised labour standards embodied in a number of ILO conventions has focussed on the following core standards: the freedom of labour to associate and to organise and bargain collectively (conventions 87 and 98); freedom from forced or compulsory labour (conventions 29 and 105); prohibition of discrimination (conventions 100 and 111); and the introduction of a minimum wage for the employment of children (convention 138).

8 Although a formal link between the WTO and core labour standards is very remote, there are several examples in which labour has been included in regional, bilateral, and preferential trade arrangements. In 1994, the entry into force of NAFTA coincided with the

establishment of the Commission for Labor Cooperation (CLC). The U.S. has entered into, or continues to pursue, bilateral free trade accords that contain labour provisions. Examples include Chile, Singapore, and Jordan. In 2002, the EU announced the revised General Scheme of Preferences, in which deeper tariff cuts were extended to developing countries that were deemed by EU inspectors to uphold basic worker rights (Polaski 2003).

9 The terms 'core labour standards' and 'human rights' are often used interchangeably. Core labour standards and universal human rights are closely intertwined, since a violation of labour standards in essence constitutes an infringement of basic human rights.

10 Article 102 states: 1) Every treaty and every international agreement entered into by any Member of the United Nations after the present Charter comes into force shall as soon as possible be registered with the Secretariat and published by it; 2) No party to any such treaty or international agreement which has not been registered in accordance with the provisions of paragraph 1 of this Article may invoke that treaty or agreement before any organ of the United Nations (UN 1945, ch. 16).

11 Perhaps a more relevant article in the UN Charter is Article 103, which states: 'In the event of a conflict between the obligations of the Members of the United Nations under the present Charter and their obligations under any other international agreement, their obligations under the present Charter shall prevail' (UN 1945).

12 Steve Charnovitz (2002) has commented on ILO supervision mechanisms covering the right to freedom of association rights, noting that because it is 'complaint driven, disproportionate attention is devoted to countries that are relatively free, rather than towards countries that forestall complaints by forbidding union'. In addition, the supervisory committee does not differentiate between 'minor infractions and major violations', and underutilises publicity to prompt changes.

13 In its history, the International Court of Justice has heard several cases involving human rights, including instances in which provisions related to the UN Commission on Human Rights were cited. However, no cases have taken place involving non-enforcement of an ILO convention. (The sole case involving the ILO was in 1955, and involved a dispute with United Nations Educational, Social, and Cultural Organization [UNESCO] over the authority of the UNESCO director general *vis-à-vis* the treatment of a member country.)

14 One survey of cases involving Latin American countries found that of the 57 cases that were heard between a Latin American member and developed country (EU, Canada, Japan, and the U.S.), 27 involved Latin America as the petitioner and 30 cases saw Latin America as the defendant. Similarly, by mid 2002, of the 59 WTO Appellate Body panel reports that have been adopted, 12 involved a Latin American country. Of these cases, five saw Latin American countries as petitioners, and seven saw them as defendants (Delich 2002).

15 Generally, increases in per capita gross domestic product (GDP) are correlated with advances in core labour standards and democratic institutions generally. Moreover, empirical work by David Dollar and Aart Kraay (2001), Dollar, William Easterley, and others suggest a roughly symmetrical relationship between average growth in income, and average rates of poverty reduction. For example, Easterley (2002) argues that 'one additional percentage point per capita growth *causes* a one percent rise in the poor's income' (see also Collier and Dollar 2002).

References

Charnovitz, Steve (1987). 'Fair Labour Standards and International Trade'. *International Trade Review* vol. 126, no. 5.

Charnovitz, Steve (2002). *Trade Law and Global Governance*. Cameron May, London.

Collier, David and David Dollar (2002). *Globalization, Growth, and Poverty*. World Bank and Oxford University Press, New York.

Convention on Biological Diversity (2000). 'Cartagena Protocol on Biosafety'.<www.biodiv.org/biosafety/protocol.asp> (November 2005).

Cosbey, Aaron and Stanley Burgiel (2000). 'The Cartagena Protocol on Biosafety: An Analysis of Results'. International Institute for Sustainable Development. <www.iisd.org/pdf/biosafety.pdf> (November 2005).

Delich, Valentina (2002). 'WTO Governance and Dispute Settlement: An Assessment from Latin American Countries'. Paper prepared for 'Integrating the Americas' Conference, Institute for International Economics, 20–21 November. <www.netamericas.net/Documents/Nov_20_2002_Papers/Delich-Pres%20Netamericas.doc> (November 2005).

Dollar, David and Aart Kraay (2001). 'Growth Is Good for the Poor'. Working Paper No. 2587. World Bank, Washington DC.

Easterley, William (2002). *The Elusive Quest for Growth*. MIT Press, Cambridge MA.

Edwards, Sebastian (1998). 'Openness, Productivity, and Growth: What Do We Really Know?' *Economics Journal* vol. 108 (March), pp. 383–398.

European Commission (2002). 'Session 2 with Nora Plaisier, Konrad von Moltke, Stephen Pursey, and Caroline Lucas, on the 'Doha Development Agenda: How Can the EU Use It to Strengthen the WTOs Engagement in Global Governance.' Seminar on Trade, Governance, and Sustainable Development. Geneva. <trade-info.cec.eu.int/doclib/ docs/2004/november/tradoc_120059.pdf> (November 2005).

Finger, J. Michael (2004). 'GATT Magic after Cancun: Finding Ways to Move Along'. *Bridges* vol. 8, no. 4, pp. 3–4.

Howse, Robert (1999). 'Democracy, Science, and Free Trade: Risk Regulation on Trial at the World Trade Organization'. *Michigan Law Review* vol. 98, no. 7, pp. 2329–2357.

Human Rights Watch (2003). 'World Report 2003: Events of 2002'. <www.hrw.org/wr2k3> (November 2005).

Hung, Veron Mei-Ying (2002). 'China's WTO Commitment on Independent Judicial Review'. *American Journal of Comparative Law* vol. 52, pp. 77–132.

International Labour Organization (2000). 'How Are International Labour Standards Enforced?' <www.ilo.org/public/english/standards/norm/enforced> (November 2005).

Jackson, John H. (1997). *The World Trading System: Law and Policy of International Economic Relations*. 2nd ed. MIT Press, Cambridge, MA.

Kapur, Devesh (2000). 'Expansive Agendas and Weak Instruments: Government-Related Conditionality of the International Financial Institutions'. In N. Woods, ed., *The Political Economy of Globalization*. Macmillan, Basingstoke.

Krugman, Paul R. (1996). 'Are Currency Crises Self-Fulfilling?' *National Bureau of Economic Research Macroeconomic Annual*.

Nolt, James (1999). 'China in the WTO: The Debate'. *Foreign Policy in Focus* vol. 4, no. 38.

Organisation for Economic Co-operation and Development (2002). 'GATS: The Case for Open Services Markets'. Organisation for Economic Co-operation and Development, Paris.

People's Decade for Human Rights Education (1999). 'A Global Movement Position Statement: Human Rights Are Not for Trading'. WTO Seattle Ministerial Conference, November. Seattle. <www.converge.org.nz/pma/apmov.htm> (November 2005).

Polaski, Sandra (2003). 'Trade and Labor Standards: A Strategy for Developing Countries'. Carnegie Endowment for International Peace. <www.carnegieendowment.org/pdf/files/Polaski_Trade_English.pdf> (November 2005).

'Populist Mayor Is President-in-Waiting'. (2003). *Financial Times*, 5 February.

Revenga, Ana (1997). 'Employment and Wage Effects of Trade Liberalization: The Case of Mexican Manufacturing'. *Journal of Labor Economics* vol. 15, no. 3 (Part 2), pp. S20–S43.

Rotterdam Convention on the Prior Informed Consent Procedure for Certain Hazardous Chemicals and Pesticides in International Trade (1998). 'Text of the Convention'. Rotterdam. <www.pic.int/en/ViewPage.asp?id=104> (November 2005).

Ruggiero, Renato (1998). 'The Trading System of the Future: Challenges and Opportunities'. 23 September. Geneva. <www.wto.org/english/news_e/sprr_e/icc_e.htm> (November 2005).

Sachs, Jeffrey and Andrew Warner (1995). 'Economic Reform and the Process of Global Integration'. Brookings Papers on Economic Activity, No. 1.

Sachs, Jeffrey (1998). 'The IMF and the Asian Flu'. *American Perspective* vol. 37 (March–April 1997).

Stiglitz, Joseph (2002). *Globalization and Its Discontents*. W.W. Norton, New York.

Stockholm Convention on Persistent Organic Pollutants (2001). 'Convention Text'. <www.pops.int/documents/convtext/convtext_en.pdf> (November 2005).

United Nations (1945). 'Charter of the United Nations'. <www.un.org/aboutun/charter> (November 2005).

Vaughan, Scott and Ali Dehlaavi (1998). 'Policy Effectiveness and Multilateral Environmental Agreements'. UNEP Environment and Trade Series No. 17. Geneva.

Victor, David, Kal Raustiala, and Eugene Skolnikoff, eds. (1998). *Implementation and Effectiveness of International Environmental Commitments: Theory and Practice*. MIT Press, Cambridge MA.

Woods, Ngaire (2001). 'Making the IMF and World Bank More Accountable'. *International Affairs* vol. 77, no. 1, pp. 83–100.

World Trade Organization (1994a). 'Marrakesh Agreement Establishing the World Trade Organization'. 15 April. <www.wto.org/english/docs_e/legal_e/04-wto_e.htm> (November 2005).

World Trade Organization (1994b). 'Relevant WTO Provisions: Text of 1994 Decision'. 14 April. Marrakesh. <www.wto.org/english/tratop_e/envir_e/issu5_e.htm> (November 2005).

World Trade Organization (1996a). 'Singapore Ministerial Declaration'. 13 December. <www.wto.org/english/thewto_e/minist_e/min96_e/wtodec_e.htm> (November 2005).

World Trade Organization (1996b). 'Report of the CTE to the Singapore Ministerial Conference'. WT/CTE/1.

World Trade Organization (2001). 'Ministerial Declaration'. Doha, 14 November. <www.wto.org/english/thewto_e/minist_e/min01_e/mindecl_e.htm> (November 2005).

Ye, Ruqiu, Wanhua Yang, Konrad von Moltke, *et al.* (2002). *Trade and Sustainability: Challenges and Opportunities for China as a WTO Member*. International Institute for Sustainable Development, Winnipeg. <www.iisd.org/pdf/2002/cciced_trade_sus.pdf> (November 2005).

Zoellick, Robert B. (2002). 'Unleashing the Trade Winds'. *Economist*, 7 December, p. 25–29.

PART V
THE G8 AND UNITED NATIONS SYSTEMS

Chapter 15

Civil Society, the United Nations, and G7/8 Summitry

Peter I. Hajnal

In today's interdependent, globalised world, no institution – whether governmental, intergovernmental, business, or civil society organisation – can exist in isolation. Governance implies complex, ever-changing interaction between and among various actors (Collenette 2002). This chapter examines and compares the relationship of nongovernmental organisations (NGOs) and other civil society organisations and coalitions with the United Nations and, in the context of summitry, with the G7/8.

Civil Society Relations with the United Nations System

Non-state actors were present at the very beginning of the UN. At the 1945 San Francisco founding conference, U.S. NGOs, trade unions, church groups, and others successfully pushed for the inclusion of human rights in the UN Charter (Humphrey 1984, 12–13). Since then, civil society–UN relations have developed in an increasingly complex though uneven manner.

Formal Relations

The UN has had a long-standing, highly structured relationship with NGOs. This relationship has taken various forms and has had as its locus several points of contact. Foremost among these is the Economic and Social Council (ECOSOC),which has set up consultative relations with NGOs under Article 71 of the UN Charter. These relations were revised by ECOSOC Resolution 1996/31 of 25 July 1996 (UN ECOSOC 1996). The 'general' consultative category consists of a small number of large, well-established NGOs that are 'concerned with most of the activities of the Council and its subsidiary bodies' (art. 22); others are termed 'special' – these tend to be smaller NGOs interested only in certain ECOSOC activities; and the largest number – more specialised, technical NGOs – are on ECOSOC's 'roster'.[1] Representatives of these NGOs participate at certain UN meetings and are able to have input into the agenda or to act as expert consultants; they also report periodically on their activities to ECOSOC. These NGOs have formed their own association, the Conference of Non-Governmental Organizations in Consultative Relationship with the United Nations (CONGO).

The UN Department of Public Information has had its own longstanding arrangements with a host of NGOs. These are expected to assist the department and the UN in general in disseminating UN-related information. They are thus essentially an extension of the information arm of the UN.[2] To bring these NGOs to the UN, the department organises annual conferences for them. The UN Secretariat has an NGO unit in the Department of Economic and Social Affairs, and an NGO section in the Department of Public Information. In addition, there is an ECOSOC Committee on Non-Governmental Organizations, which reviews NGO applications for consultative or roster status.

Besides ECOSOC and the Department of Public Information, the UN has a number of focal points throughout the secretariat for contact with NGOs relevant to various units and programmes. NGOs have come to be recognised as a source of vital experience, expertise, and information and as providers of new insights and approaches in most areas on the UN's work: development, human rights, women's issues, disarmament, peacekeeping, emergency assistance, and many others. The activities of these NGOs range from policy formulation and standard setting to operational activities and advocacy (Adams 2002).[3]

Most specialised agencies, programmes, and bodies of the larger UN system have created more or less formal mechanisms of association with NGOs. The oldest such relationship is constitutionally entrenched in the International Labour Organization (ILO). Since its establishment after the end of World War I, the ILO has featured a tripartite governance structure, incorporating representatives of governments, employers' organisations, and trade unions. To cite another example, the United Nations Educational, Scientific, and Cultural Organization (UNESCO) has long had a large number of NGOs associated with its programmes and activities, from literacy campaigns to the Man in the Biosphere programme. The Bretton Woods institutions – technically UN specialised agencies – were slower than other member organisations of the UN family to build relations with NGOs. But both the World Bank and, more recently, the International Monetary Fund (IMF) have a civil society nexus. A UN system-wide interagency institution established to assist and advise the numerous associated NGOs is the United Nations Non-Governmental Liaison Service. ECOSOC-related NGOs have also established an informal regional network (UN-NGO-IRENE) to help consolidate NGO involvement in the implementation of the Millennium Development Goals (MDGs).

The UN's Global Conferences in the 1990s and Other New Departures

NGOs and other civil society coalitions have been active at UN conferences at least since the early 1970s. For example, women's groups have used the UN as a forum for advancing women's rights since the 1975 International Women's Year, continuing with the International Women's Decade (1976–1985), the decade's mid-term World Conference on Women in Copenhagen in 1980, and the end-of-decade conference in Nairobi in 1985. But it was in the 1990s that UN-NGO relations changed drastically. The crucial turning point was the 1992 Rio de Janeiro UN Conference on Environment and Development (the Earth Summit), where civil society really came into its own. The environmental movement, development-oriented NGOs, and other civil society groups worked hard to expand their influence on the UN and its member governments. Civil society organisations learned about the preparatory process and began lobbying, monitoring events, and participating in whatever opportunities presented themselves in the lead-up to Rio. The UN was generally supportive of this process; it funded NGOs from the South and engaged in consultations.

This became the pattern for subsequent UN-organised world conferences in the 1990s; for example, the 1993 Vienna World Conference on Human Rights, or the 1998 Rome UN Conference on the Establishment of an International Criminal Court (see, for example, Weiss and Gordenker 1996; Alger 1999; Adams 2002). The pattern continued into the 21st century; there were several parallel civil society events at the 2002 Johannesburg World Summit on Sustainable Development (Rio+10).

There have been notable successes due to civil society engagement in the 'new diplomacy'. Two major examples are the Ottawa process and the resulting Landmine Ban Treaty, and the establishment of the International Criminal Court (see Rutherford 2002; Pace and Panganiban 2002). NGO involvement was a significant factor in the achievement of international consensus and government commitment on difficult policy challenges – for example, on issues of women's rights and reproductive health – at major UN conferences. Civil society participation has provided the UN not only with technical expertise but has also increased public awareness of global issues, and contributed to greater democracy, transparency, and accountability on the part of UN member governments (see Adams 2002). Indeed, one test of global governance is the degree to which state and non-state actors have been able to operate at UN conferences (Cooper 2004, 10). And, beyond the conferences, questions remain about civil society's place in the implementation of conference commitments and in subsequent developments on the global scene (Foster and Anand 1999, 9).

One institutional response of the UN to these changes was a review of consultative arrangements and rules, carried out from 1993 to 1996. It culminated in the adoption of ECOSOC Resolution 1996/31 and Decision 1996/297. The two main aims of this process were to review and update longstanding ECOSOC provisions for NGO consultative status, and, more controversially, to examine the matter of NGO participation in 'all areas of work of the UN' (UN Department of Public Information 2005b), including the General Assembly (UNGA) and the Security Council (UNSC). Resolution 1996/31 addressed the first, and dealt with such matters as the eligibility of various types of national and regional NGOs for consultative status, change in the nomenclature of consultative categories, and procedures for NGO accreditation to and participation in UN international conferences. A significant achievement here was making national, sub-regional, and regional NGOs – including the national affiliates of international NGOs – eligible for consultative status with ECOSOC (Adams 2002, 145–148). ECOSOC Decision 1996/297 dealt with the 'all areas of work of the UN' aspect of the review. However, the proposal to extend formal NGO access to UNGA and beyond ran into opposition from some member governments. It stalled for lack of political will.

UN secretary general Kofi Annan has on many occasions emphasised the importance – indeed, the necessity – of UN–civil society partnership (see, for example, UN Department of Public Information 1999). But on a practical working level the relationship has not always been easy, even though co-operation between the UN and NGOs has often been mutually beneficial. Access to UN premises, officials, and meetings has been problematic for some NGOs and their members; some UN officials and institutions have resisted. In fairness, however, the UN, with its strained resources, could not possibly cope with the potentially huge number of organisations and people involved, and with the sometimes unreasonable demands and occasionally reprehensible behaviour of certain individuals associated with a few NGOs. And while physical access to the secretariat building is in the purview of the UN administration, permission for NGOs to attend – let alone speak at – those meetings is the prerogative of governments of UN member states.

Taking up the challenge of the ECOSOC review, the Secretary General issued a report in 1998 that included proposals to enhance NGO participation throughout the UN system by various means, such as the establishment of a trust fund to help NGOs of the South to participate in UN activities. Many NGOs found this short of what they wished, such as with regard to access for NGOs to General Assembly debates (UNGA 1998). Such access has been given only on an episodic, *ad hoc* basis.

The desirability of greater UN openness toward civil society has also been raised outside the UN with increasing urgency. In its 1995 report, *Our Global Neighbourhood*, the Commission on Global Governance noted the essential contribution of civil society to global governance and the need for the UN to provide appropriate space for civil society participation. One of the commission's proposals was to convene an annual civil society forum that would consist of representatives of civil society organisations accredited to UNGA (Commission on Global Governance 1995, 258).

Five years after the commission's report, world civil society convened the Millennium Forum at the UN from 22 to 26 May 2000. It brought together some 1350 representatives of more than 1000 NGOs and other civil society organisations from 106 countries. Discussion included the broadest spectrum of concerns, including poverty eradication, the challenges of globalisation, and the democratisation of the UN and other international organisations. In his keynote address to the participants of the forum, Annan praised 'pioneering role of NGOs on a range of vital issues, from human rights to the environment, from development to disarmament'. He went on to state: 'We in the United Nations know that during the cycle of world conferences of the last decade, it was you who set the pace on many issues. You did that through advocacy and through action; by pressuring governments and by working with governments as partners and implementers' (UN Department of Public Information 2000).

The main document issued at the conclusion of the forum, 'We the Peoples Millennium Forum Declaration and Agenda for Action: Strengthening the

United Nations for the Twenty-First Century', sets forth a series of proposals for governments, for the UN and for civil society itself (UNGA 2000). Along with six thematic reports, it was subsequently submitted to the UN's own Millennium Summit in the fall of 2000 (UNGA 2000). The assembly duly received the document but has done little with it in practical terms, to the great disappointment of civil society. This is unfortunate; the MDGs, if they are to be implemented, must have active and broad civil society participation and support. This has been recognised by the Secretary General, who emphasised in his first annual report on the implementation of these goals that whatever progress has been made was by reliance on strategies 'that combine the energies of Member States, international institutions ... with those of others, notably the private sector, non-governmental organizations, philanthropic foundations, academic and cultural institutions and other parts of civil society' (UNGA 2002, 20).[4]

If regular links between civil society and UNGA are difficult politically, links between civil society and the UNSC are even more challenging and sensitive. Nevertheless, in a 1999 addendum to *Our Global Neighbourhood*, the Commission on Global Governance noted that 'members of the [Security] Council now hold regular sessions with a group of selected NGOs to discuss questions of common interest' and stated that the Council 'should take further steps towards regularising procedures for gaining the substantive and timely input of NGOs and other civil society groups with expertise on the issues on its agenda' (Commission on Global Governance 1999, 29).

The growing importance of new informal practices in UN–civil society interaction was inevitable in view of the fact that formal extension of NGO access has not been politically possible at the UN. NGO representatives participate more frequently in hearings, panels, briefings, and dialogue with governments. There are many other instances of this development: UNGA has organised panels with representatives from NGOs, academics, and business; the Commission on Social Development has begun dialogue with NGOs; the Commission on the Status of Women and other ECOSOC bodies have included NGO representatives on various panels; the Commission on Sustainable Development has organised multi-stakeholder dialogues in its work programme; various UN bodies, including the governing body of UNAIDS and the Inter-Agency Standing Committee on Humanitarian Affairs, have provided for NGO seats (Adams 2002, 148–149).

The increasingly clear phenomenon of global values shared by the UN and civil society is another factor driving these new types of informal interaction between the two actors. This is true in many areas: peace, human rights, social justice, and so forth. But the desire for institutionalisation of these relations persists, and manifests itself from time to time in proposals such as a Global People's Assembly or People's Parliament.

Responding to these concerns and to the rapidly changing global situation, the Secretary General appointed, in February 2003, a 12-member international Panel of Eminent Persons on United Nations–Civil Society Relations, led by the former president of Brazil, Fernando Henrique Cardoso, and numbering among its members several civil society representatives. In his transmittal letter, Cardoso noted that constructive engagement with civil society was no longer simply an option but a necessity for the UN if it wished to reinvigorate intergovernmental relations, and that in order to obtain civil society support the UN needed to champion meaningful reforms of global governance (UNGA 2004, 3).

The panel presented 30 proposals to enhance UN–civil society relations so that they reflect the growing capacity and influence of non-state actors, foster multistakeholder processes, and improve policy and operational partnerships. Notably, it proposed that UNGA and not ECOSOC be the NGO point of entry to the UN, and that UNGA allow carefully planned participation of non-state actors in addition to governments in its processes. It also proposed that UNGA do the following:

- engage local civil society in the UN's country-level activities;
- strengthen UNSC dialogue with civil society;
- engage representatives of national parliaments;
- streamline and depoliticise NGO accreditation and access so that it is based on expertise and competence;
- establish the requisite structural changes in the UN Secretariat; and
- redress North-South imbalances in UN–civil society relations, for example by creating a fund to enable southern NGOs to attend UN activities.

In addition to its report, the panel produced a background paper on civil society and governance, an inventory and analysis of practices in the relationship of civil society and the UN system of organisations, and informal papers on diverse actors in the UN system, on civil society–UNSC relations, and on modes of civil society influence in the UN and global governance. The 'modes' paper lists the following categories of civil society influence: operational engagement and partnership; policy advocacy, mobilisation, and dialogue; involvement in negotiations; and influencing processes of governance at the UN and in other international institutions. It remains to be seen how well the panel's ambitious proposals fare, given the UN's political, financial, institutional, and human resource constraints.

Civil Society and the G7/8

In sharp contrast with the UN, the G7/8 is a more informal, flexible, and by and large non-bureaucratic institution that lacks the two main characteristics of more structured international governmental organisations: a constitutive intergovernmental agreement and a secretariat. It follows, therefore, that civil society–G7/8 relations, too, are largely informal in nature.[5] Of course, individual G8 countries have their own G8-related bureaucracies. Practices and structures vary from country to country, and there are different government departments that incorporate units responsible for continuous monitoring, co-ordination, and follow-up of G7/8-related activities and issues, both at the summit level and at lower (ministerial and task force) levels of the broader G7/8 system. A rare example of the G7 creating a bureaucratic structure was the now-defunct G7 Support Implementation Group that had a small secretariat in Moscow. All this has implications for civil society interaction with the G7/8 system and with individual G8 member governments. The history of that interaction may be divided into four phases.

Phase 1 (1975–1980): Civil Society and the G7 More or Less Ignore Each Other

As implied above, the G7/8 saw itself from the very beginning of G7 summitry in 1975 as an informal, non-bureaucratic forum of the leaders of the most advanced market economy countries with a democratic system of governance. Recognition of civil society groups as interlocutors seems not to have entered the (publicly expressed) consciousness of the G7 leaders and their support apparatus. On the other side, the power and importance of the G7 as a discrete entity do not appear to have been widely recognised during this phase by NGOs and broader civil society, although some academic civil society organisations, notably the Trilateral Commission, started discussing the summit as early as 1978 (Sauzey 1978).

Phase 2 (1981–1994): Civil Society Recognises the G7

As the summit agenda expanded to embrace many issues beyond the early focus on macroeconomic policy co-ordination, civil society began to see the G7 as a legitimate target both for lobbying and for opposing.[6] Many of these new G7 issues have been crucial to a wide variety of NGOs and civil society coalitions. Moreover, it was becoming common public knowledge that the G7 was indeed a powerful group that had evolved into a major global institution.[7]

In addition to pre-summit lobbying of individual G7 governments by business, labour, and agricultural representatives, initial civil society reaction to the G7 took rather an undifferentiated form: the alternative summits. For some years, these counter-summits generally went by the name 'The Other Economic Summit' (TOES), and sometimes 'people's summit' or 'citizens' summit'. The first alternative summit, called the 'Popular Summit', met in Ottawa in 1981, and the first TOES proper was organised by the London-based TOES/UK – later called New Economics Foundation – and took place simultaneously with the 1984 London G7 Summit (Schroyer 1997). TOES described itself as 'an international non-governmental forum for the presentation, discussion, and advocacy of the economic ideas and practices upon which a more just and sustainable society can be built – "an economics as if people mattered"' (TOES 1997).[8] In 1985, 1986 and 1987 TOES sent delegations to the G7 summits; starting with 1988, TOES met in an event parallel with the summit. Its prominence then declined in favour of more focussed, issue-oriented civil society approaches to the G7 (and later to the G8). Each year's TOES featured a civil society coalition with varying NGO membership, meeting in the G7/8 summit city. These counter-summits ran workshops and demonstrations, and produced press releases and often a counter-communiqué critical of the official G7/8 communiqué (see, for example, People's Summit 1995). Harriet Friedmann states that 'in the 1990s, TOES morphed into teach-ins and similar gatherings under the rubric of the International Forum on Globalization' (Friedmann 2001, 88); but at least one national TOES, TOES/USA, reappeared at the time of the 2004 Sea Island Summit. A much stronger people's summit (discussed below) was to emerge later.

Civil society in many instances took issue-specific approaches. For example, the environmental movement lobbied the G7 as early as 1988. In 1990 at Houston a coalition of NGOs led by the World Wildlife Fund issued its report card on compliance with G8 environmental commitments, and in 1991 an 'Enviro-Summit' met in London a few city blocks from the official G7 summit site.

Phase 3 (1995–1997): The G7/8 Recognises Civil Society

The G7, on its part, was slower to acknowledge civil society formally. The terms 'civil society' and 'NGO' were not used in official G7 documents until the 1995 Halifax Summit. The Halifax communiqué refers to NGOs and civil society in the context of promoting sustainable development and the reform of international financial institutions (IFIs), adding that the UN and the Bretton Woods institutions should 'encourage countries to follow participatory development strategies and support governmental reforms that assure transparency and public accountability, a stable rule of law, and an active civil society' (G7 1995, para. 26). In the same document, the G7 undertakes that 'increase overall coherence, cooperation and cost effectiveness we will work with others to encourage ... improved coordination among international organizations, bilateral donors and NGOs' (para. 37).

The Halifax reference to civil society was only the beginning. The 1996 Lyon Summit, which began the fourth seven-year cycle of summitry, spoke out even more strongly about the positive role of civil society. In its economic communiqué, it underlined the need for 'a strengthened civil society' in that partnership (G7 1996, para. 34). The communiqué of the 1997 Denver Summit of the Eight went further, 'reaffirm[ing] the vital contribution of civil society' to the environment, democratic governance and poverty eradication (G8 1997, para. 13). Subsequent G7/8 summits have similarly acknowledged – at least in the language of their official documents – the increasingly important role of civil society in a number of sectors.

Other levels of the G7/8 system also took up the civil society nexus. By 1996, when G7 environment ministers met in Cabourg, France (9–10 May), they chose as one of their main themes the mobilisation of civil society; the Cabourg communiqué has several references to NGOs (G7 Environment Ministers 1996). Later, more ministerial forums (the G8 environment ministers, the Trade Ministers Quadrilateral, and others), as well as various G7/8 task forces and expert groups, have expressed their willingness to engage civil society and their appreciation of the importance of engaging all stakeholders (see Chapter 17). This marks a clear trend: the G7/8 system has recognised the increasing importance of civil society. This developing relationship reflects the evolution and maturing of both civil society and the G7/8.

Phase 4 (1998–): Civil Society Grows Stronger and More Sophisticated

Birmingham, Cologne, Okinawa The 1998 Birmingham Summit was a watershed in G7/8 interaction with civil society. It was there that the Jubilee 2000 coalition lobbied for debt relief and organised a spectacular human chain of 70 000 peaceful demonstrators who surrounded the summit site and presented a petition to the leaders, asking for debt cancellation. This prompted an unprecedented G7/8 reaction: British prime minister Tony Blair, on behalf of the G8, responded to the petition in a separate document of the summit (G8 1998). In an additional statement, Blair paid tribute to the Jubilee 2000 campaign, for the dignified manner in which it demonstrated in Birmingham, and for making a 'most persuasive case for debt relief' (cited in Dent and Peters 1999, 188). Jubilee and its successor organisations have been supported by celebrities ranging from the Irish rock star Bono and former boxing champion Muhammad Ali to Pope John Paul II, the Dalai Lama, and Archbishop Desmond Tutu.

The Jubilee movement has displayed impressive tactical and strategic savvy. It understands the workings of the G7/8 system very well. For example, in 2000, leading up to the Okinawa Summit, Jubilee followed and publicised the host leader's customary pre-summit visits by Japanese prime ministers Keizo Obuchi and then Yoshiro Mori to the other summit countries. It staged demonstrations at G7/8 ministerial meetings. It is familiar with the sherpa and sous-sherpa process.[9] It monitors and communicates the performance of G7 governments, and demands that those governments implement their past commitments.

All this has given the debt issue a high public profile that governments and intergovernmental organisations (IGOs) would find difficult to match. The idiom could not be more different from that customarily used by governments, IGOs, and the G7/8 itself. Although it is impossible to measure the precise impact of Jubilee 2000 on G7/8 governments, there is a strong perception that it is influential. A spokesperson for the World Bank stated in 1999 that Jubilee 2000 'has managed to put a relatively arcane issue – that of international finance and development – on the negotiating table throughout the world. The pledges [U.S. president] Clinton and [UK chancellor of the exchequer Gordon] Brown have made [to debt relief] would not have happened without Jubilee 2000. It's one of the most effective global lobbying campaigns I have ever seen' (Jubilee 2000 Coalition 1999b). And the *Financial Times* wrote on 17 February 1999: 'When a plea for debt relief becomes the common cause of a coalition that embraces both the Pope and the pop world, creditors should take notice' (cited in Jubilee 2000 Coalition 1999a).

The trend of largely peaceful demonstrations continued before and during the 1999 Cologne and 2000 Okinawa summits. But demonstrations and street theatre are just one aspect of civil society action, although these tend to garner the most media attention. Year-round lobbying and advocacy, as well as preparing and disseminating policy papers, are among other facets of work by NGOs and other civil society organisations. In the course of such activities, NGOs often consult governments, international organisations, academic experts, businesses, and other stakeholders.

In many cases, this type of action has allowed civil society to make a real impact on official policy.

In the lead-up to the Okinawa Summit, the Japanese government made clear its determination, as G8 chair for 2000, to reach out beyond the G8 to developing and other countries, IGOs, the private sector, and civil society. This attitude of openness was in evidence before and during the summit in several ways:

- Ahead of the summit the Japanese government appointed an official to provide regular liaison with civil society organisations during the summit planning process (Kirton 2000).
- The government sponsored a pre-summit international symposium on the role of NGOs in conflict prevention.
- There was dialogue between the Japanese government and civil society leaders, both in Europe prior to the summit, and in Japan on the opening day of the summit. Mori's meeting with representatives of nine NGOs (selected on a first-come-first-served basis) on 21 July was presented by the Japanese government as a new initiative. In fact, it was at the 1998 Birmingham Summit that civil society had its first official dialogue with the G7/8 as represented by Blair, and where Secretary of State for International Development Clare Short, on behalf of the prime minister, accepted the 1.4 million signatures amassed by the Jubilee campaign (Dent and Peters 1999, 36). Although Okinawa reconfirmed the validity of consultation and dialogue, G8 governments other than the Japanese host did not reach out to civil society sufficiently in 2000.

Genoa The 2001 Genoa Summit turned out to be a more ominous milestone in G8–civil society relations.[10] It was characterised by massive protests and marred by violence. Summit venues and activities were severely restricted by the protests outside. Out of concern for security, the local hosts of the G8 hired a luxury cruiser, the *Spirit of Europe*, to house all but one of the G8 leaders (George W. Bush). The prefecture of Genoa took various security measures: setting up a red zone and a surrounding yellow zone, and closing most transportation access to the city. Steps taken went as far as deploying anti-aircraft batteries along the runways of Genoa's Cristoforo Colombo airport. This seemed excessive at the time, but later in 2001, in the wake of the September 11 attacks against the World Trade Center in New York and the Pentagon in Washington, President Hosni Mubarak of Egypt and Italy's Deputy Prime Minister Gianfranco Fini reportedly said that Osama bin Laden's terrorist network had threatened to kill Bush and other G8 leaders (Sanger 2001).

Ahead of the summit, responsible civil society groups had made clear their intention to demonstrate and protest peacefully against economic globalisation and for more progress on debt relief. They expressed concern that anarchist and other potentially disruptive or violent groups would jeopardise peaceful, lawful, democratic protest. The Genoa Social Forum, an umbrella organisation of some 700 international, Italian, and Genoa-based NGOs and civil society coalitions, included the Jubilee Movement's Drop the Debt but also Ya Basta, an Italian anarchist organisation (although essentially a non-violent one) (Beattie 2001b). It was unclear from the start how this kind of contradiction could be resolved, especially in light of the announcement by the forum that some of its member groups 'would attempt peacefully to invade the red zone during the planned "day of civil disobedience" on Friday July 20', the first day of the summit (Beattie 2001b). The Global Social Forum as a whole planned three sets of demonstrations in the officially permitted area. The Drop the Debt met Italian national and local government representatives in June to negotiate plans for peaceful demonstrations. Drop the Debt and several other respected aid agencies had also 'drawn up contingency plans to avoid the Italian city during the summit on July 20–22 if a repeat of the violence that accompanied the recent European Union meeting in Gothenburg seem[ed] likely' (Beattie 2001b).

In the event, the demonstrations of 20 July were marred by anarchist violence (including instances of anarchists turning against peaceful demonstrators) and a similarly violent police response. The resulting death of Carlo Giuliani, the many injuries, and concern for the safety of their supporters led Drop the Debt and other groups, including the World Development Movement, to stage a vigil alongside the peaceful demonstrations still held on 21 July (World Development Movement 2001).

During the night of 21 July, Italian police stormed one of the buildings used by Genoa Social Forum without a warrant, smashing computers, confiscating computer disks, arresting about 90 people including members of the violent anarchist Black Bloc or Tute Nere (Black Overalls, to be distinguished from the generally non-violent Tute Bianche or White Overalls), and reportedly beating up protestors (many of whom were asleep) and some journalists (see, for example, 'Picking up the Pieces: After the Genoa Summit' 2001). Worse, there were eyewitness accounts of police complicity with the Black Bloc. Susan George (2001, 6) tells of a churchman, Don Vitaliano della Sala, who reported seeing Black Bloc members leaving a van of the *carabinieri* (military police), and Arthur Neslen (2001) describes a film shown after the police raid at the Genoa Social Forum press conference 'of muscular men in jeans and face-masks giving orders to "activists" on motorbikes behind police lines'.[11]

G8 leaders and most NGO groups deplored the clashes. In a special statement issued on 21 July (the first official document of the Genoa Summit), the leaders recognised and praised the role of peaceful protest and argument, but condemned unequivocally the violence and anarchy perpetrated by a small minority (G8 2001b). And the final communiqué of 22 July reaffirmed the right of peaceful protestors to have their voices heard and again deplored the violence and vandalism of those who seek to disrupt discussion and dialogue (G8 2001c, para. 35).

Civil society groups, on their part, condemned the violence in equally strong terms. Oxfam stated in a press release that 'violent disruption of international meetings doesn't help reach a solution, and it certainly doesn't help the poor. It drowns out the voice of many thousands of peaceful and serious people arguing for AIDS treatment and deeper debt relief' (Oxfam International 2001a). Adrian Lovett, director of Drop the Debt, added: 'Peaceful protest works, and it has made a hugely positive impact on recent G8 Summits. The violence we have seen in Genoa achieves nothing. Peaceful campaigners must reflect on how we make sure our concerns are addressed without the risk of hijack by violent extremists (Jubilee USA Network and Lovett 2001). Médecins Sans Frontières (MSF) put its condemnation in even stronger terms: 'MSF takes a sharp distance from every kind of violence and from those that in one way or another have chosen to manipulate these days in Genoa and created an atmosphere of violence and aggression – be it from the side of the radical demonstrators or the side of the police' (MSF 2001a).

Predictably, the media paid closest attention to the violence. Several G8 leaders expressed their frustration at this disproportionate news coverage to the detriment of reporting the actual deliberations of the G7 and G8.

A whole spectrum of issues was represented in Genoa by a variety of NGO groups, ranging from the environment to women's rights. This brief assessment focusses on just three issues: debt, health, and education. The dire consequences of unsustainable debt burdens on developing countries continued to be a major campaign objective for the Jubilee Movement. But new linkages emerged as these groups added other issues to their longstanding concern with debt: education, and HIV/AIDS and other infectious diseases. This transition led to the formation of new alliances with organisations fighting against such diseases (notably MSF) and with those promoting universal education (such as Oxfam). Civil society members of this new alliance stressed that developing countries need deeper debt relief in order to fight the HIV/AIDS pandemic more successfully and to benefit from better educational opportunities.

In a significant convergence of ideas, the Italian presidency of the G8, a few weeks before the summit, released a document entitled 'Beyond Debt Relief', setting forth the elements of an international strategy needed to stimulate growth and eradicate poverty in the poorest of the developing countries (Ministero degli Affari Esteri 2001). Italy recognised that although debt relief already given to countries eligible under the Heavily Indebted Poor Countries (HIPC) Initiative presented a significant opportunity for those countries to use more of their own resources to enhance human capital, and that every country needs a healthy and well-educated population in order to achieve greater social and economic development. The G7 finance ministers (2001), in their report to the leaders, 'Debt Relief and Beyond', revisited these themes. But civil society goals in these areas tend to exceed G8 declarations and commitments.

Although the Italian government did not set up an NGO centre in 2001 similar to the one established by the Japanese government in Okinawa in 2000, the Genoa Social Forum had several gathering points in the city. Its many activities included a public forum held 16 to 22 July entitled 'Another World Is Possible', as well as street demonstrations.

The tradition of host-government dialogue with civil society continued before and during the Genoa Summit. In the preparatory phase, the Italian government made a serious effort to communicate with NGOs, especially in the areas of development aid and poverty reduction. Four research institutes were directed to consult NGOs and solicit their recommendations in what was termed the Genoa Nongovernmental Initiative (Zupi 2001). The mayor of Genoa confirmed his intention, shared with

Italian prime minister Silvio Berlusconi, 'to open a dialogue with the movements that intend to demonstrate ... critically but peacefully during the summit'. Italy's interior minister Claudio Scajola concurred (G8 2001a).

Consultations with Italian and other G8 government leaders and ministers took place on several occasions during the summit. In a news conference on 20 July, Bono, Bob Geldof, and Lorenzo Jovanotti, pop music stars and strong supporters of the Jubilee/Drop the Debt campaign, talked of a series of meetings they had had with the British, German, Canadian, EU, and Russian leaders, as well as with George W. Bush's security advisor, Condoleezza Rice, but they expressed frustration at the Italian host's refusal to facilitate meetings with leaders from the South. The three rock musicians found the Millennium Action Plan for Africa (later the New Partnership for Africa's Development [NEPAD]) encouraging, and they welcomed the debt-forgiveness commitments of Canada and Italy as particularly praiseworthy. Nonetheless, they added that even some countries whose debt had been cancelled still had to continue to pay their rich creditors. The artists welcomed the opportunity that such meetings provided for asking the leaders hard questions such as 'Is an African life not worth the same as a European life?' They took advantage of being able to talk directly to the G7 – major shareholders of the IMF with the power to do something about debt. These widely popular musicians were articulate spokesmen and powerful symbols of the best aspirations and goals of civil society (Drop the Debt 2001a).

This kind of dialogue is no less important for the leaders of the G8. But dialogue, to be meaningful, must not consist of empty words and promises. A representative of MSF expressed disappointment at what she saw as just that kind of inadequate dialogue at Genoa, in contrast with the more upbeat assessment of Bono, Geldof, and Jovanotti.

As at other summits starting with Halifax, NGOs and civil society were reflected in several Genoa G7/8 documents; for example, the G7 Statement of 20 July, in the section concerning the launching of the new Doha round of trade negotiations, stated that 'the WTO [World Trade Organization] should continue to respond to the legitimate expectations of civil society, and ensure that the new Round supports sustainable development'(G7 2001, para. 8); and the final G8 Communiqué of 22 July, making several references to NGOs and civil society, undertook to 'promote innovative solutions based on a broad partnership with civil society and the private sector' (G8 2001c, para. 2).

Civil society's verdict on the Genoa Summit was rather negative. The Jubilee Movement noted with disappointment 'the failure of the richest nations to once again tackle the global debt crisis that is worsening the impoverishment of over 2 billion people in severely indebted countries'. Jubilee acknowledged that the number of countries eligible for debt relief under the HIPC Initiative had increased from 9 to 23 between the Okinawa and Genoa summits, but criticised the G7 for congratulating itself on progress when 'most of these countries [were] approaching unsustainable levels of debt again' (Jubilee Movement International for Economic and Social Justice 2001).

MSF criticised the Global Fund to Fight AIDS, Tuberculosis, and Malaria, noting that pledges of US$1.2 billion were 'nowhere near what is required' and were 'shamefully low'; it went on to say that 'governments call upon multinationals and the private sector to contribute. Among these are the pharmaceutical companies whose pricing policies are a fundamental part of the problem' (MSF 2001b). The initial Global Health Fund pledges fell far short of the annual funding of US$8 billion to US$10 billion Kofi Annan had asked for, and it was unclear how much of the US$1.2 billion was actually new money. And yet the initiative itself and the fact that this became a concern both to the UN and to the G8 are important, as Nicholas Bayne (2001) observes, while also noting that 'main weakness in the G8 position is that their pledges look like one-time contributions, without any assurance of continuity of funding'.

Oxfam was equally critical of the Genoa Summit's record on debt and the Global Health Fund but had a slightly more positive take on education. It stated: 'The G8 did nothing meaningful on debt relief, and announced a global AIDS fund that still needs much more resources and does nothing about the cost of drugs in poor countries. It's unacceptable that these promises remain unmet … Education breaks the cycle of poverty, and is essential in building democracy and fighting AIDS. Last year the G8 promised a global plan for education. In Genoa they said how to accomplish it … The world can't afford another unmet promise' (Oxfam International 2001b).

On energy, a joint statement issued on 22 July by the World Wildlife Fund (WWF), Greenpeace, and ECA Watch condemned the G8 leaders for refusing to adopt the action plan proposed by the Renewable Energy Task Force that had been set up the previous year in Okinawa by the G8 itself. The statement said: 'By rejecting their own findings, the G8 are actively denying people in the developing world access to clean reliable energy' (WWF, Greenpeace, and EAC Watch 2001).

The World Development Movement, assessing the Genoa G8 final communiqué of 22 July, commented on the wide gap 'that remains between the leaders and the rest of us'. It gave an almost point-by-point response to the language of the G8, welcoming certain initiatives but giving the G8 a poor mark overall. Jessica Woodroffe, head of policy at the organisation, stated: 'Ultimately these summits must be judged by the benefits they deliver to the world's poor. The result this year has been an anti-poor trade plan, nothing on debt and a feeble [global health] fund' (World Development Movement 2001).

A significant concern was expressed by Drop the Debt about the shifting priorities of the G8: 'This year the G8's big idea is to fight disease in the poorest countries. But most people are sick to death of G8 initiatives that never quite get delivered. In 1999, it was debt. Last year [in 2000], it was computers. This year it is health. Next year, we know it will be education. Every unfinished initiative is another blow to the credibility of the G8' (Drop the Debt 2001b). The G8 would do well to reflect on this perception of shifting attention to and away from crucial issues and policy initiatives. Civil society, for its part, could temper its criticism by recognising that the G7/8 has been able to deal with several issues simultaneously and has at times achieved results by an iterative process, a case in point being the conclusion of the Uruguay

Round of multilateral trade negotiations – it took several years of G7 deliberation to achieve success (Drop the Debt 2001b, 200–2001).

From Genoa to Kananaskis In the wake of the turbulent Genoa G8 Summit, many questions were raised about the future of the G8 and the way its business is conducted, as well as about civil society and other protestor groups and their *modus operandi.* For many years, the G7/8 leaders have voiced their wish to stage smaller, more intimate, and more focussed meetings, with fewer officials in attendance and perhaps fewer media personnel around. A notable advance was made at the 1998 Birmingham Summit when leaders met without their foreign and finance ministers – this practice has thereafter become established. But there continued to be much dissatisfaction with the G7/8. In a post-Genoa editorial, the *Financial Times* questioned whether 'G8 summits should exist and, if so, in what form'; it noted that 'summits have worked best when the leaders have had a chance to be separate from their national entourages ... and when there has been a crisis to try to sort out', and concludes that there 'should have been ... a commitment to hold the next G8 only when there is a burning topic to discuss' ('For Slimmer and Sporadic Summits' 2001).

G8 Dialogue with Civil Society

Before Kananaskis, there were two critical points of civil society contact with the Canadian host government. First, Canada's Standing Committee on Foreign Affairs and International Trade, whose hearings allowed ample civil society representation, produced a useful and interesting report (Standing Committee on Foreign Affairs and International Trade 2002). The report included 20 recommendations on assistance to poor countries, financial reform, debt relief, human rights, African issues, aid, health and education, international trade and investment, sustainable development, terrorism, accountability, and G8 reform. Recommendation 14, in particular, called for a true partnership with civil society in the Africa Action Plan.

Second, civil society was well represented in the series of useful consultation meetings across Canada, organised by Canadian sherpa Robert Fowler. The Canadian International Development Agency (CIDA), too, organised meetings on Africa in the lead-up to Kananaskis. But dialogue with other G8 governments was difficult, in contrast with the Quebec City Summit of the Americas in April 2002, where there had been wider-ranging civil society consultations with a number of governments (Lortie and Bédard 2001).[12]

Moderate NGOs welcomed the opportunity to meet with senior members of other G8 governments in an open process, although some NGOs found themselves unable to do so (Amnesty International 2002a). Other civil society organisations, such as Oxfam and Greenpeace, were able to establish dialogue with several or all G8 countries in the lead-up to Kananaskis. An interesting high-level dialogue, under the aegis of the Montreal International Forum (FIM), took place on 21–23 May 2002 in Montreal and Ottawa; it brought together civil society representatives from Brazil,

Canada, Colombia, France, the Netherlands, the Philippines, Senegal, UK, Uruguay, U.S., and Zimbabwe with representatives of the governments of Canada, France, Japan, and the UK. The three topics of discussion were the global democratic deficit and civil society engagement, the NEPAD consultative process, and future G8–civil society dialogue building on multi-stakeholder experiences. During this meeting the French representative expressed interest in consultations with civil society in the lead-up to the 2003 Summit, to be held in Evian-les-Bains. To this end, FIM undertook to co-ordinate preparations with members of French civil society (FIM 2002).

The Kananaskis Summit and Surrounding Events

In the lead-up to Kananaskis, the Canadian host government took a steps to promote dialogue with civil society. In addition to the series of extensive consultations with citizen groups conducted by Robert Fowler, the government made good efforts to educate the public at all levels about the G7/8 and its role. It also launched an impressive website dedicated to the summit, and provided generous funding for the G6B ('Group of Six Billion') People's Summit, held at the University of Calgary. It is an open question whether these efforts matched the British government's fruitful consultations with civil society at the time of the Birmingham Summit, the in-depth discussions (involving think tanks as well as a number of civil society groups) conducted by the Italian government prior to the Genoa Summit, or the kind of support provided by the Japanese government for the Okinawa Summit.

The record of civil society activism shows that while government initiatives toward non-state actors is important, civil society does not take its cues from government but develops strategies on its own terms. There were numerous NGO meetings in preparation for Kananaskis. Online activism was evident, attested to by several websites, such as those of G8 Activism and Partnership Africa Canada. Established websites of major international NGOs and coalitions also picked up coverage of G8-related campaigns and other activities.

Street demonstrations were largely peaceful, with an estimated 3000 to 5000 demonstrators in Calgary (and a much smaller number near Kananaskis). The pre-summit meeting of G8 foreign ministers in Whistler, British Columbia, had also passed without incident, unlike the pre-summit G7 finance ministers meeting in Halifax, Nova Scotia, where 30 demonstrators were arrested. Unlike in Genoa or Quebec City, there were no injuries. Kananaskis was a peaceful summit in part due to the remote and isolated location, the small number of protestors, the professionalism and non-threatening tactics of Canadian security forces deployed at Kananaskis and Calgary, and the Canadian political culture that tends to eschew anarchism and extremism (see Chapter 16). There is another, equally important factor: civil society's own efforts to distance itself from violent, disruptive elements and to monitor demonstrations to make sure that they remained peaceful.

The three main themes of the Kananaskis Summit (Africa, the economy, and terrorism) lent themselves to meaningful civil society participation. Amnesty

International expressed the conviction that in all three summit issues the discussion and outcome should be infused with human rights concerns and perspectives. The global economy should be strengthened in a manner that is centred on human rights. The fight against terrorism raises human rights concerns. And human rights should be a crucial aspect of NEPAD and the G8 Africa Action Plan (Amnesty International 2002b).

A 'Solidarity Village' had been planned by some segments of civil society as a camp for activists during the week of the summit. It was to be located in the foothills of the Rockies near Kananaskis Village, as a place from which to address and criticise the G8 agenda. In the event, this initiative was banned by G8 Summit officials and denied another venue in Calgary by that city's mayor.

NGOs and Civil Society Reflected in Kananaskis G7/8 Documents

For the first time in G7/8 summit history, Kananaskis produced no communiqué but only a brief, more informal chair's summary (G8 2002b). This was a result of longstanding aversion by some G8 leaders to lengthy, prescripted communiqués that, according to some, more people wrote than read. (There had been chair's summaries at earlier summits but those were issued in addition to formal communiqués.) The Kananaskis chair's summary made no direct mention of NGOs or civil society.

The statement by G7 leaders concentrated on the achievements and shortcomings of the HIPC Initiative (G7 2002). It made no reference to civil society, even though the Jubilee Movement and other civil society organisations had been instrumental in keeping the debt issue front and centre and were continuing their thrust for greater and more meaningful debt relief than had hitherto been achieved.

The Africa Action Plan (the G8's response to NEPAD) included several explicit references to civil society; other aspects of the plan implied civil society involvement (G8 2002c). The G8 leaders 'encourage South-South cooperation and collaboration with international institutions and civil society, including the business sector, in support of the NEPAD' (para. 10). Under the heading 'Promoting Peace and Security', the leaders committed to 'working with African governments, civil society and others to address the linkage between armed conflict and the exploitation of natural resources' (point 1.5); and under 'Strengthening Institutions and Governance' the leaders recorded a further commitment to support 'African efforts to involve parliamentarians and civil society in all aspects of the NEPAD process' (point 2.1).

The G8 document entitled 'A New Focus on Education for All', incorporating the report of the G8 Education Task Force, recognised that all stakeholders, including local communities, private providers, and NGOs should be 'seriously engaged in the development and implementation of education plans' (G8 2002a). In calling for a more coherent international process in the Education for All project, the report recalls UNESCO's role in bringing together on a regular basis education ministers as well as various institutions, NGOs, and representatives of developing countries, so that the political momentum may be maintained. And, to give another example of recognition of civil society's role on the ministerial level, the chair's summary of the post-Kananaskis G8 development ministers meeting points to the need for greater engagement of civil society in development strategies, especially as regards Poverty Reduction Strategy Papers (PRSPs) for developing countries (G8 Development Ministers 2002).

The G6B People's Summit

Amnesty International considered the G6B People's Summit in Calgary a success for the civil society movement. There were approximately 1400 people in attendance, more than had been expected. There were excellent presentations, and all sessions were packed. But the only connection with the official G8 Summit occurred during the open session on the final day of the G6B, with Canada's foreign minister Bill Graham and minister for international cooperation Susan Whelan present. Graham accepted the G6B's recommendations and later transmitted them to the Summit host, Prime Minister Jean Chrétien.

In his evaluation of this event, Bayne (2003) noted a generally negative attitude to the G8, with much strident criticism, especially on Africa. He added, however, that influential international NGOs such as Oxfam and MSF offered critical but more constructive comment. Interestingly, the proceedings of G6B influenced the media greatly, due to the fact that the G8 leaders themselves were not very accessible.

Civil Society Evaluation of the Kananaskis Summit and Associated Events

Many civil society organisations were represented in Calgary by North American (Canadian and U.S.) affiliates rather than people from international headquarters. This can be attributed to various causes but the cautious (perhaps over-cautious) approach of Canadian immigration and police authorities after September 11 was one major factor. Amnesty International, for one, expressed its disappointment at the refusal of Canadian authorities to grant accreditation to its observer of the policing at the G8 Summit on the grounds that he did not have 'the background and knowledge of the law required to make balanced and objective observations' (Amnesty International 2002a). The organisation disputed this claim and was nonetheless ably represented in Calgary by Amnesty Canada.

Amnesty International welcomed the G8 leaders' support of efforts by African countries and the UN to regulate activities of arms traffickers and eliminate the flow of illicit weapons to and within Africa. However, it accused the Africa Action Plan of failing to recognise the responsibility of the G8 governments themselves for the sale and transfer of arms to African countries. Amnesty International called for concrete commitments, not just inspirational sentiments. It wanted the G8 states not to approach Africa as a philanthropic concern but to take responsibility for arms trade implications: up to 80 percent of small-arms trade originates in G8 states, the U.S. and Russia being the major sources.

On conflict diamonds and other conflict commodities, Amnesty International acknowledged the G8's support of voluntary measures (notably the Kimberley Process for certifying diamonds) but demanded more: that corporate social responsibility be based on human rights standards and be binding by regulation or legislation. As for policing and law enforcement, Amnesty International asked G8 to help make police defenders of human rights, involving effective mechanisms to ensure police operational accountability, with laws governing police and law enforcement officials consistent with international human rights standards (Amnesty International 2002a, 2002b).

For Greenpeace, the overarching goals for the Kananaskis Summit and related ministerial meetings were to keep the issue of renewable energy and development in focus and to garner support for an initiative on this issue in preparation for the Johannesburg Summit. Greenpeace had not expected to see an agreement on renewables from any part of the G8 system, but considered its campaign more successful at the G8 environment ministers meeting than at the Kananaskis Summit itself. In addition, Greenpeace wanted to use the forum provided by the pre-Kananaskis G8 series of meetings to raise issues of climate change and Kyoto, especially in order to put pressure on Chrétien to announce a Canadian ratification decision either in Kananaskis or in Johannesburg. Greenpeace considered itself to have been very successful on climate change and Kyoto in the G8 environment and energy ministers meetings, not successful at all at the Kananaskis Summit, and again very successful in Johannesburg. Other Greenpeace activities included arranging for senior-level European politicians to speak to Canadian media immediately before the start of the environment ministers' pre-summit meeting in order to create a public and political dynamic that – in Greenpeace's view – forced a discussion on climate change, Canada's position on Kyoto and support for renewable energy at the meeting (see Chapter 17).

In its organisational objective to build capacity to communicate with the larger anti-corporate globalisation movement and to engage the movement's interest through the Johannesburg Summit, Greenpeace considered itself to have been moderately successful. One measure of this success was a multilingual G8 web audio project that attracted more than 1.5 million page hits during a single month. Visitors to this website stayed longer and visited more pages than usual. Greenpeace also placed its audio, video, and printed material with a whole range of alternative media, groups, listservs, and individuals.

Greenpeace presented its position throughout the G8 series of meetings leading up to Kananaskis at the national level in all G8 countries. Presentations were made in person, by correspondence and through the media. Once the summit started, given its highly choreographed nature, the only possible civil society role in Greenpeace's perception was commentary and bearing witness. It turned out, however, that interest of mainstream media was at best tangential to Greenpeace messages.

The Jubilee Movement welcomed 'the admission by the G8 countries that the levels of debt cancellation committed at Decision Point will not be sufficient to bring HIPC debt down to sustainable levels', but stated its belief that the additional US$1 billion debt cancellation offered at Kananaskis would 'fall far short of the levels needed if the HIPC countries are to meet the Millennium Development Goals'

(Jubilee Research 2002). It further commented that the G8 proposal did not provide for any further debt relief for countries already beyond completion point.

MSF admonished the G8 leaders to move from rhetoric to action in order to ensure access to effective and affordable treatments for infectious diseases in the developing world, and to 'transform political commitment into hard cash' (MSF 2002). Although the UN had called for US$10 billion for AIDS alone in the Global Health Fund, the G8 had thus far only allocated US$580 million – a shortfall of almost 96 percent. Political will and sufficient resources are needed to combat these diseases. MSF also called on the G8 to support exceptions to patent rights to allow export of medicines produced under compulsory licence, and to support research and development for effective and affordable treatments for neglected diseases affecting millions in Africa and elsewhere in the developing world.

At the close of the Kananaskis Summit, Oxfam acknowledged that the G8's Africa Action Plan contained a framework (and singled out Canada and the UK for their leadership), but cautioned that the plan contained too few concrete actions and provided too little money (Oxfam GB 2002). For six months before the summit, Oxfam had lobbied G8 governments (particularly the U.S., Britain, Germany, and Canada) in the context of NEPAD and the Africa Action Plan for a substantial aid increase, for fair trade and secure market access, and for resolution of the conflicts plaguing that continent. After the Summit, Oxfam welcomed the fact that the Africa Action Plan acknowledged the breadth of issues concerning Africa's needs, G8 endorsement of the education task force report and the resulting Education for All Action Plan, the commitment of US$1 billion to cover unsustainable debt burdens of countries suffering from a steep fall of commodity prices, and acknowledgement of the need for better and fuller consultation with African civil society in implementing NEPAD. Oxfam also pointed out the need for G8 countries to implement the pledge to increase aid to Africa, to fund the Education for All Action Plan immediately, to increase funding for the Global Health Fund, to increase debt relief, to promote fair trade, to work for an international arms trade treaty, to implement fully the guidelines for multinational enterprises set out by the Organisation for Economic Co-operation and Development (OECD), and to prevent companies under their jurisdiction from illegal or unethical exploitation of natural resources.

The reaction of African NGOs to NEPAD was particularly significant. There remained considerable opposition to a plan that many in African civil society organisations see as lacking in civil society involvement, as well as other limitations. The 50 Years Is Enough network asserted that 'Both NEPAD and the G7's action plan on Africa were devised in a vacuum, with no input from civil society organizations. Scores of prominent African civil society and academic networks have criticized NEPAD for its faithfulness to status quo "neo-liberal" economic policies and for its claim to "African ownership" in the absence of consultation beyond the inner circles of the presidents of South Africa, Nigeria, Senegal, and Algeria' (50 Years is Enough 2002).[13] Other segments of African civil society acknowledged that the G8, by consulting with African civil society organisations, was showing greater openness, and African civil society chose to engage the G8 in a reciprocal manner.

Yet, the G8 Africa Action Plan caused 'hurt surprise' among African organisations because the financial commitments were far lower than expected.[14] But the G8 cannot ignore this major initiative, however imperfect, coming from Africa and must, instead, work for improvements, including bringing African civil society on board (see Chapter 20).

Evian-les-Bains, 1–3 June 2003

Dialogue The French government expressed interest in starting consultations with civil society as early as May 2002, prior to the Kananaskis Summit and more than a year before the summit in Evian-les-Bains. Later, French president Jacques Chirac gave a prominent place on the Evian agenda to dialogue with civil society by making it one of the summit's four major themes:

- solidarity, with particular emphasis on NEPAD and access to water for all;
- the spirit of responsibility that not only governments, but all economic actors, especially business corporations, need to display in the financial, social, environmental, and ethical spheres;
- security, in order to strengthen the fight against terrorism and the proliferation of weapons of mass destruction; and
- democracy, through ongoing dialogue with civil society and with other states (G8 2003).

In the months before Evian, Chirac held a series of meetings at the Palais Elysée with civil society organisations, including some groups critical of the G8. On 30 April he met with representatives of more than 30 organisations, including Centre de Recherche et d'Information pour le Développement (CRID), Greenpeace, Friends of the Earth (FOE), ATTAC, Oxfam International, and CLAAAC, among others (Tagliabue 2003; see also CRID 2003). One journalist suggested he may well have been motivated to try 'to co-opt the participants and agenda of counter-summits staged by the antiglobalisation movement. In his desire to head off the kind of violent protests that occurred at the Genoa G8 Summit two years earlier, Mr Chirac [had] initiated meetings prior to the summit with groups such as trade unions and environmentalists. French authorities [had] provided facilities near Evian almost to formalise the counter-summit' (Graham 2003). FIM representatives met with the French sherpa as well as with officials of G8 embassies in Paris. At this meeting, held at the Elysée on 20 May 2003, FIM raised its concerns on issues of human security, NEPAD, advancing multilateralism, and democratising the G8 process.

These meetings complemented the 'enlarged dialogue' that saw the French G8 presidency invite twelve heads of state from major developing countries plus the Swiss president and the heads of the UN, the WTO, the World Bank, and the IMF.[15]

Demonstrations and Confrontation French and Swiss authorities created a 15-kilometre exclusion zone around the summit site in order to protect the assembled leaders. The centre of Evian was sealed off to all except residents, summit delegations, and security personnel, and airline flights were banned over the area during the summit period. In readiness for potential terrorist attacks, surface-to-air missiles and radars were placed around Evian and along Lake Geneva, and soldiers patrolled the Alps in case terrorists attempted to use paragliders.

On Saturday, 31 May, about 50 000 demonstrators blocked traffic on bridges and highways around Geneva, on both the Swiss and French sides, but were unable to prevent the arrival of G8 leaders or delegations at the summit site. Demonstrators also staged a peaceful march from Annemasse, France (40 kilometres west of Evian), and another from Geneva. The two demonstrations met on the Swiss side of the border and continued to march together into France.

On 1 June, the first day of the summit, some demonstrators tried to break through the cordon. Although the majority were peaceful, there was considerable anarchist violence in Geneva and Lausanne, with smashing of windows and looting of stores; for example, the Auto-Gnomes of Zurich, an anarchist group, broke into a boarded-up BP station where they stole dozens of bottles of mineral water. Geneva police struggled to control the violence and called on German police to help. Police used tear gas, water cannons, and rubber bullets, and there were several hundred arrests and injuries. Police seized four Greenpeace-owned boats with 12 banner-carrying activists on Lake Geneva.

Inevitably there were clashes between some radical groups and moderate, peaceful demonstrators. The large demonstrations were generally peaceful but, once again, the media paid much attention to the violence.

The G8's 'Take' on Civil Society Almost all meetings during the Evian Summit acknowledged civil society. The topics of the general opening meeting, which began at 13:30 on 1 June, the first day of the summit, with the participation of the enlarged dialogue partners (the G8 leaders plus leaders of the 12 invited countries, the UN, and several other international institutions), included civil society involvement, peace and security, and the environment and sustainable development. The afternoon meeting (starting at 15:15) of the G8 leaders and the UN secretary general focussed on NEPAD, received the report of the African personal representatives (APRs) of the leaders, and took stock of the G8 Africa Action Plan including aspects of official development assistance (ODA), agriculture, security, and water – all of serious concern for civil society.

The morning meeting on 2 June (starting at 9:30), restricted to the G8 leaders, discussed the state of the international economy, trade issues, corporate responsibility, debt relief, social rights, the environment, and prevention and responses to financial crises. Several of these issues interest civil society as well. The lunch meeting of G8 leaders dealt with political issues including terrorism, proliferation of weapons of mass destruction (WMD) and other weapons, as well as regional issues, notably the Middle East Peace Process (MEPP), the aftermath of the Iraq war, and North Korea. The afternoon meeting (starting at 16:00) of G8 leaders – minus George W. Bush, who left after lunch for the Sharm-el-Sheikh and Aqaba summits on the

Israeli-Palestinian conflict – discussed debt, African development, ODA, water and sanitation issues, the environment, and so forth. Finally, the leaders' closing session on the morning of 3 June was a working meeting to finalise the statement and communiqués (Colonna 2003).

Parallel Events A counter-summit, the Sommet pour un autre monde (Summit for Another World, whose French acronym, SPAM, has an odd ring for English speakers), was held in Annemasse, France, 29–31 May 2003, with about 4500 participants. It was based on the premise that although the individual heads of state or government of G8 countries are legitimate actors in their own countries and have the right to meet, the G8 summit has no place in a democratic 'global governance'; rather, it is the UN that should be strengthened and reformed, so that it can play a real part in maintaining peace, enhancing development, promoting individual and collective rights, and protecting environmental equilibrium. This parallel event was organised by the following organisations: Agir ici, Amis de la Terre (Friends of the Earth), ATTAC, Comité pour l'Annulation de la dette du tiers-monde (CADTM), Comité catholique contre la faim et pour le développement (CCFD), CRID, Dossiers et débats pour le développement durable (4D), and Greenpeace. In addition, there were several partner organisations and other supporting organisations.

The counter-summit held a number of roundtable discussions from a civil society perspective, touching on issues many of which were also dealt with by the G8 summit: NEPAD, corporate social and environmental responsibility, global taxes for financing the development, local and global effects of globalisation, rules for a global environmental governance, debt, trade and development, arms transfers, human rights, HIV/AIDS, antiterrorism, and water. The counter-summit ended with a 'debt and reparation tribunal', a concert on the theme 'for another world, drop the debt', and a communiqué entitled *'Un G8 pour rien!'* [A G8 for nothing!] (SPAM 2003b, 2003a).

As well, various civil society groups (for example, the Forum social lémanique) staged conferences, workshops, and demonstrations in Geneva, Lausanne, Annemasse, and elsewhere in the vicinity of the Evian Summit. Also at Annemasse, two camping sites were set up for protestors: an 'intergalactic village' for environmental, anti-nuclear, or other social activists, and an 'anti-capitalist, alternative, anti-war village'. Demonstrations included, on the night of 31 May, 52 bonfires lit simultaneously along the shoreline of Lake Geneva by Swiss protestors in 'a symbolic encirclement of the G8' (Keaten 2003).

Yet another parallel event, the Poor People's Summit, was organised by the Mali chapter of Jubilee 2000 and took place in the village of Siby in that country. The 400 attendees included members of NGOs, farmers, herders, women's groups, teachers, and students from six African and four non-African countries. One participant, Mohamed Thiam, a representative of Transparency International in Mali, had this message for the G8 leaders attending the Evian Summit: 'You leaders of G8, you have many riches, we have nothing. I think you can help us, not by giving money, but by being honest and equal' (Baxter 2003). He added that 'debt, unfair trade and good governance [were] themes in Siby just as ... in France, and that 'the leaders of the world have to hear the voice of African civil society'. This counter-summit issued a declaration entitled 'Consensus des peuples face au consensus du G8' [Peoples' Consensus versus G8 Consensus] (Appel du Forum des Peuples 2003).

Civil Society Evaluation In its communiqué, SPAM passed a negative verdict on the Evian Summit (SPAM 2003b). While acknowledging that the G8 leaders recognised the growing gap between rich and poor as well as the increasing number of armed conflicts and the deterioration of social conditions and the environment, the alternative summit argued that the neo-liberal, trade-centred policies of the G8 countries are in fact the cause of these global disorders. It criticised the enlarged dialogue as cosmetic, with the richest countries reserving the right to choose whom they invite. On AIDS, SPAM regretted the conditionality of U.S. funding and the lack of guaranteed access for the South to generic drugs. On debt, the alternative summit belittled the extent of debt relief granted thus far, and demanded immediate debt cancellation for the poor countries and debt relief for medium-income developing countries. On trade, SPAM disputed the assertion that liberalised trade would benefit developing countries, and noted with regret that G8 countries were prepared to strengthen liberalisation of trade in services at the forthcoming Cancun ministerial meeting of the WTO. On corruption, while acknowledging the importance the G8 countries were placing on this issue, SPAM called upon them to do something about fiscal havens instead of just concentrating on the responsibilities of the South. On corporate social and environmental responsibility, SPAM noted modest advances on the part of the G8, criticising their reliance on inadequate voluntary codes. In conclusion, SPAM called for the dissolution of the G8 and for putting in place an international architecture for peace, equity, and environmental protection, centred on the UN system.

SPAM was the single most important focal point of civil society mobilisation. But the fact that Annemasse was so distant from the G8 Summit itself and the tight control by French authorities meant that media had little or no access to transport to get to the alternative venues.[16]

The Jubilee Debt Campaign, a successor of the Jubilee 2000 coalition, reached conclusions along similar lines to SPAM's negative assessment of the G8's performance on debt forgiveness. It added that the debt relief efforts of 70 000 protestors at the 1998 Birmingham Summit and the worldwide struggle of debt campaigners since that time had not been in vain, 'for the issue of poor country debt remains formally on the agenda of the rich world ... [and a] movement has been created which remains motivated to tackle the gross injustice of debt [and to] offer a clear critique of what is going wrong – and how that can be readily rectified' (Greenhill *et al.* 2003).

Amnesty International, at the beginning of the Evian Summit, urged the G8 leaders to fulfil the promises made in Kananaskis in 2002, and address the sources of conflict plaguing Africa: arms trade and trade in natural resources used for wars. Amnesty called for the G8 to initiate a worldwide treaty on arms trade, which would help prevent arms from reaching abusers of human rights. In preparation for Evian, Amnesty published a lengthy report, 'A Catalogue of Failures: G8 Arms Exports and Human Rights Violations', in which it accused five G8 countries (U.S., Russia, France, UK, and Germany) for supplying three quarters of all global arms transfers from 1997 to 2001 (Amnesty International 2003b). The organisation also called on G8 governments to promote moves toward corporate accountability, notably by supporting the UN's draft norms on the responsibilities of multinational corporations (Amnesty International 2003a).

Jamie Drummond, executive director of Debt AIDS Trade Africa (DATA), the advocacy group formed by Bono, expressed some optimism that Evian would result in increased commitments for the Global Health Fund established at the Genoa Summit: 'There is a desire to do it, but the question is how to find the money' (Crutsinger 2003). Nathan Ford, UK medical director for MSF, pointed to the significant commitment at the Okinawa Summit in 2000 for access to affordable generic medicines for developing countries to fight AIDS, malaria, and tuberculosis but added that 'three years later, those promises were mostly unfulfilled. He said the problem with G8 summits was that they were "unaccountable" inter-governmental meetings with no institutional or legal substance to help to ensure that decisions were carried out' (Lichfield 2003).

In the matter of the environment, Greenpeace lamented that 'all controversial environment issues were either absent or diluted to nothingness at the Group of Eight (G8) summit in Evian' ('Greens Glum as World Environment Day Heads for 30th Anniversary' 2003). FOE echoed Greenpeace's dim view, asserting that the environmental outcome of the Evian Summit was weak and that the G8 pulled back from commitments it had agreed to in Johannesburg, for example with regard to corporate voluntarism (contrasted with stronger measures called for in the Johannesburg plan of implementation) (see UN 2002, para. 45). As well, Evian's outcome was weak on oil spill liability and on the voluntary 'publish what you pay' initiative. On the other hand, FOE found that the French government had listened to civil society organisations engaged in key environmental issues, making their dialogue useful.[17]

Sea Island, 8–10 June 2004

Following the post–September 11 pattern of holding summits in secluded locations, the U.S.-hosted 2004 Summit was held in the resort of Sea Island, off the coast of Georgia, with delegations housed on nearby St. Simon's Island and in Brunswick, in mainland Georgia (although earlier precedents had been set at the first summit at Rambouillet in 1975 and at Montebello in 1981). Journalists covering the event had to content themselves with being based at the International Media Centre in Savannah, some 100 kilometres from Sea Island.

Lack of Dialogue and Lack of Access Sea Island turned out to be something of an aberration in G8–civil society relations. Bayne (2004) reported that the U.S. hosts 'made no attempt to engage civil society organizations', provided no facilities for civil society in Savannah or elsewhere, and, breaking with longstanding summit tradition, did not permit even major, respected NGOs such as Oxfam and Greenpeace to distribute their literature in the media centre. Even those NGOs whose representatives are normally legitimately accredited to summits as journalists were unable to do so in Savannah. Nonetheless, some civil society organisations managed to communicate their views and literature through the good offices of friendly journalists. As well, Oxfam and DATA held a press conference outside of the media centre, and Greenpeace and other NGOs linked up with local grassroots organisations in Savannah. Other NGOs submitted articles to Georgia newspapers. So, the ability of civil society organisations to get their message out may have been hindered but could not be suppressed.

Demonstrations The very tight security in Sea Island as well as in Brunswick and Savannah turned out not to be needed against demonstrators, of whom there were very few in the streets. The total number of participants at various summit-related demonstrations plus the counter-summit in Brunswick was estimated at only 500, with only 15 arrests on minor charges, and no injury or physical damage (Kirton 2004). Demonstrators and parallel-summit participants were vastly outnumbered by some 20 000 security personnel. Partly motivated by fear of terrorist threats, the disproportionate presence of security forces nonetheless seemed to be overkill.

On 8 June, the first day of the summit, a peaceful march was organised by the International Festival for Peace and Civil Liberties to oppose the Iraq war and the *Patriot Act*. Estimates of turnout ranged from 100 to 500. Among the reasons for the very low participation was a new Georgia law, initiated by Governor Sonny Perdue, that enabled the halting of the protest at the discretion of the police or the National Guard. There was concern that the pre-emptive state of emergency in effect until 20 June, requiring a state-issued permit for any assembly of more than six people in the streets of Georgia, was curtailing civil liberties. The main organiser of the protest, Kellie Gasink of Savannah, had applied for the required permit eight months in advance but received it just the day before the march (Smith and Burnett 2004).

Parallel Event The counter-summit organised by TOES-USA was a disappointment. Trent Schroyer and Susan Hunt stated that 'efforts … to continue the TOES tradition of facilitating a critical discourse about G8 policies were systematically blocked by the Bush administration and their sycophants in Georgia … Virtually every conference venue and lodging was either placed off-limits "for security reasons" or booked by the federal government to house the over 20 000 CIA [Central Intelligence Agency], FBI [Federal Bureau of Investigation], Homeland Security, Secret Service, Army National Guard, state and local police' (Schroyer and Hunt 2004). It was only five days before the conference that Perdue gave permissions for access to a venue, at Coastal Georgia Community College in poor and badly polluted Brunswick. In addition, Schroyer and Hunt assert that the local population was intimidated by authorities and sensationalist media. The result was that despite a good intellectual line-up of speakers, the audience at the conference numbered no more than 75 for each of the 24 sessions held over three days. Ironically, according to Schroyer and Hunt, the G8 Summit was held on land to which General Sherman, at the end of the American Civil War, gave title to the Gullah Geechee people, former slaves whose descendants today live in near–developing country conditions.

One forceful speaker at the TOES meeting was Barbara Kalema. She outlined some real achievements by Africans, such as the peer review mechanism for NEPAD and greater regional integration, but criticised the G8 for failing to take real steps toward market access for Africa and for the decline of ODA. She also noted that the late invitation to the six African heads of state (only a week before the summit) showed that Africa was not on the real agenda (Lugo 2004).

Civil Society in G8 Documents There is no reference civil society in the Chair's Summary (for the first time not a full-consensus document since French president Jacques Chirac publicly disassociated himself from it) (G8 2004g). Some other Sea Island Summit documents, however, do mention NGOs and civil society. For example, the action plan on Science and Technology for Sustainable Development encourages co-operation among various stakeholders, including NGOs and communities (G8 2004f). The declaration and action plan on Fighting Corruption and Improving Transparency calls on G8 governments to foster civil society engagement, and in the associated 'national transparency and anti-corruption compacts' the governments of Georgia, Nicaragua, Nigeria, and Peru undertake to consult with or promote participation by, their civil society in some aspects of this project (G8 2004e, 2004d, 2004c, 2004b). The statement on Ending the Cycle of Famine in the Horn of Africa points up the importance of building civil society capacity and greater involvement of civil society organisations in rural development (G8 2004i). The action plan on Applying the Power of Entrepreneurship to the Eradication of Poverty similarly asks for dialogue with civil society (G8 2004e).

Notably, the Broader Middle East and North Africa initiative, the centrepiece of the U.S. agenda for the Sea Island Summit, acknowledges civil society a number of times. The declaration on Partnership for Progress and a Common Future with the Region of the Broader Middle East and North Africa welcomes reform declarations from the region's civil society and commits G8 governments to a multi-stakeholder partnership in various programmes including the proposed Forum for the Future (G8 2004h). The G8 Plan of Support for Reform in the area calls for multi-stakeholder approaches including, among other suggestions, civil society–to–civil society dialogue and civil society participation in the Forum for the Future and the also-proposed Democracy Assistance Dialogue (G8 2004a).

Civil Society Evaluation of the Sea Island Summit The trade union movement voiced strong criticism after the Sea Island Summit. The International Confederation of Free Trade Unions (ICFTU) stated that 'for the first time in 27 years the host broke with tradition and refused to meet with leaders of the international labour movement'. ICFTU characterised Sea Island as 'few modest steps but a wasted opportunity in key areas. Little was achieved as regards the much needed task of re-building multilateralism to serve the needs of the people, especially the world's poorest and most marginalized.' (ICFTU 2004).

Oxfam, at the end of the summit, acknowledged some positive points, especially the joint G8 statement on the Sudan crisis and the Global Peacekeeping Initiative by which the U.S. 'has shown at least the intent to fulfil its part of the Africa Action Plan' (Oxfam International 2004). But, asserted Mark Fried on behalf of Oxfam, 'When all's said and done, a lot more was said than done'. The leaders 'spoke welcome words, but made little progress on fulfilling the lofty promises they made ... at Kananaskis' especially on African debt relief, AIDS, trade reform, and aid.

In the lead-up to Sea Island, DATA produced a policy paper with recommendations to the G8 on Africa, the debt crisis, the HIV/AIDS crisis, the trade crisis, and democracy, accountability, and transparency (DATA 2004b). In his summing up after Sea Island, executive director Jamie Drummond was more upbeat than some other civil society organisations. He welcomed the G8 initiatives on the AIDS vaccine, on ending famine in Ethiopia, on eradicating polio, on fighting corruption, and on African peacekeeping. But he expressed disappointment at the G8 leaders' failure to commit to the complete cancellation of poor countries' debt. Looking forward to the British-hosted 2005 Gleneagles Summit, he called for an overall plan to achieve the UN's MDGs (DATA 2004a).

African civil society organisations had a small but well-informed presence in Georgia. At the conclusion of the Sea Island Summit, African NGOs and trade unions issued a joint statement criticising G8 performance but acknowledging some achievements. The statement notes that preoccupation with domestic issues and international security had displaced the G8's resolve to meet its obligations to Africa and lack of audit on implementation of G8 commitments to Africa weakened G8 accountability. Specifically, the statement comments on debt cancellation (saying that the HIPC Initiative failed to reduce the debt of eligible countries sufficiently and was not deep or fast enough, and that conditionality remained onerous), trade justice (noting that the summit failed to achieve a breakthrough on agricultural subsidies, instead referring the matter to the WTO instead, and continued to advocate trade liberalisation, which marginalises Africa's trade position), HIV/AIDS (welcoming G8 support for a global HIV vaccine enterprise but noting the continued underfunding of the Global Health Fund and the G8's failure to recognise the urgency needed); and financing for development (pointing out that this was likely the first time that the G8 and African leaders acknowledged the contribution of remittances by the African diaspora but asserting that these private contributions should not be viewed as an alternative to sufficient ODA) (African Network on Debt and Development *et al.* 2004).

Whither the G7/8-Civil Society Nexus?

Since September 11, re-examination of the future of the G7/8–civil society nexus has become particularly important. Former Canadian foreign minister Bill Graham states that 'at all levels of governance, the support of civil society is vital for ensuring the integrity and soundness of policy making' (see Chapter 20). He adds that 'international institutions must move beyond secret meetings of experts if they are to be recognised as legitimate and effective'.

In Chapter 16, John Kirton presents several proposals to improve G8 governments' interaction with civil society. As a counterpart set of ideas, the following points indicate ways in which civil society, on its part, can enhance its relations with the G7/8 in order to promote social, economic, and other global goals.

1. *Networking.* NGOs and civil society organisations have been most successful when working in co-ordination or coalition with like-minded groups. The greater impact of networks and coalitions is not merely the function of larger numbers; the whole tends to be more than a sum of its parts.

2. *Awareness of the interconnected nature of issues.* Here, too, civil society has been most effective when it recognised and exploited such links, as in the case of the interconnectedness of education, health, and debt relief, discussed earlier in the section on the Genoa Summit. Although it is natural and sensible for NGOs and civil society organisations to concentrate their energies on what they know best, it is important to avoid the 'single-issue' trap.

3. *Building on successes and learning from mistakes in using information and communication technology (ICT).* ICT has played a crucial role in transforming and empowering civil society. It has increased the scope and the speed of civil society activity tremendously. For many NGOs, ICT is the tool of choice. They have been able to use technology (the internet, videoconferencing, e-mail, text messaging, fax machines, mobile telephones, satellite hookups, and other advances) strategically in fundraising, research, advocacy, service delivery, and networking and coalition building cheaply, efficiently, and flexibly. At the same time, it is important to keep in mind that ICT can be used against civil society, or misused by mischievous or irresponsible elements within civil society itself.

4. *Knowing the G7/8 system and process as thoroughly as possible.* There still are many myths and misconceptions in civil society circles about the nature of the G7/8 institution and its place in global governance. If NGOs and other civil society organisations are to succeed in ensuring fruitful dialogue with the G7/8, it is incumbent on them to learn the structure and workings of the whole G7/8 system, including ministerial, task force, and sherpa meetings and their timing and agenda, as well as the G8 member governments' summit-supporting institutions.

5. *Starting the dialogue and lobbying early in the summit process.* G7/8 agenda building is at least a year-long process, being formulated and honed gradually from one summit to the next. The main agenda items are generally set by the host of the next summit soon after the previous summit. If civil society hopes to have any influence on the evolving summit agenda, it can do so more realistically if organisations get involved in the process early.

6. *Readiness to be reactive or proactive, according to need.* This implies, to cite just one example, taking advantage of issues that the G8 is seized of that are also of concern to civil society, as well as lobbying to try to get other civil society concerns on the G8 agenda.

7. *Isolating potentially violent or disruptive elements.* Seattle, Quebec City, Genoa, and Evian/Geneva/Lausanne showed again that violence and anarchy can do immense harm to the vast majority of civil society supporters who use peaceful and democratic methods. After September 11, it has become even more crucial for civil society to distance itself from and isolate, the 'uncivil society' of violent anarchists and others of similar bent. Civil society organisations have shown that they can succeed in this, but it is important to remain vigilant and step up self-patrolling and other efforts at future events such as G7/8 summits.

8. *Weighing carefully the costs and benefits of self-inclusion or self-exclusion.* Certain NGOs and other organisations may choose on the grounds of principle or ideology not to participate in dialogue or other constructive interaction. In view of their limited human and material resources, civil society organisations also need to reflect on whether it is worth expending time and energy on dialogue and other interaction with G8 governments before and at summits and ministerial meetings. However, it is important to recognise that this distancing exacts the price of lack of influence with or impact on the G8.

9. *Focus on other ways to exert influence.* When a host country is unwilling to interact with civil society (as at Sea Island in 2004), NGOs and other civil society organisations need to concentrate on other options to influence the G8: advocacy including the drafting and dissemination of policy papers, dialogue with receptive non-host G8 governments, and staging parallel events – in another country if necessary, following the pattern of the World Social Forum *vis-à-vis* the World Economic Forum.

Conclusion

Several lessons can be drawn from this analysis of UN–civil society and G7/8–civil society interaction. First, civil society is an increasingly important and powerful actor locally, regionally, nationally, and globally. It is an essential part of today's multi-stakeholder policy environment, including civil society relations with the UN and the G7/8 system. At its best, civil society gives voice to the plight and aspirations of those marginalised or left behind by globalisation, and it fights for the universal extension of the benefits of globalisation.

Second, distinguishing various segments of protestors is not merely an academic or journalistic exercise. Serious civil society organisations realise that in order to pursue their goals and protect their members and supporters they must isolate and prevent violent groups from sabotaging democratic rights, peaceful demonstrations, and legitimate programmes. Responsible civil society groups have found ways to police the demonstrations in which they participate, in order to prevent destructive elements from infiltrating and hijacking peaceful protest. Such self-examination is underway and is being increasingly implemented. This has become particularly important after September 11, and civil society organisations have been taking an active part to ensure peaceful protest. In Calgary, there was a team of some 40 civil society monitors out in the streets. This successful monitoring was part of the overall peaceful nature of civil society participation in the events related to the 2002 Kananaskis Summit.

Third, a crucial factor in the growing influence of civil society has been ICT. Civil society has learned fast and has used these relatively inexpensive and powerful tools purposefully and efficiently. As well, civil society has developed and employed impressive expertise in using the mass media to disseminate its message and exert its influence.

Fourth, in UN–civil society relations, recent advances in informal arrangements are perhaps more significant than the old, limited formal consultative relations that have become rather sterile. Where UN member governments were unwilling to accommodate broader and more intensive civil society participation by reforming longstanding formal arrangements, civil society has shown itself capable of flexibility and experimentation in order to enhance its role and influence in UN forums and programmes. Nonetheless, it should be noted that the longstanding ECOSOC consultative relationship has provided a model (for example, for the Organization of American States) as well as lessons to be learned (perhaps for the WTO?).

Fifth, unlike the regular, often formal arrangements with civil society found in the UN system, the OECD, and other structured, traditional IGOs, civil society relations with the G7/8 – a flexible institution largely unhampered by bureaucratic machinery – are characterised by informal practice. There is increasing mutual recognition of the desirability of dialogue and partnership among these actors, along with the inevitable tensions resulting from differing and sometimes conflicting perceptions, objectives, and tactics. Creative new ways of meeting this challenge must be found.

Civil society's dialogue with the G8, well established at Birmingham and evolved through Cologne, Okinawa, Genoa, Kananaskis, and Evian, suffered a serious setback at Sea Island but resumed at Gleneagles in 2005. Well before assuming the G8 chair on 1 January 2005, the British government gave early indications of its intention to conduct dialogue with civil society. It has been demonstrated that the G7/8 can work with responsible, constructive civil society groups in partnership rather than confronting those groups as adversaries (although peaceful confrontation is sometimes necessary). The challenge is to muster the political will and then to find ways to develop such partnerships in a meaningful and mutually beneficial manner.

Sixth, in the wake of the turbulent Genoa G8 Summit, many questions were raised about the future of the G8 and the way its business is conducted, as well as about civil society and other protester groups and their methods of operation. For many years, the G7/8 leaders have voiced their wish to stage smaller, more intimate and more focussed meetings, with fewer officials in attendance and perhaps fewer media personnel around. This process, begun at the 1998 Birmingham Summit when leaders first met without their foreign and finance ministers, led to the 2002 Summit in remote Kananaskis, where leaders came closer than ever to their preferred format. The relatively remote small French town of Evian-les-Bains, on the south shore of Lake Geneva, and the isolated Sea Island venue of the 2004 U.S.-hosted summit continued this trend; so did the 2005 Summit in Gleneagles, Scotland.

Finally, the results of civil society activity – whether positive as exemplified by bringing about the Landmine Ban Treaty or negative as in defeating the Multilateral Agreement on Investment (MAI) – cannot be achieved by NGOs and civil society groups alone or even by any combination of these actors.[18] The injustices of indebtedness of the poorest countries, environmental degradation, lack of access to affordable essential medicines to fight against devastating diseases, educational deficits – are some of the major concerns of civil society. It is civil society that plays a crucial role in campaigning for solutions, mobilising people for support of these causes, and lobbying the most powerful governments and international institutions. But, in the end, it is governments that had to sign and ratify the landmine treaty or the treaty establishing the International Criminal Court; and it is the pharmaceutical companies that must lower the price of antiretrovirals and other essential medicines in the poorest countries. Governments and IGOs may not have the political will or may be paralysed by inertia; business corporations are often motivated solely by profit rather than profit accompanied by social responsibility. Governments and corporations often cannot or will not move without civil society holding their feet to the fire. Michael Edwards (2002) observes that 'although non-governmental actors cannot replace the functions of elected governments, they do provide ideas, information, pressure for results, and the leverage required to implement solutions on the ground – all of which are necessary to solve global problems ... Acting alone, governments cannot confer legitimacy on global decisions ... [and] further engagement with ... non-state actors is inevitable'. And Kamal Malhotra asserts that 'civil society's main role is in holding both the state and the market accountable, to be ... a societal watchdog [*vis-à-vis* both the state and the market]' but cautions that civil society cannot be a substitute for the state (Canadian Broadcasting Corporation 2001, 23 June).

But here a cautionary note is in order: the legitimacy and representativeness of both the state and non-state actors can be challenged. Public goods can be produced by partnership, by patient advocacy, or, sometimes, by confrontation. Whether by willing co-operation or by intentional or unintended complementarity, civil society, government, and business need one another to achieve social, economic, and political goals. Synergy can and does occur, whether there are formal structures of interaction, well-functioning practical arrangements, or convergences of views and programmes among state and non-state actors. In this context, the 'new diplomacy' that has seen NGOs and civil society coalitions working with governments and IGOs is a significant development. Non-state actors – NGOs, business groups, nongovernmental funding agencies, and others – familiar with the situation on the ground, can tap into grassroots movements and can achieve better results than governmental entities could, working alone. At its best, civil society works in partnership with IGOs and governments for the benefit of the greatest number of people; at its worst, it acts to undermine IGOs and governments; and there are many shades of interaction along this continuum.

But governments, IGOs and the business sector cannot take it for granted that civil society will act on their terms. On 7 December 2001, in conjunction with the 100th anniversary of the Nobel Prize, 100 laureates warned in their statement that 'the most profound danger to world peace in the coming years will stem not from the irrational acts of states or individuals but from the legitimate demands of the world's dispossessed ... It cannot be expected ... that in all cases they will be content to await the beneficence of the rich' ('Our Best Point the Way' 2001). The international community must find ways to address such legitimate demands and to remedy inequalities. Responsible civil society organisations will continue to give voice to the plight and aspirations of the marginalised, and will continue to push for those goals.

The UN and other IGOs, G8 governments and civil society share the responsibility to ensure that their interaction is meaningful and productive. Meeting this difficult challenge will be a true test of the viability of both IGOs and responsible civil society movements.

Notes

1   For a full list of NGOs in consultative status, see UN ECOSOC (2005).
2   For the directory of NGOs associated with the Department of Public Information, see UN Department of Information (2005a).
3   For a discussion of the special role of religious NGOs at the UN, see Benjamin Rivlin (2002).
4   The annex to this report spells out the MDGs and associated targets (see UNGA 2002, 21–35).
5   For a more detailed discussion of the civil society–G7/8 nexus, see Peter Hajnal (2002).
6   For an account of the evolution of G7/8 agenda, see Peter Hajnal and John Kirton (2000).
7   John Kirton has termed the G7/8 'a centre of global governance'. Some disagree with this characterisation (see, for example, Baker 2000).
8   An account of the first two TOES can be found in Paul Ekins (1986). Two more recent works are by Jerry Mander and Edward Goldsmith (1996) and Trent Schroyer (1997).
9   The term 'sherpa' originates from the name of the mountain guides in the Himalayas and denotes the senior official who is the personal representative of the leader of each summit country and the European Union sherpas meet several times a year as part of their function to prepare for each summit, and sometimes to follow up on the past summit. National sherpa teams generally include, in addition to the sherpa, two sous-sherpas (one for finance, the other for foreign affairs) and a political director from each foreign ministry.
10 For a more detailed account, see Hajnal (2001).
11 Susan George is vice-president of ATTAC France ('ATTAC' stands for Association pour une Taxation des Transactions financières pour l'Aide aux Citoyens, known in English as the Association for a Taxation of Financial Transactions and for Assistance to Citizens)

and associate of the Transnational Institute (an Amsterdam-based group of scholar-activists).

12 For a different analysis of the Summit of the Americas, see Harriet Friedmann (2001).

13 Njoki Njoroge Njehu (2002), the director of 50 Years Is Enough, reiterated these concerns during the Kananaskis Summit.

14 Remarks by L. Muthoni Wanyeki, Executive Director of the African Women's Development and Communications Network (FEMNET) at the Global Governance 2002 conference, Montreal, 15 October 2002.

15 The enlarged dialogue included, in addition to the G8 heads and the EU leaders, the following: the presidents of Egypt (Hosni Mubarak), Algeria (Abdelaziz Bouteflika), Nigeria (Olusegun Obasanjo), South Africa (Thabo Mbeki), Senegal (Abdoulaye Wade), Mexico (Vicente Fox), Switzerland (Pascal Couchepin), Brazil (Luiz Inacio Lula da Silva), and China (Hu Jintao); the king of Morocco and the crown prince of Saudi Arabia (Abdallah bin Abdulaziz al Saoud); the prime ministers of Malaysia and India; and the presidents of the Group of 77 (Mohammed VI) and the Non-Aligned Movement (Mahathir bin Mohamad). The following administrative heads of international organisations also participated: UN secretary general Kofi Annan, president of the World Bank James Wolfensohn, managing director of the IMF Horst Koehler, and WTO director general Supachai Panitchpakdi. The G8-NEPAD dialogue included the G8 heads plus the presidents of Egypt, Algeria, Nigeria, South Africa, and Senegal.

16 E-mail interview with an FOE activist, August 2003.

17 E-mail interview with an FOE activist, August 2003.

18 Although the civil society community often cites its victory in bringing about the defeat of MAI, there were multiple factors at play. But the defeat illustrates the possible consequences of political processes where civil society is excluded from participation. For background information, see William Dymond (1999, 30–31) and Peter Jay Smith and Elizabeth Smythe (2000).

References

Adams, Barbara (2002). 'The United Nations and Civil Society'. In P.I. Hajnal, ed., *Civil Society in the Information Age*, pp. 141–154. Ashgate, Aldershot.

African Network on Debt and Development, African Women Development and Communication Network, Mwelekeo wa NGO, et al. (2004). 'The 2004 Summit of G8: Trick or Retreat?' Joint Statement from African NGOs and Trade Unions at the Conclusion of the 2004 Summit, 11 June. Sea Island. <www.oxfam.org.uk/what_we_do/issues/panafrica/downloads/post_g8_advisory_final.rtf>

Alger, Chadwick F. (1999). 'The United Nations System and Civil Society'. Paper presented at the International Studies Association Convention. Washington DC.

Amnesty International (2002a). 'Amnesty International Dismayed at Canadian Authorities' Refusal to Grant Accreditation to G8 Observer'. Press Release No. 107, 25 June. <web.amnesty.org/library/index/ENGAMR200042002> (November 2005).

Amnesty International (2002b). 'Show the G8 the Red Card: G8's Uncontrolled Trade in Arms and Military Aid Undermines Fundamental Human Rights'. <web.amnesty.org/g8/africa.html> (November 2005).

Amnesty International (2003a). 'G8: No Trade Off for Human Rights'. Press Release No. 132, 2 June. <web.amnesty.org/library/Index/ENGPOL300022003> (November 2005).

Amnesty International (2003b). 'A Catalogue of Failures: G8 Arms Exports and Human Rights Violations'. IOR30/003/2003, 19 May. <web.amnesty.org/library/Index/ENGIOR 300032003?open&of=ENG 366> (November 2005).

Appel du Forum des Peuples (2003). 'Consensus des peuples face au consensus du G8'. <www.attac.info/g8evian/index.php?NAVI=1016-114297-14fr> (November 2005).

Baker, Andrew (2000). 'The G7 as a Global "Ginger Group": Plurilateralism and Four Dimensional Diplomacy'. *Global Governance* vol. 6 (April-June), pp. 165–190.

Baxter, Joan (2003). 'Poor People's Summit Held in Mali'. *BBC News*, 1 June.

Bayne, Nicholas (2001). 'Impressions of the Genoa Summit, 20–22 July 2001'. <www.g8.utoronto.ca/evaluations/2001genoa/assess_summit_bayne.html> (November 2005).

Bayne, Nicholas (2003). 'Impressions of the Kananaskis Summit'. In M. Fratianni, P. Savona and J.J. Kirton, eds., *Sustaining Global Growth and Development: G7 and IMF Governance*, pp. 229–240. Ashgate, Aldershot.

Bayne, Nicholas (2004). 'Impressions of the 2004 Sea Island Summit'. 29 June. <www.g8.utoronto.ca/evaluations/2004seaisland/bayne2004.html> (November 2005).

Beattie, Alan (2001b). 'Protests Aim to Breach G8 Cordon'. *Financial Times*, 5 July.

Canadian Broadcasting Corporation (2001). 'Civil Society'. Ideas (Radio). 18, 25 June.

Centre de recherche et d'information pour le developpement (2003). 'Intervention de Gustave Massiah, président du CRID, à l'occasion de la rencontre organisée par le président de la République'. 30 April. <www.crid.asso.fr/g8/ong_gus.htm> (November 2005).

Collenette, Penny (2002). 'It's the Governance, Stupid'. *Globe and Mail*, 15 October, p. A19.

Colonna, Katherine (2003). 'Briefing with Katherine Colonna, Spokesperson for France'. 1 June. Evian. <www.g8.utoronto.ca/summit/2003evian/briefing_fr030601e.html> (November 2005).

Commission on Global Governance (1995). *Our Global Neighbourhood: The Report of the Commission on Global Governance*. Oxford University Press, Oxford.

Commission on Global Governance (1999). *The Millennium Year and the Reform Process: A Contribution from the Commission on Global Governance*. Oxford University Press, Oxford.

Cooper, Andrew Fenton (2004). *Tests of Global Governance: Canadian Diplomacy and United Nations World Conferences*. United Nations University Press, Tokyo.

Crutsinger, Martin (2003). 'G8 Heads to Tackle Various Global Issues'. *Associated Press*, 31 May.

Debt AIDS Trade Africa (2004a). 'Disappointment, But Door Left Open to Progress on Debt Relief'. 10 June. <www.data.org/archives/000527.php>

Debt AIDS Trade Africa (2004b). 'G8 and African Leadership in the War on AIDS and Extreme Poverty'. <www.data.org/archives/G82004report.pdf> (November 2005).

Dent, Martin and Bill Peters (1999). *The Crisis of Poverty and Debt in the Third World*. Ashgate, Aldershot.

Drop the Debt (2001a). 'Bono, Bob Geldof and Lorenzo Jovanotti Meet G8 Leaders in Genoa'. 27 July.

Drop the Debt (2001b). 'Verdict on Genoa Summit'. 22 July. Genoa.

Dymond, William A. (1999). 'The MAI: A Sad and Meloncholy Tale'. In F.O. Hampson, M. Hart and M. Rudner, eds., *A Big League Player? Canada Among Nations 1999*, pp. 22–54. Oxford University Press, Toronto.

Edwards, Michael (2002). 'The Mouse That Roared'. *Globe and Mail*, 3 January, p. A17.

Ekins, Paul, ed. (1986). *The Living Economy: A New Economics in the Making*. Routledge and Kegan Paul, London.

'For Slimmer and Sporadic Summits'. (2001). *Financial Times*, 23 July, p. 10.

Forum international de Montréal (2002). 'Civil Society and the G8'. <www.fimcivilsociety. org/FIM2.htm> (April 2003).

Foster, John W. and Anita Anand, eds. (1999). *Whose World Is It Anyway? Civil Society, the United Nations, and the Multilateral Future*. United Nations Association in Canada, Ottawa.

Friedmann, Harriet (2001). 'Forum: Considering the Quebec Summit, the World Social Forum at Porto Alegre, and the People's Summit at Quebec City: A View from the Ground'. *Studies in Political Economy: A Socialist Review* vol. 66, pp. 85–105.

G7 (1995). 'Halifax Summit Communiqué'. 16 June. Halifax. <www.g8.utoronto.ca/summit/ 1995halifax/communique> (November 2005).

G7 (1996). 'Economic Communiqué: Making a Success of Globalization for the Benefit of All'. 28 June, Lyon. <www.g8.utoronto.ca/summit/1996lyon/communique/> (November 2005).

G7 (2001). 'G7 Statement'. 20 July. Genoa. <www.g8.utoronto.ca/g7/summit/2001genoa/ g7statement.html> (November 2005).

G7 (2002). 'Statement by G7 Leaders: Delivering on the Promise of the Enhanced HIPC Initiative'. 27 June. Kananaskis. <www.g8.utoronto.ca/summit/2002kananaskis/ hipc.html> (November 2005).

G7 Environment Ministers (1996). 'Chairman's Summary'. Cabourg, France, 10 May. <www.g8.utoronto.ca/environment/1996cabourg/summary_index.html> (November 2005).

G7 Finance Ministers (2001). 'Debt Relief and Beyond'. Report transmitted by G7 Finance Ministers to Heads of State and Government, 21 July. Genoa. <www.g8.utoronto.ca/ summit/2001genoa/debtrelief.htm> (November 2005).

G8 (1997). 'Communiqué'. 22 June. Denver. <www.g8.utoronto.ca/summit/1997denver/ g8final.htm> (November 2005).

G8 (1998). 'Communiqué'. 15 May. Birmingham. <www.g8.utoronto.ca/summit/ 1998birmingham/finalcom.htm> (November 2005).

G8 (2001a). 'Genoa, City of Dialogue'. <www.genoa-g8.it/eng/attualita/primo_piano/primo_ piano_2.html> (October 2002).

G8 (2001b). 'Statement by the G8 Leaders (Death in Genoa)'. 21 July. Genoa. <www.g8.utoronto.ca/summit/2001genoa/g8statement1.html> (November 2005).

G8 (2001c). 'Communiqué'. 22 July. Genoa. <www.g8.utoronto.ca/summit/2001genoa> (November 2005).

G8 (2002a). 'A New Focus on Education for All'. 26 June. Kananaskis. <www.g8.utoronto. ca/summit/2002kananaskis/education.html> (November 2005).

G8 (2002b). 'The Kananaskis Summit Chair's Summary'. 27 June. Kananaskis. <www.g8.utoronto.ca/summit/2002kananaskis/summary.html> (November 2005).

G8 (2002c). 'G8's Africa Action Plan'. 27 June. Kananaskis. <www.g8.utoronto.ca/summit/ 2002kananaskis/africaplan.html> (November 2005).

G8 (2003). 'Evian Summit'. Official website. <www.g8.fr> (April 2003).

G8 (2004a). 'G8 Plan of Support for Reform'. 9 June. Sea Island. <www.g8.utoronto.ca/ summit/2004seaisland/reform.html> (November 2005).

G8 (2004b). 'Compact to Promote Transparency and Combat Corruption: A New Partnership between the G8 and Peru'. 10 June. Sea Island. <www.g8.utoronto.ca/summit/ 2004seaisland/peru.html> (November 2005).

G8 (2004c). 'Compact to Promote Transparency and Combat Corruption: A New Partnership between the G8 and Nigeria'. 10 June. Sea Island. <www.g8.utoronto.ca/summit/ 2004seaisland/nigeria.html> (November 2005).

G8 (2004d). 'Compact to Promote Transparency and Combat Corruption: A New Partnership between the G8 and Nicaragua'. 10 June. Sea Island. <www.g8.utoronto.ca/summit/2004seaisland/nicaragua.html> (November 2005).

G8 (2004e). 'G8 Action Plan: Applying the Power of Entrepreneurship to the Eradication of Poverty'. 9 June. Sea Island. <www.g8.utoronto.ca/summit/2004seaisland/poverty.html> (November 2005).

G8 (2004f). 'Science and Technology for Sustainable Development: "3R" Action Plan and Progress on Implementation'. 10 June. Sea Island. <www.g8.utoronto.ca/summit/2004seaisland/sd.html> (November 2005).

G8 (2004g). 'Chair's Summary'. 10 June. Sea Island. <www.g8.utoronto.ca/summit/2004seaisland/summary.html> (November 2005).

G8 (2004h). 'Partnership for Progress and a Common Future with the Region of the Broader Middle East and North Africa'. 9 June. Sea Island. <www.g8.utoronto.ca/summit/2004seaisland/partnership.html> (November 2005).

G8 (2004i). 'Ending the Cycle of Famine in the Horn of Africa, Raising Agricultural Productivity, and Promoting Rural Development in Food Insecure Countries'. 10 June. Sea Island. (November 2005).

G8 Development Ministers (2002). 'Chair's Summary'. 27 September. Windsor ON. <www.g8.utoronto.ca/development/09-2002-chair.html> (November 2005).

George, Susan (2001). 'L'ordre libéral et ses basses oeuvres'. *Le Monde diplomatique* vol. 48, no. 569, p. 6.

Graham, Robert (2003). '"Enlarged Dialogue" May Fall on Deaf Ears'. *Financial Times*, 29 May.

Greenhill, Romilly, Ann Pettifor, Henry Northover, *et al.* (2003). 'Did the G8 Drop the Debt? Five Years after the Birmingham Human Chain, What Has Been Achieved and What More Needs to Be Done?' May. Jubilee Research, Jubilee Debt Campaign, and CAFOD, London. <www.jubilee2000uk.org/analysis/reports/G8final.pdf> (November 2005).

'Greens Glum as World Environment Day Heads for 30th Anniversary'. (2003). *Agence France-Presse*, 4 June.

Hajnal, Peter I. and John J. Kirton (2000). 'The Evolving Role and Agenda of the G7/G8: A North American Perspective'. *NIRA Review* vol. 7, no. 2 (Spring), pp. 5–10.

Hajnal, Peter I. (2001). 'Civil Society at the 2001 Genoa G8 Summit'. *Behind the Headlines* vol. 58, no. 1.

Hajnal, Peter I., ed. (2002). *Civil Society in the Information Age*. Ashgate, Aldershot.

Humphrey, John (1984). *Human Rights and the United Nations: A Great Adventure*. Transnational Publishers, Dobbs Ferry NY.

International Confederation of Free Trade Unions (2004). 'Outcome of the Sea Island G8 Summit, 8–10 2004: Evaluation of the TUAC Secretariat'. <www.icftu.org/displaydocument.asp?Index=991220130> (November 2005).

Jubilee 2000 Coalition (1999a). 'Crumbs of Comfort: The Cologne G8 Summit and the Chains of Debt'. <www.jubilee2000uk.org/jubilee2000/news/cologne_exec.html> (November 2005).

Jubilee 2000 Coalition (1999b). 'IMF/World Bank Spring Meetings 1999'. <www.jubliee2000uk.org/jubilee2000/news/meetings1905.html> (November 2005).

Jubilee Movement International for Economic and Social Justice (2001). 'Statement on G7 Final Communiqué'. 21 July. Genoa. <www.jubileeplus.org/media/210701JMI.htm> (November 2005).

Jubilee Research (2002). 'G8 Leaders Commit a Further $1bn in Debt Relief for the HIPC Countries'. 2 July. London. <www.jubilee2000uk.org/worldnews/northamerica/debtrelief020702.htm> (November 2005).

Jubilee USA Network and Adrian Lovett (2001). 'Genoa a Bust, But Debt Campaign Still Growing'. <groups.yahoo.com/group/jubilee-usa-net/message/84> (November 2005).

Keaten, Jamey (2003). 'G8 Protesters Clash among Themselves'. *Associated Press*, 31 May.

Kirton, John J. (2000). 'Broadening Participation in Twenty-First Century Governance: The Prospective and Potential Contribution of the Okinawa Summit'. Paper presented at 'The Kyushu-Okinawa Summit: The Challenges and Opportunities for the Developing World in the 21st Century', Tokyo, United Nations University, 17 July. <www.g8.utoronto.ca/scholar/kirton20000717/> (November 2005).

Kirton, John J. (2004). 'What the G8's Sea Island Summit Means for the World Ahead'. Paper prepared for a seminar at the Canadian embassy, 27 July. Tokyo. <www.g8.utoronto.ca/scholar/kirton2004/kirton_040727.html> (November 2005).

Lichfield, John (2003). 'G8 Summit: Third World Attacks Failure of Evian to Tackle Its Problems'. *The Independent*, 4 June.

Lortie, Marc; and Sylvie Bédard (2001). 'Citizen Involvement in Canadian Foreign Policy: The Summit of the Americas Experience, Québec City, April 2001'. In P.I. Hajnal, ed., *Civil Society in the Information Age*, pp. 201–213. Ashgate, Aldershot.

Lugo, Chris (2004). 'From the G8 to Africa to You: The Other Economic Summit'. Tennessee Independent Media Center, 10 June. <www.tnimc.org/newswire/display/2189/index.php> (November 2005).

Mander, Jerry and Edward Goldsmith, eds. (1996). *The Case Against the Global Economy and for a Turn Toward the Local*. Sierra Club Books, San Francisco.

Médecins Sans Frontières (2001a). 'Violence Grants No Perspectives, Médecins Sans Frontières Schoed about War-Like Situation in Genoa'. 20 July, Genoa.

Médecins Sans Frontières (2001b). 'G8 Window Dresses While Poor Die from Lack of Medicines'. 21 July. Genoa. <www.accessmed-msf.org/prod/publications.asp?scntid=882001218145&contenttype=PARA&> (November 2005).

Médecins Sans Frontières (2002). 'G8 One Hundred Percent Talk, Five Percent Finance'. 25 June. Calgary. <www.accessmed-msf.org/prod/publications.asp?scntid=26620021717462&contenttype=PARA&> (November 2005).

Ministero degli Affari Esteri (Italy) (2001). 'Beyond Debt Release'. Published by the italian presidency. <www.g8.utoronto.ca/summit/2001genoa/pres_docs/pres1.html> (November 2005).

Neslen, Arthur (2001). 'Mean Streets: On Location, Genoa Summit'. *Now*, 26 July–1 August, p. 20.

Njehu, Njoki Njoroge (2002). 'Response to the Africa Action Plan'. Interview with G8 Online. <www.g8.utoronto.ca/g8online/2002/english/features/address4.html> (November 2005).

'Our Best Point the Way'. (2001). *Globe and Mail*, 7 December, p. A21.

Oxfam GB (2002). 'G8 Disappoints Again…'. Press release, 28 October. London.

Oxfam International (2001a). 'Violence Doesn't Help'. Press Release, 20 July. <www.oxfaminternational.com/pr010720_G8_violence_doesnt_help.htm> (April 2005).

Oxfam International (2001b). 'Genoa Fails: Big Promise for Next Year'. Press Release, 22 July.

Oxfam International (2004). 'Oxfam on G8 2004: More Said Than Done, and Not Enough Said'. Press release, 10 June. <www.oxfam.org/eng/pr040610_G8_final.htm> (November 2005).

Pace, William R. and Rik Panganiban (2002). 'The Power of Global Activist Networks: The Campaign for an International Criminal Court'. In P.I. Hajnal, ed., *Civil Society in the Information Age*, pp. 109–125. Ashgate, Aldershot.

People's Summit (1995). 'Communiqué from the People's Summit'. Halifax, 16 June. <www.igc.org/habitat/p-7/p7-comm.html> (November 2005).

'Picking up the Pieces: After the Genoa Summit' (2001). *Economist*, 28 July, p. 49–50.

Rivlin, Benjamin (2002). 'Thoughts on Religious NGOs at the UN: A Component of Global Civil Society'. In P.I. Hajnal, ed., *Civil Society in the Information Age*, pp. 155–173. Ashgate, Aldershot.

Rutherford, Kenneth R. (2002). 'Essential Partners: Landmines-Related NGOs and Information Technologies'. In P.I. Hajnal, ed., *Civil Society in the Information Age*, pp. 95–107. Ashgate, Aldershot.

Sanger, David E. (2001). 'Two Leaders Tell of Plot to Kill Bush in Genoa'. *New York Times*, 26 September, p. B1.

Sauzey, François, ed. (1978). *The London Summit Revisited*. Trilateral Commission, Washington DC.

Schroyer, Trent and Susan Hunt (2004). 'TOES 2004 Experience in Georgia'. <www.toes-usa.org/TOESBrunswick.html> (November 2005).

Schroyer, Trent, ed. (1997). *A World That Works: Building Blocks for a Just and Sustainable Society*. Bootstrap Press, New York.

Smith, Janel and Montana Burnett (2004). 'Report on Civil Society Presence at the 2004 G8 Summit'. 10 June. <www.g8.utoronto.ca/g8online/2004/english/featured-content5.html> (November 2005).

Smith, Peter Jay and Elizabeth Smythe (2000). 'Globalization, Citizenship, and Technology: The MAI Meets the Internet'. Paper prepared for the annual International Studies Association convention, 17 March. Los Angeles.

Sommet pour un autre monde (2003a). 'Summit for Another World'. Press release, no date. <www.fidh.org/ecosoc/dossiers/evian2003/spam/press11a.pdf> (November 2005).

Sommet pour un autre monde (2003b). 'Un G8 pour rien!' Press release, 3 June. <www.france.attac.org/a2033> (November 2005).

Standing Committee on Foreign Affairs and International Trade (Canada) (2002). 'Securing Progress for Africa and the World: A Report on Canadian Priorities for the 2002 G8 Summit'. <www.parl.gc.ca/InfoComDoc/37/1/FAIT/Studies/Reports/faitrp21-e.htm> (November 2005).

Tagliabue, John (2003). 'Chirac to Call for a shift from Battling Terrorism to Helping Poorer Nations'. *New York Times*, 1 June, p. YT13.

The Other Economic Summit (1997). 'Brief Introduction to TOES'. <pender.ee.upenn.edu/~rabii/toes/ToesIntro.html> (April 2005).

United Nations (2002). 'Report of the World Summit on Sustainable Development'. A/CONF.199/20. 26 August–4 September. Johannesburg. <www.johannesburgsummit.org/html/documents/documents.html> (November 2005).

United Nations Department of Public Information (1999). 'Secretary General Says "Global People-Power" Best Thing for United Nations in Long Time, Needing Response in Partnership with Civil Society'. Press Release SG/SM/7249/Rev.1, New York, 7 December. <www.un.org/News/Press/docs/1999/19991207.sgsm7249.r1.doc.html> (November 2005).

United Nations Department of Public Information (2000). 'Secretary-General, Addressing Participants at Millennium Forum, Calls for Intensified "NGO Revolution"'. Press Release SG/SM/7411 GA/9710, 22 May. <www.un.org/News/Press/docs/2000/20000522.sgsm7411.doc.html> (November 2005).

United Nations Department of Public Information (2005a). 'Directory of NGOs Associated with DPI'. <www.un.org/dpi/ngosection/ngodir.htm> (November 2005).

United Nations Department of Public Information (2005b). 'NGOs and the United Nations Department of Public Information: Some Questions and Answers'. <www.un.org/dpi/ngosection/brochure.htm> (November 2005).

United Nations Economic and Social Council (1996). 'Consultative Relationship between the United Nations and Non-Governmental Organizations'. Resolution 1996/31. 25 July. <www.un.org/documents/ecosoc/res/1996/eres1996-31.htm> (November 2005).

United Nations Economic and Social Council (2005). 'NGOs in Consultative Status with ECOSOC'. <www.un.org/esa/coordination/ngo/pdf/INF_List.pdf> (November 2005).

United Nations General Assembly (1998). 'Arrangements and Practices for the Interaction of Non-Governmental Organization in All Activities of the United Nations System'. A/53/170, 10 July. <www.un.org/documents/ga/docs/53/plenary/a53-170.htm> (November 2005).

United Nations General Assembly (2000). 'Millennium Forum held at United Nations Headquarters from 22 to 26 May 2000'. A/54/959, 8 August. <www.un.org/millennium/declaration.htm> (November 2005).

United Nations General Assembly (2002). 'Implementation of the United Nations Millennium Declaration: Report of the Secretary-General'. A/57/270, 31 July. <www.un.org/millenniumgoals/sgreport2002.pdf> (2005 November).

United Nations General Assembly (2004). 'Strengthening of the United Nations System: Note by the Secretary-General'. A/58/817, 11 June. <daccess-ods.un.org/TMP/3384112.html> (November 2005).

Weiss, Thomas George and Leon Gordenker, eds. (1996). *NGOs, the UN, and Global Governance*. Lynne Rienner, Boulder, CO.

World Development Movement (2001). 'WDM Report Back on the G8 Summit in Genoa, July 2001'. <www.wdm.org.uk/campaigns/Genoa.htm> (November 2005).

World Wildlife Fund, Greenpeace, and ECA Watch (2001). 'G8 Plan for Africa Pointless without Renewable Energy Support'. 22 July. Genoa. <archive.greenpeace.org/pressreleases/climate/2001jul222.html> (November 2005).

Zupi, Marco (2001). 'The Genoa G8 Summit: Great Expectations, Disappointing Results'. *International Spectator* vol. 36, no. 3, pp. 59.

Chapter 16

Building Democratic Partnerships: The G8–Civil Society Link

John J. Kirton

The G8 major market democracies of the United States, Japan, Germany, France, Britain, Italy, Canada, and Russia, along with the leaders of the European Union, came to Kananaskis, Alberta, for their annual summit on 26–27 June 2002. The question of who else would come was on everyone's mind in the lead-up to the event (Kirton 2001). At the previous summit in Genoa, Italy, on 20–22 July 2001, the leaders of the G8 countries and the EU had been joined by some 2000 supporting officials, 3000 journalists, the leaders and officials of several African countries and international organisations, a security force of several thousand, and 250 000 civil society protestors from around the world. Less visible were the many hundreds of civil society representatives who had worked with the host government to shape the agenda leading up to the summit, the anarchists who had sent bombs to Italian authorities in the days before it began, and the members of the al Qaeda terrorist network who had planned to murder the summit leaders and their entourage at the summit itself.

Genoa, which featured the death of an anarchist while attacking security forces, marked the culmination of a trend toward ever larger, ever more violent civil society protests at major international meetings. The trend started at the World Trade Organization (WTO) ministerial meeting in Seattle in November 1999, continued at the International Monetary Fund (IMF) meetings in Washington and Prague in 2000, and came to Canada in the summer of 2001 for the Quebec City Summit of the Americas. While Quebec City, with 25 000 civil society activists, was a quintessentially Canadian, comparatively peaceful protest, the Swedes were shocked soon after when major violence broke out at the European Council summit they hosted in Gothenburg, three weeks before the Genoa event.

As the G8 leaders witnessed the violence at Genoa, they concluded that their next summit would have to be a very different kind of affair. Thus Canadian prime minister Jean Chrétien, as host of the next summit, chose a venue in an isolated mountaintop resort in remote, rural Kananaskis. This made it possible to have small, secure, secretive summit in the style of an executive retreat, with tiny delegations of no more than 30 people per country, less visible on-site security, and a media corps kept in the medium-sized city of Calgary 100 kilometres away. Separated in such fashion from the journalists, protestors, and civil society representatives, the G8 leaders could hold their summit in splendid isolation, even more than they had when summitry first started in 1975.

Less than two months after Genoa, the massive terrorist attack on the North American homeland on 11 September 2001 put security concerns, rather than civil society dialogue, in first place at the forthcoming G8 summit. The leaders' determination was reinforced by the successful ministerial meeting of the WTO, held with minimal protest in November 2001 in remote, heavily policed, undemocratic Doha. Canada began its formal year as G8 host in January 2002 by slashing the summit's duration from the usual three days to two and squeezing its scheduled dialogue with African leaders and international organisations, its G7 economic summit, and its regular G8 summit into 48 hours in all.

At the end of the Kananaskis Summit, many thought this retreat-to-the-mountaintop model of G8 summitry had worked very well. Kananaskis was in many ways one of the most successful summits ever. Only approximately 3000 protestors assembled in Calgary and Kananaskis, and a further 4000 assembled in Canada's capital city of Ottawa. There were virtually no injuries nor was there any property damage anywhere. No one died or was injured, save for an intruding bear that fell out of a tree. Only three people were arrested in Alberta – two visiting Americans and one union official. In Ottawa, perhaps symbolically, an effort to burn the U.S. flag failed to catch fire amidst heavy rains. The 3500 journalists in Calgary, only 100 of whom were allowed to go near the leaders at Kananaskis, had little other than the substance of the summit to focus upon. While some wondered whether the estimated CA$500 million spent on the summit was a worthwhile investment, Calgarians largely welcomed the estimated CA$243 million that was directly injected into the local economy, and the much larger sums in lifetime spin-offs, that came as a result. The French, as hosts of the 2003 summit, rushed to replicate it, choosing as their site Evian-les-Bains in the isolated French Alps, where the nearest medium-sized city, Geneva, was located in another country, many kilometres away. While Evian, as a European summit, attracted far more numerous and noisy civil society activists than Kananaskis, when the summit returned to North America for the U.S.-hosted summit in Sea Island, Georgia, on 8–10 June 2004, the Kananaskis minimalist model and results were evident again. Indeed, for the Sea Island Summit, no more than 350 civil society activists showed up.

The deadly combination of the death in Genoa and the September 11 terrorism seems to have driven the G8 leaders permanently to retreat to a small, ultra-secure, secret summit, separated from civil society and the media as well. In doing so, the G8 was in danger of making a major mistake. Since the 2001 assaults on Genoa and on the World Trade Center in New York City and the Pentagon in Washington, the G8 has been in a new crisis of governability, and resulting war of persuasion and legitimacy. The primary target is no longer a few privileged leaders from once competing major powers now meeting in private in a mountain hideaway. It is the many millions of stakeholders watching, listening, or reading through the traditional media or the internet throughout the global community as a whole. After Genoa, the proliferating stories of the death, injury, protests, and police brutality at the G8 made it essential for G8 leaders to mount a much more innovative and effective effort to show that they were indeed trying to make globalisation work for the benefit of all. Two months later, with the World Trade Center destroyed and the Pentagon in flames, the need was to prove to the world that such socially sensitive globalisation was much more than just a singular crusade that predominantly white, wealthy, western, often Christian countries were imposing on Muslims or on a dispossessed developing world (Nye 2002). That need had proliferated by the time of the Sea Island Summit, when the G8 leaders began a bold new initiative to democratise and develop the Middle East and appealed for civil society leaders and citizens from the region to join with the G8 to make the initiative a success.

Private encounters on a mountaintop, cut off from civil society within the G8's own democratic societies and their partners around the world, are poorly designed to win this new, 21st-century global governance war. Better and more innovative ways must be found to connect the G8 global governors with civil society and, through the media, with citizens throughout the G8 and around the world.

This chapter presents an eleven-point programme to meet that challenge. It flows from the seminal and enduring purpose of the G7/8 summit as a unique institution led by democratically elected leaders and created to promote the values of 'open democracy, individual liberty and social advance' throughout the world (G7 1975). These proposals still allow G8 leaders to meet alone to deliberate with full frankness, set new normative directions, and take timely, well-tailored, and ambitious decisions that express their collective political will. To a large extent, the proposals are drawn from mechanisms that similar international institutions, to which G8 members belong, have already successfully employed. They have modest resource requirements. They build on the few tentative steps the G8 itself has taken in recent years (Smith 2001). Together they could transform the 21st-century G8 summit from a shrunken retreat of seemingly scared and insecure politicians into an occasion on which self-confident democratic leaders reach out in partnership with their civil societies to build a better world.

Remember Rambouillet's Rationale

In considering how to produce a G8 summit that can both connect with civil society and accomplish its ambitious agenda, the first step is to remember the reality of Rambouillet, where the summit started in 1975 (Putnam and Bayne 1987; Bayne 2000). Three elements stand out.

First, the summit was conceived and created as a global concert. Its chief architect was U.S. secretary of state Henry Kissinger, who, recognising America's new relative vulnerability, consciously sought to construct the modern equivalent of the 19th-century Concert of Europe (Kissinger 1975). The summit was thus conceived with a comprehensive, interlinked global agenda to provide effective collective global governance across the acute intra-West, East-West, and North-South divides, where America alone had already failed. Its agenda embraced and integrated both economic and political issues and concerns. Moreover, in sharp contrast to the United Nations system, the G8 proclaimed its willingness to intrude into the domestic affairs of its members to defend fundamental democratic values and to deal with pressing national concerns. G8 citizens and outsiders, as policy networks, pressure groups or protestors, thus have every right to ask the summit to take up and solve any problem they and their communities face. Unlike charter-bound and subject-specific international institutions, the G8 system – especially at the summit level – cannot legitimately ignore an issue or pass the buck.

Second, the summit was conceived and created as a democratic concert. Its common purpose was, in the discourse of 1975, to combat the political 'crisis of governability' and economic 'stagflation' – the entrenched combination of stagnant growth and high inflation – that was both cause and effect of the crisis facing the democratic world. In what might be considered the Charter of Rambouillet, the G7 leaders proudly proclaimed: 'We came together because of shared beliefs and shared responsibilities. We are each responsible for the government of an open, democratic society, dedicated to individual liberty and social advancement. Our success will strengthen, indeed is essential to, democratic societies everywhere' (G7 1975, para. 2).G7/8 leaders are thus in the first instance self-defined democrats, not self-interested plutocrats. They can thus say with confidence to citizens that theirs is not a closed club of neo-liberal devotees dedicated to ever more far-reaching financial, trade, investment, and other forms of economic liberalisation. At the same time, their seminal purpose requires them to reach out to the world's citizenry and to practice as well as to preach the principles they proclaim. Indeed, only by doing so can they accomplish their core objectives of the current generation, from combating terrorism to delivering democratically based development in Africa and the broader Middle East. As Canada's foreign minister Bill Graham told the G6B People's Summit in Calgary, 'we live in democratic societies and ultimately we respond to public opinion' (Mahoney 2002).

Third, the G7 was constructed as a public concert for the world, rather than a private club to practice democracy among itself. Beyond informal discussion, summit leaders have to produce, present, and persuade others of the value of new directions – the innovative principles and norms that would guide government policy makers and their democratic publics along different paths toward an improved global order (Kirton 2002b; Kirton 2002a; Baker 2000). They also have to take concrete decisions to put these new principles into effect. The early leaders, while tempted by the intrigue of 19th-century secret diplomacy, knew that they were popularly elected, 20th-century politicians who needed the limelight brought by the attending media to get their message out. They thus discarded the option of meeting in private, announcing only afterward that a meeting had taken place, issuing no communiqué and banishing their media from the first gathering at Rambouillet. This in part was making a public virtue of physical necessity. It was virtually impossible to move the U.S. president, his advisors, and secret service without the attending White House press corps catching wind, demanding on-site briefings, and rushing to print their conclusion in the post–Vietnam war world. But, above all, the leaders knew that if they were to be successful, they had to speak directly to their voters and to those around the world who wanted the chance to vote.

After September 11 it became even more important to use the summit to send a persuasive public message of confidence that democratic governance is possible, to identify the formula to realise this ideal, and to call upon the best of citizens' social capital to give it life. Such actions, from the collective G8 bully pulpit, are what effective democratic governance is all about. Preaching, persuasion, psychology, moral suasion, and the provision of reference points matter as much as coercion and bribery through material punishments and reward (Nye 2002). To be sure, summits may indeed seem like little more than global hot tub parties that produce little beyond a concluding piece of paper, a family photo, and surrounding photo opportunities. But G8 leaders have long known the formidable power of credible commitments encoded on paper and presented through pictures and words.

Don't Assume an Alberta Advantage

The second step is to avoid the temptation to rely on the natural 'Alberta advantage' as the recipe to produce winning summits in the years ahead. For the Kananaskis model of 2002, and the earlier Montebello model first practised in Canada in 1981, and repeated at Kananaskis in 2002, is not easily transposable outside Canada, where the political culture and geography are distinctly different.

Kananaskis proved to be such a civil summit in part because of the small numbers of protestors who arrived on site. Indeed, the few thousand civil society activists who assembled were a much smaller crowd than the 70 000 members of Jubilee 2000 who formed a human chain around the summit site in Birmingham 1998 to shout 'Drop the debt!' and launch the modern phase of civil society involvement at the summit itself (Hajnal 2002a; 2002b). With as many security personnel as protestors, it was easy for the authorities to cope, especially as the latter had the country's best and fully professional police forces carefully deployed and well trained in advance. The deliberately nonthreatening tactics adopted by the estimated 7000 police officers and military personnel mobilised at Kananaskis and Calgary further helped.

Genoa was geographically central and conveniently located for an easy, inexpensive, one-day train trip from virtually anywhere in densely populated Europe. Its location easily attracted well-organised anarchists who sponsored special trains to take the faithful, fellow travellers, and freethinkers to the summit site for a weekend of political action and tourism, replete with colour, drama, danger, and possible historic significance. Calgary, in sharp contrast, was an easy one-day train ride or drive from virtually nowhere, sitting isolated from the major metropolitan centres across a widely dispersed North American continent. Evian-les-Bains, in south-eastern France, joined Genoa in coming from a country with still consequential socialist, communist, and right-wing radical parties, as well as well-established professional anarchists with a violent bent. Canada lacked such components in its political culture, and did not even support the militia or violent fundamentalist movements that had afflicted the United States. The Sea Island Summit, in the coastal state of Georgia, shared most of Kananaskis's advantages in geography and political culture. But it also relied heavily on a massive militarised security presence, minimal government investment in civil society and media outreach, and a media core that had shrunk to only 1400, even in a U.S. presidential election year.

Subsequent summits will increasingly lack the September 11 advantage enjoyed by Kananaskis. Coming nine months after the shock of those events, Kananaskis could credibly proceed with sealed-off leaders and heavy security, to protect the leaders from the al Qaeda network that has long targeted G7/8 summits, and from the very real local terrorists that British, Russian, and other G8 leaders have long faced. Not surprisingly, a late November 2001 public opinion poll showed 77 percent of Canadians thought the summit should go ahead even with the threat of protest, disruption, and violence, 63 percent would blame protestors rather than police for any violence that took place, and 44 percent would be in favour of the police using all necessary force to control demonstrations, even if the result was loss of life ('Since September 11' 2002). Yet the September 11 shock was not as strong in politically violence-prone Europe as it was in North America, or in even more distant Japan.[1] And even with the al Qaeda and Taliban leadership still on the loose, and subsequent shocks, the September 11 effect progressively wore off. Should subsequent summits continue to isolate leaders behind legions of imperial storm trooper look-alikes, citizens will increasingly conclude that the purpose is to protect them not from death at the hands of foreign terrorists but from dissenting views from the voters at home. And with the media similarly cut off from independent, high-quality sources about what is happening at the summit, easy-to-cover, highly visual images of protests, rather than policy substance, could dominate coverage of the event.

There is thus a pressing need for a much more organised, proactive programme, in the lead-up to and at the summit, to give civil society their valuable voice. With the 21st-century summits increasingly focussing on development issues where nongovernmental organisations (NGOs) and businesses have long been centrally involved, and including leaders from the emerging democratic developing world, the need for openness and inclusion is much enhanced.

Inform the Public

The third step is to provide much more information about the G8, on the internet and in other forms (Bayne 1999). Students of soft power and communications strategy can easily recognise the enormous imbalance in information available about the G8, from its participants on the one hand and from the critics on the other, and the cumulative impact this can have in shaping public attitudes and arousing public action about the G8 and its work.

The information imbalance reached critical levels in the months immediately following Genoa when the world's media were filled with words and images about violence and death, the alleged brutality of the Italian police, and the continuing imprisonment under cruel conditions of some of the detained protesters. Hundreds of civil society groups reinforced the message by devoting their websites to the cause.

The Canadian government, as the successor host, did launch its summit-specific website immediately after Genoa, but loaded virtually no new content until it formally assumed the chair at the start of 2002. The G8, with no secretariat and website of its own, was thus left defenceless for more than six months as its reputation was assaulted in the information wars. In the world of film documentary, the opposition again struck first, with a feature film from Italy's leading leftist directors defining for the watching world what Genoa meant.

Because transparency is a basic democratic duty, the G8 collectively, perhaps through two or three successive hosts working in tandem, should devise a co-ordinated strategy to redress the imbalance. They should have a single permanent website with a continuous stream of new information to meet the needs of an interested public (Hajnal 1999). The website should include a comprehensive list of the activities of many dozens of ministerial bodies and official working groups that now make up the vast, invisible system of G7/8 governance – a system that even those inside the G8 process have difficulty tracking. It should also provide regular compliance reports on how and how well existing commitments are being met or why they are not and should not be met as circumstances change. Both insiders and outsiders have a similar need – and a common democratic obligation – to know and understand how the 'soft law' decisions of their democratically elected leaders are being fulfilled. Indeed, the leaders themselves should be the first to want to know if their summit commitments are being implemented as they intended, and, if not, why.

Include Parliamentarians

The fourth step is to put parliamentarians into the summit process. For the past half-century, the major intergovernmental institutional systems, from the UN to the North Atlantic Treaty Organization (NATO), have understood that parliamentarians are essential to their work. Canadians and Americans have learned a similar lesson in the management of their unique bilateral relationship and long ago created the Canada–United States Interparliamentary Group. More recently, under the leadership of Bill Graham, when he was chair of the House of Commons Standing Committee on Foreign Affairs and International Trade (2002), Canada founded an assembly of legislators in the Americas (see Chapter 20). The democratically and popularly elected leaders, who meet periodically in the plurilateral institutional system of the Summit of the Americas, recognise that the ongoing engagement of democratically elected legislators is essential to the realisation of their democratic purpose and development tasks.

The basic mission of strengthening democracy for its own sake and as a building block for development is no less central to the G8, especially with the high priority placed on poverty reduction in the Broader Middle East and North Africa and the shared recognition that good governance is a prerequisite for sustainable development. 'Eurocommunism' and the 'crisis of governability' in the mid 1970s, the democratic revolution in Russia in the 1990s, the need to sustain the global democratic revolution, and the new thrust to bring it to the last hold-out region of the

Middle East confirm that the democratic mission remains central to the work of the G8. As the Summit of the Americas and the G8 systems are, for Canada and the U.S., the only genuine international institutions centred on institutionalised, plurilateral summitry in which all participants are democratically and popularly elected leaders, it is clear that the G8 should join the Americas in bringing parliamentarians into the process in an organised way.

The case for including parliamentarians is clear. Legislators explain to citizens the work of, and the thinking behind, the actions of the executive branch. They act as sophisticated political sounding boards and give executive branch governors timely advance information about what the citizenry wants or will accept. Legislators are thus, in dynamic democratic practice as well as dry constitutional formula, the great connectors between executive branch governors and their citizens. They are the first line of defence in explaining to citizens and voters what the G8 is doing and why. As with foreign policy more generally, many have long thought of this issue as too specialised and of little concern to voters preoccupied with immediate domestic issues. But the events at Quebec City and at Genoa have made it a matter of broader and more active concern. Moreover, the events of September 11 and the spread of the summit's agenda to embrace once entirely domestic concerns such as health and education have given every G8 citizen an immediate interest in the G8 summit's work. And in many constituencies across multicultural Canada and in other G8 countries, the challenge of reducing poverty and combating terrorism in Africa, the Middle East, and elsewhere in the developing world is directly relevant to many voters, some of whom are recent arrivals with intense family ties to those they have left behind.

Parliamentarians are, of course, busy people with many existing interparliamentary groups to attend and fearful lest some constituents dismiss their international work as mere junketry or a perk. But the case for the G8 and its core agenda is now sufficiently compelling to bring the public on board. Parliamentarians could build on the House of Commons hearings across the country in the spring of 2002 and the recent gatherings of the speakers of the legislators in the G8. They could form a more institutionalised and inclusive G8 Interparliamentary Group, whose purposes could include the basic legislative task of monitoring compliance with the commitments that the G8's collective executive branch has made.

Generate G8 Study Centres

The fifth step moves beyond politicians to the people, beginning with a strategic elite that the Asia-Pacific Economic Co-operation Forum (APEC) has long realised can play a critical role in information wars and other tasks. The many thousands of citizens who came at their own expense to Genoa, Okinawa, Birmingham, and other summit sites did so not just to protest, but also to participate in the many 'teach-ins' and conferences sponsored by civil society organisations. Their presence reflects a pent-up demand for greater information and understanding of the issues dealt with at summits, how the G7/8 system is treating those issues, and how it might advance the common cause.

That students and citizens should have to journey to distant summits to acquire such information underscores the inadequacy of existing educational institutions in meeting these needs. If the G8 system is indeed emerging as an effective centre of global governance, just as important as the UN–Bretton Woods system constructed in 1945, then it warrants commensurate attention from the academic community, in the classroom and in regular research (Kirton 1999). Although there is a wealth of expertise and research on the subject, it is largely episodic and individual, conducted in isolation, and diffusely disseminated, rather than a dedicated, continuous enterprise mounted by teams of researchers and supported by major centres throughout and beyond the G8. It thus lacks the critical mass, cumulative quality, and visibility needed to inform the public, enrich the policy community, and contribute to an intellectual mass that could strengthen the summit system and its major thrusts. The G8 needs much more than the one endowed professorship on sustainable development that Kananaksis left behind, or the tourist-oriented historical house that Sea Island inspired Georgia's self-starting citizens to raise money for.

It is curious that the G8 still lacks the equivalent of the APEC study centre network. APEC is, like the G8, an international institutional system with a transregional membership and comprehensive agenda centred on an annual, plurilateral leaders meeting and supported by a host of ministerial meetings and official working groups. Even without the G8's democratic character and commitments, APEC has involved civil society at many levels in its work. The network of APEC study centres is a key element. (Each member country hosts at least one such centre.) The centres conduct research on APEC and the issues confronting it, contribute to the current APEC agenda, and are available to take on analytical tasks that APEC leaders may chose to entrust to them. Although the centres do not provide an analytical secretariat for APEC, they help deepen the analytical foundation and expert connections of its work in the same way that the Organisation for Economic Co-operation and Development (OECD), with its large formal secretariat, has long done for the Euro-Atlantic democratic world. The degree of direct government support for, and guidance to, the APEC centres varies considerably, depending in part on the democratic character of individual national regimes.

The G8 needs a similar analytic capability and intellectual support group. G8 leaders should announce their support for a network of G8 study centres in each G8 region or member country, offer the initial financial investment to ensure their speedy creation and operation, and suggest the initial research themes on which they would most welcome proposals. These might include establishing relationships with UN networks, reducing poverty in Africa, and monitoring the implementation of the G8's own action programme on Africa and the Middle East.

Sponsor G8 Scholarships

To build capacity for a future generation of scholarship and to give the current generation of students a much deeper understanding of the G8 system, it is important to devise the means by which the best students from within and outside G8 countries can study, on a year-round basis, the G8 community and how it can be enriched. Thus far, G8 efforts have been exceedingly fragile. At the 1998 Birmingham Summit, a small group of sponsored high school students came to the summit and conducted study sessions alongside the leaders, with whom they met briefly. The exercise was useful as a photo op to reinforce the G8's new interest in an education agenda, but left no lasting legacy – for example, national and international networks of mock G8 summits equivalent to the long-established mock UN assemblies and NATO councils. Instead, the year-round educational burden has fallen on the regular university and secondary school curricula, where there are many courses on globalisation, global governance, and the UN from a variety of perspectives but virtually none on the G8.

The required year-round educational effort must begin with the basics. The most promising students should be given first-hand, intensive exposure to the other members of the G8. Because of demographics and longstanding Commonwealth, la Francophonie, and Fulbright scholarship programmes, some students collectively have some chance to acquire a sound understanding of Britain, France, and the United States. Family ties might add Italy and perhaps Germany to the list for students from some countries of the G8. But few students have an intimate knowledge, intuitive understanding, or even initial awareness of Japan, Russia, or the EU as a whole, especially given entrenched regional and linguistic divides. Existing bilateral programmes are inadequate to the task.

An obvious solution is for the G8 leaders to create a scholarship programme, similar in structure to the Commonwealth, la Francophonie, and Fulbright programmes, which have long proven their worth. In a spirit of outreach, it should be open to students from non-G8 countries, to enlarge the understanding of the G8 beyond its members and to enrich the ability of those inside to assess the G8's impact on the global community as a whole. The G8 education ministers forum, born on the road to the Okinawa Summit of 2000, could be assigned the task of developing such a scholarship programme, in appropriate dialogue with sub-federal governments.

Educate the Citizenry

The seventh step is to reach out directly to educate students and the citizenry as a whole, with short-term measures designed to meet the immediate information and education demands. A minimal task is to devise an organised programme of information about G8 issues, institutions, and members that will secure and maintain audience interest and cumulate in a coherent whole.

One attractive vehicle for making such an educational programme readily accessible to many around the world is to place it on the internet, in video, audio, and text form, in as many G8 and world major languages as possible. The site should include a multilingual, organised, semester-long programme of serious teaching and learning. A website that merely tells schoolchildren how to say hello in all summit languages may be a useful start, but it is far from a serious response to the need. Here the major effort made by the Canadian government during the Kananaskis season, and the good work of the Georgians for Sea Island, provides a productive foundation on which to build. They included a state-of-the-art website, a programme for secondary and primary school teachers, and financial support for an internet-based, university-level course, G8 Online. Producing similar timely, well-tailored materials in all the G8's languages for every summit is the next obvious step – although still outstanding.

Massage the Media

The seventh step is to massage, as well as manage, the media. Most of the world learns about the G8 through the media, overwhelmingly from the coverage of and at annual summits. The result can be singularly limited. At Genoa, Jean Chrétien publicly complained about the media's fascination with pictures of a single burning car. When word was first heard of the death of an anarchist, virtually all of the 3000 assembled journalists abandoned their coverage of the summit to focus on that single event. The collective statement of regret about the death issued by the leaders was essentially inaudible and invisible against the full might of the media and the deluge of words and images they produced.

Newsworthy events for the mainstream media will always put bodies, bullets, bombs, and blood over politicians talking and issuing co-operative communiqués. Indeed, the elite of the summit media, from the U.S. White House press corps to their equivalents in other G8 countries, come to the summit in part on an 'assassination watch', in case their leader is assaulted and does not survive. In the face of such facts, some summit managers are occasionally tempted to limit media access in ways that might facilitate media management and communications strategy.

The disadvantages of giving in to such temptation was evident at Sea Island in 2004. In sharp contrast to every previous summit, the U.S. hosts decided to charge every journalist a sum of US$700 (initially) simply to sit down at a desk in the media centre in Savannah 100 kilometres away from the summit itself. Not surprisingly, of the 3000 journalists who had sought and secured credentials, only 1400 came, some carrying their folding chairs that could be bought at the local store for US$20. As a result, Georgia lost its one chance in a lifetime to showcase its state to the world. President George W. Bush lost his chance to get his message out to a sceptical world, beyond the rich media who could afford the privilege of covering the event.

More broadly, it is inconceivable that the public or the press in eight major democratic polities and throughout Europe would allow their leaders to gather for two or three days of public business, of potentially the highest importance, without a media presence operating with sufficient freedom to record and report on the event rapidly and accurately. The Kananaskis approach of allowing only a few pool journalists near the summit site and having only the host government rather than each national delegation brief the media throughout the summit predictably produced a media with little to cover, but the complaints of civil society critics, and strange herd mentality stories about the Kananaskis agenda being 'hijacked' by a Middle East initiative unveiled in a speech in Washington DC a few days before. It was not surprising that media judgement of the Kananaskis achievements were far more negative than more scientific analyses showed.

If a minimum democratic duty is transparency, then pondering ways to restrict media access is akin to shooting oneself in the mouth. And for the leaders themselves, limiting media access is immensely counterproductive, because it would emasculate much of the unique power of the summit. The summit offers a singular occasion for leaders – members of the world's loneliest profession – to deliberate privately and share their deepest hopes, fears, and ideas, far from the madding media and masses. But it also provides a powerful collective bully pulpit from which to set new directions for the global community – to highlight new challenges, themes, issues, and interconnections and to articulate new norms and principles in response. That it can do so is suggested by the literature on compliance with summit commitments. Leaders can get desired welfare outcomes even without mobilising their own policy instruments to implement actions themselves (von Furstenberg and Daniels 1991). In short, governments, organisations, and societies can and will respond on their own, if only they know the direction in which G8 leaders want them to go. An essential part of the dynamic – and the broader process of monitoring and mobilising pressure to ensure compliance with even hard summit commitments – is to have the media on hand to give leaders the global audience they need to get their collective message out and to help ensure that they and their partners live up to the promises made.

That is why since the beginning leaders have basked in the glow of media attention, whether from the 400 who gathered at Rambouillet in November 1975 or the more than 10 000, largely Japanese journalists accredited at]in 2000. The physical care and feeding of the attending media corps, as much as the content of the communications strategy aimed at them, is vital. At Denver in 1997, the media centre was equipped with on-site massage facilities – a useful therapy rather than a frivolous luxury for those who must work, often round the clock, for three days straight to get their information in and their messages out through all the time zones in the world. Getting enough information to deliver a useful and credible message can be a major challenge and explains why, at the margins, the media rush to cover such relatively easy alternatives as burning cars, protests, and death in the street.

To combat such tendencies, an open, easily accessible, adequately equipped media centre, fully functioning 24 hours a day is essential. The Kananaskis approach of closing portions of the facility when the local service providers reach their normal break times or at night is an act of cultural insensitivity that cripples the ability of G8 governors to get their message out. Global civil society activists with their networks of websites and more traditional media outlets do not take time off during the summit.

There is also a need for more adequate briefings, the frequency and quality of which have declined at summits of late. Following the Italian example, the process could start well before the summit with the release to the public of the major thematic paper prepared to guide summit deliberations. Following the historic leadership of Canadian sherpa Robert Fowler on the road to Kananaskis, extensive briefings by sherpas across the G8 countries and in national and media capitals in the week or two prior to the summit could contribute much. In this task, G8 ministers and leaders should also play their full part. The host and other countries should assume the burden, traditionally borne by the Japanese and EU, of providing on-site briefings immediately before the summit opens in which they outline what they expect to achieve. Documents should be available far enough in advance to allow the media to read and to digest them. Briefings by the host and all members after every working session and meal should be the norm. They should be timed and spaced to allow even small media contingents to attend as many as possible, to ensure that they are not being spun by a single source.

The briefings should also be broadcast and webcast to the world in real time, with a transcription available shortly after and ideally translated into all the relevant languages. This would allow those busy at concurrent briefings to access all briefings by archived video. It would reduce the number of journalists who have to be present at each briefing or even at the summit itself. It would also enable the whole world to hear the message more directly, without the filter of the media corps with their own and their editors' particular preoccupations at the time. Transcriptions of the webcasts would enrich, broaden, and diversify the public record of G8 summits, and translation into languages beyond the G8 would make the messages even more accessible. Traditionally only the U.S. can be counted on to provide transcripts to all of the attending media corps, and then only those briefings given by United States government spokespersons, and only in English. Transcriptions on the web would allow those on the other side of the digital divide, equipped with only first-generation internet and computer facilities, to access the information as readily as their privileged webcast counterparts. Together, this low-cost, inobtrusive innovation would do much to make the summit available to the wider world.

Clarify the Communiqué

The next step is to clarify the communiqué to give it greater credibility and to make it intelligible to all who have a stake in what it says. At the summit, the briefing programme centres around hints about the final communiqué, while the summit itself culminates with its public presentation, the ultimate moment in the great drama of every G8 summit. Not surprisingly, the communiqué has been the subject of intense debate since the beginning: what should it contain; should it even exist?

The first step is to keep the communiqué, as a minimum transparency measure, to inform citizens about the decisions of their democratically elected leaders, even if those citizens cannot participate in the deliberations that produce it. Despite the comforting rhetoric that the G8 is merely a caucus-like 'ginger group' rather than a global *directoire* (Baker 2000), the reality is that the leaders have generated a large and growing number of ambitious and significant communiqué-encoded commitments in recent years, and what is more they have complied with them to a rising and high degree. In short, communiqués and the commitments they codify do count.

Moreover, communiqués are consumed by a vast audience. Despite the prevailing cynical folklore, it is simply not true that more people are involved in preparing the communiqués than in reading them when they are unveiled. From among the 3000 members of the media on site at Genoa, the number who hit the relevant portion of the websites where the communiqués were mounted confirm that the communiqués receive at least a passing glance from millions around the world. Their contents may not always be reported in approving detail by the media or scrutinised by the mass public, but officials use them as high-level authoritative weapons to help get what they want. Here the problem is not with the inattentiveness of the audience but with the quality of the product.

Communiqués should be written with a clarity and concreteness that make them comprehensible to the average citizen. They should be more action oriented and should whenever possible specify targets and timetables for accomplishing what the leaders say they want done. They should also be more honest in identifying new or enhanced promises instead of merely repeating promises from previous years. They should acknowledge frankly where and why last year's promises were not kept. If leaders do not provide their own conscientious, self-correcting capacity and critique, then they cannot blame civil society protestors for claiming for themselves alone this part of the democratic turf. One solution, used at the Quebec City Summit of the Americas and in part by past G8 summits, is to publish with the crisp, clear communiqué a detailed action plan containing specifics of what the leaders intend to accomplish. Another useful addition, following the tentative start made by G8 foreign ministers in 2001 on the conflict prevention agenda, is to release a report card on the eve of or at the summit that lists last year's commitments, what they meant in practice, and to what extent and how they were kept.

While transparency is vital, it is not achieved by deluging the attending media with an avalanche of documents at the last minute at a summit as filing deadlines loom. The 14 separate statements that came forth in an unanticipated blizzard at Evian toward the end of the summit were impossible to digest. At Sea Island, the Americans outgunned the French by releasing 15 such statements, one of which – the chair's summary – was hard to find, and another one of which – on sustainable development – did not appear until the day after when everyone had gone home.

Include Civil Society On-Site

The tenth step is to bring civil society into the summit itself, as the Summit of the Americas did in Quebec City and as the G8 started to do at Okinawa in 2000. A multi-stakeholder civil society forum, led by and involving parliamentarians, could meet simultaneously with the leaders, or, with minimal overlap, just prior to and at the start of the summit if some fear lingers that their presence would detract from the media limelight in which the leaders want to bask alone. Whatever the precise formula, the media and the leaders interested in civil society views would have something to report on and to respond to other than those shouting slogans on the streets outside.

An important part of this innovation would be for the G8 leaders collectively, and not just the host leader or others at their individual discretion, to meet with the leaders of the civil society forum. If the leaders of Canada, the U.S., Japan, and Russia can find the time at their APEC sessions to meet with business leaders in the APEC Business Forum, they can surely find time as part of a standard-sized G8 summit to meet with civil society leaders of a much more inclusive, multi-stakeholder sort. Even as they properly reach out to leaders of international organisations and non-member countries at the start of their summit, G8 leaders should also reach down to their own citizens, to hear at first hand their views and to explain the desires, strategies, and constraints they as leaders bring to the summit.

The admirable initiative of Bill Graham in participating in the government-funded G6B People's Summit in Calgary was a minimum step forward relative to the need. It is a much better way to spend the day before the summit gets down to work than the day-long arrival ceremonies that George W. Bush chose to open with at Sea Island in 2004.

Mobilise the Ministerials

If there remain unavoidable limits to direct civil society participation at the summits, then the many ministerial meetings that have emerged in the lead-up to the summit offer an appealing opportunity for a sustained, focussed, policy-sensitive dialogue between popularly elected G8 governors and civil society representatives interested in realistic policy change. The efforts made in this direction at the spring 2002 environment ministers meeting in Banff offer a promising start, as Sheila Risbud details in Chapter 17. As the host of the 2002 G8 pre-summit foreign ministers meeting in Whistler, British Columbia, Graham took the initiative to meet for a dialogue with those few civil society activists who had come to protest. With such leadership from a traditionally closed foreign policy areas, there is no excuse for G8 ministerial meetings in more open policy areas, such as development or health, to follow the foreign ministers and environment ministers lead. Nor is there any excuse for the American decision in 2004, to cancel all of the lead up G8 meetings of ministers beyond the core portfolios of finance and (at the last minute) foreign affairs.

Conclusion

In his concluding news conference at the end of the first summit Canada attended, in Puerto Rico, Prime Minister Pierre Elliott Trudeau captured the essential purpose of the G8: 'the success of these conferences [is] … not to be judged by the solution of individual economic problems or by the setting up of new institutions or by the agreement on any particular resolution. Their success will be judged by whether we can influence the behaviour of people in our democracies and perhaps even as important the behaviour of people on the outside who are watching us, in a way in which they will have confidence that our type of economic and political freedom permits us to solve problems' (Trudeau 1976). Trudeau and his colleagues, in the first generation of G7 summitry and those that followed, succeeded in this task. They solved the crisis of governability and stagflation, stopped Eurocommunism within the G7 community, waged the new cold war of the early 1980s, and set the stage for the democratic revolution in Russia, Central and Eastern Europe, and elsewhere in the 1990s. They did so by reaching downward to their own citizens and outward to those in the global community, with dialogue and persuasion, to give their decisions the sensitivity, understanding, and legitimacy they needed for maximum effect.

The 21st century has bred a novel and equally formidable set of challenges for the current generation of G8 leaders, virtually all of whom have come to every G8 summit since they started in 2001. But the 21st century has also brought new instruments of communication and engagement and new constituencies of civil society allies to help them meet the challenge. It remains to be seen if the current generation of leaders will be as skilful as the founding fathers in mobilizing these instruments to secure equal success. Their choice will do much to determine if the G8 gatherings of the post–September 11 world become a summit in retreat or a summit reaching out.

Note

1   The 11 September 2001 terrorist attacks in the U.S. in New York, Washington, and Pennsylvania, on the ground and in the air, killed citizens from G8 countries as follows: U.S. 2800, UK 67, Canada 24, Japan 22, Germany 6, Italy 4, France 1, Russia 1. (As many bodies were never recovered and fully identified, these figures are estimates.) Thus, while the U.S. was by far the greatest victim, this was a shock fully shared throughout the G8, as citizens from all member countries died. Relative to their national populations, it was Britain across the Atlantic and Canada next door who suffered most. Japan, with a population four times that of Canada, suffered fewer deaths.

References

Baker, Andrew (2000). 'The G7 as a Global "Ginger Group": Plurilateralism and Four Dimensional Diplomacy'. *Global Governance* vol. 6 (April-June), pp. 165–190.

Bayne, Nicholas (1999). 'Continuity and Leadership in an Age of Globalisation'. In M.R. Hodges, J.J. Kirton and J.P. Daniels, eds., *The G8's Role in the New Millennium*, pp. 21–44. Ashgate, Aldershot.

Bayne, Nicholas (2000). *Hanging In There: The G7 and G8 Summit in Maturity and Renewal.* Ashgate, Aldershot.

G7 (1975). 'Declaration of Rambouillet'. 17 November. Rambouillet. <www.g8.utoronto.ca/summit/1975rambouillet/communique.html> (November 2005).

Hajnal, Peter I. (1999). *The G7/G8 System: Evolution, Role, and Documentation.* Ashgate, Aldershot.

Hajnal, Peter I. (2002a). 'The G7/G8 and Civil Society'. G8 Online 2002, Lecture 8. <www.g8.utoronto.ca/g8online/2002/english/2002/08.html> (November 2005).

Hajnal, Peter I. (2002b). 'Partners or Adversaries? The G7/8 Encounters Civil Society'. In J.J. Kirton and J. Takase, eds., *New Directions in Global Political Governance: The G8 and International Order in the Twenty-First Century*, pp. 191–208. Ashgate, Aldershot.

Kirton, John J. (1999). 'Explaining G8 Effectiveness'. In J.J. Kirton and J.P. Daniels, eds., *The G8's Role in the New Millennium*, pp. 45–68. Ashgate, Aldershot.

Kirton, John J. (2001). 'Guess Who Is Coming to Kananaskis? Civil Society and the G8 in Canada's Year as Host'. *International Journal* vol. 57, no. 1 (Winter), pp. 101–122. <www.g8.utoronto.ca/scholar/kirton2002/020507.pdf> (November 2005).

Kirton, John J. (2002a). 'Consensus and Coherence in G7 Financial Governance'. In M. Fratianni, P. Savona and J.J. Kirton, eds., *Governing Global Finance: New Challenges, G7 and IMF Contributions*, pp. 45–73. Ashgate, Aldershot.

Kirton, John J. (2002b). 'Embedded Ecologism and Institutional Inequality: Linking Trade, Environment, and Social Cohesion in the G8'. In J.J. Kirton and V.W. Maclaren, eds., *Linking Trade, Environment, and Social Cohesion: NAFTA Experiences, Global Challenges*, pp. 45–72. Ashgate, Aldershot.

Kissinger, Henry (1975). 'The Industrial Democracies and the Future'. *Department of State Bulletin* vol. 73, no. 1901 (1 December), pp. 757–764.

Mahoney, Jill (2002). 'Graham Vows to Pass on People's Message'. *Globe and Mail*, 26 June, p. A4.

Nye, Joseph S. (2002). *The Paradox of American Power: Why the World's Only Superpower Can't Go It Alone.* Oxford University Press, New York.

Putnam, Robert and Nicholas Bayne, eds. (1987). *Hanging Together: Co-operation and Conflict in the Seven-Power Summit.* Sage Publications, London.

'Since September 11' (2002). *Maclean's* 7 January, p. 39.

Smith, Gordon (2001). 'It's a Long Way from Halifax to Kananaskis'. *International Journal* vol. 57, no. 1 (Winter), pp. 123–127.

Standing Committee on Foreign Affairs and International Trade (Canada) (2002). 'Securing Progress for Africa and the World: A Report on Canadian Priorities for the 2002 G8 Summit'. <www.parl.gc.ca/InfoComDoc/37/1/FAIT/Studies/Reports/faitrp21-e.htm> (November 2005).

Trudeau, Pierre Elliott (1976). 'New Conference'. 28 June. San Juan, Puerto Rico.

von Furstenberg, George M. and Joseph P. Daniels (1991). 'Policy Undertakings by the Seven "Summit" Countries: Ascertaining the Degree of Compliance'. *Carnegie-Rochester Conference Series on Public Policy* vol. 35, pp. 267–308.

Chapter 17

Civil Society Engagement: A Case Study of the 2002 G8 Environment Ministers Meeting

Sheila Risbud

This chapter examines the Canadian-hosted G8 environment ministers meeting held in Banff, Alberta, on 12–14 April 2002 as an example of civil society engagement in the G8 process. It highlights both the successes achieved and the improvements needed in the Canadian government's outreach and engagement programme. It also addresses lessons learned from this event and how these lessons can be applied to future ministerial meetings and summits. The analysis and conclusions are based on a series of follow-up assessments and debriefings with local authorities and residents, nongovernmental organisations (NGOs), and other stakeholders.

The G8 System

The summit process comprises more than the actual gathering of G8 leaders. Ministerial-level meetings of the G8 countries take place in the months leading up to the summit. Although these meetings do not necessarily feed into the summit, their content and exchanges help to shape the leaders' discussions.

Canada, as host of the 2002 G8 Kananaskis Summit, was also host to its related ministerial meetings. While the Department of Foreign Affairs and International Trade (DFAIT) was responsible for arrangements related to the summit, individual departments were tasked with co-ordinating the ministerials Environment Canada, therefore, organised the environment ministers meeting. The logistics and content of the meeting were developed in Ottawa, and in Environment Canada's Prairie and Northern Region. The latter includes the three Prairie provinces of Manitoba, Saskatchewan, and Alberta as well as two of Canada's three territories, Nunavut and the Northwest Territories. The process led to the local outreach and engagement operations.

A New Way of Doing Business

Environment Canada's reputation for inclusiveness and progressive approaches to civil society engagement is well recognised by stakeholders. This is especially true when new legislation or major departmental initiatives are under consideration. For an event such as the G8 environment ministerial, civil society engagement entails some interaction between key stakeholders and the minister of the environment or senior government officials. Often, this takes the form of a round table or a series of smaller, focussed meetings leading up to the actual ministerial meeting.

Demonstrations around international meetings and events in recent years have raised awareness of the need to involve stakeholders in the planning of these events, partly in order to diffuse the potential for violent protest. As part of a new approach developed in the wake of violence at the 2001 Quebec City Summit of the Americas and the tragic occurrences at the G8 Genoa Summit the same year, the Royal Canadian Mounted Police (RCMP) recommended that Environment Canada engage local stakeholders in the G8 process in the early stages of planning. The G8 environment ministers meeting was the first test of this new approach, which was also applied to the subsequent summit in Kananaskis.

Banff: A Unique Setting

A distinct feature of the 2002 G8 environment ministers meeting was its location. All parties discovered quickly the different challenges involved in holding an international meeting in Banff – a close-knit community within a national park – rather than in an anonymous hotel in a large city. The town of Banff is often thought of as a picturesque, retreat-like setting for meetings. However, besides being a beautiful place, Banff is located in one of Canada's most controversial national parks. It faces serious challenges relating to sustainable development, notably the need to balance preservation of the park against growing numbers of visitors and entrepreneurs.

In 1998, Parks Canada imposed a growth cap in the park when the government realised that the current growth in the area was unsustainable. This decision was based on a 1996 study of the Bow Valley that clearly confirmed what everyone had suspected: development in Banff was having a negative impact on the environment. This growth cap divided the community between business owners who, for the most part, opposed the limit on growth, and an engaged environmental community that applauded the limit and pressures government for more restrictions on human use of the park.

When it was first announced that the G8 environment ministerial was coming to Banff, a degree of panic set in among residents. At the time of the announcement, Environment Canada did not have a presence in Banff and the RCMP did not have all of the facts at hand concerning the meeting. In the absence of information, people invented their own. The rumour mill went into overdrive.

With images of prior international meetings in mind, the residents worried that tens of thousands of protestors would invade the small town and ransack their businesses. Environmentalists were worried about the impact of such a large number of protestors on the already fragile mountain environment. Town council was concerned about financial compensation for vandalism should violence escalate.

Over the long term, the town was worried about the reputation of Banff as a tourist destination – especially since images of the meeting and the town would be broadcast into some of the town's most lucrative tourism markets. Some local activists also wondered if they could play a role in the ministers' discussions and have their issues brought to the table.

Environment Canada needed to react quickly and deliver an effective outreach strategy. The strategy had two different audiences with two different goals. The first audience was composed of business owners and local residents concerned about their personal safety and the safety of their property. These people were directly affected because of their proximity to the event. The second audience included the activists who wanted to voice their concerns directly to the Canadian environment minister and to the international community. There were six activities in Environment Canada's strategy.

Town Hall Session

Environment Canada, the RCMP, and the town of Banff were able to work collaboratively to run a 'town hall' meeting for residents. This session was well attended. It served as a first step in informing residents and other stakeholders about the upcoming meeting. This permitted the department to take the community's pulse about the event and also allowed groups to express their views and become involved in the process leading up to the actual meeting.

One-on-One Discussions

The town hall session was followed by a series of one-on-one meetings between senior officials and individuals or groups who requested more information or who wanted to provide input into the process. These individuals and groups included local environmental groups, businesses, town leaders, and the interested average individuals on the street. Their one-on-one discussions with representatives from Environment Canada and RCMP staff put a human face to the event. This helped to alleviate fears and concerns and allowed for citizen input into the organisation and content of the meeting.

Round Table Meeting

Canada's environment minister, representatives from G8 delegations, and the executive director of the United Nations Environment Programme (UNEP) met with major stakeholders from across Canada. These included environmental, development and health-oriented NGOs, representatives from business and industry, labour groups, aboriginal groups, local authorities, academics, representatives from faith communities, and youth. The G8 environment ministerial agenda and preparations for the September 2002 Johannesburg World Summit on Sustainable Development framed this sharing of views. The participants presented a wide range of issues and suggestions, and all emphasised the importance of the interrelationships central to sustainable development.

The participants also brought vision and a host of valuable ideas to the discussion. In particular, the value of good governance, and environment and health linkages – both in the developed and developing world – were noted as crucial. Specific topics such as poverty reduction, mercury contamination, climate change and the Kyoto Protocol, persistent organic pollutants (POPs), biodiversity, species at risk, renewable energy, and action at the local and corporate level were also raised. Canada, as 2002 G8 chair, reported these discussions to G8 environment ministers at the beginning of the ministerial. Generally, civil society groups were pleased to see their concerns conveyed to the Canadian environment minister and his counterparts.

Youth Forum

A youth forum was sponsored by Environment Canada and delivered through a local environmental group. It brought together 20 environmentally engaged high school students from the region to discuss the same topics that G8 environment ministers would be discussing a few days later. The youth drafted a declaration and presented it at the minister's round table meeting. The forum gave youth a new and positive relationship with the RCMP and Environment Canada. More importantly, it provided young people with an opportunity to be heard.

Involvement of Local Decision Makers

Environment Canada and the RCMP participated in the town council's G8 planning committee. The mayor and his council were given timely information about the meeting's progress. They were made to feel part of the planning process. These local decision makers, by being part of the process, ensured that the town felt more like hosts of the meeting rather than victims of it.

Working with the Local Media

A good relationship was built with the local media through both formal and informal briefing sessions. This ensured better informed coverage of the event. They provided residents with a credible local source of information on the meeting in addition to the federal government sources of information that were available.

Greening the Meeting

Environment Canada sought to make this the 'greenest' G8 environment ministers meeting ever held. As a demonstration of its commitment to sustainable development, Canada took measures to minimise the environmental impact of the meeting and for the event to serve as a hallmark for future meetings.

Every aspect of the meeting was put through a green lens to make sure that the best possible environmental choices were made. An extensive environmental management system was developed to identify all possible environmental impacts of the meeting and to plan to keep those impacts to a minimum. The first principle used was to reduce waste and pollution at the source. For example, to reduce carbon dioxide emissions from the use of multiple vehicles, delegates used shuttles powered by natural gas to travel from the airport in Calgary to the meeting in Banff. In order to designate the meeting as carbon neutral, Environment Canada purchased carbon dioxide credits from a low-income passive solar housing project in South Africa. Wind power was also purchased to offset electricity used during the meeting. Since most meetings are powered by caffeine, even the coffee served was shade grown and fair trade. While some members of the environmental community may have considered these acts to tokenism, others applauded the efforts. As one environmentalist put it: 'These meetings are going to happen whether we like it or not ... they may as well be green'.

Environment Canada shared its greening experience with the government of France in the hope that the 2003 ministerial meetings and summit would build on the environmental leadership displayed in Banff and Kananaskis. While the French expressed interest in Canada's approach, their efforts to green the environment ministerial in Paris and the summit in Evian-les-Bains were not as rigorous as those employed in Banff.

Evaluation and Future Considerations

The G8 environment ministers meeting was successful in several ways. First, ministers were able to discuss in detail the three themes of the meeting (environment and development, environment and health, and environmental governance). They also managed to exchange views on climate change. Second, civil society engagement was high, although tempered by heightened post–September 11 security. Third, the only protest was peaceful and small. It comprised 22 protestors dressed as endangered spotted owls.

The environment ministerial engaged citizens in a positive manner, but opportunities were nonetheless lost as a result of short planning time, coupled with financial constraints. In Chapter 16, John Kirton proposes 11 steps to improve the G8–civil society link, including the suggestion of including civil society on site in a multi-stakeholder forum. The 2002 stakeholder round table only partially met this recommendation. While it was certainly a step in the right direction, civil society did not have the time to discuss important issues in depth, nor were groups given an opportunity to do so. A full two-day meeting, parallel to the environment ministerial, might have resulted in more effective participation.

The only direct interface that civil society had with ministers, however, was during that round table. A large number of participants from varied backgrounds were asked to provide statements to the minister within a two-hour period, which limited the level of their engagement. The themes discussed by ministers were broad and multidisciplinary in nature, but more focussed discussion topics with civil society participants might have been more effective. Although the civil society participants were Canadian, other G8 ministers would likely have benefited from the discussions and should have been strongly encouraged to participate personally instead of sending representatives.

Local outreach was successful on the security front, as residents were made to feel safe and secure about the event. However, in terms of reaching out to local citizens and involving them in the ministerial's content, the outreach strategy was not as effective as it could have been. Ministerial meetings should make room for the community that is hosting their event. After all, given the security risks that the community perceives it is taking when one of these meetings comes to town, it is only fair to have local residents be part of the organisation of the meeting.

Environment Canada set up a website to keep people informed about the meeting and its related documents. But the site was launched late in the process and was not as up to date as it could have been. This frustrated local residents and activists who were eager to find out more about the meeting's themes. As Kirton (2001) suggests, 'a single permanent website with a continuous stream of new information' is an important vehicle for engaging citizens.

Conclusion

The environment ministers meeting held in Banff represented a significant step forward for civil society engagement. However, it was but the first step. Groups want to be heard and want to be part of the process. There is value in having them involved. It is important, however, to ensure that outreach and engagement not be seen as attempts on the part of governments simply to placate civil society, but as a genuine commitment to citizen involvement.

Citizen participation helps inform deliberations at the ministerial level and serves to diffuse the propensity for violent protest. Indeed, if future summits follow the trend of smaller, retreat-style meetings with limited delegations, it will be even more important for civil society to be involved at these ministerial-level meetings. In particular, further thought should be given to the role that host communities can play in planning future meetings.

Reference

Kirton, John J. (2001). 'Guess Who Is Coming to Kananaskis? Civil Society and the G8 in Canada's Year as Host'. *International Journal* vol. 57, no. 1 (Winter), pp. 101–122. <www.g8.utoronto.ca/scholar/kirton2002/020507.pdf> (November 2005).

Chapter 18

Canada and the Kyoto Protocol: Beyond Ratification to Implementation

Désirée M. McGraw[1]

In June 1992, more than 100 heads of state and government as well as 30 000 activists and journalists gathered in Rio de Janeiro for the first ever Earth Summit.[2] The meeting was widely heralded as the highest-level gathering in human history. Participants produced ground-breaking agreements to combat climate change and stem the loss of biological diversity, and in the process galvanised world attention to environmental issues. The Rio meeting also created Agenda 21, a global blueprint for implementing sustainable development, which involves a balanced and integrated approach to ecological, economic, and social concerns.

Rio not only established a new regime of international law on sustainable development, but also institutionalised what Steven Bernstein (2002) labels the 'compromise of liberal environmentalism', namely 'the predication of international environmental protection on the promotion and maintenance of liberal economic order'. Indeed, the very term 'sustainable development' remains controversial today: some perceive it as an attempt to legitimate economic growth within the concept of environmental protection. It was originally defined by the 1987 report of the World Commission on Environment and Development (also known as the Brundtland Report) as 'development that meets the needs of the present without compromising the ability of future generations to meet their own needs' (World Commission on Environment and Development 1987). In Canada, this definition has been integrated into federal legislation and into the amendments to the *Auditor General Act* (1995), which established the Commissioner of the Environment and Sustainable Development.[3]

This chapter will examine the adoption of a key and current instrument of sustainable development and international governance – the Kyoto Protocol to the UN Framework Convention on Climate Change that emerged from the Earth Summit – from a Canadian perspective. In particular, it will address Canada's debate surrounding the accord's ratification and implementation according to five themes (or '5Cs'): competitiveness, credibility, consultations, commitment, and consistency in public and foreign policy (McGraw 2003).

Canada and the Environment: From Leader to Laggard

The United Nations designated the 1990s as the 'turn-around decade' on sustainable development. Instead, the decade was characterised by some as the lost decade in this regard, and countries such as Canada have contributed to this reality. Indeed, since the 1992 Earth Summit, Canada is widely considered to have turned from environmental leader to environmental laggard, both at home and abroad (McGraw 2002d) (see also Toner 2000).

It is true that in Rio Canada readily signed onto general agreements on biodiversity and climate change – commitments that environment minister David Anderson later characterised as 'immodest'. There is no doubt that the main agreements of the Earth Summit – the Convention on Biological Diversity (CBD), the UN Framework Convention on Climate Change (UNFCCC), a Statement of Forest Principles, and Agenda 21 – were lofty. Unfortunately, many of the outputs that emerged from the ten-year follow-up conference to Rio, the World Summit on Sustainable Development (WSSD) held in Johannesburg in September 2002, were headed for the same ineffectual fate as their predecessors.[4] Indeed, many view the Earth Summit as constituting a step back from the 1992 one. Because Canadian negotiators were instructed by their political masters to resist specific targets and timelines on a broad range of issues, Canada bears some responsibility for this outcome. At the Johannesburg Summit, Canada earned a place alongside Australia and the U.S. to form what Greenpeace and other well-established nongovernmental organisations (NGOs) dubbed the 'Axis of Environmental Evil'.

Although such rhetoric is undoubtedly excessive, it is clear that Canada no longer holds the mantle of international environmental leadership it once did. While Canada was one of the leading member countries of the Organisation for Economic Co-operation and Development (OECD) to sign and ratify the original Rio conventions on biodiversity and climate change, it has subsequently stalled on stricter and more substantive sub-agreements. Perhaps the most compelling illustration of Canada's evolution from environmental leader to laggard is in the area of biodiversity. Canada was the first industrialised country to sign the CBD, thereby creating the 'biodiversity bandwagon' at Rio that convinced most of the rest of the G7 countries to sign on – despite overt opposition by the George H. Bush's administration. Canada had been viewed by North and South alike as a champion of the biodiversity issue. As a result, it managed to beat out countries such as Spain, Switzerland, and Kenya in its bid to host the CBD secretariat, which has been headquartered in Montreal since 1996. However, Canada's support for the CBD has slipped in more recent years. Most notably, Canada has signed but not yet ratified the first legally binding sub-agreement to the CBD: the Cartagena Protocol on Biosafety addressing transboundary movement of genetically modified organisms (GMOs). During these negotiations, Canada served as the spokesperson for the so-called 'Miami Group' of major agricultural exporters, which resisted any binding agreement regarding the trade in or labelling of products containing GMOs.[5]

At the domestic level, after commissioning an arm's-length assessment of Canada's environmental performance since Rio, the government stalled on releasing the critical outcome: Canada's national report to the WSSD, 'Sustainable Development: A Canadian Perspective', was made public only weeks before the conference started, several months past the due date set by the UN (Environment Canada 2002).

A comprehensive review of Canada's environmental performance over the last decade is well beyond the scope of this chapter.[6] Instead, this overview will focus on a single case as an illustration of Canada's environmental record from 1993 to 2003: the Kyoto Protocol to the 1992 UNFCCC.

The Kyoto Protocol

In 1992, Canada was one of the first industrialised countries to both sign and ratify the UNFCCC, one of two treaties to emerge from the Earth Summit.[7] The Kyoto Protocol, named after the Japanese city in which it was adopted on 11 December 1997, constitutes the first substantive treaty aimed at reinforcing and operationalising the principles embodied in the original framework agreement on climate change. Specifically, the accord calls for industrialised countries to reduce their greenhouse gas (GHG) emissions by at least 5 percent below 1990 levels within the 2008–2012 timeframe (the first commitment period).[8] Canada was to achieve a 6 percent reduction below the 1990 base year. Kyoto represents the first critical step to meeting global climate change commitments: these entail a total reduction of between 50 percent and 75 percent in global GHG in this century alone.

In light of its reduced environmental reputation in the decade since Rio, Canada did not go into WSSD from a position of strength. Therefore, Chrétien's pledge at Johannesberg that Parliament would ratify the Kyoto Protocol by year's end came as a surprise to the UN community, to Canadians, and, it would appear, to his own Cabinet.[9] Nonetheless, it was a critical announcement at a critical time. Kyoto now stood poised to become legally binding. To be operational, the accord requires ratification by a minimum of 55 countries responsible for at least 55 percent of the globe's GHG emissions. Although Kyoto had long surpassed the first criterion for entry into force, the second remained elusive – especially in light of the Bush administration's refusal to ratify the agreement – until 16 February 2005 when it entered into force. All members of the G8, with the exception of the U.S., had ratified it. While the U.S. contributes roughly 25 percent to global GHG emissions, Canada produces a mere 3 percent. But person for person, Canadians – along with Australians and Americans – are the biggest energy consumers in the world. Thus, the country has a unique opportunity and responsibility to contribute to the global fight against climate change. Canada should compensate for its vast size and cold climate not with more GHG emissions, but with greater innovation and investment in efficient sources of energy.

Kyoto: A Question of Competitiveness

Opponents of Kyoto claimed that Canada could not afford to implement the accord because it would damage Canada's economic competitiveness. However, the policy uncertainty created by the government's protracted hesitation regarding ratification and subsequent lack of a clear implementation plan was costly for corporate decision making. Canadian corporations were legitimately concerned about the negative effects of uncertainty on their competitiveness and ability to attract investment. Following ratification of the accord, efficient negotiation of details of the implementation plan in conjunction with key industrial sectors as well as the provinces and territories would provide the best way to address such uncertainty. Clear and credible targets would allow corporations to make more informed investment and other business decisions.

Kyoto will provide very substantial opportunities to make a transition to a more efficient and competitive economy. According to the Pembina Institute for Appropriate Technology, Canada's competitiveness was likely to benefit, not suffer, from Parliament's vote to ratify the Kyoto Protocol (Boustie, Raynolds, and Bramley 2002). Its report found that by government taking a lead on environmental policy, firms could be more efficient and competitive. In a survey of corporations in several key sectors (including oil and gas, electricity, chemicals, transportation, and manufacturing) with major operations in Canada, those firms that took early action to improve efficiency and effect emission-reduction strategies in anticipation of Kyoto ratification also increased their competitiveness. For example, from 1990 to 2000, Dupont reduced its GHG emissions by 60 percent while production increased by 10 percent and shareholder return quadrupled. Between 1995 and 2001, Interface, a flooring products firm, reduced GHG emissions per unit of production by 64 percent in its Canadian operations while the company's waste reduction programme produced savings of more than CA$185 million worldwide. British Petroleum, one of the world's largest oil companies, dubbed itself 'Beyond Petroleum', which was more than an advertising gimmick: in 1997, the company committed to reducing its GHG emissions by 10 percent below 1990 levels by 2010. Not only did BP already achieved this target eight years ahead of schedule (in March 2002), but it also did so at no net economic cost (savings from increased efficiency outweighed expenditures) while more than doubling its basic earnings per share (from US$0.17 in 1998 to US$0.36 in 2001).

The editor of Canadian business magazine *Corporate Knights* described Kyoto as 'an Innovation Agenda in disguise' with the following explanation:

New technologies that make sense in a world that puts cost constraints on emitters of greenhouse gases will emerge ... Firms that invest in cleaner ways of doing business will gain market share and reduce costs. By aligning firms with price signals that send a clear message (pollution costs), Kyoto will stir up a critical mass of activity establishing a business web of innovative firms that will act as a reinforcing network for developing ever-cleaner and more efficient processes. Those firms that continue to waste energy will waste away (Heaps 2002).

Opportunities for trade in clean technologies are not limited to OECD countries. The emergence of markets in the developing world and economies in transition – China, India, Latin America, and Africa, as well as Eastern and Central Europe – will provide those who move quickly with tremendous economic opportunity. Indeed, over the next 20 years alone, the global market for climate-related technologies will be valued in the trillions of dollars. As developing countries continue to grow in the coming decades, Canada will be poised to export the very technologies that these economies will urgently need to develop in an environmentally sustainable way.

Developing countries' demand for clean technology will significantly increase if they are required to grow in an environmentally sustainable way, for example by decreasing their GHG emissions and other measures. By leading on Kyoto, Canada would have a greater say at the negotiation table about whether and when countries such as Brazil, China, and India come on board the global climate change regime. Ratification by industrialised countries such as Canada also creates an additional incentive for developing economies to commit to their own targets. In this way, Canada's commitment to Kyoto supports both its environmental and economic objectives. By ratifying Kyoto, Canada sent an important political signal that strengthens future markets for its environmentally friendly economic goods and services. Thus, in meeting its Kyoto targets, Canada will not only be contributing to emissions reductions and global sustainability; it will be at the forefront of an emerging world market and a fundamental transition of the global economy.

Also prominent in the rhetoric of Kyoto critics is the notion that Canada cannot afford to implement the agreement because its largest trading partner has rejected it. This argument confuses lack of leadership by the Bush administration on climate change with lack of action by American states, cities, companies, and citizens. Indeed, state and municipal governments in the U.S. are moving faster and further than their Canadian counterparts in reducing GHG emissions (Bramley 2002). Moreover, despite the Bush team's opposition to Kyoto, Washington still administers a much more substantial body of GHG-reducing measures than does Ottawa. At every level of government, Canada lags behind its U.S. counterparts in its efforts to curb climate change. If these trends continue, the U.S. may well shrink its GHG emissions in line with Kyoto targets despite not having formally ratified the accord. And although it is unlikely to do so under the Bush administration's watch, the U.S. may well ratify under a future administration. With U.S. ratification would come a stronger push for enforcement mechanisms, and thus potentially costly trade measures. So Canada has a choice: it can pay now or pay more later.

Although the U.S. appears to be making progress on climate change outside the Kyoto framework, Canada's track record remains very poor. In the absence of legally binding targets, Canada invoked the voluntary Rio pledge to stabilise its GHG emissions at the 1990 level by 2000. Instead, despite a slew of federal and provincial plans purporting to address climate change, Canada's emissions levels grew by 20 percent in the last decade and, in 1997, it abandoned the voluntary target altogether. Given the country's ever-growing emissions levels, the federal government estimates that Canada will need to reduce its current levels by 25 percent in order to meet its Kyoto target by 2010.

In short, implementing Kyoto will not only allow Canada to contribute to the global effort to curb climate change, it will have the practical effect of narrowing

– not widening – the gap with the United States. Moreover, Kyoto does not preclude Canada from strengthening its global commitments with national or indeed regional ones, such as under the North American Free Trade Agreement (NAFTA), provided these enhance rather than erase its Kyoto targets.

Currently, while the U.S. remains outside the global climate change regime, the demand for special emissions permits (which signatories to Kyoto can purchase to offset their excess emissions) will be lower, thereby reducing the price of such permits and thus the cost of complying with Kyoto targets.

The sale of emissions permits is one of several global market-based mechanisms under Kyoto that increase flexibility and reduce costs in terms of meeting targets. Other Kyoto schemes such as Joint Implementation and the Clean Development Mechanism also allow industrialised countries such as Canada to work with other countries so that not all implementation must be carried out domestically.

Kyoto: A Question of Credibility

Despite the initial praise it inspired in some international and environmental circles, Chrétien's commitment in Johannesburg was not clear-cut: for too long, Canada's position remained contingent upon two additional and improbable conditions, one national, the other international. This equivocation undermined Canada's credibility on this critical issue both at home and abroad. Far from re-establishing the country's credentials as an environmental champion, the confusion following the prime minister's remarks in Johannesburg alienated important stakeholders on all sides of this issue.

The international community, especially the European Union, would likely block any additional amendments to Kyoto, particularly those proposed by a country widely seen to have already watered down the accord. Indeed, Canada played an influential role throughout the Kyoto and other global climate negotiations by successfully securing a number of concessions which reflect its national interests. One such example is the inclusion of 'carbon sinks' in the Bonn agreement of November 2001: Canada helped to negotiate credits for expanding the size and carbon storage of its managed forests. The increased range and flexibility of mechanisms countries may employ to meet their commitments must be acknowledged as a diplomatic success for Canada. However, this same initiative has been criticised as a substantive weakness from an environmental perspective given that it effectively entails fewer real reductions in greenhouse gas emissions.

In this light, the position – long held by several prominent Canadian political and business leaders – that Canada should not ratify Kyoto because it is too feeble proves perverse. If Kyoto does not do enough to curb climate change, it is in part because countries such as Canada have consistently negotiated additional concessions (such as getting credits for its forests as carbon sinks) that have served to weaken the protocol's effect in terms of real reductions in GHG emissions. Having successfully softened the accord, Canada's walking away from it would have been viewed by the international community as an act of bad faith, if not betrayal. All too often, this is the U.S. approach to international treaties, not the Canadian one.

Concretely, rejection of Kyoto would have weakened Canada's influence in future rounds of global climate negotiations, which could eventually to bring key countries such as India, China, and Brazil into the fold. Thus, from an international perspective, non-ratification would have damaged Canada's reputation and its leverage in future international negotiations on critical issues beyond climate change.

Environmentalists who strongly support Kyoto viewed the Johannesburg announcement as a last-ditch, legacy-driven effort to reverse the country's decade-long slide from environmental leader to laggard. Many perceived the belated support for the accord as an act of 'ecological opportunism' stemming from Chrétien's preoccupation with his legacy rather than from a real concern for the environment.[10] Nonetheless, despite private musings regarding the motivation and timing of the Johannesburg pledge, most environmentalists expressed public support for the decision.

Business may resent the added burden of having to scramble to meet Kyoto targets within a much tighter timeframe. Had Canada not only signed but also ratified the Protocol following its adoption in 1997, energy producers and consumers would have had more time to transition to a cleaner, less carbon-dependent economy. As noted above, the policy confusion created by the government's protracted hesitation regarding Kyoto also proved problematic for corporate decision making, which thrives in conditions of certainty. It is time to bring clarity and get on with the business of implementation, which is what the corporate community does well: set clear rules, and it will work to meet them.

Some provinces decried the federal government's breech of public trust in changing the focus of its consultations on Kyoto from ratification to implementation. Alberta even threatened to challenge the federal government's authority legally in this regard. There is little doubt that the federal government circumvented a public consultation process that it had itself laid out. However, as will be argued below, this process was ill conceived and over-extended from the start. Consent of the provinces is not required for ratification of international agreements; this authority rests strictly with the federal government. Still, given the provinces' shared jurisdiction over natural resources, the federal government has a responsibility to consult its provincial and territorial counterparts on how to implement these treaties. It must work to involve the provinces, particularly in areas of action under their jurisdiction. Indeed, without securing the full co-operation of the provinces, a number of key instruments may be unavailable for implementation.

Therefore, if one views ratification as a matter of foreign policy (to be exercised by the federal government for the common good) and implementation as a matter of domestic environmental and economic policy (to be jointly agreed by the federal and provincial governments), the revised focus of the deliberations – from consultations on whether to ratify to real negotiations on how to implement – is not only more acceptable, but is preferable (notwithstanding the delay in moving forward with both ratification and, now, implementation).

Kyoto: A Question of Consultations

Contrary to popular belief, Canada's commitment to ratify the Kyoto Protocol did not come with the Chrétien's pledge at the Johannesburg Summit in September 2002. The government initially signalled its intent to ratify Kyoto when it signed the accord on 29 April 1998.[11] It was not until November 2002 that the government released its draft Climate Change Plan for Canada was published (Canada 2002a), with the final plan, Project Green, published on 13 April 2005. Why then did it take so long for the government to produce a viable national action plan to implement the agreement? This failure is not, as some would have it, due to lack of consultations or technical know-how; Canada has some of world's best people in both the private and public sectors working on climate change issues. The failure to craft a clear, comprehensive, and timely implementation programme was due purely to a lack of political will.

Complaints regarding the federal government's failure to consult fully with the provinces, key sectors, and stakeholders are disingenuous in light of the real record. There have been more extensive consultations on Kyoto than on any other treaty signed by Canada. The objection here is not to consultations *per se*, but to their selective use for purely opportunistic or public relations purposes. As decisions once enacted by elected representatives in national legislatures are increasingly made by non-elected officials at international summits, it is critical that citizens and parliamentarians become more informed and involved at all levels and stages of the policy-making process. But tackling the so-called democratic deficit in international decision making should not be a discriminatory undertaking; nor should it be used as a delay tactic regarding matters on which the government would rather avoid taking decisive action.

Ottawa's mistake lies not in its failure to consult but, rather, in its failure to consult the right people on the right question at the right time. Selective discussions with elites, experts, and special interest groups were often framed by whether to ratify Kyoto, when instead the government should have been consulting Canadians directly on how to implement the accord from the start. The delay between ratification and the announcement of the implementation plan late in 2002 prolonged a decade of policy confusion, procrastination, and vacillation on the critical issue of climate change.

Although Canada's ratification readiness would have been greatly enhanced by having an implementation plan in place, the foot-dragging of the previous decade made it clear that no such plan would materialise until ratification was assured (McGraw 2002c). This argument was based on the practical concern that the protracted debate on ratification was running out the clock on implementation. The logical conclusion was that, for better or worse, implementation was contingent upon ratification. However, the Canadian government's lack of follow-up after the December 2002 decision to adopt Kyoto lent credence to the opposite conclusion. It may have been more responsible to insist on a clear action plan to ensure Canada could meet its climate change targets before making such an important commitment.

Kyoto: A Question of Commitment

Once Canada was legally committed to Kyoto, implementation of the plan that followed ratification was of central importance. With ratification, Kyoto became domestic law and Canada has until between 2008 and 2012 as its deadline for achieving the plan, not for developing it. This reality check led some to want to abandon Kyoto altogether. It led others to the opposite conclusion: Canada must elevate Kyoto as a matter of national priority, and actively engage stakeholders on how – not whether – to achieve its implementation.

Whatever side of the issue one espouses, it is clear that the government mismanaged Kyoto from the beginning. No doubt, the protocol is a political and technical minefield, but Ottawa exacerbated the issue's inherent complexity and controversy through continued confusion. Instead of addressing Kyoto as a matter of public policy, federal and provincial governments have treated it as a matter of public relations. In the case of Kyoto, the federal government broke many basic rules of crafting and selling public policy: it should define the problem and get the public to accept it; it should propose a solution and consult on it; it should develop and negotiate plan to implement it, and accept the consequences.

For Canada to meet its Kyoto targets, it needed a national plan based on a truly national effort: a renewed federal, provincial, territorial, and municipal undertaking that would involve stakeholders from industry and labour as well as environmental and consumer groups. Demand for public information and stakeholder engagement is high. In the first three weeks after the draft climate change plan was released in 2002, the federal government received more than 1000 written submissions by individuals and its website had roughly 100 000 downloads. A cross-Canada 'Commission on Climate Change' might have been an effective way to engage concerned citizens and their elected representatives directly in the process.

Perhaps Canada should follow the example of Norway and other parties to Kyoto. After assembling a team of high-profile and well-respected individuals both to champion the accord with domestic audiences and to co-ordinate its implementation, Norway produced a solid national action plan in a matter of six weeks.

For Canada to reach its Kyoto targets it requires not only effective actions and measures to reduce GHG emissions, but also effective governance systems to guide the implementation process. Building on core democratic principles such as leadership, transparency, accountability, enforcement, and engagement, the first task in the post-ratification process should have been rebuilding confidence among key stakeholders so that implementation would be both credible and predictable. Indeed, national stakeholder workshops on climate change were held in June 2002, involving 14 day-long meetings in every province and territory with more 900 participants, to discuss four broad policy options for achieving the targets (Canada 2002b). Two key co-ordinating mechanisms were proposed, the first being an efficient, central focal point for the federal government. Given that responsibilities for climate change lie with many agencies, and that accountabilities need to be assigned to these same agencies, a federal climate change coordination office is needed that would have the necessary authority and the technical knowledge. Second, an effective inter-jurisdictional body is needed to operate at the political level as well as the bureaucratic level. The National Air Issues Coordinating Committee served this role until 2001 and could have been resurrected, or a new one – a 'National Climate Change Action Committee' – could be created.

During a special presentation to parliamentarians during the ratification debate, George Greene (2002) concluded that an effective governance system would need clear and transparent decision making, accountability for delivering on commitments and obligations, and oversight and monitoring to ensure progress is made. He called for effective engagement of the public and key interests in moving forward.

Any national initiative must also go beyond Kyoto *per se* to address global climate change. The continuing rise in Canada's GHG emissions places the country on a path that is far from sustainable. This trend must be reversed: the consensus of international scientists is that global emissions must fall by up to 75 percent in this century alone if we are to avoid dangerous human-caused disruption of our climate. Such projections underscore the importance of Kyoto's modest 6 percent target as a vital first step in bringing Canada into the carbon-constrained world of the new millennium.

In recent years, however, the Canadian government has proven it can muster the massive political will and resources to tackle seemingly intractable problems successfully: the country's fiscal deficit provides a compelling case in point. The rationale presented was short-term pain for long-term gain: it would be irresponsible to leave such a burden on future generations. The same logic applies, if not more so, to the ecological debt. If Canada can mobilise political will for something as seemingly mundane as a fiscal deficit, surely it can make headway on the environmental deficit.

In public opinion polls, the environment consistently ranks as a core value among Canadians. It is central to both its national economy and its national identity. Citizens are experiencing the effects of environmental deterioration – from increasingly volatile weather patterns to suffocating smog and poisoned water – all around them, and they want action. Among a broad range of worthy ecological issues and initiatives, Kyoto has become the litmus test on the environment. Any government, sector, or individual seen to be stalling on Kyoto will be seen to be stalling on the environment.

In a survey of Canadian values conducted by Michael Marzolini (2002), a majority of Canadians expressed strong support for state action on the environment and a preference for government's role in helping to equip them for the future. This challenge raises a question posed by Thomas Homer-Dixon (2001): 'Can we generate and implement useful ideas fast enough to solve the very problems – environmental, social and technological – we've created?'

Ultimately, curbing climate change will constitute an unprecedented test not only of technical know-how, but also of public will and political leadership. Kyoto will help determine whether Canada's citizens and leaders are up to the challenge of bringing our country and our economy into the 21st century.

Kyoto: A Question of Consistency

Having ratified the Kyoto Protocol does not preclude Canadians from developing a made-in-Canada action plan on climate change; it compels us to do so. Kyoto provides an internationally agreed framework for meeting targets on GHG reductions within a specified timeframe. It does not dictate how countries are to meet these objectives. In fact, through a series of global market-based mechanisms, the accord augments, not diminishes, the flexibility with which individual countries can meet their climate change commitments. In short, Kyoto sets the context for action on climate change, but does not dictate how a country meets its international commitments.

The real issue is whether Canada will address climate change within a global framework, or whether it will adopt a strictly national (or indeed provincial or sectoral) approach to what is a global problem. In adopting Kyoto, Canada opted to extend its general preference for multilateralism to climate change.

Canada has consistently expressed strong support for a multilateral approach to solving international problems, such as Iraq and its potential use of weapons of mass destruction (WMD) beyond its own borders. Just as it opposed the U.S. unilateral stance *vis-à-vis* Iraq, so too has it rejected strictly unilateral approaches to curbing climate change. On both the issues of Iraq and climate change, anything short of globally sanctioned action represent not only diplomatic defeats, but sub-optimal solutions to what are ultimately global security threats.[12]

In the context of international relations, 'hard' security and trade matters have traditionally trumped 'soft' social and environmental ones. The reality, however, is that ecological degradation is a growing source of conflict in the world, and thus represents a real threat to collective security. Pervasive climate change has been described as second only to nuclear war in terms of its catastrophic effects globally. In this sense, climate change is far more than a matter of environmental policy; it is increasingly a matter of national security.

The evidence underlying global climate change is objective, far-reaching, and compelling. Indeed, few issues on the global agenda have galvanised such widespread consensus within political and scientific communities. The Intergovernmental Panel on Climate Change (IPCC), representing 1500 of the world's leading atmospheric scientists, economists, and technologists, has repeatedly concluded that the current scope, scale, and pace of climate change are unprecedented, and that human activity – mainly through the production of GHGs such as carbon dioxide – is increasingly influential in this regard.[13] Canadian scientists from across the country have been active in their areas of expertise in the work of this international panel. And even sceptical nations find the science convincing. Thirteen national academies of science, including the U.S. counterpart with members hand-picked by George Bush himself, concur with these findings.

Still, international affairs are not susceptible to courtroom proofs beyond reasonable doubt. It is precisely for this reason that a precautionary principle underlies many environmental agreements such as the Kyoto Protocol. While the U.S. (and to some extent Canada) has sought to expel direct reference to this principle in international treaties, its intent is straightforward: where there is a threat of serious or irreversible harm, lack of scientific certainty should not preclude action. Otherwise, positive proof would come too late. The principle essentially asserts that it is better to err on the side of action that turns out to be unnecessary than to expose ourselves to preventable devastation through inaction.

According to this logic, Kyoto (as a first, albeit far more timid, global step) in a way is to climate change what an internationally sanctioned pre-emptive attack might be to Iraq's use of WMD. Such an analogy will undoubtedly irritate environmentalists and military strategists alike, but it serves to highlight the need to apply a consistent standard of evidence as a basis for action across a range of international issues. Indeed, it could be argued that the burden of proof needed to justify a military action, which may involve loss of human life, should be higher than that required for a nonviolent response to an environmental danger: implementing Kyoto may cost jobs (although it may also create some), but it will not cost lives (indeed, it may save some, particularly in small-island developing states that do not have the means to adapt to climate change).

Conclusion

The Kyoto Protocol represents the most important international initiative to date for combating rising GHG emissions. Indeed, Kyoto is the only global game in town for addressing global warming and other consequences of climate change. The result of ten years of tough negotiations in which Canada played an influential role, the accord reflects tradeoffs among more than 150 states with divergent interests at vastly different stages of their economic development.[14] Significantly, Kyoto recognises that it is industrialised countries that have been producing the majority of the globe's anthropogenic GHG emissions, and that it is these countries that must lead the global effort to reduce these. Kyoto also acknowledges that developing countries must have room to grow their economies while preparing to assume their own targets in the future. As such, for critics of Kyoto to suggest that developing and least-developed countries are somehow getting a free ride is simply misguided.

Domestic disagreements within Canada about how to address climate change only serve to reinforce Kyoto's value as an international agreement. Indeed, the protocol embodies liberal principles – such as intergenerational equity, common but differentiated responsibility, the polluter pays principle and the precautionary principle – that may prove instructive for Canada as it seeks establish a fair and equitable national climate change regime that does not unduly burden particular provinces, sectors, or stakeholders.[15]

After more than a decade of international negotiations and national consultations on climate change, Canada's Parliament voted overwhelmingly in favour of ratifying the Kyoto Protocol on 9 December 2002. The prime minister signed an executive order-in-council that finalised the ratification process on 16 December 2002. The following day, environment minister David Anderson deposed the instrument of ratification with the UN for formal international recognition of Canada's legally binding commitment to the Kyoto Protocol. With this act, Canada became the 100th country to become a party to the protocol; it provided positive encouragement to countries such as Russia, which in turn ratified the protocol on 18 November 2004. Canada's international efforts should focus on securing the support of uncommitted countries, particularly major GHG-producing ones – without which an effective climate change regime cannot operate effectively. Domestic efforts should be devoted to building credibility and certainty into implementation initiatives. Although Canada's ratification of the Kyoto Protocol is now complete, the contentious nature of the debate surrounding this decision guarantees that the domestic implementation process will be dynamic, if not divisive.

However, the longer Canada postpones effective implementation, the more difficult – if not impossible – it will be to meet its Kyoto targets. Failure to meet global climate change commitments could well become a self-fulfilling prophecy.

Notes

1   An earlier version of this chapter was published in Axworthy and Aster (2003). A revised and update version of the publication is used here with their permission.

2   The Earth Summit – known officially at the United Nations Conference on Environment and Development (UNCED) – marked the 20th anniversary of the United Nations Conference on the Human Environment held in Stockholm. Canadian businessman and diplomat Maurice Strong spearheaded both summits.

3   For analyses of sustainable development in the Canadian context, see O.P. Dwivedi, Patrick Kyba, Peter Stoett, and Rebecca Tiessen (2001) and Environment Canada (2003).

4   For a survey of national initiatives to implement commitments made in at the Johannesburg Summit, see Désirée McGraw (2003).

5   For an examination of the biosafety negotiations, see John Vogler and Désirée McGraw (2000). For an overview of the biodiversity negotiations, see McGraw (2002a). See also McGraw (2002b).

6   For a more complete analysis of Canada's environmental performance throughout the 1990s, a special report by Canada's Commissioner on Environment and Sustainable Development (2002) entitled 'The Commissioner's Perspective: 2002 – The Decade after Rio' as well as reports from 1997 to 2001. See also nongovernmental publications, such as 'Rio Reports' by the Sierra Club of Canada (annual) and 'Shadow Reports' by the Canadian Environmental Network (Skuce 2002).

7   Ratification is one of several formal processes (alongside acceptance, approval, and accession) by which an international treaty becomes domestic law. For an excellent analysis of Canada's domestic application of international law, see Jutta Brunnée and Stephen Toope (2002). It has been argued that Canada's legal obligations to combat climate change stem not only from its adherence to the UNFCCC but also to other treaties in the fields of environment, human rights, trade, and investment. See Carlsson (2002).

8   According to Article 3(1) of the Kyoto Protocol, parties included in Annex I (industrialised countries and those in transition to market-based economies) 'shall, individually or jointly, ensure that their aggregate anthropogenic carbon dioxide equivalent emissions of

the greenhouse gases ... do not exceed their assigned amounts ... with a view to reducing their overall emissions of such gases by at least 5 per cent below 1990 levels in the commitment period 2008 to 2012' (UNFCCC 1992). Moreover, paragraph 2 states that 'each Party included in Annex I shall, by 2005, have made demonstrable progress in achieving its commitments under this Protocol', although Article 4(6) provides that those countries listed in Annex I that are moving to a market economy are accorded a 'certain degree of flexibility' in meeting their commitments.

9   Canada ratified the Kyoto Protocol on 17 December 2002.

10 In August 2002 – just days before the Kyoto pledge in Johannesburg – Chrétien announced that he would retire as prime minister in February 2004, although in fact Paul Martin took over as prime minister on 12 December 2003.

11 Although a treaty is adopted collectively by the international community (for example, via the UN), it is signed by individual countries. In international law, signature represents the first formal step on the road to ratification. Ratification by a requisite number of countries (normally specified in the treaty itself) ensures that a treaty enters into force, and thus becomes legally binding on all parties (that is, all countries that have ratified the agreement). Transforming an international agreement into domestic law is done differently in different countries. In Canada, this occurs through the adoption of legislation at the federal or provincial levels (and sometimes both levels) that creates domestic legal obligations consistent with the agreement. In some cases, the agreement as a whole can also be included in a statute that is adopted by the legislative or executive branch of government. Domestic implementation can also be accomplished in whole or in part by administrative acts of the governments of the individual parties, such as the elaboration of national action plans.

12 Similarly, as there is little doubt that the U.S. would prevail militarily against Iraq, a made-in-the-U.S. alternative to Kyoto could undoubtedly help address climate change. But international relations are about means, not just ends. Let it be stated emphatically that there is no moral equivalence between the potential deployment of WMD by Saddam Hussein and the dangers posed by climate change. While the former would represent the deliberately evil act of a single despot, the latter reflects the seemingly benign actions of countless producers and consumers throughout the world (mainly in industrialised countries). Notwithstanding this important distinction, there is a clear double standard in international affairs: the burden of proof for taking collective action against an environmental threat appears to exceed that required for responding to a military one.

13 The World Meteorological Organization (WMO) and the United Nations Environment Programme (UNEP) established the IPCC in 1988. The role of the panel is to assess the scientific, technical, and socioeconomic information relevant for the understanding of the risk of human-induced climate change. The panel has produced three key reports: the 'First Assessment Report', released in 1990, was instrumental informing the negotiations leading to the adoption of the UNFCC in 1992; the 'Second Assessment Report: Climate Change 1995' provided key input to the negotiations that led to the adoption of the Kyoto Protocol in 1997 (IPCC 1995b); the 'Third Assessment Report: Climate Change 2001', published the results of findings on climate change in relation to scientific basis, mitigation, and impacts, adaptation, and vulnerability (IPCC 1995a).

14 For an examination of these negotiations, see Irving Mintzer and J.A. Leonard (1994) and Matthew Patterson (1996).

15 Many of these principles are enshrined in the 1992 Rio Declaration (UNCED 1992). See also Philippe Sands (1996).

References

Axworthy, Thomas and Howard Aster, eds. (2003). *Searching for the New Liberalism*. Mosaic Press, Oakville ON.

Bernstein, Steven (2002). 'Liberal Environmentalism and Global Environmental Governance'. *Global Environmental Politics* vol. 2, no. 3, pp. 1–16.

Boustie, Sylvie, Marlo Raynolds, and Matthew Bramley (2002). 'How Ratifying the Kyoto Protocol Will Benefit Canada's Competitiveness'. Pembina Institute, <www.pembina.org/pdf/publications/competitiveness_report.pdf> (November 2005).

Bramley, Matthew (2002). 'A Comparison of Current Government Action on Climate Change in the U.S. and Canada'. Pembina Institute, Drayton Valley AB. <www.pembina.org/pdf/publications/reportcard_020517.pdf> (November 2005).

Brunnée, Jutta and Stephen J. Toope (2002). 'A Hesitant Embrace: The Application of International Law by Canadian Courts'. In D.M. McRae, ed., *Canadian Yearbook of International Law*, vol. 40. University of British Columbia Press, Vancouver.

Canada (2002a). 'Climate Change Plan for Canada'. 21 November. <www.climatechange.gc.ca/english/publications/plan_for_canada> (November 2005).

Canada (2002b). 'A Discussion Paper on Canada's Contribution to Addressing Climate Change'. <www.climatechange.gc.ca/english/publications/canadascontribution> (November 2005).

Carlsson, Lina, Ahsfaq Khalfan, Marie-Claire Cordonnier Segger, et al. (2002). 'International Legal Obligations and Sustainable Climate Change in Canada'. Legal brief for the consideration of the ratification and implementation of the Kyoto Protocol in Canada. Centre for International Sustainable Development Law, Montreal. <www.cisdl.org/pdf/brief_climate.pdf> (November 2005).

Commissioner of the Environment and Sustainable Development (Canada) (2002). 'The Commissioner's Perspective: 2002 – The Decade After Rio'. Report of the Commissioner of the Environment and Sustainable Development. <www.oag-bvg.gc.ca/domino/reports.nsf/html/c20021000ce.html> (November 2005).

Dwivedi, O.P., Patrick Kyba, Peter Stoett, et al. (2001). *Sustainable Development and Canada: National and International Perspectives*. Broadview Press, Toronto.

Environment Canada (2002). 'Sustainable Development: A Canadian Perspective'. <www.wssd.gc.ca/canada_at_wssd/canadian_perspective_e.pdf> (November 2005).

Environment Canada (2003). 'Sustainable Development Strategy 2001–2003'. <www.ec.gc.ca/sd-dd_consult/index_e.cfm> (November 2005).

Greene, George (2002). 'Putting in Place Governance and Engagement Processes for Implementation'. Notes for presentation to 'Beyond Kyoto: A Win-Win Climate Change Action Plan for Canada', Citizen-Government Dialogue, 4 December. Ottawa.

Heaps, Toby A.A. (2002). 'Kyoto: An Innovation Agenda in Disguise'. *Corporate Knights* November, pp. 10–14. <www.corporateknights.ca/content/page.asp?name=Kyoto_innovation_agenda> (November 2005).

Homer-Dixon, Thomas (2001). *The Ingenuity Gap: Can We Solve the Problems of the Future?* Vintage, Toronto.

Intergovernmental Panel on Climate Change (1995a). 'IPCC Third Assessment Report: Climate Change 2001'. <www.ipcc.ch/pub/un/syreng/spm.pdf> (November 2005).

Intergovernmental Panel on Climate Change (1995b). 'IPCC Second Assessment: Climate Change 1995'. <www.ipcc.ch/pub/sarsyn.htm> (November 2005).

Marzolini, Michael (2002). 'Polling Alone: Canadian Values and Liberalism'. Paper presented to 'Searching for the New Liberalism' conference, Munk Centre for International

Studies, 27–29 September. Toronto. <www.pollara.ca/new/Library/SURVEYS/newliberalism-feb203.pdf> (November 2005).

McGraw, Désirée (2002a). 'The Convention on Biological Diversity: Key Characteristics and Implications for Implementation'. *Review of European Community and International Law* vol. 11, no. 1, pp. 17–28.

McGraw, Désirée (2002b). 'The Story of the Biodiversity Convention: From Negotiation to Implementation'. In P. Le Prestre, ed., *Governing Global Biodiversity: The Evolution and Implementaiton of the Convention on Biological Diversity.* Ashgate, Aldershot.

McGraw, Désirée (2002c). 'How Fast Should We Go on Kyoto?' *Globe and Mail*, 22 October, p. A19.

McGraw, Désirée (2002d). 'Ten Years after the Earth Summit'. *Montreal Gazette*, 1 June, p. B7.

McGraw, Désirée (2003). 'The Case for Kyoto: A Question of Competitiveness, Consultations, Credibility, Commitment, and Consistency'. *Policy Options* vol. December-January, pp. 35–39. <www.irpp.org/po/archive/dec02/mcgraw.pdf> (November 2005).

McGraw, Désirée and Johannah Bernstein (2003). 'WSSD Follow-Up Approaches in Select OECD Countries: An Analytical Overview'. Report commissioned by Stratos Inc. for the Earth Summit 2002 Canadian Secretariat.

Mintzer, Irving M. and J.A. Leonard (1994). *Negotiating Climate Change.* Cambridge University Press and Stockholm Environment Institute, Cambridge.

Patterson, Matthew (1996). *Global Warming and Global Politics.* Routledge, London.

Sands, Philippe (1996). *Principles of International Environmental Law: Frameworks, Standards, and Implementation.* Vol. 1. Manchester University Press, Mancheseter.

Sierra Club of Canada (annual). 'Rio Report'. <www.sierraclub.ca/national/rio> (November 2005).

Skuce, Nikki (2002). 'Summit or Plummit: A Call for Canadian Leadership 10 Years after Rio'. Canadian Environmental Network's Forum on the World Summit for Sustainable Development, <www.cen-rce.org/wssd/reporteng.html> (November 2005).

Toner, Glen (2000). 'Canada: From Early Frontrunner to Plodding Anchorman'. In W.M. Lafferty and J. Meadowcroft, eds., *Implementing Sustainable Development: Strategies and Initiatives in High Consumption Societies*, pp. 53–84. Oxford University Press, New York.

United Nations Conference on Environment and Development (1992). 'Rio Declaration on Environment and Development'. 14 June. Rio. <www.unep.org/Documents/Default.asp?DocumentID=78 &ArticleID=1163> (November 2005).

United Nations Framework Convention on Climate Change (1992). 'Text of the Convention'. Kyoto Protocol to the United Nations Framework Convention on Climate Change. <unfccc.int/essential_background/kyoto_protocol/items/1678.php> (November 2005).

Vogler, John and Désirée McGraw (2000). 'An International Environmental Regime for Biotechnology'. In A. Russell and J. Vogler, eds., *The International Politics of Biotechnology: Investigating Global Futures*, pp. 123–141. Manchester University Press, Manchester.

World Commission on Environment and Development (1987). *Our Common Future* (Brundtland Report). Oxford University Press, Oxford.

Chapter 19

Globalisation of the Marketplace

Michael E. Cloghesy

Is the globalisation of the marketplace a positive factor in improving the quality of the environment in developing countries? Clearly, this is not a given. Nor is it an automatic consequence of opening a national marketplace to the world. Rather, it is an issue of some complexity.

Although there is evidence that suggests that industrialisation can degrade the environment in developing countries, especially in its early stages, it has also been demonstrated that the quantity of pollutants decreases as the per capita gross domestic product (GDP) increases. For globalisation to help improve the quality of the environment, other factors must be present. Of particular importance are good governance, stable government, realistic legislation, an appropriate regulatory infrastructure, and resources to enforce the law. Responsible corporate behaviour from multinational corporations (MNCs) often helps. This is especially the case if the local government has endorsed the concept of sustainable development and is prepared to work with industry and civil society to set objectives that will enhance the quality of the environment and ensure a viable economy at the same time. Civil society, both within and beyond the business community, has an important role to play in developing countries to ensure that the national government moves in the direction of sustainability.

Environmental Quality and Economic Development

Jean-Yves Duclos (2001) has suggested that environmental degradation is usually a consequence of demographics, in particular, population density. He also suggests that the relation between environmental quality and standard of living is a bell-shaped curve, referred to as an environmental Kuznets curve (see Figure 19.1). At one end of the horizontal axis is the early industrial state, and at the other end is the economically developed state. The vertical axis relates to the degree of degradation from an environmental perspective. According to Duclos, both the early industrial and developed countries would have a relatively higher level of environmental quality, whereas countries in transition would have the greatest level of environmental degradation. The environmental Kuznets curve shows the beginning of an improvement in environmental quality once the per capita GDP increases past a certain level, in this case US$5000.

An example of this pattern was given at a meeting on sustainable development that took place prior to the Summit of the Americas in Quebec City in April 2002. There, a government representative from a South American country indicated that most of the pollution stemming from mining in that country was related to very small-scale (artisanal) mining operations rather than from multinational state-of-the-art operations.

In most instances, the environment is not a major priority with poor countries. Environment becomes an important issue only when a certain level of quality of life – the basics of food, health, clean water, and shelter – is attained and there are sufficient resources available to address environmental problems. Clearly, there is a direct relationship between the desire to improve the quality of the environment and the standard of living in a particular country.

The Economist (2001) suggests that pressure from environmental groups and other market forces provide the critical link in this transition. They compel companies to clean up their act. Thus, there is a trend toward basic standards of environmental quality on an international level:

each environmental impact is mitigated by far more powerful forces. For a start, trade spurs economic growth, which is the ultimate guarantor of greater environmental protection: history shows that, as people get richer, they begin to demand a cleaner environment – and can afford to pay for it. What is more, trade liberalisation exposes filthy and inefficient domestic industries to competition, and attracts foreign direct investment; these in turn spur investment in newer, and therefore cleaner, technologies.

Figure 19.1 Environmental Kuznets Curve

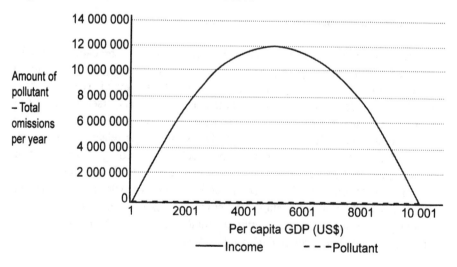

The Role of the Private Sector and National Government

Permanent and durable solutions are needed to develop the economy in poorer countries. For private sector investments and job creation to occur, there must be good governance, democracy, good legal infrastructure, absence of corruption, and a stable government. The priorities of private firms are survival and maximising profits. Major corporations and multinationals have made significant progress in the area of responsible corporate governance over the past 20 to 30 years. They have been influenced by market forces and have developed codes of ethics and defined corporate social responsibilities.

Antiglobalists fear that globalisation will make governments disappear. Today 51 percent of the biggest economies in the world are corporations. Noreena Hertz (2001) implies that sales equate with power. This view can be contested in that governments always retain their power over the people.

The role of government in developing countries is essential to ensuring that globalisation works for them, not against them. Supachai Panitchpakdi (2002), the director general of the World Trade Organization (WTO), states that

> while there is incontrovertible economic evidence that open markets and free trade hold great benefits, it is equally true that trade can create losers. If the global trading system is to continue to progress along the path of trade liberalization – as I believe it must – governments must take adequate measures to ensure that those who have lost out are looked after.
>
> Without such measures political support for trade liberalization will become increasingly unsustainable.

He goes on to say that bodies such as the WTO should not impose global rules regarding social measures, which should be left to governments to implement according to their own circumstances.

Small and medium-sized enterprises are the most at risk. They require support during transition. Environmental legislation and regulations must be put in place in the context of sustainable development and there must be open dialogue between corporations and government.

A good example of progress is the case of the *maquiladoras* in Mexico. Initially, there was little or no existent legislation on environment. Then legislation was put in place, but there were no resources to enforce it. Currently, there is more enforcement and conditions have improved.

Philippe Legrain (2002) shows that economic integration is the only hope for many of the world's poorest people, providing illustrations from Vietnam, South Korea, Mexico, and many other developing countries. Thomas Friedman (2000) suggests that globalisation is not a choice but a reality. However, Legrain shows that government has great sway over both the extent and the forces of economic integration. According to the World Bank, in 2002 GDP per person rose by 5 percent per year in those developing countries that had opened their economies the most to international trade and investments ('GDP per Person' 2002). Thus, there is sufficient evidence to demonstrate that once poorer countries satisfy their primary objectives of providing food, basic health, and shelter to their people, economic development is their next objective, which equates to increased wealth and quality of life, and raising environmental standards.

Globalisation in the context of open markets will provide investments to develop industries and create jobs and wealth, which will allow for addressing environmental problems. MNCs, mainly because of global market forces, will generally raise living standards in developing countries and conduct their business in a responsible way. These firms will be in a position to assist local governments in setting up an infrastructure in the context of sustainable development. The key to achieve success in implementing a viable economy and enjoy all its social benefits is good governance and willingness on the part of the developing country's government to commit to reform and the elimination of corruption.

Toward Public-Private Partnerships

Industrialisation has the potential to degrade the environment in developing countries, especially in its early stages. Globalisation of the marketplace does not guarantee that the quality of the environment will improve. Other factors must be present. The most important are good governance, implying a stable government devoid of corruption with realistic legislation, and a regulatory infrastructure and resources to enforce the law. Responsible corporate behaviour from MNCs will, in most cases, provide a constructive context to move ahead. This is the case especially if the local government has endorsed the concept of sustainable development and is prepared to work with industry and civil society to set objectives that will enhance the quality of the environment and, at the same time, ensure a vibrant economy. To a large extent, responsible firms are prepared to work as partners with government to achieve these goals.

The main problem is that a number of developing nations, particularly in Africa, are not interested in seeing the good governance agenda move forward. This is in part because they want to preserve the *status quo* and retain power in the hands of a few corrupt officials. At the World Summit on Sustainable Development (WSSD) in Johannesburg in 2002, certain developing countries were reluctant to move ahead with the good governance proposal. Their main objective was to obtain funding from rich countries without any such preconditions. This was viewed by most countries present as being no longer acceptable. Governments of developed countries are no longer prepared to hand out funds that end up in private bank accounts. As Canadian environment minister David Anderson stated clearly at one of the Canadian delegation's meetings at the WSSD, Canada tried to implement government-to-government programmes but they did not produce the expected results. Now, the federal government wants to work with the private sector to achieve sustainable development on a worldwide basis. This implies that although the private sector may have the resources, it needs a good governance context in which to operate.

In short, globalisation offers an opportunity to improve the quality of life, including the environment. But without a good governance context this process will not occur. Few companies will invest in a country that is unstable politically and corrupt. The biggest disappointment that came out of the Johannesburg Summit was that a number of developing countries did not want to commit to the good governance process. Thus, progress for these countries is at a standstill.

Given the appropriate context – where good governance is in place – globalisation of the marketplace can indeed improve the quality of life including the environment in developing countries. But it is not a perfect world. Eradicating corruption and ensuring responsible behaviour on the part of the private sector is more easily said than done.

There are perhaps other means of accomplishing the objective of providing a better quality of life for all. In the meantime, globalisation can provide a tangible means to achieve progress in this area. However, civil society, including the private sector, has an important role to play in developing countries to ensure that the government in place moves in the right direction, which in this case, is sustainability.

References

Duclos, Jean-Yves (2001). 'La croissance protège l'environnement'. *La Press*, 25 November, p. A13.

Economist (2001). 'Economic Man, Cleaner Planet'. *Economist* 29 September, p. 103.

Friedman, Thomas L. (2000). *The Lexus and the Olive Tree*. Rev. ed. Farrar Straus Giroux, New York.

'GDP per Person' (2002). *Economist*, 24 November, p. 74.

Hertz, Noreena (2001). *The Silent Takeover: Global Capitalism and the Death of Democracy*. Free Press, New York.

Legrain, Philippe (2002). *Open World: The Truth about Globalization*. Abacus, London.

Panitchpakdi, Supachai (2002). 'Open Markets, But Look After the Losers'. *International Herald Tribune*, 21 October, p. 10.

PART VI
CONCLUSION

Chapter 20

Civil Society and Institutions of Global Governance

Bill Graham

Throughout a long political career, the American congressman Tip O'Neill was known for his maxim 'All politics is local'. More recently, the American journalist Thomas Friedman has pronounced that 'all politics is global'. In a typically Canadian spirit of conciliation and diplomacy, one can conclude that both of them are right.

Problems of global scope are being felt locally around the world. The political burdens and challenges they create are local as well as global. Such conditions of interdependence and complexity highlight the need for strong institutions of global governance, which alone are capable of guiding and coordinating efforts to address global crises. At all levels of governance, the support of civil society is vital for ensuring the integrity and soundness of policy making. At the international level, civil society plays a key role both in supporting institutions of global governance and in fostering the climate of public opinion necessary for these institutions to succeed.

The Interdependence of Local and Global Concerns

In an increasingly interdependent world it is amply clear that all politics is local and global at the same time. On virtually every level of every public concern, problems and opportunities of global scope intersect with local realities.

Take two prominent issues in the Canadian news: the proposed ratification of the Kyoto Protocol and the treatment of Canadian residents at the U.S. border. In both of these cases, issues facing people in their daily lives intersect with environmental, economic, and security conditions of global scope. In fact, domestic political issues today can seldom be addressed without considering the foreign context framing them.

Conversely, it is also clear that problems on a global scale can be tackled only by taking international strategies down to the national, regional, and local levels. If one considers some of the most urgent crises now facing the world, one sees vast environmental degradation, endemic poverty in Africa and elsewhere in contrast with the great wealth in North America and Europe, health pandemics such as HIV/AIDS, the existence of weapons of mass destruction (WMD), and organised crime and terrorism on an international scale.

The Need for Strong Global Governance Institutions

Such conditions of interdependence and complexity highlight the need for strong institutions of global governance, which alone are capable of guiding and co-ordinating efforts to address global crises. The terrorist attacks in New York and Washington in 2001, and subsequent events in Bali, Moscow, the Middle East, Madrid, and London have brought home a new awareness of the world's interdependence.

All citizens have a new sense of their vulnerability to forces and events beyond their borders and beyond their nation's control. In this critical area of security, as well as in others such as trade, health, and the environment, Canadians are committed to a multilateral approach. They and their government believe that working through global institutions is the best way to pursue a safer, healthier and more prosperous world both for Canadians at home and for people everywhere.

On the security front, Canadians recognise that military and law enforcement capacity must be multilateral in order to be effective. They also know that they must work multilaterally to build institutions capable of addressing the social, political, and economic instabilities that may fuel conflict and unrest. Canadians need to explore ways to ensure their security with a long-term view – one that recognises that where there is good governance, democracy, and respect for human rights, there are stable, prosperous, and secure states.

On the economic front, the Canadian government sees the same need for effective international rules and institutions in working to expand prosperity at home and abroad. While there may be disagreement over how equitably growth is occurring in the world today, it is clear to most that the benefits of an open, rules-based trading system far outweigh the disadvantages. The Canadian government will continue to approach international trade issues with Canadian values in mind. It will try to help spread opportunities for growth so as to expand prosperity among Canada's trading partners, including those in the developing world.

Here too, one sees the benefits of multilateralism. Canada will continue to assign top priority to the World Trade Organization (WTO) and the Doha Development Agenda. If handled properly, the WTO can build relationships of trust so that developing countries can fully participate in both the process and benefits of the multilateral trading system. Canada sent a strong and appreciated signal to this effect at the 2002 Kananaskis Summit, when Prime Minister Jean Chrétien announced unilateral reductions in most tariff items for least-developed countries.

These tools and others will be needed as the international community begins to address the interdependent nature of economic, environmental, and social issues. In order to promote international trade and prosperity, it will have to deal with issues such as governance, regulatory balance, competitiveness, and environmental standards. Canada made a start in 2001 in Quebec City, when the Summit of the Americas linked free trade to an agenda that also addressed broader concerns.

Civil Society and Global Governance Institutions

There is a key role for civil society both in supporting institutions of global governance and in fostering the climate of public opinion necessary for these institutions to succeed. At all levels of governance, the support of civil society is vital for ensuring the integrity and soundness of policy making.

In the area of Canadian foreign policy, the government takes seriously its obligation to seek out the best advice, information, and resources that Canadian citizens have to offer. It looks to interested Canadians from all parts of the country – analysts, scholars, and activists – to bring new insights on a range of crucial problems.

Several years ago, the Canadian government set up a new institution, the Canadian Centre for Foreign Policy Development, to consult citizens about a range of international issues. When the centre was created, its board decided not to limit its clients to traditional foreign affairs stakeholders such as academics and think tanks. Instead, using internet-based technology, the centre reached out to groups that had not previously been much engaged in foreign affairs – youth, civic organisations, minorities, indigenous peoples, and local officials, to name a few. The experience has been useful in learning about the concerns of a range of citizens and in developing a broader constituency for international relations. Prior to the Kananaskis Summit, the centre held a nationwide series of public round tables on African issues in order to hear from people interested in development, trade, multiculturalism, and foreign policy.

As the Minister of Foreign Affairs at the time, I met with several groups organised by the centre to canvass them on topics such as Canadian-European relations and relations with Muslim communities both in Canada and abroad. These meetings tended to be with experts in the field, but I believed in searching for more representative voices as well. Meetings in my constituency office gave me insights into the concerns of individuals. I also met with groups organised according to a shared focus. For example, I met with a group of Afghan Canadian women to receive their report containing recommendations on how Canada can best serve the interests of Afghan women and girls as Canada aids their country's reconstruction. Such meetings give me personal, concrete insights into far-away events that would otherwise be abstract and remote.

Beyond the national level, it is also vital for civil society to be engaged in the international institutions that have been so painstakingly constructed since World War II. In this sphere in particular, one sees the truth of what John Kenneth Galbraith said some decades ago: 'The worst policy is one made in secrecy by the experts.' Civil society groups have always embraced this view in acting as the conscience to government, ensuring that its policies are decent, fair, and representative.

In recent decades, however, the role of civil society has greatly expanded into more consultative and collaborative dimensions as well. As governments around the world are coming to realise, policies made in secrecy by experts cannot be substantively informed enough, or executed effectively enough, to succeed.

More bluntly, international institutions must move beyond secret meetings of experts if they are to be recognised as legitimate and effective. The increasingly vigorous protests at international meetings in recent years reflect a real need for these institutions to become more responsive to and less remote from the people whose interests they are supposed to serve. Current levels of popular disaffection are not surprising, given the secrecy, isolation, and technocratic agendas that have characterised such organisations in the past.

That is why the Canadian government has been committed to invigorating institutions of global governance and making them more responsive to citizens' concerns about issues such as labour, the environment, culture, and human rights. The government has addressed what is referred to as the democratic deficit of these institutions on two fronts. First, it has supported the increased involvement of parliamentarians, who are the democratically elected representatives of popular interests. Involving parliamentarians in existing forums, and creating new parliamentary assemblies to complement them, can bring the concerns of ordinary citizens to bear more directly on the agendas of international discussions.

Second, the Canadian government also strongly supports increasing the participation of civil society and nongovernmental organisations (NGOs) in the mechanisms of global governance. Their expertise and grassroots participation are also indispensable for reform.

In this effort at reform, parliamentarians and members of civil society are natural allies, who have no need for the turf wars that sometimes arise. Their respective functions and expertise – elected legitimacy, on one hand, and specialised knowledge, on the other – each contribute to the pursuit of goals they hold in common. As a result, they, as often as not, work together.

Recent Advances in Civil Society Participation in Global Governance Institutions

Some notable steps have recently taken in the direction of reform, often through the efforts of parliamentarians and civil society groups acting in concert.

At the Quebec City Summit of the Americas in April 2001, I was pleased to act as a parliamentarian in fostering communication between civil society groups and the government leaders gathered for the summit. As then Chair of Canada's House of Commons Standing Committee on Foreign Affairs and International Trade, I arranged for that committee to hold public hearings before and after the summit, in order to involve citizens and parliamentarians alike in the summit process.

In the lead-up to the summit, the government conducted extensive consultations with civil society groups such as aboriginal peoples, youth, churches, and the business community. These were not just Canadian groups, but were representative voices from throughout the Americas. During the summit itself, there was a very constructive meeting between 60 or so Canadian civil society organisations and

15 ministers from the Americas. The civil society groups offered views about the summit's agenda, and the government's response at least partly addressed their fears about leaders' unresponsiveness to popular concerns. In the end, Prime Minister Chrétien put a 8-centimetre-thick book of consultation reports on the summit table of each minister in attendance.

The following year, at the 2002 G8 Summit in Kananaskis, international co-operation minister Susan Whelan and I attended the G6B (Group of Six Billion) People's Summit in Calgary, an alternative gathering at which civil society activists discussed issues they felt were not being adequately addressed by G8 leaders. After meeting with the G6B representatives, I transmitted their thoughtful comments to the prime minister at Kananaskis itself.

At the meetings for the Free Trade Agreement of the Americas (FTAA), Canada succeeded despite strong resistance from certain countries in having civil society representatives consulted by the negotiating group. This was a clash between cultures that view civil society with suspicion, as the opposition, and Canadian culture, which recognises that NGO groups can be critical of government and yet be important in forming policy. Canada's perspective on these matters is gaining influence in Mexico and other Latin American countries, where at first it was met with considerable hostility.

A real engagement of civil society presumes that it has genuine access and opportunity to participate. It is a triumph for the increasing transparency of this organisation that it now publishes the negotiating texts of its agreements. This practice that was initiated in Buenos Aires by Pierre Pettigrew as Canada's Minister for International Trade. At the Organization of American States (OAS), the creation of the Inter-Parliamentary Forum of the Americas (FIPA) has made that institution freshly relevant by engaging parliamentarians from member states in discussion of popular concerns such as health, democracy, human rights, and the environment.

I was proud to be elected the first president of FIPA at its inaugural meeting in Ottawa in 2001. I greatly appreciated the chance to share my constituents' views with parliamentarians from throughout the hemisphere as we discussed how to deal with the consequences of integrating the Americas. It was genuinely exciting to be part of this process of articulating a collective political vision of the hemisphere's future. The Americas is about far more than free trade.

At the WTO, Canada has worked with civil society groups to try to create a parliamentary assembly capable of ensuring that social, cultural, and environmental issues are included on the WTO agenda. At the Doha ministerial in 2001, I worked on this effort with colleagues from the European Parliament, the Inter-Parliamentary Union, and interested NGOs. While the assembly still faces many challenges before it can become a reality, Pettigrew insisted that the parliamentary assembly be placed on the Doha ministerial agenda.

The initiative owes its genesis to Senator Bill Roth, who proposed it three years ago at the WTO ministerial meeting in Seattle. At that time there was a meeting of parliamentarians representing some 60 countries, all of which supported the idea. But the idea, and the impetus for this initiative, first came from NGOs such as the

World Federalists and others, which started working on it some time ago. Indeed, I attended a meeting to discuss this idea at the Geneva ministerial in 1998. Of the 60 or so people in the room only one or two of us were politicians. So NGOs and parliamentarians do collaborate effectively on such issues.

Thus many small steps have been taken in the right direction. Canada will continue to promote these changes in global governance, and will continue to encourage all national governments to see parliamentarians and civil society groups as their allies in the ongoing process of reform.

Civil Society and Global Issues

Moving from the global organisations to particular issues of global concern, many civil society partnerships have also contributed to human security initiatives in Canada's foreign policy. Both parliamentarians and NGOs have been crucial on issues such as landmines, the International Criminal Court, and the Kimberley Process on conflict diamonds.

The International Committee of the Red Cross became an equal partner with Canada in the process to eradicate landmines. We worked closely together in the years leading to the establishment of the 1997 Ottawa Convention banning antipersonnel mines. Since then, the Red Cross has played an invaluable role in supporting initiatives such as community-based mine-awareness programmes and medical assistance for mine victims. In turn, Canada has provided funding for mine action programmes implemented by the Red Cross and other partners.

Another successful collaboration with civil society led to the creation of the International Criminal Court. The court was itself a reaction by governments to popular demand around the world for an end to impunity for war crimes. Canada took a leading role in developing this crucial international instrument, and its parliamentarians were immensely helpful in the effort, promoting the court with their counterparts bilaterally and through forums such as the Inter-Parliamentary Union and Parliamentarians for Global Action. Many of our partners in civil society share in this landmark achievement. Canada is committed to promoting civil society involvement in our ongoing campaign to ensure that the International Criminal Court gains universal acceptance and that it functions fairly and effectively in delivering truly impartial justice.

Canada has hosted a meeting of Parliamentarians for Global Action to consider two items significant for the future of our global architecture: the International Criminal Court and a recent report on humanitarian intervention titled 'The Responsibility to Protect' (International Commission on Intervention and State Sovereignty 2001). It is pursuing a similar approach with regard to the Kimberley Process, an intergovernmental effort led by South Africa and aimed at keeping conflict diamonds out of legitimate markets. Canada hosted the 2002 plenary meeting, which involved government representatives, the private sector, and NGOs. It also provided support to a Canadian NGO, Partnership Africa Canada, which authored a major study on conflict diamonds in Sierra Leone and undertook a project on 'just mining' practices.

The most important international organisation for global governance today is the United Nations. It is there that much of our efforts to increase transparency, accountability, and effectiveness are directed. It is truly vital to secure the effectiveness of this institution. Like the other multilateral institutions noted above, the UN cannot successfully undertake the reforms necessary to maintain its legitimacy and relevance unless it has support from all levels of civil society.

Conclusion

Internationalism is a fragile thing. It depends on a foundation of cultural attitudes that make it possible for peaceful and inclusive dialogue to happen. The Canadian government believes that Canadians can make an important contribution on the world stage through the model they provide of a culture in which, by and large, internationalism works in a national context. As Janice Stein has remarked: 'Canada is a society of diversity whose members are internationalized through ties of kinship and attachment to every society in the globe.' As Canada becomes a microcosm of the world, whether we can succeed in constructing a broad architecture of security within Canada will become a litmus test for others.

Canada has something unique to offer the world: its experience in working and living together in a vast multicultural country and, in so doing, promoting mutual respect, understanding and tolerance. Canadians are often their own most vocal critics. That is of fundamental importance in a free and democratic society. But it is always striking to travel abroad and to realise that, by just about any standard, Canadians are greatly admired as a truly vibrant and successful society.

When I travel abroad, I often tell the story of my own constituency in Toronto. I represent an area that includes St. James Town, where some 12 000 people speak 57 different languages. We would not have peace, harmony, social justice, and cooperation with one another in that intensely crowded space if we did not have respect for one another and a willingness to work together to solve our problems. Indeed, my own riding and the people I represent are an illustration of our history as a country of immigration. Canada was originally populated by aboriginal peoples. The first wave of immigration was largely European. Successive waves of immigrants have come from all parts of the globe. In this respect, Canada is like the United States, the country closest to Canada in values and culture. With each wave of immigration, Canada has grown stronger. Today, its cultural diversity is the hallmark of its national identity. It gives Canada strength in the world because, the world is in Canada.

But in offering Canada as an exemplar of global possibilities, Canadians cannot afford to be complacent about the condition of their own society. Having the world within Canada's borders means that when things get ugly abroad, Canadians see the reverberations at home. When Benjamin Netanyahu attempted to speak at Concordia

University in the summer of 2002, the riots that broke out were an alarming sign of how fragile a commitment to dialogue can be. They underline that Canadians must all be vigilant to ensure that this type of conduct is not tolerated in Canada.

So not all elements or tendencies of civil society are ones to be encouraged. As Canadians keep in mind the urgent global problems facing them, as they try to strengthen and reform the multilateral institutions needed to address these problems, as they foster the involvement of NGOs and parliamentarians in that process – in all of this, they need to be mindful of the larger cultural context that will either promote or oppose the values of pluralism, inclusiveness, civility, and mutual respect. In the course of my mandate as foreign affairs minister and now as defence minister, it was my experience that Canadian civil society representatives are generally motivated to promote those quintessentially Canadian values. Our society is enriched by their active participation and I, for one, will continue to urge government to take advantage of this important resource.

References

International Commission on Intervention and State Sovereignty (2001). 'The Responsibility to Protect: Report of the International Commission on Intervention and State Sovereignty'. <www.iciss.ca/report-en.asp> (November 2005).

Index